Lecture Notes in Computer Science

Vol. 379: A. Kreczmar, G. Mirkowska (Eds.), Mathematical Foundations of Computer Science 1989. Proceedings, 1989. VIII, 605 pages. 1989.

Vol. 380: J. Csirik, J. Demetrovics, F. Gécseg (Eds.), Fundamentals of Computation Theory. Proceedings, 1989. XI, 493 pages. 1989.

Vol. 381: J. Dassow, J. Kelemen (Eds.), Machines, Languages, and Complexity. Proceedings, 1988. VI, 244 pages. 1989.

Vol. 382: F. Dehne, J.-R. Sack, N. Santoro (Eds.), Algorithms and Data Structures. WADS '89. Proceedings, 1989. IX, 592 pages. 1989.

Vol. 383: K. Furukawa, H. Tanaka, T. Fujisaki (Eds.), Logic Programming '88. Proceedings, 1988. VII, 251 pages. 1989 (Subseries LNAI).

Vol. 384: G.A. van Zee, J.G.G. van de Vorst (Eds.), Parallel Computing 1988. Proceedings, 1988. V, 135 pages. 1989.

Vol. 385: E. Börger, H. Kleine Büning, M.M. Richter (Eds.), CSL '88. Proceedings, 1988. VI, 399 pages. 1989.

Vol. 386: J.E. Pin (Ed.), Formal Properties of Finite Automata and Applications. Proceedings, 1988. VIII, 260 pages. 1989.

Vol. 387: C. Ghezzi, J. A. McDermid (Eds.), ESEC '89. 2nd European Software Engineering Conference. Proceedings, 1989. VI, 496 pages. 1989.

Vol. 388: G. Cohen, J. Wolfmann (Eds.), Coding Theory and Applications. Proceedings, 1988. IX, 329 pages. 1989.

Vol. 389: D.H. Pitt, D.E. Rydeheard, P. Dybjer, A.M. Pitts, A. Poigné (Eds.), Category Theory and Computer Science. Proceedings, 1989. VI, 365 pages. 1989.

Vol. 390: J.P. Martins, E.M. Morgado (Eds.), EPIA 89. Proceedings, 1989. XII, 400 pages. 1989 (Subseries LNAI).

Vol. 391: J.-D. Boissonnat, J.-P. Laumond (Eds.), Geometry and Robotics. Proceedings, 1988. VI, 413 pages. 1989.

Vol. 392: J.-C. Bermond, M. Raynal (Eds.), Distributed Algorithms. Proceedings, 1989. VI, 315 pages. 1989.

Vol. 393: H. Ehrig, H. Herrlich, H.-J. Kreowski, G. Preuß (Eds.), Categorical Methods in Computer Science. VI, 350 pages. 1989.

Vol. 394: M. Wirsing, J.A. Bergstra (Eds.), Algebraic Methods: Theory, Tools and Applications. VI, 558 pages. 1989.

Vol. 395: M. Schmidt-Schauß, Computational Aspects of an Order-Sorted Logic with Term Declarations. VIII, 171 pages. 1989 (Subseries LNAI).

Vol. 396: T.A. Berson, T. Beth (Eds.), Local Area Network Security. Proceedings, 1989. IX, 152 pages. 1989.

Vol. 397: K.P. Jantke (Ed.), Analogical and Inductive Inference. Proceedings, 1989. IX, 338 pages. 1989 (Subseries LNAI).

Vol. 398: B. Banieqbal, H. Barringer, A. Pnueli (Eds.), Temporal Logic in Specification. Proceedings, 1987. VI, 448 pages. 1989.

Vol. 399: V. Cantoni, R. Creutzburg, S. Levialdi, G. Wolf (Eds.), Recent Issues in Pattern Analysis and Recognition. VII, 400 pages. 1989.

Vol. 400: R. Klein, Concrete and Abstract Voronoi Diagrams. IV, 167 pages. 1989.

Vol. 401: H. Djidjev (Ed.), Optimal Algorithms. Proceedings, 1989. VI, 308 pages. 1989.

Vol. 402: T.P. Bagchi, V.K. Chaudhri, Interactive Relational Database Design. XI, 186 pages. 1989.

Vol. 403: S. Goldwasser (Ed.), Advances in Cryptology – CRYPTO '88. Proceedings, 1988. XI, 591 pages. 1990.

Vol. 404: J. Beer, Concepts, Design, and Performance Analysis of a Parallel Prolog Machine. VI, 128 pages. 1989.

Vol. 405: C.E. Veni Madhavan (Ed.), Foundations of Software Technology and Theoretical Computer Science. Proceedings, 1989. VIII, 339 pages. 1989.

Vol. 406: C.J. Barter, M.J. Brooks (Eds.), AI '88. Proceedings, 1988. VIII, 463 pages. 1990 (Subseries LNAI).

Vol. 407: J. Sifakis (Ed.), Automatic Verification Methods for Finite State Systems. Proceedings, 1989. VII, 382 pages. 1990.

Vol. 408: M. Leeser, G. Brown (Eds.), Hardware Specification, Verification and Synthesis: Mathematical Aspects. Proceedings, 1989. VI, 402 pages. 1990.

Vol. 409: A. Buchmann, O. Günther, T.R. Smith, Y.-F. Wang (Eds.), Design and Implementation of Large Spatial Databases. Proceedings, 1989. IX, 364 pages. 1990.

Vol. 410: F. Pichler, R. Moreno-Diaz (Eds.), Computer Aided Systems Theory – EUROCAST '89. Proceedings, 1989. VII, 427 pages. 1990.

Vol. 411: M. Nagl (Ed.), Graph-Theoretic Concepts in Computer Science. Proceedings, 1989. VII, 374 pages. 1990.

Vol. 412: L.B. Almeida, C.J. Wellekens (Eds.), Neural Networks. Proceedings, 1990. IX, 276 pages. 1990.

Vol. 413: R. Lenz, Group Theoretical Methods in Image Processing. VIII, 139 pages. 1990.

Vol. 414: A. Kreczmar, A. Salwicki, M. Warpechowski, LOGLAN '88 – Report on the Programming Language. X, 133 pages. 1990.

Vol. 415: C. Choffrut, T. Lengauer (Eds.), STACS 90. Proceedings, 1990. VI, 312 pages. 1990.

Vol. 416: F. Bancilhon, C. Thanos, D. Tsichritzis (Eds.), Advances in Database Technology – EDBT '90. Proceedings, 1990. IX, 452 pages. 1990.

Vol. 417: P. Martin-Löf, G. Mints (Eds.), COLOG-88. International Conference on Computer Logic. Proceedings, 1988. VI, 338 pages. 1990.

Vol. 418: K.H. Bläsius, U. Hedtstück, C.-R. Rollinger (Eds.), Sorts and Types in Artificial Intelligence. Proceedings, 1989. VIII, 307 pages. 1990. (Subseries LNAI).

Vol. 419: K. Weichselberger, S. Pöhlmann, A Methodology for Uncertainty in Knowledge-Based Systems. VIII, 136 pages. 1990 (Subseries LNAI).

Vol. 420: Z. Michalewicz (Ed.), Statistical and Scientific Database Management, V SSDBM. Proceedings, 1990. V, 256 pages. 1990.

Vol. 421: T. Onodera, S. Kawai, A Formal Model of Visualization in Computer Graphics Systems. X, 100 pages. 1990.

Vol. 422: B. Nebel, Reasoning and Revision in Hybrid Representation Systems. XII, 270 pages. 1990 (Subseries LNAI).

Vol. 423: L. E. Deimel (Ed.), Software Engineering Education. Proceedings, 1990. VI, 164 pages. 1990.

Vol. 424: G. Rozenberg (Ed.), Advances in Petri Nets 1989. VI, 524 pages. 1990.

Vol. 425: C.H. Bergman, R.D. Maddux, D.L. Pigozzi (Eds.), Algebraic Logic and Universal Algebra in Computer Science. Proceedings, 1988. XI, 292 pages. 1990.

Vol. 426: N. Houbak, SIL – a Simulation Language. VII, 192 pages. 1990.

Vol. 427: O. Faugeras (Ed.), Computer Vision – ECCV 90. Proceedings, 1990. XII, 619 pages. 1990.

Vol. 428: D. Bjørner, C.A.R. Hoare, H. Langmaack (Eds.), VDM '90. VDM and Z – Formal Methods in Software Development. Proceedings, 1990. XVII, 580 pages. 1990.

Vol. 429: A. Miola (Ed.), Design and Implementation of Symbolic Computation Systems. Proceedings, 1990. XII, 284 pages. 1990.

Vol. 430: J.W. de Bakker, W.-P. de Roever, G. Rozenberg (Eds.), Stepwise Refinement of Distributed Systems. Models, Formalisms, Correctness. Proceedings, 1989. X, 808 pages. 1990.

Vol. 431: A. Arnold (Ed.), CAAP '90. Proceedings, 1990. VI, 285 pages 1990.

Vol. 432: N. Jones (Ed.), ESOP '90. Proceedings, 1990. IX, 436 pages 1990.

Vol. 433: W. Schröder-Preikschat, W. Zimmer (Eds.), Progress in Distributed Operating Systems and Distributed Systems Management. Proceedings, 1989. V, 206 pages. 1990.

Vol. 434: J.-J. Quisquater, J. Vandewalle (Eds.), Advances in Cryptology – EUROCRYPT '89. Proceedings, 1989. X, 710 pages. 1990.

Vol. 435: G. Brassard (Ed.), Advances in Cryptology – CRYPTO '89. Proceedings, 1989. XIII, 634 pages. 1990.

Vol. 436: B. Steinholtz, A. Sølvberg, L. Bergman (Eds.), Advanced Information Systems Engineering. Proceedings, 1990. X, 392 pages. 1990.

Lecture Notes in Computer Science

Edited by G. Goos and J. Hartmanis

472

K.V. Nori C.E. Veni Madhavan (Eds.)

FST and TCS 10

Foundations of Software Technology and Theoretical Computer Science

Tenth Conference, Bangalore, India
December 17–19, 1990
Proceedings

Springer-Verlag
Berlin Heidelberg New York London
Paris Tokyo Hong Kong Barcelona

Volume Editors
Kesav V. Nori
Tata Research Development and Design Centre
1, Mangaldas Road, Pune 411 001, India

C. E. Veni Madhavan
Department of Computer Science and Automation
Indian Institute of Science
Bangalore 560 012, India

Conference Sponsors
Centre for Development of Advanced Computing
Computer Maintenance Corporation
Indian Institute of Science
Tata Consultancy Services
Tata Institute of Fundamental Research
Tata Research Development and Design Centre

CR Subject Classification (1987): B.7.2, F.2.2, F.3.1–2, F.4.1–3, G.2.1–2, H.2.4, I.2.2–4, I.2.7, I.2.10, I.3.5

ISBN 3-540-53487-3 Springer-Verlag Berlin Heidelberg New York
ISBN 0-387-53487-3 Springer-Verlag New York Berlin Heidelberg

Printing and binding: Druckhaus Beltz, Hemsbach/Bergstr.
2145/3140-543210 – Printed on acid-free paper

PROFESSOR R. NARASIMHAN

DEDICATION

There are many reasons to celebrate in this tenth year of FST&TCS conferences. This conference is organised and run by the Computer Science Research community in India without support from any professional societies. It is an expression of solidarity of this community to find effective means of exposure to the quality of research elsewhere, and to be visible on account of merit. Its purpose has been to provide a forum for professional interaction between members of this research community and their counterparts in different parts of the world. The effects of this sustained exposure is locally visible: the quality of teaching in theoretical aspects of Computer Science has uniformly improved in all the major Departments of Computer Science in India; also, the number and quality of papers in Theoretical Computer Science reporting on original research carried out in India has steadily increased.

The Tenth Conference on Foundations of Software Technology and Theoretical Computer Science is dedicated to Professor R. Narasimhan on the eve of his retirement from the Computer Science Group at TIFR. It was his vision of finding means to integrate individual researchers into a community, his emphasis on quality, his ideas on methods of maintaining quality in a visible manner, and his constant support to the Conference Committees in their endeavours to implement his ideas, which have helped make this conference an accepted annual event. We will always be beholden to him for having helped us believe in ourselves.

Technical Programme Committee, FST&TCS 10

ACKNOWLEDGEMENTS

We owe a debt of gratitude to many who have contributed to this conference:

- to all the authors of the 116 submitted papers for providing us with delectable material;

- to all the authors of the 26 selected papers for giving us an excellent programme;

- to all the reviewers for their discerning comments;

- to all Invited Speakers for accepting our invitations;

- to Patricia Lobo, Deenaz Bulsara, A. M. Farooqi, P. R. Naik, and Y. Pajnigar, S. Shelar, C. Kumbhar for efficiently managing the Conference Secretariat;

- to Faculty and Students of the Department of Computer Science and Automation of IISc for providing organisational support;

- to the funding agencies for their encouragement and support.

December, 1990

K. V. Nori
C. E. Veni Madhavan

Conference Advisory Committee

D Bjorner (Denmark)

A Chandra (IBM Resarch)

S Crespi Reghizzi (Milan)

Z Galil (Columbia)

D Gries (Cornell)

M Joseph (Warwick)

A Joshi (Pennsylvania)

R Kannan (CMU)

U Montanari (Pisa)

R Narasimhan (TIFR)

M Nivat (Paris)

R Parikh (New York)

S Rao Kosaraju (Johns Hopkins)

S Sahni (Minnesota)

W A Wulf (Virginia)

Technical Programme Committee

G P Bhattacharjee (IIT Kharagpur)

S Biswas (IIT Kanpur)

K Krithivasan (IIT Madras)

S N Maheshwari (IIT Delhi)

K V Nori (TRDDC Pune)

R K Shyamasundar (TIFR)

Y N Srikant (IISc Bangalore)

P S Thiagarajan (SPIC Foundation)

C E Veni Madhavan (IISc Bangalore)

G Venkatesh (IIT Bombay)

LIST OF REVIEWERS

G S Adhar, Univ. of North Carolina, USA
W R Adrion, Univ. of Massachusetts, USA
A Aggarwal, IBM-T J Watson Res Ctr, USA
A Aggarwal, Univ. of Maryland, USA
R K Ahuja, IIT Kanpur, India
M Ahuja, Ohio State Univ., USA
J Anderson, Comp Resources Int'l, Denmark
A Arora, MCTC, USA
K Bagchi, Aalborg Univ., Denmark
S Balaji, ISRO B'lore, India
S Banerjee, IISc B'lore, India
R Barua, ISI Calcutta, India
G Barua, IIT Kanpur, India
K Berkling, Syracuse Univ., USA
S Bettayeb, Louisiana State Univ., USA
P Bonatti, Corso Italia, Pisa, Italy
E Bevers, Univ. of Leuven, Belgium
B Bhargava, Purdue Univ., USA
P C P Bhatt, IIT Delhi, India
B K Bhattacharya, Simon Fraser Univ., Canada
B B Bhattacharya, ISI Calcutta, India
S Biswas, IIT Kanpur, India
D Bjorner, Tech Univ. of Denmark, Denmark
J R S Blair, Univ. of Tennessee, USA
J Camilleri, Computel Labs, Cambridge, UK
D M Campbell, Brigham Young Univ., USA
D L Carver, Louisiana State Univ., USA
J Case, Univ. of Delaware, USA
M Cerioli, Univ. of Genoa, Italy
D R Chand, Framingham, MA, USA
V Chandru, IISc B'lore, India
S Chaudhari, Rutgers NJ, USA
J Cheriyan, Univ. of Saarland, FRG
B Courcelle, France
K Culik II, Univ. of South Carolina, USA
D D'Souza, R M I T, Australia
P Dasgupta, Georgia Inst. of Tech., USA
A Datta, IIT Madras, India
R W Dawes, Queen's Univ., Canada
A Dawar, Univ. of Pennsylvania, USA
P J de Bruin, Univ. of Saarland, FRG
W P de Roever, Kiel Univ., FRG
A Deb, Memorial Univ., Canada
N C Debnath, Winona State Univ., USA
S K Debray, Univ. of Arizona, USA
A H Dekker, Griffith Univ., Australia
N Deo, Univ. of Central Florida, USA
J S Deogun, Univ. of Nebraska-Lincoln, USA
S C Desarkar, IIT Kharagpur, India
J Desharnais, Univ. Laval, Canada
T K Dey, Purdue Univ., USA
A A Diwan, TIFR Bombay, India
Dubashi, Cornell Univ., USA
P Dublish, Univ. of Hildesheim, FRG
R Dwyer, St. Univ. of North Carolina, USA
W Fey, Univ. of Berlin, FRG
J Fiadeiro, Imperial College, UK
M. Gabbrielli, Univ. of Pisa, Italy
G Gambosi, IASI-CNR, Italy
A V Ganapati, IISc B'lore, India
M Garzon, Memphis State Univ., USA
E V Gestel Univ. of Leuven, Belgium
S K Ghosh, TIFR Bombay, India
D Goelman, Villanova Univ., USA
Md Gouda, MCTC, USA
R Greenlaw, College of Eng., Durham, NH, USA
J Gunawardena, Hewlett-Packard Labs, UK
R Gupta, Simon Fraser Univ., Canada
K Havelund, Tech Univ. of Denmark, Denmark
A Haxthauser, Louisiana State Univ., USA
L S Heath, Virginia PI & State Univ., USA
H Heller, Siemens, FRG
M Hermann, CRIN, France
Z Hong, Nanjing Univ., PR China
G Hotz, Univ. of Saarland, FRG
W J Hsu, Michigan State Univ., USA
S S Iyengar, Louisiana State Univ., USA
S Jain, Univ. of Rochester, USA
R Janardan, Univ. of Minnesota, USA
J M Janas, Bundeswehr Univ. Munich, FRG
L S Jensen, Univ. of Denmark, Denmark
Y J Jiang, Imperial College, UK
M Joseph, Univ. of Warwick, UK
A K Joshi, Univ. of Pennsylvania, USA
J Kamper, IBM, FRG
K Kanchanasut, Univ. of Melbourne, Australia
R Kannan, CMU, USA
S Kapoor, IIT Delhi, India
H Karnick, IIT Kanpur, India
V N Kasyanov, USSR Academy of Sc., USSR
V B Kaujalgi, IIM B'lore, India
C Kenyon, Laboratoire d'Informatique, France
S Khuller, Cornell Univ., USA
C M R Kintala, AT & T Bell Labs, USA
S Krishnamoorthy, Georgia Tech, USA
K Krithivasan, IIT Madras, India
S Kumar, IIT Kanpur, India
A Kumar, IIT Delhi, India

V S Lakshmanan, IISc B'lore, India
C Levcopoulos, Lund Univ., Sweden
G Levi, Corso Italia, Pisa, Italy
C P Lewington, Univ. of Essex, UK
A Lingas, Lund Univ., Sweden
K Lodaya, Matscience Madras, India
H H Lovengreen, Univ. of Denmark, Denmark
S M Mahajan, BARC Bombay, India
S Mahajan, Simon Fraser Univ., Canada
A Mahanti, Univ. of Maryland, USA
M Maher, IBM-TJ Watson Res Ctr, USA
S N Maheshwari, IIT Delhi
A K Majumdar, IIT Kharagpur
F M Malvestuto, Studi-DOC, ENEA Italy
A Marchetti, Rome, Italy
Mehndiratta, IIT Bombay, India
A K Mittal, IIT Kanpur, India
C K Mohan, New York, USA
S Morasca, Milan Polytechnic, Italy
A Moslemie, Univ. of Helsinki, Finland
R Motwani, Stanford Univ., USA
I S Mumick, Stanford Univ. USA
D V J Murphy, Univ. of Glasgow, UK
C R Muthukrishnan, IIT Madras, India
K N R Nair, Univ. of Poona, India
A Nakamura, Hiroshima Univ., Japan
N K Nanda, AIT Bangkok, Thailand
G Narasimhan, Memphis State Univ., USA
K V Nori, TRDDC Pune, India
L Narayan, Univ. of Rochester, USA
S Olariu, Old Dominion Univ., USA
B J Oommen, Carleton Univ., USA
A K Pal, IIM Calcutta, India
S P Pal, IISc B'lore, India
M Palis, Univ. of Pennsylvania, USA
C P Rangan, IIT Madras, India
G E Pantziou, Computer Tech. Inst., Greece
M A Papalaskari, Villanova Univ., USA
J Paredaens, Univ. of Antwerp, Belgium
A Paulraj, C-DAC, B'lore, India
A Pettorosi, IASI-CNR, Italy
M Pezze, Milan Polytechnic, Italy
I Phillips, Imperial College, UK
B C Pierce, IBM-TJ Watson Res Ctr, USA
B Plateau, INPG, France
S K Prasad, Univ. of Central Florida, USA
M Protasi, Univ. of Rome, Italy
S Purushothaman, Penn. State Univ., USA
P Raghavan, IBM-TJ Watson Res Ctr, USA
C S Raghavendra, USC, USA
V Rajasekar, IISc B'lore, India
S Rajasekaran, Univ. of Penn., USA
K S Rajasethupathy, SUNY-Brockport, USA
S Ramakrishnan, Bowling Green Univ., USA
R Raman, Univ. of Rochester, USA
R Ramanujam, IMSc Madras, India
S Ramesh, IIT Bombay, India
E Ritter, Univ. of Cambridge, UK
N S V Rao, Old Dominion Univ., USA
K S Rao, John Hopkins Univ., USA
S Rengarajan, IISc B'lore, India
C Retore, Imperial College, UK
K Ross, IBM-TJ Watson Res Ctr, USA
H V Sahasrabuddhe, Univ. of Poona, India
R Sangal, IIT Kanpur, India
A Saoudi, Univ. of Paris VII, France
H Saran, Univ. of California, USA
S Sarkar, IBM Corporation, USA
S Saxena, IIT Kanpur, India
B Schieber, IBM-TJ Watson Res. Ctr., USA
S Sen, Duke Univ., USA
A S Sethi, Univ. of Delaware, USA
S G Shiva, Univ. of Alabama, USA
S Singh, IIT Delhi, India
M Sinha, IIT Delhi, India
G Sivakumar, Univ. of Delaware, USA
A Somani, Univ. of Washington, USA
N Sopankar, Univ. of Texas, USA
N Soundarajan, Ohio State Univ., USA
P Spirakis, Computer Tech. Inst., Greece
P Sreenivasa Kumar, IISc B'lore, India
Y N Srikant, IISc B'lore, India
P K Srimani, Colorado State Univ., USA
M Subramaniam, TRDDC Pune, India
V S Sunderam, Emory Univ., USA
R Sunderraman, Wichita State Univ., USA
S Sur-Kolay, ISI Calcutta, India
R K Shyamasundar, TIFR Bombay, India
G Taubenfeld, Yale Univ., USA
P S Thiagarajan, SPIC Sc Foundn., India
P Tiwari, IBM-TJ Watson Res Ctr, USA
A Tyagi, Univ. of North Carolina, USA
R S Valiveti, Carleton Univ., USA
V Vazarani, Cornell Univ., USA
C E Veni Madhavan, IISc B'lore, India
S Venkatesan, Univ. of Texas, USA
G Venkatesh, IIT Bombay, India
K Vidyasankar, Memorial Univ., USA
V Vinay, IISc B'lore, India
D S L Wei, Univ. of Pennsylvania, USA
R Wilkinson, RMIT, Australia
M F Worboys, Univ. of Leicester, UK
R Yerneni, Tandem Computers, USA
J H You, Univ. of Alberta, Canada
C D Zaroliagis, CTI, Greece
E Zucca, Univ. of Genoa, Italy

TABLE OF CONTENTS

Reasoning About Linear Constraints Using Parametric Queries

Tien Huynh Leo Joskowicz Catherine Lassez Jean-Louis Lassez
IBM T.J. Watson Research Center
P.O.Box 704
Yorktown Heights, NY 10598

Abstract

We address the problem of building intelligent query systems to reason about linear arithmetic constraints. The central issue is the development of tools for testing solvability, for constraints representation, for incremental updates and for intelligent feedback. The concept of parametric queries introduced in the context of constraint logic programming provides the starting point for this study. The relevance of this approach is illustrated by examples from the domain of spatial reasoning.

1 Introduction

Linear arithmetic constraints are key elements in applications such as Operations Research, Constructive Solid Geometry, Robotics, CAD/CAM, Spreadsheets, Model-based Reasoning, Theorem Proving and Program Verification. Constraints handling techniques have been incorporated in a number of programming systems including CLP($\Re$), CHIP, CAL, Prolog III, BNR-Prolog, Mathematica and Trilogy. More recently constraints have been introduced in committed choice languages [M], [S] and in database querying languages [KKR]. Here we address the general problem of designing systems to reason about linear arithmetic using the constraints as the basic entity. The domain knowledge is expressed as constraints, and queries are asked on these constraints to extract new information. These queries are asked in an interactive context where the constraints in store can be dynamically added and deleted. Apart from the problem of finding suitable query-answering mechanisms, this raises the complex problem of coordinating the various operations.

To answer queries, efficient mechanisms are required to deal with subsumption, implicit equalities, redundancy, canonical representation, projections, and incrementally updating. For each of these problems, one can import algorithms from Symbolic Computation, Computational Geometry, Automated Reasoning and Operations Research. However, a collection of disconnected algorithms only makes an ad-hoc system. A general system requires a coherent underlying theory and an integrated implementation. In this paper, we informally present an integrated framework based on the concept of *parametric queries* which provides a unifying formalism and leads to a general query-answering method.

The rest of the paper is organized as follows. In the next section, we present examples of the use of constraints in the domain of spatial reasoning. These examples illustrate how the various kinds of information in this particular domain translate naturally into constraints and what the required constraint-handling operations are. In section 3 we define the general concept of parametric queries that provides a framework to express the different aspects of reasoning with constraints. We also show how a basic but somewhat ignored result of Linear Programming leads to a method to answer these queries. In section 4, we discuss the key issue of constraints representation and present a natural canonical form that fits the requirements of both the interaction and the processing of queries. In section 5, we address the problem of dynamically updating the constraints in store and we show the importance of proper feedback information for maintaining a coherent system of constraints. In the last section, we show how linear programming generalizes naturally into a symbolic computation method to answer parametric queries. As a particular case, we show how a variant of the dual simplex leads to a solver which provides, for free, information on the algebraic properties of the constraints and the geometric structure of the associated polyhedron.

2 Spatial reasoning: a case study

Spatial reasoning covers a wide spectrum of tasks and domains, such as planning the motion of a robot's arm, analyzing and designing machines, and solving commonsense problems. The fundamental question underlying these tasks is: given an assembly of rigid objects, determine how they move and interact with each other in space. Object geometry determines the motion properties of an assembly. For example, Figure 1 shows a simple puzzle consisting of an enclosing frame containing three identical red and blue blocks. Given that the blocks have opposite orientations, we want to determine if the blocks can move, how many blocks can move at a time or if the blue and red blocks can exchange positions.

Finding the motion properties of objects in an assembly can be formulated as a constraint

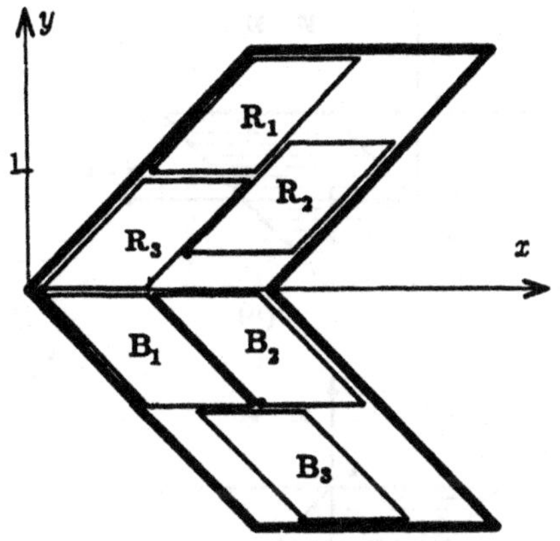

Figure 1: Geometric description of a puzzle consisting of a fixed frame containing three identical red R_i (upper) and blue (lower) B_i unit length diamond-shape blocks.

satisfaction problem [Ja]. Every moving object is assigned a reference point and one motion parameter for each of its potential degrees of freedom. Specific parameter values define the objects' *configuration*, i.e., its position and orientation in space. The space generated by all objects' motion parameters is called a *configuration space*. For example, each block in the puzzle has its reference point attached to its lower left corner and two translational parameters: x_i and y_i for the red blocks, and u_i and v_i for the blue blocks. The parameters' axes are aligned with the cartesian x-y coordinate frame and define a 12-dimensional configuration space. The configuration depicted in Figure 1 corresponds to the point:

$$\{x_1 = 1, \quad y_1 = 1, \quad x_2 = 1.5, \quad y_2 = 0.5, \quad x_3 = 0, \quad y_3 = 0,$$
$$u_1 = 1, \quad v_1 = -1, \quad u_2 = 2, \quad v_2 = -1, \quad u_3 = 2.5, \quad v_3 = -2\}.$$

Since rigid objects cannot deform or interpenetrate, their motions are constrained by the contacts between them. Each pairwise contact defines a *motion constraint* on the objects' degrees of freedom. Motion constraints are non-linear inequality functions on the objects' motion parameters. Their exact form is determined by the object geometry and degrees of freedom. Translating polyhedral objects generate linear constraints[1]. The set of motion constraints for each object pair is computed by examining all possible contacts between the objects' faces, edges, and vertices [LW].

In the puzzle, the frame restricts red blocks to slide along its edges. The corresponding motion constraints are graphically depicted in Figure 2(a). The axes are the motion parameters

[1]Other non-linear constraints of curved geometry and rotations can sometimes be approximated by linear inequalities [Jb].

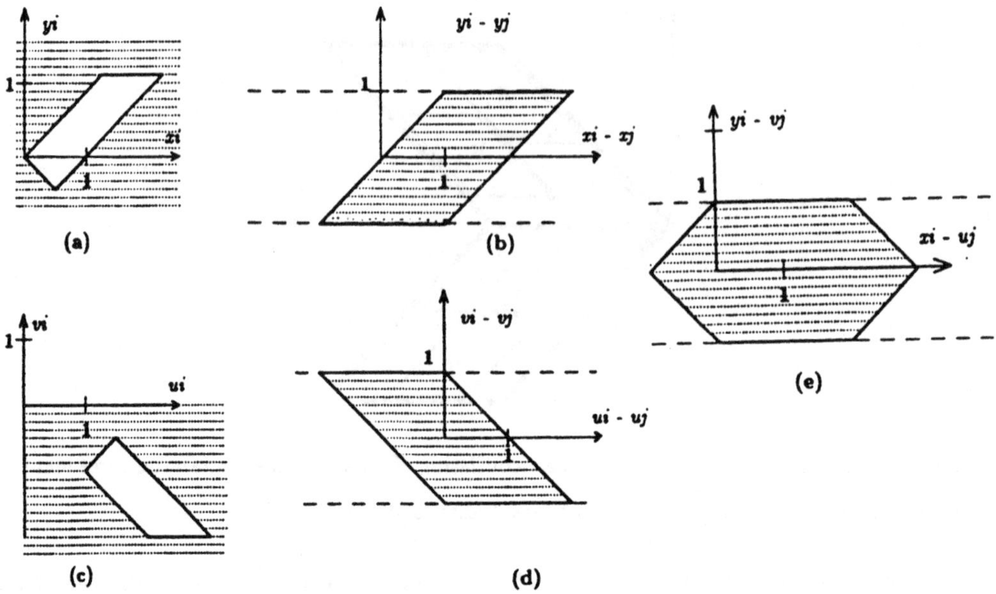

Figure 2: Graphical representation of the local motion constraints: (a) the frame and a red block; (b) two red blocks; (c) the frame and a blue block; (d) two blue blocks, and (e) a red and a blue block. Shaded areas correspond to forbidden object configurations.

of block R_i, x_i and y_i. Each of the trapezoid's boundaries corresponds to a contact: the left line corresponds to the red block's left edge sliding along the frame's upper left edge. The red blocks are constrained to slide around each others' contours, as shown in Figure 2(b). Motion constraints are described by disjunctions and conjunctions of linear constraints. Each conjunctive clause defines a convex region. The union of all conjunctive clauses defines the set of legal configurations. The frame and red block motion constraints are described by a single region:

$$\{y_i \leq 1, \quad x_i - y_i \geq 0, \quad x_i + y_i \geq 0, \quad x_i - y_i \leq 1\}$$

for $i = 1,2,3$, whereas the motion constraints of two red blocks R_i and R_j are described by four regions, partitioned as indicated by the dashed lines in the figure:

$$\{(x_i - x_j) - (y_i - y_j) \geq 1, \quad y_i - y_j > -1, \quad y_i - y_j > -1\} \;\vee\; y_i - y_j \geq 1 \;\vee$$
$$\{(x_i - x_j) - (y_i - y_j) \leq -1, \quad y_i - y_j > -1, \quad y_i - y_j > -1\} \;\vee\; y_i - y_j \leq -1$$

for $i, j = 1,2,3$ and $i \neq j$. Similar sets of constraints describe the remaining three interactions, shown in Figure 2. Physical object motions must be within the pairwise object contacts. That is, they must satisfy the set of all pairwise motion constraints.

Properties of the objects' motions can be extracted from queries on the set S of all motion constraints. These questions include, among many others:

1. *Assembly:* can the objects be assembled? If not, which object must be removed?
2. *Freedom:* is an object fixed? How many degrees of freedom does it have? Can an object move in a fixed direction?
3. *Planning:* can we get from one assembly configuration to another?
4. *Editing:* what happens if the shape of an object is modified, or a new object is added? Do the assembly's motion properties change?

To determine if objects can be assembled, we test if S is solvable. A solvable S is a non-empty configuration space which contains at least one point corresponding to a feasible object configuration. If S is unsolvable, the constraints causing its unsolvability define the objects that interpenetrate. Removing one of these objects deletes the problematic constraints. To determine an objects' degrees of freedom, we find the values of its motion parameters. Each constant parameter removes a degree of freedom. When they are all constant, the object is fixed. To find the motion range, we project S on the space of the variable motion parameters. Equality relations of the type $\alpha x + \beta y = \gamma$ where x and y are the motion parameters of an object define an axis of motion. To determine if we can go from one configuration to another, we test if the corresponding configuration space points belong to the same connected region. Finally, to determine what happens as a consequence of a structural change, we must replace the motion constraints of the original object with the motion constraints of the new object. To test for assembly equivalence, we must test if their constraints are equivalent.

The set S generally contains many redundant inequalities and implicit equalities. Removing them and putting S in a canonical form directly answers many of the above questions. For example, the region of the puzzle's configuration space containing the configuration in Figure 1 is defined by the set S of 45 inequalities:

$$\bigcap_{i\neq j}\{y_i \leq 1,\ x_i - y_i \geq 0,\ x_i + y_i \geq 0,\ x_i - y_i \leq 1,$$
$$v_i \geq -2,\ u_i + v_i \leq 1,\ u_i - v_i \geq 2,\ u_i + v_i \geq 0,\ y_i - v_j \geq 1\}$$
$$\cap\ \{y_1 - y_2 > -1,\ \ y_1 - y_2 < 1,\ \ (x_1 - x_2) - (y_1 - y_2) \leq -1,$$
$$y_1 - y_3 \geq 1,$$
$$y_2 - y_3 > -1,\ \ y_2 - y_3 < 1,\ \ (x_2 - x_3) - (y_2 - y_3) \geq 1,$$
$$v_1 - v_2 > -1,\ \ v_1 - v_2 < 1,\ \ (u_1 - u_2) + (v_1 - v_2) \leq -1,$$
$$v_1 - v_3 \geq 1,$$
$$v_2 - v_3 \geq 1\}$$

for $i, j = 1, 2, 3$. The canonical representation S' is much more compact and informative:

$$\{x_1 = 1,\ \ y_1 = 1,\ \ x_3 = 0,\ \ y_3 = 0,$$
$$u_1 = 1,\ \ v_1 = -1,\ \ u_2 = 2,\ \ v_2 = -1,$$
$$x_2 \leq 2,\ \ y_2 \geq 0,\ \ x_2 - y_2 = 1,$$
$$u_3 \geq 2,\ \ u_3 \leq 3,\ \ v_3 = -2\}$$

These 10 equalities and 6 inequalities provide direct answers to some of the above queries. First, S is solvable and thus contains feasible object configurations. All blocks except R_2 and B_3 are fixed. B_3 has a single degree of freedom, whereas R_2 moves along the axis defined by $x_2 - y_2 = 1$. Further, since there is no functional relationship between the parameters of R_2 and B_3, their motions are independent. The other configuration space regions are similar and can be constructed incrementally [JS]. By examining them, we conclude that only one red and one blue object can move independently at a time, that the red and blue blocks do not mix, and that the clockwise order of the blocks cannot be reversed.

Editing queries require updating the motion constraints. Suppose we remove block R_3 and want to know if this affects the motion range of B_2. We delete all the motion constraints related to R_3 from S, and project the result onto the u_2-v_2 plane. The resulting projection is:

$$\{u_2 \geq 1.5,\ \ u_2 \leq 2,\ \ u_2 = 1 - v_2\}$$

that is, B_2 is no longer fixed but can slide into the upper part of the puzzle.

The following sections show how the various operations discussed here naturally translate into basic operations of the proposed constraint based system and the importance of a suitable canonical form for the constraints.

3 Parametric Queries

Given a set S of constraints as a conjunction of linear equalities, inequalities and negative constraints (disjunctions of inequations), we consider the following queries:

1. Is S solvable?
2. If S is not solvable, what are the causes of unsolvability?
3. Does S contain any redundancy or implicit equalities?
4. Is S equivalent to another given set S'?
5. Does S imply $x = 2$?
6. Does there exist α such that S implies $x = \alpha$?
7. Does there exist $\alpha, \beta, \ldots, \gamma$ such that S implies $\alpha x + \beta y \ldots = \gamma$.
8. Does there exist $\alpha, \beta, \ldots, \gamma$ such that S implies $\alpha x + \beta y \ldots \leq \gamma$ and $\alpha = 2\beta - 1$?

The first query is a typical problem of Linear Programming as it corresponds to the first phase of the simplex. The second query is characteristic of constraints manipulating system where the constraints in store can be modified to restore solvability using feedback information provided by the solver. Query 3 deals with the simplification of the constraints representation. Redundancy is a major factor of complexity in constraints processing. The removal of redundancy and of implicit equalities are key steps in building a suitable canonical representation for the constraints. Query 4 addresses the problem of constraint representation. Queries 5 and 6 are classic Constraint Satisfaction Problems (CSP) which look for variables with grounded value. Query 7 is a generalization of CSP to linear relations: variables are bound to satisfy given linear relations. Finally, the last query generalizes the above with an inequality relation.

A priori, there does not seem to be any real connections between, for instance, testing for solvability and finding implicit equalities or finding whether a given relation is implied by the constraints in store. It is, however, possible to express these various problems within a general framework whose foundation is the concept of *parametric query*.

Definition 1 *A parametric query Q is of the form*

$$\exists \alpha, \beta, \gamma, \ldots, \forall x, y, \ldots : S \Rightarrow \alpha x + \beta y + \ldots \leq \gamma \wedge R(\alpha, \beta, \ldots, \gamma)?$$

where S is the set of constraints in store and R is a set of linear relations on the parameters $\alpha, \beta, \ldots, \gamma$.

A parametric query asks under what conditions on $\alpha, \beta, \ldots, \gamma$, the constraint in Q is implied by the constraints in store. Specific queries can be formulated in this framework by varying the parameters. For instance,

- *Is x bound to a specific value a?*
  $\exists \alpha, \beta, \ldots, \gamma, \forall x, y, \ldots, S \Rightarrow \alpha x + \beta y + \ldots = \gamma$ with $\alpha = 1, \beta = 0, \delta = 0, \ldots, \gamma = a$.

- *Is x ground?*
  Same as above but with γ unconstrained.

- *Does S imply $2x + 3y \leq 0$?*
  All parameters set to 0 except $\alpha = 2$ and $\beta = 3$.

- *What are the constraints implied by the projection of S on the $\{x,y\}$-plane?*
  All parameters except α, β, and γ are set to 0 and there is no relation R.

The test for solvability and the classic optimization problem can also be expressed in this way:

- *Is S solvable?*
  All parameters except γ are set to 0 and there is no relation R. By Fourier's theorem [F] S will be solvable iff the answer does not allow γ to be negative.

- *What is the maximum of $x + y$?*
  With the objective function $f = x + y$ we set $\alpha = 1$ and $\beta = 1$. All other parameters are set to 0 except γ. The answer will give a lower bound for γ which corresponds to the maximum of f. That is $min(\gamma) = max(f)$ which is essentially the duality theorem of Linear Programming.

Parametric queries are analogous to Logic Programming queries which ask if there exists an assignment to the variables in the query so that the query becomes a logical consequence of the program clauses and generalize CSP's which are restricted to constraints of the type $x = a$.

The method to get answers for parametric queries is derived from the following result

Theorem 1 (The Subsumption Theorem [A]) *A constraint C is implied by a set of constraints S iff C is a quasi-linear combination of constraints in S.*

A *quasi-linear* combination of constraints is a positive linear combination with the addition of a positive constant on the righ-hand side. For instance, let S be the set

$$\{2x + 3y - z \leq 1,\ x - y + 2z \leq 2,\ x - y + z \leq 0\}$$

and Q be the query

$$\exists \alpha, \beta, \forall x, y, S \Rightarrow \alpha x + \beta y \leq 1?$$

The following relations express that the constraint in Q is a quasi-linear combination of the constraints in S.

$$\begin{aligned}
&2\lambda_1 + \lambda_2 + \lambda_3 = \alpha\\
&3\lambda_1 - \lambda_2 - \lambda_3 = \beta\\
&-\lambda_1 + 2\lambda_2 + \lambda_3 = 0\\
&\lambda_1 + 2\lambda_2 + q = 1\\
&\lambda_1 \geq 0, \lambda_2 \geq 0, \lambda_3 \geq 0, q \geq 0
\end{aligned}$$

where the λ_i's are the multipliers of the constraints in S. Once the solvability of this system is established, the answer to Q is the set of relations

$$\{2\alpha - 3\beta \leq 0,\ -\alpha = +\beta \leq 0,\ -3\alpha + 7\beta \leq 5\}$$

on the parameters α, β obtained by eliminating the λ's and q via Fourier's algorithm.

In section 6, we present a more efficient method to answer parametric queries based on this result and a generalization of classic Linear Programming techniques. In [HLL] one will find further applications of projection in Symbolic Computation such as constructing the convex hull of a given set of points, computing the image of a polyhedral set by a linear function, etc.

4 Canonical constraint representation

An appropriate constraint representation is a key factor for a practical system. Given an arbitrary set of constraints, there exists an infinite number of equivalent representations. Some of these representations can be very different, as illustrated by the following example.

$$(S_1): \begin{cases} x - 3y - z \leq 1 \\ x - 2y + z \leq 1 \\ 2x - y + z - u \geq 0 \\ -2y - 2z + u \geq 1 \\ -x + 3y + u \geq 1 \\ 2y - z \geq 1 \\ x + u \neq 0 \\ y \neq 2 \end{cases} \qquad (S_1'): \begin{cases} x = 0 \\ y = -\frac{2}{5} \\ z = \frac{1}{5} \\ u = \frac{3}{5} \end{cases}$$

S_1 and S_1' are equivalent but it is not obvious that S_1 represents a point. This can lead to irrelevant interaction and to unnecessary computation. Answering a query requires processing the inequalities in S_1, whereas this is a straightforward verification in S_1'. Clearly, S_1' is better. However, the situation is not always that clear cut. For instance consider:

$$(S_2): \begin{cases} x + z \leq u \\ x + z \leq 10 \\ u \leq z \\ y \leq z + u \\ z \leq x + u \\ 0 \leq y \\ u \neq 0 \end{cases} \qquad (S_2'): \begin{cases} x = 0 \\ z = u \\ y \leq 10 \\ y - 2u \leq 0 \\ -y \leq 0 \\ y \neq 0 \vee u \neq 0 \end{cases}$$

Here also, S_2 and S_2' are equivalent but making a choice is not obvious. S_2' contains equalities and the inequalities are simpler than in S_2 but it also contains a disjunction of inequations whereas S_2 has only one inequation and no disjunction.

Different representations may be more efficient for comparison between sets, for solvability, for efficiency of execution and for incremental updates. Examples in section 2 have shown how many queries are answered automatically when the constraints are put into an appropriate canonical form. What we need is a representation that optimizes both the interaction and the computation. From the interaction side, we want a representation that fits the semantics of the object it describes. For processing, apart from the obvious problem of redundancy, the other major issue is implicit equalities. As the bulk of the computation is the processing of inequalities, it is essential to use equations, including implicit equalities, to simplify the constraints and to process remaining inequalities only when necessary. These considerations lead to the definition of a canonical form [LMc89a] characterized by:

- Equations in solved form, representing the affine hull,
- Inequalities representing a full-dimensional polyhedral set and free of redundancy
- Disjunctions of inequations in solved form

Important properties of this canonical form are:

- Unicity
- Separability into equations, inequalites and inequations

Unicity provides a simple syntactic equivalence test as two sets are equivalent if and only if they have the same canonical form. Separability is a direct consequence of the following result.

Theorem 2 (Constraint Propagation Theorem) *A set S of constraints in canonical form is partioned into a set of equations E, a set of inequalities I and a set of precise[2] inequations N such that:*

1. $S \models ax + by + \ldots = c$ *iff* $E \models ax + by + \ldots = c$
2. $S \models ax + by + \ldots \leq c$ *iff* $I \models ax + by + \ldots \leq c$
3. $S \models ax + by + \ldots \neq c$ *iff* $N \models ax + by + \ldots \neq c$

This means that if a query contains only equalities, it is sufficient to look at the equality part of the canonical form and the same is true for inequalities and for inequations. The case of inequations is more complex as negative constraints introduce disjunctions. A result on the independence of negative constraints provides a way to handle this problem, see [LMc89b]. A full treatment is to be found in [LMc89a].

The process of transforming efficiently an arbitrary set of constraints into its equivalent canonical form is complex. The main problem is the elimination of redundancy and the detection of implicit equalities. A naive method to test for redundancy requires running a linear program for each constraint. However, it is possible to classify redundancy according to their complexity

[2] A negative constraint is *precise* if it is not implied by the other constraints and if it is expressed in terms of its smallest possible dimension, see [LMc88].

so that simple redundancy can be eliminated in a straitghforward way. For instance, syntactic redundancy such as

$$\{x + y \leq 2,\ 2x + 2y \leq 8\}$$

or

$$\{x - y + 2z \leq 0,\ 2x - 2y + 4z \leq 5\}$$

require only a simple syntactic check. More complex types can be transformed into simpler ones. For instance, in

$$\{-x = y - z \leq 0,\ x - y + 2z \leq 0,\ -x + y - 3z \leq 0,\ x - y \leq 1\}$$

the last constraint is hull redundant, that is, its corresponding hyperplane is parallel to the affine hull of the polyhedral set. The detection of hull redundancy requires a linear program. However, by using the affine hull which is $\{x = y,\ z = 0\}$, the redundancy becomes the tautology $0 \leq 1$ which is straightforward to remove. This problem is addressed more thoroughly in [LHM]. Also one should note that various properties of the canonical form proposed for linear constraints also hold for other constraints in term algebra, geometry, logic and other domains. An axiomatization of this phenomenon is to be found in [LMc90].

5 Updates with feedback

Adding and deleting constraints, apart from the obvious problem of incrementality, raises several key issues about the management of the constraints in store. The first one is what to do in case of unsolvability. In an interactive setting, unsolvability does not always mean the end of the interaction. On the contrary, further action is usually required to restore solvability. When the last added constraint introduces an inconsistency, simply removing this constraint, although an obvious solution, may not be acceptable from an application point of view. As one cannot work with an unsolvable set, other constraints must then be removed or modified. Performing these changes as efficiently as possible requires feedback knowledge on the causes of unsolvability. A similar situation arises when implicit equalities or redundant inequalities are introduced.

The second major issue concerns the deletion of constraints. Removing a constraint cannot introduce unsolvability, but it can modify the semantic integrity of the constraints in store. Such a problem arises when the removed constraint is part of an implicit equality or a cause of redundancy. For instance, we consider the set

$$\{-x - y \leq 0,\ -x + v \leq 0,\ -x + z - u \leq 0,\ x + z - u \leq 0,\ 2x + y - v \leq 0,\ -z + u \leq 0\}$$

where all the constraints are implicit equalities and which reduce to

$$\{x = 0,\ y = 0,\ z - u = 0,\ v = 0\}.$$

If a constraint is removed from the initial set, the status of some, but not all, constraints changes. For instance, removing $-x - y \leq 0$ leads to the new set

$$\{x = 0,\ y - u = 0,\ v \leq 0,\ y - v \leq 0\}.$$

The original constraints $-x + v \leq 0$ and $2x + y - v \leq 0$ are no longer implicit equalities, they are only simplified by the other equalities. We see later in this section how to solve this problem algorithmically.

Another problem arises with equations. Assume that the above set also contains the equation $y = x + w$. Because of the presence of the implicit equalities, w is bound to 0. When the constraint $-x - y \leq 0$ is removed, w is no longer bound to 0 but to y. Here again, specific information is necessary in order to carry out meaningful modifications. To perform these changes correctly and efficiently, the system must keep a log of the status of the constraints involved including information on the group of implicit equalties this constraint belongs to.

Feedback on both the causes of unsolvability and of implicit equalities can be obtained for free as a side-effect of the test for solvability with Fourier's algorithm. To test for solvability, Fourier's algorithm generates linear combinations of constraints that eliminate all the variables. Unsolvability is detected when a combination gives a contradiction. For instance, with

$$\begin{array}{ll} (C_1) & x - y \leq 0 \\ (C_2) & y - u \leq 0 \\ (C_3) & z - u \leq 0 \\ (C_4) & v - u \leq 0 \\ (C_5) & x - v \leq 0 \\ (C_6) & -x + v \leq -1 \end{array}$$

the existence of the combination

$$C_4 + C_5 + C_6 = 0 \leq -1$$

proves that the set is unsolvable. This contradiction can be eliminated by removing either C_4, C_5 or C_6. This gives some flexibility to restore a solvable set during interaction. Without this feedback information, we could either remove the last constraint introduced (the obvious cause of the unsolvability) or test each constraint individually. Removing the last constraint may be unacceptable from an application point of view, whereas testing constraints individually is in most cases too costly.

The same technique applies to implicit equalities using the result that implicit equalities exist if and only if Fourier's algorithm generates the tautology $0 \leq 0$ [LM]. Like in the case of unsolvability, feedback information is readily available as the constraints which are part of the combination that gives the tautology are all implicit equalities. For instance, with

$$\begin{array}{ll} (C_1) & -2x + y \leq 0 \\ (C_2) & x + y + z \leq 2 \\ (C_3) & x + 2y \leq 1 \\ (C_4) & -x + 3z - w \leq 0 \\ (C_5) & 3x - 4y \leq -1 \end{array}$$

the combination

$$2C_1 + C_3 + C_5 = 0 \leq 0$$

shows that $-2x + y \leq 0$, $x + 2y \leq 1$, and $3x - 4y \leq -1$ are implicit equalities. Once a group of implicit equalities are identified, the set of constraints can be simplified. Here the implicit equalities reduce to

$$\{x = \frac{1}{5},\ y = \frac{2}{5}\}$$

and the remaining inequalities become

$$\{z \leq \frac{7}{5},\ 3z - w \leq \frac{1}{5}\}.$$

As we see Fourier's algorithm not only tells us which inequalities are implicit equalities, but we are provided also with a grouping which is useful for updating. If an inequality in a group is removed, the remaining inequalities in that group are no longer implicit equalities while the implicit equalities outside that group are not affected. A more practical method than Fourier's algorithm will be found in section 6.

The canonical form can also facilitate the updating. Adding new constraints may result in a much simpler canonical form instead of increasing the size and complexity of the constraints in store. For instance, adding $x_4 + x_2 \leq 30$ to the set

$$\{x = 0,\ y = u,\ u \leq 10,\ y - 2u \leq 0,\ -x \leq 0,\ y \neq 0 \lor u \neq 0\}$$

in canonical form results in the new canonical form

$$\{x = 0,\ y = 20,\ z = 10,\ u = 10\}$$

6 Updates with feedback

Let $S = \{Ax \leq b\}$ be the set of constraints in store. We want to find a finite representation of the answers to the parametric query:

$$\exists \alpha_1, \ldots, \alpha_n, \beta \, \forall x_1, \ldots, x_n : S \Rightarrow (\alpha_1 x_1 + \ldots + \alpha_n x_n \leq \beta) \wedge R(\alpha_1, \ldots, \alpha_n, \beta) \, ?$$

where $R(\alpha_1, \ldots, \alpha_n, \beta)$ represents a set of linear relations on the parameters. The apparent technical difficulty of computing the answers is due to the non-linearity of the query. However, using the Subsumption theorem mentioned earlier as a basis and variable elimination as the underlying operation, one can derive the set of answer. Namely, if

$$\alpha_1 x_1 + \ldots + \alpha_n x_n \leq \beta.$$

is a quasi-linear combination of the constraints in S, then by eliminating the μ_i's and q from the system

$$\{\alpha_j = A_{.j}{}^T \mu, \; \beta = b^T \mu + q, \; \mu_i \geq 0, \; q \geq 0, \; i = 1, \ldots, m, \; j = 1, \ldots, n\}$$

(where $A_{.j}$ denotes the j column of the $m \times n$ matrix A, μ_i's are the non-negative multipliers to the constraints of S) we obtain a set of relations between the α_j's and the β which forms the answer to the query.

For example, let S be the set

$$\{x + 2y + 2z \leq 1, \; -2x - 2y + z \leq 2, \; x + 2y - 2z \leq 3, \; -x - y - z \leq 4, \; 2x + y + z \leq 5\}$$

and Q be the query

$$\exists \alpha, \beta \forall x, y, z : S \Rightarrow \alpha x + \beta y \leq 1?$$

We first verify whether Q is a quasi-linear combination of the constraints in S by solving the system

$$(I) \begin{cases} \mu_1 - 2\mu_2 + \mu_3 - \mu_4 + 2\mu 5 = \alpha \\ 2\mu_1 - 2\mu_2 + 2\mu_3 - \mu_4 + \mu 5 = \beta \\ 2\mu_1 + \mu_2 - 2\mu_3 - \mu_4 + \mu 5 = 0 \\ \mu_1 + 2\mu_2 + 3\mu_3 + 4\mu_4 + 5\mu 5 + q = 1 \\ q \geq 0 \\ \mu_i \geq 0 \;\; \text{where } i = 1, \ldots, 5 \end{cases}$$

If (I) is solvable, then by eliminating the μ_i's and q we have

$$B = \{-3\alpha + \beta \leq 1, \; 9\alpha - 8\beta \leq 1, \; 9\alpha - 11\beta \leq 1, \; -18\alpha + 13\beta \leq 4, \; 6\alpha - \beta \leq 2\}$$

as the answer to the parametric query Q. Otherwise, Q is not implied by S.

The key operation to answer linear parametric queries is variable elimination. Eliminating variables in equalities is straightforward. However, eliminating variables in inequalities is more complex as the process tends to introduce substantial redundancy. A classic technique for eliminating variables in inequalities is Fourier's elimination procedure. Although there are various variants for improving this procedure with additional heuristics, none of them can avoid the (sometimes doubly) exponential growth of intermediate results. An important factor in this complexity is the fact that variables are eliminated one by one. This bottleneck can be bypassed using the so called *quasi-dual* formulation proposed in [L].

6.1 Quasi-dual formulation

Let V be the set of variables to be eliminated from $S = \{Ax \leq b\}$. The quasi-dual formulation for this problem is given as follows:

$$\Delta : \begin{cases} A_{.j}{}^T \lambda = 0 \quad \forall j : x_j \in V \\ \Sigma \lambda_i = 1 \\ \lambda_i \geq 0 \end{cases}$$
$$\Phi : \begin{cases} \alpha_k = A_{.k}{}^T \lambda \quad \forall k : x_k \notin V \\ \beta = b^T \lambda \end{cases}$$

This formulation is in fact a generalized linear program where Δ is the polyhedron associated with the constraints and Φ is the objective function which maps $\Re^m$ to $\Re^{n-e+1}$, where e is the number of variables to be eliminated. The solutions to finding $extr(\Phi(\Delta))$, where *extr()* denotes the set of extreme points, determine a finite set of constraints which defines the projection of the polyhedron represented by S. Since Δ is bounded, $\Phi(\Delta)$ has a finite number of extreme points. In case when Δ is empty, that is if the system representing Δ is unsolvable, the projection is the whole space. This alternative to Fourier's elimination procedure is called the *extreme point method.*

One way to compute $extr(\Phi(\Delta))$ is to first enumerate the extreme points of Δ and then map them by Φ. However, not all extreme points of Δ map into an extreme point of $\Phi(\Delta)$, some correspond to redundant constraints in the projection. The implementation of the extreme point method and related practical issues are discussed in [HL].

In the last example, after eliminating μ_1, μ_2, μ_3 and μ_4 using the equalities we are left with the following system of inequalities

$$(II)\begin{cases} 12\mu_5 + q - 3\alpha + \beta \leq 1 \\ -36\mu_5 - 2q + 18\alpha - 11\beta \leq -2 \\ -18\mu_5 - q + 9\alpha - 7\beta \leq -1 \\ 45\mu_5 + 4q - 18\alpha + 13\beta \leq 4 \\ \mu_5 \geq 0 \\ q \geq 0 \end{cases}$$

To generate the relations between α and β we need to eliminate μ_5 and q from (II). Of course in this small problem Fourier's procedure is the best choice. But our goal here is to illustrate the use of the quasi-dual formulation and the extreme point method. Hence, the quasi-dual formulation for (II) is

$$\Delta : \begin{cases} 12\lambda_1 - 36\lambda_2 - 18\lambda_3 + 45\lambda_4 - \lambda_5 = 0 \\ \lambda_1 - 2\lambda_2 - \lambda_3 + 4\lambda_4 - \lambda_6 = 0 \\ \lambda_1 + \lambda_2 + \lambda_3 + \lambda_4 + \lambda_5 + \lambda_6 = 1 \\ \lambda_i \geq 0 \text{ where } i = 1, ..., 6 \end{cases}$$

$$\Phi : \begin{cases} \gamma_1 = -3\lambda_1 + 18\lambda_2 + 9\lambda_3 - 18\lambda_4 \\ \gamma_2 = \lambda_1 - 11\lambda_2 - 7\lambda_3 + 13\lambda_4 \\ \delta = \lambda_1 - 2\lambda_2 - \lambda_3 + 4\lambda_4 \end{cases}$$

In this example Δ has six extreme points

$$\lambda_A = \{\tfrac{1}{14}, 0, 0, 0, \tfrac{6}{7}, \tfrac{1}{14}\}, \ \lambda_B = \{\tfrac{3}{5}, \tfrac{1}{5}, 0, 0, 0, \tfrac{1}{5}\}, \ \lambda_C = \{\tfrac{1}{2}, 0, \tfrac{1}{3}, 0, 0, \tfrac{1}{6}\},$$
$$\lambda_D = \{0, 0, 0, \tfrac{1}{50}, \tfrac{9}{10}, \tfrac{2}{25}\}, \ \lambda_E = \{0, \tfrac{1}{3}, 0, \tfrac{4}{15}, 0, \tfrac{2}{5}\}, \ \lambda_F = \{0, 0, \tfrac{1}{2}, \tfrac{1}{5}, 0, \tfrac{3}{10}\}$$

which give

$$\Phi(\lambda_A) = \{\gamma_1 = -\tfrac{3}{14}, \ \gamma_2 = \tfrac{1}{14}, \ \delta = \tfrac{1}{14}\}, \quad \Phi(\lambda_B) = \{\gamma_1 = \tfrac{9}{5}, \ \gamma_2 = -\tfrac{8}{5}, \ \delta = \tfrac{1}{5}\},$$
$$\Phi(\lambda_C) = \{\gamma_1 = \tfrac{9}{6}, \ \gamma_2 = -\tfrac{11}{6}, \ \delta = \tfrac{1}{6}\}, \quad \Phi(\lambda_D) = \{\gamma_1 = -\tfrac{18}{50}, \ \gamma_2 = \tfrac{13}{50}, \ \delta = \tfrac{4}{50}\},$$
$$\Phi(\lambda_E) = \{\gamma_1 = \tfrac{54}{45}, \ \gamma_2 = -\tfrac{9}{45}, \ \delta = \tfrac{18}{45}\}, \quad \Phi(\lambda_F) = \{\gamma_1 = \tfrac{9}{10}, \ \gamma_2 = -\tfrac{9}{10}, \ \delta = \tfrac{3}{10}\}$$

respectively. All but $\Phi(\lambda_F)$ correspond to the extreme points of $\Phi(\Delta)$ which give the set B. For example, the coordinates of $\Phi(\lambda_A)$ corresponds to the constraint $-\frac{3}{14}\alpha + \frac{1}{14}\beta \leq \frac{1}{14}$ which is equivalent to $-3\alpha + \beta \leq 1$.

6.2 Solvability, implicit equalities and unsolvability

Systematic applications of Fourier's elimination procedure to all variables of a set $S = \{Ax \leq b\}$ gives Fourier's algorithm for solving S. If S is unsolvable, from Fourier's algorithm one can trace all subsets of constraints in S that cause the contradiction. More recently, [LM] proved that Fourier's algorithm also provides pointers to those constraints in S that are indeed the implicit equalities if there are any. Here we show how to utilize the quasi-dual formulation to achieve these discriminating characteristics of Fourier's algorithm within the same framework, but more efficiently. Essentially the quasi-dual formulation is an implementation of Fourier's algorithm where all variables are eliminated simultaneously rather than step by step.

The quasi-dual formulation for eliminating all variables from S is

$$\Delta : \begin{cases} A^T\lambda = 0 \\ \Sigma\lambda_i = 1 \\ \lambda_i \geq 0 \end{cases}$$

$$\Phi : \quad \beta = b^T\lambda$$

In this particular case, Φ maps $\Re^m$ to $\Re$ which is related to the linear program D:

$$\begin{aligned} \text{minimize} \quad & b^T\lambda \\ \text{subject to} \quad & A^T\lambda = 0 \\ & \Sigma\lambda_i = 1 \\ & \lambda_i \geq 0. \end{aligned}$$

S is solvable iff β cannot take strictly negative values. It is obvious that in general solving S in this manner is far more efficient than using Fourier's algorithm. Since D is a variant of the dual simplex in Linear Programming, it inherits nice properties from the standard dual simplex such as good incremental behavior, no need to introduce slack variables and no restriction to positive variables. More importantly as a side effect of the solvability test we obtain information about the algebraic properties of the constraints and about the geometric structure of the associated polyhedron. This information is essential for all the problems we have addressed in this paper. Some properties of D are summarized in the following theorem, others are to be found in [HLL].

Theorem 3

1. Δ unsolvable $\Rightarrow$ S solvable $\wedge$ $\nexists$ implicit equalites

   else:

2. $min(b^T\lambda) > 0$ $\Rightarrow$ S solvable $\wedge$ $\nexists$ implicit equalites

3. $min(b^T\lambda) = 0$ $\Rightarrow$ S solvable $\wedge$ $\exists$ implicit equalites

4. $\exists\lambda : b^T\lambda < 0$ $\Rightarrow$ S unsolvable

A main advantage of this method is that we know a priori if there exists any implicit equalities in S before searching for them. In case where $min(b^T\lambda) = 0$, the corresponding extreme point for this minimal value gives us a first minimal subset of implicit equalities in S. Therefore we can compute these equalities and use them to simplify the remaining inequalities. Once this is done, we set up another linear program D from the updated inequalities and apply the above theorem again. This process is repeated until the set of inequalities becomes full dimensional.

Another alternative to identify all the implicit equalities in S is to first augment the representation of Δ with the constraint $\Sigma b^T = 0$ to form the new polytope

$$\Delta' : \begin{cases} b^T\lambda = 0 \\ A^T\lambda = 0 \\ \Sigma\lambda_i = 1 \\ \lambda_i \geq 0 \end{cases}$$

Then by simply enumerating the extreme points of Δ' one will obtain all the indices of the constraints in S that are implicit equalities. Each extreme point associate with a group of implicit equalities for updating.

In the course of minimization, if $b^T\lambda$ becomes negative then we can stop the process immediately as we know that S is not solvable. Again, the corresponding extreme point that gives this negative value provides us a first minimal infeasible subset in S. To extract all the minimal infeasible subsets in S one also first augments the representation of Δ. For the sake of simplicity, the additional constraint is an weak inequality $b^T \leq 0$ rather than a strict one. Hence, the new polytope becomes

$$\Delta' : \begin{cases} b^T\lambda \leq 0 \\ A^T\lambda = 0 \\ \Sigma\lambda_i = 1 \\ \lambda_i \geq 0 \end{cases}$$

Each minimal infeasible subset of S is associated with an extreme point of Δ' which corresponds to a strictly negative value of $b^T\lambda$.

References

[A] S. Achmanov, *Programmation Linéaire*, Editions Mir, Moscou 1984.

[F] J.B.J. Fourier, reported in: Analyse des travaux de l'Académie Royale des Sciences, pendant l'année 1824, Partie Mathématique, *Histoire de l'Académie Royale des Sciences de l'Institut de*

France 7 (1827) xlvii-lv. (Partial English translation in: D.A. Kohler, Translation of a Report by Fourier on his work on Linear Inequalities, *Opsearch* 10(1973) 38-42.)

[HL] T. Huynh and J-L. Lassez, "Practical Issues on the Projection of Polyhedral Sets," IBM Research Report, T.J. Watson Research Center, 1990.

[HLL] T. Huynh, C. Lassez and J-L. Lassez, "Fourier Algorithm Revisited," *2nd International Conference on Algebraic and Logic Programming*, Springer-Verlag Lecture Notes in Computer Sciences, 1990.

[Ja] L. Joskowicz, "Reasoning about the Kinematics of Mechanical Devices," *International Journal of Artificial Intelligence in Engineering*, Vol 4 No. 1, 1989.

[Jb] L. Joskowicz, "Simplification and Abstraction of Kinematic Behaviors," *Proceedings of the 11th International Joint Conference on Artificial Intelligence*, Detroit, 1989.

[JS] L. Joskowicz and E. Sacks, "Incremental Kinematic Analysis of Machines," forthcoming, 1990.

[KKR] P. Kanellakis, G. Kuper and P. Revesz, "Constraint Query Languages," *PODS 90*, Nashville.

[L] J-L Lassez, "Parametric Queries, Linear Constraints and Variable Elimination," *DISCO 90*, Springer-Verlag Lecture Notes in Computer Sciences, 1990.

[LHM] J-L. Lassez, T. Huynh and K. McAloon, "Simplification and Elimination of Redundant Arithmetic Constraints," *Proceedings of NACLP 89*, MIT Press.

[LM] J-L. Lassez and M.J. Maher, "On Fourier's Algorithm for Linear Arithmetic Constraints," IBM Research Report, T.J. Watson Research Center, 1988.

[LMc88] J-L. Lassez and K. McAloon, "Applications of a Canonical Form for Generalized Linear Constraints," *Proceedings of the FGCS Conference*, Tokyo, December 1988, 703-710.

[LMc89a] J-L. Lassez and K. McAloon, "A Canonical Form for Generalized Linear Constraints," IBM Research Report, T.J. Watson Research Center, 1989.

[LMc89b] J-L. Lassez and K. McAloon, "Independence of Negative Constraints," *TAPSOFT 89*, Advanced Seminar on Foundations of Innovative Software Development, LNCS 351 Springer Verlag 89.

[LMc90] J-L Lassez, K. McAloon, "A Constraint Sequent Calculus," *LICS 90*. Philadelphia.

[LW] T. Lozano-Pérez, and M. Wesley, "An algorithm for Planning Collision-Free Paths among Polyhedral Obstacles," *Communications of the ACM*, Vol. 22, 1979.

[M] M. Maher, "A Logic Semantics for a class of Committed Choice Languages," *Proceedings of ICLP4*, MIT Press, 1987.

[S] V. Saraswat, "Concurrent Constraint Logic Programming," MIT Press, to appear.

Discriminant Circumscription

Li Yan Yuan   *Jia-Huai You*

Department of Computing Science
University of Alberta
Edmonton, Alberta, Canada, T6G 2H1

Abstract

We present a new circumscription method, called *discriminant circumscription*, for first order theories described by clauses whose orientations are of primary importance in their applications. These applications have been primarily dominated by deductive databases and logic programs. We show that discriminant circumscription is equivalent to the stable model semantics of deductive databases. This method is therefore strictly more powerful than those previously proposed by Przymusinski and by Lifschitz.

Key Words: *Logic Programming with Negation, Deductive Databases, Nonmonotonic Reasoning.*

1. Introduction

An oriented clause theory is a set of clauses whose body may contain negative literals and whose head is a disjunction of atoms. The intended meanings of these clauses are closely related to their implication orientations. Oriented clause theories find their applications in deductive databases and logic programs where different orientations of clauses often result in completely different semantics. Throughout this paper, we will refer to an oriented clause theory as a deductive database (DB).

A challenging problem in the field of deductive databases and logic programs has been a declarative semantics and a proof theory for an arbitrary set of such clauses.

One approach to the problem is to establish relationships between deductive database semantics and nonmonotonic formalisms such as predicate completion [1] and circumscription [10]. On the one hand, since predicate completion yields a first order formula and circumscription of clauses can be computed by resolution-like algorithms [16], proof theories for query-answering in DB's can be directly supported by the rich reservoir of first order theorem-proving tools. On the other hand, deductive database query-answering procedures, if developed, may serve as proof procedures for answering queries in those nonmonotonic formalisms.

The relationship between deductive database semantics and circumscription has been studied by Przymusinski and Lifschitz. Przymusinski showed the equivalence of the perfect model semantics with prioritized circumscription for stratified and locally stratified deductive databases [13, 14]. Lifschitz obtained a similar result for stratified logic programs by using pointwise circumscription [9].

A fundamental assumption in these works has been that the intended meaning of a deductive database depends on clause orientations, which can in fact be completely characterized by a priority relation for stratified DB's. Consider a DB consisting of a single clause $\neg a \rightarrow b$, for example. The intended meaning of the DB is represented by model $\{b\}$, since $\neg a \rightarrow b$ is no longer considered equivalent to $a \vee b$, and the orientation of the implication determines that a should be minimized before b.

It was soon discovered that deductive databases lying outside of the locally stratified make practical sense and deductive database semantics should be extended to allow a wider class of programs [6]. The two dominant approaches so far have been a two-valued formalization—the stable model semantics [6], and a three-valued formalization—the well-founded model semantics [18]. Przymusinski gave an elegant definition of three-valued circumscription and showed its relation with the well-founded semantics [15]. The relation between McCarthy's two-valued circumscription and the stable model semantics remains unknown. There is an urgent need, from the proof-theoretic point of view, for an investigation of the relationship, as there has been no formally defined procedural semantics for the stable model semantics. As a matter of fact, it seems doubtful whether such a relation can be established in some way at all, since once a DB goes beyond the locally stratified it appears there is no way one can capture the intended meaning of a DB determined by clause orientations.

To answer this question, this paper presents a new method of circumscription which is based on the idea of circumscribing over a *working program*. A working program is obtained from the given deductive database by syntactically distinguishing positive information and negative information embedded in a predicate (i.e., a relation). The central mechanism resembles that of predicate renaming, which has seen its applications in a number of places (see, for example, [5]). Surprisingly, this mechanism works nicely for DB's under an extended stable model semantics. By the fact that there exist query-answering algorithms for circumscriptive theories, such as *MILO–resolution* [16], our result provides a complete and formal proof-theoretic characterization of the stable model semantics.

In the next section we recall some basic definitions. Section 3 introduces the method of working program and its circumscription formula. In Section 4, we provide an extension of Gelfond and Lifschitz's stable model semantics for deductive databases. We show in Section 5 that the models of the circumscription formula of a deductive database correspond to the stable models of that database. Section 6 contains final remarks.

2. Preliminaries

A *deductive database (DB)* is a set of clauses of the form

$$L_1 \wedge \cdots \wedge L_n \rightarrow A_1 \vee \cdots \vee A_m$$

where $m \geq 1$, $n \geq 0$, A_i are atoms and L_i are literals. A *logic program* is a special case of DB with $m = 1$ for all clauses. The notions of *interpretation* and *model* are defined as usual.

We consider a first order language L. Let Π denote a first order theory consisting of a finite number of clauses. To capture the feature of common-sense reasoning that no objects should have a property unless it has to, McCarthy [10, 11] developed a nonmonotonic reasoning technique, called circumscription. Suppose $P = \{P_1, \cdots, P_n\}$ is a tuple of predicates to be minimized. The circumscription of P in Π is defined as:

$$CIRC(\Pi; P) \equiv \Pi(P) \wedge (\forall P')\,[(\Pi(P') \wedge P' \rightarrow P) \rightarrow P' \equiv P]$$

where $P' = \{P_1', \cdots, P_n'\}$ is a tuple of predicate variables similar to P, and $P' \rightarrow P$ is an abbreviation of "for every tuple of variables x and for every $i \leq n$, $P_i'(x) \rightarrow P_i(x)$."

Circumscription is based on the notion of minimal model. A model M of theory Π is *P-minimal* iff there is no model N, such that M and N differ only in how they interpret predicates from P, and the extension of every predicate in P from N is a subset of its extension in M. It has been shown by McCarthy and Lifschitz [8, 10] that for a first order theory Π and a formula F, $CIRC(\Pi; P) \models F$ iff $M \models F$ for every P-minimal model M of Π. When P is the set of all predicates, we simply use the term *minimal model.*

Throughout this paper, we consider only Herbrand models. Herbrand base will be denoted by H_L. An *instantiated* clause is a ground clause obtained by substituting terms from the Herbrand universe of the language. We call an atom *a positive literal* and an atom with the negation sign in front *a negative literal.*

Extensive studies have been carried out around so-called *stratified databases*. A database is *stratified* if the clauses therein can be partitioned into ordered sets of clauses such that if a negated atom appears in the body of a clause in a partition, then the definition of the atom (i.e., the clauses whose instances contain the atom in their heads) must appear in a previous partition, and if a positive atom appears in the body of a clause, then its definition appears either in the same partition or in a previous partition. Thus a stratification is actually a priority relation determined by clause orientations.

The definition of the stable model semantics [6] is based on an argument from autoepistemic logic that an intended model of a logic program should be a possible set of beliefs that a *rational* agent might hold. Let Π be a set of ground clauses. For any subset M of Herbrand base, let Π_M be the program obtained from Π by deleting (i) each rule that has a negative literal $\neg B$ in its body with $B \in M$; and (ii) all negative literals in the bodies of the remaining rules. Let M' be the least model of the modified program. If $M' = M$, then M is said to be a stable model of Π.

3. Discriminant Circumscription

We first discuss the difficulties of describing a non-stratified deductive database in terms of circumscription. We then provide a solution based on the idea of working program.

3.1 Priority Conflict Does Not Mean Equal

The coincidence of the perfect models of a DB with the models of prioritized circumscription can be explained by using a simple example.

Consider $\neg a \rightarrow b$ again. The perfect model of this program is $M = \{b\}$; this is the same as assigning the task of minimizing a a higher priority than that of minimizing b. This priority is determined by the clause orientation which again determines a stratification (unique in this example) of predicate symbols. Since this priority relation can be *completely* determined for stratified DB's, the priority of these minimization tasks corresponds precisely to the mechanism of prioritized circumscription (for locally stratified DB's, a complete determination has to be done over the entire Herbrand base; this fact leaves the established relationship in [14] to be of mainly theoretical interest). When this priority relation involves conflict, one possible solution is to make all involved parties "equal." In terms of stratification, this can be viewed as putting all the involved into the same stratum.

Example 3.1. Suppose Π is $\{\neg a \rightarrow b, \neg b \rightarrow a\}$. Then treating a and b as "equal"; i.e., minimizing them in parallel, denoted by $CIRC(\Pi; \{a, b\})$, works nicely, as models $M_1 = \{a\}$ and $M_1 = \{b\}$ of the circumscriptive expression indeed capture the intended meaning of an indefinite situation in which $a \vee b$ is a true sentence. □

However, the problem is not as straightforward as what the above example seems to suggest, because the correspondence between the suggested stratification and the order of minimization determined by clause orientations can be destroyed in the general case.

Example 3.2. Consider Π as consisting of

$$a$$
$$a \wedge \neg p \rightarrow q$$
$$b \wedge \neg q \rightarrow p$$

q has higher priority than p to be minimized by the second clause, but p should be minimized before q according to the third clause; hence a conflict results. Treating p and q as "equal" (i.e., putting them into the same stratum) can be expressed as $CIRC(\Pi; \{a,b\} > \{p,q\})$, where $\{a,b\} > \{p,q\}$ means a and b should be minimized in parallel first before p and q are minimized in parallel. This circumscription formula has two models: $M_1 = \{a, q\}$ and $M_2 = \{a, p\}$. M_2 is unwanted since the conclusion p is not supported by any clause. In other words, there is no way the conclusion can be justified by the orientation of the clauses. Note that M_2 is rejected both by the well-founded semantics and by the stable model semantics. □

The more careful reader may have noticed that the behavior we would like to capture is actually a dynamic one; whether M_2 in the above example is desired or unwanted depends upon whether b turns out to be true or false; desired if it is and unwanted otherwise.

3.2 Working Program

An interpretation of a predicate is a set of tuples. The difficulty of treating conflicting predicates "equal" stems from the fact that in circumscription such a relation is minimized as a complete unit. The idea of working program is to separate negative and positive information by a method of "renaming," so that the minimization process within a relation can be dealt with.

Definition 3.1. Let $\Pi(P)$ denote a DB where $P = \{P_1, \cdots, P_n\}$ is the set of all predicate symbols in Π. Let $N = \{N_{P_1}, \cdots, N_{P_n}\}$ be a set of *new* predicate symbols where each N_{P_i} has the same arity as that of P_i.

The working program of Π, denoted as $\Pi_\omega(N, P)$, is a deductive database obtained from Π by replacing each positive occurrence† $P_i(t_1, \cdots, t_k)$ in any clause in Π with $N_{P_i}(t_1, \cdots, t_k)$.

The predicates in N are called *internal* and the predicates in Π are called *external*. □

Example 3.3 The working program of Example 4.2 is

$$N_a$$
$$N_a \wedge \neg p \rightarrow N_q$$
$$N_b \wedge \neg q \rightarrow N_p \quad \square$$

† By a positive occurrence, we mean either a positive literal in the body, or an atom in the head.

From the programming environment point of view, the mechanism of the working program corresponds to division of knowledge in a knowledge base into *internal* part and *external* part. The existence of internal data items which are opaque to the user of the system is often for the convenience of implementation only. In the preceding example, the new predicates in N, i.e., $\{N_a, N_a, N_p, N_q\}$, represent internal data items while only the predicates in P, i.e., $\{a, b, p, q\}$ are of interest to the user.

A note on the notation: the working program $\Pi_\omega(N, P)$ itself may not contain all predicate symbols in N and P. This discrepancy will not impose any technical problem since the circumscription formula to be given shortly involves all predicates from N and P.

Definition 3.2. Let $\Pi(P)$ be a DB. Suppose $T(P, N)$ is a logical formula containing the working program of Π, P is the set of external predicates and N is the set of internal predicates. Let also M be a set of ground atoms whose predicates are from P. Then, M is said to be an *external* model of the formula $T(P, N)$ if there exists a set M_N of ground atoms whose predicates are from N such that $M \cup M_N$ is a model of $T(P, N)$. □

From the logic point of view, one can always emphasize the satisfiability of a subset of predicates in a formula. The proof of the following lemma is straightforward.

Lemma 3.1. Let $\Pi(P)$ be a DB. Let $T(N, P)$ be a logical formula containing the working program of Π, where P is the set of external predicates and N is the set of internal predicates. Let also ξ be a sentence whose predicates occur in the formula but are not from N. Then, $T(N, P) \models \xi$ iff ξ is true in every external model of $T(N, P)$. □

Definition 3.3. Let $\Pi(P)$ be a DB and $\Pi_\omega(N, P)$ its working program, where $P = \{P_1, \cdots, P_n\}$ and $N = \{N_{P_1}, \cdots, N_{P_n}\}$. Define *discriminant circumscription* of $\Pi(P)$ as $CIRC(\Pi_\omega(N, P); N) \wedge (N \equiv P)$, where $N \equiv P$ is an abbreviation of "for every tuple of variables x and for every $i \le n$, $N_{P_i}(x) \equiv P_i(x)$. □

Example 3.4. Consider a DB of a single clause: $\neg b \rightarrow a$. Its working program is $\neg b \rightarrow N_a$. There are total 16 ways to assign truth values to the entire set of the predicates $\{N_a, N_b, a, b\}$. Let us denote the truth value *false* by 0 and *true* by 1, and use a sequence of 0's and 1's to represent an assignment corresponding to $\{N_a, N_b, a, b\}$. For example, 0100 corresponds to N_a being false, N_b being true, a being false, and b being false. It is clear that only those that have 1 for N_a or 1 for b can be models of $\neg b \rightarrow N_a$. Then, there are only four models of $CIRC(\Pi_\omega(N, P); N)$, where $P = \{a, b\}$ and $N = \{N_a, N_b\}$: 1000, 0001, 0011, 1010; of which only 1010 satisfies $N \equiv P$. The model 1010 corresponds to the stable model $\{a\}$ of the original program $\neg b \rightarrow a$.

The difference between $CIRC(\Pi; P)$ and $CIRC(\Pi_\omega(N, P); N)$ (under the restriction that $N \equiv P$) can be illustrated by the same example above. Because of the requirement that $N \equiv P$, we only list below those combinations of assignments which can possibly satisfy $CIRC(\Pi_\omega(N, P); N)$ and $N \equiv P$ simultaneously:

a	b	N_a	N_b
0	0	0	0
0	1	0	1
1	1	1	1
1	0	1	0

The first row is not even a model of $\neg b \rightarrow N_a$. The second row is a model (corresponding to a P-minimal model of the original program $\neg b \rightarrow a$). It is eliminated by the fact there is another model of $\neg b \rightarrow N_a$, i.e., 0100, which is N-smaller than 0101. The model 0100 itself is eliminated by the requirement $N \equiv P$. The third row is similarly eliminated. This leaves the fourth row as the only model corresponding to the stable model of $\neg b \rightarrow a$. □

Example 3.5. Consider the working program in Example 3.3. Recall from Example 3.2 that the original DB has $M_1 = \{a, q\}$ and $M_2 = \{a, p\}$ as its minimal models where $M_2 = \{a, p\}$ is unwanted because p is not justifiable. In the following table, the first row of truth value corresponds to M_1 and the reason that it remains to be a model of the discriminant circumscription formula is because it satisfies the requirement $N \equiv P$ in the formula. The second row, which corresponds to M_2, fails to remain to be a model because $N \equiv P$ is not satisfied.

N_a	N_b	N_p	N_q	a	b	p	q
1	0	0	1	1	0	0	1
1	0	0	0	1	0	1	0

By examing all possible assignments of truth values that satisfy the discriminant circumscription formula, it is not difficult to show that the first row is the only model of the formula. Its projected external model is then the desired model of the original DB. It can be verified that this model is also stable.

□

It follows from Definition 3.3 that

Proposition 3.2. Any external model of $CIRC(\Pi_\omega(N, P); N) \wedge (N \equiv P)$ is a minimal model of Π. The reverse, however, is not always true. □

Discriminant circumscription may not always possess a model. For example, consider $\neg a \rightarrow a$, which fails to possess a stable model, and its working program $\neg a \rightarrow N_a$. The N-minimal models of $\neg a \rightarrow N_a$ are: $\{a\}$ and $\{N_a\}$, both of which are eliminated by the requirement $a \equiv N_a$.

4. A Stable Model Semantics for Deductive Databases

In this section we extend the stable model semantics to handle deductive databases.

Definition 4.1. Let Π be a DB and M be a model of Π. An atom Q in M is said to be justifiable iff

(i) there exists an instantiated clause from Π

$$\neg B_1 \wedge \cdots \wedge \neg B_m \rightarrow C_1 \vee \cdots \vee C_n$$

where $m \geq 0$ and $n \geq 1$, such that $\neg B_1 \wedge \cdots \wedge \neg B_m$ is true in M, and there exists i, $1 \leq i \leq n$, such that $C_i = Q$ and for all $C_j \neq Q$, C_j is false in M; or inductively

(ii) there exists an instantiated clause from Π

$$A_1 \wedge \cdots \wedge A_k \wedge \neg B_1 \wedge \cdots \wedge \neg B_m \rightarrow C_1 \vee \cdots \vee C_n$$

such that all A_i are justifiable, $A_1 \wedge \cdots \wedge A_k \wedge \neg B_1 \wedge \cdots \wedge \neg B_m$ is true in M, and there exists i, $1 \leq i \leq n$, such that $C_i = Q$ and for all $C_j \neq Q$, C_j is false in M.

M is said to be *justifiable* iff every atom in M is justifiable. □

The concept of justifiability defined here is intimately related to the concept of labeling-based justification in Doyle's truth maintenance system [2]. It essentially says that any positive conclusion should be able to be demonstrated by the reasoning that follows the orientation of the rules, because this orientation reflects one's intuition about the way the reasoning should be performed. An atom can be assumed false if it leads to a consistent argument. It was shown in [19] that the unintuitive extension in the Hanks-McDermott shooting problem [7] (also see [12]) resulted from a violation of this principle.

Let Π be a DB. By the *extended stable model semantics* of Π, we mean that Π denotes the first order theory that contains all sentences true in every justifiable model of Π.

Not only is the extended stable model semantics a genuine extension of the stable model semantics, but it can also be used to describe some other proposed semantics of more restricted DB's. The following proposition is easy to prove.

Proposition 4.1 Let Π be a DB. Then,

(i) every justifiable model of Π is a minimal model of Π;

(ii) if the head of every clause consists of a single atom, then a model of Π is a stable model iff it is a justifiable model of Π; and

(iii) if Π is stratified, then a model of Π is a perfect model of Π iff it is a justifiable model of Π; the conclusion also holds for locally stratified DB's. □

As a matter of fact, the extended stable model semantics can be defined in terms of the stable model semantics of a transformed program.

Definition 4.2. Let $L_1 \wedge \cdots \vee L_n \rightarrow A_1 \vee \cdots \vee A_m$ be a clause. A *factor* of $\{A_1, ..., A_m\}$ is defined to be $\sigma\{A_1, ..., A_m\}$ such that σ is the most general unifier of a subset of $\{A_1, ..., A_m\}$.

Π_f is said to be the *factored* version of Π if $\Pi_f = \Pi \cup \{\sigma\{L_1 \wedge \cdots \wedge L_n\} \rightarrow \sigma\{A_1 \wedge \cdots \vee A_m\}$ | for each clause $L_1 \wedge \cdots \vee L_n \rightarrow A_1 \vee \cdots \vee A_m$ in Π and each factor $\sigma\{A_1, ..., A_m\}\}$. □

For example, the factored version of $\{\rightarrow p(a,x) \vee p(x,a)\}$ is

$$\rightarrow p(a,x) \vee p(x,a)$$
$$\rightarrow p(a,a).$$

Definition 4.3. Let Π_f be a factored version of a DB Π. Let Π'_f be obtained by replacing each oriented clause

$$L_1 \wedge \cdots \wedge L_n \rightarrow A_1 \vee \cdots \vee A_m$$

in Π_f, where L_i are literals, by m clauses with each A_i serving as the head:

$$L_1 \wedge \cdots \wedge L_n \wedge \neg A_1 \wedge \cdots \wedge \neg A_{i-1} \wedge \neg A_{i+1} \wedge \cdots \wedge \neg A_m \rightarrow A_i$$

We call Π'_f so obtained a *normal* DB of Π_f and denote it as $NORM(\Pi_f)$. □

Using relevant definitions, we can show the following result.

Proposition 4.2. Let Π be a DB. Then, a justifiable model of Π is a justifiable model of $NORM(\Pi_f)$, and vice versa. □

A similar technique of obtaining a normal DB has been employed in [4] for non-Horn logic programs without negation.

For notational convenience, we assume from now on that a given DB is already factored, so we can drop the subscript f.

5. Equivalence of Stable Model Semantics with Discriminant Circumscription

In this section, we show the main result of this paper: the discriminant circumscription of a DB coincides with the extended stable model semantics defined in Section 4.

First, we define Clark's predicate completion [1] and fixpoint completion proposed by Dung and Kanchanasut [3], which shows that the models of fixpoint completion are in fact stable models of the original program. We extend the method of fixpoint completion to deductive databases under the extended stable model semantics. We then show this extended fixpoint completion is equivalent to discriminant circumscription. This leads to the conclusion that the extended stable models are external models of the discriminant circumscription.

It is sufficient for the purpose of this paper to consider predicate completion over instantiated (thus ground) DB's.

Definition 5.1. (Clark 1978 [1]): Let Π be a ground normal DB, S be a set of ground atoms, and for each atom A in S, $E_{A_i} \rightarrow A$, where $i = 1, ..., n$, be all clauses in Π with A as a head. Then the predicate completion of Π over S, denoted as $COMP(\Pi; S)$, is defined as:

$$COMP(\Pi; S) \equiv \Pi \wedge (\wedge_{A \in S} E_{A_1} \vee \cdots \vee E_{A_n} \leftarrow A)$$

We will take the liberty of using a set of predicates in the place of S to denote the set of all ground instances of these predicates. □

We give below an alternative definition of quasi fixpoint of [3].

Definition 5.2. A clause is said to be *non-positive* if it is an instantiated clause of the form: $\neg D_1 \wedge \cdots \wedge \neg D_n \rightarrow A$, where $n \geq 0$.

Let Π be a normal DB. A *quasi clause* of Π is defined inductively as follows:

(i) A non-positive clause in Π is a quasi clause of Π; and inductively,

(ii) $\neg D_1 \wedge \cdots \wedge \neg D_k \rightarrow A$ is a quasi clause of Π if there exists an instantiated clause of Π $B_1 \wedge \cdots \wedge B_m \wedge \neg C_1 \wedge \cdots \wedge \neg C_n \rightarrow A$, where $n, m \geq 0$, and the following are quasi clauses of Π:

$$\neg C_{11} \wedge \cdots \wedge \neg C_{1q_1} \rightarrow B_1$$

$$\cdots\cdots$$

$$\neg C_{m1} \wedge \cdots \wedge \neg C_{mq_m} \rightarrow B_m$$

such that $\{D_1, ..., D_k\} = \{C_{11}, ..., C_{1q_1}, ..., C_{m1} ..., C_{mq_q}, C_1, ..., C_n\}$.

We will use $QUA\,(\Pi)$ to denote the set of all quasi clauses of Π and call it a quasi clause DB. □

Proposition 5.1. (Dung and Kanchanasut 1989 [3]) Let Π be a normal DB. Then, a stable model of Π is a model of $COMP\,(QUA\,(\Pi); H_L)$, where H_L is the Herbrand base, and vice versa. □

This result can be extended to deductive databases.

Lemma 5.2. Let Π be a DB. Then, a justifiable model of Π is a model of $COMP\,(QUA\,(NORM\,(\Pi)); H_L)$, and vice versa.

Proof: It follows from Propositions 4.2 and 5.1. □

The next two lemmas describe the equivalences of discriminant circumscription of a DB with those of the two special forms.

Lemma 5.3. Let Π be a DB, and $\Pi' = NORM\,(\Pi)$. Let P be the set of external predicates of Π and N the set of internal predicates of Π. Then,

$$(CIRC\,(\Pi_\omega(N, P); N) \wedge P \equiv N) \equiv (CIRC\,(\Pi'_\omega(N, P); N) \wedge P \equiv N).$$

Proof: To show the equality, we first observe that $NORM\,(\Pi)$ and Π are logically equivalent. By Definition 4.3, any clause ξ

$$L_1 \wedge \cdots \wedge L_n \rightarrow A_1 \vee \cdots \vee A_m$$

in Π corresponds to the set Φ of clauses

$$L_1 \wedge \cdots \wedge L_n \wedge \neg A_1 \wedge \cdots \wedge \neg A_{i-1} \wedge \neg A_{i+1} \wedge \cdots \wedge \neg A_m \rightarrow A_i$$

for every $i \leq m$. Although their working programs, i.e., ξ_ω and Φ_ω, may not be logically equivalent in general, with the restriction $P \equiv N$, we can substitute any occurrence of A_i in Φ_ω by N_{A_i}, and vice versa. With this, it is a straightforward task to show that Φ_ω can reduce to ξ_ω; hence $\xi_\omega \wedge (P \equiv N)$ and $\Phi_\omega \wedge (P \equiv N)$ are logically equivalent. Since the clause ξ is arbitrary, we conclude that the equality holds. □

Lemma 5.4. Let Π be a DB where each clause head is singleton. Let P be the set of external predicates of Π and N the set of internal predicates of Π. Then,

$$CIRC(\Pi_\omega(N,P);N) \equiv CIRC(QUA(\Pi_\omega(N,P);N)).$$

Proof: Although the complete proof is nontrivial, the whole idea is that since $QUA(\Pi_\omega(N,P);N))$ is obtained by eliminating *positive circulars*, an interpretation M is an N-minimal model of $QUA(\Pi_\omega(N,P);N))$ iff it is an N-minimal model of $\Pi_\omega(N,P);N)$. We omit the details here. A complete proof can be found in the full version of this paper [20]. □

Lemma 5.5. Let Π be a quasi clause DB, P the set of external predicates in Π, and N the set of internal predicates. Then,

$$CIRC(\Pi_\omega(N,P);N) \equiv COMP(\Pi_\omega(N,P);N).$$

Proof: The proof is quite straightforward due to the fact that the working program of a quasi clause DB is still a quasi clause DB in which no atom appears both positively and negatively. □

We now give the main theorem.

Theorem 5.6. Let Π be a DB and $\Pi_\omega(N,P)$ be the working program of Π, where P is the set of external predicates in Π and N is the set of internal predicates. Then, an external model of $CIRC(\Pi_\omega(N,P);N) \wedge (N \equiv P)$ is a justifiable model of Π, and vice versa.

Proof: Let Π' be $NORM(\Pi)$. We then have

$CIRC(\Pi_\omega(N,P));N) \wedge (N \equiv P)$

$\equiv CIRC(\Pi'_\omega(N,P));N) \wedge (N \equiv P)$	by Lemma 5.3
$\equiv CIRC(QUA(\Pi'_\omega(N,P));N) \wedge (N \equiv P)$	by Lemma 5.4
$\equiv COMP(QUA(\Pi'_\omega(N,P));N) \wedge (N \equiv P)$	by Lemma 5.5
$\equiv COMP(QUA(\Pi'_\omega(P,P));P) \wedge (N \equiv P)$	by equal substitution

It follows from Lemma 4.1 that an external model of the last expression above is a model of $COMP(QUA(\Pi'_\omega(P,P));P)$, and vice versa. By Lemma 5.2, we conclude that any external model of $CIRC(\Pi'_\omega(N,P);N) \wedge (N \equiv P)$ is a justifiable model of Π, and vice versa. □

6. Final Remarks

Investigations of relationships among various non-monotonic reasoning formalisms may lead to a deeper understanding of common-sense reasoning. The results of the past few years have shown that non-monotonic reasoning, logic programming with negation, deductive databases with incomplete information in various senses are intimately related.

This paper answers an outstanding question about the relationship between circumscription and stable model-based deductive databases. Our method is based on a simple renaming mechanism of predicates in order to separate positive and negative information embedded in a given deductive database. The result is somehow surprising, since predicate renaming, which is purely syntactic and which is among the very first methods to be considered but almost immediately abandoned when dealing with negation in logic programs (see [17]), has been shown to be able to capture the dynamic behaviors of non-stratified deductive databases.

We believe that this method deserves further investigation. This is based on our observation that circumscription can only treat an extension (an interpretation for a predicate) as a complete unit, and there are certain applications, such as the one shown in this paper concerning DB semantics that relies on clause orientations, that need to handle certain non-standard minimization processes.

Acknowledgment

We thank the referees for useful comments. This work is supported by the Natural Sciences and Engineering Research Council of Canada.

References

1. Clark K., Negation as Failure, in *Logic and Databases*, H. Gallaire and J. Minker (ed.), Plenum Press, New York, 1978, 293-322.
2. Doyle J., A Truth Maintenance System, *Artificial Intelligence Vol. 12*, (1979), 231-272.
3. Dung P. and K. Kanchanasut, A Fixpoint Approach to Declarative Semantics of Logic Programs, in *Proc. North American Conference on Logic Programming*, E. Lust and R. Overbeek (ed.), MIT Press, 1989, 604-625.
4. Dung P. and K. Kanchanasut, On the Generalized Predicate Completion of Non-Horn Program, in *Proc. North American Conference on Logic Programming*, E. Lust and R. Overbeek (ed.), MIT Press, 1989, 587-603.
5. Gelfond M. and V. Lifschitz, Compiling Circumscriptive Theories into Logic Programs, in *Proc. 7th AAAI*, 1988, 455-459.
6. Gelfond M. and V. Lifschitz, The Stable Model Semantics for Logic Programming, in *Proc. 5th Symposium/Conference on Logic Programming*, R. A. Kowalski and K. A. Bowen (ed.), MIT Press, 1988, 1070-1080.
7. Hanks S. and D. McDermott, Nonmonotonic Logic and Temporal Projection, *Artificial Intelligence Vol. 33*, (1987), 379-412.
8. Lifschitz V., Computing Circumscription, *Proc. IJCAI-85*, Los Angeles, CA, 1985, 121-127.
9. Lifschitz V., On the Declarative Semantics of Logic Programs with Negation, in *Foundations of Deductive Databases and Logic Programming*, J. Minker (ed.), Morgan Kaufman Publishers, 1988, 177-192.
10. McCarthy J., Circumscription—A Form of Non-monotonic Reasoning, *Artificial Intelligence Vol. 13*, (1980), 27-39.
11. McCarthy J., Applications of Circumscription to Formalizing Common-Sense Reasoning, *Artificial Intelligence Vol. 28*, (1986), 86-116.
12. Morris P. H., The Anomalous Extension Problem in Default Reasoning, *Artificial Intelligence Vol. 35*, (1988), 383-399.

13. Przymusinski T., Non-monotonic Reasoning vs. Logic Programming: a New Perspective, in *Formal Foundations of Artificial Intelligence*, D. Patridge and Y. Wilks (ed.), 1988.

14. Przymusinski T., On the Declarative Semantics of Deductive Databases and Logic Programs, in *Foundations of Deductive Databases and Logic Programming*, J. Minker (ed.), Morgan Kaufman Publishers, 1988, 193-216.

15. Przymusinski T., Three-Valued Formalizations of Non-monotonic Reasoning and Logic Programming, in *Proc. First Int'l Conference on Principles of Knowledge, Representation, and Reasoning*, Morgan Kaufmann, 1989, 341-348.

16. Przymusinski T. C., An Algorithm to Compute Circumscription, *Artificial Intelligence Vol. 38*, (1989), 47-73.

17. Shepherson J., Negation in Logic Programs, in *Foundations of Deductive Databases and Logic Programming*, J. Minker (ed.), Morgan Kaufman Publishers, 1988, 19-88.

18. Van Gelder A., K. Ross and J. Schlipf, Unfounded Sets and Well-founded Semantics for General Logic Programs, in *Proc. the 7th ACM PODS*, 1988, 221-230.

19. You J. and L. Li, Supported Circumscription and Its Relation to Logic Programming with Negation, in *Proc. North American Conference on Logic Programming*, MIT Press, 1989.

20. Yuan L. and J. You, A New Circumscription Method for Stable Model Semantics, unpublished manuscript, 1990.

Complexity of Algebraic Specifications *

Ramesh Subrahmanyam
Department of Computer and Information Science
University of Pennsylvania
Philadelphia, PA 19104 U.S.A.

ABSTRACT

In the field of algebraic specification, the semantics of an equationally specified datatype is given by the initial algebra of the specifications. We show in this paper that in general the theory of the initial algebra of a given set of equations is Π^0_2-complete. The impossibility of complete finite axiomatization of equations as well as inequations true in the initial algebra is therefore established. We, further, establish that the decision problem is, in general, Π^0_1-complete if the equational theory is decidable. We extend the investigation to a certain semantics of parameterized specifications (the so-called *free extension functor semantics*) that has been proposed in the literature. We present some results characterizing the recursion-theoretic properties of (a) the theory of the free extension algebras of parameter algebras relative to the the theory of the parameter algebras, and (b) the theory of the models of a parameterized specification relative to the theory axiomatized by the specification itself.

1 Introduction

Abstract Data Types (ADT's) are available in modern programming languages belonging to as diverse families as those of ML and MODULA and they are an essential ingredient in the programming-in-the-large paradigm. ADT's allow the programmer to restrict access to data through a specified collection of operations while hiding the actual data structures and the code that achieve the implementation of these operations. In this paper we study the computational complexity of reasoning about ADT's [Goguen 1978, Guttag 1978, Ehrig & Mahr 1985] with respect to the initial algebra semantics for unparameterized equational specifications (see section 2) and the free extension functor semantics for parameterized equational specifications(see section 4). Conventional equational reasoning, using the equations in the specification as axioms, is *not* complete for deriving the equalities that hold in the initial algebra. Indeed, consider the one-sorted specification in Figure 1. It is easy to see that its initial algebra (see Section 2) is isomorphic to the natural numbers with zero, successor, and addition, hence

*This research was supported by U.S. Army Research Office grant DAAL03-89-C-0031PRI.

Signature: $\{0, s, +\}$
$x + 0 = x$
$x + s(y) = s(x + y)$

Figure 1

it validates, for example, the equation

$$0 + x = x$$

But this equation is not provable by equational reasoning from the axioms in Figure 1, as an easy analysis using canonical rewriting shows.

To prove more of the equations that hold in initial algebras, one can use various *induction principles*(see [Goguen 1984],[Huet & Hullot 1982], [Goguen & Meseguer 1985], and [Zhang 1988]). The problem is that all of these proof systems, or any other recursive axiomatization for that matter, are (in general) necessarily *incomplete*. In [F.Nourani 1981] (see also [MacQueen & Sannella 1985]) it is noted that, as a consequence of Matijasevič's result on the recursive unsolvability of Hilbert's Tenth Problem (see p. 356 of [Davis 1976]), one can describe a finite specification such that validity of equations in the initial algebra (which is isomorphic to the natural numbers) is Π_1^0-complete. The unsolvability of Hilbert's Tenth is a deep result, and it is not really necessary to appeal to it: in the proof of Theorem 8 we construct a specification for which the Π_1^0-hardness of the validity of equations in the initial algebra is obtained via a simple reduction from the complement of the Halting Problem.

We address, in section 2 of this paper, the following general problem: given a specification $SPEC$ and an equation e, is e valid in the initial algebra of $SPEC$? By the previous comments, this problem is Π_1^0-hard. But what is the tight bound here? Is the problem also in Π_1^0, thus leaving open the possibility of perspicuous axiomatization of the validity of *inequations*? We prove that in fact the problem is Π_2^0-complete (see Theorem 3); thus we cannot hope for complete reasoning about inequations either. We also prove that even assuming the decidability of equational reasoning from a given set of axioms, complexity can be Π_1^0-complete, in the worst case (Theorem 8), and thus complete reasoning about equations is still impossible in general.

Next, we consider the complications that arise in the case of parameterized ADT specifications. The "standard semantics" here is the so-called free extension functor and we are interested in reasoning about equations that hold in the free extensions of all the algebras satisfying the parameter specification. With this modification we establish that the theory of the free extension of an algebra is Π_1^0-complete relative to the equational theory of the algebra in the language of the parameter specification augmented with a set of new constants,one per element of the algebra. We also establish that the theory of the class of free extensions of all algebras satisfying the parameter specification is Π_1^0-complete with respect to the equational theory of the entire specification. for the analogs of the results that we have obtained in the unparameterized case. We obtain some of these analogs while some are still open.

The paper is organized as follows : In Section 2 we define some concepts that we will later refer to in the paper. Section 3 discusses the decision problem of equality of terms in the initial algebra, and its ramifications. Section 4 introduces the notion of Parameterized Datatype Specifications and the *free extension functor* semantics . Section 5 is devoted to some results pertaining to decision problems and related characterizations. We conclude in Section 6 pointing out some questions that need to be answered to complete the picture. For details omitted in the paper, [Subrahmanyam 1990] may be consulted.

2 Basic Definitions

We review some basic concepts in Universal Algebra and Equational Logic (for more details, see [Burris & Sankappanavar 1981]), and Recursion Theory (see [Rogers 1967]).

Let E be a given set of equations over algebraic terms constituted from a signature Σ. In general, we could consider a many-sorted theory : such a theory(or a specification , as we will refer to it later) will be given by a triple(S,Σ,E), where S is a set of sorts, Σ is a signature of function symbols over these sorts, and E is a set of equations, the terms appearing in which are well-typed. Since, the consideration of multiple sorts adds no interest to the problem at hand, we will restrict ourselves to a single sort.

A Σ-algebra consists of a domain D associated with an interpretation function $[\![\cdot]\!]$. This function associates each n-ary function symbol in the signature with a function from D^n to D. We define environments and term evaluation in a given environment as in first-order models. Further,we take the notion of satisfaction of an equation in a given algebra to mean satisfaction of the corresponding universally closed formula. Thus if SPEC ($\equiv$ (S,Σ,E)) is a specification, a Σ-algebra with sorts S satisfying the equations E will be called a SPEC-algebra.

We define the semantic entailment relation $\models$ between a set of equations E and an equation e as is usual in logic: E$\models$e iff e is satisfied in every algebra that satisfies E.

The logic of equations is a proof system consisting of the reflexivity axiom and four rules : symmetry, transitivity, substitutivity and replacement. We say that E$\vdash$ e iff there is a finite proof tree with either the equations in E or the reflexivity axiom at the leaves, and the aforementioned rules of inference at the internal nodes. It is well-known that every equational proof can be written as a chain of replacements. Further, the logic imposes an equivalence relation (corresponding to provable equality) on the set of all terms (that we denote $T_\Sigma(X)$, where Σ is the signature and X is a countably infinite set of variable symbols).

The following completeness result due to Birkhoff is an important result.

Theorem 1 E$\vdash$e *iff* E$\models$e

A Σ-homomorphism between Σ-algebras A and B, is a function h:$D_A \rightarrow D_B$ such that for every n-ary function symbol f $\forall a_1 \in D_A \cdots \forall a_n \in D_A h(f_A(a_1 \cdots a_n)) = f_B(h(a_1), \cdots, h(a_n))$.

Here f_A and f_B denote the interpretation of the symbol f in the algebras A and B respectively. It is well-known in universal algebra that the category of Σ-algebras that satisfy a given set of equations E, with Σ-homomorphisms as arrows , has a (unique) initial object. In other words there is an algebra I unique up to Σ-isomorphism , such that there is a unique Σ-homomorphism from I to any other algebra satisfying E. This algebra I is called the initial algebra of the given set of equations E. We now state a well-known lemma:

Lemma.2 *Let* I *be the initial algebra of a given set of equations over a signature* Σ. *Then, for any equation* **e**,

$$\mathbf{I} \models \mathbf{e} \leftrightarrow \forall\theta \mathbf{I} \models \theta(\mathbf{e}) \leftrightarrow \forall\theta E \vdash \theta(e)$$

where θ ranges over ground substitutions. Consequently every ground equation true in the initial algebra is provable by equational reasoning (from the given set of equations).

We briefly (and informally) review some concepts from recursion theory that are needed in this paper (for details, see [Rogers 1967]. In this paragraph, sets will mean sets of natural numbers. A Turing reduction from **A** to **B** is given by the index x of the A-relative total recursive function ϕ_x^A (if it exists) that computes membership in B. Informally an A-relative recursive function is a function computed by a Turing machine which operates with the set A as an oracle. A is Turing reducible to B (denoted A $\leq_T$ B) if and only if there is a Turing reduction from A to B. A set is X said to be (Turing) complete relative to a class of sets if for every set Y in the class there is a Turing Reduction from Y to X. In such an event, X is *computationally* the most complex set in the class. The arithmetical hierarchy is defined by an inductive definition . It is a sequence of pairs of sets (Σ_n^0, Π_n^0) such that

(a) Σ_0^0 and Π_0^0 are both the class of total recursive sets

(b) For every X and n, $X \in \Sigma_n^0 \leftrightarrow \overline{X} \in \Pi_n^0$

(c) $B \in \Sigma_{n+1}^0$ if and only if $\exists A.(A \in \Sigma_n^0$ and $\forall x.(x \in B \leftrightarrow \exists y.(<x,y> \in A)))$

Here, the operator <> denotes the canonical bijective encoding of ordered pairs of natural numbers, into natural numbers. It follows from the above definitions that:

(d) $B \in \Pi_{n+1}^0$ if and only if $\exists A.$ (A $\in \Pi_n^0$ and $\forall x.(x \in B \leftrightarrow \forall y.(<x,y> \in A)))$

A set is Σ_n^0-complete(Π_n^0-complete) if it is in $\Sigma_n^0(\Pi_n^0)$, and is complete relative to the class Σ_n^0 (Π_n^0).

3 Complexity of Truth in Initial Algebras

In this section we determine the (recursion-theoretic) complexity of equality in the initial algebra of a given set of equations. The following is the main result of this section.

(r1) $U(x,y,z,t) = AU(\epsilon, q_0, \langle x,y\rangle, t, z)$

(r2) $AU(s,q,cons(c_2,cons(c_3,s_2)),succ(t),z) = AU(snoc(s,c_0),q_1,cons(c_3,s_2),t,z)$, iff $\delta(q,c_2) = (q_1,c_0,r)$.

(r3) $AU(snoc(s_1,c_1),q,cons(c_2,s_2),succ(t),z) = AU(s_1,q_1,cons(c_1,cons(c_3,s_2)),t,z)$, iff $\delta(q,c_2) = (q_1,c_3,l)$.

(r4) $AU(\epsilon,q_f,snoc(cons(x,z),x),t,z) = \mathbf{true}$, for every $q_f \in f$.

Figure 2

Theorem 3 *Given a finite(or recursive) set of equations E over a signature Σ, the theory of the initial algebra of E, denoted by $I(\Sigma,e)$, is Π^0_2-complete.*

Proof: First, we will establish the problem is indeed in Π^0_2. For fixed (Σ,E), let us abbreviate the initial algebra by I. Then for any equation e,

$$I \models e \leftrightarrow \forall\theta\exists p \cdot A(\theta) \wedge B(\theta,e) \rightarrow C(p, subst(\theta,e)),$$

where the intended meanings of the three predicates are as follows:

$A(\theta)$ iff θ is an encoding of a valid ground substitution with a finite set of support.

$B(\theta,e)$ iff every free variable in equation e is in the set of support of the substitution θ

$C(p,e))$ iff e is a ground equation , and p is a proof of e.

To show the Π^0_2 hardness of the problem, we provide a reduction from $\{x \mid W_x \text{ is infinite}\}$,(we use standard notation in recursion theory : W_x denotes the domain of the partial function encoded by x, and ϕ_x is the function corresponding to the index x) which is known to be Π^0_2-hard [Rogers 1967]. Towards this end, we define some relations:

$U(x,y,z,t)$ iff ϕ_x yields output z on input y in fewer than t time steps.

$AU(u,q,v,t,z)$ iff the universal Turing Machine will terminate in fewer than t time steps from the configuration uqvb, and upon termination the contents of the tape would be the string z. Figure 2 shows the axiomatization of these relations. [1] We now define some more relations and add the rules shown in

[1] We also need to add to these the axioms for cons and snoc (which we do not list there). The list function snoc accepts a list and element as arguments and attaches the element to the end of the list. Further, we need to include the sort Bool

(r5) AuxAccept(x,cons(⟨y,p⟩,L)) = AuxAccept(x,snoc(⟨y+1,p⟩,snoc(⟨y,p+1⟩,L)))

(r6) AuxAccept(x,cons(⟨y,p⟩,L)) = Γ(x,y,p,L)

(r7) Γ(x,y,p,L) = **true** iff either ∃z U(x,y,z,p),or ∃⟨m,n⟩∃z U(x,m,z,n)

(r8) Accept(x,y) = AuxAccept(x,cons(⟨y,1⟩,nil))

Figure 3

Figure 3:

Accept(x,y) iff ϕ_x accepts some z>y.

AuxAccept(x,L) . Let L be a list of pairs of the form ⟨input,time⟩. If there exists an input i such that it is less than the first component of some pair in L, and ϕ_x defined on i, then this relation is true. To simulate the computation of this relation by rewriting, we remove the head pair ⟨a,t⟩ from L, simulate (t+1) steps of the execution of ϕ_x on a, after queuing ⟨a,t+1⟩ and ⟨a+1,t⟩ at the end of the list L.

What remains is merely an axiomatization of Γ. This is very similar to that for U. Rules (r2)-(r4) carry over with the fifth argument added as a dummy argument.(Figure 4)

It is easy to see that for any ground a and y, as a consequence of the supplied axioms, Accept(a,y) is provable equal to **true** iff ϕ_a accepts some z>y in a finite number of steps. Whence, the domain of ϕ_a is infinite iff every ground instance of the equation Accept(a,y) for fixed a and variable y is true. By the definition of the initial algebra, this must be a theorem in the theory of the initial algebra. This demonstrates the Π_2^0-hardness of the theory of an arbitrary initial algebra. ∎

We can further establish the following theorem:

Theorem 4 *For any specification E, if the theory of the initial algebra of E is Π_2^0-hard then the provable ground theory is Σ_1^0-hard.*

Proof: Consider the equational axiomatization(call it E_1,say) described in Theorem 3. The theory of the initial algebra of E_1 is known to be Π_2^0 hard, and its equational theory is known to be Σ_1^0-hard. We will show a reduction from the equational theory of E_1 to the equational theory of E, thereby

and constants true and false in our specifications. We ignore such details here.

(r9) Γ(x,y,p,k) = $\Lambda\Gamma(\epsilon, q_0, \langle x,y \rangle$,p,k)

(r10)Γ(x,y,p,cons($\langle$l,m$\rangle$,rest)) = $\Lambda\Gamma(\epsilon, q_0, \langle x,l \rangle$,m,cons($\langle$y,p$\rangle$,rest))

(r11) $\Lambda\Gamma$(s,q,cons(c_2,cons(c_3,s_2)),succ(t),k) = $\Lambda\Gamma$(snoc(s,c_0),q_1,cons(c_3,s_2),t,k), iff $\delta(q,c_2)=(q_1,c_0,r)$

(r12) $\Lambda\Gamma$(*snoc*(s_1,c_1),q,cons(s_2,c_2),succ(t),k) = $\Lambda\Gamma$(s_1,q_1,cons(c_1,cons(c_3,s_2)),t,k), iff $\delta(q,c_2)=(q_1,c_3,l)$

(r13) $\Lambda\Gamma$ (s,q_f,b,t,k) = **true**, iff $q_f \in$f.

Figure 4

establishing our claim. Since the theory of the initial algebra of E is assumed to be Π_2^0-hard and that of E_1 is in Π_2^0, there is a many-one reduction f from the latter to the former. Given any ground equation $e(\equiv t_1 = t_2)$, e is provable from E_1 iff e is true in the initial algebra of E_1 iff $f(t_1) = f(t_2)$ is true in the initial algebra of E iff $f(t_1) = f(t_2)$ is provable from E. Thus f is also a many-one reduction from the equational theory of E_1 to the equational theory of E∎

Lemma 5 *If* **E** *is a decidable equational theory then the equational theory of the initial algebra of* **E** *is co-recursively enumerable.*

Proof: As mentioned in Lemma 2, every ground equation that is true in the initial algebra of a given set of equations is provable in equational logic from the equational axioms. By assumption truth of ground equations in the initial algebra is decidable. By lemma 2, an equation is true in the initial algebra if and only if every ground instance of the equation is true. Whence it follows the equational theory of the initial algebra of E is co-recursively enumerable.

But is there an axiomatization which is decidable, for which equality in the initial algebra is Π_1^0− complete?. Consider the axiomatization of (N,0,+,*,exp), given by the corresponding primitive recursive defining equations $\mathbf{E_1}$ in Figure 5(s stands for successor). The following are easily established:

Lemma 6 *(N,0,s,+,*,exp) is the initial algebra of* $\mathbf{E_1}$.

Lemma 7 *There are primitive recursive equations* **F** *the terms in which contain an additional three-place function symbol T, such that the initial algebra of* $E_1 \oplus$**F** *is the structure (N,0,s,+,*,exp,T) where*

$$E_1$$

$$x + 0 = x$$

$$x + s(y) = s(x + y)$$

$$x * 0 = 0$$

$$x * s(y) = x * y + x$$

$$exp(x, 0) = s(0)$$

$$exp(x, s(y)) = exp(x, y) * x$$

Figure 5

T is a three-place function which takes only the values 0 and 1, with the property that, for the canonical gödel numbering of Turing machines

$$T(x, y, z) = \begin{cases} 1 & \text{if machine x on input y halts in less than or equal to z steps} \\ 0 & \text{otherwise.} \end{cases}$$

Theorem 8 *The theory of the initial algebra of $E_1 \oplus$F is Π_1^0-complete.*

Proof: Membership in Π_1^0 follows from lemma 2. This is because , all the equations in the theory are primitive recursive. It can be shown that by orienting the equations from left to right one obtains a canonical rewrite system the reflexive t, symmetric and transitive closure of the rewriting relation of which is identical to the equivalence relation associated with the equational theory. Consequently, the entailment of such a theory is a decidable relation.

Given the gödel number x of a machine the decision problem whether the machine x does not halt when given its own index as input is known to be Π_1^0- complete. This is equivalent to the truth of the equation

T(x,x,y) = 0

Thus the decision problem of truth in the initial algebra is Π_1^0- complete. ∎

Corollary 9 *In general, the theory of the initial algebra of a given set* **E** *of equations is not recursively axiomatizable.*

This is because the logical consequences of a recursively axiomatized theory are recursively enumerable. We have shown however that (even with equations of a restricted form, namely, where the equational theory is decidable) this is not the case.

4 Parameterized Datatype Specifications

Parameterized datatype specifications are very common in computer science: lists, stacks and sets are some of the most common examples of parameterized datatypes. As an example Figure 6 gives a specification of the **SET** datatype.

$$\Sigma = \{\text{insert}, \text{nil}\}$$

$$insert(x, insert(y, z)) = insert(y, insert(x, z)) \quad insert(x, insert(x, y)) = insert(x, y)$$

Figure 6

A parameterized datatype specification can also include specifications for the parameter type. Such a specification is thus an ordered pair (SPEC1,SPEC2), with SPEC1 $\subseteq$ SPEC2 (The relation $\subseteq$ between specifications means component-wise containment). Thus, we may specify a set datatype which requires of its parameter an "equality" symbol eq:, and require of the parameter that the **eq** be an equivalence relation.

The semantics of parameterized abstract datatypes is defined along lines similar to the initiality definition of the semantics of non-parameterized datatypes. If SPEC is an unparameterized specification and n is the number of sorts in it, its initial algebra is given by firstly computing the left-adjoint $\mathcal{F}$ to the forgetful functor $\mathcal{U}$ from the category of SPEC-algebras to the category of $\mathbf{SET}^n$(which can be seen as the category of objects satisfying the null specification), and subsequently evaluating $\mathcal{F}$ on the empty set. The following definition of the semantics of a parameterized specification (taken from [Ehrig & Mahr 1985]) is easily seen as a natural generalization of this idea:

Definition. Let CAT1 and CAT2 be the categories of algebras satisfying specifications SPEC1 and SPEC2 respectively, with morphisms the Σ_1- and Σ_2- homomorphisms respectively (Σ_i is the signature of the specification SPECi). Let U be the forgetful functor from CAT2 to CAT1. Then the left adjoint to U is the semantics of the parameterized specification SPEC $\equiv$ (SPEC1,SPEC2). To be more precise one may define the semantics of SPEC to be the class of all left adjoints(which as we have observed, are naturally isomorphic) to the forgetful functor from CAT2 to CAT1.

For this definition to be meaningful, two results need to be mentioned. Firstly, if SPEC1 and SPEC2 are equational specifications, then the aforementioned left adjoint always exists ([Lawvere 1963]) Secondly this left adjoint functor is unique up to natural isomorphism.

A simple algebraic characterization of one of these left adjoint functors (also taken from [Ehrig & Mahr 1985]), will prove useful for proving the theorems in the sequel. Given specification SPEC $\equiv$ (SPEC1,SPEC2), and a SPEC1-algebra $\mathcal{A}$ we define an algebra F($\mathcal{A}$) (also called the $\mathcal{A}$-quotient algebra). Define:

const($\mathcal{A}$) = {a :→ s: a ∈ $\mathcal{A}_s$, s∈S}

eqn($\mathcal{A}$) = $\{ (t_1,t_2) : t_1,t_2 \in T_{\Sigma_1 \cup const(\mathcal{A})}, eval_{\mathcal{A}}(t_1) = eval_{\mathcal{A}}(t_2) \}$

SPEC2($\mathcal{A}$) = SPEC2 $\oplus$ (ϕ,const($\mathcal{A}$),eqn($\mathcal{A}$)).

F($\mathcal{A}$) = $V_{\mathcal{A}}(T_{SPEC2(\mathcal{A})})$.

Here, $eval_{\mathcal{A}}$(t) evaluates the term t under the obvious assignment of elements of $\mathcal{A}$ to the constant symbols in const($\mathcal{A}$); further $T_{SPEC2(\mathcal{A})}$, is the initial algebra of the specification $SPEC2(\mathcal{A})$, and $V_{\mathcal{A}}$ is the forgetful functor from the category of SPEC2($\mathcal{A}$) algebras to the category of SPEC2-algebras.

F($\mathcal{A}$) is called the free extension of $\mathcal{A}$ with respect to the specification SPEC. The object function F can be extended naturally to morphisms making it a functor.

Since $T_{SPEC2(\mathcal{A})}$ is the initial algebra of the specification SPEC2($\mathcal{A}$), by Lemma 2, all ground equations (true in it) between terms over the signature $\Sigma_2 \cup const(\mathcal{A})$ are provable from eqn($\mathcal{A}$) and E_2 via pure equational reasoning.

5 Complexity of Parameterization

We now state a lemma about semantic equality of Σ_2-terms over $T_{SPEC2(\mathcal{A})}$.

Lemma 10 *Given a countable SPEC1-algebra $\mathcal{A}$ whose elements are enumerable by a recursive function, and an oracle for equality of terms over the signature Σ_2 in F($\mathcal{A}$)(, with respect to a variable assignment whose range is the* parameter algebra*) the decision problem of testing equality of two Σ_2 terms in F($\mathcal{A}$) is Π_1^0.*

Proof: To determine the truth of a given equation between Σ_2-terms in the algebra F($\mathcal{A}$) ,we proceed as follows: firstly, observe that every element of the algebra $F(\mathcal{A})$ is of the form [t] where t$\in \Sigma_2 \cup const(\mathcal{A})$ ([t] stands for the equivalence class containing t with respect to the congruence imposed by the equations in SPEC2($\mathcal{A}$)). Thus, the given equation **e** is true in the algebra with respect to the given assignment θ if and only if the modified equation **e1** is true in the same algebra under assignment θ_1, where we define **e1** and θ_1 as follows: For every variable **x** such that θ(x) = c, let c = [t]σ_x, where t$\in T_{\Sigma_2 \cup X}$ and σ_x has only elements of $\mathcal{A}$ in its range. Here X is a set of completely new variables. Call the substitution consisting of all such ordered pairs (x,t) σ. Choose the t's and σ_x's in such a way that σ_x's have disjoint domains; let θ_1 be the disjoint sum of the σ_x's. Let **e1** be obtained by applying the substitution σ to the equation **e**.

We can now use the given oracle to decide the truth of **e1** with respect to the assignment θ_1 in the algebra SPEC2($\mathcal{A}$). Since we can, for every assignment (and there are only countably infinite such) decide the truth of the given equation, the decision problem is Π_1^0∎

The Π_1^0 completeness of the decision problem is a straightforward adaptation of Theorem 3.

Lemma 11 *The problem stated in Lemma 10 is Π_1^0- hard relative to the problem of testing equality of $\Sigma_1 \cup const(\mathcal{A})$-terms in $\mathcal{A}$.*

If the given SPEC1-algebra $\mathcal{A}$ is surjective (meaning that the initial map from the initial SPEC1-algebra is surjective), then every element is named by some variable-free Σ_1 term. An initial algebra, in particular, is an initial algebra. In such a case the argument in the proof of Lemma 10 can be trivially modified to yield the following:

Lemma 12 *The decision problem of testing equality of Σ_2 terms over the SPEC2(A)-algebra is Π^0_1-complete relative to the equality of ground Σ_2 terms over SPEC2(A)[2], if the algebra A is surjective.*

We now present a characterization analogous to the π^0_2- completeness result in section 3. This characterization is for the case of the parameterized specifications.

Given an equational specification SPEC1 ($\equiv(S_1,\Sigma_1,E_1)$) and a S_1-indexed family of countably infinite sets of generators , there is a model M of SPEC1 which is called the free algebra of the specification with respect to the family of generators. Consider given an infinite set of (many-sorted) variables X. Let $\equiv$ be the congruence on the set of terms $T_{\Sigma_1}(X)$ generated by the equations E_1. Then, M is defined to have carrier sets whose elements are the equivalence classes of $\equiv$. The interpretation of an n-ary function symbol f is given to be the function which carries the tuple $([t_1],..,[t_n])$ to $[f(t_1,..,t_n)]$, where [t] denotes the equivalence class of $\equiv$ that contains the term t.

The following is a well known result (and in point of fact is used in the proof of Birkhoff's Completeness Theorem (Theorem 1)):

Lemma 13 *Any equation* e *over the signature Σ_1 is true in* M *if and only if it is provable from the equations in E_1 by pure equational reasoning.*

One might look for an analogous result in two ways : one possibility is to look for the complexity of reduction of the decision problem of equational truth in the F($\mathcal{A}$)-algebra to the problem of truth of Σ_1-equations in $\mathcal{A}$. Another possibility is to obtain a characterization of the reduction of the the theory of all F($\mathcal{A}$) algebras(where $\mathcal{A}$ is a SPEC1-algebra) to the equational theory E_2.

The first possibility is unworkable because the Σ_1-theory of $\mathcal{A}$ does not determine the Σ_2-theory of F($\mathcal{A}$). For an example, see [Subrahmanyam 1990]. In what follows, we look at the second possibility.

Theorem 14 *If* M *is the free algebra of the specification SPEC1 , then the Σ_2-theory of F(*M*) is Π^0_1 relative to E_2.* [3]

Proof: Let $t_1 = t_2$ be a given equation with $t_i \in T_{\Sigma_2}(X)$. By definition, $F(M) \models t_1 = t_2$ if and only if for every assignment σ the equation is true in F(M). By the very construction of F(M), every element is an equivalence class under the aforementioned congruence: further each such equivalence class has a term of the form $T[s_1,..,s_n]$,where T is a Σ_2-context containing no variable occurrence, and having n holes, and each of the s_i are variables. Clearly, therefore, the value of any term t with respect to an assignment σ is equal to the value of a term (with assignment σ_2 defined as follows : each variable x

[2]..or equivalently relative to E_2 and equality of Σ_1 ground terms over $\mathcal{A}$

[3]If the specification SPEC2 is assumed to have no more sorts than the specification SPEC1, one can use the well-known fact that adjunctions compose to yield adjunctions [MacLane 1988] to observe that the F(M) is the free algebra in the category of SPEC2-algebras. Thus equality of Σ_2-terms is actually axiomatized by E_2 [Subrahmanyam 1990]. The assumption of SPEC2 introducing no additional sorts is unusual in practice, however.

is assigned the equivalence class containing the constant $a_{[x]}$, where [x] is the equivalence class in the algebra M containing the term x) of the form just described. Now, note that two terms of this form are (by the definition of F(M) equal under assignment σ_2 if and only if they are provably equal by equational reasoning from E_2. This establishes that the problem is Π_1^0 relative to E_2∎

Theorem 15 *Let $t_1 = t_2$ be a $T_{\Sigma_2}(X)$ equation true in F(M). Then, for any other model $\mathcal{A}$ of E_1, it is true in F($\mathcal{A}$).*

Proof: Let σ be any assignment to the variables occurring in t_1 and t_2 with range the elements of F($\mathcal{A}$). We will show that for any such assignment $(F(\mathcal{A}), \sigma) \models t_1 = t_2$. Let $(\mathbf{b}_i)_{i \in I}$ (I is some index set) be an indexing of the constants in const($\mathcal{A}$). Then there are ground Σ_2-contexts T_1 and T_2 such that

$$[t_i\sigma\ ] = [T_i[b_1^i,..,b_n^i]] \qquad\qquad i = 1,2$$

(the right hand side has a ground term; the assignment is irrelevant). Let B denote the set of elements of const($\mathcal{A}$) occurring inside the contexts T_1 and T_2 above. Consider a 1-1 mapping θ from B into the set of elements $\{a_x \mid x \in X\}$ (a subset of const(M). Since $t_1 = t_2$ holds in F(M), we know that

$$F(M) \models T_1[\theta(b_1^1),..,\theta(b_n^1)] = T_2[\theta(b_1^2),..,\theta(b_n^2)]$$

As observed in Lemma 10, this has an equational proof Ξ (a chain of replacements) from E_2 and eqns(M). Consider the replacement of every a_x in the range of θ by $\theta^{-1}(a_x)$, and every other a_x by some arbitrary constant $\mathbf{b}_k$. Further every symbol $a_{t[x_1,..,x_n]}$ is replaced by $t[\theta^{-1}(x_1),..,\theta^{-1}(x_n)]$. We will abuse notation and call this replacement θ^{-1}. Let Ξ_1 be the result of applying θ_{-1} to Ξ.

It is easily seen that the equational steps in Ξ that involve equations in E_2 translate into valid equational steps in Ξ_1. However the case of equational steps in Ξ where the equation occurs in eqns(M) is trickier. Suppose the equational step is:

$$t_1[y_1,..,y_k,a_{s_1},..,a_{s_n}] = t_2[y_1,..,y_k,a_{s_1},..,a_{s_n}]$$

This means that :

$$t_1[y_1,..,y_k,s_1,..,s_n] = t_2[y_1,..,y_k,s_1,..,s_n]$$

is follows from E_1 by equational reasoning. The corresponding equational step in Ξ_1 is

$$t_1[y_1,..,y_k,\theta^{-1}(a_{s_1}),..,\theta^{-1}(a_{s_n})] = t_2[y_1,..,y_k,\theta^{-1}(a_{s_1}),..,\theta^{-1}(a_{s_n})]$$

which is an instance of the preceding equation. Thus Ξ_1 is a legitimate proof as well. Thus $t_1 = t_2$ is true in F($\mathcal{A}$)∎

We have shown herewith that

$$\bigcap_{\mathcal{A} \models E_1} \text{Theory}(F(\mathcal{A})) = \text{Theory}(F(M))$$

It is easy, now, to arrive at the following result:

Theorem 16 *The theory of the class of all free extensions(with respect to a parameterized specification (SPEC1,SPEC2)) of models of a given parameter specification SPEC1 is Π_1^0 relative to the theory of SPEC2. Furthermore, there are specifications (SPEC1,SPEC2) where the theory of SPEC2 is decidable and the theory of the abovementioned class is Π_1^0-complete.*

6 Conclusions

We have shown that the recursion theoretic complexity of the theory of the initial algebra of a given equational theory is , in general, Π_2^0-complete. This result points to the impossibility of any effective complete axiomatization of the theory of initial algebras. We have, further, obtained a series of characterizations of the recursion-theoretic relationships between the specifying equations and the theories of the free extensions of parameter algebras. We have established the existence of a Π_1^0 reduction (relative to the equational theory of the specification) to the theory of the class of free extensions of the algebras satisfying the parameter extensions, and shown that in the case of decidable specifications this decision problem is Π_1^0-complete. We conjecture that , more generally, there are specifications whose equational theory is undecidable (some r.e. degree) , and the complexity of the class of free extensions of parameter algebras is Π_1^0-complete *relative to the theory of the specification.* The issue of specifications whose equational theories are non-recursive enumerable are of little interest (since we are only interested in finite specifications).

By highlighting the cause of the high complexity, we expect that these results will shed light on useful and interesting ways of constraining the complexity of algebraic specifications. Further, these results are also foundational for the analysis of decision problems concerning truth of higher order equations in the full type hierarchy with a given initial algebra as a base type, which has obvious importance in the area of reasoning about recursion-free functional programs.

Acknowledgements: I thank the following for their contributions to this work: Val Breazu-Tannen for very insightful discussions, advice and encouragement; Aravind Joshi for material and moral support; the anonymous referees for pointing out errors in an earlier draft, and Vijay Gehlot for discussions and for help with the document preparation.

References

[Burris & Sankappanavar 1981] S. Burris and H. P. Sankappanavar. *A course in universal algebra*. Volume 78 of *Graduate Texts in Mathematics*, Springer-Verlag, 1981.

[Davis 1976] M. Davis, Y. Matijasevič, and J. Robinson. Hilbert's tenth problem, diophantine equations: positive aspects of a negative solution. In *Proceedings of Symposia in Pure mathematics, Vol. 28*, pages 323–378, American Mathematical Society, 1976.

[Ehrig & Mahr 1985] H. Ehrig and B. Mahr. *Fundamentals of algebraic specification 1: equations and initial semantics*. Springer-Verlag, 1985.

[F.Nourani 1981] F.Nourani. On induction for programming logic : syntax, semantics and inductive closure. *Bulletin of the EATCS*, (13):51–64, February 1981.

[Goguen & Meseguer 1985] J. Goguen and J. Meseguer. Initiality, induction, and computability. In *Algebraic Methods in Semantics*, Cambridge Univ. Press, 1985.

[Goguen 1978] J. A. Goguen, J. W. Thatcher, and E. G. Wagner. An initial algebra approach to the specification, correctness, and implementation of abstract data types. In R.T. Yeh, editor, *Current Trends in Programming Methodology*, Prentice-Hall, 1978.

[Goguen 1984] J. A. Goguen. How to prove algebraic inductive hypotheses without induction. In *Proceedings of the Conference on Automated Deduction*, pages 356–373, Springer-Verlag, 1984.

[Guttag 1978] J. V. Guttag, E. Horowitz, and D. R. Musser. Abstract data types and software validation. *Communications of the ACM*, 21:1048–1064, 1978.

[Huet & Hullot 1982] G. Huet and J-M. Hullot. Proofs by induction in equatioanl theories with constructors. *Journal of Computer and System Sciences*, 25:239–266, 1982.

[Lawvere 1963] F. W. Lawvere. Functorial semantics of algebraic theories. In *Proc. Nat. Acad. Sci. Vol.50*, pages 869–872, 1963.

[MacLane 1988] S. MacLane. *Categories for the Working Mathematician*. Volume 5 of *Graduate Texts in Mathematics*, Springer-Verlag, 1988.

[MacQueen & Sannella 1985] D. MacQueen and D. T. Sannella. Completeness of proof systems for equational specifications. *IEEE Transactions on Software Engineering*, SE-11:454–461, 1985.

[Rogers 1967] H. Rogers. *Theory of Recursive Functions and Effective Computability*. New York: McGraw-Hill, 1967.

[Subrahmanyam 1990] R. Subrahmanyam. *Theory of the initial algebra of a set of equations*. Technical Report, University of Pennsylvania, Philadelphia, 1990.

[Zhang 1988] H. Zhang, D. Kapur, and M. S. Krishnamoorthy. A mechanizable induction principle for equational specifications. 1988. Manuscript.

A New Method for Undecidability Proofs of First Order Theories

Ralf Treinen*

Abstract: We claim that the reduction of Post's Correspondence Problem to the decision problem of a theory provides a useful tool for proving undecidability of first order theories given by an interpretation. The goal of this paper is to propose a framework for such reduction proofs. The method proposed is illustrated by proving the undecidability of the theory of a term algebra modulo AC and the theory of a partial lexicographic path ordering.

1 Introduction

The interest of this paper is twofold. First it proposes a general methodology for proving results of the kind:

The first order theory of the predicate logic model $\mathcal{I} = \cdots$ is undecidable.

Second, besides examples that serve just for the illustration of the method proposed, we show some applications that are interesting in their own right.

We only consider theories of given models, in contrast to theories defined by some sets of axioms that are not necessarily complete. When applied to (the theory of) a given model $\mathcal{I}$, the method leads to an effective mechanism that yields for each Post Correspondence Problem P over the alphabet $\{a, b\}$ a formula, denoted $\underline{\texttt{solvable}}_P$, such that

$$P \text{ is solvable} \quad \Leftrightarrow \quad \mathcal{I} \models \underline{\texttt{solvable}}_P \tag{1}$$

Because of the effectiveness of the construction of this formula we immediately get the undecidability result for the theory from the well-known undecidability of Post's Correspondence Problem. Furthermore we are interested in showing not only undecidability of the whole theory of $\mathcal{I}$, but of a smallest possible fragment of this theory. In the construction of $\underline{\texttt{solvable}}_P$ we will therefore try to avoid alternations of quantifiers as far as possible.

The basic principle of the proof method proposed is the simulation of the two data types involved in Post's Correspondence Problem: strings and sequences (resp. sets). The representation of the objects of these data types is performed by appropriate representation functions mapping the carrier sets into the universe of the model under consideration. The representation does not reflect directly in the theory of the model, especially there is no need for formulas characterizing the images of the representation functions. The operations on the data types are expressed by first order formulas that are to be designed in regard to the properties of the model.

The target formula $\underline{\texttt{solvable}}_P$ consists of a "frame" that is independent of the model under consideration but uses subformulas representing the operations on the data types. We present the frame formula

*Address: FB14 – Departement of Computer Science, Universität des Saarlandes, D6600 Saarbrücken, West Germany; email: treinen@cs.uni-sb.de

and formulate the requirements that guarantee the "correctness" of the representation of the carrier sets and the pertaining operations.

To a large extent we constrain the meaning of the formulas only for those elements of the universe that represent objects of the data types. Moreover, beyond the correctness of data type representation we have to make sure that a certain relation on the universe is Noetherian. This is an inherent property of the model, since the well-foundedness of a relation is not expressible in first order logic[1].

The method proposed here exploits the properties of the model instead of properties of the *theory of* the model as it has been done in [Tar53] and [Rab65]. The logic is not involved in the definition of the representation functions: The intended applications concern universes constituting a formal language, such that the representation may often be performed on a purely symbolic level. The logic is only used in the realization of the operations of the data types. We will demonstrate some applications where this technique yields very simple reduction proofs.

A first set of applications illustrating the method proposed is concerned with equational problems, that is validity of formulas with equality as the only predicate symbol in the initial, respectively the free algebra of an equational specification (see [BS89] for an introduction to equational problems). The first example (A) treats the decision problem for the theory of ground term algebras modulo the axioms of associativity and commutativity (AC for short) and has been given as open problem in [Com88]. In this paper the existential fragment has been shown decidable thus extending the results for AC unification ([Sti81] and [Kir85] for the case of additional free function symbols). The generalization of this result to the free algebra refutes a conjecture of [BS89] where general equational problems are claimed to be decidable provided unification with free function symbols is decidable. The extension by the axiom of idempotency to ACI in Example (B) is straightforward.

To the author's knowledge the undecidability of the theory of ground terms modulo associativity alone (Example (F)) has not been stated before, but since Quine ([Qui46]) has proved the undecidability of the theory of concatenation this is not a surprising result. A unification algorithm for this theory has been given by Plotkin ([Plo72]). In contrast to the AC case, associativity without commutativity is of unification type ω (see [BHS86] for the classification of unification problems), this coincides with the observation that our technique yields undecidability of the Σ_3 fragment in the AC case but Σ_2 in the case of associativity.

The second field of application is the theory of ground terms equipped with some ordering relation. The undecidability of the "theory of subterm relation" has been shown in [Ven87] but without the extension to possibly infinite trees. Furthermore [Ven87] shows the decidability of the existential fragment. We mention this application in order to illustrate the benefit gained from a systematic study of reduction proofs.

The question of decidability of the theory of a total simplification ordering has been posed in [Com88]. The decidability of the existential fragment of a total lexicographic path ordering (lpo for short) is shown in [Com90b]. We prove in Example (C) the undecidability of the Σ_4 fragment of a partial lpo. Unfortunately there still remain two big gaps between these results (see Section 5).

The undecidability of the Σ_2 fragment of complete number theory (Example (G)) is of course by no means a new result; it is presented here merely for demonstrating some aspects of the method proposed. The undecidability of the Σ_1 fragment has been shown in [Mat70].

The separation of Post's Correspondence Problem into two datatypes induces the structure of the paper: After a survey of the mathematical framework in Section 2 the simulation of the data type "strings" is discussed in Section 3. In the applications this part will always be the trivial one. Section 4 describes the construction of the sentence $\underline{\texttt{solvable}}_P$ while presenting two alternative methods for the representation of construction sequences. In the first method sequences are viewed as sets. This

[1]Not even by a sentence of the extension $L_{\omega_1,\omega}$ containg countably infinite disjunctions and conjunctions ([Kei71]).

method is easier to use than the second one representing sequences directely but is less powerful, since in some applications the second method can yield a smaller number of quantifier alternations in the formula $\underline{\texttt{solvable}}_P$.

2 Preliminaries

In this paper we consider unsorted first order logic where equality is not required. For the basic notions according syntax and semantics of first order logic the reader is referred to textbooks on mathematical logic, for instance [End72]. We specify a predicate logic basis as a pair (P, F) where the set of function symbols F is given in the form $\langle f(n_f), g(n_g), \ldots\rangle$ and the set of predicate symbols $P = \langle \oplus(n_\oplus), \odot(n_\odot), \ldots\rangle$. The numbers in parantheses are not part of the syntax but indicate the arity of the symbols. If $=(2)$ is present in P it is always interpreted as equality. We will frequently use symbolic names for formulas, and in defining one formula we will often refer to other formulas via their symbolic "macro" names without giving an exact semantics of macro expansion for formulas. We only mention the following notions:

$w(x_1, \ldots, x_n)$ where w is a symbolic name for a formula stands for a formula the free variables of which are (possibly as proper subset) among $\{x_1, \ldots, x_n\}$. As usual $w(t_1, \ldots, t_n)$ denotes the result of simultanously substituting in $w(x_1, \ldots, x_n)$ the x_i by the corresponding t_i. We write $\mathcal{I} \models w[r_1, \ldots, r_n]$ if w is satisfied in $\mathcal{I}$ by the assignement $\{x_i \leftarrow r_i\}$. For the sake of convenience we allow infix notion, for instance $(x)w(y)$ instead of $w(x, y)$. Furthermore, in the examples, we will sometimes use tuples of variables instead of a single variables. In this case of course we have to replace the corresponding quantifiers by quantifier strings of the same kind.

The set of formulas over a given basis is split up into fragments. According to [Rog87] the *number of quantifier alternations* of a formula in prenex normal form ([Gal86]) is "the number of pairs of adjacent but unlike quantifiers". If this number is n and the outermost quantifier is $\exists$ (resp. $\forall$) the formula belongs to the Σ_{n+1}- (resp. Π_{n+1}-) fragment. $\Sigma_0 = \Pi_0$ denotes the set of quantifier-free formulas. An abitrary formula belongs to a certain fragment if it is logically equivalent to a prenex normal form formula contained in this fragment.

Given a set Σ of symbols Σ^* denotes the set of finite and Σ^+ the set of finite nonempty strings over Σ. $\triangleleft$ is the prefix ordering on strings. A *Post Correspondence Problem* P over an alphabet Σ ([Pos46]) is given by a finite set of the form

$$\{(p_i, q_i) \mid 0 \leq i \leq m; p_i, q_i \in \Sigma^+\}$$

A *P-construction sequence* for $(u, v) \in \Sigma^* \times \Sigma^*$ is a sequence $((u_j, v_j))_{j=1\ldots n}$ with $u_j, v_j \in \Sigma^*$ for all j, $u_1 = v_1 = \epsilon$, $u_n = u$ and $v_n = v$, and for each $1 \leq j \leq n-1$ there is a $0 \leq i \leq m$ with $u_{j+1} = u_j p_i$ and $v_{j+1} = v_j q_i$ where juxtaposition denotes the concatenation of strings. In this case (u, v) is called *P-constructable*. P is *solvable* if there is a $u \in \Sigma^+$ such that (u, u) is P-constructable.

Equational problems emerged from the study of unification problems that can now be considered as a special case of equational problems (see [Sie89] for a survey on unification). For a set F of ranked function symbols let $T(F)$ denote the set of F-ground terms and $T(F, X)$ the set of F-terms that contain variables from the set X. $T(F)$ and $T(F, X)$ will also be considered as F-algebras where the symbols from F are given their Herbrand interpretation ([Gal86]). The basis and the model for equational problems are defined by an equational specification (F, E) in the sense of [EM85], here restricted to the one-sorted case, that is F is a ranked set of function symbols and E is a set of implicitly universally quantified equations of F-terms. The only predicate symbol is the equality symbol, the set of function symbols is given by the specification. [BS89] designate the following models of a specification (F, E):

- the *initial algebra* is the quotient of the ground term algebra $T(F)$ by the congruence generated by E.

- the *E-free algebra* is the quotient of the term algebra $T(F,X)$ by the congruence generated by E where X is a not further specified infinite set of variables.

A discussion of term algebras can be found in [EM85]. In this context [BS89] call the Π_3 fragment *special equational problems* and the Σ_2 fragment *special equational problems without independent parameters.*

The *lexicographic path ordering* on $T(F)$ has been described in [Der87][2] as a tool for proving termination of term rewriting systems. For a given partial order[3] $<_F$ on the set F of function symbols the lexicographic path ordering $\preceq_{\mathrm{lpo}}$ is recursively defined by

$$t = g(t_1, \dots, t_n) \preceq_{\mathrm{lpo}} f(s_1, \dots, s_m) = s$$

iff $t = s$ or one of the following holds

- $t \preceq_{\mathrm{lpo}} s_i$ for some i
- $g <_F f$ and $t_j \prec_{\mathrm{lpo}} s$ for all j
- $f = g$ and there is a $j \leq n$ with
  - $t_i = s_i$ for all $i < j$
  - $t_j \prec_{\mathrm{lpo}} s_j$
  - $t_i \prec_{\mathrm{lpo}} s$ for all $i > j$

where $x \prec_{\mathrm{lpo}} y$ is an abbreviation for $x \preceq_{\mathrm{lpo}} y \wedge x \neq y$. $\preceq_{\mathrm{lpo}}$ is a simplification ordering ([Der87]), especially it is a partial order containing the subterm ordering. $\preceq_{\mathrm{lpo}}$ is total iff the underlying precedence $<_F$ is total.

$f^n(t)$ means n applications of the unary function symbol f to the term t. $lth(s)$ denotes the length of the sequence s. □ designates the end of a proof, the end of an example will be marked by ◇.

3 Simulation of Strings

The first thing we need for the representation of the data type string is a coding function

$$\phi: \{a, b\}^* \to \mathcal{I}$$

We will use the symbol ϕ also to denote the corresponding function $\phi: \{a,b\}^* \times \{a,b\}^* \to \mathcal{I}^2$. The operations that will be used in the simulation of Post's Correspondence Problem are the test for emptiness and for each single nonempty string a unary function that appends this fixed string to its argument. For the sake of generality this function will be represented as a formula instead of a term. More precisely, we need:

- $\underline{\texttt{is-}\epsilon}(x)$
- $(y)\underline{v}(x)$ for each $v \in \{a, b\}^+$

such that

[INJ] ϕ is injective

[EPS] For all $r \in \mathcal{I}$: $\mathcal{I} \models \underline{\texttt{is-}\epsilon}[r]$ iff $r = \phi(\epsilon)$

[2] referring to an unpublished paper of Kamin and Lévy.

[3] The definition in [Der87] (precedence) is slightly more general in using quasi-orderings.

[CON] For all $r \in \mathcal{I}$, $v \in \{a,b\}^+$, $w \in \{a,b\}^*$: $\mathcal{I} \models [r]\underline{v}[\phi(w)]$ iff $r = \phi(wv)$

Definition 1 *$\sqsubset$ is the relation on $\mathcal{I}$ defined by: $x \sqsubset y$ iff there is a $v \in \{a,b\}^+$ with $\mathcal{I} \models [y]\underline{v}[x]$. As usual $\sqsubset^*$ denotes the reflexive transitive closure of $\sqsubset$. Furthermore $\sqsubset$ generalizes to pairs of objects by $(x_1,x_2) \sqsubset (y_1,y_2)$ iff $x_1 \sqsubset y_1$ and $x_2 \sqsubset y_2$.*

If $r_1 = \phi(w_1)$ and $r_2 = \phi(w_2)$ then $r_1 \sqsubset r_2$ expresses the prefix relationship between w_1 and w_2. However the definition is not restricted to representatives of strings, we will need this definition and the pertaining requirement in its full generality later. The formula $\underline{\texttt{finite}}$ characterizes the set of elements of the universe where $\sqsubset$ is a Noetherian relation. This set has to contain *at least* (but may not be equal to) the image of ϕ.

[NOE] There is no infinite descending $\sqsubset$-chain $(r_i)_{i\geq 0}$ in $\mathcal{I}$ with $\mathcal{I} \models \underline{\texttt{finite}}[r_0]$.

[FIN] For all $w \in \{a,b\}^+$: $\mathcal{I} \models \underline{\texttt{finite}}[\phi(w)]$

Example (1): The basis B contains at least the function symbols $\epsilon(0), a(1), b(1)$ and the equality symbol $=(2)$. Let $\mathcal{I}$ be the algebra of B-ground terms modulo some set of equations that do not involve any of the symbols ϵ, a, b.

Deliberately confusing the characters a, b from the alphabet with the unary function symbols a, b we define

$$\begin{aligned} \phi(\sigma_0 \cdots \sigma_n) &:= \sigma_n(\cdots(\sigma_0(\epsilon))\cdots) \\ \underline{\texttt{is-}\epsilon}(x) &:= x = \epsilon \\ (y)\underline{\sigma_0 \cdots \sigma_n}(x) &:= y = \sigma_n(\cdots(\sigma_0(x))\cdots) \\ \underline{\texttt{finite}}(x) &:= \text{TRUE} \end{aligned}$$

The reader might easily check that these definitions fulfill the requirements. ◇

Example (2): The basis B contains at least the function symbols $\epsilon(0), f(2)$ and the equality symbol $=(2)$. Analogously to Example (1) let $\mathcal{I}$ denote the algebra of B-ground terms modulo some set of equations that do not involve any of ϵ, f. With the temporary definitions $\overline{a}(t) := f(\epsilon, t)$ and $overlineb(t) := f(f(\epsilon,\epsilon),t)$ we define

$$\begin{aligned} \phi(\sigma_0 \cdots \sigma_n) &:= \overline{\sigma_n}(\cdots(\overline{\sigma_0}(\epsilon))\cdots) \\ \underline{\texttt{is-}\epsilon}(x) &:= x = \epsilon \\ (y)\underline{\sigma_0 \cdots \sigma_n}(x) &:= y = \overline{\sigma_n}(\cdots(\overline{\sigma_0}(x))\cdots) \\ \underline{\texttt{finite}}(x) &:= \text{TRUE} \end{aligned}$$

The above definitions still constitute a correct representation of strings when we enlarge the model $\mathcal{I}$ to the free algebra $T(F,X)$ modulo E. ◇

The next example shows a nontrivial $\underline{\texttt{finite}}$ formula.

Example (3): B contains at least the function symbols $\epsilon(0), a(1), b(1)$ and the predicate symbols $=(2), \leq(2)$. Consider the algebra $\mathcal{I}$ of finite and infinite B-ground terms where $\leq$ is interpreted as the subterm relation.[4] We choose ϕ, $\underline{\texttt{is-}\epsilon}$ and $\underline{v}$ as in Example (1). The set of finite objects consists now of the terms built only with unary function symbols and containing the symbol ϵ.

$$\underline{\texttt{finite}}(x) := \epsilon \leq x \wedge \forall x'.x' \leq x \supset \{x' = \epsilon \vee \exists x''.x' = a(x'') \vee x' = b(x'')\}$$

[4]Note that the case of finite terms only is covered by Example (1).

If the set of nonunary function symbols $B' \subseteq B$ is finite we can transform the conclusion of the above implication into a Π_1-formula, thus saving one alternation of quantifiers:

$$\underline{\texttt{finite}}(x) := \epsilon \leq x \wedge \forall x'.x' \leq x \supset \bigwedge_{f \in B'} \forall \vec{z}.x' \neq f(\vec{z}) \qquad \diamond$$

4 Solutions of P

We are now ready to define the subformula $\underline{\texttt{one-step}}_P$. The intended meaning of $\underline{\texttt{one-step}}_P(y_1, y_2, y_3, y_4)$ is: "The pair of strings represented by (y_1, y_2) is obtained from the pair of strings represented by (y_3, y_4) by the application of one P-construction step." This is the only subformula that depends directly on the Post Correspondence Problem P:

$$\underline{\texttt{one-step}}_P(y_1, y_2, y_3, y_4) \quad := \quad \bigvee_{i=0,\ldots,m} ((y_1)\underline{p_i}(y_3) \wedge (y_2)\underline{q_i}(y_4))$$

where $P = \{(p_i, q_i) \mid i = 0, \ldots, m\}$.

4.1 Simulation of Sequences as Sets

In order to construct the sentence $\underline{\texttt{solvable}}_P$ we have to formulate something like "there is a P-construction sequence such that $\cdots$". How can we express as a formula the fact that something represents a P-construction sequence? The key idea we are going to explore now is: Instead of talking directly about sequences we may view a P-construction sequence as a *set* of pairs of strings. Since by definition a P-construction sequence is strictly ordered by the prefix relation on (pairs of) strings we are able to recover the sequence from the set.

With this idea we can now define the subformula $\underline{\texttt{constr}}_P(x)$ meaning that x represents a P-construction sequence. $\underline{\texttt{constr}}_P$ uses the subformula $(y_1, y_2)\underline{\texttt{in}}(x)$ reflecting the element relationship, the definition of which depends again on the model under consideration. From now on let a fixed Post Correspondence Problem P be given.

$$\begin{aligned} \underline{\texttt{constr}}_P(x) := \forall y_1, y_2.(y_1, y_2)\underline{\texttt{in}}(x) \supset & \\ & \{\underline{\texttt{is-}\epsilon}(y_1) \wedge \underline{\texttt{is-}\epsilon}(y_2)\} \vee & (2) \\ & \exists y_3, y_4.(y_3, y_4)\underline{\texttt{in}}(x) \wedge \underline{\texttt{one-step}}_P(y_1, y_2, y_3, y_4) & (3) \end{aligned}$$

Still leaving pending the definition of $\underline{\texttt{in}}$ we can now show

Lemma 1 *For all $r_1, r_2, u, s \in \mathcal{I}$ with $(r_1, r_2) \sqsubset^* (u, u)$ and*

$$\mathcal{I} \models \underline{\texttt{finite}}[u]$$
$$\mathcal{I} \models \underline{\texttt{constr}}_P[s]$$
$$\mathcal{I} \models [r_1, r_2]\underline{\texttt{in}}[s]$$

If [INJ], [EPS], [CON] and [NOE] are fulfilled then $(r_1, r_2) \in \text{IM}(\phi) \times \text{IM}(\phi)$ and the associated pair of strings $\phi^{-1}(r_1, r_2)$ is P-constructable.

Proof: We fix u and s with the above properties. Because of [NOE] there can not exist an infinite descending (w.r.t. $\sqsubset$) chain of pairs $(r_1, r_2) \sqsubset^* (u, u)$. We can therefore perform Noetherian induction on (r_1, r_2).

If $\mathcal{I} \models \underline{\texttt{is-}\epsilon}[r_1] \wedge \underline{\texttt{is-}\epsilon}[r_2]$ then [EPS] yields $(r_1, r_2) = \phi(\epsilon, \epsilon)$ and we are done.

Otherwise case (3) from the definition of $\underline{\texttt{constr}}_P$ applies, so there exist r_3, r_4 with $\mathcal{I} \models [r_3, r_4]\underline{\texttt{in}}[s]$ and $\mathcal{I} \models \underline{\texttt{one-step}}_P[r_1, r_2, r_3, r_4]$. From the definition of $\underline{\texttt{one-step}}_P$ follows $(r_3, r_4) \sqsubset (r_1, r_2) \sqsubset^* (u, u)$. The induction hypothesis yields that $(r_3, r_4) \in \text{IM}(\phi) \times \text{IM}(\phi)$ and $\phi^{-1}(r_3, r_4)$ is P-constructable, and because of [CON] and the definition of $\underline{\texttt{one-step}}_P$ the same holds for (r_1, r_2). □

We are now ready to define $\underline{\texttt{solvable}}_P$.

$$\underline{\texttt{solvable}}_P \quad := \quad \exists x, y. \underline{\texttt{constr}}_P(x) \wedge \underline{\texttt{finite}}(y) \wedge (y, y)\underline{\texttt{in}}(x) \wedge \neg \underline{\texttt{is-}\epsilon}(y)$$

From the above lemma we get immediately

Corollary 1 *If [INJ], [EPS], [CON] and [NOE] are fulfilled then*

$$\mathcal{I} \models \underline{\texttt{solvable}}_P \quad \Rightarrow \quad P \textit{ is solvable}$$

The reader should note that up to now we did not need any constraints on the subformula $\underline{\texttt{in}}$. We made use of the special properties of the model only in order to fulfill the requirements in connection with the simulation of strings. Once the representation of strings with the subformulas $\underline{\texttt{is-}\epsilon}, \underline{v}, \underline{\texttt{finite}}$ is found we get the first direction of our "goal"-theorem (1) for free — that is without worrying about the representation of sequences.

In order to prove the opposite direction of (1) we now have to choose a representation function for P-construction sequences and a corresponding formula $(y_1, y_2)\underline{\texttt{in}}(x)$. M denotes the domain of the representation function $\psi: M \to \mathcal{I}$:

$$M := \{(u_i, v_i)_{i=1\dots n} \mid u_i, v_i \in \{a, b\}^*, n \geq 2, u_i \triangleleft u_{i+1}, v_i \triangleleft v_{i+1}, (u_1, v_1) = (\epsilon, \epsilon)\}$$

Our last requirement relates the representation function ψ with the subformula $\underline{\texttt{in}}$ that is supposed to express the element relationship:

[IN] For all $s \in M$: $\mathcal{I} \models [r_1, r_2]\underline{\texttt{in}}[\psi(s)]$ iff there exits $j \in \{1, \dots, lth(s)\}$ with $(r_1, r_2) = \phi(s(j))$

Lemma 2 *If [EPS], [CON], [FIN], [IN] are fulfilled then*

$$P \textit{ is solvable} \quad \Rightarrow \quad \mathcal{I} \models \underline{\texttt{solvable}}_P$$

The next theorem summarizes the method as it stands now:

Theorem 1 *Let B be a predicate logic basis and $\mathcal{I}$ a model for B. If we can find representation functions ϕ, ψ and formulas $\underline{\texttt{is-}\epsilon}, \underline{v}, \underline{\texttt{finite}}, \underline{\texttt{in}}$ such that [INJ], [EPS], [CON], [FIN], [NOE] and [IN] are fulfilled then the first order theory of $\mathcal{I}$ is undecidable.*

Now we can complete the examples started in Section 3:

Example (A): Consider equational problems for the equational specification $(F_A, AC(+))$ where $F_A := \langle \epsilon(0), a(1), b(2), f(2), +(2) \rangle$ and $AC(+)$ denotes the axioms of associativity and commutativity for $+$:

$$\begin{aligned} x + y &= y + x \\ (x + y) + z &= x + (y + z) \end{aligned}$$

We take the representation of strings from Example (1). It is easy to see that with the following definitions [IN] is fulfilled in the initial and in the free algebra:

$$\begin{aligned} \psi((u_i, v_i)_{i=1,\dots,n}) \quad &:= \quad f(\phi(u_1), \phi(v_1)) + \dots + f(\phi(u_n), \phi(v_n)) \\ (y_1, y_2)\underline{\texttt{in}}(x) \quad &:= \quad \exists x'. x = f(y_1, y_2) + x' \end{aligned}$$

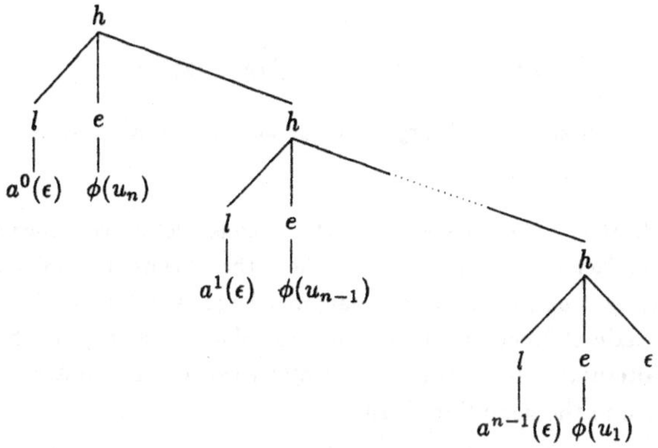

Figure 1: The term $\delta((u_i)_{i=1\ldots n})$ representing the sequence $(u_i)_{i=1\ldots n}$

Theorem 2 *The (Σ_3 fragment of the) first order theory of a ground term algebra (resp. term algebra) modulo associativity and commutativity is undecidable.*

We can improve this result by restricting the base to $F_{A'} := \langle\epsilon(0), f(2), +(2)\rangle$ and $P_{A'} := \langle=(2)\rangle$. With the representation of strings as in example (2) and ψ, $\underline{\text{in}}$ as above we obtain undecidability of the first order theory of $T(F_{A'})/_{AC(+)}$ and of $T(F_{A'}, X)/_{AC(+)}$.

We can also show that undecidability holds when + *and* f are associative and commutative, and also in the case of the simpler signature $\langle\epsilon(0), f(1), +(2)\rangle$. These are the simplest cases where the first order theory is undecidable: [Com88] remarks that the case of one AC function symbol and one constant is equivalent to Presburger arithmetic and therefore decidable. Using this idea the case of one AC function symbol plus a finite set of constants (called the "theory of finitely generated multisets" in [Com90a]) can as well be reduced to the theory of Presburger arithmetic. ◇

Example (B): Theorem 2 still holds when the set of axioms is enlarged by the axiom of idempotency: $x + x = x$.

Example (C): Let $F_C := \langle\epsilon(0), a(1), b(1), e(1), l(1), h(3)\rangle$ and $P_C := \langle=(2), \leq(2)\rangle$. $\mathcal{I}_C$ is the ground term algebra $T(F_C)$ where $\leq$ is interpreted as the lexicographic path ordering $\preceq_{\text{lpo}}$ generated by the following precedence on F_C:

$$\epsilon <_F a <_F b <_F h <_F \begin{cases} l \\ e \end{cases}$$

e and l are uncomparable in the order $<_F$.

ϕ, $\underline{\texttt{is-}\epsilon}$, $\underline{\texttt{finite}}$ and $\underline{v}$ can be copied from example (1). A P construction sequence will be represented by two lists of labeleld strings, one for the first component and one for the second. The labels associate the corresponding components of a pair, moreover they will be essential for the formulation of the membership relation.

We associate to each nonempty sequence $s = (u_i)_{i=1,\ldots,n}$ the term $\delta(s)$ as shown in Figure 1 and choose

$$\psi((u_i, v_i)_{i=1,\ldots,n}) := (\delta((u_i)_{i=1,\ldots,n}), \delta((v_i)_{i=1,\ldots,n}))$$

In order to formulate the subformula $\underline{\text{in}}$ we use the following temporary definition:

$$(y)\underline{\texttt{in}}(x)\underline{\texttt{at}}(z) \quad := \quad h(l(z), e(y), \epsilon) \leq x \land \tag{4}$$

$$\forall y'.h(l(z), e(y'), \epsilon) \leq x \supset y' \leq y \tag{5}$$

Finally we define

$$(y_1, y_2)\underline{\mathtt{in}}(x_1, x_2) \quad := \quad \exists z.(y_1)\underline{\mathtt{in}}(x_1)\underline{\mathtt{at}}(z) \wedge (y_2)\underline{\mathtt{in}}(x_2)\underline{\mathtt{at}}(z)$$

Theorem 3 *The (Σ_4 fragment of the) first order theory of a partial lexicographic path ordering is undecidable.*

The proof of [IN] can be found in [Tre90]. The separation of the P-construction sequence into two lists is not essential for the proof. In fact an analogous proof where the P-construction sequence is represented by one list of pairs of strings is also possible (by changing the arity of h to 4). The price of this variant is the need for another maximal function symbol uncomparable to e and l, thereby leading to a "less total" ordering. In this alternative proof the labels $l(a^i(\epsilon))$ can not be omitted, they are necessary for the maximality condition in the definition of $\underline{\mathtt{in}}$.

We remark that the same construction can be used to show that the Σ_4 fragment of the first order theory of a recursive path ordering([Der82]) is undecidable. ◇

Counting the quantifiers involved in the above construction we find that the formula $\underline{\mathtt{solvable}}_P$ is at least in the Σ_3 fragment. This is an inherent drawback of this method since $\underline{\mathtt{solvable}}_P$ follows the pattern

$$\exists s \cdots \forall (s_1, s_2) \in s \cdots \exists (s_3, s_4) \in s \cdots$$

In general the formula $\underline{\mathtt{in}}$ is the most "expensive" one (in terms of alternations of quantifiers). We will always try to find a formula $\underline{\mathtt{in}}$ in Σ_1, if we do not succeed we get undecidability only for a fragment larger than Σ_3.

4.2 Direct Simulation of Sequences

In some applications it is possible to overcome this limitation by using a direct simulation technique for sequences. In this case we have to perform three different operations on the data type sequence, and we have to work a little bit harder to regulate the correlation of the pertaining formulas. We will come back to a comparison of these two methods at the end of this section.

The formulas that are to be designed for the model under consideration are

- $\underline{\mathtt{nonempty}}(x)$
- $(y_1, y_2, x')\underline{\mathtt{sub\text{-}of}}(x)$
- $(y_1, y_2)\underline{\mathtt{head\text{-}of}}(x)$

The intended meaning of the first formula should be clear, $(y_1, y_2, x')\underline{\mathtt{sub\text{-}of}}(x)$ is supposed to express that the sequence with first element (y_1, y_2) and tail x' is a suffix of the sequence x, and $(y_1, y_2)\underline{\mathtt{head\text{-}of}}(x)$ is intended to express that (y_1, y_2) is the head of the sequence x.

The analogous definition of $\underline{\mathtt{constr}}_P$ is now

$$\begin{aligned}
&\underline{\mathtt{constr}}_P(x) := \forall y_1, y_2, x'.(y_1, y_2, x')\underline{\mathtt{sub\text{-}of}}(x) \supset \\
&\quad \{\underline{\mathtt{is\text{-}\epsilon}}(y_1) \wedge \underline{\mathtt{is\text{-}\epsilon}}(y_2)\} \vee \\
&\quad \{\underline{\mathtt{nonempty}}(x') \wedge \forall y_3, y_4.(y_3, y_4)\underline{\mathtt{head\text{-}of}}(x') \supset \underline{\mathtt{one\text{-}step}}_P(y_1, y_2, y_3, y_4)\}
\end{aligned}$$

and finally the formula $\underline{\mathtt{solvable}}_P$ reads

$$\underline{\mathtt{solvable}}_P := \exists x, y.\underline{\mathtt{constr}}_P(x) \wedge (y, y)\underline{\mathtt{head\text{-}of}}(x) \wedge \underline{\mathtt{finite}}(y) \wedge \neg\underline{\mathtt{is\text{-}\epsilon}}(y)$$

In contrast to section 4.1 where we obtained the first direction of (1) just from the representation of strings we now have to state additional requirements on the newly introduced formulas:

[NH] $\mathcal{I} \models \forall x.\underline{\texttt{nonempty}}(x) \supset \exists y_1, y_2.(y_1, y_2)\underline{\texttt{head-of}}(x)$

[HS] $\mathcal{I} \models \forall x, y_1, y_2.(y_1, y_2)\underline{\texttt{head-of}}(x) \supset \exists x'.(y_1, y_2, x')\underline{\texttt{sub-of}}(x)$

[HSH] $\mathcal{I} \models \forall x, x', y_1, y_2, y_3, y_4.(y_1, y_2, x')\underline{\texttt{sub-of}}(x) \wedge (y_3, y_4)\underline{\texttt{head-of}}(x') \supset \exists x''.(y_3, y_4, x'')\underline{\texttt{sub-of}}(x)$

At this point the reader might remark that we could have used [NH] as a definition of nonempty by turning the implication sign into an equivalence. In this case only the requirement [HS] and [HSH] remain relating head-of to sub-of. We do not choose this approach in order to avoid the introduction of extra quantifiers. Example (D) shows how a model specific argument leads to the elimination of an unwanted existential quantifier in the definition of nonempty.

With the help of these properties we can now prove a lemma analogous to Lemma 1:

Lemma 3 *For all* $r_1, r_2, u, s, s' \in \mathcal{I}$ *with* $(r_1, r_2) \sqsubset^* (u, u)$ *and*

$$\mathcal{I} \models \underline{\texttt{finite}}[u]$$
$$\mathcal{I} \models \underline{\texttt{constr}_P}[s]$$
$$\mathcal{I} \models [r_1, r_2, s']\underline{\texttt{sub-of}}[s]$$

If [INJ], [EPS], [CON], [NOE], [NH] and [HSH] are fulfilled then $(r_1, r_2) \in \text{IM}(\phi) \times \text{IM}(\phi)$ *and* $\phi^{-1}(r_1, r_2)$ *is P-constructable.*

Proof: By Noetherian induction on (r_1, r_2) similar to the proof of Lemma 1. □

Corollary 2 *If [INJ], [EPS], [CON], [NOE], [NH], [HSH] and [HS] are fulfilled then*

$$\mathcal{I} \models \underline{\texttt{solvable}_P} \quad \Rightarrow \quad P \textit{ is solvable}$$

In a first attempt we could require as in Section 4.1 a coding function mapping the set M into $\mathcal{I}$. This will suffice in some examples, but we can be more liberal and allow for each sequence s a "private" coding function for the set of the subsequences of s:

$$\psi \in \prod_{s \in M} (\{0, \ldots, lth(s)\} \rightarrow \mathcal{I})$$

The subformulas nonempty, sub-of and head-of have to work properly for the codings of subsequences: For all $s \in M, n \leq lth(s)$:

[NIL] $\mathcal{I} \models \underline{\texttt{nonempty}}[\psi(s)(n)]$ iff $n \neq 0$

[HEA] $\mathcal{I} \models [r_1, r_2]\underline{\texttt{head-of}}[\psi(s)(n)]$ iff $n \geq 1$ and $(r_1, r_2) = \phi(s(n))$

[SUB] $\mathcal{I} \models [r_1, r_2, t]\underline{\texttt{sub-of}}[\psi(s)(lth(s))]$ iff there is $i \in \{1, \ldots, lth(s)\}$ with $(r_1, r_2) = \phi(s(i))$ and $t = \psi(s)(i-1)$

Lemma 4 *If [EPS], [CON], [FIN], [NIL], [HEA] and [SUB] are fulfilled then*

$$P \textit{ is solvable} \quad \Rightarrow \quad \mathcal{I} \models \underline{\texttt{solvable}_P}$$

Theorem 4 gives the complete method developed in this section:

Theorem 4 *Let B be a predicate logic basis and* $\mathcal{I}$ *a model for B. If we can find representations* ϕ, ψ *and formulas* is-ϵ, v, finite, head-of *and* sub-of *such that [INJ], [EPS], [CON], [NOE], [NH], [HS], [HSH], [FIN], [NIL], [HEA] and [SUB] are fulfilled, then the first order theory of* $\mathcal{I}$ *is undecidable.*

Example (D): Let us now see how the undecidability result for the theory of subterm ordering from [Ven87] fits into our framework:

Let $F_D := \langle \epsilon(0), a(1), b(1), f(3) \rangle$ and $P_D := \langle =(2), \leq(2) \rangle$. $\mathcal{I}_D$ is the algebra of F_D-ground terms where $\leq$ is interpreted as the subterm relation. The representation of strings has been given in Example (1). We choose $\psi(s)(i)$ as follows:

$$\psi(s)(i) := \begin{cases} \epsilon & \text{if } i = 0 \\ f(\phi(u_i), \phi(v_i), \psi(s)(i-1)) & \text{otherwise} \end{cases}$$

and define the remaining formulas:

$$\begin{aligned} (y_1, y_2)\underline{\texttt{head-of}}(x) &:= \exists x'.x = f(y_1, y_2, x') \\ (y_1, y_2, x')\underline{\texttt{sub-of}}(x) &:= f(y_1, y_2, x') \leq x \\ \underline{\texttt{nonempty}}(x) &:= \exists y_1, y_2, x'.x = f(y_1, y_2, x') \end{aligned}$$

We can save one alternation of quantifiers in $\underline{\texttt{solvable}}_P$ by transforming $\underline{\texttt{nonempty}}$ into a Π_1 formula[5].

$$\underline{\texttt{nonempty}}(x) \quad := \quad x \neq \epsilon \wedge \forall x'.x \neq a(x') \wedge x \neq b(x')$$

Theorem 5 ([Ven87]) *The (Σ_2-fragment of the) first order theory of the subterm ordering is undecidable.* ◇

Example (E): We can modify the above example by enlarging the model to the algebra of finite and infinite ground terms. We can use exactly the same proof as above but with the $\underline{\texttt{finite}}$ formula as in Example (3) to show

Theorem 6 *The (Σ_2 fragment of the) first order theory of the subterm ordering in the algebra of finite and infinite trees in undecidable.* ◇

Example (F): If we drop commutativity from example (A) we can now show undecidability even of the Σ_2 fragment:

Consider the equational specification $(F_F, A(+))$ where $F_F = \langle \epsilon(0), f(2), +(2) \rangle$ and $A(+)$ denotes the axiom of associativity for $+$:

$$(x + y) + z \quad = \quad x + (y + z)$$

For the initial algebra we take the representation of strings from Example (2) and ψ similar to Example (A):

$$\begin{aligned} \psi((u_i, v_i)_{i=1,\ldots,m})(j) &:= f(\phi(u_j), \phi(v_j)) + \cdots + f(\phi(u_1), \phi(v_1)) + \epsilon \quad (j \geq 1) \\ \psi((u_i, v_i)_{i=1,\ldots,m})(0) &:= \epsilon \\ (y_1, y_2)\underline{\texttt{head-of}}(x) &:= \exists x'.x = f(y_1, y_2) + x' \\ (y_1, y_2, x')\underline{\texttt{sub-of}}(x) &:= x = f(y_1, y_2) + x' \vee \exists x''.x = x'' + f(y_1, y_2) + x' \\ \underline{\texttt{nonempty}}(x) &:= x \neq \epsilon \wedge \forall y_1, y_2.x \neq f(y_1, y_2) \wedge x \neq \epsilon + y_1 \end{aligned}$$

Here the formula $\underline{\texttt{nonempty}}$ is again obtained by a quantifier elimination analogous to Example (D).

Theorem 7 *The (Σ_2 fragment of the) theory of a ground term algebra modulo associativity is undecidable.* ◇

[5] In ground term algebras over a finite alphabet it is always possible to transform a purely equational formula into a Π_1 (or Σ_1) formula, see [CL89].

In the examples (D) to (F) we gave uniform codings for the sequences. The last example (G) shows the use of "private" coding functions for the subsequences of a given sequence. As mentioned in the introduction this is an artificial example that serves just for the purpose of demonstrating the usage of our method in its full generality.

Example (G): Let $F_G := \langle 0(0), 1(0), +(2), *(2) \rangle$ and $P_G := \langle =(2), \leq(2) \rangle$. Our interpretation $\mathcal{I}_G$ is the model of natural numbers. In order to define the representation of strings we introduce two abreviations:

$$\begin{aligned} \overline{a}(t) &:= t+t \\ \overline{b}(t) &:= t+t+1 \end{aligned}$$

It is easy to see that the following representation of strings fulfills the requirements since there is an obvious correspondence between strings and the binary representation of natural numbers.

$$\begin{aligned} \phi(\sigma_0 \cdots \sigma_n) &:= \overline{\sigma_n}(\cdots \overline{\sigma_0}(1)) \cdots) \\ \underline{\texttt{is-}\epsilon}(x) &:= x = 1 \\ (y)\underline{\sigma_0 \cdots \sigma_n}(x) &:= y = \overline{\sigma_n}(\cdots \overline{\sigma_0}(x)) \cdots) \\ \underline{\texttt{finite}}(x) &:= \text{TRUE} \end{aligned}$$

We use Gödel's β-predicate ([God31], see also [End72]) to represent sequences in the domain of natural numbers. The existence of the representation ψ is a consequence of the fundamental property of the β-predicate.

$$\begin{aligned} \underline{\texttt{nonempty}}(c,d,n) &:= n \geq 1 \\ (y_1,y_2)\underline{\texttt{head-of}}(c,d,n) &:= \beta(c,d,n+n,y_1) \wedge \beta(c,d,n+n+1,y_2) \\ (y_1,y_2,(c',d',n'))\underline{\texttt{sub-of}}(c,d,n) &:= c'=c \wedge d'=d \wedge n' \leq n \wedge (y_1,y_2)\underline{\texttt{head-of}}(c',d',n') \end{aligned}$$

As a result we obtain the undecidability of the Σ_2 fragment of complete number theory. The reader should note that $\text{IM}(\phi) = \mathcal{I} \setminus \{0\}$ — especially the images of ϕ and ψ are not disjoint. ◇

In this section we have finished the presentation of the two methods for proving the undecidability of the first order theory of a model. The first method is appropriate for models that miss a concept of ordering (for instance term algebras modulo associativity and commutativity), while the second is applicable to models where some kind of ordering is present. In view of the fact that the second method can yield undecidability of a more simple fragment than the first one, the question arises why we did not use the second method for proving undecidability of the theory of a partial recursive path ordering in order to find a formula $\underline{\texttt{solvable}}_P$ in a smaller fragment than Σ_4.

The reason is that we can benefit from the simpler quantification structure of $\underline{\texttt{solvable}}_P$ in the second method only if we succeed in finding *simple* formulas $\underline{\texttt{nonempty}}$, $\underline{\texttt{sub-of}}$ and $\underline{\texttt{head-of}}$ fulfilling the requirements. More precisely, we get a formula $\underline{\texttt{solvable}}_P$ in Σ_3 iff $\underline{\texttt{nonempty}}$ is in $\Pi_2 \cup \Sigma_1$ and both $\underline{\texttt{sub-of}}$ and $\underline{\texttt{head-of}}$ are in $\Pi_1 \cup \Sigma_2$, provided that $\underline{\texttt{is-}\epsilon}$, $\underline{v}$ and $\underline{\texttt{finite}}$ do not induce any further alternation of quantifiers. This is usually the case, in all applications we found the expensive operations belong to the datatype set, resp. sequence. Using representations of sequences in the spirit of Example (C) one could try to define $\underline{\texttt{sub-of}}$ with the help of a maximality condition as it has been done in the definition of $\underline{\texttt{in}}$, but we did not succeed in finding a formula $\underline{\texttt{sub-of}} \in \Pi_1 \cup \Sigma_2$ fullfilling [HSH].

5 Conclusions

We have presented two methods for proving the undecidability of the first order theory of a model. In order to apply one of these methods to a given model we have to find appropriate representations of the data types "string" and "sequence" and formulas expressing the operations on these data types. The two main theorems (Theorem 1 and Theorem 4) state that the proof of undecidability is completed if the pertaining set of requirements is fulfilled. We would like to point out some statements that at a first glance one might expect to be essential for a reduction proof but that in fact are not. With the presentation of this list we claim that applications benefit from a systematic study of reduction proofs since it localizes the crucial points where the special properties of a model are involved.

- A general binary concatenation operation is not necessary. The reader might try to find such a formula in the case of representation of strings by unary function symbols (Example (1)).
- The codings of strings and sequences may be non-disjoint.
- Formulas characterizing the images of the representations ϕ and ψ are not needed. In particular, it is not necessary to express that the elements of some set (sequence) are indeed pairs of strings.
- One should not worry about an *explicit* characterization of the finiteness of sequences in terms of first order logic.

In the undecidability proof of [Ven87] there exist subformulas in his construction that *explicitly* specify the shape of the objects that are intended to express P-construction sequences. In the approach presented here this is not necessary, we therefore yield a simpler formula $\texttt{solvable}_P$.

There is a potentially useful extension to the method that was not carried out since there are no applications at hand. Strings have been coded in the universe of the model by a representation *function*, instead we could associate an equivalence class of the universe to each string. This implies the need for further restrictions that guarantee the congruence property of the operations on strings.

The starting point of the method proposed is the undecidability of Post's Correspondence Problem. Of course there are many other undecidable problems that might serve for reduction to the decision problem of a theory (see [Dav77]). One may, for instance, take the uniform halting problem for Turing machines and perform a reduction proof in the above style: A Turing machine halts iff there is a finite sequence of configurations such that the first and the last one are in some special form and such that each adjacent pair is related by some "local transformation". A configuration can be interpreted as a pair of strings (the part of the tape to the left, resp. to the right of the head). Hence the data types involved here are the same. Our choice of Post's Correspondence Problem is somewhat arbitrary but leads to a technically simpler proof.

Another popular candidate for reduction is complete number theory. One may use the result of [Mat70] on the unsolvability of Hilberts Tenth Problem and reduce the Σ_1-fragment hoping to obtain a formula $\texttt{solvable}_P$ in a pretty small fragment. In fact [Qui46] gives a reduction of complete number theory to the theory of concatenation of strings over the alphabet $\{a, b\}$. The number n is coded by the string consisting of n a's, such that addition of numbers corresponds to the concatenation of strings. Multiplication is expressed with the help of lists that can be viewed as computation sequences for an iterative version of the multiplication algorithm. So it seems that this approach yields equally small fragments as ours, but the special point in Quine's proof is that a general concatenation operation is available in the logic, such that no quantifiers are needed for expressing addition. In most of the applications presented here we have just some kind of successor function given, in which case we need a list construction for expressing the addition operation. In order to optimize the alternations of quantifiers the iterative processes of addition and multiplication has to be performed in one list apparatus, thus yielding a more complex reduction proof.

In the introduction we mentioned some decidability results related to our applications, but there are still some gaps between these results and ours. We conclude with some open problems:

- The decidability of the Σ_1-fragment of the theory of ground term algebra modulo associativity and commutativity has been proved in [Com88]. While we have shown the undecidability of the

Σ_3-fragment the Σ_2-case is still unsolved.

- [Com90b] shows the decidability of the Σ_1-fragment of a total lexicographic path ordering, but the same question for the partial case remains open. On the other hand we have shown the undecidability of the Σ_4-fragment of the theory of *partial* lexicographic path ordering. We gave the proof for a precedence that is "as total as possible" but did not succeed in applying the technique to the total case. The reason is that at least two uncomparable function symbols are needed in order to distinguish between the two components of a pair. A proof of undecidability in the style presented here seems only to be possible beyond a purely symbolic level of representation, as illustrated in Example (G).

I am grateful to Jacques Loeckx, Stephan Uhrig, Hans-Jürgen Bürckert, Hubert Comon and one of the referees for their comments on earlier versions of this paper.

References

[BHS86] Hans-Jürgen Bürckert, Alexander Herold, and Manfred Schmidt-Schauß. *On Equational Theories, Unification and Decidability.* SEKI-Report SR-86-20, Universität Kaiserslautern, 1986.

[BS89] Hans-Jürgen Bürckert and Manfred Schmidt-Schauß. *On the Solvability of Equational Problems.* SEKI Report SR-89-07, Universität Kaiserslautern, 1989.

[CL89] Hubert Comon and Pierre Lescanne. Equational problems and disunification. *Journal of Symbolic Computation*, 7(3,4):371–425, 1989.

[Com88] Hubert Comon. *Unification et Disunification. Théorie et Applications.* PhD thesis, Institut National Polytechnique de Grenoble, Grenoble, France, 1988.

[Com90a] Hubert Comon. *Disunification:A Survey.* Rapport de Recherche no. 540, LRI, Université de Pairs Sud, january 1990.

[Com90b] Hubert Comon. Solving inequations in term algebras. In *5th Symposium on Logic in Computer Science*, 1990.

[Dav77] Martin Davis. Unsolvable problems. In Jon Barwise, editor, *Handbook of Mathematical Logic*, chapter C.2, pages 567–594, North-Holland, 1977.

[Der82] Nachum Dershowitz. Orderings for term-rewriting systems. *Theoretical Computer Science*, 7:279–301, 1982.

[Der87] Nachum Dershowitz. Termination of rewriting. *Journal of Symbolic Computation*, 3:69–116, 1987.

[EM85] H. Ehrig and B. Mahr. *Fundamentals of Algebraic Specification, vol. 1. EATCS-Monographs on Theoretical Computer Science*, Springer-Verlag, 1985.

[End72] Herbert B. Enderton. *Mathematical Introduction to Logic.* Academic Press, 1972.

[Gal86] Jean H. Gallier. *Logic for Computer Science.* Harper & Row, publishers, 1986.

[God31] Kurt Gödel. Über Formal Unentscheidbare Sätze der Pricipia Mathematica und Verwandter Systeme I. *Monatsheftc für Mathematik und Physik*, 38:173–198, 1931.

[Kei71] H. Jerome Keisler. *Model Theory for Infinitary Logic. Studies in Logic and the Foundations of Mathematics, vol. 62*, North-Holland Publishing Company, 1971.

[Kir85] Claude Kirchner. *Méthodes et Outils de Conception Systématique d'Algorithmes d'Unification dans les Théories Équationelles.* PhD thesis, Centre de Récherche en Informatique de Nancy, 1985.

[Mat70] Yu Matijacevič. Enumerable sets are diophantine. *Dokl. Akad. Nauk. SSSR*, 191:279–282, 1970.

[Plo72] G. D. Plotkin. Building-in equational theories. In Bernard Meltzer and Donald Michie, editors, *Machine Intelligence 7*, pages 73–90, Edinburgh University Press, 1972.

[Pos46] Emil L. Post. A variant of a recursively unsolvable problem. *Bulletin of the AMS*, 52:264–268, 1946.

[Qui46] W. V. Quine. Concatenation as a basis for arithmetic. *Journal of Symbolic Logic*, 11(4):105–114, 1946.

[Rab65] M. O. Rabin. A simple method for undecidability proofs and some applications. In Yehoshua Bar-Hillel, editor, *Logic, Methodology and Philosophy of Science*, pages 58–68, North-Holland, 1965.

[Rog87] Hartley Rogers, Jr. *Theory of Recursive Functions and Effective Computability.* MIT Press, second edition, 1987.

[Sie89] Jörg H. Siekmann. Unification theory. A survey. *Journal of Symbolic Logic*, 1989.

[Sti81] Mark E. Stickel. A unification algorithm for associative-commutative functions. *Journal of the ACM*, 28(3):423–434, 1981.

[Tar53] Alfred Tarski. A general method in proofs of undecidability. In Alfred Tarski, Andrzej Mostowski, and Raphael M. Robinson, editors, *Undecidable Theories*, pages 1–35, North-Holland, 1953.

[Tre90] Ralf Treinen. *A new method for undecidability proof of first order theories.* Technical Report A 09/90, Universität des Saarlandes, Saarbrücken, may 1990.

[Ven87] K. N. Venkataraman. Decidability of the purely existential fragment of the theory of term algebra. *Journal of the ACM*, 34(2):492–510, april 1987.

GENERATING PLANS IN LINEAR LOGIC

M. Masseron* C. Tollu J. Vauzeilles
L.I.P.N./C.S.P.
C.N.R.S. & Université Paris-Nord
93430 VILLETANEUSE
(*) and Equipe de Logique, Université de Paris VII, C.N.R.S. UA 753

1-Introduction

The logical characterization of the concept of action has already been investigated in a fruitful way by many authors (see for example : [Nilsson 80], [Bibel 86], [Fronhöfer 87], [Bibel&al. 88], and their references) but, while it is relatively easy to represent a sequence of actions by a proof, the converse operation has not yet been achieved in a satisfactory way. The attempts made in order to correct the flows inherent to the logic employed (most of the time a fragment of the classical or intuitionistic predicate calculus or some modal logic system) can be roughly splitted into two groups (not rigorously delineated) :

a) either introducing a "situation predicate" and/or a temporal parameter, along with an appropriate semantic apparatus. Even if the latter semantics enjoys good properties, nothing enables us to say what its exact relation to the initial problem is, since the only known link is the logical translation, which is not regarded as really adequate. Though these methods have turned out to be efficient for treating simple problems of planification, their lack of flexibility and robustness seems crippling for dealing with more complex questions.

b) or restricting the use of tautologies such as $\mathbf{A \wedge B \Rightarrow A}$ or $\mathbf{A \Rightarrow A \wedge A}$. That restriction is strikingly necessary, as it appears by a simple look at the classical example of the domain : the problem of a robot which takes and stacks blocks with a single hand. At the beginning, the hand is empty, blocks a and b are on a table and c is on top of b. The application of the tautology $\mathbf{A \wedge B \Rightarrow A}$ would for instance lead to forget that block b is present ; the application of the tautology $\mathbf{A \Rightarrow A \wedge A}$ could make believe that the robot has two hands, at least ! (see 2.1 and 4.1.3 below for an accurate description of this example).

The deduction rules responsible for the above tautologies were isolated in 1934/35 when Gentzen introduced sequent calculus [Gentzen 34] : they are known as **contraction** and **weakening**. It had not been realized to what extent classical logic was affected by discarding such rules until Girard proposed **linear logic** [Girard 87a]. Amongst other phenomena, let us just mention the fact that conjunction (resp. disjunction) splits into two distinct connectives, namely $\otimes$ and & (resp. $\oplus$ and ⅋).

In the present work, we adopt position b) by using an appropriate fragment of Girard's linear logic (essentially, the fragment corrresponding to $\otimes$ and $\oplus$), and we give a simple proof of the equivalence between actions and their assigned proofs : it is indeed possible to translate, in a natural way, a formal proof into a sequence of actions, without using any ingredient extraneous to the logical system.

2- How to specify problems of planification

We refer the reader to the numerous articles written on the subject for a detailed exposition of this point (for example [Bibel 86], [Chapman 87] or [GinSmith 88]) (see also our technical report [Gallia 90]). Our aim is merely to give an accurate set-theoretic description of the planification problems which are coped with in this work. We are given the following data :

- a set of constants, representing the objects on which the system acts : in our example, these are the three blocks a, b and c.

- a set of predicates, capable of characterizing the system : in our example, this means characterizing the relative positions of the blocks and the state of the hand of the robot :

OTA(x) : x is on the table,
ON(x,y) : x is on top of y,
CL(x) : x is clear, i.e. there is nothing on top of it,
HOLD(x) : the robot holds x,
EMPTY : the hand of the robot is empty.

A state of the system is a set of occurrences of closed atomic formulas : for instance, {OTA(**a**), OTA(**b**), ON(**c**,**a**), CL(**b**), CL(**c**), EMPTY}.
An action system is a set of occurrences of rules of the kind :

$$\{A_{1,1}, ..., A_{1,m_1}\}\text{or} ... \text{or}\{A_r, ..., A_{r,m_r}\} \rightarrow \{B_{1,1}, ..., B_{1,n_1}\}\text{or} ... \text{or}\{B_{s,1}, ..., B_{s,n_s}\}.$$

In particular, in the "deterministic" case, one gets : $\{A_1, ..., A_m\} \rightarrow \{B_1, ..., B_n\}$. Such rules are generally written with variables, although we shall only use here the closed variants, obtained by substituting constants to the variables.
Such a rule transforms a state compatible with its first member into a new state obtained by replacing the part of the state described by one of the sets $\{A_{i,1}, ..., A_{i,m_i}\}$, by the state partially described by one of the sets $\{B_{j,1}, ..., B_{j,n_j}\}$ (the choice of i and j is the "responsibility" of the machine). The analogy with the so-called "add lists" and "delete lists" of STRIPS is obvious (see [Nilsson 80]). The main improvement due to our treatment is, as will appear later, that all this information can be compiled **within** the logic.
Here is the action system of our specific problem :

Take(x) : {EMPTY, CL(x), OTA(x)} → {HOLD(x)}
Remove(x,y) : {EMPTY, CL(x), ON(x,y)} → {HOLD(x), CL(y)}
Put(x) : {HOLD(x)} → {EMPTY, CL(x), OTA(x)}
Stack(x,y) : {HOLD(x), CL(y)} → {EMPTY, CL(x), ON(x,y)}

For the sake of clarity and homogeneity of the vocabulary, we shall call *elementary action* what is usually referred to as an action and *concrete action* a sequence of elementary actions.

3- Linear theories

The deductive system is a linear sequent calculus, similar to the one G. Gentzen introduced in 1934 [Gentzen 34] : this tool has for long revealed extremely efficient in proof theory, but it remains somewhat unpopular among potential users such as computer scientists or even logicians. Readers unfamiliar with Gentzen's sequent calculus will find in the appendix of our technical report [Gallia 90] a short guide - elementary remarks and general principles- to this formalism. In the body of our text, we shall sometimes refer to this appendix by using the symbol (†) (for a textbook presentation of Gentzen's sequent calculus, see [Girard 87] or [Girard&alii 89]).

3.1- Presentation of a linear sequent calculus

A sequent is an expression of the form $\Gamma \vdash \Delta$ where Γ and Δ are **finite** sets of occurrences of formulas of the considered language : the order of the elements is immaterial, but two occurrences of the same formula are regarded as distinct (it is often talked of "multisets" in this context) ; on the other hand, the same occurrence of a given formula may appear simultaneously in two distinct multisets (see for instance the identity group below). This last remark is the basis for the (obvious) definition of the intersection and of the union of multisets (as used in **4.2**).

A set $\{A\}$ composed of a single formula is simply written A, and the comma indicates union ; for example : Γ, A, B is short for $\Gamma \cup \{A,B\}$. For the sake of simplicity, we shall often write "formula" instead of "occurrence of a formula", but this will never be ambiguous as far as an element of a sequent is concerned. We limit ourselves to sequents with only one formula on the right side (in the spirit of minimal logic).

The logical axioms and rules we shall use are best presented in the following way:

Identity group

(Axiom) $\underline{A} \vdash \underline{A}$
(A is atomic)

$$\frac{\Gamma \vdash \underline{A} \qquad \Delta, \underline{A} \vdash B}{\Gamma, \Delta \vdash B}\ (\text{Cut})$$

Group of the multiplicative conjunction (⊗) and 1

$$(\otimes\text{-l})\ \frac{\Gamma, \underline{A}, \underline{B} \vdash C}{\Gamma, \underline{A \otimes B} \vdash C} \qquad\qquad \frac{\Gamma \vdash \underline{A} \qquad \Delta \vdash \underline{B}}{\Gamma, \Delta \vdash \underline{A \otimes B}}\ (\otimes\text{-r})$$

$$(1\text{-l})\ \frac{\Gamma \vdash A}{\Gamma, \underline{\mathbf{1}} \vdash A} \qquad\qquad \vdash \underline{\mathbf{1}} \quad (1\text{-r})$$

Group of the additive disjunction (⊕) and 0

$$(\oplus\text{-l})\ \frac{\Gamma, \underline{A} \vdash C \quad \Gamma, \underline{B} \vdash C}{\Gamma, \underline{A \oplus B} \vdash C} \qquad \frac{\Gamma \vdash \underline{A}}{\Gamma \vdash \underline{A \oplus B}}\ (\oplus\text{-r1}) \qquad \frac{\Gamma \vdash \underline{B}}{\Gamma \vdash \underline{A \oplus B}}\ (\oplus\text{-r2})$$

(0-l) $\Gamma, \underline{\mathbf{0}} \vdash A$
(the formulas of Γ are atomic)

(nothing on the right for **0**)

Remarks : every rule or axiom contains **active** formulas : they are the ones on which the rule effectively acts, and we have underlined them ; we will explicitly indicate the active formulas only when necessary. In each sequent, the non-active formulas constitute the context : managing the context is an important part of the rule.

a) The relation "A |— B is provable" is reflexive (because A |— A is provable for any A) and transitive (because of the cut-rule) ; thus, "A |— B and B |— A are provable" is an equivalence relation over the set of all formulas and "A |— B is provable" defines a partial ordering (modulo the above equivalence relation).

Because of this equivalence relation, the set of formulas equipped with (⊗, **1**) (resp. with (⊕, **0**)) can be considered a commutative monoid; furthermore, ⊗ is distributive with respect to ⊕, and **0**⊗A is equivalent to **0**.

Those purely algebraic properties will be freely used throughout the paper ; for example, we shall often assume that a formula is in the (disjunctive normal) form of a "sum of monomials". We must once again stress that we are chiefly interested in the proofs.

b) A⊗B is correctly interpreted as the simultaneous presence of A and B. We therefore get a conjunction in a very strong sense : as a matter of fact, one cannot generally prove A⊗B |— A !

It must be noticed that the sequent $A_1, ..., A_m$ |— B means that B is a (linear) consequence of $A_1 \otimes ... \otimes A_m$. Our paper can be viewed as an attempt at explaining this notion of linear consequence in terms of actions.

c) A⊕B is a disjunction, with an exclusive meaning which will be stressed later.

d) **0** plays the role of absurdity : if |— **0** is provable, every sequent is provable. **0** will not be taken into account in this work : its appearance in the transition axioms corresponds to "impossible" situations which, for sake of readability, we have excluded.

3.2- Linear theories

The theories we shall study in this work will be expressed in a language composed of free variables, constants and predicates. The logical symbols are those we have just introduced. A *closed sequent* is a sequent exclusively composed of closed formulas.

A *linear theory* contains two sets of proper axioms, which are all closed sequents :

1) the *current state axioms* are occurrences of closed atomic formulas, the current state axiom corresponding to A being written |— A ;

2) the *transition axioms* correspond to the actual *action system*.

Every transition axiom is a closed sequent $A_1, ..., A_m$ |— B where :

- $A_1, ..., A_m$ are atomic formulas ;
- B is a formula of the language, written as a sum of monomials.

The set of transition axioms is closed under substitution of a tuple of constants to another.

A proof of a sequent S, in such a theory, is a proof in the usual meaning of sequent calculus (†), with S as its end-sequent, and **managing the current state axioms in a niggardly way** : in each rule, this management is exactly copied from the management of the contexts. More accurately, one defines a proof **D** of the sequent S, and the set AU(**D**) of the current state axioms it uses, by the following inductive clauses :

1) a current state axiom |— A is a proof **D** of this sequent, with AU(**D**) = {A} ;

2) a logical axiom (**Identity axiom, 1-r, 0-l**) or a transition axiom is a proof **D** of the sequent expressing this axiom, with AU(**D**) = ∅ ;

3) if **D** is a proof of S, then the application of a unary (i.e. one premise) rule (**⊗-l, 1-l, ⊕-r1, ⊕-r2**) with premise S and conclusion S', gives a proof **D'** of S' with AU(**D'**) = AU(**D**) ;

4) if **D** and **E** are proofs, respectively of S and T, such that AU(**D**) $\cap$ AU(**E**) = $\varnothing$, then an application of the cut rule or of the **$\otimes$-r** rule with premises S and T, and conclusion S', gives a proof **D'** of S' with AU(**D'**) = AU(**D**) $\cup$ AU(**E**) ;

5) if **D** and **E** are proofs, respectively of S and T, such that AU(**D**) = AU(**E**), then an application of the **$\oplus$-l** rule with premises S and T, and conclusion S', gives a proof **D'** of S' with AU(**D'**) = AU(**D**) = AU(**E**).

Remark : the inductive definition of the proofs enables us to use to a large extent constructions or demonstrations by induction, which we shall designate by the expression "induction on proofs" ; for instance :

Definition. The *height* h(**D**) of a proof **D** is defined, by induction on proofs, in the following way :

- h(**D**) = 0 when **D** is an axiom ;
- h(**D**) = h(**E**)+1 when **D** is obtained from **E**, by application of a unary rule ;
- h(**D**) = h(**E**)+h(**F**)+1 when **D** is obtained from **E** and **F** by application of a binary (i.e. two premises) rule.

All demonstrations in this work are done (or are to be done) by induction on the proofs or on the height of the proofs.

The following lemma is useful to characterize the proofs in a linear theory :

Lemma 1 (†) : *If* **D** *is a proof of* $\Gamma \vdash C$ *such that* $A \in$ AU(**D**), *then there exists a proof* **D'** *of* $A, \Gamma \vdash C$ *such that* AU(**D'**) = AU(**D**) - {A}. *An inverse transformation can be obtained by applying the cut rule between* **D** *and the current state axiom* $\vdash A$.

A proof **D** of $\Gamma \vdash C$ can thus be "normalized" in the following way :

- a proof **D'** of the sequent AU(**D**), $\Gamma \vdash C$, with AU(**D'**) = $\varnothing$, by a repeated application of lemma 1,
- then, by applications of the cut rule, a proof **D"** of the initial sequent $\Gamma \vdash C$, with AU(**D"**) = AU(**D**).

The niggardly use of the current state axioms is, in this case, perfectly clear : they are used at most once and as late as possible !

Definition : A *formal* action is a proof **D** of a sequent of the form $A_1, ..., A_m \vdash B$, satisfying the following conditions :

- AU(**D**) = $\varnothing$;
- the set $\{A_1 , ..., A_m\}$ **is a subset of the set of current state axioms** (they are sets of occurrences of formulas): in particular, all A_i are atomic ;
- B is a formula of the language, written as a sum of monomials.

For example, the transition axioms are formal actions.

Lemma 1 means that a formal action $A_1, ..., A_m \vdash B$ is equivalent to a proof **D'** of $\vdash B$ such that AU(**D'**) = $\{A_1 , ..., A_m\}$ whose intuitive meaning is to consume $A_1, ..., A_m$ and produce B.

3.3- Cut elimination theorem (†)

Gentzen's "**Hauptsatz**" [Gentzen 34](discussed in [Girard 87]), which one adapts without difficulty to the present situation, can be stated as follows :

Let T *be a linear theory and* S *a sequent written in the language of* T, *then, for each proof* **D** *of* S, *one can construct a proof* **D'** *of* S, ***all the active formulas of the cut rules of which belong to proper axioms of T*** *(such cuts are called* ***proper cuts****). Moreover* AU(**D'**) = AU(**D**) *and* h(**D'**) $\leq$ h(**D**).

This property of the height is peculiar to linear logic (in the original case, where there are weakening and contraction rules, the height of the proof grows dramatically during the cut elimination process).
It might seem useless to write proofs containing "logical cuts" that we later get rid of, but it is to a large extent inevitable, as it will appear in almost all proofs written down in the present paper. Indeed, the cut elimination procedure requires an accurate knowledge of the proof, which is not generally accessible. It is nonetheless possible to draw a natural and useful consequence from the preceding theorem (this consequence is known as the **subformula property**) :
One observes, in every rule except for the cut rule, that each formula appearing in a premise sequent is a subformula of a formula appearing in the conclusion sequent (A is a subformula of itself, A et B are subformulas of A⊗B, ...). Therefore, if a theory uses a set **Op** of logical operators, the other operators of linear logic can be discarded from all proofs.

4- Conjunctive planification

Conjunctive planification is dealt with in the framework of the linear theories where the only logical symbol is ⊗ (along with **1**) : the cut elimination theorem thus enables us to strictly limit ourselves, as for the logical rules, to the ones of the corresponding group; from now on, we shall speak of "conjunctive linear theories". In the following paragraphs, it will be noticeable that the formalization we propose only takes into account the altered part of the initial situation. We do not have to specify what happens to the remainig part; therefore our treatment provides us with an appropriate framework for coping with the famous **frame problem** [MacHayes 69] in an elegant way.

4.1- An example of conjunctive linear theory : it is a formalization of the problem of a robot that we have already described in (**2.**).

- the language we shall use contains three distinct constants **a**, **b**, **c** and five predicates: OTA(x), ON(x,y), CL(x), HOLD(x), EMPTY ;
- the transition axioms are all closed sequents obtained from the following sequents by substituting constants to variables :

Take(x) : EMPTY, CL(x), OTA(x) |— HOLD(x)
Remove(x,y) : EMPTY, CL(x), ON(x,y) |— HOLD(x)⊗CL(y)
Put(x) : HOLD(x) |— EMPTY⊗CL(x)⊗OTA(x)
Stack(x,y) : HOLD(x), CL(y) |— EMPTY⊗CL(x)⊗ON(x,y).

- the current state axioms :

|— OTA(**a**), |— OTA(**b**), |— ON(**c**,**a**), |— CL(**b**), |— CL(**c**), |— EMPTY correspond to the already mentioned initial state.

4.2- THEOREM. Let T be a conjunctive linear theory.
Every concrete action can be represented by a formal action and, vice versa, every formal action can be interpreted as a concrete action.
It is obviously the second part of the theorem which constitute the principal novelty of the present work. We shall give a complete demonstration in a precise framework.

Soundness property : *Every concrete action can be represented by a formal action.*

Demonstration : We prove it by induction on the number of elemetary actions performed in order to achieve the concrete action.
If this number is 0, the formal action is the axiom $\vdash \mathbf{1}$;
otherwise, let us consider the concrete action $\mathbb{E}'$ which consists in performing at first the concrete action $\mathbb{D}$ then the concrete action $\mathbb{E}$: by induction hypothesis, $\mathbb{D}$ et $\mathbb{E}$ can be respectively represented by:

- **D**, a formal action proving $A_1, ..., A_m \vdash B_1 \otimes ... \otimes B_n$;
- E, a formal action proving $C_1, ..., C_p \vdash D$.

Let AE be the initial set of current state axioms. After $\mathbb{D}$ has been performed, the state is the union of the following disjoint sets :

- $F = AE - \{A_1, ..., A_m\}$;
- $G = \{B_1, ..., B_n\}$.

Thus, the fact that $\mathbb{E}$ can be performed after $\mathbb{D}$ means that the set $H = \{C_1, ..., C_p\}$ is composed of two disjoint sets :

- $F \cap H$ which we shall denote $\{C_1, ..., C_r\}$, giving new indices to the C_k if necessary ;
- $G \cap H$ which we shall denote $\{B_1, ..., B_q\}$, giving new indices to the B_j if necessary.

The formal action corresponding to "perform $\mathbb{D}$ then $\mathbb{E}$" must therefore prove the sequent :

(*) $$A_1, ..., A_m, C_1, ..., C_r \vdash D \otimes B_{q+1} \otimes ... \otimes B_n.$$

We still have to construct such a formal action.

- Starting with **E**, a repeated use of the **⊗-r** rule with the identity axioms for $B_{q+1}, ..., B_n$, gives a proof **E'** of $B_1, ..., B_q, B_{q+1}, ..., B_n, C_1, ..., C_r \vdash D \otimes B_{q+1} \otimes ... \otimes B_n$; then a repeated use of the **⊗-l** rule beginning with **E'**, gives a proof **E"** of

$$B_1 \otimes ... \otimes B_n, C_1, ..., C_r \vdash D \otimes B_{q+1} \otimes ... \otimes B_n$$

- By applying the cut rule between **D** et **E"** with main formula $B_1 \otimes ... \otimes B_n$, one obtains a proof of the sequent (*), which is the formal action we sought.

Completeness property : *Every formal action represents a concrete action.*
We need the following technical result, based on the fact that the left members of the axioms we manipulate contain only atomic formulas.
Lemma 2 (†).
If **D** *is a proof of the sequent* $A \otimes B, \Gamma \vdash C$, *then there exists a proof of* $A, B, \Gamma \vdash C$ *using the same proper axioms as* **D** *and such that* $h(\mathbf{D}') \leq h(\mathbf{D})$.

Demonstration of the completeness property : Let **D** be a formal action : we shall associate to it a concrete action by induction on the height.

- If **D** is an axiom, the concrete action is immediately known : it is the identical action in the case of a logical axiom (an identity axiom for some atomic formula or axiom **1-d**), and, in the case of a proper axiom, it is the elementary action corresponding to it ;
- if the last rule applied is a **⊗-r** rule, **D** has the following form:

$$\frac{\begin{array}{cc}\ldots\mathbf{E}\ldots & \ldots\mathbf{F}\ldots \\ A_1, \ldots, A_p \vdash B & A_{p+1}, \ldots, A_m \vdash C\end{array}}{A_1, \ldots, A_p, A_{p+1}, \ldots, A_m \vdash B \otimes C}\ (\otimes\text{-}\mathbf{r})$$

the induction hypothesis applies to **E** and to **F** and to their "achievements" : the concrete action associated to **D** is the concrete action associated to **E** followed by the concrete action associated to **F** (the order does not matter in this case) ;

- finally, if the last rule is a cut rule, **D** has the following form :

$$\frac{\begin{array}{cc}\ldots\mathbf{E}\ldots & \ldots\mathbf{F}\ldots \\ A_1, \ldots, A_p \vdash B & A_{p+1}, \ldots, A_m, B \vdash C\end{array}}{A_1, \ldots, A_p, A_{p+1}, \ldots, A_m \vdash C}\ (\mathbf{cut})$$

where $B = B_1 \otimes \ldots \otimes B_n$. Thanks to lemma 2, we have a proof **F'** of the sequent $A_{p+1}, \ldots, A_m, B_1, \ldots, B_n \vdash C$, which is a formal action whose height is lesser than the height of **F**. One can apply the induction hypothesis to **E** and **F'** : the succession, in this order, of the concrete action associated to **E**, and of the concrete action associated to **F'** is the concrete action we sought.

4.3- Example

Figure 1 shows a formal action, in the linear theory presented at the beginning, corresponding to the following sequence of elementary actions :

Remove(**c**,**a**), put(**c**), take(**b**), stack(**b**,**a**) ;

moreover, since it demonstrates the sequent :

EMPTY, CL(**c**), ON(**c**,**a**), CL(**b**), OTA(**b**)
|—EMPTY⊗CL(**b**)⊗ON(**b**,**a**)⊗CL(**c**)⊗OTA(**c**),

the final sate is described by EMPTY, CL(**b**), ON(**b**,**a**), CL(**c**), OTA(**c**), along with OTA(**a**) which has not been modified.

4.4- Plans

A proof contains a lot of superfluous information which we are now going to eliminate in order to obtain diagrams similar to Bibel's ones [Bibel 83] : these diagrams will be, in our case, given an orientation, which is a very precious piece of information that will turn out to be useful in our theorem.

Definitions :

A *pseudo-plan* is a graph composed of vertices and oriented edges :

- each *vertex* is labelled by the name of an axiom (the same axiom can generate several labels) ; a vertex labelled by the axiom $A_1, \ldots, A_m \vdash B_1 \otimes \ldots \otimes B_n$ is provided with the entries $eA_1, \ldots, eA_m$ and the exits $sB_1, \ldots, sB_n$;

- an *oriented edge* admits an exit sA as its origin and an entry of the same type eA as its end ; it is convenient to label such an edge by A itself.

The *entries and exits of a pseudo-plan* are the ones which are not the origin or the end of an edge.

Take(x) : $EMPTY, CL(x), OTA(x) \vdash HOLD(x)$

Remove(x,y) : $EMPTY, CL(x), ON(x,y) \vdash HOLD(x) \otimes CL(y)$

Put(x) : $HOLD(x) \vdash EMPTY \otimes CL(x) \otimes OTA(x)$

Stack(x,y) : $HOLD(x), CL(y) \vdash EMPTY \otimes CL(x) \otimes ON(x,y)$

x := **a** , y := **b** , z := **c**

$$EMPTY, CL(y), OTA(y) \vdash \underline{HOLD(y)} \qquad \underline{HOLD(y)}, CL(x) \vdash EMPTY \otimes CL(y) \otimes ON(y,x)$$

-- **(cut)**

$$CL(z) \vdash CL(z) \qquad EMPTY, CL(y), OTA(y), CL(x) \vdash EMPTY \otimes CL(y) \otimes ON(y,x)$$

-- **(⊗-r)**

$$OTA(z) \vdash OTA(z) \qquad EMPTY, CL(y), OTA(y), CL(x), CL(z) \vdash EMPTY \otimes CL(y) \otimes ON(y,x) \otimes CL(z)$$

-- **(⊗-r)**

$$EMPTY, CL(y), OTA(y), CL(x), \underline{CL(z)}, \underline{OTA(z)} \vdash EMPTY \otimes CL(y) \otimes ON(y,x) \otimes CL(z) \otimes OTA(z)$$

-- **(⊗-l)**

$$\underline{EMPTY}, CL(y), OTA(y), CL(x), \underline{CL(z) \otimes OTA(z)} \vdash EMPTY \otimes CL(y) \otimes ON(y,x) \otimes CL(z) \otimes OTA(z)$$

-- **(⊗-l)**

$$HOLD(z) \vdash \underline{EMPTY \otimes CL(z) \otimes OTA(z)} \qquad \underline{EMPTY \otimes CL(z) \otimes OTA(z)}, CL(y), OTA(y), CL(x) \vdash EMPTY \otimes CL(y) \otimes ON(y,x) \otimes CL(z) \otimes OTA(z)$$

-- **(cut)**

$$\underline{HOLD(z)}, CL(y), OTA(y), \underline{CL(x)} \vdash EMPTY \otimes CL(y) \otimes ON(y,x) \otimes CL(z) \otimes OTA(z)$$

-- **(⊗-l)**

$$EMPTY, CL(z), ON(z,x) \vdash \underline{HOLD(z) \otimes CL(x)} \qquad \underline{HOLD(z) \otimes CL(x)}, CL(y), OTA(y) \vdash EMPTY \otimes CL(y) \otimes ON(y,x) \otimes CL(z) \otimes OTA(z)$$

-- **(cut)**

$$EMPTY, CL(z), ON(z,x), CL(y), OTA(y) \vdash EMPTY \otimes CL(y) \otimes ON(y,x) \otimes CL(z) \otimes OTA(z)$$

(We have underlined a few active formulas to make the reading of the proof easier)

Figure 1 : an example of a formal action

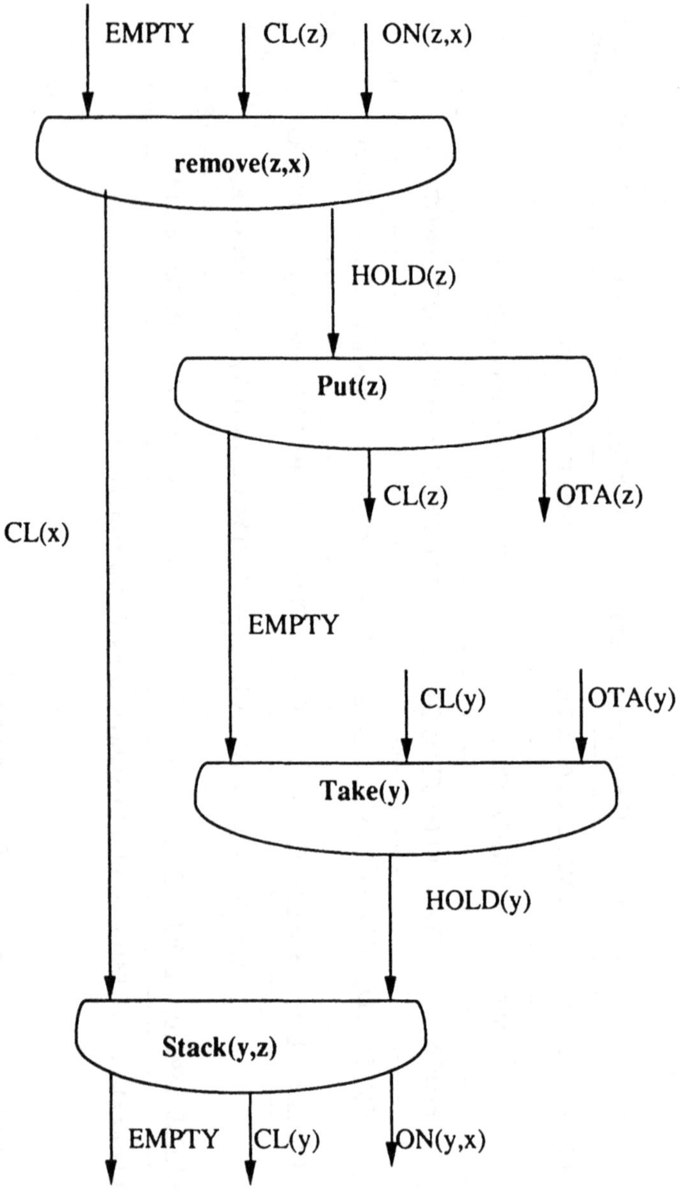
EMPTY
CL(z)
ON(z,x)
remove(z,x)
HOLD(z)
Put(z)
CL(z)
OTA(z)
CL(x)
EMPTY
CL(y)
OTA(y)
Take(y)
HOLD(y)
Stack(y,z)
EMPTY
CL(y)
ON(y,x)

Figure 2

The *orientation of a pseudo-plan* is the transitive closure of the relation defined over the set of all entries and exits by :

- eA < sB if eA and sB are attached to the same vertex ;
- sA < eA if there exists an edge between sA and eA.

That defines as well a relation between the vertices, on the basis of : $\mathbb{E} < \mathbb{F}$ if and only if there exists an edge whose origin is an exit of $\mathbb{E}$ and whose end is an entry of $\mathbb{F}$.

One constructs a pseudo-plan $\mathbb{D}$ associated to a proof **D** by induction over the proofs:

- if **D** is a proper axiom, $\mathbb{D}$ is reduced to a vertex, labelled by an occurrence of the name of that axiom, provided with the entries and exits corresponding to it ;
- if **D** is another kind of axiom, $\mathbb{D}$ is empty ;
- if **D** is obtained from **E** by an application of the ($\otimes$-l) rule, $\mathbb{D}$ is identical to $\mathbb{E}$;
- if **D** is obtained from **E** and **F** by an application of the ($\otimes$-r) rule, $\mathbb{D}$ is the union of $\mathbb{E}$ and $\mathbb{F}$;
- if **D** is obtained from **E** and **F** by an application of the cut rule on the formula $B_1\otimes...\otimes B_n$, $\mathbb{D}$ is obtained from the union of $\mathbb{E}$ and $\mathbb{F}$ by linking sB_j to eB_j for each j such that sB_j is an exit of $\mathbb{E}$ and eB_j is an entry of $\mathbb{F}$. We note that , in the latter case, there may be no link added to the union : from the action point of view, that corresponds to the independence condition ; from the proof-theoretic point of view, it can be interpreted as the elimination of a logical cut, which is an interesting property of the present construction.

One easily checks that the entries of the pseudo-plan constructed from a proof of the sequent $\Gamma \vdash \Delta$ correspond to some atomic components of Γ and that its exits correspond to some atomic components of Δ.

A **plan** is a pseudo-plan constructed from a formal action.

Figure 2 gives the plan associated to the formal action of figure 1.

THEOREM

Let $\mathbb{D}$ be a pseudo-plan whose entries constitute a subset of the current state. $\mathbb{D}$ is a plan if and only if its orientation is a partial ordering.

Demonstration : The construction of a plan gives, in an obvious way, a partial ordering. Vice versa, let $\mathbb{D}$ be a pseudo-plan whose orientation is a partial ordering. Let us choose a label which is minimal with respect to the partial ordering over $\mathbb{D}$: this minimality condition entails the absence of any edge entering this vertex ; thus, if we cut off the edges which go out of this vertex, we obtain the pseudo-plan $\mathbb{E}$ that corresponds to the proper axiom $A_1, ..., A_m \vdash B_1\otimes...\otimes B_n$, itself corresponding to the label, and the pseudo-plan $\mathbb{F}$ containing the other vertices and edges. Let us draw up the statement of accounts for the entries and exits :

- all entries $eA_1, ..., eA_m$ of $\mathbb{E}$ are entries of $\mathbb{D}$ (this is still a matter of minimality) ;
- by giving if necessary new indices to the B_j, one can designate by $sB_1, ..., sB_p$ the exits of $\mathbb{E}$ freed by the cutting off of the edges, and by $sB_{p+1}, ..., sB_n$ the ones that already were exits of $\mathbb{D}$;
- in the same way, let us designate by $eC_1, ..., eC_q$ the other entries and by D the conjunction of the formulas of the remaining exits of $\mathbb{D}$.

The induction hypothesis apply to both pseudo-plans: the first one gives the formal action reduced to the axiom concerned, the second one gives a formal action leading to the sequent $B_1, \ldots, B_p, C_1, \ldots, C_q \vdash D$: one then concludes with the method used in the demonstration of the soundness property for the formal actions : it enables us to construct a proof of the sequent which we were aiming at. It is quite easy to check that the plan constructed from the obtained formal action is the original plan.

5- Disjunctive planification

Disjunctive planification, which is dealt with in the framework of the linear theories using as logical symbols $\otimes$, $\oplus$ and **1** (see **3.1.**) includes conjunctive planification. In this new context, one can also make an interesting use of the constant **0**.
The problems treated by disjunctive planification involve a kind of non-determinism: it does not depend on the current state of the system but on the way the concrete actions are performed by the machine (there is a classical example of such a non-deterministic action in [Bibel 86]). This helps to understand why we use the additive disjunction connective to grasp such a sort of non-determinism (see [Gallia 90] and [Girard 87b] where an intuitive semantics of $\oplus$ in terms of inner non-determinism is discussed and a few examples are analysed).
Disjunctive planification can very well be handled by our formalism, but it requires additional technical refinements. That is the reason why we shall not bother in the present paper with a lengthy presentation of this topic (for a thorough treatment and the complete demonstrations of the corresponding soundness and completeness properties, see [Gallia 90]).

6. Conclusion

We dealt with a well-delineated domain of planning and, thanks to linear logic,we gave it an adequate logical characterization, so that we managed to solve the completeness problem. Although this domain may appear restricting at first glance, it seems that it includes most of the examples in the literature on plan analysis and it gives rise to important questions which are quite satisfactorily handled by the formalism we proposed. On the other hand, we hope that our work modestly contributed to a deeper intuitive understanding of linear logic. Besides, we think that integrating other features of linear logic, such as the ones attached to linear implication (--o) or the bounded modalities $?_n$ and $!_n$ will enable to cope with more realistic situations.

Aknowledgements : we are deeply indebted to Jean-Yves Girard for having encouraged us to attack the problem and to the anonymous referees for their careful reading of our paper and their numerous comments and indications.

References

[Bibel 83] **W. Bibel** : Matings in Matrices, *Communications of the ACM* Volume **26**(1983) 844-852

[Bibel 86] **W. Bibel** : A Deductive Solution for Plan Generation, *New Generation Computing* **4**(1986) 115-132

[Bibel & alii 88] **W. Bibel, L. Farinas del Cerro, B. Fronhöfer, A. Herzig** : Plan Generation by Linear Proofs : on semantics (draft, 13 pp.)

[Chapman 87] **D. Chapman** : Planning for conjunctive goals, *Artificial Intelligence* **32**(1987) 333-377

[Fronhöfer 87] **B. Fronhöfer** : Linearity and Plan Generation, *New Generation Computing* **5**(1987) 213-225

[Gallia 90] **M. Masseron, C. Tollu and J. Vauzeilles** : Planification et logique linéaire, *Technical report, Laboratoire d'Informatique de Paris-Nord*,(1990)

[Gentzen 34] **G. Gentzen** : *The Collected Papers of Gerhard Gentzen*, Ed. E. Szabo, North-Holland, Amsterdam (1969)

[GinSmith 88] **M.L. Ginsberg, D.E. Smith** : Reasoning about Action I : A Possible Worlds Approach, *Artificial Intelligence* **35**(1988) 165-195

[Girard 87] **J.-Y. Girard** : *Proof theory and logical complexity*, Bibliopolis, Napoli(1987)

[Girard 87a] **J.-Y. Girard** : Linear logic, *Theoretical Computer Science* **50**(1987) 1-102.

[Girard 87b] **J.-Y. Girard** : Towards a Geometry of Interaction, *Proc. AMS Conference on Categories, Logic and Computer Science*, Boulder, CO(1987)

[Girard&alii 89] **J.-Y. Girard, Y. Lafont and P. Taylor** : *Proofs and Types*, Cambridge Tracks in Computer Science, CUP(1989)

[MacHayes 69] **J. McCarthy, P.J. Hayes** : Some Philosophical Problems from the Standpoint of Artificial Intelligence, *Machine Intelligence* **4**(1969) 463-502

[Nilsson 80] **N.J. Nilsson** : *Principles of Artificial Intelligence*, Springer (1980)

Automata-Theoretic Techniques for Image Generation and Compression *

Karel Culik II
Dept. of Computer Science
University of South Carolina
Columbia, SC 29208, USA

Simant Dube
Dept. of Computer Science
University of South Carolina
Columbia, SC 29208, USA

Abstract

In this paper, the representation, generation and inference of images using automata theoretic techniques is investigated. It is shown that highly complex images, including "fractal" (self-similar) images, can be manipulated by the application of these techniques. Languages and relations over some alphabet are interpreted as images by treating strings as rational coordinates. In particular, the rational relations, specified by rational expressions, are considered. It is shown how texture of an image can be defined by probabilistic finite generators. Iterative generators are also considered.

1 Introduction

Since the study of fractal geometry was pioneered by B. Mandelbrot [13], considerable progress has been made in its application to diverse areas—ranging from image compression [1] to new "chaos" physics [10]. Classical geometry provides a first approximation to the structure of physical objects, and especially "man-made" objects. The new "fractal" geometry is an extension of classical geometry. It can be used to make precise models of physical structures from ferns to galaxies.

Here we study automata-theoretic methods of image generation and compression. Images here are sets of points in n-dimensional space (or sometimes functions on this space specifying the level of grey or color). Points are represented by coordinates, i.e. n-tuples of rational numbers. In turn, rational numbers are represented by strings of bits usually in binary notation (e.g. string 011 represents number 0.011 in binary notation). Hence an n-tuple of strings can be interpreted as a point in the n-dimensional space $< 0,1 >^n$, and a relation $\rho \subseteq \underbrace{\Sigma^* \times \ldots \times \Sigma^*}_{n-times}$ as a set of points, i.e. an object (image). Similarly, an ω-string is interpreted as a real number in the interval $< 0,1 >$. A similar approach to represent patterns by finite automata has been independently taken in [2]. Our approach is more general as we have defined images in terms of languages of infinite words, rather than finite words, and we have also considered textures.

It has been known for more than twenty years that, for example, the Cantor Set (as subset of $[0,1]$) can be represented in ternary notation by regular expression $\{0+2\}^+$ [9,11]. We can show how most "regular" 2-dimensional geometrical objects (both classical and fractal) can be represented by simple rational expressions. The rational expressions allow to build complex images from simple ones by set and other operations. We can convert the rational expressions into probabilistic finite generators that are used to generate images. We also have a method to automatically infer the probabilistic generator from an arbitrary given image, which we briefly describe here, the details are in a forthcoming paper. This is based on the quad tree representation of images that has already been used in Computer Graphics for compressing data [12] and computing the Hausdorff dimension of images [14]. Hence we can concisely represent objects (both fractal and classical) and regenerate them in the original or modified version.

Our representation by rational expressions or probabilistic finite generators has some specific advantages. For example, zooming corresponds to a simple language operation. So if we want to zoom to some subarea we can compute first the expression corresponding to that subarea and then use it to generate the zoomed picture. This is even simpler in the case of the probabilistic generator when we just restrict the first few bits to those specifying the zoomed area.

Using the automata-theoretic methods we can show a number of results about this representation, as the following. Given a rational point (as an ω-word) and an image (compact set) representation, it is decidable whether the point is in the image. Using the decidability of the equivalence problem for ω languages we can decide the image equivalence problem, i.e. whether two rational expressions describe the same image.

We finally mention that IFS method, as studied in [1], to generate fractals and to compress images has been generalized in [5] using a technique called affine automaton. Rational expressions also happen to be a special case of affine automata and this allows an efficient implementation of rational expressions on standard numerically-oriented (not using bit-by-bit approach) hardware and software. Iterative generators as introduced briefly in this paper also generalize IFS.

We omit some of the proofs, they can be found in [7].

2 Preliminaries

A *language* is a set of strings over some alphabet of symbols. In this paper, a language will be over an alphabet, denoted by Σ, of n symbols $\{0,1,\ldots,n-1\}$ where $n \geq 2$. In this section, we present some of the relevant definitions.

(Binary) rational expressions are defined inductively as follows:
(1) ϕ is a rational expression denoting empty set.
(2) For $u,v \in \Sigma^*$, (u,v) is a rational expression denoting the relation $\{(u,v)\}$.
(3) If ρ and σ are rational expressions, then $\rho+\sigma, \rho\sigma$ and ρ^* are rational expressions denoting the union, concatenation of ρ and σ, or the Kleene closure of ρ, respectively.
For example, $(0,0)^*(1,\varepsilon)^*(1,1)$ is a rational expression denoting the relation $\{(0^n1^m, 0^n1) | n \geq 0, m \geq 1\}$. A relation defined by a rational expression is called a *rational relation.*

A *generalized sequential machine* (GSM) is a 6-tuple $M = (Q,\Sigma,\Delta,\delta,q_0,F)$, where Q,Σ and Δ are the states, input alphabet and output alphabet, respectively, δ is a mapping from $Q \times \Sigma$ to finite subsets of $Q \times \Delta^*$, q_0 is the initial state, and F is the set of final states. The interpretation of (p, w) in $\delta(q, a)$ is that M in state q with input symbol a may, as one possible choice of move, enter state p and output the string w. The domain of the transition function δ can be extended to $Q \times \Sigma^*$ in the straightforward manner. Let $M(x)$, where M is a GSM as defined above, denote the set

$$M(x) = \{y | (p, y) \text{ is in } \delta(\mathrm{q}_0, \mathrm{x}) \text{ for some p in F}\}.$$

A GSM defines a relation $\rho \subseteq \Sigma^* \times \Delta^*$

$$\rho = \{(x, y) | x \in \Sigma^*, y \in M(x)\}.$$

Regular languages are preserved under GSM mapping i.e. if L is a regular language then $M(L)$ is also regular.

A *finite transducer* is a generalization of GSM in which the transition function δ is a mapping from $Q \times (\Sigma \cup \{\varepsilon\})$ to finite subsets of $Q \times \Delta^*$. The relations over Σ defined by finite transducers are exactly the rational relations.

In formal language theory, the computation domain is the free monoid Σ^* over a finite alphabet Σ. This domain can be extended by adding the set of infinite strings Σ^ω [4,8]. Formally, Σ^ω denotes all infinite (ω-length) strings $\sigma = \prod_{i=1}^{\infty} a_i, a_i \in \Sigma$, over Σ. An element σ of Σ^ω is called an *ω-word* or *ω-string*. An *ω-language* is any subset of Σ^ω. The set of both finite and infinite strings is denoted by $\Sigma^\infty = \Sigma^* \cup \Sigma^\omega$. The superscript ω means infinite repitition, e.g. $(00)^*1^\omega$ denotes a ω-set of strings which have an even number of zeroes followed by an infinite number of consecutive ones. Later we will interpret finite strings as rational numbers and ω-strings as real numbers.

An *ω-finite automaton*(ω-FA) is a 5-tuple $(Q, \Sigma, \delta, q_0, F)$, where Q is the finite set of states, Σ is the input alphabet, δ is a mapping from $Q \times \Sigma$ to 2^Q, q_0 is the initial state and F is the set of final states.

An ω-word is accepted by a ω-FA if on reading the input ω-word the ω-FA enters a final state infinitely many times. Formally, let $M = (Q, \Sigma, \delta, q_0, F)$ be a ω-FA and let $\sigma = \prod_{i=1}^{\infty} a_i \in \Sigma^\omega$ be the input ω-word, where $a_i \in \Sigma$, for all $i \geq 1$. A sequence of states $\{p_i\}, i = 1, 2, \ldots, \omega$ is called a *run of M on σ* iff $p_1 = q_0$ and for each $2 \leq i \geq \omega, p_i \in \delta(p_{i-1}, a_{i-1})$. The ω-regular language accepted by M, denoted by $L(M)$ is the set of all such ω-strings $\sigma \in \Sigma^\omega$ such that for each such σ there exists a run of M on σ such that some final state is entered infinitely many times.

A language is ω-regular if it is accepted by an ω-finite automaton. The class of ω-regular languages is closed under all Boolean operations. For any ω-regular languages L_1 and L_2, effectively given, it is decidable whether (1) L_1 is empty, finite or infinite; (2) $L_1 = L_2$; (3) $L_1 \subseteq L_2$; (4) $L_1 \cap L_2 = \phi$ [4].

An ω-word τ is an output on an input ω-word σ under ω-finite transducer T if there exists a run of T on σ which produces τ. The relation defined by an ω-finite transducer is called an *ω-rational relation*. The ω-rational relations are exactly the relations defined by the ω-rational expressions. The family of ω-regular sets is closed under ω-rational relations [8].

Let $x, y \in \Sigma^*$. If there exists $u \in \Sigma^+$ such that $xu = y$, then y is called an extension of x, denoted by $x \prec y$ or $y \succ x$. An ω-word τ is called the algebraic limit of an infinite sequence of finite words $x_1, x_2, \ldots, x_n, \ldots$ if $x_1 \prec x_2 \prec \ldots \prec x_n \prec \ldots$ and x_i is a prefix of

τ for all $i \geq 1$. An ω-word τ is called an *adherence* of a language L if there is an infinite sequence of words $x_1, x_2, \ldots, x_n, \ldots$ such that each $x_i, i \geq 1$, is a prefix of a word in L and τ is the algebraic limit of the sequence.

3 Interpretation of Languages and Relations as Images

Let $\Sigma = \{0, 1, \ldots, n-1\}$ be an alphabet of n symbols. A word in Σ^* can be interpreted as a rational number in the interval $[0,1]$. More precisely, a string $w = w_1 w_2 \ldots w_m$ represents a coordinate with "numeric value" equal to the rational number $(.w_1 w_2 \ldots w_m)_n$, which is nothing but the number obtained by placing the radix point to the left of the word and treating the number in notation with radix n. For example, if $\Sigma = \{0, 1\}$, then the string $w = 0110$ represents the binary number $(.0110)_2$, which is equal to 0.375 in decimal notation. In a similar manner, an ω-word in Σ^ω can be interpreted as a real number e.g. the ω-word $(01)^\omega$ over $\Sigma = \{0, 1\}$ represents the binary number 0.010101... in binary notation.

Formally, we define an *interpretation function* $I : \Sigma^\infty \to [0,1] \times [0,1]$ which maps a finite or infinite string to its "numeric value." An n-tuple of words can be interpreted as a point in $[0,1]^n$, where each component word is interpreted individually as a coordinate value i.e. $I(x_1, x_2, \ldots, x_n) = (I(x_1), I(x_2), \ldots, I(x_n))$, where $n \geq 1$.

A compact subset of n-dimensional Euclidean space, where $n \geq 1$, is a formalization of an n-dimensional image (without texture). Therefore, a topologically closed ω-relation $L \subseteq \underbrace{\Sigma^\omega \times \ldots \times \Sigma^\omega}_{n-times}$ can be interpreted as an image $X = I(L) \subseteq [0,1]^n$.

The notion of adherence allows one to specify an image by a language of finite words. Let $L \subseteq \Sigma^*$. Then the image represented by L, denoted by $A(L) \subseteq [0,1]$, is given by

$$A(L) = \{I(\sigma) | \sigma \in \text{adherence}(L)\}.$$

In other words, $A(L) = I(\text{adherence}(L))$.

To represent images in more than one dimension, we consider n-ary relations and extend the definition of adherence from languages to relations. We need to only extend the definition of the Prefix operation from finite words to ω-words. An n-tuple $(x_1, x_2, \ldots, x_n)$, where $x_i \in \Sigma^*$ is a prefix of $(y_1, y_2, \ldots, y_n)$, where all y_i's are in Σ^* or all y_i's are in Σ^ω, if x_i is a prefix of y_i, $1 \leq i \leq n$. Also, if ρ is an n-ary relation, we will denote $\rho.\underbrace{(0, 0, \ldots, 0)}_{n-times}{}^*$ by shorthand $\rho.0^*$.

In this paper, we will focus on 1-D and 2-D images, and therefore, be dealing with languages and binary relations. However, all the results hold for any arbitrary number of dimensions.

Note that the interpretation function I may not be injective, when its domain is restricted to some language $L \subseteq \Sigma^\omega$. For example, $I(01^\omega)$ and $I(10^\omega)$ both are equal to the same binary number 0.1. In general, a number might have two different representations. If $\Sigma = \{0, 1, \ldots, n-1\}$, then the *left canonical representation* is the one with trailing 0's, while the *right canonical representation* is the one with trailing $(n-1)$'s. If for every point which is in the image represented by a given language and which has two representations, the language has both the representations then the language is called to be in the *canonical form*.

Example: The Cantor Set is obtained by starting with the interval $[0,1]$ and successively deleting the middle third open subinterval. The n-th iteration is represented by the regular language $\{0+2\}^n\Sigma^*$, where $\Sigma = \{0,1,2\}$. The Cantor Set C is the limit of this recursive process. This set can be represented by languages as follows.

$$C = A(\{0+2\}^*) = I(\{0+2\}^\omega).$$

Note that $\{0+2\}^\omega$ represents the Cantor Set but is not canonical because the point $x = 0.333\ldots$ has two representations—02^ω and 10^ω, and only the first representation is in the language.

4 Representation of Images by Rational Expressions

A remarkable variety of images can be represented by considering rational expressions (and topologically closed ω-rational relations).

We consider only a normal length-preserving form of rational expressions (rational relations), as this allows us to treat a (binary) rational relation ρ over alphabet Σ as a language over alphabet $\Sigma \times \Sigma$. This is not an essential restriction because practically one does not specify the value of one coordinate much more precisely than that of the other coordinate. Moreover, if there is a bounded difference in the precision of different coordinate values, then the lengths of their representations can be made exactly equal by suffixing zeroes.

A rational relation ρ is called *almost length-preserving* if for every $(x_1, x_2) \in \rho$, $||x_1| - |x_2|| < c$, where c is a fixed positive constant. Alternatively, let M be a finite transducer. If every loop in M is exactly length-preserving, then M is called almost length-preserving. A rational relation is almost length-preserving if there exists an almost length-preserving finite transducer accepting the rational relation.

A rational relation ρ is called *(exactly) length-preserving* if for each $(x_1, x_2) \in \rho$, $|x_1| = |x_2|$. A length-preserving finite transducer is a Mealy machine (which produces exactly one output symbol for every input symbol).

These definitions can be generalized to ω-rational relations in a straightforward manner. An ω-rational relation is almost length-preserving if it is accepted by an ω-finite transducer which is exactly length-preserving on all of its loops. An ω-rational relation is (exactly) length-preserving if it is accepted by an ω-finite transducer which is length-preserving on all of its transitions.

Now we show a normal form of our rational relations.

Theorem 1 *Let ρ be an almost length-preserving ω-rational relation. Then, there exists another ω-rational relation δ, such that δ is exactly length-preserving and both ρ and δ represent the same image.*

The following theorem states that if one wants to include $I(\rho)$, besides its limit points, in the represented image, then one needs to concatenate ρ with 0^*.

Theorem 2 *Let ρ be an n-ary length-preserving relation over some alphabet Σ. Then $A(\rho.0^*)$ is the closure of $I(\rho)$ i.e. $A(\rho) = I(\rho) \cup \{$limit points of I$(\rho)\}$.*

Since adherence set of a regular set is an ω-regular set, we may work only with ω-regular sets as image representations. The following lemma states that this holds for relations too.

Lemma 1 *Let ρ be an almost length-preserving rational relation. Then, the adherence set of ρ is a length-preserving ω-rational relation.*

Moreover, we can work with canonical representations.

Lemma 2. *Let an image be represented by a length-preserving ω-rational relation. Then, there exists an ω-rational relation which is a canonical representation of the same image.*

Proof: Without loss of generality, let the alphabet be $\{0,1\}$. Construct an ω-finite transducer T which on an input ω-word σ does the following at every step:
(1) it copies the input symbol into the output.
(2) it guesses that the remaining portion of the input is an infinite sequence of 0's (and therefore σ is in the left canonical form), and converts it into the right canonical form.
(3) it guesses that the remaining portion of the input is an infinite sequence of 1's (and therefore σ is in the right canonical form), and converts it into the left canonical form.
Clearly, T converts every length-preserving ω-rational relation into an equivalent canonical length-preserving ω-rational relation. □

Several results from the theory of ω-regular languages can be used to show the decidability of different questions about images.

Theorem 3 *The membership problem of a rational point, effectively given as an ω-word, in a given image is decidable.*

Proof: Let the given rational point be x. Now x can be represented by an ω-rational relation R_x, such that $I(R_x) = \{x\}$. Let ρ be the length-preserving rational relation representing the given image. Let T be the ω-finite transducer in the proof of Lemma 2. Then, the point x is in the image iff $T(R_x) \subseteq T(\text{adherence}(\rho))$. Since, the inclusion problem for ω-regular sets is decidable [4], the proof follows. □

Theorem 4 *It is decidable whether two image representations are equivalent i.e. whether they represent the same image.*

Several results from the theory of ω-regular languages can be used to show the decidability of different questions about images.

Theorem 5 *The membership problem of a rational point, effectively given as an ω-word, in an image given by a rational expression, is decidable.*

Theorem 6 *For two images A and B (compact sets) given by rational expressions it is decidable whether:*
(i) $A = B$ (equivalence problem)
(ii) $A \subseteq B$ (inclusion problem)
(iii) $A \cap B = \phi$ (overlap problem)

Theorem 7 *Given two images A and B, effectively given, it is decidable whether the Hausdorff distance $h(A, B)$ between them is less than or equal to ϵ.*

In the above proof, the underlying metric d for the Hausdorff metric is assumed to be $d((x_1, y_1), (x_2, y_2)) = \max\{|x_1 - x_2|, |y_1 - y_2|\}$. This metric is topologically equivalent to the Euclidean metric.

5 Operations on Images

One of the reasons why the representation of images by languages turns out to be concise is that a number of operations on images can be concisely described by language operations. First note that the boolean operations of union and intersection have straightforward graphical interpretation. Therefore, for example, the parts of an image lying outside a window can be clipped by intersecting the language representing the image with the language defining the window. Also note that the k-th *approximation* to any image represented by a language L is given by $(L \cap \Sigma^{\leq k}).\Sigma^*$. If L is an ω-language, then the approximation is given by $(\text{Prefix}(L) \cap \Sigma^{\leq k}).\Sigma^\omega$. However note that if one is defining images as the interpretation of arbitrary languages then the closure under Boolean operations holds, but in our definition images are compact sets and, therefore, are not closed under complementation.

In this section, we focus mainly on three interesting operations on images—zooming operation, placement operation, and more complicated operations performed by GSM.

We will illustrate these operations on 2-D images. Let $R(x,y), x,y \in \Sigma^*$, denote the rectangular subarea (window) in $[0,1]^2$ which has its lower left corner at the point $I(x,y)$, and which has sides of lengths $\frac{1}{n^{|x|}}$ and $\frac{1}{n^{|y|}}$, where $n = |\Sigma|$, in the horizontal and vertical directions, respectively i.e.

$$R(x,y) = \{(a,b) \in [0,1] \times [0,1] | I(x) \leq a \leq I(x) + \frac{1}{n^{|x|}}, I(y) \leq b \leq I(y) + \frac{1}{n^{|y|}}\}.$$

It is assumed, for the purpose of this definition, that $I(\varepsilon) = 0$.

Zooming: Suppose we are given an image being represented by a language L, and it is desired to zoom into the window $R(x,y)$, for some $x,y \in \Sigma^*$. This operation is accomplished with the *quotient* operation on the relation L,

$$L_{zoom}^{R(x,y)} = (x,y) \setminus L = \{(u,v) \mid (xu, yv) \in L\}.$$

Clearly, this operation zooms into the image enclosed in the rectangular area $R(x,y)$. One disadvantage of this simple zooming is that the dimensions of the zoomed window are dependent upon the lengths of the strings x and y. To perform more advanced zooming, one may use concatenation and union operation in conjunction with quotient operation. For example, suppose the language is over the binary alphabet, and we want to zoom into the window W given by

$$W = \{(a,b) \in [0,1]^2 \mid 0.25 \leq a,b \leq 0.75\}.$$

This zooming is performed by the following more complicated language operation

$$L_{zoom}^W = (0,0)((01,01) \setminus L) \cup (0,1)((01,10) \setminus L) \cup (1,0)((10,01) \setminus L) \cup (1,1)((10,10) \setminus L)$$

See Fig. 1 which shows an example of this zooming operation. Some simple images defined by rational expressions are also shown in the figure.

The zooming operation provides one with a sufficient condition to test the "self-similarity" of an image. Clearly, if $L_{zoom}^W = L$ for some window W, then it implies that there is a scaled down copy of the image in the window W, and therefore the image is self-similar.

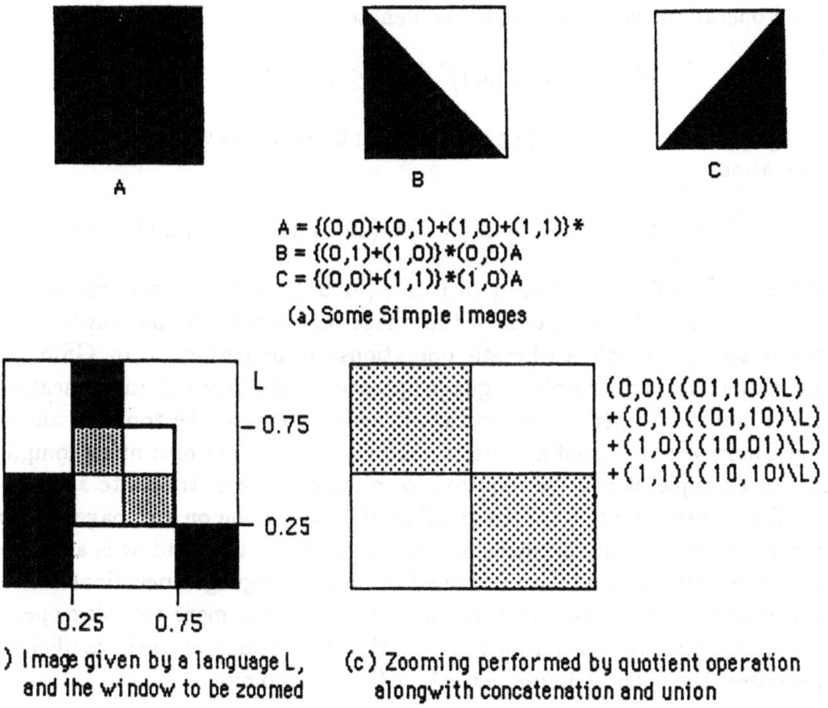

Figure 1: Some Simple Images and An Example of Zooming Operation

Placement: Placement can be viewed as an operation inverse to zooming. We are given an image and a window, and it is desired to place a scaled down copy of the image in the window.

Suppose the given image is represented by a relation L and the window where the image is to be placed is $R(x,y)$ for some $x, y \in \Sigma^*$. Then, concatenating (x,y) with L results in the placement operation

$$L_{place}^{R(x,y)} = \{(x,y)\}.L = \{(xu, yv) \mid (u,v) \in L\}.$$

Therefore, the simple concatenation operation provides us a mechanism to place images at various positions.

Moreover, it is possible to generate "fractal" images, by placing the copies of a basic image at infinitely many places i.e. by concatenating the language L, which is a representation of the basic image, with an infinite language L', which gives these infinitely many places where the copies of the basic image will be placed.

For example, if $L' = \{(0,0),(0,1),(1,0)\}^*$ then the operation $L'.L$ creates a Sierpinski Triangle type fractal image. Actually, the well-known Sierpinski Triangle happens to be a special case, when $L = L'$.

Note that concatenating an image with a string (x,y) scales it down by a factor which is $\frac{1}{n^{|x|}}$ and $\frac{1}{n^{|y|}}$, along the horizontal and vertical directions respectively. To perform more advanced placement, one may use quotient and union operations in conjunction with concatenation operation. For example, let W denote the window

$$W = \{(a,b) \in [0,1]^2 \mid 0.25 \leq a,b \leq 0.75\}$$

Then, an image represented by a language L can be placed in this window by the following language operation

$$L^W_{place} = (01,01)((0,0) \setminus L) \cup (01,01)((0,1) \setminus L) \cup (10,01)((1,0) \setminus L) \cup (10,10)((1,1) \setminus L).$$

This operation can be also performed by $(0,0).L + (01,01)$, where $+$ is arithmetic addition i.e. (0.25,0.25) is added to every point of the image represented by the relation $(0,0).L$. We will shortly see that simple arithmetic operations can be performed by GSM.

GSM operations: Though, simple language operations, like quotient and concatenation operations, can be used to perform important image operations, like zooming and placement, we need more sophisticated automata-theoretic tools to perform more complicated operations. For example, it may be required to rotate or scale or translate an image. In general, it will be interesting to perform an affine transformation on an image. Moreover, for most general zooming and placement operations, in which the window is arbitrary, we need more complex mechanisms than provided by simple language operations.

GSM mappings provide a powerful mechanism to perform more complex operations on images. Since affine transformations have rational constants as their coefficients for practical purposes, they can be implemented by GSM mappings.

Theorem 8 *Let $\tau : [0,1]^2 \to [0,1]^2$ be an arbitrary affine transformation. Then τ can be implemented with a GSM M such that*

$$\tau(A(\rho)) = A(M(\rho)),$$

where $\rho \subseteq \Sigma^* \times \Sigma^*$ (and ρ is length-preserving).

The following result extends the result to ω-languages.

Theorem 9 *Let $\tau : [0,1]^n \to [0,1]^n$ be an arbitrary affine transformation. Then τ can be implemented with an ω-finite transducer M such that*

$$\tau(I(\rho)) = I(M(\rho)),$$

where $\rho \subseteq \Sigma^\omega \times \Sigma^\omega$ (and ρ is length-preserving).

In the above proof, the ω-finite transducer that implements the given affine transformation is synchronous i.e. it reads the two input bits synchronously and produces two output bits synchronously. Such an ω-transducer is called a simple one.

To summarize, the images represented by rational expressions have the following important closure properties:

Theorem 10 *The class of images represented by length-preserving rational relations is closed under union, intersection, zooming, placement and (simple) GSM operations.*

6 Texture Images Defined by Finite Generators

So far we have considered only images as compact subsets of n-dimensional Euclidean subspace $[0,1]^n, n \geq 1$, and have used rational expressions as their representations. But in real-world images, an important characteristic of images is their *texture*. An image for which texture is defined will be refered as a texture image. In this section, we show how texture images can be defined by (length-preserving) rational expressions.

From now onwards, we will call a finite automaton accepting a rational expression as a *finite generator*.

A straightforward method of defining texture is by assigning probabilities to the transitions of the finite generator such that, for each state, outgoing transitions' probabilities sum to unity. Such a generator is nothing but a probabilistic finite generator which generates a point with some probability. The image which is represented by such a generator and is given by the adherence of the rational relation, is generated by the ω-finite automaton obtained from the original finite generator by making every state a final state.

We will illustrate the notion of texture by considering 2-D images, which are subsets of $[0,1]^2$. Let $x, y \in \Sigma^*$ and let $|x| = |y| = n$. Define

$$B(x,y) = \{(a,b) \in [0,1]^2 | I(x) \leq a < I(x) + 1/|\Sigma|^n, I(y) \leq b < I(y) + 1/|\Sigma|^n\}$$

where I, as usual, is the interpretation function. In other words, $B(x,y)$ is the window which has as its lower left corner at the point $(I(x), I(y))$ and has horizontal and vertical dimensions equal to $\frac{1}{|\Sigma|^n}$.

Let $\mathcal{G} = \{B(x,y) | x, y \in \Sigma^*, |x| = |y|\}$.

Mathematically, a *measure* is a real non-negative additive function μ defined on a countable base of Borel sets [1].

Let $\mu(B(x,y))$, where $B(x,y) \in \mathcal{G}$ be the probability of generating the tuple (x,y) by the given finite generator. Note that μ so defined is a normalized measure as $\mu([0,1]^2) = 1$ [1].

Define *measure density* $\lambda : \mathcal{G} \to [0,\infty]$ as follows

$$\lambda(B(x,y)) = \mu((B(x,y)) / \text{ area of B(x, y)}$$

where area of $B(x,y)$ is $1/|\Sigma|^{2n}, n = |x| = |y|$.

Now we are in a position to define the texture of an image, effectively given as a finite generator. (Note that the final states of the generator are immaterial as the ω-FA accepting the adherence of the rational relation accepted by the generator as all its states as final).

The *texture* of an image, represented by a probabilistic finite generator M, is the measure density function $\lambda : \mathcal{G} \to [0,\infty]$ defined by M.

An important theoretical result about the problem of testing the equivalence of two texture images follows from the decidability of the equivalence of probabilistic finite automata [15]. A probabilistic finite automaton is an automaton in which for every state s and every input symbol a, the probabilities on the outgoing transitions of the state s on input symbol a sum to unity.

Lemma 3 *Every probabilistic finite generator can be simulated by a probabilistic finite automaton.*

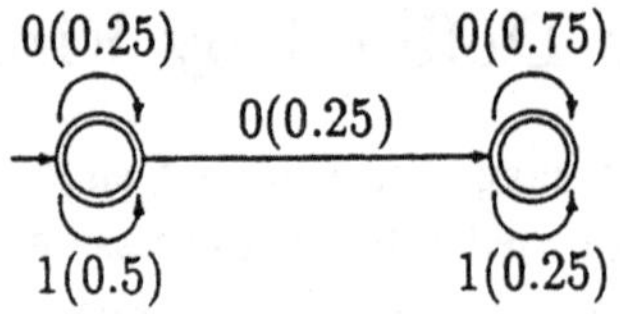

Figure 2: Finite Generator from the Proof of Theorem 13

Theorem 11 *It is decidable whether two texture images, effectively given as probabilistic finite generators, are equivalent.*

Proof: The proof follows from Lemma 3 and the decidability of the equivalence problem for probabilistic finite automata [15]. □

Finally, we show that nondeterminism allows one to define a wider variety of texture images. A deterministic generator below is a probabilistic generator whose underlying finite automaton is deterministic. In a similar way the pumping lemma for regular sets enables us to show proper containment of regular sets in CFL, this following lemma will help us to show the proper containment of texture images defined by deterministic generators in those defined by nondeterministic ones.

Lemma 4 *Let A be a (texture) image defined by a deterministic generator. Then there exists $n \geq 0$, such that by zooming into the window $R(u,v)$ for all possible $(u,v) \in \Sigma^* \times \Sigma^*$, $|u| = |v|$ we get at most n distinct (texture) images. Moreover, n can be chosen to be the number of states of the minimal deterministic generator of A.*

Proof: Let $M = (K, \ldots)$ be the minimal deterministic generator of A. Given $(u,v) \in \Sigma^* \times \Sigma^*$, $|u| = |v|$, the image obtained by zooming into the window $R(u,v)$ is defined by the deterministic generator obtained from M by replacing its initial state by the one reached by (u,v). Clearly, there is at most $|K|$ distinct automata obtained this way. In the case of black and white images (compact sets) we ignore the probabilities. □

Theorem 12 *The class of texture images defined by nondeterministic generators is strictly greater than that defined by deterministic generators.*

Proof: In Fig. 2 an example of a probabilistic nondeterministic finite generator is shown. The texture image defined by it obviously does not satisfy the Lemma 4. Thus it cannot be defined by any deterministic generator. □

7 Examples of Images Defined by Rational Relations

In this section, we present a number of examples illustrating the power of the rational expressions to represent images.

Example: Consider the following three rational expressions:

$$\begin{aligned}\Delta_1 &= \{(0,0)+(0,1)+(1,0)+(1,1)\}^*,\\ \Delta_2 &= \{(0,1)+(1,0)\}^*(0,0)\Delta_1,\\ \Delta_3 &= \{(0,0)+(1,1)\}^*(1,0)\Delta_1.\end{aligned}$$

These expressions represent three simple images X_1, X_2, and X_3, respectively, one being the unit filled square, and the other two being filled triangles (see Fig. 1(a)).
Example: The Sierpinski Triangle is represented by the regular expression $\{(0,0)+(0,1)+(1,0)\}^*$ over $\Sigma = \{0,1\}$.
Example: In Fig. 3, self-similar image of diminishing triangles is shown. This image too has a simple rational expression as its representation. Basically, we are placing infinite number of copies of the triangle at the points in the language $\{(0,1)+(1,0)\}^*(0,0)$. The corresponding finite generator is also shown. The probabilities in this generator is chosen in such a way that we obtain a uniform texture.
Example: In Fig. 4, the representation of H-tree VLSI layout by a rational expression is shown. Note that the rational expressions H and V represent the horizontal line and vertical line, respectively. In the figure, we have shown the image upto a finite depth $n(=5)$, represented by a rational expression, which is prefixed by $\Sigma^n \times \Sigma^n$, where $\Sigma = \{0,1\}$. The limiting case, when $n \to \infty$, defines a space-filling layout.
Example: In Fig. 5, an image with fractal dimension $D = 1.79$ is shown. It is interesting to note that D is exactly between the fractal dimension of Sierpinski Triangle ($D = 1.58$) and that of filled square ($D = 2$). The fractal dimension is computed using the result in [14], according to which it is $\log_2 |\lambda|$, where λ is an eigenvalue, of maximum modulus, of the connection matrix C of the underlying finite automaton (C_{ij} is the number of transitions from state i to state j). In our example, $\lambda = \sqrt{12}$, which gives a dimension of 1.79.

8 Inference of a Generator from an Image

We briefly describe the idea based on which an algorithm to automatically infer a finite generator for a given image can be devised [7]. We will illustrate the idea by considering a "human" approach which can be employed to infer the finite generator shown in Fig. 3(c) for the image of diminishing triangles shown in Fig. 3(a). Denote the image of diminishing triangles by A. Create a state s_0 (which will be the initial state of the resulting finite generator) representing A. Now subdivide the image into four subimages, corresponding to four quadrants. Identify a quadrant by its lower left corner i.e. by (0,0),(0,1),(1,0) and (1,1) (in binary notation). The four subimages are as follows:
B: A filled triangle in quadrant (0,0).
C: Images of diminishing triangles in quadrant (0,1) and (1,0).
D: A totally blank image in quadrant (1,1).
We ignore D as it is totally blank. Since B is not similar to A, an already existing image, we create a new state s_1 for it. We put a transition to s_1 from s_0 labeled (0,0), as B corresponds to quadrant (0,0) of image A. Image C is similar to A, and therefore we do not create any new state for it, and instead have two self-loops at s_0 labeled (0,1) and (1,0). Repeating the above method for image B, results in an image of filled square

(a) Image

$I = \{(0,1) + (1,0)\}$
$\Delta = \{I + (0,0) + (1,1)\}$

$I^*(0,0)I^*(0,0)\Delta^*$

(b) Rational Expression

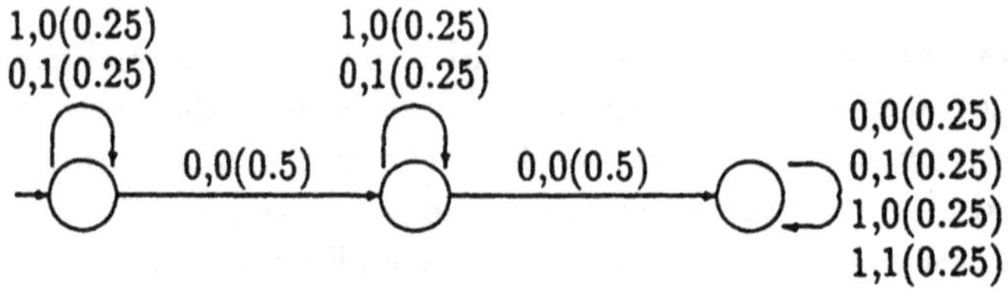

(c) Probabilistic Finite Generator

Figure 3: Diminishing Triangles

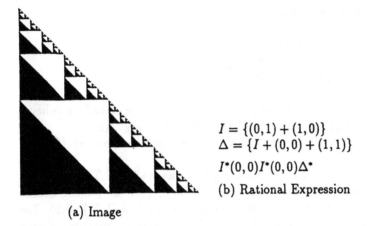

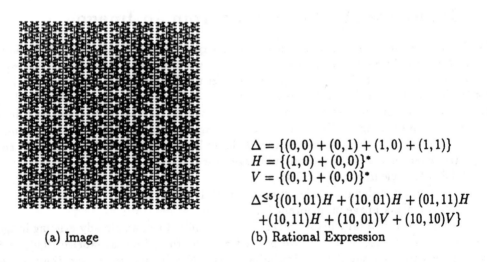

(a) Image

$\Delta = \{(0,0) + (0,1) + (1,0) + (1,1)\}$
$H = \{(1,0) + (0,0)\}^*$
$V = \{(0,1) + (0,0)\}^*$

$\Delta^{\leq 5}\{(01,01)H + (10,01)H + (01,11)H$
$+ (10,11)H + (10,01)V + (10,10)V\}$

(b) Rational Expression

Figure 4: H-Tree VLSI layout

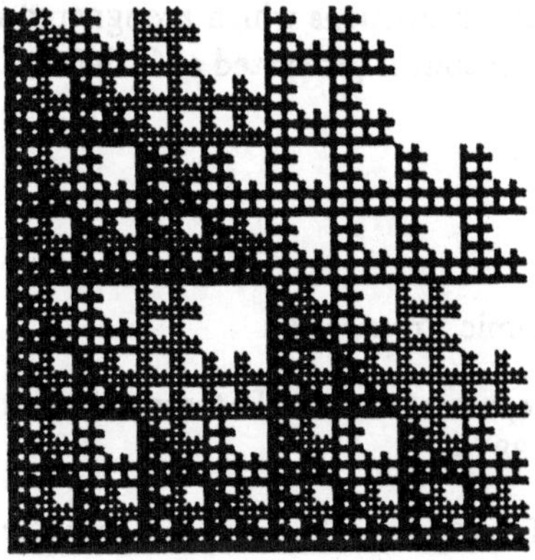

$$I = \{(0,0) + (0,1) + (1,0)\}^*$$
$$\Delta = \{I + (1,1)\}^*$$
$$(\Delta I)^* + (I\Delta)^*$$

(a) Image

(b) Rational Expression

Figure 5: A Variation of Sierpinski Triangle, with fractal dimension = 1.79

different from the existing ones (A and B). A new state s_2 is created. Repeating the method once more for s_2, however does not result in any new images, and the algorithm terminates giving us the finite generator as shown in Fig. 3(c).

9 Iterative Finite Generators

In this section, we briefly introduce iterative finite generators, which are studied in detail in [6].

Let T be an ω-finite transducer. Define

$$\Omega^{(0)} = \Sigma^\omega,$$

$$\Omega^{(i)} = T(\Omega^{(i-1)}), i \geq 1.$$

Define the *limit set* of T as,

$$\Omega = \cap_{i=0}^{\infty} \Omega^{(i)}.$$

The image generated by T is $I(\Omega)$ (where I is the usual interpretation function). An ω-finite transducer defined in such a manner to generate images is called an *iterative finite generator*. In a similar fashion, we may define iterative generators for languages of finite strings, in which case T is a finite transducer.

Theorem 13 *The class of images defined by iterative finite generators is strictly greater than that defined by (noniterative) finite generators.*

The above result follows from the observation that a finite generator can be implemented by an iterative finite generator which has the same state transition diagram as the finite generator, but with additional input symbols on the transitions which are ignored i.e. for each transition, irrespective of the input the same output is generated as is defined by the finite generator.

References

[1] M. F. Barnsley, *Fractals Everywhere*, Academic Press, 1988.

[2] J. Berstel and M. Morcrette, "Compact Representation of Patterns by Finite Automata," Proceedings Pixim'89, Paris, pp. 387-402.

[3] L. Boasson and M. Nivat, "Adherences of Languages," *Jour. of Computer. Syst. Sci.*, **20**, 285-309 (1980).

[4] R. Cohen and A. Gold, "Theory of ω-languages," Part I and II, *Jour. of Computer Syst. Sc.*, **15**, 169-208 (1977).

[5] K. Culik II and S. Dube, "Affine Automata: A Technique to Generate Complex Images," accepted for presentation at the Fifteenth International Symposium on *Mathematical Foundations of Computer Science*, Czechoslovakia (1990).

[6] K. Culik II and S. Dube, "A Comparison of Some Automata-Theoretic Techniques to Generate Images," under preparation.

[7] K. Culik II and S. Dube, "Image Synthesis Using Rational Relations", Research Report TR90001, Dept. of Computer Science, University of South Carolina (1990).

[8] K. Culik II and S. Yu, "Cellular Automata, $\omega\omega$-Regular Sets, and Sofic Systems," to appear in *Discrete Applied Mathematics*.

[9] S. Even, "Rational Numbers and Regular Events," *IEEE Transactions on Electronic Computers*, **EC-13**, No. 6, 740-741 (1964).

[10] J.Gleick, *Chaos–Making a New Science*, Penguin Books, 1988.

[11] J. Hartmanis and R. E. Stearns, "Sets of Numbers Defined By Finite Automata," *American Mathematical Monthly*, **74** 539-542 (1967).

[12] G. M. Hunter and K. Steiglitz, Operations on Images Using Quadtrees, *IEEE Trans. on Pattern Analysis and Machine Intell.*, **1** 145-153 (1979).

[13] B. Mandelbrot, *The Fractal Geometry of Nature*, W. H. Freeman and Co., San Francisco, 1982.

[14] L. Staiger, "Quadtrees and the Hausdorff Dimension of Pictures," Workshop on Geometrical Problems of Image Processing, Georgenthal GDR, 173-178 (1989).

[15] W. G. Tzeng, "The Equivalence and Learning of Probabilistic Automata," *FOCS proceedings*, 268-273 (1989).

Recognizable Infinite Tree Sets and their Complexity

A. Saoudi

L.I.T.P †
Univ. Paris VII
2, place Jussieu 75252 Paris
FRANCE

D. E. Muller P. E. Schupp
Univ. of Illinois at Urbana-Champaign
Department of Mathematics
1409 West Green street
Urbana, Illinois 61801
U. S. A

Abstract

In this paper we consider the extension of Nerode theorem to infinite trees. Unfortunately, we prove that this extension is not possible. We give some characterisations of Recognizable and Rational ω-tree sets in terms of ω-tree automata. We consider some complexity measures of Recognizable and Rational ω-tree sets and prove that these measures define infinite hierarchies□

Keywords : Tree automata, Büchi automata, Muller automata, and Rabin automata .

Introduction

The theory of automata has many applications such as in compiling, logic, and parallel processing. This theory has been extended to infinite words by defining various generating and recognizing devices (see L. Boasson and M. Nivat [1] and J. R. Büchi [2]). The above theory has been extended to infinite trees , first by M. O. Rabin [16,17] and then by Y. Gurevich and L. Harrington

† Laboratoire d'Informatique Théorique et Programmation. This research was supported by PRC Maths-Info, France.

[7], T. Hayashi and S. Miyano [8], D. Muller and P. Schupp [9], D. E. Muller et al. [10], M. Nivat et al. [12], M. Takahashi [20], W. Thomas [21]. M. O. Rabin [16] gives a characterization of S2S in terms of automata on infinite trees and then proves that S2S is decidable , where S2S is the monadic second order theory of the binary tree. In [7], Y. Gurevich and L. Harrington used a special game reduce the complementation to a determinancy result. This allows them to simplify the proof of the decidability of S2S. Likwise, D. Muller and P. Schupp [9] introduce alternating automata on infinite trees and then give an alternative proof. In another example M. Y. Vardi and P. Wolper [22] consrtruct decision procedures for temporal logic of fair concurrent programs using automata on infinite trees. It is well known from D. E. Muller et al. [10] and M. Y. Vardi et al. [22] that the complexity of decision procedures for most Temporal and Dynamic Logics depend on the complexity of tree automata. Recently, A. Emerson and C. Jutla [6] have obtained essentially optimal decision procedures for various modal logics using an optimal algorithm for testing non-emptiness of tree automata.

The first aim of this work is the simplification of Rabin's proof of the decidability of S2S. For this, we will try to simplify the proof of the closure under complementation of sets accepted by Rabin's tree automata. This can be done by extending Nerode Theorem to infinite trees. By using Nerode's theorem only a non-constructive proof of complementation lemma is attainable. The second aim is to study the complexity of recognizable and rational ω-tree sets.

For this, we define some natural complexity measures of recognizable infinite tree sets, where the measure of a set is defined in terms of tree automata which accept it. Here, we consider the following measures: the minimal number of states, the minimal number of transitions, the minimal number of designated states(i.e. Büchi's index), and the minimal number of designated sets(i.e. Muller's index). We define also the size of a rational set(i.e. set accepted by Büchi tree automata) as the minimal number of rational finite tree sets required to describe it.

The organisation of this paper is as follows:

In the first section, we give some basic definitions. In the second section, we introduce new acceptance conditions and compare them with Muller's and Büchi's conditions. We prove that each recognizable set is union of some classes of an invariant relation of finite index. Unfortunately, we prove that Nerode theorem cannot be extended to infinite trees In the third section, we prove that each measure of the above measures define a strict hierarchy. In the last section, we prove that the introduced measures for both deterministic and pseudo-deterministic sets define a strict hierarchies.

1. Notations and definitions

Let Σ be a finite alphabet. Then the set of k-ary finite trees over Σ, called finite trees for short, denoted by T_Σ is defined inductively as follows :

(i) If $a \in \Sigma$ then $a \in T_\Sigma$.

(ii) If $t_1, t_2, \ldots, t_k \in T_\Sigma$ and $a \in \Sigma$ then $a(t_1, \ldots, t_k) \in T_\Sigma$.

Let$t$ be a k-ary finite tree, called tree for short, then the domain of t, denoted by $dom(t)$, is defined inductively as follows :

(i) If $t \in \Sigma$ then $dom(t)=\{\lambda\}$,where λ denotes the empty word.

(ii) If $t=a(t_1,\ldots,t_k)$ then $dom(t)=\{\lambda\}\cup(\bigcup_{i=1}^{k} i.dom(t_i))$.

Note that a tree t can be viewed as a mapping from $dom(t)$ to Σ. Here trees are denoted as terms. An infinite tree (i.e. k-ary ω-tree) over Σ is a mapping from $D_k=\{1,\ldots,k\}^*$ to Σ . We denote by T_Σ^ω (resp. T_Σ) the set of infinite (resp. finite) k-ary trees over Σ. We define an infinite branch of the tree t, starting at the root, as an infinite word $(t(u_i))_{i\geq 0}$, where :

(i) $u_0=\lambda$, and

(ii) For each i, there exists a $j_i \in \{1,\ldots,k\}$ such that $u_{i+1}=u_i j_i$.

Let t_i (i=1,2) be a finite k-ary tree with F_i (i.e. $Fr(t_i)$) as a frontier (i.e. $F_i=\{u : u\in dom(t_i)$ and uj is not in $dom(t_i)$, for $1\leq j\leq k\}$). We define the relation < between two frontiers as : $F_1 < F_2$ if for each node y $\in F_2$ there exists a node x $\in F_1$ such that x < y . t_1 is an **initial tree** of t_2 ($t_1\leq t_2$) iff (i) $dom(t_1) \subseteq dom(t_2)$, and (ii)for each u$\in dom(t_1)$: $t_1(u)= t_2(u)$. Then t_1 is called a **proper initial tree** of t_2 (i.e $t_1<t_2$) if t_1 is an initial tree of t_2 and $F_1 < F_2$. Let L be a set of finite k-ary trees; we define the limit of L in the sense of Rabin as:

$Rlim$(L)= { t / there is an infinite sequence $(t_i)_{i\geq 0}$ *with* $t_i\in L$, $t_i < t_{i+1}$, and $t_i<t$} .

Let $X=\{x_1,\ldots,x_n\}$ be a set of variables such that $X\cap\Sigma=\emptyset$ and let $(L_i)_{0\leq i\leq n}$ be a sequence of sets of finite k-ary trees over $\Sigma\cup X$ such that $L_i\cap X=\emptyset$ and L_i contains finite k-ary tree such that all variables occur as values of frontier nodes. If $a \in \Sigma$ and L_i is a set of finite trees then $a(L_1,\ldots L_k)=\{a(t_1,\ldots,t_k):t_i\in L_i\}$. We define $L_0.<L_1,\ldots,L_n>$ as the set of trees that are obtained by taking t in L_0 and grafting elements of L_i at the nodes of t valued by x_i. $L_0<L_1,\ldots,L_n>$ is formally defined as follows :

(i) If t = x_i then $t.<L_1,\ldots L_n> =L_i$

(ii) If $t = a(t_1,\ldots,t_k)$ then $t<L_1,\ldots L_n> =a(t_1<L_1,\ldots L_n>,\ldots,t_k<L_1,\ldots L_n>)$

(iii) $L.<L_1,\ldots,L_n>=\bigcup_{t\in L} t.<L_1,\ldots L_n>$.

Let $L_0.<L_1,\ldots,L_n>^p=(L_0.<L_1,\ldots L_n>^{p-1}).<L_1,\ldots L_n>$,where $L_0.<L_1,\ldots L_n>^0=L_0$

$L_0.<L_1,\ldots,L_n>^{\omega} = \{ t\in T^{\omega}_{\Sigma}: \exists\ (t_n)_{0\le n\le\omega}$ *such that*

$t\ = Rlim\ \{t_n: 0\le n\le\omega\}\ , t_o\in L_o$ and $t_p\in t_{p-1}.<L_1,..,L_n>\}$.

A set L of infinite trees is said to be *rational*(i.e. regular) if there is a sequence $(L_i)_{0\le i\le n}$ of rational finite tree sets such that L is equal to $L_0<L_1,\ldots,L_n>^{\omega}$.

A **projection** is a mapping from a set Σ to a set Δ . A projection determines a mapping from the set of trees on Σ to the set of trees on Δ . For more details about properties of trees the reader can consult B. Courcelle [4].

2 . Recognizable ω-tree sets

Let L be a set of infinite trees over Σ, L is called **omega-rational** if and only if there is a sequence $(L_i)_{0\le i\le n}$ of rational(i.e. regular) sets of finite trees such that $L=L_0.<L_1,\ldots,L_n>^{\omega}$.

Now, we will introduce new types of infinite tree automata and then characterize both recognizable and rational ω-tree sets.

A **Büchi k-ary ω-tree automaton** , a Büchi tree automaton for short, is a structure $M=<Q,\Sigma,I,\delta,F>$, where Q is a set of finite states, Σ is a finite set of input symbols, I is the set of initial states, $\delta:Q\times\Sigma\rightarrow 2^{Q^k}$ is the transition function and F is a set of a designated states of Q. A computation of M on the tree t is a tree C on Q with $C(\lambda)=q_0$ and for each node u $(C(u1),\ldots,C(uk))\ \in\ \delta\ (C(u),t(u))$. The tree t is accepted by the Büchi tree automaton M, if for some computation of M on t, and for each branch of this computation, a state from F occurs infinitely often in this branch.

A **Büchi k-ary ω-tree T-automaton** , a Büchi tree T-automaton for short, is a structure $M=<Q,\Sigma,I,\delta,T>$, where Q,Σ,δ,I are defined as before and T is a set of designated transitions. An infinite tree t is accepted by a Büchi tree T-automaton M, if there is a computation of M on t such that each branch of this computation meets T infinitly many time .

For each set L of infinite trees, the following conditions are equivalent :

(i) L is accepted by a Büchi tree automaton,

(ii) L is accepted by a Büchi tree T-automaton, and

(iii) L is an omega-rational set.

The equivalence between (i) and (iii) is due to M. Nivat and A. Saoudi [12,13]. The equivalence between (i) and (ii) can be done easily by coding computation with transitions. Intuitively, the equivalence between (i) and (ii) that every set of infinite trees accepted bu a Büchi tree automaton can be denoted by an omega-rational tree expression. This can be viewed as a generalization of Kleene theorem to automata on infinite trees.

Let us mention that M. Nivat et al. [13] characterize omega-rational tree sets in terms of tree grammars. In [20], M. Takahashi characterizes the family of omega-rational tree sets in terms of fixed points.

A **Muller k-ary ω-tree automaton** , a Muller tree automaton for short, is a structure $M=<Q,\Sigma,I,\delta,F>$, where Q, Σ,*I* , δ are defined as before, and $F \subseteq 2^Q$ is a collection of designated sets of states.

A **Muller k-ary ω-tree T-automaton** , a Muller tree T-automaton for short, is a structure $M=<Q,\Sigma,I,\delta,T>$,where Q,Σ,I,δ are defined as before and T is a family of designated sets of transitions. The tree t is accepted by the Muller tree automaton (resp. T-automaton) M iff there is a computation of M on t such that for each infinite branch of this computation, the set of states(resp. transitions) occurring infinitely often in this branch belongs to F(resp. T).

A **generalized Muller k-ary ω-tree automaton** , a Generalized Muller tree automaton, is a structure $M=<Q,\Sigma,I,\delta,F>$, where Q,Σ , I , δ are defined as before, and $F \subseteq 2^{2^Q}$ is a collection of designated sets.

A **generalized Muller k-ary ω-tree T-automaton** , a generalized Muller tree automaton for short, is a structure $M=<Q,\Sigma,I,\delta,T>$, where Q,Σ,I,δ are defined as before and T is a family of sets of sets of transitions. The generalized (resp. T-automaton) Muller tree automaton M accepts t iff there is a computation of M on t such that the set of all sets of states(resp. transitions), occurring infinitely often on infinite branches belongs to F(resp. T).

For each set of infinite trees K, the following conditions are equivalent :

(i) K is accepted by a Muller tree automaton,

(ii) K is accepted by a Muller tree T-automaton,

(iii) K is accepted by a genralized Muller tree automaton, and

(iv) K is accepted by a generalized Muller tree T-automaton.

The equivalence between (i) and (iii) is due to M. Nivat and A. Saoudi [13]. This equivalence is due to the fact that the generalized Muller condition is a boolean combination of the Muller condition . By using the same technique as for Büchi tree automata, one can easily prove that (i) is equivalent to (ii) and (iii) is equivalent to (iv). □

In [12], M. Nivat and A. Saoudi characterize recognizable ω-tree sets, where a recognizable set is a set accepted by a Muller tree automaton, in terms of tree grammars.

Next we show that each recognizable ω-tree set is union of some of the equivalence classes of an invariant relation of finite index. For this, we first recall some definitions and results.

Definition 2.1

A **bottom-up Muller k-ary ω-tree automaton is a structure** $M=<Q,\Sigma,\delta,Fin,F>$, where Q,Σ,F are defined as for a Muller tree automaton, $\delta: Q^k \times \Sigma \rightarrow 2^Q$ is the transition function, and $Fin \subseteq Q$ is the set of terminal states. □

A computation of the bottom-up automaton M on the tree t is a tree C over Q with $C(\lambda) \in Fin$ and for each node u, $C(u) \in \delta(<C(u1),...,C(uk)>,t(u))$. M accepts t iff there is a computation C of M on t such that for each infinite branch of this computation, the set of states occurring infinitely often in this branch belongs to F.

M is said to be deterministic (resp. total) iff for each $<q_1,\ldots,q_k> \in Q^k$ and $f \in \Sigma$, $Card(\delta(<q_1,\ldots,q_k>,f)) \leq 1$ (resp. $Card(\delta(<q_1,..,q_k>,f)) \geq 1$).

Theorem 2.2(M. Nivat and A. Saoudi)

For each set L of infinite trees, the following conditions are equivalent:

(i) L is accepted by a deterministic bottom-up Muller k-ary tree automaton, and

(ii) L is recognizable. □

Let R be an equivalence relation over T_Σ^ω then R is said to be k-invariant if $t_i \, R \, t'_i$, where $i=1,k$, then $f(t_1,\ldots,t_k) \, R \, f(t'_1,\ldots,t'_k)$ for all $f \in \Sigma$. The index of R is the number of its equivalence classes.

Theorem 2.3

Let L be a recognizable set of k-ary ω-trees. Then L is the union of some of the equivalence classes of a k-invariant equivalence relation of finite index. □

Proof:

Let L be a recognizable set of k-ary ω-trees then one can exhibit a deterministic and total bottom-up Muller tree automaton $M=<Q,\Sigma,\delta,Fin,F>$ accepting L. Let R_M be the relation defined by : tR_Mt' iff for each $q \in Q$ the followwing sets are equal :

- $\{Inf(C)$: *C is a computation of M on t* , and $C(\lambda)=q\}$, and
- $\{Inf(C)$: *C is a computation of M on t'* , and $C(\lambda)=q\}$.

$Inf(C)$ denotes the set of sets of states occurring infinitely often on some infinite branch of C.

R_M is an eqivalence relation. Since Q is finite, the index of R_M is also finite.

$L = \bigcup_{i=1}^{n} [t_i]$, where $[t_i]=\{t: \exists q \in Fin \; \exists H \subseteq F \; \exists C$ such that $C(\lambda)=q$ and $Inf(C)=H\}$.

Now we shall prove that the converse of the last theorem is not true in general (i.e. $Card(\Sigma)\geq 2$). But, if Σ contains one symbole the converse of the last theorem is true. Let t be an infinite tree over $\{a,b\}$, then $t|_{1^*}=a^{n_1}b^{k_1}a^{n_2}b^{k_2}$....., where $t|_{1^*}$ is the ω-word lying on the first branch (i.e. 1^*). Let $A(t)$ denotes the set $\{n_i : i\geq 1\}$.

Let R be the relation over T^{ω}_{Σ} such that tRt' iff $A(t)$ and $A(t')$ are recursively enumerable .

R is an equivalence relation of finite index which is k-invariant. Let L_0 be the set of k-ary infinite trees t over $\{a,b\}$ such that $A(t)$ is recursively enumerable. Since bottom-up Muller tree automaton are not able to count arbitrarily large, L_0 cannot be accepted by a bottom-up Muller tree automaton. This shows that Nerode theorem cannot be extended to infinite trees.

3. Hierarchies of Recognoizable ω-tree sets

Now we shall define an infinite hierarchy of omega-rational sets in terms of the minimal size of omega-rational expressions. Let $E=E_0.<E_1,...,E_n>^{\omega}$ be an omega-rational expression then the size of E is n. We define the regular index of L, where L is an omega-rational set, by the minimal size of omega-rational expressions denoting L. Let $R_n(\Sigma)$ be the family of omega-rational sets L, such that the regular index of L is less or equal to n. From now on, we assume that Σ contains at least two symbols.

Examples:

Let Π_n defined by the set of nodes 2^n1^*. Let s_n be the k-ary ω-tree with :

(i) $s_n|_{\Pi_i}=(ba^i)^{\omega}$, where $0\leq i\leq n$, where $s_n|_{\Pi_i}$ denotes the restriction of s_n to Π_i.

(ii) $s_n(u)=b$ if $u \in \{1,...,k\}^* - \bigcup_{i=1}^{n}\Pi_i$.

Let $T_n=\{s_n\}_{n\geq 0}$ then T_0 and T_1 can be denoted by the following omega-rational tree expressions:

- $T_0=b(x_1,....,x_1)<b(x_1, . . . ,x_1)>^{\omega}$.
- $T_1=b(x_1,x_2,x_1,..,x_1)<b(x_1, . . . ,x_1),a(b(x_2,x_1,..,x_1),x_1,..,x_1)>^{\omega}$.

Note that T_{n-1} can be denoted by an omega-rational tree expression of size n.

Let $BS_n(\Sigma)$ (resp. $MS_n(\Sigma)$) be the family of sets accepted by Büchi (resp. Muller) tree automata with at least p states, where $1\leq p\leq n$.

Proposition 3.1

For each $n\geq 1$, the family $BS_n(\Sigma)$ (resp. $MS_n(\Sigma)$) is properly included in $BS_{n+1}(\Sigma)$ (resp. $MS_{n+1}(\Sigma)$).

Proof:

Let $(t_n)_{n\geq 1}$ be the sequence such that $t_0=b^\omega$, where b^ω is the infinite tree over $\{b\}$, and $t_{n+1}=a(t_n, \ldots, t_n)$.

Let $H_n=\{t_{n-1}\}$ and $X \in \{B,M\}$. We shall exhibit an X-automaton M_n accepting H_n. $M_n=<Q_n,\{a,b\},q_n,\delta_n,F_n=\{q_0\}or\{\{q_0\}\}>$ is defined inductively by:

(i) $\delta_0(q_0,b)=(q_0,\ldots,q_0)$;

(ii) $\delta_{n+1}(q,a)=\delta_n(q,a)$ if $q\neq q_{n+1}$;

(iii) $\delta_{n+1}(q_{n+1},a)=(q_n,\ldots,q_n)$;

(iv) If $X=B$ then $F_n=\{q_0\}$ else $F_n=\{\{q_0\}\}$.

Then M_n accepts H_n. Assume that H_n is accepted by the tree automaton M with at most $n-1$ states. Let p be the finite path $(\lambda,1,\ldots,1^{n-1})$ and C be a successful computation of M on t_{n-1}. Then there are two nodes u and v from p, which are labelled by the same state in C. Let $t=t_{n-1}/u$ and $t'=t_{n-1}/v$, where t/u denotes the subtree descending from u. Now consider the tree τ obtained from t_{n-1} by substituting the subtree t, occurring at the node u, by the tree t'. τ is an infinite tree accepted by M. This leads to a contradiction. □

We now establish a similar result by considering transitions instead of states.

Let $BT_n(\Sigma)$ (resp. $MT_n(\Sigma)$) be the family of sets accepted by Büchi (resp. Muller) tree automata with at least p transitions, where $1\leq p\leq n$.

Proposition 3.2

For each $n\geq 1$, the family $BT_n(\Sigma)$ (resp. $MT_n(\Sigma)$) is properly included in $BT_{n+1}(\Sigma)$ (resp. $MT_{n+1}(\Sigma)$)□

Using the previous examples(i.e. H_n), one can code computations by trees over the set of transitions transitions and then apply the same technique used in the precedent proof.

Remark:

The last two propositions are valid for Büchi tree automata, Muller tree T-automata, and generalized Muller tree automata.

Let L be a set accepted by a Büchi tree automaton then the Büchi index of L, denoted by $\beta(L)$, is the minimal number of designated states of Büchi automata accepting L. This formally means that :

$\beta(L)= Min\{k:L=L^\omega(M),M=<Q,\Sigma,I,\delta,F>$, and $|F|= k\}$

Let L be a set accepted by a Muller tree automaton then the Muller index of L , denoted by $\mu(L)$, is the minimal number of designated sets of states of Muller tree automata accepting L.

Examples :

Let $L_1=a(b^\omega,b^\omega)=a(x_1,x_1)<b(x_1,x_1)>^\omega$, then $\beta(L_1)=\mu(L_1)=1$.

Let $L_2=a(b^\omega,c^\omega)+a(c^\omega,b^\omega)$, then $\beta(L_2)=2$. □

Let $MI_n(\Sigma)$ (resp. $BI_n(\Sigma)$) be the family of sets with Muller (resp. Büchi) index less or equal to n.

Theorem 3.3

For $n\geq 1$, and each set L of infinite trees, the following statements are equivalent :

(i) L belongs to $BI_n(\Sigma)$, and

(ii) L belongs to $R_n(\Sigma)$ □

The proof straitforward the construction used in M. Nivat and A. Saoudi [13] to prove the equality between omega-rational sets and sets accepted by Büchi tree automata.

Note that T. Hayashi and S. Miyano [8] prove that $MI_n(\Sigma)$ is properly included in $MI_{n+1}(\Sigma)$. As another related work, A. Mostowski [11] and D. Niwinski [14] prove that Rabin's pair indices define a strict hierarchy.

Let t be an infinite tree over Σ. Then we define $B^\omega(t)$ as the set of infinite words over Σ lying on some infinite branch of t.

Proposition 3.4:

Let L be a set of infinite trees accepted by a Muller tree automaton. Then the ω-language $B^\omega(L)$ is regular. □

Proof:

Let $M=<Q,\Sigma,q_0,\delta,F>$ be a reduced Muller tree automaton accepting L, where reduced means that each state q is reachable from the initial state and M accepts at least one tree from q. This reduction is possible since the emptiness problem for Muller tree automata is decidable (see M. O. Rabin [16]).

Let $M'=<Q,\Sigma,q_0,\delta',F>$ be a Muller string automaton such that if $(q,a)\in Q\times\Sigma$ and $(q_1,\ldots,q_k)\in\delta(q,a)$ then $\{q_1,\ldots,q_k\}\subseteq\delta'(q,a)$. M' accepts $B^\omega(L)$. □

Before proving that for each n, there is a set of infinite trees which cannot be denoted by an omega-rational tree expression with a size less than n, we will give some technical lemma.

Lemma 3.5

Let $(t_i)_{0\leq i\leq n}$ be a sequence of finite trees and t be an infinite tree denoted by $t_0<t_1,\ldots,t_n>^\omega$.

Then $B^\omega(t)=\bigcup_{i=1}^{n}A_iB_i^\omega$, where A_i and B_i are regular languages. □

Proof sketch:

Using the construction of M. Nivat et al.[13], one can obtain a Büchi tree automaton M with n states accepting $\{t\}$. To complete the proof it suffices to use the proposition 3.4 □

Proposition 3.6

For each integer $n \geq 1$, the family $R_n(\Sigma)$ is properly included in $R_{n+1}(\Sigma)$. □

Proof:

It suffices to prove that T_n cannot be denoted by an omega-rational tree expression of size n. Assume that $T_n \in R_n(\Sigma)$. Then $T_n = t_0 < t_1, \ldots, t_n >^\omega$, for some sequence of finte trees $(t_i)_{0 \leq i \leq n}$. Then we have :

(i) $\bigcup_{i=0}^{n} (ba^i)^\omega \subset B^\omega(T_n)$ (by definition of T_n).

(ii) $B^\omega(T_n) = \bigcup_{j=1}^{n} A_j B_j^\omega$ (by lemma 3.5).

(i) and (ii) implie that there are three integers $l,k,r \in \{1,\ldots,n\}$ such that $(ba^l)^\omega$ and $(ba^k)^\omega$ belong to $A_r B_r^\omega$. That means that $(ba^l)^\omega$ (resp. $(ba^k)^\omega$) is of the form $xy_1y_2\ldots$ (resp. $uv_1v_2\ldots$), where x and u (resp. y_i and v_i) belong to A_r (resp. B_r). Let h (resp. j) be the smallest integer such that $y_1 \ldots y_h$ (resp. $v_1 \ldots v_j$) contains $(ba^l)^2$ (resp. $(ba^k)^2$) as a factor (i.e. segment). Then $x(y_1 \ldots y_h v_1 \ldots v_j)^\omega$ is an infinite branch of s_n containing $(ba^l)^2$ and $(ba^k)^2$ as factors. This leads to a contradiction. □

4. The Complexity of Deterministic Classes

In this section, we define a similar hierarchies of deterministic classes, in other hand those accepted by deterministic tree automata. We denote by DG, the family of sets belong to G which are accepted by deterministic tree automata.

Theorem 4.1 (A. Saoudi [19])

A set L is accepted by a Muller (resp. Büchi) tree automaton iff it is a projection of a set K accepted by a deterministic Muller (resp. Büchi) tree automaton. □

Remarks :

Note that the proof of the theorem 4.1 has the following properties:

(i) L is accepted by a tree automaton with n states iff K is accepted by a tree automaton with n states.

(ii) L is accepted by a Büchi (resp. Muller) tree automaton with $|F|=n$ iff K is accepted by a Büchi (resp. Muller) tree automaton with $|F|=n$ □

Theorem 4.2

For each $n \geq 1$ and $X \in \{B,M\}$, the following statements hold:

(i) $DXS_n(\Sigma) \subset DXS_{n+1}(\Sigma)$,

(ii) $DXT_n(\Sigma) \subset DXT_{n+1}(\Sigma)$,

(iii) $DXI_n(\Sigma) \subset DXI_{n+1}(\Sigma)$, and

(iv) $DR_n(\Sigma) \subset DR_{n+1}(\Sigma)$. □

Proof Sketch :

One can prove the statements (i) and (ii) using the last remarks and the above results on the nondeterministic hierarchies. For the statement (iii), one can remark that H_n is accepted by a deterministic tree automaton with n transitions but not accepted by a deterministic automaton with $(n-1)$ transitions. For the statement (iv), one can remark that T_n is deterministic.

A tree automaton $M=<Q,\Sigma,I,\delta,F>$ is said to be pseudo-deterministic if for each $(q,a) \in Q \times \Sigma$, $|\delta(q,a)| \leq 1$.

Let $PDB_n(\Sigma)$ (resp. $PDM_n(\Sigma)$) be the family of sets accepted by Büchi (resp. Muller automata) with at least p initial states, where $1 \leq p \leq n$.

Theorem 4.3

For each $n \geq 1$ and $X \in \{B,M\}$, the family $PDX_n(\Sigma)$ is properly included in $PDX_{n+1}(\Sigma)$. □

Proof :

Let $T_p=\{t_1, \ldots ,t_p\}$, where $(t_n)_{n\geq 1}$ is the sequence of infinite trees defined in the proof of Proposition 3.1 . Let $M=<Q,\Sigma,I,\delta,F>$ be the tree automaton such that: $I=\{q,q_1, \cdots ,q_p\}$, $\delta(q,b)=(q,\ldots,q)$, $\delta(q_1,a)=(q,\ldots,q)$, and $\delta(q_i,a)=(q_{i-1}, \ldots ,q_{i-1})$ for each $i \in \{1,..,p\}$, then M accepts T_{p+1}. Assume that T_{p+1} is accepted by the pseudo-deterministic tree automaton M with p initial states, then there is two infinite trees t_i and t_j which are accepted from the same initial state q. Since $t_k=a(t_{k-1},\ldots,t_{k-1})$ and M is pseudo-deterministic, then M accepts also the tree $a(t_{i-1}, \ldots ,t_{i-1},t_{j-1})$ which is not in T_{p+1} . □

Acknowledgment. We thank Prof. M. Nivat for many fruitful discussions.

References :

[1] **L. Boasson and M. Nivat,** " Adherences of context-free languages ", J. Comput. Syst. Sci. 20(1980)285-309.

[2] **J. R. Büchi,** " On a decision method in restricted second order arithmetic", Proc. Cong. Logic in Methodology and Phil. of Sci., Standford University Press, Calif. (1960)1-11.

[3] **S. S. Cosmadakis, H. Gaifman, P. C. Kanellakis, M. Y. Vardi** " Decidable Optimization

Problems for Database Logic Programs ", Proc. 20th ACM Symp. on Theory of Computing (1988)477-490.

[4] **B. Courcelle**, " Fundamentals of infinite trees", Theoret. Comput. Sci. no. 25(1983)95-169.

[5] **A. E. Emerson**. "Automata, tableaux, and temporal logics", Proc. Workshop on Logics of Programs, Brooklyn (1985).

[6] **A. E. Emerson, and C. Jutla**. "The complexity of tree automata and logics of programs", Proc. 29th IEEE Symp. on Foundations of Comput. Sci. (1988)328-336.

[7] **Y. Gurevich and L. Harrington** , "Trees, Automata, and Games", Proc. 14th ACM Symp. on Theory of Computing (1982)237-263.

[8] **T. Hayashi and S. Miyano**, "Finite tree automata on infinite trees", Bull. of Informatics and Cybernitics,(1985) 71-82.

[9] **D.E. Muller and P. E Schupp**, "Alternating automata on infinite objects,determinancy, and Rabin's theorem", in "Automata on infinite words"(M. Nivat and D. Perrin, eds) LNCS 192(1985)100-107.

[10] **D. E. Muller, A. Saoudi, and P. E. Schupp**, "Weak alternating Automaton give a Simple Explanation of Why Most Temporal and Dynamic Logic are Decidable in Exponential Time", Proc. of the third IEEE Symposium on Logic in Computer Science(1988).

[11] **A. Mostowski**, "Determinancy of sinking automata and various Rabin's pair indices", Inf. Proc. Letters 15(1982)153-183.

[12] **M. Nivat and A. Saoudi**,"Automata on infinite trees and Kleene closure of regular tree sets", Bulletin of the E.A.T.C.S no. 36(1988)131-136.

[13] **M. Nivat and A. Saoudi**, "Rational, Recognizable and computable languages", Univ. Paris VII, L.I.T.P. publication no. 85-75.

[14] **D. Niwinski**, "A note on Indices of Rabin's Pairs Automata", manuscript, The University of Warsaw (1986).

[15] **R. Parikh**. "Propositional Game Logic", Proc. 25th IEEE Symp. on Foundations of Comput. Sci. (1983)195-200.

[16] **M. O. Rabin**, "Decidability of second order theories and automata on infinite trees", Trans. Amer. Math. Soc. 141(1969)1-35.

[17] **M. O. Rabin**, "Weakly definable relations and special automata, Math. Logic and Foundation of set theory", Y.Bar Hillel, Edit. Amsterdam North Holland (1970)1-23.

[18] **S. Safra** , "On the complexity of ω-automata", Proc. 29th Symp. on Foundations of Computer Sci. (1988)319-327.

[19] **A. Saoudi**, "Variétés d'automates d'arbres infinis", Theoret. Comput. Sci. 44(1986)1-21.

[20] **M. Takahashi** , "The greatest fixed point and Rational ω-tree languages", rapport L.I.T.P 85-69.

[21] **W. Thomas**, "A Hierarchy of sets of infinite trees", G.I Conference, L.N.C.S no 145, Springer-Verlag, Berlin(1982)335-342.

[22] **M. Y. Vardi and P. Wolper**, "Reasoning about Fair Concurrent programs", Proc. 18th Symp. on Theory of Computing, Berkeley (1986).

[23] **M. Y. Vardi**. "Verification of Concurrent Programs: The Automata-Theoretic Framework", Logic in Computer Science (1987).

The Expressibility of Nondeterministic Auxiliary Stack Automata and its relation to Treesize Bounded Alternating Auxiliary Pushdown Automata

V.Vinay
Computer Science and Automation
Indian Institute of Science
Bangalore 560012, India

V.Chandru*
Industrial Engineering
Purdue University
W.Lafayette IN 47907, U.S.A.

Abstract

Two aspects of nondeterministic auxiliary stack automata (NAuxSA) are studied in this paper. The first is regarding the *expressibility* of NAuxSA. More specifically, it is shown that the polynomial hierarchy can be characterised in terms of AuxSA with resource bounds. The second aspect is a *duality* relation between NAuxSA and alternating auxiliary pushdown automata (Alt-AuxPDA) connecting time bounds on the former with treesize bounds on the latter.

1 Introduction

Ibarra [Ib 71] proved that nondeterministic auxiliary stack automata (NAuxSA) are extremely powerful machines. He showed that NAuxSA (S(n)) equals DTIME $(2^{2^{O(S(n))}})$. Alternating Turing machines were introduced in [CKS 81]. Ladner, Lipton and Stockmeyer [LLS 84] studied the effects of alternation on a variety of models including auxiliary pushdown and stack automata. They characterised space bounds on these models in terms of deterministic time. However, the effects of simultaneous resource bounds on stack automata has not received much attention. Here, we show that despite their power, NAuxSA are sensitive enough to capture $\mathcal{NP}$. We do so, by introducing a new resource called *scan* to denote the number of times a NAuxSA alternates between the pushdown and scan modes.

The class $\mathcal{LOGCFL}$ (class of languages NC^1 reducible to $CFLs$) was first characterised in [Su 78] as the class of languages accepted by NAuxPDA space,time $(\log n, n^{O(1)})$. It is known that $\mathcal{LOGCFL}$ and $\mathcal{NP}$ have similar behaviour, i.e. they have similar characterisations on a variety of models. For example, Russo [Ru 80] showed that both have polynomial treesize on ATMs (they differ in the space they use), Venkateswaran [Ve 87, Ve 88] proved that both have semi-unbounded circuit characterizations with identical depth, O(log n) (they differ in the size of the circuit). Not surprisingly they also have similar pebbling characterizations [VVV 90]. Jenner and Kersig [JK 88] showed that the difference between $\mathcal{NP}$ and $\mathcal{LOGCFL}$

*Visiting Professor, Computer Science and Automation, Indian Institute of Science, 1989. Research supported by O.N.R. grant number N00014-86-K-0689, I.I.Sc. (GARP) Visiting Scientists Grant, and Ministry of Human Resources and Development Grant IMS-NV.

is *one alternation*, i.e. $\mathcal{NP} = A\Sigma_2 - AuxPDA\,space, time\,(\log n, n^{O(1)})$. We prove that the difference between $\mathcal{LOGCFL}$ and $\mathcal{NP}$ is *one scan* ! In fact, we prove something stronger - the NAuxSA are nonerasing.

- $\mathcal{NP} \;=\; NAuxSA\,space, time, scan(\log n, n^{O(1)}, 1)$

So $\mathcal{NP}$ is an NLOG machine with a pushdown store whose contents can be read once. We believe this is one of the first characterizations of $\mathcal{NP}$ in terms of NLOG machines with additional power. We also prove that

- $\mathcal{P} \;=\; DAuxSA\,space, time(\log n, n^{O(1)})$

This reveals the connection between $\mathcal{P}$ and DLOG. In general, we show

- $\Sigma_k^p \;=\; A\Sigma_k - AuxSA\,space, time, scan(\log n, n^{O(1)}, 1)$ *for* $k \geq 1$

Motivated by Ruzzo's result [Ru 80] we show that

- *For* $S(n) \geq \log n$ *and* $Z(n) = \Omega(2^{O(S(n))})$,

$$NAuxSA\,space, time(S(n), Z^{O(1)}(n)) \;=\; Alt - AuxPDA\,space, tsz(S(n), Z^{O(1)}(n))$$

This leads to yet another characterization of $\mathcal{NP}$

- $\mathcal{NP} \;=\; Alt - AuxPDA\,space, tsz(\log n, n^{O(1)})$

2 Preliminaries

2.1 Alternating Auxiliary Pushdown Automata

An alternating auxiliary pushdown automaton (Alt-AuxPDA) is an alternating turing machine (ATM) with an additional pushdown store. The space used by the machine corresponds to space on the worktape only. A more formal definition is given in [LLS 84]. We assume that the Alt-AuxPDA behaves deterministically while pushing or popping. So a configuration could be universal, existential, push, pop or accepting.

By a *surface configuration*, v, of an Alt-AuxPDA machine M on input x, we mean v = (q,i,α,j,z) where q is the current state of M, i is the input head position, α is the worktape contents, j is the worktape head postion and z is the top of stack symbol. A surface configuration has information only about the stack top rather than the whole stack. We use *top* to extract the top of stack symbol from a surface configuration (top(v) = z).

By a *surface computation tree* of M on $x \in L(M)$ we mean a tree S(x) whose vertices are labelled with surface configurations such that a vertex labelled by an *existential (push,pop)* surface configuration has exactly one child, the universal surface configuration has both children and all leaves are accepting.

Note that every push configuration r has a balancing pop configuration along every path in the subtree rooted at the push configuration. We call these pop configurations $v_1, v_2, \cdots, v_k$ as *mates* of r and vice-versa [Ve 87]. We call their children $z_1, z_2, \cdots, z_k$ as *restarts* of r.

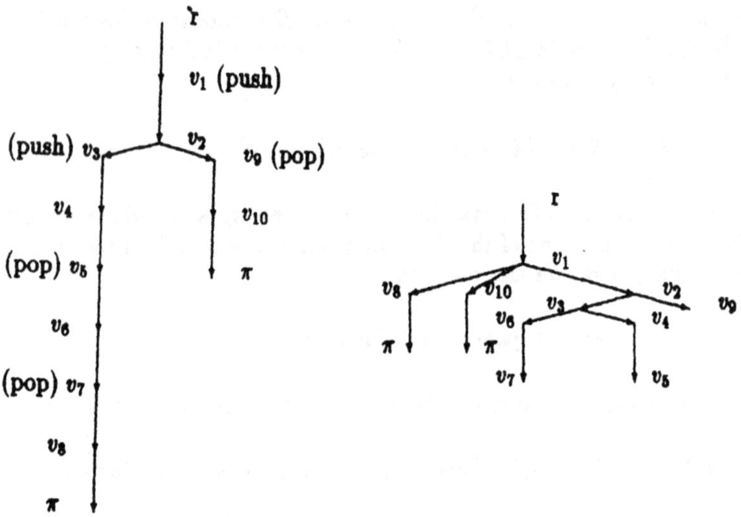

Figure 1: (a) Surface Computation Tree (b) Accepting Tree

Note also that top(r) = $top(z_i)$, $1 \leq i \leq k$. To reconstruct the top of stack information in z_i from v_i, v_i needs the top of stack information from its mate r. To emphasize this dependency, we define an *accepting tree*.

For any $x \in L(M)$, let S(x) be a surface computation tree. Let r be a push vertex; $q_1, q_2, \cdots, q_k$ be its mates and $z_1, z_2, \cdots, z_k$ be the restarts of r. Then add an edge (r, z_i) $1 \leq i \leq k$ and delete the edge (q_i, z_i) $1 \leq i \leq k$. We call the transformed tree the accepting tree of M on input x. Figure 1, on the next page, shows this transformation. It is apparent that $x \in L(M)$ if and only if there is such an accepting tree.

The labels of the leaves of any accepting tree are either popping or accepting configurations. Note that the notion of an accepting tree can be used to give a straight forward proof of the containment [Ru 80]

$$NAuxPDA\,space, time(S(n), Z(n)) \subseteq ASPACE, TSZ(S(n), Z(n)$$

The accepting tree may be looked upon as an abstraction of realizable pairs [Co 71]. The treesize of an input $x \in L(M)$ is the number of vertices in the corresponding accepting tree. $Alt\text{-}AuxPDA\,space, tsz(S(n), Z(n))$ denotes all languages accepted by an Alt-AuxPDA within space S(n) and treesize Z(n), where n is the length of the input.

2.2 Nondeterministic Auxiliary Stack Automata

A *nondeterministic auxiliary stack automaton* (NAuxSA) is a nondeterministic auxiliary pushdown automaton with the additional power that the stack head can read the stack contents without popping but cannot overwrite the contents of the stack except by pushing or popping. The states (and hence the configations) of the stack machine are said to be in pushdown mode if the machine may push or pop but cannot read the contents of the stack. To read the contents of the stack, the machine enters the scan mode. Till such time as the machine enters the pushdown mode, the stack can be looked upon as a read only input. The machine remains in the scan mode until it reads the first blank (i.e. to the right of the top of stack). Then it shifts its head back to the top of stack and enters the pushdown mode. As usual, we assume that the push and pop moves are deterministic and the machine never accepts while in the scan mode.

By a *nonerasing auxiliary stack automaton* (NAuxNESA) we mean one where pop moves are disallowed. By *space* used by an NAuxSA we mean the work-tape space. *Scan* denotes the number of alternations between the pushdown and the scan modes.

$NAuxSA\,space, time, scan(S(n), T(n), Sc(n))$ denotes the class of languages accepted by NAuxSA within space S(n), time T(n) and scan alternation Sc(n). Similar definitions hold for non-erasing stack automata.

Finally, we could allow the NAuxSA to alternate by introducing a universal state. $A\Sigma_k - AuxSA$ denotes AuxSA wherein (k-1) alternations are allowed, starting with an existential configuration. $A\Sigma_1 - AuxSA$ is evidently just NAuxSA.

3 Characterizing the Polynomial Hierarchy

In this section we prove a characterization of the polynomial hierarchy. The proof is very similar to the one in [JK 88]. We trade off a *scan* for one alternation.

Lemma 1 $\Sigma_k^p \subseteq A\Sigma_k - AuxNESAspace, time, scan(\log n, n^{O(1)}, 1)$

Proof: We know from [So 76] that the following language is complete for Σ_k^p.

$$L_k = \{F(x_1, x_2, \cdots, x_k) : \exists x_1 \forall x_2 \cdots Q_k x_k F(x_1, x_2, \cdots, x_k) = 1\}$$

Naturally Q_k is $\exists$ if k is odd and $\forall$ if k is even. Each x_i is itself a sequence of variables $x_{i1}, x_{i2}, \cdots, x_{il}$. Assume, with no loss of generality, that $F(x_1, x_2, \cdots, x_k)$ is in 3 CNF (3 DNF) when k is odd (even). Verify the correctness of the encoding using log space. Then guess assignments for variables x_1 existentially, x_2 universally, etc. and push them onto the pushdown stack. To guess existentially (universally), the stack automaton uses its own alternation. When the assignments of all the k variables $x_1, x_2, \cdots, x_k$ have been guessed, the stack automaton enters the *scan mode*. It verifies each clause in the formula sequentially by scanning the stack repeatedly (but never again enters the pushdown mode). Clearly, this verification takes no more than polynomial time. Noting that the stack never pops anything from the stack and that *scan* alternation is used only once, the result follows. □

Lemma 2 $A\Sigma_k - AuxSA\,space, time(n^{O(1)}, n^{O(1)}) \subseteq \mathcal{NP}(\Pi_{k-1}^p) = \Sigma_k^p$

Proof: *Basis* (k=1):$NAuxSA\ space, time(n^{O(1)}, n^{O(1)}) \subseteq \mathcal{NP}$. This is clearly true as an $\mathcal{NP}$ machine can use its nondeterminism to simulate the nondeterminism of the NAuxSA. The stack can be simulated by the $\mathcal{NP}$ machine on its worktape. Since the time used is atmost polynomial, the result holds for the basis case.

Induction ($k > 1$): Assume the result is true for k-1. Consider an $A\Sigma_k - AuxSA$ M. Define

$$L_M = \{c : \ c \ is\ a\ universal\ configuration\ of\ M\ that\ is\ accepting\}$$

Clearly $L_M \in A\Pi_{k-1} - AuxSA\ space, time(n^{O(1)}, n^{O(1)}) \subseteq \Pi^p_{k-1}$, by induction hypothesis. So an $\mathcal{NP}$ machine can simulate M until it alternates (we may assume it always does). Then the $\mathcal{NP}$ machine writes the universal configuration on the oracle query tape and questions a Π^p_{k-1} oracle. The $\mathcal{NP}$ machine accepts if and only if the oracle answers "yes". The induction is complete. □

Combining lemmata 1 and 2 we get

Theorem 3

$$\begin{aligned}\Sigma^p_k &= A\Sigma_k - AuxNESA\ space, time, scan(\log n, n^{O(1)}, 1)\\ &= A\Sigma_k - AuxSA\ space, time, scan(n^{O(1)}, n^{O(1)}, n^{O(1)})\end{aligned}$$ □

Corollary 4

$$\begin{aligned}\mathcal{NP} &= NAuxNESA\ space, time, scan(\log n, n^{O(1)}, 1)\\ &= NAuxSA\ space, time, scan(n^{O(1)}, n^{O(1)}, n^{O(1)})\end{aligned}$$ □

We now characterize the class $\mathcal{UP}$. This is the class of languages that are accepted by polynomial time nondeterministic turing machine unambiguoslyi.e., has exactly one accepting path.

Theorem 5 $\mathcal{UP} = UAuxNESA\ space, time, scan(\log n, n^{O(1)}, 1)$

Proof: The containment ($\supseteq$) is trivial. To show ($\subseteq$) assume that any configuration is of length n^c for some constant $c > 0$. Guess the unique accepting path and push it onto the stack. Then enter the scan mode and verify that the guess is correct. This is done by using a $c\log n$ space counter (to come down a polynomial number of steps in the stack) to verify that a ith symbol in a configuration comes from the corresponding $i-1^{st}, i^{th}$ & $i+1^{st}$ symbols in the previous configuration. □

Remarks:

1. Note that Lemma 1 could have been proved as in Theorem 5. The advantage of doing so is that no complete language would be needed.
2. We have shown in Corollary 1 (Theorem 1) that $\mathcal{LOGCFL}$ and $\mathcal{NP}$ differ by only one scan. Surprisingly, we find that adding more space or scan resources does not increase the power of the stack automaton.
3. Note that NLOG equals $\mathcal{NP}$ if and only if the additional stack with scanning power does not help.

4. The $\mathcal{NP}$ result above may be interpreted in the frame-work of reducibilities as $\mathcal{LOGCFL}$ closure of $\mathcal{DLOG}$, i.e., $\mathcal{NP} = \mathcal{LOGCFL}(\mathcal{DLOG})$. However, more "stringent" characterizations of $\mathcal{NP}$ are known [AJ 90]. They show $\mathcal{NP} = \mathcal{NLOG}(\mathcal{CO} - 1\mathcal{NLOG})$ where $1\mathcal{NLOG}$ is a one-way NLOG machine.

Given the characterizations of $\mathcal{NP}$ and $\mathcal{UP}$, the next result is not surprising.

Theorem 6 $\mathcal{P} = DAuxNESA(\log n, n^{O(1)}) = DAuxSA(n^{O(1)}, n^{O(1)})$

Proof: ($\subseteq$) We show ASPACE ($\log n$) $\subseteq$ DAuxNESA ($\log n, n^{O(1)}$). The number of distinct configurations of the log space bounded ATM, M, is n^c for some constant $c \geq 0$. The DAuxNESA, $\tilde{M}$, simulates M as follows.
Initially, all accepting configurations of M are pushed onto the stack (with a \$ sign separating them). A counter is initialized to count the number of new configurations added to the stack in each cycle. If no new elements are added in a cycle and if the initial configuration has not been pushed, then $\tilde{M}$ rejects.
In any one cycle, $\tilde{M}$ cycles through all configurations of length $\log n$, in lexicographic order, on its work tape. After fixing a target configuration, $\tilde{M}$ enters the scan mode and makes sure that the target configuration is not already in the stack. This takes polynomial time. If the target configuration is in the stack, $\tilde{M}$ generates the next configuration. Otherwise $\tilde{M}$ deterministically generates the two children of the target configuration, say c_1 and c_2. It then checks if c_1 and c_2 are present in the stack. If the target configuration is a universal (existential) configuration and both its children are in the stack then it is pushed onto the stack (after entering the pushdown mode) and the counter is incremented by one. If the target configuration is the initial configuration then $\tilde{M}$ halts and accepts. The maximum number of cycles is obviously n^c. So $\tilde{M}$ uses no more than $\log n$ space and polynomial time.
($\supseteq$) DAuxSA($n^{O(1)}, n^{O(1)}$) $\subseteq \mathcal{P}$, trivially. □

Remarks:

1. We are unable to show that one scan is sufficient to capture $\mathcal{P}$. Therefore it is interesting to study the nature of languages in *DAuxSA space, time, scan*($\log n, n^{O(1)}, 1$). Note that it contains the class $\mathcal{LOGDCFL}$.

2. Contrast the results of this section with [JK 88] where the polynomial hierarchy starts with $\mathcal{LOGCFL}$. It would appear that to capture $\mathcal{LOGCFL}$, we need no more than $\log\log n$ space and polynomial time on a NAuxSA.

4 NTIME & Alternating Treesize

Cook [Co 71] showed that NAuxPDA space(S(n)) equals ASPACE(S(n)). Ruzzo [Ru 80] extended this relationship by showing that time on NAuxPDA is equivalent to treesize on ATM's. We show a similar connection between NAuxSA and AltAuxPDA. We would like to reiterate that *"proofsizes of machines that alternate correspond to time on some nondeterministic machine"*. As a consequence it would seem that alternation can always be replaced by nondeterminism by making the machine more powerful in some other way. Thus an ASPACE machine is equivalent to an NSPACE machine with a pushdown and an AltAuxPDA is equivalent to a NAuxSA (a NAuxPDA which can read the contents of its pushdown stack). We leave it as an open problem to find a NAuxSA space(S(n)) with some additional power to capture AltAuxSA space(S(n)) (and what is alternation on that machine equivalent to ?and so on!).

Theorem 7
The following are equivalent
for $S(n) \geq \log n$ $Z(n) = \Omega(2^{\mathcal{O}(S(n))})$

(1) *Alt-AuxPDA space,tsz*$(S(n), Z^{\mathcal{O}(1)}(n))$
(2) *ASPACE,TSZ*$(2^{\mathcal{O}(S(n))}, Z^{\mathcal{O}(1)}(n))$
(3) *NAuxPDA space,time*$(2^{\mathcal{O}(S(n))}, Z^{\mathcal{O}(1)}(n))$
(4) *NAuxSA space,time*$(S(n), Z^{\mathcal{O}(1)}(n))$

Proof: (1) $\subseteq$ (2)
On input x, consider an accepting tree of an AltAuxPDA machine M. The nodes of the tree are labelled by surface configurations (of size S(n)) with the number of nodes in the tree bounded by Z(n). The simulating ATM $\tilde{M}$ uses its alternation to match the alternation of the AltAuxPDA. Note that the number of distinct surface configurations are at most $2^{cS(n)}$ for some constant $c > 0$. The machine $\tilde{M}$ initially writes down the accepting configuration of M (which may be assumed to be unique). We will call this the ACLIST. In particular, every configuration of M has an associated ACLIST- the leaves of the subtree rooted at that configuration in the accepting tree. The ATM, $\tilde{M}$, starts with the initial configuration and simulates the machine M as follows

- If the current configuration "*(cc)*" is existential then $\tilde{M}$ existentially guesses the next configuration (by simulating one move of M). This configuration inherits the ACLIST of its parent.
- If the current configuration is universal then $\tilde{M}$ universally guesses its successor configuration. The successor inherits the ACLIST of its parent configuration.
- If the current configuration is PUSH then $\tilde{M}$ guesses existentially the leaves $v_1, v_2, \cdots, v_k$ of its unique successor in the accepting subtree i.e., the corresponding popping configurations (this may require $2^{\mathcal{O}(S(n))}$ space). It then finds the successor of each of these popping configurations $z_1, z_2, \cdots, z_k$ respectively. Next $\tilde{M}$ alternates to a universal state and does the following
  - It verifies that for the current configuration (cc) that top(cc) = top(z_i) for all i: $1 \leq i \leq k$.
  - The other branches proceed as if the above property holds- there is a branch for each z_i such that the z_i's become the current configuration and the ACLIST is inherited from the PUSH configuration.(The other items on tape may be erased).
  - One branch corresponds to the successor of the PUSH configuration which now becomes the current configuration. The ACLIST of this configuration is the list of k popping vertices that have been guessed.
- If the current configuration is POP then check if cc is on the ACLIST. If it is then accept, else reject.

The above simulation is faithful to the accepting tree of M on input x.
The space used by $\tilde{M}$ is $2^{\mathcal{O}(S(n))}$ and simulating a step of M involves $2^{\mathcal{O}(S(N))}$ time in the worst case. Since there are no more than Z(n) nodes in the accepting tree of M on x, the treesize of $\tilde{M}$ is bounded by $2^{\mathcal{O}(S(n))}.Z(n)$.
(2) $\subseteq$ (3)
This follows from Russo's theorem [Ru 80].

(3) $\subseteq$ (4)
We will actually show, for some d=O(1), that

$$NAuxPDA\,space,time(2^{S(n)}, T(n)) \subseteq NAuxSA\,space,time(S(n), d^{2S(n)}T^2(n))$$

It is well known that if $\alpha \vdash_m \beta$ then the ith symbol in β, β_i, is completely determined by $\alpha_{i-1}, \alpha_i, \alpha_{i+1}$ *and* m (where $m \in \{L, R\}$ denotes the two choices at α if it is existential). The procedure below describes the simulation.

PUSH(initial configuration) /* onto stack */
(use S(n) workspace to ensure that the length is $c^{S(n)}$)
if initial configuration is accepting *then* acc := true
else acc:= false;

do $\neg$*acc*
Case of top(ID)
Existential: PUSH(L) *or* PUSH(R)
l=0;
do $l \neq c^{S(n)}$
guess $\gamma \in \Gamma \cup Q \times \Gamma$
Enter *scan* mode. Remember γ in the finite control.
Go back $c^{S(n)}$ steps (use S(n) space counter).
Remember whether m is L or R.
Remember $\gamma_1, \gamma_2, \gamma_3$ appropriately from the previous ID.
Check that γ follows from $\gamma_1, \gamma_2, \gamma_3$ and m in one step.
If not *reject*.
od
PUSH:
Push #. Guess the mate of the top ID
and push it onto stack. Push($), push this stack
symbol on top of the guessed mate. Guess the succeeding
configuration of the top ID (as done above) and verify
(only that you have to go back $2c^{S(n)}$ steps).
POP:
/* Check if the configuration of the machine on top
matches with the last guessed configuration - a guessed
configuration is sandwiched between # and $ signs */
Match the guessed ID with the top ID, symbol by symbol,
using a counter to denote the number of symbols checked backwards
from $ and deleting the top of stack symbol after it has checked
(it can be remembered in the finite control) and enter the *scan*
mode. If the ID's are not identical then *reject* else pop all
symbols upto and including #. Guess and verify the
next configuration (as above).
end case
If top(ID) is accepting *then* acc := true;
od

Analysis: Clearly, S(n) space is sufficient (this space is only used to maintain a counter). To analyze time, notice that the stack cannot have more than $2c^{S(n)}.T(n)$ symbols. So, at worst, it takes $d^{S(n)}.T(n)$ (constant $d > 1$) time to simulate any one move. Hence the total time taken is no more than $d^{S(n)}.T^2(n)$. The correctness of the procedure is self evident.

(4) $\subseteq$ (1)

We will show that

$$NAuxSA\ space, time(S(n), T(n)) \subseteq Alt - AuxPDA\ space, treesize(S(n), 2^{O(S(n))}.T(n))$$

The key to the proof is the treesize required to compute the transition table (to be explained later). The alternating, auxilliary PDA simulates the stack automaton as follows:

- It uses its existential move to simulate the SA's nondeterminism.
- If the SA pushes a symbol x_m, the alternating AuxPDA guesses a transition table and pushes it onto the stack. It then pushes the symbol x_m. The machine alternates to a universal state and takes one of two courses of action. One branch verifies the validity of the guessed transition table while the other proceeds as if the guess is correct.
- When the stack automaton pops, the simulating machine pops the top of stack symbol along with the corresponding transition table.
- When the stack automaton enters the *scan* mode then the alternating AuxPDA guesses the transition and writes on the storage tape (it takes S(n) space to do this). Then universally verify the guess (using the transition table) along one path and continue simulation along the other as if the guess is correct (in which case the space used by the original configuration can be reused).

There are two aspects of the simulation above that need explanation. One is the nature of the transition table and the other is the procedure for validating of the guessed transition table.

When the stack automaton enters the *scan* mode, we could look upon the stack as a read only input tape. We know that, for the SA to quit the *scan* mode, the stack head should point to the first blank above the top of stack. But the alternating AuxPDA cannot examine the contents of the pushdown without popping it. We therefore maintain a transition table which contains the following information. For each quadruple $< q, i, \alpha, j >$ (where q is the machine state, i the position of the input head, α the worktape contents and j the head position on the input tape when entering the *scan* mode) and a fixed sequence of stack symbols, the transition table contains $< \tilde{q}, \tilde{i}, \tilde{\alpha}, \tilde{j} >$ indicating the state of the machine, the input head position etc. when the *SA quits the scan mode*. We write $< q, i, \alpha, j > \rightarrow < \tilde{q}, \tilde{i}, \tilde{\alpha}, \tilde{j} >$ and refer to $< \tilde{q}, \tilde{i}, \tilde{\alpha}, \tilde{j} >$ as a valid successor of $< q, i, \alpha, j >$. In the nondeterministic case a quadruple could have more than one valid successor. Nevertheless, any transition table will contain, for every quadruple, some valid successor (if there are no valid successors we think of an appropriate distinguished symbol to indicate this).

We are ready to explain the details of the PUSH move.

- Clearly any quadruple occupies cS(n) space and therefore there are atmost $2^{cS(n)}$ distinct quadruples. It is also clear that any transition table can be coded with $2^{dS(n)}$ bits.

The consistency of the transition table is verified as follows:

- Universally verify, over all $2^{cS(n)}$ quadruples of length cS(n), the following:

- Let the quadruple be $< q, i, \alpha, j >$. Pop the stack and write x_m on the work tape. Then pop the stack to extract the successor of the quadruple from the guessed transition table.
- The validity of the successor remains to be verified, i.e., $< q, i, \alpha, j > \rightarrow < \tilde{q}, \tilde{i}, \tilde{\alpha}, \tilde{j} >$. Clearly the number of quadruples that can occur intermediately in proving the above cannot exceed $2^{cS(n)}$ (otherwise there is a loop). Also notice that successive transitions in the above chain can be verified by either (a) one move of the SA with x_m under the "stack head" or (b) a reference to the transition table corresponding to $x_{m-1}, \cdots, x_1$. A divide and conquer argument (or a two-person uninterpreted pebbling argument) shows that the verification can be carried out by the simulating machine within time $\log(2^{cS(n)})$ and treesize of $2^{d'S(n)}$ nodes.

Analysis: The correctness of the simulation is self-evident. It is easy to see that no more than O(S(n)) workspace was used by the simulating machine. To bound the treesize, note that the simulation of the PUSH is most involved. We have already noted that verification of the validity of any one transition takes no more than $2^{O(S(n))}$ nodes. Since there are $2^{cS(n)}$ transitions to be checked, universally, this can be done with $2^{O(S(n))}$ nodes. All other moves are bounded by $2^{O(S(n))}$ nodes in the simulation. So any one move of the stack automaton needs no more than $2^{O(S(n))}$ nodes to simulate and the result follows. □

5 Conclusion

We have characterized $\mathcal{NP}$ in two different models. The NAuxSA characterization elucidates the difference between $\mathcal{NP}$ and NLOG.

However there are certain interesting questions left unanswered. For example, is there a natural two-person auxilliary pebbling game that captures the computation of an Alt-AuxPDA ? Is there a characterization of AC^1 in terms of the Alt-AuxPDA resources ?

6 Addendum

After the submission of this paper, Birgit Jenner [J 90] drew the first author's attention to the fact that a checking stack automata is identical to a pushdown with scan one. She pointed out that the checking stack characterization of the polynomial hierarchy was noted in their paper [JK 88]. We thank Birgit Jenner for bringing this fact to our notice. The blame for re-inventing the wheel is entirely ours. However our result is slightly stronger than theirs: we show that increasing space to a polynomial and \ or increasing scan to a polynomial does not help. We also believe our motivations were different.

Acknowledgements

We are thankful to H.Venkateswaran for encouraging us in this research. We are also grateful to C.E.Veni Madhavan for useful discussions on this subject.

References

[AJ 90] Alvarez,C., and Jenner,B., A Very Hard LOG Space Counting Class, *Proceedings 5th Annual Conference on Structure in Complexity Theory*, (1990),154-168.

[CKS 81] Chandra,A.K., Kozen,D.C. and Stockmeyer,L., Alternation, *JACM* 28 (1981), 114-133.

[Co 71] Cook,S.A. Characterizations of pushdown machines in terms of time-bounded computers, *JACM* 18(1971), 4-18

[Ib 71] Ibarra,O.H.,Characterizations of some tape and time complexity classes of Turing machines in terms of multihead and auxiliary stack automata, *JCSS* 5(1971), 88-117.

[J 90] Jenner,B.,*personal communication*.

[JK 88] Jenner,B. and Kersig,B., Characterizing the polynomial hierarchy by alternating Auxiliary pushdown automata, *STACS(1988)*, LNCS 294, 118-125. Also *RAIRO Theoretical Informatics and Applications* 23(1989) 93-99.

[LLS 84] Ladner,R.E., Lipton,R.J. and Stockmeyer,L.J., Alternating pushdown and stack automata, *SIAM J. on Computing* 13(1984), 135-155.

[Ru 80] Russo,W.L., Tree-size bounded alternation, *JCSS* 21(1980), 218-235.

[So 76] Stockmeyer,L.J., The polynomial-time hierarchy, *TCS* 3(1976), 1-22.

[Su 78] Sudborough,I.H., On the tape complexity of deterministic context free languages, *JACM* 25(1978), 405-414.

[Ve 87] Venkateswaran,H., Properties that characterise $\mathcal{LOGCFL}$, *Proceedings* 19th *Annual ACM STOC* (1987), 141-150.

[Ve 88] Venkateswaran,H., Circuit definitions and nondeterministic complexity classes, *Proceedings* 8th *FST & TCS* (1988), LNCS 338, 175-192.

[VVV 90] Vinay,V.,Venkateswaran, H. and Veni Madhavan,C.E., Circuits, Pebbling and Expressibility,*Proceedings 5th Annual Conference on Structure in Complexity Theory*, (1990), 223-230.

Towards Constructive Program Derivation in VDM

Christopher P. Lewington
British Telecom Research Labs
Ipswich
Suffolk
England

1 Abstract

Formal specification methods and constructive theories are generally considered to be alternative approaches to software development. In this paper we demonstrate that the two paradigms in fact have much to offer one another. The shortcomings of the two approaches include inadequate program derivation techniques for formal methods and poor specification facilities in constructive theories. Here we examine how the program extraction power of the constructive theory TK may be coupled with simple specifications written in VDM to suggest the possibility of a more coherent approach to software development.

2 Introduction

Current opinion has it that software development techniques known as 'formal methods' (for example VDM [Jon 86]) are alternative approaches to the constructive methods (such as Martin-Lof's Type Theory [Mar 82], PX [HaN 87] and TK [HeT 88]) for software development. Both approaches have their relative merits and disadvantages; for example the constructive theories lack sufficiently rich methods of specification, and specifications are often expressed in what amounts to (intuitionistic) predicate calculus. A distinct advantage of the constructive paradigms is that they do however possess powerful methods for program extraction. Conversely, software development techniques such as VDM have particular strengths with regard to the process of specification and data reification; but ultimately one is still forced to write a program and verify that it meets a sufficiently refined specification, using methods such as Hoare logics for total correctness.

It appears then that, far from being *alternative* approaches to software development, formal methods and constructive theories may in fact have much to offer one another. The work covered in this paper is intended to support this claim. By interpreting a simple VDM operation specification into the constructive theory TK and providing a proof of the interpreted specification one may obtain via realizability a program which meets the TK specification. Provided that the rules used in such a proof are sound with respect to the interpretation, the extracted program will also meet the original VDM specification. The process therefore amounts to a *specification transformation* using a correctness-preserving 'transformation package' consisting of the interpretation itself (the *eureka step*, to borrow terminology from the functional programming community) and a collection of sound inference rules. The work in this paper may therefore be seen as an initial examination of this concept with a view to hopefully motivating further research in this direction.

The paper is organised as follows. In section 3 we provide the simple form of a VDM operation specification that we intend to consider, together with a propositional language for expressing pre and postconditions. In section 4 we provide a brief summary for a subtheory of TK suitable for our purposes.

An interpretation of the pre/postcondition language into TK is given in section 5, which requires an examination of the VDM concept of hooked variables in detail. Section 5 also contains the TK interpretation of a simple VDM operation, together with a detailed discussion of the development of suitable transformation rules and a soundness theorem for the 'transformation package'. In section 6 we briefly illustrate that under the transformation the correct denotational semantics are provided by realizability for TK. Section 7 contains our conclusions and possible future work areas, and finally section 9 contains references to the relevant literature.

3 A Simple Fragment of VDM

VDM is a well-known formal specification methodology which allows for both the specification of functions and operations using a pre/postcondition format. A detailed knowledge of VDM is unnecessary for this study, and the interested reader is referred to [Jon 86]. We merely note that, ultimately, a program still needs to be *written* and then verified; this is the problem that we shall attempt to overcome in a modest way. For now, we turn to the form of specification we intend to consider.

3.1 Operations and a Language for Pre and Postconditions

First of all we provide an assertion language which we shall use to express the pre and postconditions of the simple VDM operations we intend to consider. The language may be thought of as a propositional subset of the VDM assertion language. The target programming language is given by the following grammar:

Expressions: $e \in E; e \rightarrow n \mid v \mid e_1 \oplus e_2$

Commands: $S \rightarrow v := e \mid S_1 ; S_2 \mid$ **if** B **then** S_1 **else** S_2 **fi** $\mid$ **while** B **do** S **od**

Booleans: $B \rightarrow e_1$ **eq** $e_2 \mid B_1$ **and** $B_2 \mid B_1$ **or** $B_2 \mid$ **not** B $\mid$ True $\mid$ False

where n and v range over suitable sets of numerals and program variables respectively, and $\oplus$ is any binary arithmetic operator. The assertion language for expressing the pre and postconditions is given by:

Terms: $t \in VT$; $t \rightarrow e \mid e \mid B \mid \underline{v} \mid \underline{v}$
Assertions: $\Phi \in VA$; $\Phi \rightarrow R_n(t_1, \ldots, t_n) \mid \text{true} \mid \text{false} \mid \neg \Phi \mid \Phi_1 \wedge \Phi_2 \mid \Phi_1 \Rightarrow \Phi_2$

where R_n denotes any decidable relation symbol.

Remarks:

(i) Note that we use italics to represent hooked variables; we shall adopt this convention throughout the paper.
(ii) The term '*e*' is merely the programming language expression 'e' with all of its program variables replaced by their corresponding hooked variables; note that such expressions may only play a part in the logic, since hooked variables are only intended to have a logical function. Similarly, '$\underline{v}$' is a tuple of hooked program variables.
(iii) When necessary we shall use P, Q, P1, Q1 and so on to represent assertions which do not contain hooked variables. Assertions which may contain hooked variables will be denoted by R, R1 and so on, following the VDM convention.
(iv) We shall adopt the conventions of ***T***(t) and ***F***(t) for 't = True' and 't = False' respectively when required. ◊

Having provided the pre/postcondition language, we turn our attention to the general form of a VDM operation specification that we intend to consider.

We shall keep the specification of operations as simple as possible; thus we consider them to be of the form

OP()
ext rd x : T_1, **wr** z : T_2
pre P(....., x, ..., z, ...)
post Q(......, x, ..., z, ...) $\wedge$ R(......., *z* ,......)

Note that in a postcondition we distinguish between the part of the assertion which contains hooked variables and that which does not; this convention will make our subsequent discussions slightly more elegant.

In the next section we provide a brief presentation of the subtheory of TK that we require.

4 The Constructive Theory TKS

The paradigm in which we shall work is a sub-theory of TK [HeT 88]. Full details of TK itself may be found in that paper, but for our purposes we shall only require a simpler theory, which we shall call TKS. The papers [Hen 89a], [Hen 89b] cover the aspects of program derivation in general within TK, and [Hen 90] examines the topic of information loss in more detail.

4.1 The Language

The language of the theory is given by the following grammar:

Terms: $t \rightarrow x \mid c \mid \lambda x.t \mid t_1 t_2$

Formulae: $\alpha \rightarrow t \in T \mid t_1 = t_2 \mid t\downarrow \mid \bot$

$$\Phi \rightarrow \alpha \mid \Phi_1 \wedge \Phi_2 \mid \Phi_1 \vee \Phi_2 \mid \Phi_1 \Rightarrow \Phi_2 \mid \forall x\, \Phi \mid \exists x\, \Phi$$

Types: $T \rightarrow \{x \mid \Phi\} \mid I(T, \Phi)$

The atomic assertion $t\downarrow$ is intended to signify that the term t denotes a value, and $\bot$ denotes falsdum. Note that where appropriate we shall use standard unpackings for bounded quantification; thus

$$(\forall x \in T)\Phi \Leftrightarrow (\forall x)(x \in T \Rightarrow \Phi) \text{ and } (\exists x \in T)\, \Phi \Leftrightarrow (\exists x)(x \in T \wedge \Phi)$$

The type structure given by the grammar will be explained when we come to the introduction and elimination rules for type membership in due course.

4.2 The Rule System of TKS

The axioms and rules of the system are just the rules for the logic of partial terms [Bee 85], which is essentially a version of intuitionistic predicate calculus with modifications to the rules for universal elimination and existential introduction to ensure that certain terms are defined:

$$(\forall\text{- Elim})\quad \frac{\forall x\Phi \qquad t\downarrow}{\Phi(t)} \qquad\qquad (\exists\text{ – Intro})\quad \frac{\Phi(t) \qquad t\downarrow}{\exists x\, \Phi}$$

The terms of the theory are governed by a theory of partial lambda calculus, and the types by the following rules:

$$(\text{T-Elim})\quad \frac{z \in \{x \mid \Phi\}}{\Phi(z)} \qquad\qquad (\text{T-Intro})\quad \frac{\Phi(z)}{z \in \{x \mid \Phi\}}$$

The above rules relate to types that are defined essentially by the use of comprehension; a simple example of such a type that we shall use is the type of total functions:

$$T_1 \rightarrow T_2 =_{def} \{f \mid (\forall z \in T_1)((f\, z) \in T_2)\}$$

The introduction and elimination rules for membership of inductive types are:

$$(\text{I - Intro (i)})\quad \frac{z \in A}{z \in I(A, \Phi)} \qquad\qquad (\text{I - Intro (ii)})\quad \frac{\forall x\, (\Phi(z,x) \Rightarrow x \in I(A, \Phi))}{z \in I(A, \Phi)}$$

(I-Elim)

$$\frac{(\forall z \in A)\,\Psi(z) \qquad (\forall z \in \mathrm{Clos}(I(A,\Phi)))\,((\forall x \in \{w \mid \Phi(z,w)\})\,\Psi(x) \Rightarrow \Psi(z))}{(\forall z \in I(A,\Phi))\,\Psi(z)}$$

where Clos(I(A, Φ)) denotes the closure of the set generated by Φ, and which is disjoint from the base set A. The inductive type introduction rules essentially determine the closure conditions for the inductive type I(A, Φ). The elimination rule given above is the induction rule associated with the inductive type scheme I(A, Φ), and the type itself is essentially given by the base type, A, together with an assertion Φ which tells us how to build up the type from preceding values; for example, the inductive type of natural numbers has the base set {0}, and the assertion Φ is given by $\Phi(x,y) \Leftrightarrow x = \mathbf{succ}\ y$, where **succ** is the usual successor function.

4.3 Realizability for the theory TKS

The original concept of realizability was developed by Kleene [Kle 45] in an attempt to relate the constructive meaning of logical operations to recursive functions. His objective was to provide a framework for carrying out metamathematics, and the functions obtained were of no real consequence. However, from a computer science point of view they are rather interesting, since they may be considered as 'programs' which make the computational content of logical derivations explicit (loosely: the assertion to be proved is taken to be a specification, and the term which realizes it is a program which meets that specification). All of this is well known, and some research has been undertaken to examine the possibilities of program development using such a framework ([Hen 89a], [HaN 87]). The theory TK of Henson and Turner is such an approach, and programs are extracted from proofs of assertions in the logic via an algorithm which arises from the proof of soundness of the realizability interpretation. The realizability interpretation gives us a way of associating terms of the theory to assertions; the interpretation itself is given inductively by associating formulae of the form 'e ρ Φ', which is to be read 'e realizes Φ' , to each formula Φ. The free variables of e ρ Φ are those of Φ together with the 'fresh' variable e. It is worth stating at this stage that the formula 'e ρ Φ' is in fact a meta notation; the symbol ρ does not appear as part of the language (although the formula which e ρ Φ represents is a TKS assertion).

Before we give the definition of the realizability interpretation, we shall define what is meant by a *safe* formula; such formulae are particularly useful for certain optimizations of realizability applications, as we shall see when we come to the soundness of the interpretation itself.

Definition 4.1 - Safe Formulae

Let α denote any atomic assertion, and Φ and Ψ be any other assertions. Then we define *safe formulae* via a predicate *safe* as follows:

(i) *safe*(α)

(ii) If *safe*(Φ) and *safe*(Ψ) then *safe*(Φ ∧ Ψ)

(iii) If *safe*(Ψ) then *safe*(Φ ⇒ Ψ)

(iv) If *safe*(Φ) then *safe*((∀x)Φ)

(v) If *safe*(Φ) then *safe*($\{x \mid \Phi\}$)

(vi) If *safe*(T) and *safe*(Φ) then *safe*($I(T, \Phi)$).

(vii) If *safe*(T) then *safe*($x \in T$). ◊

Safe formulae are analogous to, for example, negative, almost negative formulae[Bee 85] and type zero formulae [HaN 87]. Essentially the notion of a safe formula extends the notion of almost negative by allowing arbitrary antecedents for implicational formulae; their main use is in allowing us to ignore irrelevant information when we use our realizability interpretation. Finally we note the important point that decidable formulae are also safe formulae; this fact shall prove to be of use in our subsequent work.

The definition of realizability that we shall give here is (more or less) just a smaller version than the interpretation given in [Hen 89b], since we only require an interpretation for our particular subtheory TKS. Note that in the definition, $(e)_0$ and $(e)_1$ refer to the usual selector functions on the pair e.

Definition 4.2 - Realizability Interpretation

(i)	$e \rho \Phi$	is	Φ	(*safe*(Φ))
(ii)	$e \rho\ t \in \{x \mid \Phi\}$	is	$e \rho \Phi(t)$	
(iii)	$e \rho\ x \in I(A, \Phi)$	is	$x \in I(A, \Phi)$	(*safe*(A) and *safe*(Φ))
(iv)	$e \rho\ \Phi \wedge \Psi$	is	$\Phi \wedge (e \rho \Psi)$	(*safe*(Φ))
(v)	$e \rho\ \Phi \wedge \Psi$	is	$(e \rho \Phi) \wedge \Psi$	(*safe*(Ψ))
(vi)	$e \rho\ \Phi \wedge \Psi$	is	$(e)_0 \rho \Phi \wedge (e)_1 \rho \Psi$	(otherwise)
(vii)	$e \rho\ \Phi \vee \Psi$	is	$(e)_0 \rightarrow \Phi \wedge (e)_1 \rho \Phi , \Psi \wedge (e)_1 \rho \Psi$	
(viii)	$e \rho\ \Phi \vee \Psi$	is	$(e)_1 \rightarrow \Phi, \Psi$	(*safe*(Φ) and *safe*(Ψ))
(ix)	$e \rho\ \Phi \Rightarrow \Psi$	is	$\forall x((x \rho \Phi) \wedge \Phi \Rightarrow (e\,x)\downarrow \wedge (e\,x) \rho \Psi)$	
(x)	$e \rho\ (\forall x) \Phi$	is	$\forall x((e\,x)\downarrow \wedge (e\,x) \rho \Phi)$	
(xi)	$e \rho\ (\forall x \in T)\Phi$	is	$(\forall x \in T)((e\,x) \rho \Phi)$	(*safe*(T))
(xii)	$e \rho\ (\exists x) \Phi$	is	$\Phi((e)_1) \wedge (e)_0 \rho \Phi((e)_1)$	
(xiii)	$e \rho\ (\exists x) \Phi$	is	$\Phi(e)$	(*safe*(Φ)) ◊

Note that in definition 4.2 we only refer to realizability for inductive types given by safe sets and formulae; as we shall see, these are the only inductive types that we shall consider here, and so we merely give the relevant clause. The interested reader is referred to [Hen 90] for a further discussion.

The *soundness* of a realizability interpretation essentially means that we can find some term t of our term language which will make the computational content of a constructive proof in TKS explicit. This idea is stated formally by the following (meta) theorem.

Theorem 4.3 - Soundness of Realizability

If TKS $\vdash \Phi$, then there is a term , t , of the term language such that $t\downarrow$ and

TKS $\vdash t \rho \Phi$.

Proof:

The proof proceeds by induction on the length of the derivation of the formula Φ. In general the proof involves associating a term to the conclusion of each of the TKS inference rules, inductively assuming realizers of the hypotheses; one particular term which we shall have occasion to use is the **irec** combinator, which is the realizer for the (I-Elim) rule. In the case when I(A, Φ) is safe, **irec** is of the form

$$\mathbf{irec}\ f\ g\ x = f\ x \qquad (x \in A)$$
$$\mathbf{irec}\ f\ g\ x = g\ x\ (\mathbf{irec}\ f\ g)$$

where f and g are the realizers of the hypotheses of the rule. Note that the sets A and Clos(I(A, Φ)) must be recursively separable in order that **irec** suffices as a realizer; this will be the case for the application covered in this paper. A further discussion on the role of safe formulae may be found in [Hen 90]. ◊

This concludes our remarks concerning the theory TKS. In the next section we shall examine how one might interpret the pre/postcondition language of section 3 in TK. With such an interpretation in place, we shall see how some transformation rules may be obtained by extending some of the intuitions behind the verification rules given in this section, and how the concept of a hooked variable affects the structure of our constructed 'transformation package' that facilitates program derivation.

5 Interpreting VDM Specifications in TKS: A Transformation Package

First of all we provide interpretations of the pre/postcondition language in TKS. Two such interpretations are given; one which is a single-state function and another which is a two-state function. This enables us to make simplifications in certain cases when we examine the interpretation of a VDM operation, as we shall see shortly.

The first topic to address is that of the interpretation of program variables in TKS. As has been noted and explored elsewhere [TuZ 88] program variables are not variables at all in the conventional sense. We make this explicit by interpreting them as TKS term constants.

Given that we intend to interpret program variables as constants, we assume the existence of a basic type, Ide, of identifiers in TKS. We shall use emboldening to represent the bijection between the set of program variables, PV, and Ide. Note that tuples of program variables are treated in the same way. We will also use emboldening for the bijection between numerals in the Hoare logic and the TKS set Nat.

We shall also need a set of states mapping program variables to numbers. This is simply the set of all total functions from identifiers to numbers. Hence we define

$$\Sigma =_{def} \text{Ide} \rightarrow \text{Nat}$$

and we shall use σ to denote typical elements of this set. Note that state update is defined as usual, namely

$$\sigma[\mathbf{x} \leftarrow e]y = \textit{if } x{=}y \textit{ then } e \textit{ else } \sigma(y)$$

5.1 Translating Pre and Postconditions into TKS

Now that we have a notion of state in TKS, we can give a semantic function for programming language expressions which, given an expression and a state yields an element of Nat in TKS. The definition of this function is as expected, but we give it here for completeness. Note that in all of the following definitions, the symbol '—»' is used to represent meta-level functionality.

Definition 5.1 - Semantics of Programming Language Expressions

We define the following semantic function

$[]_E \in E \twoheadrightarrow (\Sigma \rightarrow \text{Nat})$

as follows:

(i) $[v]_E\sigma = \sigma(v)$

(ii) $[n]_E\sigma = n$

(iii) $[e_1 \oplus e_2]_E\sigma = [e_1]_E\sigma \oplus [e_2]_E\sigma$. ◊

Now we provide a single-state function which maps terms of the pre/postcondition language, *L*(VDM), that do *not* contain hooked variables to TKS terms written in *L*(TKS), the language of TKS. The definition of the function is as follows.

Definition 5.2 - Term Mapping (single state)

Let *true* and *false* be TKS constants, and let *and, or, not* and *eq* be TKS functions implementing the appropriate truth tables over *true*and *false*. Then we define

$[]_T \in L(\text{VDM}) \twoheadrightarrow (\Sigma \twoheadrightarrow L(\text{TKS}))$

as follows:

(i) $[\,e\,]_T\sigma = [\,e\,]_E\sigma$

(ii) $[\,\underline{v}\,]_T\sigma = <\sigma(v_1), \ldots, \sigma(v_n)>$, where $\underline{v}$ is the tuple $< v_1, \ldots, v_n >$

(iii) $[\,e_1 \text{ eq } e_2]_T\sigma = eq([\,e_1]_E\sigma, [e_2]_E\sigma)$

(iv) $[B1 \text{ and } B2]_T\sigma = and([B1]_T\sigma, [B2]_T\sigma)$

(v) $[\,B1 \text{ or } B2]_T\sigma = or([B1]_T\sigma, [B2]_T\sigma)$

(vi) $[\text{not } B]_T\sigma = not([B]_T\sigma)$

(vii) $[\,\text{True}\,]_T\sigma = true$

(viii) $[\,\text{False}\,]_T\sigma = false$. ◊

With the single-state term function in place we may provide a single-state assertion mapping; note that we use the abbreviation *T* to represent any trivially true assertion (such as 0 = 0).

Definition 5.3 - Assertion Mapping (single state)

Define the mapping

$[]_A \in L(\text{VDM}) \twoheadrightarrow (\Sigma \twoheadrightarrow L(\text{TKS}))$

as follows:

(i) $[\, R_n(t_1, \ldots, t_n)\,]_A\sigma = R_n([t_1]_T\sigma, \ldots, [t_n]_T\sigma)$

(ii) $[\,\mathrm{true}\,]_A\sigma = T$

(iii) $[\,\mathrm{false}\,]_A\sigma = \bot$

(iv) $[\,\neg\Phi\,]_A\sigma = [\Phi]_A\sigma \Rightarrow \bot$

(v) $[\,\Phi_1 \wedge \Phi_2]_A\sigma = [\Phi_1]_A\sigma \wedge [\Phi_2]_A\sigma$

(vi) $[\Phi_1 \Rightarrow \Phi_2]_A\sigma = [\Phi_1]_A\sigma \Rightarrow [\Phi_2]_A\sigma$ ◊

Using definition 5.3, we may collect all of the states satisfying a particular assertion into one set by means of the following definition.

Definition 5.4 - State Satisfaction (single-state)

The set of states which satisfy an assertion P containing no hooked variables is defined as follows:

$$\Sigma_P = \{\sigma \in \Sigma \mid [P]_A\sigma\}.$$ ◊

Note also that for any assertion P without hooked variables, the set Σ_P is decidable. This is clear, since the TKS assertion $[P]_A\sigma$ is decidable, and hence Σ_P is a decidable TKS set.

The above definitions do not allow us to capture the intuitive notion of a hooked variable, i.e. that such a variable refers to the value of a program variable before execution of some operation. Such a notion may at least partially be captured by appealing to a two-state interpretation for the language, as we shall now discuss.

Under the usual 'free variable' interpretation of a free hooked variable, the *intuitive* meaning of a hooked variable is lost; to treat such a variable as merely a free variable destroys the 'value in the initial state' intuition. For this reason, we have chosen to provide a further interpretation for the assertion language which is a *two state* function; this at least goes some way to preserving the specification meaning of a hooked variable within the logic itself. This interpretation is given by the following definitions; note that we expand the definition more than might be expected in order to highlight the changes that hooked variables necessitate.

Definition 5.5 - Term Mapping (two state)

We define

$[]_{VT} \in VT \longrightarrow\!\!\!\!\!\rightarrow (\Sigma \longrightarrow\!\!\!\!\!\rightarrow (\Sigma \longrightarrow\!\!\!\!\!\rightarrow \mathcal{L}(\mathrm{TKS})))$

as follows:

(i) $[\mathrm{v}]_{VT}\sigma\sigma' = \sigma'(\mathrm{v})$

(ii) $[\mathit{v}]_{VT}\sigma\sigma' = \sigma(\mathrm{v})$

(iii) $[\mathrm{e}_1 \oplus \mathrm{e}_2]_{VT}\sigma\sigma' = [\mathrm{e}_1]_E\sigma' \oplus [\mathrm{e}_2]_E\sigma'$

(iv) $[e_1 \oplus e_2]_{VT}\sigma\sigma' = [e_1]_E\sigma \oplus [e_2]_E\sigma$

(v) $[\mathrm{n}]_{VT}\sigma\sigma' = \mathbf{n}$

(vi) $[\,\underline{\mathrm{v}}\,]_{VT}\sigma\sigma' = [\,\underline{\mathrm{v}}\,]_T\sigma'$

(vii) $[\underline{\mathit{v}}]_{VT}\sigma\sigma' = [\underline{\mathrm{v}}]_T\sigma$

(viii) $[\,\mathrm{e}_1\ \mathbf{eq}\ \mathrm{e}_2]_{VT}\sigma\sigma' = eq([\,\mathrm{e}_1]_E\sigma', [\mathrm{e}_2]_E\sigma')$

(ix) $[\mathbf{B1\ and\ B2}]_{VT}\sigma\sigma' = \mathit{and}([\mathrm{B1}]_T]\sigma', [\mathrm{B2}]_T\sigma')$

(x) $[\mathbf{B1\ or\ B2}]_{VT}\sigma\sigma' = \mathit{or}([\mathrm{B1}]_T\sigma', [\mathrm{B2}]_T\sigma')$

(xi) $[\mathbf{not\ B}]_{VT}\sigma\sigma' = \mathit{not}([\mathrm{B}]_T\sigma')$

(xii) $[\mathrm{True}]_{VT}\sigma\sigma' = \mathit{true}$

(xiii) $[\mathrm{False}]_{VT}\sigma\sigma' = \mathit{false}$. ◊

Definition 5.6 - Assertion Mapping (two state)

Define the mapping

$[]_{VA} \in \mathrm{VA} \twoheadrightarrow (\Sigma \twoheadrightarrow (\Sigma \twoheadrightarrow L(\mathrm{TKS})))$

as follows:

(i) $[R_n(t_1, ..., t_n)]_{VA}\sigma\sigma' = R_n([t_1]_{VT}\sigma\sigma', ..., [t_n]_{VT}\sigma\sigma')$

(ii) $[\mathrm{true}]_{VA}\sigma\sigma' = \mathcal{T}$

(iii) $[\mathrm{false}]_{VA}\sigma\sigma' = \perp$

(iv) $[\neg\Phi]_{VA}\sigma\sigma' = [\Phi]_{VA}\sigma\sigma' \Rightarrow \perp$

(v) $[\Phi_1 \wedge \Phi_2]_{VA}\sigma\sigma' = [\Phi_1]_{VA}\sigma\sigma' \wedge [\Phi_2]_{VA}\sigma\sigma'$

(vi) $[\Phi_1 \Rightarrow \Phi_2]_{VA}\sigma\sigma' = [\Phi_1]_{VA}\sigma\sigma' \Rightarrow [\Phi_2]_{VA}\sigma\sigma'$ ◊

In these definitions, the first state is used to provide 'initial' values to program variables, and the second state provides 'current' values. This point shall become clearer when we discuss the eureka step for the interpretation of operations in the next subsection.

We may again collect all of the states satisfying a particular assertion into one set and provide a further notion of state satisfaction.

Definition 5.7 - State Satisfaction (two-state)

The set of states which satisfy an assertion R with hooked variables given by some state $\sigma \in \Sigma$ is defined as follows:

$$\Sigma_{R(\sigma)} = \{\sigma' \in \Sigma \mid \sigma \in \Sigma \wedge [R]_{VA}\sigma\sigma'\}. \qquad ◊$$

Note that we take the second ('current') state, as that is really what we did in our earlier definitions.

Some simple properties that we may have occasion to use are given in the following proposition.

Proposition 5.1

(i) $\underline{\Sigma}_X \equiv \Sigma_{\neg X}$, for any assertion X.

(ii) $(\forall\sigma \in \Sigma)((\Sigma_P \cap \Sigma_{R(\sigma)}) \equiv \Sigma_{(P \wedge R(\sigma))})$

(iii) $(\forall\sigma \in \Sigma)([P \Rightarrow Q]_A\sigma) \Rightarrow \Sigma_P \subseteq \Sigma_Q$

(iv) $(\sigma \in \Sigma_{P[v \leftarrow e]}) \Rightarrow \sigma[v \leftarrow [e]_E\,\sigma] \in \Sigma_P$ ◊

Armed with these interpretation functions we may provide a eureka definition which can be used to interpret VDM operations into TKS specifications.

5.2 The Eureka Definition and Transformation Rules

We concern ourselves with total correctness; thus intuitively, given any state which satisfies the precondition P of an operation there is another which satisfies the postcondition $(Q \wedge R)$, and the hooked variables in R are given values by the state satisfying P. Wrapping this up into a TKS assertion gives us

$$(\forall\sigma \in \Sigma)(\exists\sigma' \in \Sigma)(\sigma \in \Sigma_P \Rightarrow \sigma' \in \Sigma_{(Q \wedge R(\sigma))})$$

as a eureka definition for a state interpretation. Notice that the free occurrences of σ in the unpacking of $\sigma' \in \Sigma_{R(\sigma)}$ are bound to states satisfying the precondition P, as required by the intuitive meaning of a VDM operation specification. Furthermore, it may be seen that the eureka definition captures a similar requirement to that expressed by the implementability proof obligation for operations [Jon 86]; this is to be expected, since the provision of a constructive proof of implementability will yield a program to meet the specification.

The next stage in the development of our 'transformation package' is to provide the correctness-preserving rules associated with the state interpretation. We shall need rules for each of the constructs available in the target programming language, which in our case is very simple. Further, we need a rule for consequence to facilitate strengthening and weakening of pre and postconditions. In the case of the while rule, we will provide a rule that amounts mainly to an interpretation of the usual VDM verification rule under the eureka definition.

First of all we require a rule which represents an assignment in some way. The rule that we propose is

$$(\forall\sigma \in \Sigma)(\exists\sigma' \in \Sigma)(\sigma \in \Sigma_{P[v \leftarrow e]} \Rightarrow \sigma' \in \Sigma_{(P \wedge R(\sigma))}) \quad \text{(Assignment)}$$

where R is the assertion $(v = e) \wedge \underline{v} = \underline{v}$ and the tuple $\underline{v}$ contains all of the program variables of P, other than v. The intuition is that after execution of an assignment, the program variable v contains the value of the expression e as given by the precondition $P[v \leftarrow e]$, and the other program variables in P retain the values that they had under the precondition $P[v \leftarrow e]$.

Next we require a rule for sequencing. We shall take as obvious hypotheses to the rule the assertions relating to the specifications that we wish to compose; thus we take

$$(\forall\sigma \in \Sigma)(\exists\sigma' \in \Sigma)(\sigma \in \Sigma_{P1} \Rightarrow \sigma' \in \Sigma_{(P2 \wedge R1(\sigma))}) \text{ and}$$
$$(\forall\sigma \in \Sigma)(\exists\sigma' \in \Sigma)(\sigma \in \Sigma_{P2} \Rightarrow \sigma' \in \Sigma_{(Q \wedge R2(\sigma))})$$

Consider three arbitrary states $\sigma_1 \in \Sigma_{P1}$, $\sigma_2 \in \Sigma_{(P2 \wedge R1(\sigma1))}$ and $\sigma_3 \in \Sigma_{(Q \wedge R2(\sigma2))}$. Unpacking these using the state satisfaction definition yields $[R1]_{VA}\sigma_1\sigma_2 \wedge [R2]_{VA}\sigma_2\sigma_3$. Now, suppose we can prove $[R3]_{VA}\sigma_1\sigma_3$ from this, for some hooked variable assertion R3. Then it follows that $[Q \wedge R3]_{VA}\sigma_1\sigma_3$, as Q is an assertion which contains no hooked variables. Since $\sigma_1 \in \Sigma_{P1}$ and $\sigma_3 \in \Sigma_Q$ it seems reasonable to infer the conclusion

$$(\forall\sigma \in \Sigma)(\exists\sigma' \in \Sigma)(\sigma \in \Sigma_{P1} \Rightarrow \sigma' \in \Sigma_{(Q \wedge R3(\sigma))})$$

We may wrap up all of this intuition into a general inference rule for sequencing, which we shall denote by (Sequence); the hypotheses of the rule are

$$(\forall\sigma \in \Sigma)(\exists\sigma' \in \Sigma)(\sigma \in \Sigma_{P1} \Rightarrow \sigma' \in \Sigma_{(P2 \wedge R1(\sigma))}),$$

$$(\forall\sigma\in\Sigma)(\exists\sigma'\in\Sigma)(\sigma\in\Sigma_{P2}\Rightarrow\sigma'\in\Sigma_{(Q\wedge R2(\sigma))})\text{ and}$$
$$(\forall\sigma_1\in\Sigma_{P1})(\forall\sigma_2\in\Sigma_{P2})(\forall\sigma_3\in\Sigma_Q)([R1]_{VA}\sigma_1\sigma_2\wedge[R2]_{VA}\sigma_2\sigma_3\Rightarrow[R3]_{VA}\sigma_1\sigma_3)$$

and the conclusion of the rule is

$$(\forall\sigma\in\Sigma)(\exists\sigma'\in\Sigma)(\sigma\in\Sigma_{P1}\Rightarrow\sigma'\in\Sigma_{(Q\wedge R3(\sigma))})$$

This form of sequencing rule, compared to the interpretation of the usual VDM verification rule [Jon 86], remains as consistent as possible to the standard single-state rule and allows for more general hooked variable assertions in the conclusion. Moreover it is a useful technique for introducing new hooked variable assertions; such assertions cannot be dealt with adequately using the consequence rule, as we shall discuss shortly.

The transformation rule for a conditional is precisely as one might expect, since it does not involve any difficulties with hooked variable assertions. Thus the hypotheses of the rule, which we denote by (Conditional), are

$$(\forall\sigma\in\Sigma)(\exists\sigma'\in\Sigma)(\sigma\in\Sigma_{(P\wedge\mathcal{T}(B))}\Rightarrow\sigma'\in\Sigma_{(Q\wedge R(\sigma))})\text{ and}$$
$$(\forall\sigma\in\Sigma)(\exists\sigma'\in\Sigma)(\sigma\in\Sigma_{(P\wedge\mathcal{F}(B))}\Rightarrow\sigma'\in\Sigma_{(Q\wedge R(\sigma))})$$

and the conclusion of the rule is

$$(\forall\sigma\in\Sigma)(\exists\sigma'\in\Sigma)(\sigma\in\Sigma_{P}\Rightarrow\sigma'\in\Sigma_{(Q\wedge R(\sigma))})$$

Now we turn our attention to a form of consequence rule. The rule that we propose, called (Consequence), has the hypotheses

$$(\forall\sigma\in\Sigma)([P\Rightarrow P1]_A\sigma)\,,\,(\forall\sigma\in\Sigma)([Q1\Rightarrow Q]_A\sigma)\text{ and}$$
$$(\forall\sigma\in\Sigma)(\exists\sigma'\in\Sigma)(\sigma\in\Sigma_{P1}\Rightarrow\sigma'\in\Sigma_{(Q1\wedge R(\sigma))})$$

and its conclusion is

$$(\forall\sigma\in\Sigma)(\exists\sigma'\in\Sigma)(\sigma\in\Sigma_{P}\Rightarrow\sigma'\in\Sigma_{(Q\wedge R(\sigma))})$$

This rule is clearly different from the one that we might expect; it is only applicable to those assertions which do not contain hooked variables. The reason for this choice may be seen by considering the VDM consequence rule, i.e.

$$\frac{P\Rightarrow P1\quad\{P1\}\,S\,\{R1\}\quad R1\Rightarrow R}{\{P\}\,S\,\{R\}}$$

The VDM rule as it stands requires a proof of R1 ⇒ R, and it is perfectly possible that R1 and R may contain free hooked variables. However when one is required to prove the assertion R1 ⇒ R, the intuitive meaning of a hooked variable is lost. The reason that we avoid the problem here is due to the fact that the sequencing rule makes the state information *explicit*, and so we are able to preserve the intuitive meaning of hooked variables; namely, we can use them in a specific context.

The final transformation rule that we provide concerns the representation of an iteration construct. The structure of this rule is broadly that of an interpretation of the VDM iteration rule, i.e. an interpretation of

$$\frac{\{P \wedge \mathcal{T}(B)\}\ S\ \{P \wedge R\}}{\{P\}\ \textbf{while}\ B\ \textbf{do}\ S\ \textbf{od}\ \{P \wedge \mathcal{F}(B) \wedge R^*\}}$$

where R is the hooked variable assertion expressing a well-foundedness relation with regard to some bound function, and R^* is the same assertion as R, but containing the reflexive closure of the relation present in the assertion R. To interpret this adequately, we need to define an inductive type in TKS which captures the well-foundedness information.

We shall insist that the set of states satisfying the loop invariant can be well-ordered, and further that R^* holds upon termination. We are therefore led to define the base set of our inductive type by

$$A =_{def} \{\sigma' \in \Sigma \mid (\forall \sigma \in \Sigma_P)(\sigma' \in \Sigma_{(P \wedge \mathcal{F}(B) \wedge R^*(\sigma))})\}$$

The assertion that we use to generate the type is based on the well-ordering over states. If we denote the bound function articulated in R by f we can define the ordering over states by

$$\forall \sigma, \sigma' \in \Sigma :\ \sigma <^s \sigma' \ \text{ iff } \ [f(v_1, ..., v_n)]_T\sigma < [f(v_1, ..., v_n)]_T\sigma'$$

where $v_1, ..., v_n$ are the program variables appearing in the bound function, and '<' is the ordering appearing in the assertion R. We therefore define our assertion Φ by:

$$\Phi(\sigma_1, \sigma_2) \ \Leftrightarrow \ \sigma_2 <^s \sigma_1 \wedge \sigma_1 \in \Sigma_{(P \wedge \mathcal{T}(B))} \wedge \sigma_2 \in \Sigma_P$$

The structure of the induction rule for $I(A, \Phi)$ will therefore merely be an instance of the general TKS induction rule. Thus having defined an inductive type to make the well-ordering information in the assertion R explicit, we arrive at a rule for iteration:

$$\frac{(\forall \sigma \in \Sigma)(\exists \sigma' \in \Sigma)(\sigma \in \Sigma_{(P \wedge \mathcal{T}(B))} \Rightarrow \sigma' \in \Sigma_{(P \wedge R(\sigma))}) \qquad \Sigma_P \equiv I(A, \Phi)}{(\forall \sigma \in \Sigma)(\exists \sigma' \in \Sigma)(\sigma \in \Sigma_P \Rightarrow \sigma' \in \Sigma_{(P \wedge \mathcal{F}(B) \wedge R^*(\sigma))})}$$

There is a proposition which holds regarding this rule which we shall find useful in the next section when we examine the question of realizability for the rules. Essentially it ensures that any program which is extracted from the proof of the first hypothesis of the iteration rule yields a state lower down in the ordering imposed on the set Σ_P, when given a state already in Σ_P.

Proposition 5.2

Suppose that, for some term t, with P, B , and R as given in the iteration transformation rule:

$$t\ \rho\ (\forall \sigma \in \Sigma)(\exists \sigma' \in \Sigma)(\sigma \in \Sigma_{(P \wedge \mathcal{T}(B)} \Rightarrow \sigma' \in \Sigma_{(P \wedge R(\sigma))})$$

Then for any $\sigma \in \Sigma_{(P \wedge \mathcal{T}(B))}$, $(t\ \sigma) \in \Sigma_P$ and $t\sigma <^s \sigma$.

Proof:

Straightforward; the details may be found in [Lew 90]. ◊

This completes the discussion of our 'transformation package' for a eureka definition based on a state interpretation. In the next subsection we demonstrate that our rules are sound with respect to the eureka definition, and hence that they suffice as correctness-preserving transformation rules.

5.3 The Correctness of the Package

The following theorem tells us that the rules of the transformation package are correctness-preserving.

Theorem 5.1 - Transformation Correctness

Under a state interpretation, the transformation rules with respect to the eureka definition are correctness-preserving.

Proof:

The proof proceeds by induction over the length of the derivation of an interpreted specification. We consider the iteration rule by way of example.

We assume by hypothesis that

$$(\forall \sigma \in \Sigma)(\exists \sigma' \in \Sigma)(\sigma \in \Sigma_{(P \wedge T(B))} \Rightarrow \sigma' \in \Sigma_{(P \wedge R(\sigma))}) \text{ and } \Sigma_P \equiv I(A, <^S)$$

where

$$A =_{def} \{\sigma' \in \Sigma \mid (\forall \sigma \in \Sigma_P)(\sigma' \in \Sigma_{(P \wedge F(B) \wedge R^*(\sigma))})\}$$

We need to prove that

$$(\forall \sigma \in \Sigma)(\exists \sigma' \in \Sigma)(\sigma \in \Sigma_P \Rightarrow \sigma' \in \Sigma_{(P \wedge F(B) \wedge R^*(\sigma))})$$

We first prove by $I(A, \Phi)$-induction that

$$(\forall \sigma \in I(A, \Phi))(\exists \sigma' \in \Sigma)(\sigma \in \Sigma_P \Rightarrow \sigma' \in \Sigma_{(P \wedge F(B) \wedge R^*(\sigma))})$$

as follows.

Base Case: $\sigma \in A$

Trivial; we know by the definition of A that $\sigma \in \Sigma_{(P \wedge F(B) \wedge R^*(\sigma))}$, and so the result follows by simple predicate logic.

Induction Case: $\sigma \in Clos(I(A, \Phi))$

Our induction hypothesis is

$$(\exists \sigma' \in \Sigma)(s \in \Sigma_P \Rightarrow \sigma' \in \Sigma_{(P \wedge F(B) \wedge R^*(s))})$$

for any $s \in I(A, \Phi)$ such that $s <^S \sigma$, $\sigma \in \Sigma_{(P \wedge T(B))}$ and $s \in \Sigma_P$. So, assume $\sigma \in \Sigma_P$. Since B is decidable, and we know that $\sigma \notin \Sigma_{(P \wedge F(B))}$, we must have that $\sigma \in \Sigma_{(P \wedge T(B))}$.

Now, from our 'main proof' induction hypothesis we obtain, since $\sigma \in \Sigma$, $(\exists \sigma' \in \Sigma)(\sigma' \in \Sigma_{(P \wedge R(\sigma))})$. Now assume $s \in \Sigma_{(P \wedge R(\sigma))}$ for some arbitrary state s. Then by part (ii) of proposition 5.1 we have $s \in \Sigma_P$ and $s \in \Sigma_{R(\sigma)}$. If f is the bound function, we may then obtain

$$[f(v_1, \ldots, v_n)]_A s < [f(v_1, \ldots, v_n)]_A \sigma ,$$

which by definition of the well-ordering over states gives us $s <^{s} \sigma$. By $I(A, \Phi)$-induction and as $s \in \Sigma_P$ also, we get $(\exists\sigma' \in \Sigma)(\sigma' \in \Sigma_{(P \wedge F(B) \wedge R^*(s))})$. Assume $\sigma' \in \Sigma_{(P \wedge F(B) \wedge R^*(s))}$, for some arbitrary state σ'. By the definition of state update we get $[R^*]_{VA} s\sigma'$. As R^* contains the reflexive closure information regarding the bound function f, we must have that $[f(v_1, ..., v_n)]_A\sigma' \leq [f(v_1, ..., v_n)]_A s$. We already know $[f(v_1, ..., v_n)]_A s < [f(v_1, ..., v_n)]_A\sigma$, therefore by simple relational algebra we get $[f(v_1, ..., v_n)]_A\sigma' \leq [f(v_1, ..., v_n)]_A\sigma$.

So, by the definition of state update we obtain $\sigma' \in \Sigma_{R^*(\sigma)}$ and so by proposition 5.1 part (ii) we obtain $(\exists\sigma' \in \Sigma)(\sigma' \in \Sigma_{(P \wedge F(B) \wedge R^*(\sigma))})$. Since $\sigma \in \Sigma_P$ we obtain $(\exists\sigma' \in \Sigma)(\sigma \in \Sigma_P \Rightarrow (\sigma' \in \Sigma_{(P \wedge F(B) \wedge R^*(\sigma))})$.

(End of $I(A, \Phi)$-induction)

Thus by $I(A, \Phi)$-induction we can prove that

$$(\forall\sigma \in I(A, \Phi))(\exists\sigma' \in \Sigma)(\sigma \in \Sigma_P \Rightarrow \sigma' \in \Sigma_{(P \wedge F(B) \wedge R^*(\sigma))})$$

Since we know from our well-ordering assumption that $\Sigma_P \equiv I(A, \Phi)$, this just becomes

$$(\forall\sigma \in \Sigma_P)(\exists\sigma' \in \Sigma)(\sigma \in \Sigma_P \Rightarrow \sigma' \in \Sigma_{(P \wedge F(B) \wedge R^*(\sigma))})$$

Further, it is a trivial matter to prove by contradiction that

$$(\forall\sigma \in \underline{\Sigma}_P)(\exists\sigma' \in \Sigma)(\sigma \in \Sigma_P \Rightarrow \sigma' \in \Sigma_{(P \wedge F(B) \wedge R^*(\sigma))})$$

and hence we may conclude, since$(\underline{\Sigma}_P \cup \Sigma_P) \equiv \Sigma$, that

$$(\forall\sigma \in \Sigma)(\exists\sigma' \in \Sigma)(\sigma \in \Sigma_P \Rightarrow \sigma' \in \Sigma_{(P \wedge F(B) \wedge R^*(\sigma))}),$$

as required. ◊

Thus theorem 5.1 verifies that our rules preserve correctness in the sense that the correspondence between the interpretation and the VDM operations is preserved under application of the rules.

In this section we have provided a 'transformation package', consisting of a language interpretation, a eureka definition and some correctness-preserving transformation rules. This package enables us to transform simple VDM operations into TKS specifications; proofs of such specifications in TKS allow us to then extract programs which meet the original VDM specifications, rather than performing *post hoc* verification. In the next section we discuss the role of realizability with regard to the transformation rules.

6 Obtaining Denotational Semantics from Transformation Proofs

The correct denotational semantics arise from our transformation rules as a direct consequence of the soundness of realizability for TKS. Thus performing a specification transformation using our 'transformation package' amounts to proving the interpreted VDM specification in TK using the transformation rules and hence obtaining a program which meets it via the soundness of realizability. Such a program is the denotational semantics of an imperative program which (since the transformation is correct) meets the original VDM specification; this was earlier observed in [LeH 90], in the context of denotational semantics derivation from Hoare logics.

To demonstrate that the correct program semantics are indeed obtained from our transformation rules via realizability we shall again consider the iteration rule.

The semantics of a terminating **while** loop is given by

$$\mathbf{loop}\ t\ \sigma = \sigma \qquad ([F(B)]_A\sigma)$$

$$\mathbf{loop}\ t\ \sigma = \mathbf{loop}\ t\ (t\,\sigma)$$

where **loop** is an instance of the **irec** combinator defined by

$$\mathbf{loop}\ t\ \sigma = \mathbf{irec}\ (\lambda\sigma.\sigma)\ \ (\lambda xy.y(t\,x))\ \sigma$$

and the term t is the term extracted from the proof of the first hypothesis of the iteration rule, i.e. t realizes

$$(\forall\sigma \in \Sigma)(\exists\sigma' \in \Sigma)(\sigma \in \Sigma_{(P \wedge T(B))} \Rightarrow \sigma' \in \Sigma_{(P \wedge R(\sigma))})$$

The term $\lambda\sigma.(\mathbf{loop}\ t\ \sigma)$ is the realizer obtained from the soundness of realizability for the iteration transformation rule. In other words, it realizes the conclusion of the iteration rule, i.e. it is the case that

$$(\forall\sigma \in \Sigma)(\ (\mathbf{loop}\ t\ \sigma) \in \Sigma \wedge (\sigma \in \Sigma_P \Rightarrow (\ \mathbf{loop}\ t\ \sigma) \in \Sigma_{(P \wedge F(B) \wedge R^*(\sigma))})$$

The verification of the above assertion in reality arises from the soundness of realizability for TK together with the soundness proof for the iteration rule. Thus, the term (**loop** t σ) is a witness to the truth of the existential assertion

$$(\exists\sigma' \in \Sigma)(\sigma \in \Sigma_P \Rightarrow \sigma' \in \Sigma_{(P \wedge F(B) \wedge R^*(\sigma))})$$

which we proved earlier by I(A, Φ)-induction. So, to demonstrate that $\lambda\sigma.(\mathbf{loop}\ t\ \sigma)$ really is the realizer we obtain by the soundness of realizability, we merely need to re-examine our earlier I(A, Φ)-induction proof, since (**loop** t σ) is certainly defined for any state σ. Thus in the base case, for any $\sigma \in A$, it should be the case that

$$\sigma \in \Sigma_P \Rightarrow (\mathbf{loop}\ t\ \sigma) \in \Sigma_{(P \wedge F(B) \wedge R^*(\sigma))}$$

when $(\mathbf{loop}\ t\ \sigma) = \sigma$; this is clear. Now, in the induction case we know from proposition 5.2 that $(t\,\sigma) <^S \sigma$ and $(t\,\sigma) \in \Sigma_P$, and so the induction hypothesis of the soundness proof tells us that $(\mathbf{loop}\ t\ (t\,\sigma)) \in \Sigma_{(P \wedge F(B) \wedge R^*((t\,\sigma)))}$. If $\sigma \in \Sigma_P$ and B *holds* under σ then we should expect, by the definition of **loop**, that $(\mathbf{loop}\ t\ (t\,\sigma)) \in \Sigma_{(P \wedge F(B) \wedge R^*(\sigma))}$. But we know that $(\mathbf{loop}\ t\ (t\,\sigma)) \in \Sigma_{(P \wedge F(B))}$ and $(\mathbf{loop}\ t\ (t\,\sigma)) \in \Sigma_{R^*((t\,\sigma))}$. Now, if we were to re-examine our soundness proof for the iteration rule we would see that $(\mathbf{loop}\ t\ (t\,\sigma)) \in \Sigma_{(P \wedge F(B))}$ and $(\mathbf{loop}\ t\ (t\,\sigma)) \in \Sigma_{R^*(\sigma)}$, from our argument concerning the reflexive closure of the well-ordering for the bound function. Hence we do indeed have $(\ \mathbf{loop}\ t\ \sigma) \in \Sigma_{(P \wedge F(B) \wedge R^*(\sigma))}$.

Therefore $\lambda\sigma.(\mathbf{loop}\ t\ \sigma)$ is a realizer for any state in the inductive type I(A, Φ), and hence for any state in Σ_P. The affirmation that it is also a realizer for the conclusion of the iteration rule is then immediate from the fact it suffices as a realizer for sets in the complement of Σ_P, since that part of the soundness proof is carried out via a contradiction and so any term serves as a realizer for it.

We have demonstrated in this section that if we were to use our 'transformation package' we would obtain, as a consequence of the soundness of realizability for the transformation rules, imperative programs in the form of their denotational semantics which satisfy specifications as interpreted into TK. Since the transformation rules preserve correctness, such programs will also meet the original VDM specifications that are transformed. In the next section we shall draw some conclusions and discuss some future objectives.

7 Conclusions and Future Work

In this paper we hope to have demonstrated that constructive methodologies and formal specification methods (in particular VDM) do indeed have much to offer one another in terms of providing a more coherent framework for the software development process. That process may, for example, follow the following pattern. At the top level a sufficiently abstract VDM specification is developed, which is then reified (discharging the proof obligations where appropriate) down to a suitable level for implementation. To ensure that the overall development process remains a formal one, the last level of VDM specification may be transformed via a eureka definition to a TK specification, which may then be proved (if possible) using the correctness-preserving transformation rules from the transformation package chosen. One may envisage various different transformation packages being available, with each one corresponding to a different eureka definition (the interpretation of a VDM specification) and containing (possibly) different rules reflecting the program constructs required. Having proved the TK specification, the soundness of realizability provides (via the transformation rules) an imperative program which meets the original specification (though this cannot , of course, be true of VDM specifications which are not implementable; such specifications could not be proved in TK since it is a sound theory). These points are elaborated on further in [Lew 90].

Our work on VDM has provided an initial insight into the way in which constructive theories and formal methods may interact to yield a more satisfactory approach to software specification and development. Of course our investigation has been a fairly modest one, and there are many aspects which require further investigation; for example, more complex states need to be considered, and some example derivations may prove to be instructive (although some of this work is considered in [Lew 90]). Deeper aspects to be examined include the introduction of quantifiers in the VDM specification fragment; this would then enable a treatment of topics such as sorting, using arrays for example. Even the correct introduction of array constructs is philosophically problematic, and this is clearly another area for further investigation.In summary, we feel that the possible benefits of a unified development approach using formal methods and constructive theories merit the subject worthy of future examination, and we hope that others may share our interest.

8 Acknowledgements

I would like to thank Martin Henson for many interesting discussions and suggestions regarding the research presented in this paper, and also the anonymous referees for their valuable comments. The research was conducted at the University of Essex, Colchester, England, and the work was supported by the Science and Engineering Research Council (SERC), with a SERC research studentship and a research grant, no. GR/F/02809.

9 References

[Bee 85] Beeson, M. J., **Foundations of Constructive Mathematics** , Springer-Verlag : New York , 1985

[BMJ 88] Bloomfield, R., *et al* (eds.), **VDM 88 : VDM - The Way Ahead**, Proceedings of the 2nd VDM symposium, Dublin, Ireland, Lecture Notes in Computer Science **328**, 1988.

[HaN 87] Hayashi, S. and Nakano, T. , **PX : A Computational Logic** , Publications of Research Institute for Mathematical Sciences, Kyoto University, Tokyo, 1987.

[Hen 89a] Henson, M. C. **Program Development in the Constructive Theory TK** , Formal Aspects of Computing 1, pp. 173 - 189, 1989.

[Hen 89b] Henson, M. C., **Realizability Models for Program Construction**, Proceedings of Groningen conference on Mathematics of Program Construction, Lecture Notes in Computer Science 375, pp. 256 - 272, 1989.

[Hen 90] Henson , M. C. , **Information Loss in the Constructive Theory TK**, Proc. IFIP WC2 working conference on programming concepts and methods, Israel, 1990.

[HeT 88] Henson, M. C. and Turner, R. **A Constructive Set Theory for Program Development** , Proc. 8th Conference on FST and TCS, Pune, India 1988.

[Jon 86] Jones, C. B. , **Systematic Software Development using VDM**, Prentice-Hall International (U. K.), 1986.

[Kle 45] Kleene , S. C. **On the Interpretation of Intuitionistic Number Theory** , Journal of Symbolic Logic Vol. 10, pp. 109 - 124 , 1945.

[Lew 90] Lewington, C. P., **Towards Constructive Specification Transformation,** PhD thesis, University of Essex Department of Computer Science, 1990.

[LeH 90] Lewington, C. P. and Henson, M. C. , **Deriving Denotational Semantics from Axiomatic Semantics in Constructive Set Theory**, submitted to 'Formal Aspects of Computing', April 1990.

[Mar 82] Martin-Löf, P., **Constructive Mathematics and Computer Programming,** *in:* Logic, Methodology and Philosophy of Science VI, pp. 153 - 175, North Holland, 1982.

[Sto 77] Stoy, J. E., **Denotational Semantics : The Scott-Strachey Approach To Programming Language Theory** , M. I. T. Press : London , 1977.

[TuZ 88] Tucker, J. V. and Zucker, J. **Program Correctness Over Abstract Data Types, with Error-state Semantics** , North-Holland : Amsterdam , 1988.

A New Method for Proving Termination of AC-Rewrite Systems

Deepak Kapur*
Computer Science Dept.
State University of New York
Albany, NY 12222
kapur@cs.albany.edu

G. Sivakumar†
Computer Science Dept.
University of Delware
Newark, DE 19716
siva@cis.udel.edu

Hantao Zhang‡
Computer Science Dept.
The University of Iowa
Iowa City, IA 52242
hzhang@herky.cs.uiowa.edu

Abstract

A new method, which extends the lexicographic recursive path ordering of Dershowitz and Kamin and Levy, to prove termination of associative-commutative (AC) rewrite systems is proposed. Instead of comparing the arguments of an AC-operator using the multiset extension, we *partition* them into disjoint subsets and each subset is used only once for comparison. To preserve transitivity, we introduce two techniques— *pseudocopying* and *elevating* of arguments of an AC operator. This method imposes *no restrictions at all* on the underlying precedence relation on function symbols. It can therefore prove termination of a much more extensive class of AC rewrite systems, than previous methods such as associative path ordering which restrict AC operators to be minimal or sub-minimal in precedence. A number of examples illustrating the power of the approach are discussed. The method has been implemented in *SUTRA* (formerly called *RRL*, *Rewrite Rule Laboratory*), a theorem proving environment based on rewrite techniques and completion.

1 Introduction

Rewrite systems provide an interesting and useful model of computation based on the simple inference rule of "replacing equals by equals." This elegant paradigm uniformly integrates logic and functional programming. Rewrite techniques have also proved successful in many other areas including theorem proving, specification and verification, and proof by induction.

The power of the rewriting approach stems from the ability to "orient" equality ($\leftrightarrow$), which is symmetric, into a directed "rewrite" relation ($\rightarrow$), which is anti-symmetric, using a "well-founded ordering." The rules are used for "simplifying" expressions by repeatedly replacing instances of left-hand sides by the corresponding right-hand sides. For example, the rules below express addition

*Partially supported by the National Science Foundation Grant no. CCR-8906678.
†Partially supported by the National Science Foundation Grant no. CCR-9009755.
‡Partially supported by the National Science Foundation Grant no. CCR-9009414.

and multiplication over natural numbers.

$$\begin{array}{|rcl|} 0+x & \rightarrow & x \\ s(x)+y & \rightarrow & s(x+y) \\ 0*x & \rightarrow & 0 \\ s(x)*y & \rightarrow & y+(x*y) \end{array}$$

A sample derivation chain is $s(0)*s(0) \rightarrow s(0)+(0*s(0)) \rightarrow s(0)+0 \rightarrow s(0+0) \rightarrow s(0)$.

Termination of such derivations is crucial for using rewriting in proofs and computations. Syntactic "path orderings," based on a precedence relation $\succ_f$ on function symbols, have been developed to prove termination of a set of rewrite rules. A comprehensive survey is [3].

Many functions that are of interest (like $*$ and $+$ above) also have the properties of *associativity* and *commutativity* (AC for short) expressed by the following equations.

$$\begin{array}{|rcl|} (x+y)+z & = & x+(y+z) \\ x+y & = & y+x \end{array}$$

The second equation above cannot be oriented as a rewrite rule in either direction without losing termination. A solution for handling such AC operators has been to not explicitly orient the above equations, but to redefine the rewriting relation itself to be modulo AC ($\rightarrow_{AC}$) and use this instead [14, 16].

Extending the "path orderings" to show termination of $\rightarrow_{AC}$ has proven surprisingly difficult. Approaches [2, 4] so far have had only limited success by imposing very strong restrictions on the allowable precedence relation $\succ_f$ on function symbols [18]. Any AC-operator is either minimal in the precedence relation, or can be bigger than at most one other distinct minimal operator that is also AC or unary [18]. In particular, these restrictions will not allow us to orient rules needed in the Boolean-ring like $x+x \rightarrow 0$ (where we need $*$ to be of higher precedence than $+$ and $+$ to be of higher precedence than the constant 0) or handle a system with two unary operators f and g and rules

$$\begin{array}{rcl} f(x)+f(y) & \rightarrow & f(x+y) \\ g(x)+g(y) & \rightarrow & g(x+y) \end{array}$$

Because of these limitations, polynomial orderings [1, 13] remain the most popular way of exhibiting termination of ac-rewrite systems. However, this approach requires, in general, much more expertise from the user to find an appropriate polynomial interpretation of terms.

In this paper we develop a new solution to this problem, and present a well-founded ordering ACRPO ($\succ_{ac}$) that imposes *no restrictions* at all on the preçedence relation between function symbols. We have implemented this in both *RRL* — *Rewrite Rule Laboratory* [10, 11], and *SUTRA* (a common Lisp version of *RRL*) and used it to prove termination of all the usual systems that have AC-functions.

The rest of the paper is organized as follows. In Section 2, we give a brief introduction to rewrite systems, and remind the reader of the definition and use of the recursive path ordering (*RPO*). Section 3 illustrates the main difficulties *RPO* has in handling AC-rewriting. We also motivate and develop the main ideas needed in our approach— *partitioning*, *elevating* and *pseudo-copying*. In Section 4, we give the formal definition of $\succ_{ac}$ and illustrative examples. The proof of well-foundedness is given in Section 5. We conclude in Section 6, by suggesting extensions of this idea to more powerful syntactic orderings than *RPO*.

2 Rewrite Systems and the Recursive Path Ordering

We first briefly explain the basic notions of rewrite systems. We give the definition of the recursive path ordering (RPO) and its use in proving termination.

2.1 Rewrite Systems and Termination

We work with a set $T(F,X)$ of terms constructed from a (finite) set F of function symbols and a (countable) set X of variables. We normally use the letters a through h for function symbols; s, t, and u through w for arbitrary terms; x, y, and z for variables. Each function symbol $f \in F$ has an *arity* $n \geq 0$ which is the number of arguments (immediate subterms) that it has in a well-formed term. *Constants* are function symbols of arity zero. Variable-free terms are called *ground*.

A term t in $T(F,X)$ may be viewed as a finite ordered tree. Internal nodes are labeled with function symbols (from F) of arity greater than 0. The outdegree of an internal node is the same as the arity of the label. Leaves are labeled with either variables (from X) or constants. The size of a term is the number of nodes in the tree. We use $u[t]_\pi$ to denote a term that has t as a subterm at position π. We use $u[\cdot]$ to denote the *context* in which t occurs in the term $u[t]_\pi$. The context is the tree obtained by deleting t from the tree. By $t\mid_\pi$, we denote the *subterm* of t rooted at *position* π. A subterm of t is called *proper* if it is distinct from t.

A substitution σ is a mapping from variables to terms such that $x\sigma \neq x$ for a finite number of variables x's. A substitution can be extended to be a mapping from terms (equations) to terms (equations).

A rewrite *rule* over a set T of terms is an ordered pair (l,r) of terms such that the variables in r also appear in l, and is written $l \to r$. A *rewrite system* (or *term rewriting system*) R is a set of such rules. Rules can be used to replace instances of l by corresponding instances of r.

We use $\to$ (sometimes $\to_R$) to denote the rewrite relation associated with a rewriting system R. A term s *rewrites* to another term t, denoted $s \to t$, if $s\mid_\pi = l\sigma$ and $t = s[r\sigma]_\pi$, for some rule $l \to r$ in R, position π in s, and substitution σ. The rewrite relation $\to$ over T is *terminating* (or *well-founded*) if there is no infinite sequence of terms t_i in T such that $t \to t_1 \to t_2 \cdots$.

One approach to proving termination of rewrite systems is to show the rewrite relation $\to$ is contained in a well-founded partial ordering (transitive and irreflexive) $\succ$ on terms that has the following properties:

1. **Subterm Property**: $u[t] \succ t$ for any term t and a non-empty context $u[\cdot]$.
2. **Deletion Property**: $f(\ldots t \ldots) \succ f(\ldots\ldots)$ for any operator f that has variable arity, and any term t.
3. **Monotonicity**: $s \succ t$ implies that $u[s]_\pi \succ u[t]_\pi$, for all contexts $u[\cdot]$, terms s and t, and positions π.
4. **Stability**: $s \succ t$ implies that $s\sigma \succ t\sigma$ for all terms s and t, and substitutions σ.

Any ordering having the first three properties is called a *simplification* ordering, and is well-founded [3]. If it also has the stability property it is a *reduction* ordering and can be used for proving termination of rewrite systems. If for every rule $l \to r$ in R, $l \succ r$ in a reduction ordering $\succ$, then $\to$ is terminating. We use $\succ_{mul}$ to denote the extension of $\succ$ to multisets and $\succ_{lex}$ to sequences [3].

2.2 Recursive Path Ordering

Let $\succ_f$ be a well-founded precedence relation (partial ordering) on a set of function symbols F. Each operator is also assigned a *status* which is one of { *multiset, left-to-right, right-to-left* }. This status is used to decide in what order (if any) to compare subterms of terms having the same root operator. Any operator that is of variable arity must have multiset status. We also require that if f and g are equivalent ($f \sim_f g$), then f and g must have the same status.

The recursive path ordering $\succ_{rpo}$ extends $\succ_f$ to a well-founded (partial) ordering on terms as follows.

Definition 2.1 [3, 7] *A non-variable term $t = f(t_1, \ldots, t_n) \succ_{rpo} x$ (a variable) iff x occurs in t. Otherwise, $t = f(t_1, \ldots, t_n) \succ_{rpo} g(s_1, \ldots, s_m) = s$ iff one of the following holds.*

1. *$f \succ_f g$, and $t \succ_{rpo} s_j$ for all j, $1 \leq j \leq m$.*
2. *$f \sim_f g$, and either*
   - *f has multiset status, and $\{\!\{t_1, \ldots, t_n\}\!\} \succ_{mul} \{\!\{s_1, \ldots, s_m\}\!\}$, Or,*
   - *f has left-to-right (similarly, right-to-left) status, and*
     - *$(t_1, \ldots, t_n) \succ_{lex} (s_1, \ldots, s_m)$, and*
     - *$t \succ_{rpo} s_j$ for all j, $1 \leq j \leq m$.*
3. *$t_i \underset{\sim rpo}{\succ} s$ for some i, $1 \leq i \leq n$.*

Example 2.2 *If $F = \{f, g, a, b\}$, with $f \succ_f g$ and $a \succ_f b$, then*

$$t = f(g(a,b),b) \underset{rpo}{\succ} g(f(b,b), f(g(b,b),a)) = s$$

Since $f \succ_f g$, we have to compare each top-level subterm of s with t and assuming multiset status for f, this leads to the comparison of the multiset $\{\!\{g(a,b), b\}\!\}$ with $\{\!\{b, b\}\!\}$ in one case and $\{\!\{g(b,b), a\}\!\}$ in the other, and in both cases we have the desired relation.

Theorem 2.3 [3] *$\succ_{rpo}$ is a reduction ordering, i.e., it is a simplification ordering and is stable under substitution.*

This basic scheme can be extended a little (mainly in case 2 of the definition) by using *decompositions* [15, 6] or *paths* [8]. See [17] for a good survey of the power and efficiency of these extensions.

3 AC-Rewriting and Motivation for New Techniques

In this Section we illustrate difficulties encountered in extending RPO to AC-rewriting, and motivate the ideas needed for our new ordering.

With operators that are associative and commutative, the definition of rewriting needs to be modified to include the consequences of these two properties which are not explicitly added as rules (since $x * y = y * x$ cannot be oriented). Let $\mathcal{F}_{AC}$ denote the set of such operators.

Consider a rule $a * b \rightarrow c$, where $* \in \mathcal{F}_{AC}$. The term $t = (b * c) * a$ cannot be rewritten directly if we use the definition of $\rightarrow$ given earlier, as no subterm of t is of the form $a * b$. But t is equivalent to the term $s = (a * b) * c$ (using the AC properties of $*$) and $s \rightarrow c * c$. AC-rewriting ($\rightarrow_{AC}$) is defined to cover such cases as follows.

Definition 3.1 *$u[t] \rightarrow_{AC} u[s']$ if $t \leftrightarrow_{AC} \cdots \leftrightarrow_{AC} s$ (re-arranging arguments of AC operators) and $s \rightarrow s'$ using $l \rightarrow r$ in R.*

A key idea that figures in many approaches to AC-rewriting is to treat AC operators not as strictly binary functions (arity = 2) but to let them be variadic and use *flattening* (of AC operators) to convert terms like $(a * b) * c$ to $*(a, b, c)$. We use $\bar{t}$ to denote the flattened form of a term t.

Definition 3.2 *The flattened form $\bar{t}$ of a term t is defined below.*

$$\bar{t} = \begin{cases} x & \text{if } t = x, \text{ a variable} \\ f(\bar{t_1}, \ldots, \bar{t_n}) & \text{if } t = f(t_1, \ldots, t_n) \text{ and } f \notin \mathcal{F}_{AC} \\ f(T_1 \cup \ldots \cup T_n) & \text{if } t = f(t_1, \ldots, t_n), f \in \mathcal{F}_{AC} \text{ and } T_i = \begin{cases} \{\!\{s_1, \ldots, s_m\}\!\} & \text{if } \bar{t_i} = f(s_1, \ldots, s_m) \\ \{\!\{\bar{t_i}\}\!\} & \text{otherwise} \end{cases} \end{cases}$$

The important question that arises is, whether the termination of $\rightarrow_{AC}$ can be proved using $\succ_{rpo}$ and treating AC operators just like other function symbols (except that they have variable arity), and using flattened terms always. That is, we may attempt to define an ordering $\succ_{ac}$ on AC-terms using $s \succ_{ac} t$ iff $\bar{s} \succ_{rpo} \bar{t}$. As the following simple example shows, this does not work. Consider the two rule system with AC operator f (hence varying arity for f),

$$\begin{array}{rcl} f(a, b) & \rightarrow & g(a, b) \\ f(x, g(y, z)) & \rightarrow & f(x, y, z) \end{array}$$

This is clearly not terminating, since $f(a, b, c) \rightarrow_{AC} f(c, g(a, b)) \rightarrow_{AC} f(a, b, c) \ldots$
But with the precedence relation $f \succ_f g$, we have for each rule $l \rightarrow r$ that $\bar{l} \succ_{rpo} \bar{r}$. Thus $\succ_{rpo}$, by itself, is not well-founded when AC operators are used and handled only by flattening. Note that if an operator were only commutative, then RPO would work, if such operators are given multiset status.

A closer analysis of the example reveals that the major problem is because of using multiset comparison after flattening to compare terms with the same AC operator as root. Although the multiset $M_1 = \{\!\{x, g(y, z)\}\!\}$ is bigger than the multiset $\{\!\{x, y, z\}\!\} = M_2$[1], we should really be comparing M_1 with one of the following candidates $M_{31} = \{\!\{x, f(y, z)\}\!\}$ or $M_{32} = \{\!\{y, f(x, z)\}\!\}$ or $M_{33} = \{\!\{z, f(x, y)\}\!\}$ to make up for the f that disappeared because of flattening.

3.1 Partitioning is a Sufficient Condition

Since we need an ordering on terms to be monotonic, a sufficient condition for defining $\bar{t} = f(t_1, \ldots, t_n) \succ_{ac} f(s_1, \ldots, s_m) = \bar{s}$ (in any AC-ordering $\succ_{ac}$ based on RPO) would be to check if there is some way to partition into two distinct parts the multisets of arguments $T = \{\!\{t_1, \ldots, t_n\}\!\} = T_1 \cup T_2$ and $S = \{\!\{t_1, \ldots, t_n\}\!\} = S_1 \cup S_2$ such that $f(T_i) \succ_{ac} f(S_i)$ (we abuse notation slightly if one of the partitions is a singleton and in this case $f(u)$ really means u). That is, we do not use multiset comparison of arguments which will allow a single subterm on the left-hand side term to account for many different subterms on the right-hand side term. Conversely, for every subterm in the right-hand side term we may want a distinct partition on the left-hand side to "take care" of it.

The main problem with defining $\succ_{ac}$ on flattened terms using only partitioning is that this alone does not guarantee transitivity as illustrated in two revealing examples below.

[1]The reader would notice that if $f(M_1) > f(M_2)$, where f is an AC operator, then the ordering will not be stable under substitutions.

Example 1. We have one AC operator f, and precedence relation $g \succ_f f \succ_f c$.
Let $t_1 = f(g(x), g(y))$, $t_2 = f(x, x, y, y)$ and $t_3 = f(c(x, y), c(x, y))$.

First note that $g(x) \succ_{ac} f(x, x)$ because $g \succ_f f$ and $f(x, y) \succ_{ac} c(x, y)$ since $f \succ_f c$. So, $t_1 \succ_{ac} t_2$ is necessarily true because the arguments of t_2 can be partitioned as $\{\!\{x, x\}\!\} \cup \{\!\{y, y\}\!\}$ and each partition ($f(x, x)$ or $f(y, y)$) is smaller than the corresponding partition in t_1 ($g(x)$ or $g(y)$). With a different partitioning of the arguments of t_2 into $\{\!\{x, y\}\!\} \cup \{\!\{x, y\}\!\}$ we have that each partition ($f(x, y)$) is bigger ($\succ_{ac}$) than the corresponding partition in t_3 ($c(x, y)$). Thus we necessarily have that $t_1 \succ_{ac} t_2$ and $t_2 \succ_{ac} t_3$. But, by partitioning alone, there is no way to show that $t_1 \succ_{ac} t_3$, which must be the case because of transitivity.

Example 2. Let us replace the term t_1 in example 1 by $f(c(g(x), x), c(f(y, y), y))$. Let the precedence relation $\succ_f$, and the terms $t_2 = f(x, x, y, y)$, and $t_3 = f(c(x, y), c(x, y))$ be as before. A similar problem arises in this example because the c (which is smaller than f in precedence) masks the subterm $g(x)$ (or $f(y, y)$) which needs to contribute to both partitions.

3.2 Pseudocopying Big-Terms and Elevating Small-Terms

The above two examples illustrate the problem with basing $\succ_{ac}$ only on partitioning. In the first example, the argument $g(x)$ has the root-operator g which is bigger in the precedence than the AC operator f (let us call such subterms Big-Terms). The subterm $g(x)$ is forced to be in only *one* partition, even though $g(t) \succ_{rpo} f(t, t, \ldots, t)$ for any number of t's.

We fix this by *pseudocopying* in our new ordering. With each operator $f \in F$, we associate a new pseudo-operator ff which is not in F. A pseudocopy of a term $t = f(t_1, \ldots, t_n)$ is denoted $ff(t_1, \ldots, t_n)$. It is a version of t that behaves exactly like t when compared with any term different from t. Conceptually, we intend a pseudo-copy to be a term *very slightly smaller* than the original. A pseudo-copy of a term t may be thought of as the term $pc(t)$, where pc looks like a unary function symbol but serves exclusively as a pseudocopy mark. Thus, $ff(\ldots)$ is just an abbreviation for $pc(f(\ldots))$ to make clear the distinction that a term t is not to be thought of a subterm of its pseudo-copy $pc(t)$. Note that pseudo-operators like ff are not related in precedence relation to other function symbols. They are merely used as marks to denote that a subterm is a pseudo-copy, and we go back to the original for doing comparisons.

Before attempting to partition the multiset of arguments, we may replace a subterm that is a Big-Term by a finite number of its pseudocopies, so that it can be used in different partitions. The reason for using pseudocopies, instead of just duplicating Big-Terms, is to preserve the irreflexivity of the ordering.

The problem in example 2, is in the case when an argument has a root operator c which is not greater than the AC operator f. We call such terms *Small-Terms*. The only reason a Small-Term may be needed to "take care" of more than one argument on the right-hand side term, is when it conceals some (one) subterm that is a Big-Term (as in the case above in the first argument) or a subterm that begins with the same AC operator (as in the second argument). We fix this case by *elevating* Small-Terms. That is, before attempting partitioning, we can replace a Small-Term by *one* of its arguments.

Thus, the main new ideas in the ordering that we formally define in the next section are the following.

- When comparing terms with the same (or equivalent) AC operator as root, find a suitable partitioning of the arguments on each side that works. The base case for this recursion is when either partition becomes size 1. In our definition in the next section, we refine this further by insisting that each argument of the smaller term (i.e., the right-hand side) be in a partition by itself.

- Before attempting partitioning, a Big-Term may be (optionally) replaced by a finite number of its pseudocopies. We give a simple crude bound on this number later.
- Before attempting partitioning, a Small-Term may be (optionally) replaced by any one of its arguments.

We will prove that these ideas are powerful enough to ensure transitivity and well-foundedness of the ordering, which can therefore be used to show termination of $\rightarrow_{AC}$.

4 Definitions and Examples

In this section we define our new ordering $\succ_{ac}$ on AC-terms. Note that henceforth all terms (in all definitions/proofs) are always kept in flattened form. That is, AC operators are variadic, and no argument to an AC-operator f also has top-level operator f. We also sometimes use $f(T)$, where $f \in \mathcal{F}_{AC}$, T is an appropriate multiset of terms $\{\!\{t_1, \ldots, t_n\}\!\}$ to denote the (flattened) term $f(t_1, \ldots, t_n)$. If T is a singleton, as in $f(\{\!\{t_1\}\!\})$, we really mean the term t_1 itself, without the f.

We assume a precedence relation $\underset{\sim f}{\succ}$ on the set of function symbols, with the only restrictions being that a function can be equivalent ($\sim_f$) only to another with the same status. AC-operators have neither multiset nor lexicographical status. It is convenient to think that each AC-operator has a new status called *AC*. In particular, two different AC-operators may be equivalent ($\sim_f$), an AC-operator cannot be equivalent to a non-AC one.

4.1 Definitions

First, we define a binary relation $\Rightarrow$ on terms with the same (or equivalent) AC operator f as root. Case 1 pseudocopies subterms with root function symbol bigger than f (Big-Terms). Case 2 replaces a subterm, whose root function symbol is not greater than f (Small-Terms), by one of its arguments and flattens. Case 3 allows "flattening" of an operator equivalent to f.

Definition 4.1 *Let $f \in \mathcal{F}_{AC}$, $t = f(T)$ be a flattened term, where $T = \{\!\{t_1, \ldots, t_n\}\!\}$. $t \Rightarrow \overline{f(T_1)}$ in one step iff there is a $t_i = g(r_1, \ldots, r_k)$ in T, $T_1 = T - \{\!\{t_i\}\!\} \cup T_2$, and one of the following holds.*

1. **Pseudocopying** $g \succ_f f$, *and* $T_2 = \{\!\{gg(r_1, \ldots, r_k), \ldots, gg(r_1, \ldots, r_k)\}\!\}$ *for some finite number of pseudocopies* $gg(r_1, \ldots, r_k)$.
2. **Elevating** $g \not\succ_f f$, *and* $T_2 = \{r_j\}$ *for some* j.
3. **Flattening** $g \sim_f f$, *and* $T_2 = \{\!\{r_1, \ldots, r_k\}\!\}$.

This relation $\Rightarrow$ applies only to terms that have a top-level AC-operator. Intuitively, if t is a term with the outermost operator in $\mathcal{F}_{AC}$, and $t \Rightarrow^* t_1$, then t_1 is a "candidate" term that needs to be considered for partitioning when comparing t with another term s having the same (or equivalent) outermost AC-operator. That is t is "bigger" than s, if t itself, or a candidate t_1 derivable from t, can be partitioned suitably to show it to be bigger than s. For example, if $f \in \mathcal{F}_{AC}$, and $g \succ_f f \succ_f c$, we have the derivation chain

$$f(g(x), c(g(y), y)) \Rightarrow f(gg(x), gg(x), c(g(y), y)) \Rightarrow f(gg(x), gg(x), g(y)).$$

Two (flattened) terms are *equivalent* ($\sim_{ac}$) if they satisfy the following definition.

Definition 4.2 *A term $t = f(t_1,\ldots,t_n) \sim_{ac} g(s_1,\ldots,s_m) = s$ iff $f \in F$ (i.e., f or g is not a pseudocopy of an operator), $f \sim_f g$, $n = m$, and one of the following holds.*

1. *f has left-to-right or right-to-left status, $t_i \sim_{ac} s_i$ for all i $(1 \le i \le n)$.*
2. *$f \in \mathcal{F}_{AC}$ or f has the multiset status, and there is a permutation p of $(1,\ldots,n)$ such that $t_i \sim_{ac} s_{p(i)}$.*

It should be easy to see that $\sim_{ac}$ is an equivalence relation. The above definition implies that a pseudo-copy is not equivalent to any other term. In particular, it is not equivalent to its original.

The definition of $\succ_{ac}$ is given below. Cases 1, 2, and 3 are identical to the corresponding cases in RPO. Case 4 is the new interesting one, which compares two terms that begin with the same or equivalent AC operators. We first eliminate common arguments, and then partition the remaining arguments in the bigger term (directly, or after transforming to a suitable candidate) to account for each remaining argument in the smaller term. Note that pseudo-operators occur only in candidate terms. If we need to compare a term starting with a pseduo-operator, we go back to the original. That is, a pseudo-copy $ff(t_1,\ldots,t_n) \succ_{ac} s$ for any term s only if $f(t_1,\ldots,t_n) \succ_{ac} s$. As noted before, a pseudo-copy is not equivalent to its original.

Definition 4.3 *A non-variable term $t \succ_{ac} x$ (a variable) iff x occurs in t. Otherwise, $t = f(t_1,\ldots,t_n) \succ_{ac} g(s_1,\ldots,s_m) = s$, iff one of the following holds.*

1. *$f \succ_f g$, and $t \succ_{ac} s_j$ for all j $(1 \le j \le m)$.*
2. *$f \sim_f g$, $f, g \notin \mathcal{F}_{AC}$, f and g have the same status, and either*
   - *f has multiset status, and $\{\!\{t_1,\ldots,t_n\}\!\} \succ_{mul} \{\!\{s_1,\ldots,s_m\}\!\}$, or*
   - *f has left-to-right (similarly, right-to-left) status, and*
     - *$(t_1,\ldots,t_n) \succ_{lex} (s_1,\ldots,s_m)$, and*
     - *$t \succ_{ac} s_j$ for all j, $(1 \le j \le m)$.*
3. *$t_i \underset{\sim ac}{\succ} s$ for some i $(1 \le i \le n)$, where $t_i \underset{\sim ac}{\succ} s$ if and only if $t_i \sim_{ac} s$ or $t_i \succ_{ac} s$.*
4. *$f \sim_f g$, $f, g \in \mathcal{F}_{AC}$, $t = f(T)$, $s = g(S)$, $S' = S - T = \{\!\{s'_1,\ldots,s'_k\}\!\}$ (where "$-$" denotes the multiset difference performed using $\sim_{ac}$, i.e., terms equivalent with respect to $\sim_{ac}$ can be dropped from T and S), either*
   - *$k = 0$ and $n > m$ (i.e., $S - T = \emptyset$ and $T - S \neq \emptyset$), or*
   - *$f(T - S) \Rightarrow^* f(T')$, and $T' = T_1 \cup \ldots \cup T_k$ and for all i $(1 \le i \le k)$ either*
     - *$T_i = \{u\}$ and $u \underset{\sim ac}{\succ} s'_i$, or*
     - *$T_i = \{\!\{u_1,\ldots,u_l\}\!\}$ and $f(u_1,\ldots,u_l) \underset{\sim ac}{\succ} s'_i$.*

   Also, in this case, either $t \Rightarrow^+ f(T')$, or for at least one i, the $\underset{\sim ac}{\succ}$ is strict.

4.2 Examples

Consider the two examples in the previous section that demonstrated the lack of transitivity based on partitioning alone.

In example 1, to prove $t_1 = f(g(x), g(y)) \succ_{ac} f(c(x,y), c(x,y)) = t_3$, we make two pseudocopies of each argument

$$\begin{aligned} t_1 = f(g(x), g(y)) &\Rightarrow f(gg(x), gg(x), g(y)) \\ &\Rightarrow f(gg(x), gg(x), gg(y), gg(y)) \\ &= f(\{\!\{gg(x), gg(y)\}\!\} \cup \{\!\{gg(x), gg(y)\}\!\}) \end{aligned}$$

and the partitioning shown can be used to prove $t_1 \succ_{ac} t_3$ since $f(gg(x), gg(y)) \succ_{ac} c(x, y)$.

Similarly, in example 2, from $t_1 = f(c(g(x), x), c(f(y, y), y))$, we elevate (and then pseudocopy) subterms of each argument

$$\begin{aligned} t_1 = f(c(g(x), x), c(f(y,y), y)) &\Rightarrow f(g(x), c(f(y,y), y)) \\ &\Rightarrow f(g(x), y, y) \quad \text{Elevating } f(y,y) \text{ causes flattening} \\ &\Rightarrow f(gg(x), gg(x), y, y) \\ &= f(\{\!\{gg(x), y\}\!\} \cup \{\!\{gg(x), y\}\!\}) \end{aligned}$$

and the partitioning shown can be used to prove $t_1 \succ_{ac} t_3$ since $f(gg(x), y) \succ_{ac} c(x, y)$.

Example 3. Suppose $t_1 = f(a, c)$ and $t_2 = f(b, b, b)$, with $a \succ_f b \succ_f c$. If we wish $t_1 \succ_{ac} t_2$, we may add the precedence relation $a \succ_f f$. If we wish $t_2 \succ_{ac} t_1$, we may add $f \succ_f a$. That is, without the restriction on precedence relations, we have higher flexibility to orient equations. Note that the precedence relation $f \succ_f a$ is not allowed in [2].

Example 4. Suppose $*, + \in \mathcal{F}_{AC}$, $* \sim_f +$ and $+ \succ_f 1 \succ_f 0$. It can be shown that $1 * x \succ_{ac} x + 0$. When x is substituted by $1 * 1$ in both $1 * x$ and $x + 0$, we can still show that $*(1, 1, 1) \succ_{ac} (1 * 1) + 0$, because $\succ_{ac}$ is stable under substitution. A similar example is given in [18] for illustrating that any ordering based on the associative pair condition will lose the stability if two AC operators are equivalent.

The ordering $\succ_{ac}$ can easily show (with appropriate choice of precedence relation $\succ_f$) that all well-known AC-systems terminate. For instance, it is easy to show that, for each of the rules given in the following examples, the left-hand side is greater than the right-hand side by $\succ_{ac}$.

Example 5. *Free commutative rings.* $+, * \in \mathcal{F}_{AC}$ and $* \succ_f I \succ_f + \succ_f 0$.

$$\begin{array}{lll} (r1) & x + 0 & \rightarrow x \\ (r2) & x + I(x) & \rightarrow 0 \\ (r3) & I(0) & \rightarrow 0 \\ (r4) & I(I(x)) & \rightarrow x \\ (r5) & I(x + y) & \rightarrow I(x) + I(y) \\ (r6) & x * 0 & \rightarrow 0 \\ (r7) & x * I(y) & \rightarrow I(x * y) \\ (r8) & x * (y + z) & \rightarrow (x * y) + (x * z) \end{array}$$

$* \succ_f I \succ_f +$, which violates the associative pair condition [2], is needed for proving the termination of $(r5)$ and $(r7)$. Note that the same precedence relation can be used to prove the termination of the canonical systems for free rings with the unit or noncommutative free rings with or without the unit. Similarly, $\succ_{ac}$ can be used to prove the termination of the canonical systems for free commutative groups, multiple-units multiple-inverses free groups, homomorphisms of free groups and rings, free distribute lattices (with or without units), and most of the examples listed in [18] and [5].

Example 6. *Free boolean rings.* $+, * \in \mathcal{F}_{AC}$ and $* \succ_f + \succ_f 0$.

$$
\begin{array}{lll}
(r1) & x + 0 & \rightarrow x \\
(r2) & x * 0 & \rightarrow 0 \\
(r3) & x * 1 & \rightarrow x \\
(r4) & x * x & \rightarrow x \\
(r5) & (x + y) * z & \rightarrow (x * z) + (y * z) \\
(r6) & x + x & \rightarrow 0
\end{array}
$$

$+ \succ_f 0$ is needed to prove the termination of $(r6)$. [2]

Example 7. *Addition modulo 2.* $+ \in \mathcal{F}_{AC}$ and $+ \succ_f s \succ_f 0$.

$$
\begin{array}{lll}
(r1) & x + 0 & \rightarrow x \\
(r2) & x + s(y) & \rightarrow s(x + y) \\
(r3) & s(s(x)) & \rightarrow x \\
(r4) & x + x & \rightarrow 0
\end{array}
$$

$+ \succ_f s$ is needed for $(r2)$ and $+ \succ_f 0$ for $(r4)$.

Example 8. *Arithmetic theories.* $*, + \in \mathcal{F}_{AC}$ and $* \succ_f + \succ_f s \succ_f 0$.

$$
\begin{array}{lll}
(r1) & x + 0 & \rightarrow x \\
(r2) & x + s(y) & \rightarrow s(x + y) \\
(r3) & x * 0 & \rightarrow 0 \\
(r4) & x * s(y) & \rightarrow x + (x * y) \\
(r5) & (x + y) * z & \rightarrow (x * z) + (y * z)
\end{array}
$$

$+ \succ_f s$ is needed for $(r2)$ and $* \succ_f +$ for $(r4)$ and $(r5)$.

Example 9. *Milner's nondeterministic machines.* $+ \in \mathcal{F}_{AC}$ and $L \succ_f + \succ_f T \succ_f 0$.

$$
\begin{array}{lll}
(r1) & x + 0 & \rightarrow x \\
(r2) & x + x & \rightarrow x \\
(r3) & T(x) + x & \rightarrow T(x) \\
(r4) & T(x + y) + T(y) & \rightarrow T(x + T(y)) \\
(r5) & L(x + T(y)) & \rightarrow L(x + y) + L(y) \\
(r6) & T(x + y) + x & \rightarrow T(x + y) \\
(r7) & T(T(x)) & \rightarrow T(x) \\
(r8) & L(T(x)) & \rightarrow L(x)
\end{array}
$$

As shown above, there is no restriction on the number of AC operators or its precedence relation with other operators.

5 Proof of Well-Foundedness of $\succ_{ac}$

In this section we prove first that $\succ_{ac}$ is a well-defined, partial ordering. The most interesting part of this proof is in showing that $\succ_{ac}$ is transitive. Then we show that it is a monotonic simplification ordering, which is stable under substitutions. This proves that it is well-founded.

Because $\succ_{ac}$ is an extension of RPO (if there are no AC operators, it is identical to RPO) and is defined based on the tree structure of terms, most lemmas or theorems of this section will be proved

[2] The associative path ordering cannot accept $+ \succ_f 0$; though it is said in [2] (pp.345) that $(r6)$ can be oriented by the relation $+ \succ_f 0$.

by structural induction (or on the size of terms), and we often skip most cases except the one when the root operators of the both terms are equivalent AC operators; the skipped cases follow directly from the similar proof for RPO.

First we show that there are only a finite number of candidates to try (in Case 5) while checking if $t \succ_{ac} s$. We give a loose upper bound here, just to make the proof easy. This ensures that $\succ_{ac}$ is well-defined. That is, for any two terms t and s, we can check in finite time if $t \succ_{ac} s$ or not.

Lemma 5.1 *Let $f \in \mathcal{F}_{AC}$, $t = f(T) = f(t_1, \ldots, t_n)$ a flattened term. If $t \succ_{ac} s$, and if we need to use the derivation $t \Rightarrow^* f(T')$, in showing that $t \succ_{ac} s$, then T' needs at most k pseudocopies of any subterm of t, where k is the total number of arguments appearing under all operators equivalent to the operator f in s (which is flattened).*

Proof. We prove this by induction on the sum of the sizes of t and s. The interesting case is when $s = f(S) = f(s_1, \ldots, s_m)$, which is when pseudocopies are needed. Assuming, without loss of generality, $T \cap S = \emptyset$, this means that we have $T' = T_1 \cup \ldots \cup T_m$ and $f(T_i) \succsim_{ac} s_i$. By induction, if the total number of arguments below any operator equivalent to f in s_i is k_i, then at most $max\{k_i, 1\}$ pseudocopies are needed in T_i for the term s_i. □

An illustrative example for the reader to try is to compare $f(g(x), g(y))$ with $f(c(f(x, x, x, y, y)), c(f(x, x, y, y, y)))$ assuming $g \succ_f f$.

Property 5.2 *$\succ_{ac}$ is irreflexive. That is, $t \not\succ_{ac} t$, for any term t.*

Proof. From the definiton of $\succ_{ac}$. The case when t's outermost operator is not in $\mathcal{F}_{AC}$, is the same as RPO [3]. When t starts with an AC-operator, by definition we eliminate equivalent arguments before partitioning. So it is not the case that $t \succ_{ac} t$. □

Lemma 5.3 *If $t = f(t_1, \ldots, t_n) \succsim_{ac} g(s_1, \ldots, s_m) = s$, there must be a position λ in t such that, the $t|_\lambda = h(r_1, \ldots, r_k)$, with $h \succsim_f g$ and $h(r_1, \ldots, r_k) \succsim_{ac} s$*

Proof. From the definition of $\succ_{ac}$ and $\sim_{ac}$, this is true whichever case is used to show $t \succsim_{ac} s$. □

Lemma 5.4 *Let $f, g \in \mathcal{F}_{AC}$, $f \sim_f g$, and $t = f(t_1, \ldots, t_n) \succ_{ac} g(s_1, \ldots, s_m) = s$. If some $s_i = h(r_1, \ldots, r_k)$ is a Big-Term (i.e. $h \succ_f g$), in s (wlog not also in t), then there is a suitable candidate $t' = f(T_1 \cup \ldots \cup T_i \cup \ldots \cup T_m)$ derivable from t, in which T_i has only a single term in it (a Big-Term or its pseudo-copy).*

Proof. Since $t \succ_{ac} s$, there is some candidate with $f(T_i) \succsim_{ac} h(r_1, \ldots, r_k) = s_i$. But, we know $h \succ_f f$. Also from Lemma 5.3, there must be a single subterm t_{i_1} of $f(T_i)$, with root symbol atleast as big as h, such that $t_{i_1} \succsim_{ac} s_i$. It is sufficient to leave only t_{i_1} in T_i, and distribute any extra terms in T_i among other pieces of the partition. □

Lemma 5.5 *Any derivation chain $t = f(t_1, \ldots, t_n) \Rightarrow \ldots \Rightarrow f(T') = t'$ to obtain a candidate t' for t, can be rearranged into two parts $t \Rightarrow^* t_1 \Rightarrow^* t'$, such that only elevation and flattening are used in $t \Rightarrow^* t_1$, and only pseudo-copying is used in $t_1 \Rightarrow^* t'$.*

Proof. Pseudo-copying of a subterm happens only when it is at the top-level and has a root symbol bigger ($\succ_f$) than the AC-root of the term being transformed. Once a subterm is pseudo-copied, it can neither be flattened or elevated. So, it is possible to do all the elevating and flattening first. □

Note that if $t \Rightarrow^+ t_1$ using only flattening and elevating, then the size of t_1 must be less than the size of t.

Property 5.6 *If $t \succ_{ac} s = g(s_1, \ldots, s_m)$, then $t \succ_{ac} s_i$ for all i.*

Proof. Using induction on the size of t. □

Lemma 5.7 *Let $t = f(t_1, \ldots, t_n) \succ_{ac} g(s_1, \ldots, s_m) = s$, $f \sim_f g$ and f, g are AC. If $s \Rightarrow^* s'$ using only elevation and flattening, then $t \succ_{ac} s'$.*

Proof. By induction on the number of steps in $s \Rightarrow^* s'$. The base case when $s = s'$ is trivial. Otherwise, let $s \Rightarrow s'' \Rightarrow^* s'$ Let $t \Rightarrow^* f(T_1 \cup \ldots \cup T_m)$ be the candidate used, with $f(T_i) \succsim_{ac} s_i$, to show $t \succ_{ac} s$. If $s \Rightarrow s''$ is an elevation step, then by the previous property, the same candidate can be used to show $t \succsim_{ac} s''$. Otherwise, $s \Rightarrow s''$ must be a flattening step of some $s_i = h(r_1, \ldots, r_k)$ with $h \sim_f g$. From $f(T_i) \succsim_{ac} h(r_1, \ldots, r_k) = s_i$, there must a partitioning of a candidate $f(T_i)'$ obtainable from $f(T_i)$ to handle each r_j separately. This same derivation can be used to obtain a suitable candidate to show $t \succ_{ac} s''$. By induction, the Lemma is proved. □

Lemma 5.8 *Let $f \in \mathcal{F}_{AC}$, $g \succ_f f$, $gg(r_1, \ldots, r_k)$ a pseudo-copy of $g(r_1, \ldots, r_k)$, s a term with no pseudo-operators in it, and T a multiset of terms and pseudo-copies such that $gg(r_1, \ldots, r_k)$ is not in T. Then $f(gg(r_1, \ldots, r_k), \ldots, gg(r_1, \ldots, r_k), \cup T) \succsim_{ac} s$ implies $f(g(r_1, \ldots, r_k) \cup T) \succsim_{ac} s$.*

Proof. Any candidate derivable from $f(gg(r_1, \ldots, r_k), \ldots, gg(r_1, \ldots, r_k), \cup T)$ is derivable from $f(g(r_1, \ldots, r_k) \cup T)$. □

This reversal of pseudo-copying is used in the proof of transitivity.

Property 5.9 *$\succ_{ac}$ is transitive. That is, for any terms t, s and r, if $t \succ_{ac} s$, $s \succ_{ac} r$, then $t \succ_{ac} r$.*

Sketch of Proof: This is proved using induction on the sum of the sizes of t, s and r and considering the various possiblities for t, s and r. All the cases except the one where $t = f(t_1, \ldots, t_n) = f(T)$, $s = g(s_1, \ldots, s_m) = g(S)$, and $r = h(r_1, \ldots, r_k) = h(R)$, with $f \sim_f g \sim_f h$ and $f \in \mathcal{F}_{AC}$ (which implies $g, h \in \mathcal{F}_{AC}$ too), are similar to the proof of transitivity of RPO with status [3].

The case when all three terms have the equivalent AC operators as root is proved below. Let $t \Rightarrow^* f(T') = t'$ be used to show $t \succ_{ac} s$, and $s \Rightarrow^* f(S') = s'$ be used to show $s \succ_{ac} r$. For convenience, we assume that any common arguments in t and s (or s and r) are not dropped or changed in any way in the derivations and are only removed finally before comparing $f(T')$ with s (similarly $f(S')$ with r). We have the following cases.

1. **At least one step of elevating or flattening in $t \Rightarrow^* t'$.**
   By Lemma 5.5 such steps, which reduce the size of t, can be moved ahead of any pseudo-copying. So, let $t \Rightarrow t_1 \Rightarrow^* t'$, with the first step being elevation or flattening. We have then that $t_1 \succ_{ac} s$ (using the same candidate $f(T')$) and $s \succ_{ac} r$. By induction $t_1 \succ_{ac} r$. This implies $t \succ_{ac} r$ since any candidate derivable from t_1 is also derivable from t.

2. **At least one step of elevating or flattening in $s \Rightarrow^* s'$.**
As above, let $s \Rightarrow s_1$ be the first elevation or flatenning. We have $s_1 \succ_{ac} r$ and size of s_1 less than that of s. By Lemma 5.7 $t \succ_{ac} s_1$. By induction $t \succ_{ac} r$.

3. **All steps in $t \Rightarrow^* t'$ and $s \Rightarrow^* s'$ are only pseudo-copying.**
Let $s' = f(S')$. S' can be partitioned into k parts $S_1' \cup \ldots \cup S_k'$ (note that $k \geq 2$) and each part "takes care" of one r_j. That is, for all j, $1 \leq j \leq k$, $g(S_j') \underset{\sim ac}{\succ} r_j$. Since only pseudo-copying happens in $s \Rightarrow^* s'$, each S_j' consists only of some original top-level subterms of s and some number of pseudo-copies of other top-level subterms of s. Let $S_{j_1}' = \{\!\{s_l \mid s_l \in S_j' \textit{ and } s_l \textit{ is not a pseudocopy}\}\!\}$, $S_{j_2}' = \{s_l \mid \textit{pseudocopy}(s_l) \in S_j'\}$ (Note: S_{j_2}' is a set with only one copy of each original.) Since $g(S_j') \underset{\sim ac}{\succ} r_j$, we have by Lemma 5.8 that $s_j' = g(S_{j_1} \cup S_{j_2}) \underset{\sim ac}{\succ} r_j$. Note that s_j' is a pure term (no pseudo-operators) embedded in $s = g(S)$. That is, $s_j' = g(s_{i_1}, \ldots, s_{i_l}) = g(S_j'')$ with $s_{i_l} \in S$.

Corresponding to each s_j' in the construction above, we similarly construct a pure term t_j' embedded in t (hence not bigger in size). This is done by first combining the pieces T_l' that takes care of each $s_l \in S_j''$, and replacing all pseudo-copies by one copy of each corresponding original. Again by Lemma 5.8 we have $t_j' \underset{\sim ac}{\succ} s_j'$. Since $s_j' \underset{\sim ac}{\succ} r_j$, by induction hypothesis we have $t_j' \underset{\sim ac}{\succ} r_j$ for all $1 \leq j \leq k$.

Note that the only subterms t_l of t that may be used in more than one t_j' are ones that are BigTerms that have been pseudo-copied when showing that $t \succ_{ac} s$. Therefore, we can derive from t a candidate $t'' = f(T'')$ (T'' corresponds to the union of candidates used to show $t_j' \underset{\sim ac}{\succ} r_j$), which demonstrates that $t \succ_{ac} r$, since one of the $\underset{\sim ac}{\succ}$ must be strict. □

Thus, $\succ_{ac}$ is a well-defined, partial term ordering. Next we show that $\succ_{ac}$ is well-founded (assuming $\succ_f$ is well-founded). We show this by checking that it is a simplification ordering (has subterm, and deletion properties and is monotonic) [3].

Property 5.10 $\succ_{ac}$ *has the subterm property. That is,* $u[s] \succ_{ac} s$ *for any term* s *and any non-empty context* $u[\cdot]$

Proof. From Case 3 of the definition, the subterm property of $\succ_{ac}$ follows easily. □

Case 4 for AC-operators and the fact that varying arity operators can have only multiset status guarantees that $\succ_{ac}$ has the deletion property.

Property 5.11 $\succ_{ac}$ *has the replacement property. That is, if* s *and* t *are terms such that* $t \succ_{ac} s$, *then* $f(\ldots, t, \ldots) \succ_{ac} f(\ldots, s, \ldots)$ *for any operator* f, *where the missing arguments are assumed to be the same in both sides.*

Proof. If $f \in \mathcal{F}_{AC}$, because of the use of the multiset difference (dropping common arguments) in Case 4 of the definition, this property holds. If f is not AC, we may prove by cases according to the status of f that the property holds. □

Property 5.12 $\succ_{ac}$ *is monotonic. That is, if* $t \succ_{ac} s$ *then* $u[t] \succ_{ac} u[s]$ *for any context* $u[\cdot]$.

Proof. This is a corrollary of the replacement property proved by induction on the size of $u[\cdot]$. □

The subterm, deletion, and monotonicity properties imply that $\succ_{ac}$ is a simplification ordering, which implies it is well-founded, provided $\succ_f$ is a well-founded precedence relation [3]. To use $\succ_{ac}$

for proving termination of AC-rewriting we also need the property of stability under substitutions, and the property that it is compatible with $\sim_{ac}$ both of which are easy to show.

Property 5.13 *$\succ_{ac}$ is stable (has the substitution property). That is, $t \succ_{ac} s$ implies $t\sigma \succ_{ac} s\sigma$ for any substitution σ.*

Proof. By induction on the sum of sizes of s and t. The AC-case does not cause difficulty here, because of the use of partitioning. Since each subterm is accounted for by a separate partition, the induction is not difficult. □

Property 5.14 *$\succ_{ac}$ is AC-compatible. That is, for any terms t, t_1, s, and s_1, if $t \sim_{ac}^{*} t_1$, $s \sim_{ac}^{*} s_1$, and $t \succ_{ac} s$, then $t_1 \succ_{ac} s_1$.*

Proof. This follows directly because $\succ_{ac}$ uses only flattened terms and the order of arguments in flattened terms does not matter for Case 4. □

Putting all this together, we have the main theorem.

Theorem 5.15 *$\succ_{ac}$ is a well-founded reduction ordering that can be used to prove termination of AC-rewrite systems.*

6 Conclusion

In this paper we have developed a new ordering $\succ_{ac}$ (based on RPO) for proving termination of rewrite systems that include operators which are associative and commutative. It improves previous attempts considerably by not imposing any restrictions at all on the number of AC operators or their precedence relation with other operators, while retaining lexicographic status for non-AC operators.

But, RPO itself has been extended in several ways even for the non-AC case. Among such extensions is one based on paths $\succ_p$.[8] that can prove (unlike RPO) that $a(g(x), g(y)) \succ_p c(x, y)$ with the precedence relation $g \succ_f c$. We sketch below a simple and direct way to extend the ideas of *pseudocopying*, *elevating*, and *partitioning* to develop an ordering $\succ_{ac-p}$ that is based on $\succ_p$ instead of RPO and is correspondingly more powerful.

The path ordering shows that $t \succ s$ by showing that for every path in s, there is a path in t that is "bigger". Paths themselves are sequences of 2-tuples ending possibly in a variable, corresponding to a distinct path from root to leaf in the tree structure of a term. Each 2-tuple $\langle f, t\rangle$ corresponds to a position in a path, and has the function symbol f and the subterm t at that position. Paths are compared by showing that each 2-tuple in the "smaller" path is "taken care of" by a 2-tuple in the "bigger" path. 2-tuples in different paths are compared by first comparing the function symbols, then the suffix string of 2-tuples in the corresponding paths, then the terms in the 2-tuple, and finally the prefix string (or context). See [8] for more details.

To extend $\succ_p$ to AC-terms, the main ideas are essentially the same as for extending *RPO* to $\succ_{ac}$. We have to *a priori* do pseudocopying, elevating and flattening, and then when comparing 2-tuples with the same AC operator as the first component, partition the paths (in the suffixes) into distinct parts.

In the following system for boolean implication ($\supset$) from [18], with AC operator $\wedge$

$$\begin{array}{rcl} ff \supset y & \rightarrow & \neg ff \\ x \supset ff & \rightarrow & \neg x \\ \neg x \supset \neg y & \rightarrow & y \supset (x \wedge y) \end{array}$$

the third rule cannot be oriented in the direction shown with any choice on precedence relations. But, if we choose $\neg \succ_f \wedge$, then all the paths in the term $s = y \supset (x \wedge y)$ can be taken care of by paths in the term $t = \neg x \supset \neg y$. For example, the path

$$\langle \supset,\ s\rangle\ \langle \wedge,\ x \wedge y\rangle\ y$$

in s is smaller than the path

$$\langle \supset,\ t\rangle\ \langle \neg,\ y\rangle\ y$$

in t, since they both end in the same variable y, and the 2-tuple $\langle \neg,\ y\rangle$ is bigger than the 2-tuple $\langle \wedge,\ x \wedge y\rangle$ since $\neg \succ_f \wedge$, and the 2-tuple $\langle \supset,\ t\rangle$ is bigger than $\langle \wedge,\ s\rangle$ since it has a bigger right-context (suffix). Details of the definition of $\succ_{ac-p}$ and proofs will be included in an expanded version of this paper [9].

The ordering $\succ_{ac}$ has been implemented in both *RRL — Rewrite Rule Laboratory*, and *SUTRA* (a common Lisp version of *RRL*) and used to prove termination of AC-systems, including all the examples mentioned in Section 3. For efficiency, it is useful to develop heuristics to decide which terms to elevate, when to make pseudo-copies, and how to do the partitioning. The details about the implementation and experimentation will also be given in [9].

Acknowledgment: The authors thank Joachim Steinbach for helpful comments on an earlier draft of this paper.

References

[1] Ben Cherifa, A., and Lescanne, P. (1987). Termination of rewriting systems by polynomial interpretations and its implementation. *Science of Computer Programming,* 9, 2, 137-160.

[2] Bachmair, L., and Plaisted, D.A. (1985). Termination orderings for associative-commutative rewriting systems. *J. of Symbolic Computation,* 1, 329-349

[3] Dershowitz, N. (1987). Termination of rewriting. *J. of Symbolic Computation,* 3, 69-116.

[4] Gnaeding, I., and Lescanne, P. (1986). Proving termination of associative-commutative rewriting systems by rewriting. Proc. of *8th International Conference on Automated Deduction (CADE-8),* Oxford, Lecture Notes in Computer Science 230 (ed. Siekmann), Springer Verlag, 52-60.

[5] Hullot, J.-M. (1980). *A catalogue of canonical term rewriting systems.* Technical Report CSL-113, SRI International, Menlo Park, CA.

[6] Jouannaud, J.-P., Lescanne, P., and Reinig, F. (1982). Recursive decomposition ordering. IFIP Working Conference on *Formal Description of Programming Concepts,* (ed. D. Bjorner), W. Germany, 331-348.

[7] Kamin, S., and Levy, J-J. (1980). Attempts for generalizing the recursive path ordering. Unpublished Manuscript, INRIA, France.

[8] Kapur, D., Narendran, P., and Sivakumar, G. (1985). A path ordering for proving termination of term rewriting systems. Proc. *10th CAAP,* Berlin, LNCS 185, 173-187.

[9] Kapur, D., Sivakumar, G., and Zhang, H. (1990). *Termination of AC-Rewrite Systems.* Technical Report, Computer Science Dept., University of Delaware, in preparation.

[10] Kapur, D., and Zhang, H. (1987). *RRL: A Rewrite Rule Laboratory - User's Manual.* GE Corporate Research and Development Report, Schenectady, NY. (Revised May 1989, Tech. Report 89-03, Dept. of Computer Science, Univ. of Iowa.)

[11] Kapur, D., and Zhang, H. (1988). *RRL*: A Rewrite Rule Laboratory, Proc. of *9th International Conference on Automated Deduction (CADE-9)*, Argonne, Lecture Notes in Computer Science 310 (eds. Lusk and Overbeek), Springer Verlag, 768-769.

[12] Knuth, D.E. and Bendix, P.B. (1970). Simple word problems in universal algebras. In: *Computational Problems in Abstract Algebras.* (ed. J. Leech), Pergamon Press, 263-297.

[13] Lankford, D.S. (1979). On proving term rewriting systems are noetherian. Memo MTP-3, Lousiana State University.

[14] Lankford, D.S., and Ballantyne, A.M. (1977). Decision procedures for simple equational theories with commutative-associative axioms: complete sets of commutative-associative reductions. Automatic Theorem Proving Project, Dept. of Math. and Computer Science, University of Texas, Austin, Texas, Report ATP-39.

[15] Lescanne, P., (1990). On the recursive decomposition ordering with lexicographical status and other related orderings, *J. Automated Reasoning,* 6, 1, 39-49.

[16] Peterson, G.L., and Stickel, M.E. (1981). Complete sets of reductions for some equational theories. *J. ACM,* 28, 2, 233-264.

[17] Steinbach, J. (1989). Extensions and comparison of simplification orderings. Proc. *3rd International Conf. on Rewriting Techniques and Applications (RTA-89),* Chapel Hill, NC, 434-448.

[18] Steinbach, J. (1989). Path and decomposition orderings for proving AC-termination. Seki-Report, SR-89-18, University of Kaiserslautern. See also "Improving associative path orderings," in: Proc. of *10th International Conference on Automated Deduction (CADE-10),* Kaiserslautern, Lecture Notes in Computer Science 449 (ed. Stickel), Springer Verlag, 411-425.

Efficient Parallel Algorithms for Optical Computing with the DFT Primitive*

JOHN REIF
Department of Computer Science
Duke University
Durham, NC 27706

AKHILESH TYAGI
Department of Computer Science
University of North Carolina
Chapel Hill, NC 27599-3175

Abstract

The optical computing technology offers new challenges to the algorithm designers since it can perform an n-point DFT computation in only unit time. Note that DFT is a non-trivial computation in the PRAM model. We develop two new models, DFT-VLSIO and DFT-Circuit, to capture this characteristic of optical computing. We also provide two paradigms for developing parallel algorithms in these models. Efficient parallel algorithms for many problems including polynomial and matrix computations, sorting and string matching are presented. The sorting and string matching algorithms are particularly noteworthy. Almost all of these algorithms are within a polylog factor of the optical computing (VLSIO) lower bounds derived in [BR87] and [TR90].

1 Introduction

Over the last 15 years, VLSI has moved from being a theoretical abstraction to being a practical reality. As VLSI design tools and VLSI fabrication facilities such as MOSIS became widely available, the algorithm design paradigms such as systolic algorithms [Kun79], that were thought to be of theoretical interest only, have been used in high performance VLSI hardware. Along the same lines, the theoretical limitations of VLSI predicted by area-time tradeoff lower bounds [Tho79] have been found to be important limitations in practice. The field of electro-optical computing is at its infancy, comparable to the state of VLSI technology, say, 10 years ago. Fabrication facilities are not widely available – instead, the crucial electro-optical devices must be specially made in the laboratories. However, a number of prototype electro-optical computing systems – perhaps most notably at Bell Laboratories under Wong, as well as optical message routing devices at Boulder [MJR89], Stanford and USC, have been built recently. The technology for electro-optical computing is likely to advance rapidly in the 90s, just as VLSI technology advanced in the late 70s and 80s. Therefore, following our past experience with VLSI, it seems likely that the theoretical underpinnings for optical computing technology – namely the discovery of efficient algorithms and of resource lower bounds, are crucial to guide its development.

What are the specific capabilities of optical computing that offer room for new paradigms in algorithm design? It is well known that optical devices exist that can compute a two-dimensional Fourier transform or its inverse in unit time, see Goodman [Goo82], or any of [Hor87], [Iiz83], [Fei88], [KF86], which describe the fundamentals of optical computing. This is a natural characteristic of light. This opens up exciting opportunities for the algorithm designers. In the widely accepted model of parallel computation – PRAM, not many interesting problems can be solved in $O(1)$ time. In particular, the best known parallel algorithm for Discrete Fourier Transform – FFT, takes time $O(\log n)$ for an $n-$point DFT. Given this powerful technology, the question we address in this paper is, "which problems can use the DFT computation primitive gainfully?". It is not immediately clear that given a problem, apparently disparate from DFT, such as sorting, how one reduces it to several instances of DFT to derive an efficient algorithm. We identify two general techniques that benefit a host of problems. First, we show a way to compute 1-dimensional

*The research of J. Reif was supported in part by DARPA/ARO contract DAAL03-88-K-0195, Air Force Contract AFOSR-87-0386, DARPA/ISTO contract N00014-88-K-0458, NASA subcontract 550-63 of primecontract NAS5-30428. A. Tyagi was supported by NSF Grant #MIP-8806169, NCBS&T Grant #89SE04 and a Junior Faculty Development award from UNC, Chapel Hill.

n-point DFT efficiently using a series of 2-dimensional DFTs. Note that the optical devices compute a 2-dimensional DFT. However, the 1-dimensional DFT seems to be the one which is more naturally usable in most of the problems. Secondly, we demonstrate an efficient way to perform a parallel-prefix computation with DFT primitives. Equipped with these two techniques, we propose constant time solutions for a variety of problems including sorting, several matrix computations and string matching.

In this paper, we consider discrete models for optical computing with a DFT primitive. In particular, an n-point DFT operation or its inverse can be computed in unit time using n processors. The development of a new model of computation is a task full of trade-offs. Only the essential characteristics of the underlying computing medium should be reflected in the model. Any unnecessary characteristics only serve to undermine the usefulness of such a model. PRAM (parallel random access machine) [FW78], [SS79] has provided a much needed model for the development of parallel algorithms for some time now. The algorithm designers do not have to worry about underlying networks and the details of timing inherent in the VLSI technology used to implement the processors. In a similar vein, our objective is to develop a model that captures the essence of optical computing medium with respect to algorithm design. We believe that the most important characteristic that distinguishes the optical technology from the VLSI technology is the ability to compute a powerful primitive, DFT, in unit time. Not surprisingly then, this is the focus of our models. Our new models are:

DFT-Circuit Model: where we allow an n-point DFT primitive gate along with the usual scalar operations of bounded fanin.

DFT-VLSIO: which extends the standard VLSI model to 3-dimensional optical computing devices that compute the 2-D DFT as a primitive operation. We refer to an electro-optical computation as VLSIO, where O stands for *optics* [described in detail in Section 2].

Note that although we did not mention a PRAM-DFT model where a set of n processors can perform a DFT in unit time; all the algorithms in DFT-Circuit model work for such a PRAM-DFT model. A PRAM-DFT can simulate a DFT-Circuit of size $s(n)$ and time $t(n)$ with $s(n)$ processors in time $O(t(n))$. Hence, a PRAM-DFT model is an equally acceptable choice for the development of parallel algorithms in optical computing.

Our main results are efficient parallel algorithms for solving a number of fundamental problems in these models. The problems solved include:

1. prefix sum
2. shifting
3. polynomial multiplication and division
4. matrix multiplication, inversion and transitive closure.
5. Toeplitz matrix multiplication, polynomial GCD, interpolation and inversion.
6. sorting
7. 1 and 2 dimensional string matching

The sorting and string matching algorithms were not at all obvious. Although, we don't have any lower bounds in the DFT-circuit model, many of these parallel algorithms are optimal with respect to the VLSIO model. The known lower bound results in VLSIO are as follows. Barakat and Reif [BR87] showed a lower bound of $\Omega\left(I_f^{3/2}\right)$ on $VT^{3/2}$ of a VLSIO computation for a function f with information complexity I_f. V denotes the volume of the VLSIO system computing f. We [TR90] proved a lower bound of $\Omega\left(I_f f(\sqrt{I_f})\right)$ on the energy-time product for a VLSIO model with the energy function $f(x)$. Table 1 compares our results with the best-known PRAM algorithms for the corresponding problems. All the bounds are in Big-Oh notation (O).

A summary of related work follows. VLSIO (electro-optical VLSI, introduced in Barakat, Reif [BR87]) is the more general model of optical computing [described in Section 2.2]. They considered volume-time trade-offs and lower bounds in this model. We [TR90] demonstrated energy and energy-time product lower and upper bounds for optical computations. We are not aware of any algorithm design work in this model. This is a new model of computation and we expect that the growth in the optical technology during this decade would spur growth in algorithm research.

This paper is organized as follows. Section 2 introduces the two models of computation – VLSIO and DFT-Circuit. The algorithms for a set of direct applications of DFT are described in Section 3. Section 4 describes two sorting algorithms and an algorithm for the element distinctness problem in these models. Both one dimensional and two-dimensional string matching algorithms are sketched in Section 5. We compare the performance of DFT-VLSIO algorithms with the known VLSIO lower bounds in Section 6. Section 7 describes a generalization of these models where the model is parametrized by the displacement rank d. Due to space limitations, some of the algorithm descriptions are very brief. More details will be provided in a latter version.

2 DFT-VLSIO and DFT-Circuit Models

2.1 VLSI Model

It has been observed many times that the conventional electronic devices are inherently constrained by 2-dimensional limitations. Indeed, this was the original motivation for the VLSI model of Thompson [Tho80] which has been successfully applied to model such circuits. The widely accepted VLSI model allowed us both to compare the properties of algorithms such as area and time, and also to determine the ultimate limitations of such devices.

An entry $f(n) : g(n)$ stands for $O(f(n)) : O(g(n))$.			
	DFT-Circuit Size : Time	DFT-VLSIO Volume : Time	PRAM-CRCW # Processors : Time
1-D DFT	$n : 1$	$n^{3/2} : 1$	$n : \log n$
Poly Mult	$n : 1$	$n^{3/2+\epsilon} : 1$ or $n^{3/2} : \log^* n$	$n : \log n$
Barrel Shift	$n : 1$	$n^{3/2+\epsilon} : 1$ or $n^{3/2} : \log^* n$	$n : \log n$
Prefix Sum	$n : 1$	$n^{3/2+\epsilon} : 1$ or $n^{3/2} : \log^* n$	$n : \log n$
Poly Div	$n^3 : 1$ or $O(n) : O(\log\log n)$		$n : \log n$ [RT87]
Toeplitz Matrix Multiplication; Inverse and Poly GCD & Interpolation	$n^3 : 1$ or $n : \log\log n$ $n : \log n$	$n^{3/2+\epsilon} : \log n$ or $n^{3/2} : \log n \log^* n$	$n^2 : \log n$ [PR85], [PR85]
Matrix Mult	$n^{2.376} : 1$	$n^{7/2} : 1$	$n^3 : \log n$
Matrix Inversion Transitive Closure	$n^3 : \log n$	$n^{7/2} : \log n$	$n^{2.376} : \log^2 n$ [CW87]
Sorting	$n^2 : 1$ or *(probabilistic)* $n^{1+\epsilon} : 1$ or $\frac{n^{1+\epsilon}}{\log n} : \log\log n$	$n^{5/2} : 1$ or *(probabilistic)* $n^{1+\frac{3\epsilon}{2}} : 1$ or $\frac{n^{1+\frac{3\epsilon}{2}}}{\log^{3/2} n} : \log\log n$	$n : \log n$ [Col88], [AKS83]
Element Distinctness	same as sorting	same as sorting	same as sorting
1-Dimensional String Matching	$n : 1$	$n^{3/2+\epsilon} : 1$ or $n^{3/2} : \log^* n$	$\frac{n}{\log\log n} : \log\log n$ [BBG+89]
2-Dimensional String Matching	$n : 1$	$n^{3/2+\epsilon} : 1$ or $n^{3/2} : \log^* n$	$\frac{n}{\log\log n} : \log\log n$

Table 1: Comparison of DFT-Circuit and DFT-VLSIO Algorithms with PRAM Algorithms

Let us first summarize the $2-D$ VLSI model, which is essentially the same as the one described by Thompson [Tho79]. A computation is abstracted as a communication graph. A communication graph is very much like a flow graph with the primitives being some basic operators that are realizable as electrical devices. Two communicating nodes are adjacent in this graph. A layout can be viewed as a convex embedding of the communication graph in a Cartesian grid. Each grid point can either have a processor or a wire passing through. A wire cannot go through a grid point with a processor unless it is a terminal of the processor at that grid point. The number of layers is limited to some constant γ. Thus both the fanin and fanout are bounded by 4γ. Wires have unit width and bandwidth and processors have unit area. The initial data values are localized to some constant area, to preclude an encoding of the results. The input words are read at the designated nodes called input ports. The input and subsequent computation are synchronous and each input bit is available only once. The input and output conventions are where-determinate but need not be when-determinate.

2.2 VLSIO Model

The recent development of high speed electro-optical computing devices [Jor89], [HJP88] allows us to overcome the 2-D limitations of traditional VLSI. In particular, the optical computing devices allow computation to be done in 3 dimensions, with full resolution in all the dimensions.

A rather different model for 3-D electro-optical computation is described in [BR87], which combines use of optics and electronics components in ways that models currently feasible devices. This model is known as the VLSIO model, with the O standing for optics. In this model, the fundamental building block is the optical box, consisting of a rectilinear parallelepiped whose surface consists of electronic devices modeled by the 2-D VLSI model and whose interior consists of optical devices. Communication from the surface is assumed to be done via electrical-optical transducers on the surface. Given specified inputs on the surface of the optical box, it is assumed that the output to the surface is produced in 1 time unit. Note that we do not rule out the possibility of two wide optical beams crossing, while still transmitting distinct information. However, there is an assumption (justified by a theorem of Gabor [Gab61]) that a beam of cross section A can transmit at most $O(A)$ bits per unit time. This is the only assumption made about the power of the optical boxes.

For the purposes of upper bounds, we would have to be more specific about the computational power of optical boxes. The use of electro-optical devices will certainly allow us to overcome the 2-D limitations. The VLSIO potentially has more advantages over 2-D VLSI than just 3-dimensional interconnections of 3-D VLSI [LR86], [Pre83]. In particular, it is well known that a 2 dimensional Fourier transform or its inverse can be computed by an optical device in unit time. In our discrete model, we assume that an optical box of size $\sqrt{n} \times \sqrt{n} \times \sqrt{n}$ with an input image of size $\sqrt{n} \times \sqrt{n}$ can compute a 2-D Discrete Fourier Transform (DFT) in unit time. We call this the DFT-VLSIO model.

This is consistent with the capabilities of the electro-optical components constructed in practice. In this case, the VLSIO model is clearly more powerful than the 3-D VLSI model, *e.g.* since in that model we cannot do a DFT in constant time. A VLSIO device consists of a convex volume with a packing of optical boxes whose interiors do not intersect, but may be connected by wires between their surfaces. This allows for communication between two optical boxes. *Note that the VLSIO model encompasses the 3-D VLSI model as a subcase: the particular subcase where each optical box is just a 2-D surface with no volume.*

A VLSIO circuit is an embedding of a communication graph with the nodes corresponding to optical boxes in a three dimensional grid. The volume of a VLSIO circuit is the volume of the smallest convex box enclosing it. Due to Gabor's theorem [Gab61] establishing a finite bound on the bandwidth of an optical beam, without any loss of generality, we assume that only binary values are used in transmitting information.

2.3 The DFT-Circuit Model

Let R be an ordered ring. A circuit over R consists of an acyclic graph with a distinguished set of input nodes, and a labeling of all the non-input nodes with a ring operation. In the DFT circuit model, we allow:

1. scalar operations such as $\times$, $+$ and comparison with 2 inputs, and
2. DFT gates with n inputs and n outputs.

The *size* of the DFT circuit is the sum of the number of edges and the number of nodes. Recall from Parberry, Schnitger [PS88] that a *threshold* circuit is a Boolean circuit of unbounded fanin, where each gate computes the threshold operation. Threshold circuits are shown in Reif and Tate [RT87] to compute a large number of algebraic problems such as polynomial division, triangular Toeplitz inverse, integer division, sin, cosine etc. in $n^{O(1)}$ size and simultaneous $O(1)$ depth.

Since the first output of a DFT gate is the sum of the inputs, and since comparison operations are allowed, a DFT circuit clearly has at least the power of a threshold circuit of the same size and depth. The question we address in this paper is the power of the DFT operation above and beyond its power to compute threshold. Note that no non-trivial lower bounds on a threshold circuit computing a DFT are known. But, just by its definition, at least n threshold gates are required for a DFT computation.

3 Algorithms

We use the following scheme to describe the algorithms. For each problem, we state the problem, followed by the DFT circuit algorithm which in turn is followed by the DFT-VLSIO algorithm.

Before we sketch the algorithms, let us demonstrate a computation of 1-D DFT using a 2-D DFT primitive. After this, we would assume that a 1-D DFT can also be done in unit time in both DFT-circuit and DFT-VLSIO models.

For DFT the input is a vector $x = [x_0\ x_1 \dots x_{n-1}]$ and the output is $\vec{y} = A\vec{x}$. A is a $n \times n$ DFT matrix whose ijth element is ω^{ij} where ω is a principal nth root of unity.

The following algorithm, a variant of Agarwal and Burrus algorithm [AB74], uses a series of two-dimensional DFT operations to realize a one-dimensional DFT. We assume a commutative ring R with a principal nth root of unity ω such that $x_i \in R$. Without loss of generality, let us also assume that $\sqrt{n}$ is a power of two. Let us define the following.

$$\begin{aligned} < i,j > &= i\sqrt{n} + j \\ < i,- > &= (i\sqrt{n},\ i\sqrt{n}+1, \dots, i\sqrt{n}) \\ < -,j > &= (j,\ j+\sqrt{n}, \dots, j+n-\sqrt{n}) \end{aligned}$$

Let $\overline{A}^{(\sqrt{n})}$ be the $\sqrt{n} \times \sqrt{n}$ circulant matrix such that $\overline{A}^{(\sqrt{n})}_{ij} = \omega^{\sqrt{n}ij}$.

Algorithm:

1. **for** $j = 0, \dots, \sqrt{n}-1$ in parallel **do** $y_{< j,- >} = \overline{A}^{(\sqrt{n})} x_{< -,j >}$.
2. **for** $j = 0, \dots, \sqrt{n}-1$ and $v = 0, \dots, \sqrt{n}-1$ in parallel **do** $z_{< j,v >} = y_{< j,v >}\, \omega^{jv}$.
3. **for** $v = 0, \dots, \sqrt{n}-1$ in parallel **do** $f_{< -,v >} = \overline{A}^{(\sqrt{n})} z_{< -,v >}$.

The output is $\vec{f} = [f_0\ f_1 \dots f_{n-1}]$.

Proof of Correctness:

$$\begin{aligned} f_{< u,v >} &= \textstyle\sum_{j=0}^{\sqrt{n}-1} z_{< j,v >}\,\omega^{\sqrt{n}ju} && \text{by step 3} \\ &= \textstyle\sum_{j=0}^{\sqrt{n}-1} \left(y_{< j,v >}\omega^{jv}\right)\omega^{\sqrt{n}ju} && \text{by step 2} \\ &= \textstyle\sum_{i=0}^{\sqrt{n}-1}\sum_{j=0}^{\sqrt{n}-1} \left(\left(x_{< i,j >}\omega^{\sqrt{n}iv}\right)\omega^{jv}\right)\omega^{\sqrt{n}ju} \\ &= \textstyle\sum_{i=0}^{\sqrt{n}-1}\sum_{j=0}^{\sqrt{n}-1} x_{< i,j >}\,\omega^{\sqrt{n}iv+jv+\sqrt{n}ju} \\ &= \textstyle\sum_{i=0}^{\sqrt{n}-1}\sum_{j=0}^{\sqrt{n}-1} x_{< i,j >}\,\omega^{< i,j > \cdot < u,v >} \end{aligned}$$

Hence for all $s = 0, \dots, n-1$, $f_s = \sum_{k=0}^{n-1} x_k \omega^{ks}$.

□

Recall that in DFT-VLSIO a n-point DFT takes time $O(1)$ and volume $n^{3/2}$. In this algorithm, the first and third steps perform $\sqrt{n}$, $\sqrt{n}$-point DFT computations and hence take time $O(1)$ and volume $n^{1/4}$. But the second step performs a n-point DFT and hence takes time $O(1)$ and volume $n^{3/2}$. It takes $O(1)$ gates, $O(1)$ depth and $O(n)$ size in DFT-circuit model. The following are some well known applications of DFT, we will just survey.

3.1 Polynomial Multiplication

The input is two $(n-1)$st degree polynomials $p(x) = \sum_{i=0}^{n-1} a_i x^i$ and $q(x) = \sum_{j=0}^{n-1} b_j x^j$. The product of $p(x)$ and $q(x)$ is the $(2n-2)$nd polynomial $p(x)\,q(x) = \sum_{i=0}^{2n-2}\left[\sum_{j=0}^{i} a_j b_{i-j}\right] x^i$. Note that we had shown in the 2-D DFT to 1-D DFT discussion (Section 3) that if the coefficients of a polynomial $p(x)$, a_i are from an underlying ring R, then the DFT of its coefficients can be performed in time $O(1)$ with $O(n^{3/2})$ volume. Let us assume this ring R to be the domain of the coefficients of $p(x)$ and $q(x)$. The principal difficulty in polynomial multiplication is that several multiplications of the coefficients also need to be performed.

DFT-Circuit: First perform the $2n-1$ point DFT of the two input polynomials $p(x)$ and $q(x)$ with $2n-1$ size gates and in $O(1)$ time. This is followed by a dot-product of the two *DFT* vectors in unit time, which involves multiplication of the ith coefficients. Notice that the scalar operations can be performed in unit time using a single scalar gate. The dot-product can, then, be performed in unit time with n gates of size 2 each. This is followed by an inverse DFT of this vector, which is derived in much the same way as a DFT computation. The whole process takes $2n-1$ size and $O(1)$ time.

DFT-VLSIO Model: The one dimensional DFTs can be done in the way described in the previous section in volume $n^{3/2}$ and time $O(1)$. The dot-product of the two DFT vectors is not as trivial in DFT-VLSIO as in DFT-Circuit, as no scalar gates performing multiplication in unit time are available. To multiply $2n-1$ coefficients of $\log n$ bits each, we can use a Wallace tree type of multiplier realized in VLSI [[HP90], pages A46-49]. Such a multiplier takes volume $O(\log^2 n)$ volume with time $O(\log\log n)$. For n such multiplications, the total volume is $O(n\log^2 n)$ with time $O(\log\log n)$.

However, we can do even better if we reduce the integer multiplication of two $\log n$ bit numbers to a polynomial multiplication. A modulo p ring, for an appropriate prime p, will have this property. A $\log n$ bit integer $A = a_{\log n-1}, \ldots, a_1, a_0$ can be considered as a polynomial $\sum_{i=0}^{\log n-1} a_i x^i$ with $x=2$. To multiply the two $\log n$ bit integers A and B, multiply A and B as polynomials. For the polynomial multiplication, take their DFT in volume $O(\log^{3/2} n)$ and time $O(1)$. The dot-product of these $2\log n - 1$-bit DFT vectors can again be done recursively as a polynomial multiplication of two $\log\log n$ bit numbers. This recursive procedure for polynomial multiplication takes time $O(\log^* n)$, where $k = \log^* n$ if $\lfloor \log^{(k)} n \rfloor = 1$. Here $\log^{(k)} n$ stands for k repeated applications of the log function as in log log ... $\log n$. The resource requirement of this algorithm is also $O(n^{3/2})$ volume. To see this, consider the ith level of recursion for $i = 1, \ldots, \log^* n$. At this point, there are $n \log n \log\log n \ldots \log^{(i)} n$ instances of $\log^{(i+1)} n$-bit multiplications. The volume required for this step, then, is $n \log n \log\log n \ldots \log^{(i)} n\, [\log^{(i+1)} n]^{3/2}$. This is $O(n^{3/2})$. Most of this analysis is very simplistic to elaborate the point. A more exact analysis arriving at the same answer can be provided.

There is a third way to do the integer multiplication so as to perform polynomial multiplication in $O(1)$ time with $O(n^{3/2})$ volume. However, the hardware is used more inefficiently in this algorithm, which might argue for using one of the previous algorithms in practice. As we had shown in Section 2.3, a DFT gate can perform thresholding in a trivial way. The first bit of the DFT vector is the sum of all the input bits. A comparison corresponds to an addition, which can also be performed with one DFT operation. Reif and Tate [RT87] show that the integer multiplication can be done in constant depth $[O(f(\epsilon)1)$ for any $\epsilon > 0]$ with threshold gates of total size $O(n^{1+\epsilon})$. A threshold circuit of size $O(n^{1+\epsilon})$ corresponds to a VLSIO circuit of volume $O(n^{\frac{3}{2}+\frac{3\epsilon}{2}})$. Hence, to perform polynomial multiplication in $O(1)$ time, $O(n^{3/2+\epsilon})$ volume is required, for some $\epsilon > 0$.

3.2 Barrel Shifting

The input to this problem is a vector $\vec{x} = [x_0\, x_1 \ldots x_{n-1}]$. The output vector is cyclically shifted by $0 \le c \le n-1$: $\vec{y} = [y_0\, y_1 \cdots y_{n-1}]$ where $y_i = x_{(i-c) \bmod n}$.

DFT-Circuit: A cyclic shift can be reduced to a right shift by doubling the vector size as described in Vuillemin [Vui83]. Let vector $\vec{X}$ be the concatenation of $\vec{x}$ to itself $\vec{x}\vec{x}$. A right shift by c on $\vec{X}$ is equivalent to multiplying the polynomial corresponding to $\vec{X}$ by the polynomial x^c. The multiplication of two $2n$ degree polynomials can be done in time $O(1)$ and with $O(n)$ size.

DFT-VLSIO Model: This is also equivalent to polynomial multiplication and hence can be done in either volume $O(n^{3/2})$ and time $O(\log^* n)$ or $O(n^{3/2+\epsilon})$ volume with $O(1)$ time.

3.3 Prefix Sum

The input is $n+1$ elements $x_0, x_1, \ldots x_n$. The output is all the prefix sums: $\sum_{j=0}^{i} x_j$ for all $0 \leq i \leq n$.

DFT-Circuit: The prefix sum can be reduced to a polynomial multiplication. In particular, consider the multiplication of two polynomials – $\sum_{i=0}^{n} x_i y^i$ and $\sum_{j=o}^{n} y^j$. The multiplication of these two polynomials is $\sum_{i=0}^{2n} \left(\sum_{j=0}^{i} x_j\right) x^i$. Thus the ith coefficient of this product is the ith prefix sum for $0 \leq i \leq n$. This computation takes $O(n)$ size with $O(1)$ time.

DFT-VLSIO Model: Once again, this takes either volume $O(n^{3/2})$ with time $O(\log^* n)$ or $O(n^{3/2+\epsilon})$ volume with $O(1)$ time.

3.4 Polynomial Division

The inputs to this problem are two n and m degree polynomials $p(x)$ and $q(x)$. The output is two polynomials $d(x)$ and $r(x)$ such that $p(x) = d(x)\,q(x) + r(x)$ where degree($r(x)$) < degree($q(x)$).

DFT-Circuit: The polynomial division can be done either with n^3 size in time $O(1)$ or with n size in time $O(\log\log n)$. In the first case, the reciprocal is found by the expression $\frac{1}{1-p(x)} = \sum_{i=0}^{n-1} p(x)^i$. To find the reciprocal of $q(x)$, use $p(x) = 1 - q(x)$. For computing $p(x)^i$, perform the DFT on $p(x)$. In the Fourier domain, every component of DFT($p(x)$) is raised to i to derive the DFT of $p(x)^i$. These powers of the coefficients can be read from a lookup table. An inverse DFT then gives $p(x)^i$. Since we need to compute upto $p(x)^{n-1}$, these DFTs are n^2-point transforms. Computation of each $p(x)^i$ requires n^2 size. Thus the whole computation takes n^3 size with $O(1)$ time. In the second case, a variation of Tate and Reif [RT87] algorithm is used.

3.5 Toeplitz Matrix Multiplication, Inverse and Polynomial GCD and Interpolation

An $n \times n$ matrix M is *Toeplitz* if $M[i,j] = M[i-k, j-k]$ for all $1 \leq i,j \leq n$ and $\forall k$ such that $1 \leq i-k,\ j-k \leq n$. Note that an upper or lower triangular Toeplitz matrix can be multiplied by a vector by use of a single convolution, which reduces it to the polynomial multiplication. The Toeplitz matrix multiplication can be reduced to 4 triangular Toeplitz matrix multiplications. This gives the same DFT-Circuit and DFT-VLSIO complexity for Toeplitz matrix multiplication as the complexity of polynomial multiplication in Section 3.1.

THE TRIANGULAR TOEPLITZ INVERSE is reducible to polynomial division. The general Toeplitz inverse has the same complexity as GCD and POLYNOMIAL INTERPOLATION. All these problems require $\log n$ stages of Toeplitz steps as shown in Pan, Reif [PR87]. Hence they all take time $O(\log n)$ with $O(n)$ size on DFT-Circuit. In DFT-VLSIO, we have two choices for polynomial multiplication. Thus, it either takes time $O(\log n)$ with $O(n^{3/2+\epsilon})$ volume or time $O(\log n \log^* n)$ is needed with volume $O(n^{3/2})$.

3.6 Matrix Multiplication

The input here is two $n \times n$ matrices A and B. The output is another $n \times n$ matrix C, such that $c_{i,j} = \sum_{k=0}^{n-1} a_{i,k} b_{k,j}$.

DFT-Circuit: There are n^2 n-point inner products to be performed. Each inner product is the first component of the DFT of the two vectors. This is equivalent to a n^3-point DFT and hence takes time $O(1)$ with n^3 size.

DFT-VLSIO Model: The matrix multiplication requires n^2 n-point DFT computations. Each n-point DFT takes time $O(1)$ with $n^{3/2}$ volume. Hence the complete computation takes time $O(1)$ with volume $O(n^{7/2})$.

3.7 Matrix Inversion

Given a nonsingular $n \times n$ matrix A, compute its inverse matrix.

DFT-Circuit: By Pan and Reif [PR85], the matrix inversion takes time $O(\log n)$ with n^3 size.

DFT-VLSIO Model: This can be done in time $O(\log n)$ with $n^{7/2}$ volume.

3.8 Transitive Closure

Given an input $n \times n$ matrix A, its transitive closure is to be computed.

DFT-Circuit: The transitive closure takes time $O(\log n)$ with n^3 size.

DFT-VLSIO Model: This can be done in time $O(\log n)$ with $n^{7/2}$ volume.

4 Sorting

In this section, we describe sorting algorithms in the DFT-circuit and DFT-VLSIO models. We show that the sorting can be performed in size n^2 in time $O(1)$ deterministically. A randomized algorithm sorts with size $O(n^{1+\epsilon})$ in time $O(1)$ or in time $O(\log\log n)$ with size $O(n^{1+\epsilon}/\log n)$.

The input is a sequence S of n values $a_1, a_2, \ldots, a_n$, where each value is $\log n$ bits long. The output is a sequence of the same values in an non-descending order.

DFT-Circuit: The algorithm is a variation of Flashsort reported in Reif, Valiant [RV87]. Let us first show that a sequence of n numbers can be rank-sorted in time $O(1)$ with n^2 size. The gate $p_{i,j}$ compares a_i and a_j and outputs a 1 if $a_i > a_j$. It outputs a 0 otherwise. The rank of a_i is the sum of the output values of the gates $p_{i,1}, p_{i,2}, \ldots, p_{i,n}$. The 0th component of the DFT of these n values gives this sum. Let us present the Flashsort based sorting algorithm.

1. Take a random sample of n^ϵ elements of S to form a sample set S' of size n^ϵ, for $0 < \epsilon < 1/2$.
2. Rank sort S' in time $O(1)$ with n size.
3. Form a set S'' by choosing every $(\log n)$th element from S'. A result in Reif and Valiant [RV87] shows that S'' splits S into the subsets of expected size $n^{1-\epsilon}c\log n$ and with a high probability, $1 - \frac{1}{\log^c n}$, of size at most $(1+\mu)\, n^{1-\epsilon}c\log n$ where μ is of the order of $\frac{d}{\log n}$ where $c, d \geq 2$.
4. Separate S into the sets $S_0, S_1, \ldots, S_t$ on the basis of S'', where t is in the range from $\frac{n^\epsilon}{(1+\mu)c\log n} + 1$ to $\frac{n^\epsilon}{c\log n} + 1$. This split can be done with rank-ordering using $c\frac{n^\epsilon}{\log n}$ size circuit for each element in S in time $O(1)$ for a total size of $c\frac{n^{1+\epsilon}}{\log n}$.
5. Use the algorithm recursively for each S_i in parallel until the subproblems are reduced to size n^ϵ each. Then the $n^{1-\epsilon}$ instances of n^ϵ subproblems can be ranksorted with $n^{1+\epsilon}$ size in time $O(1)$. In this case, the whole algorithm takes expected time $O(\frac{1-\epsilon}{\epsilon})$ with $O(n^{1+\epsilon})$ size. Or the recursion can terminate when the subproblems have size $O(1)$*. Then the total time is $O(\log\log n)$ with size $O(n^{1+\epsilon}/\log n)$.

The straight rank-ordering gives an $O(1)$ time algorithm with n^2 size.

DFT-VLSIO Model: The rank sorting algorithm can be implemented in DFT-VLSIO in volume $n^{5/2}$ in time $O(1)$. While the Flashsort based algorithm has expected time $O(1)$ with volume $O(n^{1+\frac{3\epsilon}{2}})$. When the recursion terminates at unit sized subproblems, then the time is $O(\log\log n)$ with volume $O(n^{1+\frac{3\epsilon}{2}}/\log^{3/2} n)$.

4.1 Element Distinctness

The input to this problem is a set of n, $\log n$-bit values. The problem is to determine if all of the n words are distinct.

DFT-Circuit: Sort the n elements of the set. Then compare each element in the sorted list with its left and right neighbors. The complexity is dominated by the sorting algorithm. Hence this is a $O(1)$ time algorithm with size $O(n^{1+\epsilon})$. All the other bounds from sorting also hold.

DFT-VLSIO Model: Once again, the sorting part has the complexity derived in the previous subsection. This is followed by $3n$ comparisons. Each comparison can be done in time $O(1)$ and $O(\log^{3/2} n)$ volume.

*Technically, for the probabilistic analysis of Flashsort to work, the problem size should be at least a polynomial in log (polylog). At that point a less efficient deterministic algorithm can be used. However, for the simplicity of exposition we have chosen to give this *inaccurate* version, as they both lead to the same amount of resources.

Hence the $O(\log\log n)$ time, $O(n^{1+\frac{3\epsilon}{2}}/\log^{3/2} n)$ volume algorithm still works. For a unit time algorithm, use the unit time sorting algorithm followed by the unit time comparisons. The volume requirements of the comparison phase are dominated by $O(n^{1+\frac{3\epsilon}{2}})$, the volume requirements of the sorting phase. Thus the $O(1)$ time, $O(n^{1+\frac{3\epsilon}{2}})$ volume sorting algorithm also works.

5 String Matching

5.1 One Dimensional String Matching

Given a binary string $A = a_0a_1a_2\ldots a_n$ and a binary pattern $B = b_0b_1b_2\ldots b_m$ with $m \leq n$, find all the occurrences of B in A.

DFT-Circuit: We reduce the problem of string matching to that of polynomial multiplication. The reduction of string matching to the integer multiplication was known to Kosaraju [Kos89] and is due to Mike Fischer. This provides a $O(1)$ time algorithm with n size. Consider two polynomials derived from the strings A and B: $A(x) = \sum_{i=0}^{n} a_i x^i$ and $B(x) = \sum_{j=0}^{m} b_j x^j$. The product of two polynomials $C(x) = A(x)\,B(x)$ can be written as $\sum_{i=0}^{m+n} c_i x^i$ where $c_i = \sum_{j=0}^{n} a_j b_{i-j}$. Note that a coefficient c_i, for $m \leq i \leq n$, equals the number of places where $b_0b_1\ldots b_m$ 1-matches the substring $a_ia_{i+1}\ldots a_{i+m}$, *i.e.* the number of places both the strings have a 1. Repeat the same process for the complementary strings of A and B. The sum of c_i and $\bar{c}_i$ is $m+1$ iff $b_0b_1\ldots b_m$ matches the substring $a_ia_{i+1}\ldots a_{i+m}$. This procedure requires two polynomial multiplications and $O(n)$ scalar operations. Hence it takes time $O(1)$ with $O(n)$ size.

DFT-VLSIO Model: The same reduction gives a $O(1)$ time $n^{3/2+\epsilon}$ volume VLSIO circuit. It can also be done in time $O(\log^* n)$ using $O(n^{3/2})$ volume.

5.2 Two Dimensional String Matching

This idea can be extended to **two dimensional string matching** as well. Here the input is $A = (a_{i,j} \mid 0 \leq i,j \leq n)$ and $B = (b_{i,j} \mid 0 \leq i,j \leq m)$. We wish to find a match of B in A, that is if $\exists i,j,\ \forall k,l \in (0,\ldots m)$

$a_{i+k,\,j+l} = b_{k,l}$.

DFT-Circuit: The solution uses 2-D DFT in a way similar to the one dimensional string matching. The 2-dimensional string matching problem can be reduced to a multiplication of two polynomials in two variables. Let us form a polynomial $A(x,y) = \sum_{i=0}^{n}\sum_{j=0}^{n} a_{i,j}x^iy^j$ and $B(x,y) = \sum_{k=0}^{m}\sum_{l=0}^{m} b_{k,l}x^ky^l$. Let the product of $A(x,y)$ and $B(x,y)$ be given by $\sum_{i=0}^{mn}\sum_{j=0}^{mn} c_{i,j}x^iy^j$ where $c_{i,j} = \sum_{k=0}^{n}\sum_{l=0}^{n} a_{i,j}b_{i-k,\,j-l}$. Similarly let $\left(\sum_{i,j=0}^{n}(1-a_{i,j})\,x^iy^j\right)\left(\sum_{k,l=0}^{m}(1-b_{k,l})x^ky^l\right) = \left(\sum_{i',j'=0}^{mn}\bar{c}_{i',j'}x^{i'}y^{j'}\right)$. Then there is a match at i',j' iff $c_{i',j'} + \bar{c}_{i',j'} = (m+1)^2$.

This requires two n^2-point 2-D DFT operations. The resource requirements are $O(1)$ time with linear size - $O(n)$.

DFT-VLSIO Model: The previous approach gives a $O(1)$ time $n^{3/2+\epsilon}$ volume VLSIO circuit for two dimensional string matching as well. The second approach to polynomial multiplication takes time $O(\log^* n)$ with volume $n^{3/2}$.

6 Comparison with VLSIO Lower Bounds

As we had stated earlier, we do not have lower bounds in the DFT-Circuit model to compare the optimality of our algorithms. However, Barakat and Reif [BR87] showed a lower bound of $\Omega\left(I^{3/2}\right)$ on $VT^{3/2}$ of a VLSIO computation, where V is the volume and T is the time of the computation. This lower bound applies to the DFT-VLSIO model as well. In [TR90], we derive a lower bound of $\Omega(I^{3/2})$ on the uniswitch energy of a VLSIO computation. All these algorithms can be realized as uniswitch computations. Then the uniswitch energy is equivalent to volume. Hence the other useful lower bound on these problems in DFT-VLSIO is $V = \Omega(I^{3/2})$. For most of the problems in Sections 3, 4 and 5, the information complexity I is $\Omega(n)$. Table 2 compares our algorithms with respect to these lower bounds.

All the algorithms except the ones for matrix multiplication, inversion and transitive closure are within a polylog factor of the lower bounds. Deterministic sorting algorithm is also off by a factor of $\sqrt{n}$. Since

	Lower Bound E and $VT^{3/2}$	Upper Bounds $E : VT^{3/2}$
1-D DFT	$\Omega(n^{3/2})$	$O(n^{3/2}) : O(n^{3/2})$
Poly Mult	$\Omega(n^{3/2})$	$O(n^{3/2+\epsilon}) : O(n^{3/2+\epsilon})$ or $O(n^{3/2}\log^* n) : O(n^{3/2}(\log^* n)^{3/2})$
Barrel Shift	$\Omega(n^{3/2})$	$O(n^{3/2+\epsilon}) : O(n^{3/2+\epsilon})$ or $O(n^{3/2}\log^* n) : O(n^{3/2}(\log^* n)^{3/2})$
Prefix Sum	$\Omega(n^{3/2})$	$O(n^{3/2+\epsilon}) : O(n^{3/2+\epsilon})$ or $O(n^{3/2}\log^* n) : O(n^{3/2}(\log^* n)^{3/2})$
Toeplitz Matrix Inverse and Poly GCD & Interpolation	$\Omega(n^{3/2})$	$O(n^{3/2+\epsilon}\log n) : O(n^{3/2+\epsilon}\log^{3/2} n)$ or $O(n^{3/2}\log n\log^* n) : O(n^{3/2}(\log n\log^* n)^{3/2})$
Matrix Mult	$\Omega(n^3)$	$O(n^{7/2}) : O(n^{7/2})$
Matrix Inversion Transitive Closure	$\Omega(n^3)$	$O(n^{7/2}) : O(n^{7/2}\log^{3/2} n)$
Sorting	$\Omega(n^{3/2})$	$O(n^{5/2}) : O(n^{5/2})$ or *(probabilistic)* $O(n^{1+\frac{3\epsilon}{2}}) : O(n^{1+\frac{3\epsilon}{2}})$ or $O(\frac{n^{1+\frac{3\epsilon}{2}}}{\log^{3/2} n}) : O\left(\frac{n^{1+\frac{3\epsilon}{2}}(\log\log n)^{3/2}}{\log^{3/2} n}\right)$
Element Distinctness	same as sorting	same as sorting
1-Dimensional String Matching	$\Omega(n^{3/2})$	$O(n^{3/2+\epsilon}) : O(n^{3/2+\epsilon})$ or $O(n^{3/2}\log^* n) : O(n^{3/2}(\log^* n)^{3/2})$
2-Dimensional String Matching	$\Omega(n^{3/2})$	$O(n^{3/2+\epsilon}) : O(n^{3/2+\epsilon})$ or $O(n^{3/2}\log^* n) : O(n^{3/2}(\log^* n)^{3/2})$

Table 2: Comparison of DFT-VLSIO Algorithms with the VLSIO Lower Bounds

the algorithms for DFT-Circuit and DFT-VLSIO models are identical, in the absence of lower bounds in DFT-Circuit model, we conjecture that the same type of optimality is achieved in the DFT-Circuit model as well.

7 Generalization of the DFT Model

Our assumption that an optical box can compute only a 2-D DFT in unit time is appropriate for many thin (linear) optical filters. But this assumption may be too restrictive to model *thick* optical components (such as volume holograms). In this case, we generalize our models so that an optical box or gate can compute a matrix multiplication of *displacement rank* d in unit time using n size circuit (or n processors). The resulting model will be called DFT_d model.

A matrix A has *displacement rank* d if $A = \sum_{i=1}^{d} U_i L_i$, where U_i, L_i are upper and lower triangular Toeplitz matrices [defined in Subsection 3.5] respectively. The notion of displacement rank was first introduced in [MK77] and is restated in [KKM79]. Note that if A has displacement rank d, then it can be multiplied in $2d$ triangular Toeplitz matrix multiplications, and thus $2d$ convolutions. Thus the DFT_d model can be simulated by the DFT_1 model within a factor of $2d$ slowdown.

8 Conclusions

VLSI is, perhaps, the most commonly used technology to build parallel processors. However, we do not write our algorithms at that level of abstraction. PRAM (parallel random access machine) has proved to be a nice abstraction for writing the algorithms. With the advent of optical computers, we have a need for a similar clean model for the parallel algorithm development removed from the details of the technology, and yet capturing all the essential features. In this paper, we proposed two such models, namely DFT-Circuit and DFT-VLSIO. The DFT-Circuit model can very well be used as DFT-PRAM model. The salient characteristic of these models is that they can compute a non-trivial operation – DFT, in unit time.

We investigated the fundamental paradigms for algorithm design in such a novel medium. In particular, we used two algorithms very frequently. We provide an efficient algorithm to compute 1-dimensional DFT from the physically available 2-dimensional DFT. We also provide an efficient solution to the parallel-prefix computation. Using these two techniques, we have provided constant-time or near constant time algorithms for many problems including matrix computations, sorting and string matching. The string matching algorithm is particularly new. We also showed that most of these algorithms are optimal within a polylog factor with respect to VLSIO lower bounds.

This paper is just a beginning. We hope that our model would provide an incentive for many computer scientists to be interested in the algorithm design task for the now emerging field of optical computing. It is not at all clear how one tackles classes of problems, such as geometric computations, in an efficient way in this model. Similarly, some non-trivial lower bounds in this model would be desirable.

References

[AB74] R. C. Agarwal and C. S. Burrus. Fast One-Dimensional Digital Convolution by Multidimensional Techniques. *IEEE Trans. on Acoustics, Speech and Signal Processing*, ASSP-22(1):1–10, February 1974.

[AKS83] M. Ajtai, J. Komlos, and E. Szemeredi. An $O(n \log n)$ Sorting Network. *Combinatorica*, 3:1–19, 1983.

[BBG+89] O. Berkman, D. Breslauer, Z. Galil, B. Schieber, and U. Vishkin. Highly Parallelizable Problems. In *Proceedings of ACM Symposium on Theory of Computing*, pages 309–319. ACM-SIGACT, 1989.

[BR87] R. Barakat and J. Reif. Lower Bounds on the Computational Efficiency of Optical Computing Systems. *Applied Optics*, 26:1015–1018, March 1987.

[Col88] R. Cole. Parallel Merge Sort. *SIAM Journal of Computing*, 17(4):770–785, August 1988.

[CW87] D. Coppersmith and S. Winograd. Matrix Multiplication via Arithmetic Progressions. In *Proceedings of ACM Symposium on Theory of Computing*, pages 1–6. ACM-SIGACT, 1987.

[Fei88] D. G. Feitelson. *Optical Computing, A Survey for Computer Scientists.* MIT Press, 1988.

[FW78] S. Fortune and J. Wyllie. Parallelism in Random Access Machines. In *Proceedings of ACM Symposium on Theory of Computing*, pages 114–118. ACM-SIGACT, 1978.

[Gab61] D. Gabor. Light and Information. In E. Wolf, editor, *Progress in Optics*, pages 111–153. North-Holland, Amsterdam, Holland., 1961.

[Goo82] J. W. Goodman. Architectural Development of Optical Data Processing Systems. *Journal of Electrical and Electronics Engineering - IE Aust. and IREE Aust.*, 2(3):139–149, September 1982.

[HJP88] V. P. Heuring, H. F. Jordan, and J. Pratt. A Bit-Serial Architecture for Optical Computing. Technical Report OCS Technical Report 88-01a, Optoelectronic Computing Center, University of Colorado, Boulder, March 1988.

[Hor87] J. L. Horner. *Optical Signal Processing.* Academic Press, 1987.

[HP90] J. L. Hennessy and D. Patterson. *Computer Architecture: A Quantitative Approach.* Morgan-Kaufmann, 1990.

[Iiz83] K. Iizuka. *Engineering Optics*, volume 35 of Springer Series in Optical Sciences. Springer-Verlag, second edition, 1983.

[Jor89] H. F. Jordan. Pipelined Digital Optical Computing. Technical Report OCS Technical Report 89-34, Optoelectronic Computing Center, University of Colorado, Boulder, 1989.

[KF86] M. V. Klein and T. E. Furtak. *Optics.* John Wiley & Sons: New York, second edition, 1986.

[KKM79] T. Kailath, S. Y. Kung, and M. Morf. Displacement Ranks of Matrices and Linear Equations. *J. Math. Anal. Appl.*, 68(2):395–407, April 1979.

[Kos89] S. R. Kosaraju, October 1989. personal communication.

[Kun79] H.T. Kung. Let's Design Algorithms for VLSI Systems. In *Proceedings of the Caltech Conference on Advanced Research in VLSI: Architecture, Design, Fabrication*, pages 65–90. Caltech, January 1979.

[LR86] F. T. Leighton and A. L. Rosenberg. Three-Dimensional Circuit Layouts. *SIAM Journal on Computing*, 15(3):793–813, March 1986.

[MJR89] E. S. Maniloff, K. M. Johnson, and J. Reif. Holographic Routing Network for Parallel Processing Machines. In *Proceedings of SPIE International Congress on Optical Science and Engineering.* SPIE, April 1989.

[MK77] M. Morf and T. Kailath. Recent Results in Least-Squares Estimation Theory. *Ann. Econ. and Soc. Meas.*, 6(3):261–274, 1977.

[PR85] V. Pan and J. Reif. Efficient Parallel Solution of Linear Systems. In *Proceedings of the ACM Symposium on Theory of Computing*, pages 143–152. ACM-SIGACT, 1985. also to appear as Fast and efficient parallel solution of dense linear systems in Computers and Mathematics with Applications.

[PR87] V. Pan and J. Reif. Some Polynomial and Toeplitz Matrix Computations. In *Proceedings of the 27th IEEE Symposium on Foundations of Computer Science*, pages 173–184. IEEE, 1987.

[Pre83] F. P. Preparata. Optimal Three-Dimensional VLSI Layouts. *Math. Systems Theory*, 16:1–8, 1983.

[PS88] I. Parberry and G. Schnitger. Parallel Computation with Threshold Functions. *Journal of Computer and System Sciences*, 36(3):278–301, June 1988.

[RT87] J. Reif and S. Tate. On Threshold Circuits and Polynomial Computation. In *Proceedings of 2nd Structure in Complexity Theory Conference.* ACM-SIGACT, 1987. Revised version: On Threshold Circuits and Efficient, Constant Depth Polynomial Computation, August 1988.

[RV87] J. Reif and L. Valiant. A Logarithmic Time Sort on Linear Size Networks. *Journal of the Association for Computing Machinery*, 34(1):60–76, January 1987.

[SS79] W. J. Savitch and M. Stimson. Time Bounded Random Access Machines with Parallel Processing. *Journal of the ACM*, 26:103–118, 1979.

[Tho79] C.D. Thompson. Area-Time Complexity for VLSI. In *Proceedings of ACM Symposium on Theory of Computing.* ACM-SIGACT, 1979.

[Tho80] C. D. Thompson. *A Complexity Theory for VLSI.* PhD thesis, Department of Computer Science, Carnegie-Mellon University, Pittsburgh, 1980.

[TR90] A. Tyagi and J. Reif. Energy Complexity of Optical Computations. In *Proceedings of the Second IEEE Symposium on Parallel and Distributed Processing.* IEEE, December 1990. to appear.

[Vui83] J. Vuillemin. A Combinatorial Limit to the Computing Power of VLSI Circuits. *IEEE Transactions on Computers*, pages 294–300, March 1983.

The Power of Collision: Randomized Parallel Algorithms for Chaining and Integer Sorting

Rajeev Raman

Computer Science Department
University of Rochester
Rochester,NY 14627
email: raman@cs.rochester.edu

Abstract

We address the problem of sorting n integers each in the range $\{0,\ldots,m-1\}$ in parallel on the PRAM model of computation. We present a randomized algorithm that runs with very high probability in time $O(\lg n/\lg\lg n + \lg\lg m)$ with a processor-time product of $O(n \lg\lg m)$ and $O(n)$ space on the CRCW (COLLISION) PRAM [7]. The main features of this algorithm is that it matches the run-time and processor requirements of the algorithms in the existing literature [2, 10], while it assumes a weaker model of computation and uses a *linear* amount of space. The techniques used extend to improved randomized algorithms for the problem of *chaining* [11, 15], which is the following: given an array $x_1,\ldots,x_n$, such that m of the locations contain non-zero elements, to chain together all the non-zero elements into a linked list. We give randomized algorithms that run in $O(1)$ time using n processors, whenever m is not too close to n. A byproduct of our research is the weakening of the model of computation required by some other sorting algorithms.

1 Introduction and Previous Work

The problem of *integer sorting* in parallel has received a lot of attention in recent years. This is a restricted version of sorting where the keys are integers that are known to lie within a range that is not too large compared to the size of the set to be sorted. This problem is apparently simpler than *general* (comparison-based) sorting, where the keys are not known to have any particular structure. A special case called the *polynomial* integer sorting problem is of special interest: this is the problem of sorting n integers each in the range $\{0,\ldots,n^{O(1)}\}$. This problem can be solved sequentially in linear time on a RAM using radix sorting [13], in contrast to the well-known $\Omega(n \lg n)$ lower bound on comparison-based sorting. This difference in complexity shows up in the case of parallel sorting algorithms as well. For parallel algorithms, a fast run-time achieved without excessive use of processors is desired. Therefore, we say that a parallel algorithm achieves *optimal speedup* if its processor-time product is within a constant factor of the best known sequential algorithm (for convenience, we say that a parallel algorithm that achieves optimal speedup is *optimal*). Since the best sequential algorithm for any problem is trivially an optimal parallel algorithm, we are interested in parallel algorithms that optimally achieve a run time that is polylogarithmic in n.

Efforts at finding optimal parallel algorithms for sorting problems have met with mixed success. While an optimal logarithmic time PRAM algorithm has been discovered for the general sorting problem [4], the best known parallel algorithm for solving the polynomial integer sorting problem has processor time product of $O(n \lg\lg n)$ with a run time of $O(\lg n/\lg\lg n)$ [2]. Hagerup [10] had previously obtained a similar processor-time product and logarithmic run time for this problem. An optimal algorithm is known for the special case of sorting n integers in the range $\{0,\ldots,n-1\}$ [16]. This algorithm is not *stable*, *i.e.*, the order of records with equal keys may not remain the same in the output as in the input, so this procedure cannot be used to solve the polynomial integer sorting problem in general. A stable sorting procedure for keys in the range $\{0,\ldots,\lg n-1\}$ was also given in [16]. The algorithm of Bhatt *et. al.* also sorts integers in the range $\{0,\ldots,m-1\}$ in in $O(\lg n/\lg\lg n + \lg\lg m)$ time with a processor time product of $O(n \lg\lg m)$. The best sequential RAM algorithm for this problem is that of Kirkpatrick and Reisch [12] whose algorithm runs in $O(n(\lg\lg m - \lg\lg n))$ time. The algorithm of Bhatt *et. al.* thus achieves optimal speedup whenever $\lg\lg m = (1+\Omega(1))\lg\lg n$. When $\lg\lg m = O(\lg n/\lg\lg n)$, no faster algorithm can be obtained for this problem, by using any polynomial number of processors. However, there are shortcomings in the algorithm of Bhatt *et. al.*: besides being non-optimal, it runs on a strong model of parallel computation and uses a large amount ($O(nm^{\epsilon})$) of space.

While we are unable to achieve the primary goal of optimality in this paper, we do address the latter criticisms (strength of model and large amounts of space) to some extent. There are reasons (besides the obvious reason of obtaining a stronger result) for attempting to weaken model of computation used. Such an endeavor gives insight into how much of the properties of the model of computation used are necessary for the purposes of the result. In addition, current parallel computer technology is at a stage where even the assumptions of the weakest PRAM model seem unrealistic, and so weakening the model is another step in the direction of practicality. The algorithm of Bhatt *et. al.* runs on the CRCW (ARBITRARY) PRAM (abbreviated by ARBITRARY) model of computation. This model was introduced by Vishkin [18] and is a concurrent-write PRAM with the property that if several processors attempt simultaneously to write to a location, an arbitrary one succeeds. Our algorithm works on the CRCW (COLLISION) PRAM (abbreviated by COLLISION) introduced in [8] as a synchronous version of the conflict resolution scheme used by Ethernet. This model has the property that in case of a write conflict, the contents of the memory location being written into are erased and a special collision symbol appears in the location instead. It was shown in [8, 7] that COLLISION was strictly weaker than ARBITRARY, *i.e.*, COLLISION cannot simulate ARBITRARY without loss of time or without increasing the number of processors. The algorithm of Bhatt *et. al.* repeatedly uses the power of ARBITRARY to do precisely what was proved to be difficult for COLLISION in [7]. Our algorithm sorts integers from $\{0,\ldots,m-1\}$ on the COLLISION model of computation and runs with very high probability within $O(\lg n/\lg\lg n + \lg\lg m)$ time using *linear* space. The processor-time product of our algorithm is $O(n \lg\lg m)$, which, like the algorithm of Bhatt *et. al.*, matches the efficiency of Kirkpatrick and Reisch's sequential algorithm whenever $\lg\lg m = (1+\Omega(1))\lg\lg n$. Our algorithm is randomized, however, and runs with probability $1-n^{-\beta}$ within the stated time, for any prespecified integer β. Using the notation from [16], when an algorithm runs within time $O(T(n))$ with probability $1-n^{-\beta}$, for any prespecified integer β, we say that the algorithm runs in time $\tilde{O}(T(n))$.

Given an array of elements $x_1,\ldots,x_n$, m of which are non-zero, the *(unordered) chaining* problem is to chain all the non-zero elements into a linked list. If the order of the elements in the list is required to be the same as their order of occurence in the original array, then we get the *ordered chaining* problem. The version of the problem where an upper bound k on the number of non-zero elements as part is given of the input is called the *k-chaining* problem. To perform this task, either m processors, one for each non-zero element, or n processors, one for each element of the array are given. This problem is motivated by the fact that typically, database operations involve more than just finding all the records that satisfy a particular predicate: usually they have to be retrieved as well, in order to process them. In the parallel context, we might suppose that one processor is associated with each record, and when a query is presented, each processor determines whether the record it has matches the query predicate or not, following which the processors, in parallel, chain the records so found for further operations. This problem also has applications to processor reallocation and has been studied before in [11, 15]. Ragde [15] gives a CRCW PRAM algorithm for ordered chaining that runs in $O(\alpha(n))$ time using n processors (here $\alpha(n)$ is a functional inverse of Ackermann's function, and grows very slowly indeed). Ragde posed the problem of whether or not algorithms for chaining can be found which run in constant time using a linear number of processors, and was able to show that whenever $m < n^{1/4-\epsilon}$, unordered chaining can be done in constant time. We address this problem, and show that even for values of m which are very close to n, chaining can be done in $\tilde{O}(1)$ time. More precisely, we show that whenever $m < n/\lg^{(i)} n$, for any fixed i, *ordered* chaining can be done in $\tilde{O}(1)$ time using n processors. We also investigate a natural generalization of the chaining problem, and give a constant time algorithm that is not implied by any of the existing chaining algorithms.

Remark: We would like to point out some similarities between our work and that in the existing literature. Our sorting algorithm is similar to a randomized simulation of an algorithm for simulating the execution of an algorithm for the PRIORITY model on a model called COLLISION$^+$ [3] (which is stronger than COLLISION). The idea of hashing to reduce the space required by a parallel sorting algorithm was recently used independently by Matias and Vishkin [14] to obtain a linear-space sorting algorithm, but our algorithm is superior to theirs in all respects, since while it uses the same amount of resources, it runs on a weaker model of computation, and guarantees its time bounds with much higher probability. Besides, their algorithm cannot be sped up to sublogarithmic speeds. (It is possible that by applying some of our ideas their algorithm may be modified to have properties similar to ours.)

2 Preliminaries

2.1 Existing Tools and Techniques Used

The *prefix sum problem* is the following: given n integers $x_1, \ldots, x_n$ in an array, to evaluate all of the sums $ps_i = \sum_{j=1}^{i} x_i$, for $1 \leq i \leq n$. Cole and Vishkin [5] prove that the prefix sum problem can be solved optimally in $O(\lg n/\lg\lg n)$ time on the COMMON model of computation. However, their result only needs the ability to compute the logical OR function in constant time. Since COLLISION permits this as well, we have the following lemma:

Lemma 1 ([5], Theorem 2.2.2) *The prefix-sum computation of n integers, each of $O(\log n)$ bits, can be done optimally in $O(\lg n/\lg\lg n)$ time on the* COLLISION *model of computation.*

We can modify the following algorithm in [16] to run on the COLLISION model of computation (the proof can be found in the appendix):

Lemma 2 *A set of n general keys can be sorted in $\tilde{O}(\lg n/\lg\lg n)$ time using $n(\lg n)^\epsilon$* COLLISION *processors, for any constant $\epsilon > 0$.*

Using the above lemma, we see that the following results due to Rajasekaran and Reif [16], which are claimed for the ARBITRARY model, also work on the COLLISION model:

Lemma 3 ([16], Theorems 3.1 and 4.2) *A set of n integers in the range* $\{0, \ldots, n(\lg n)^{O(1)}\}$ *can be sorted in* $\tilde{O}(\lg n)$ *time using* $n/\lg n$ *processors, and in* $\tilde{O}(\lg n/\lg\lg n)$ *time using* $n(\lg\lg n)^2/\lg n$ *processors on the* COLLISION *model of computation.*

The "leftmost one in memory" problem can be stated as follows: given n consecutive memory locations $M_1, \ldots, M_n$, each containing a 0 or a 1, find the least index i such that $M_i = 1$. Fich *et. al.* [7] prove the following:

Lemma 4 ([7], pp. 609–610) *"Leftmost one in memory" problems can be solved in* $O(1)$ *time by n* COLLISION *processors, each associated with one memory location.*

Finally, we will use the following result due to Ragde related to the chaining problem. The original result used the COMMON model of computation, but it is clear that COLLISION could be substituted to obtain the same result.

Lemma 5 ([15], Theorem 1) *Given n memory locations,* $M_1, \ldots, M_n$, *and a number m, we can in constant time using n* COLLISION *processors, for any value of m, either conclude that there are more than m non-zero items in the memory location, or move the items into* M_1 *through* $M_{m^4 \lg n}$.

2.2 Bounds on Tails of Distributions

We now prove or state bounds on the tails of certain distributions. We say that X is $B(n,p)$-distributed if X is a binomially distributed variable with parameters n and p, *i.e.*, X is the random variable that corresponds to the number of successes in n trials, each of which independently has probability of success p. Then:

Lemma 6 (Chernoff bounds, [1]) *Let X a random variable that is* $B(n,p)$*-distributed, and let* $LE(\epsilon, n, p) = \Pr[X \leq (1-\epsilon)np]$. *Then:*

$$LE(\epsilon, n, p) \leq e^{-\epsilon^2 np/3}. \tag{1}$$

Similarly, if $GE(\epsilon, n, p) = \Pr[X \geq (1+\epsilon)np]$, *then:*

$$GE(\epsilon, n, p) \leq e^{-\epsilon^2 np/2}. \tag{2}$$

Sometimes it is necessary to bound the number of 'successes' in a collection of trials that are not stochastically independent but are *negatively correlated*, *i.e.*, the success of one trial only decreases the probability of success of another trial. The following lemma, used without proof in several places in the existing literature of parallel randomized sorting algorithms, allows us to apply Chernoff bounds in these cases as well: (this proof is due to Sanjay Jain):

Lemma 7 *Let* $a_1, a_2, \ldots, a_n$ *be n random trials (not necessarily independent) such that the probability that trial* a_i *'succeeds' is bounded above by p regardless of the outcomes of the other trials. Then if X is the random variable that represents the number of 'successes' in these n trials, and Y is a binomial variable with parameters* (n, p), *then:*

$$\Pr[X \geq k] \leq \Pr[Y \geq k], \quad 0 \leq k \leq n.$$

PROOF. The proof is by induction on n. Let Y_i be a binomial variate with parameters (i, p) and let X_i denote the random variable that represents the number of successes in the first i trials $a_1, \ldots, a_i$. For the base case $i = 1$ it is obvious that $\Pr[X_1 \geq k] \leq \Pr[Y_1 \geq k]$, for any k. For $i = m + 1$, we have that, for all $k \geq 1$:

$$\Pr[Y_{m+1} \geq k] = \Pr[Y_m \geq k] + p\Pr[Y_m = k-1] = (1-p)\Pr[Y_m \geq k] + p\Pr[Y_m \geq k-1]. \quad (3)$$

Also,

$$\begin{aligned}
\Pr[X_{m+1} \geq k] &= \Pr[X_m \geq k] + \Pr[(X_m = k-1) \wedge a_{m+1} \text{ succeeds}] \\
&= \Pr[X_m \geq k] + \Pr[X_m = k-1]\Pr[a_{m+1} \text{ succeeds} \mid X_m = k-1] \\
&\leq \Pr[X_m \geq k] + p\Pr[X_m = k-1] \\
&= (1-p)\Pr[X_m \geq k] + p\Pr[X_m \geq k-1] \quad (4)
\end{aligned}$$

Comparing equations 3 and 4 and using the inductive hypothesis, we have the proof.□

3 Parallel Construction of a Fast Priority Queue

This section reviews a variant of the priority queue described by van Emde Boas *et. al.* [17] (hereafter referred to as the EKZ data structure), and describes methods of constructing this data structure in parallel.

3.1 A Fast Priority Queue

The EKZ data structure stores a set $S \subseteq \{0, \ldots, N-1\}$, (the elements in S are all distinct), such that predecessor queries can be answered in $O(\lg\lg N)$ time. The EKZ data structure for $\{0, \ldots, N-1\}$, N a power of 2, is a complete binary tree with depth $\lg N$, with all leaves at the same level. The edge leading to the left child of each internal node is labeled with a 0, and the one to the right node with a 1. Every leaf corresponds to the integer that is obtained by concatenating the bits obtained by traversing the path from the root to it (the edges incident upon the root are the MSB's). Every leaf node that corresponds to an integer in S is marked, and an internal node is marked iff one of its children is marked. Every internal node also contains the maximum and minimum element from S stored in the subtree rooted at it. The data structure is stored in an array A of size $O(N)$ in the usual way, with the children of a node stored at $A[i]$ being located at $A[2i]$ and $A[2i+1]$. In addition, all elements in S are linked together in an ordered list.

This data structure can be used to find *Pred*(x) and *Succ*(x) in $O(\lg\lg N)$ time by doing a binary search on the path from x to the root to find the first marked node along the path. Either the maximum value in the subtree rooted at this node will be *Pred*(x) or the minimum value in the subtree rooted at this node will be *Succ*(x). As the elements of S are linked together in a linked list, finding either the predecessor or the successor will enable us to get the other.

Some vertices on a marked path from a leaf to a root are the *left* or *right join* vertices of that path. The left join vertices of a path p are all the vertices v such that p goes to the right child of v and the left child of v is marked (*i.e.*, p is joined by another path from the left at v). The right join vertices of a path are defined similarly. The set of *join* vertices of a path is the union of the sets of its right and left join vertices. Let p be the path from $x \in S$ to the root. The predecessor of x is the maximum element stored at the left child of the deepest left join vertex l along p. Also note that exactly all vertices from x to l will have x as the minimum value in the subtree rooted at them.

3.2 Perfect Hashing

In this section we will review the perfect hashing scheme proposed by Fredman *et. al.* [9]. An EKZ data structure for a set $S \subseteq \{0, \ldots, N-1\}$ stored in an array of size $O(N)$ may have many elements that are zero: only $O(|S| \lg N)$ locations will contain non-zero values. By storing the useful portions of the array in a hash table, such that the array index is used as a key to retreive the value stored there, the space requirement can be considerably reduced. Dietzfelbinger *et. al.* have used this idea in a sequential context [6].

Suppose that $S \subseteq \{1, \ldots, N\}$, and $|S| = n$. Let p be the smallest prime such that $p > N$ and let $s \geq n$. Fredman *et. al.* consider the class of hash functions defined by $\mathcal{H}_{p,s} = \{h^k_{p,s}(x) = (kx \bmod p) \bmod s | 1 \leq k \leq p\}$. They prove the following:

Lemma 8 *Let p and s be as above, and let W^k_i be the number of times the value i is achieved by $h^k_{p,s}$ when restricted to S, that is, $W^k_i = |\{y \in S | h^k_{p,s}(y) = i\}|$. Then*

1. *With probability at least a half, a function $h^k_{p,s}$ chosen uniformly at random from $\mathcal{H}_{p,s}$ satisfies $\sum_{i=1}^{s}(W^k_i)^2 < 5n$.*

2. *With probability at least a half, a function $h^k_{p,2s^2}$ chosen uniformly at random from $\mathcal{H}_{p,2s^2}$ is injective on S.*

These facts are then used to obtain a linear space static data structure for answering membership queries about S. A 'top-level' hash function is chosen that satisfies condition 1 above, which partitions S into at most s buckets. For each bucket containing $m > 1$ elements, $2m^2$ locations are allocated, and a second level hash function is chosen from $\mathcal{H}_{p,2m^2}$ which satisfies condition 2. Thus the composition of the top level function with the appropriate second level hash function is an injective mapping, and membership queries can be answered in $O(1)$ time. Note that the second level tables require a total of $O(n)$ space, since the top-level function is chosen to satisfy condition 1 above.

3.3 Constructing the EKZ Data Structure in Parallel

Theorem 9 *An EKZ data structure on $S \subseteq \{0, \ldots, n^c - 1\}$, $|S| = n$ can be constructed in:*

1. *$\tilde{O}(\lg n)$ time using $n \lg n$ COLLISION processors, $O(n \lg n)$ space, assuming S is presented as a sorted array.*

2. *$O(1)$ time using $n \lg n$ COLLISION processors, using $O(n^c)$ space, assuming only that the items are distinct and $\lg n$ processors are associated with each.*

PROOF. The algorithms are as follows:

ALGORITHM 1: The idea here is basically that instead of writing information directly into the array that represents the data structure, the processors will determine what to write by looking at the input and write (array index,value) pairs in an auxiliary array instead. Then these values are stored in a hash table using the array index as key.

Step 1: Let the given input be $x_1, \ldots, x_n$. Assign one processor to each input element. Let $l = \lceil \lg n^c \rceil$ and let $x_i = b_{i,l} \ldots b_{i,1}$. For each x_i, let $d_i = \max\{j | b_{i,j} \neq b_{i+1,j}\}$. Then if the path from x_i to the root is $v_0, \ldots, v_l$, then exactly the nodes $v_0, \ldots, v_{d_i}$ will have x_i as the maximum value in their subtree. Similarly, each processor can determine the portion of the path along which the value assigned to it is the minimum value stored. This takes $O(l)$ time by a straightforward implementation (note that $l = O(\lg n)$).

Step 2: Let B be an array of size nl. Processor i writes the (at most) l pairs $\langle loc, x_i \rangle$ pairs such that in the actual EKZ structure, location loc would have contained x_i as the subtree maximum, into locations $B[il]$ through $B[(i+1)l - 1]$. (A similar procedure is followed for subtree minima.) Let the set of pairs stored in B be E. (Note that $|E| = O(n \lg n)$.) The time taken is $O(l)$.

Step 3: Using a standard parallel prefix algorithm the processors compact E into $|E|$ consecutive locations in memory, in time $O(\lg n)$.

Step 4: Let p be the smallest prime such that $p > nl$. The processors divide up into $d_1 \lg n$ groups of $O(n)$ each. In parallel, the processors in each group choose a 'top-level' hash function h independently at random from $\mathcal{H}_{p,|E|}$. Each group then checks to see if its choice is 'good', *i.e.*, without too many collisions at the top level. This is done by first evaluating h at all the elements of E, which takes $O(|E|/n) = O(l)$ time using n processors. The value of the hash function is an integer in the range $\{0, \ldots, |E| - 1\}$. Counting the number of elements mapped on to each bucket can be accomplished by sorting $h(E)$ using the known optimal algorithm (lemma 3). This takes $\tilde{O}(\lg n)$ time using $O(|E|/\lg n)$ processors per group, for a total of $|E|$ processors. If good function(s) are found, an arbitrary one is chosen using "leftmost one in memory" (lemma 4). Similarly, for each bucket that has a collision, the processors try $d_2 \lg n$ different 'second-level' hash functions, trying to find one which is injective. If none is found, then the computation is aborted. Note that checking a function for injectiveness takes $O(1)$ time on the COLLISION model.

Analysis: Now we fix the constants d_1 and d_2. If at the first stage we try $d_1 \lg n = \beta \lg n$ different hash functions, then since each one independently has a probability $1/2$ of being good, with probability at least $1 - n^{-\beta}$ at least one good hash function will be found. At the second level, we try $d_2 \lg n = (\beta + 1) \lg n$ different functions for each bucket, so that an injective second level hash function will be found for all buckets with probability at least $1 - n \cdot n^{-(1+\beta)} = 1 - n^{-\beta}$.

Remark: By using a "bucketing" scheme, the space requirements can be reduced to $O(|S|)$ without increasing the asymptotic query time. The details are easy and are omitted.

ALGORITHM 2: Here we assume that the $\lg n$ processors associated with each element are numbered $1, 2, \ldots, \lg n$. Let the given input be $x_1, \ldots, x_n$, $x_i \in \{0, \ldots, n^c - 1\}$ for some $c > 1$, and all the x_i's be distinct. Let $path_i$ be the path from x_i to the root.

Step 1: The $\lg n$ processors associated with x_i mark all nodes along $path_i$. In constant time the processors determine for each node along $path_i$ whether it is a join vertex or not. Using the "leftmost one in memory" algorithm, in constant time the $\lg n$ processors determine the deepest left join and right join vertices along $path_i$.

Step 2: In constant time the processors write the pair $\langle i, x_i \rangle$ as the subtree minimum (maximum) for all vertices below the the deepest left (right) join vertex. Finally, in constant time the processor associated with the deepest left (right) join vertex v looks at v's left (right) child and reads the pair $\langle k, x_k \rangle$ which is the subtree maximum (minimum) there and sets $Pred(x_i) = k$ ($Succ(x_i) = k$).□

4 Applications

4.1 Integer Sorting

We will now prove our results on integer sorting. For the sake of clarity, we will present a less general algorithm first and then show how to successively modify it to obtain our final result.

Theorem 10 *Integers in the range* $\{0,\ldots,n^c-1\}$, *for any constant* c, *can be sorted in* $\tilde{O}(\lg n)$ *time using* $n \lg\lg n/\lg n$ COLLISION *processors and* $O(n)$ *space.*

PROOF. We assume the input is given in an array $X[1..n]$. The algorithm is as follows.

Step 1: For each i in parallel, the processors compute $Y[i] = nX[i] + i$. The $Y[i]$'s are distinct and are in the range $\{0,\ldots,n^{c+1}-1\}$. Let S be the set of values in the array Y.

Step 2: The processors construct $S' \subseteq S$ by placing $x \in S$ independently in S' with probability $\lg^{-2} n$. By doing this, we can ensure that $|S| \leq d_1 n/\lg^2 n$ and that at most $d_2 \lg^3 n$ elements of S have a value that lies in between two consecutive elements of S' with high probability, if d_1 and d_2 are chosen appropriately.

Step 3: Using standard parallel prefix, the processors compact S' into an array using $n/\lg n$ processors and $O(\lg n)$ time, and sort S' using $|S'|$ processors in time $O(\lg n)$ using Cole's merge sort.

Step 4: Using Algorithm 1 from theorem 9, an EKZ data structure on S' is made. This stage uses $|S'|\lg n$ processors and runs with high probability in time $O(\lg n)$. The data structure so constructed will occupy $O(|S'|\lg n)$ space.

Step 5: For each element of S, the processors determine its predecessor in S', as well as the rank of its predecessor in S'. This step is computationally the most expensive, needing a processor time product of $O(n\lg\lg n)$.

Step 6: S' partitions S into $|S'|+1$ subcollections in the following way: if the elements of S' are $z_1,\ldots,z_{|S'|}$ in sorted order, then the ith collection $C_i = \{x \in S | z_i \leq x < z_{i+1}\}$, $0 \leq i \leq |S'|$. Associate with each element x of S the index i such that $x \in C_i$, and sort S using these indices as keys. Since these indices are integers in the range $\{0,\ldots,n-1\}$, the algorithm of lemma 3 can be used for this purpose.

Step 7: The processors now sort the individual subcollections. If the ith collection C_i is assigned $\lceil |C_i|/\lg n\rceil \lg\lg n$ processors, sorting it will take $O(\lg n \lg(|C_i|)/\lg\lg n)$ time, which is $O(\lg n)$ time since $\max_i\{|C_i|\} \leq d_2 \lg^3 n$ with very high probability.

Analysis: The size of the set S' is a binomial variable with parameters $(n, \lg^{-2} n)$. By a routine application of lemma 6 (Chernoff bounds for binomial distributions), we see that for any $d_1 \geq 1+\epsilon$, the probability that $|S'| > d_1 n/\lg^2 n$ is no more than $e^{-\epsilon^2 n/3\lg^2 n}$, which is sufficient for our purposes. Now we fix the value of d_2. Consider S in sorted order. The probability that k consecutive elements of S are not in S' is $(1-\lg^{-2} n)^k$, and hence $\mathrm{Prob}[|C_i| \geq k] \leq (1-\lg^{-2} n)^k$. Setting $k = (\beta+1)\lg^2 n \ln n$ and using the standard inequality $(1-1/x)^x < 1/e$ we find that the probability that $|C_i|$ exceeds $\ln 2(\beta+1)\lg^3 n$ is less than $1 - n^{-(\beta+1)}$. Thus choosing $d_2 = \ln 2(\beta+1)$ we can ensure that no collection is larger than $d_2 \lg^3 n$ with the required probability. □

We now show how to extend our algorithm to handle integers in the range $\{0, \ldots, m-1\}$, where m is superpolynomial in n. Only the modifications that need to be made to theorem 9 and theorem 10 will be given as proof. The assumptions are that evaluating hash functions on integers in the given range as well as comparing them, take constant time.

Theorem 11 *Integers in the range* $\{0, \ldots, m-1\}$, *for any* $m > n$, *can be sorted in* $\tilde{O}(\lg n)$ *time using* $n \lg\lg m / \lg n$ COLLISION *processors and* $O(n)$ *space.*

PROOF. Assume $\lg\lg m$ is $o(\lg n)$ (if $\lg\lg m/\lg n$ is $\Omega(1)$ using Cole's merge sort will suffice for the result). Choose $S' \subseteq S$ by putting $x \in S$ in S' with probability $(\lg m \lg^2 n)^{-1}$. We compact S' into an array as before, and sort it using Cole's merge sort, which takes $O(\lg n)$ time since comparisons between keys can be done in constant time. Now we dedicate $\lg m$ processors to each element of S' to aid in the construction of the EKZ data structure. Using these $\lg m$ processors, the values d_i in theorem 9 can be calculated in constant time using "leftmost one in memory". These values can be written into the auxiliary array B in theorem 9 in $O(1)$ time. The rest of the EKZ construction proceeds as before.

Now with $O(n \lg\lg m)$ work we divide the set up into the collections C_i. As before, with high probability $\max_i\{|C_i|\} = O(\lg m \lg^3 n)$. We assign $\lceil |C_i|/\lg n \rceil \lg\lg m$ processors to each collection to sort it in $O(\lg n \lg |C_i|/\lg\lg m) = O(\lg n)$ time.□

Now we sketch the modifications that need to be made to theorem 11 to obtain our most general result:

Theorem 12 *Integers in the range* $\{0, \ldots, m-1\}$, *for any* $m > n$, *can be sorted in* $\tilde{O}(\lg n/\lg\lg n + \lg\lg m)$ *time using* $\min(n, n \lg\lg m \lg\lg n/\lg n)$ COLLISION *processors and* $O(n)$ *space.*

PROOF. We eliminate all the $\lg n$-time 'bottlenecks' in theorem 11 simply by replacing all the logarithmic time algorithms there by sublogarithmic ones from section 2. We list the replacements performed below:

1. While compacting the sample S' use the fast parallel prefix algorithm.
2. Sorting S' is done by using $|S'| \lg n$ processors and applying the sublogarithmic algorithm of lemma 2 instead of Cole's merge sort.
3. During the hashing phase in the construction of the EKZ data structures, counting the collisions is done by sorting the output of the hash function using the (non-optimal) sublogarithmic algorithm of lemma 3. The work done during this stage now increases to $O(n \lg\lg n)$ but this is subsumed by later more expensive phases.
4. Creating the collections C_i is done using the sublogarithmic algorithm again. To sort the C_i's we allocate $\min(|C_i|, \lceil |C_i|/\lg n \rceil \lg\lg m \lg\lg n)$ processors to C_i to sort it in $O(\lg n/\lg\lg n + \lg\lg m)$ time.□

4.2 The Chaining Problem

Now we turn to the chaining problem. Recall that the parameters here are n, the size of the array, m, the number of non-zero elements and k, which is an (optional) upper bound on m. Since constructing an EKZ data structure on a set S also permits us to chain the elements of S together, we obtain as an immediate corollary of theorem 9:

Corollary 13 *Ordered chaining can be done in $O(1)$ time using $m \lg n$ processors on the* COLLISION *model of computation, provided there are $\lg n$ processors numbered 1 through $\lg n$ at each non-zero location.*

Though the number of processors used is $O(n)$ whenever $m = O(n/\lg n)$, this algorithm cannot be said to solve the chaining problem, since it makes the strong assumption that each non-zero element has $\lg n$ associated auxiliary processors that are consecutively numbered as well. However, using this algorithm as a subroutine, we are able to get processor- and time-efficient algorithms for the chaining problem. To do so we have to solve the processor allocation problem. Let the set of indices associated with non-zero elements be NZ ($|NZ| = m$).

Let $\lg^{(i)} n$ be the ith iterate of the lg function (*i.e.*, $\lg^{(0)} n = n$, and for $i > 0$, $\lg^{(i)} n = \lg(\lg^{(i-1)} n)$). For the problem of ordered chaining we show the following:

Theorem 14 *Ordered chaining can be done in $\tilde{O}(1)$ time using n* COLLISION *processors provided $m < n/(\lg^{(t)} n)^6$, for any fixed $t > 0$.*

PROOF. The proof is inductive. For the base case $t = 1$ we will solve the allocation problem by grouping the given processors into $G = n/\lg n$ groups of size $\lg n$, and then creating a mapping $A : NZ \mapsto \{1, \ldots, G\}$, such that for each $g \in G$, at most two distinct $i \in NZ$ will have $A(i) = g$. The mapping will be constructed in two phases: the first will be randomized and.the next, deterministic. In the,first step, all non-zero elements will be assigned to a group at random, and those that get hold of a unique group will allocate that group to themselves. A substantial number of non-zero elements will remain unallocated, but the remainder will be "uniformly scattered" in the input array. In particular, it will be the case that with very high probability, every sufficiently large chunk of the input array will contain only a "polynomially sparse" number of unsatisfied non-zero elements. The compaction algorithm of lemma 5 can now be used to locally solve the allocation problem.

Step 1: Each processor $p \in NZ$ chooses a random integer $g(p)$ from $\{1, \ldots, n/\lg n\}$. Let U be the set of processors with unique integers $g(p)$, *i.e.*, $U = \{p \in NZ | (\forall p' \in NZ \backslash \{p\})\ g(p) \neq g(p')\}$. Every $p \in U$ sets $A(p) = g(p)$. Let $NZ_1 = NZ \setminus U$.

Step 2: Now divide the input array into contiguous chunks of size $s = \lg^6 n$, with the ith chunk $C(i)$ consisting of the indices $si + 1, \ldots, s(i+1)$, for $1 \le i \le n/s$. Let $NZ_1(i) = NZ_1 \cap C(i)$. For each i, s processors attempt to compress $NZ_1(i)$ into locations $si + 1, \ldots, si + s/\lg n$ using the algorithm of lemma 5. This will work iff $C(i)$ is *sparse*, *i.e.*, $(|NZ_1(i)|)^4 \lg s < s/\lg n$.

Thus in each chunk $C(j)$ that is sparse, every $p \in NZ_1(j)$ is assigned a unique integer $g_1(p)$ in the range $1, \ldots, s/\lg n$, and sets $A(p) = sj/\lg n + g_1(p)$. We will show that with high probability all the chunks $C(j)$ are sparse.

Step 3: For each $p \in NZ$, the $\lg n$ processors $A(p)$ are used to solve the ordered chaining problem using corollary 13.

Analysis: Since each index in NZ is in NZ_1 with probability at most $\lg^{-5} n$ independently of all other indices, lemma 7 implies that $|NZ_1(i)|$ is upperbounded by a random variable that is binomially distributed with parameters $(s, \lg^{-5} n)$. Lemma 6 now states that $|NZ_1(i)| > d_1 \lg n$ with probability at most $2^{-d_2 \lg n} = n^{-d_2}$ for any prespecified number d_2, if d_1 is large enough. This implies that all chunks will be sparse with the required probability, if d_2 is large enough.

For the inductive step we assume that the proposition is true for $t = 1, \ldots, r$. During steps 1 and 2, an attempt is made to allocate $\Omega(\lg^{(r+1)} n)$ processors with each index in NZ, in a manner similar to steps 1 and 2 in the base case. Then the input array is divided into segments, and the ordered chaining problem is solved locally within these segments. Then representatives are chosen from within each segment. With high probability, the number of representatives will be small enough so that a recursive call can be made to the algorithm of the inductive hypothesis. We divide the n processors into $G = n/\lg^{(r+1)} n$ groups of $\lg^{(r+1)} n$ each.

Step 1: Each processor $p \in NZ$ chooses a random integer $g(p)$ from $\{1, \ldots, n/\lg^{(r+1)} n\}$. Let U be the set of processors with unique integers $g(p)$: each $p \in U$ sets $A(p) = g(p)$. Let $NZ_1 = NZ \setminus U$.

Step 2: The input array is divided into contiguous chunks $C(i)$ of size $s = (\lg^{(r+1)} n)^6$ and we let $NZ_1(i) = NZ_1 \cap C(i)$ as before. Using s processors, for each i, an attempt is made to compress $NZ_1(i)$ into locations $si + 1, \ldots, si + s/\lg^{(r+1)} n$ by running the algorithm of lemma 5. This will work iff $C(j)$ is *sparse*, *i.e.*, iff $|NZ_1(j)|^4 \lg s < s/\lg^{(r+1)} n$. Let $S = \{j | C(j) \text{ is sparse}\}$. Thus for every $j \in S$, every $p \in NZ_1(j)$ is assigned a unique integer $g_1(p)$ in the range $1, \ldots, s/\lg^{(r+1)} n$, and sets $A(p) = sj/\lg^{(r+1)} n + g_1(p)$. Let $NZ_2 = NZ_1 \setminus \cup_{j \in S} NZ_1(j)$.

Step 3: Now we divide the input array into contiguous segments $S(i)$, $1 \le i \le n/(\lg^{(r)} n)^7$ of size $(\lg^{(r)} n)^7$. Call a segment $S(i)$ *allocated* if $S(i) \cap NZ_2 = \emptyset$, and *non-allocated* otherwise. For any $S(i)$, let $T(i) = S(i) \cap NZ$ be the set of non-zero elements within $S(i)$. Let A be the set of indices that represent allocated segments and NA the set of indices representing non-allocated segments. By the definition of A, we know that for each $i \in A$, each $p \in T(i)$ has $\Omega(\lg^{(r+1)} n)$ processors allocated to it, and so we can use the algorithm of corollary 13 to link each element in $T(i)$ to its successor in $T(i)$. After this is done, the first and last elements from $T(i)$, $i \in A$, are chosen to be *representatives* for that segment. Let the set of all representatives be R.

Step 4: Note that $|R| \le 2n/(\lg^{(r)} n)^7$. We will show that $|NZ_2| = o(n/(\lg^{(r)} n)^{13})$ with very high probability. Since $|NA| \le |NZ_2|$, this implies that $|\cup_{i \in NA} T(i)|$ is $o(n/(\lg^{r} n)^7)$ and hence a recursive call suffices to chain the elements of $R \cup (\cup_{i \in NA} T(i))$ together in order. A little care must be taken in the recursive call not to reset successors for non-zero elements whose successors are already known from a previous higher-level invocation, and corollary 13 can easily be modified to handle this. (Otherwise, the representatives may end up not pointing to their successors after this recursive call.)

Analysis: Consider each chunk $C(i)$, which has at most $s = (\lg^{(r+1)} n)^6$ non-zero elements in it initially. The probability that each $p \in NZ$ is also in NZ_1 is at most $(\lg^{(r+1)} n)^{-5}$, and so the probability that $|NZ_1(i)| > d_1 \lg^{(r+1)} n$ is at most $2^{-d_2 \lg^{(r+1)} n} = (\lg^{(r)} n)^{-d_2}$, for any d_2, if d_1 is large enough. Thus, for any chunk i, $\Pr[i \notin S] \le (\lg^{(r)} n)^{-d_2}$, which implies $|\{i | i \notin S\}| < n/(\lg^{(r)} n)^{14}$ with the required probability, if d_2 is large enough, and thus $|NZ_2|$ is $o(n/(\lg^{(r)} n)^{13})$ with high probability. □

Corollary 15 *Unordered chaining can be done in $O(1)$ time with probability at least $1 - n^{-\beta}$, using n COLLISION processors, for any prespecified constant β, provided $m < n/\lg^{(i)} n$, for any fixed i.*

We would like to point out here that the technique above can be used to solve a generalized version of the chaining problem. Define the *c-color* chaining problem to be the following: suppose we are given an array of values $x_1, \ldots, x_n$, such that each array element has a value in the range $\{0, \ldots, c\}$. Let S_k, $k \in \{1, \ldots, c\}$, be the set of array indices i such that $x_i = k$. The c-color chaining problem is then to output c linked lists $l_1, \ldots, l_c$ such that l_i contains all the elements in S_i exactly once. This generalization has a natural interpretation in the context of database operations: it enables us find all the records that match a particular predicate and then subclassify them based on a secondary field as well. Ragde's algorithm gives only a $O(c)$ time solution to this problem and the algorithm of Hagerup and Nowak [11] has a run time of $O(\lg\lg n)$, independent of c. The algorithm for the 'base case' of theorem 14 above can clearly be used to solve the c-color chaining problem as well, and thus we can solve the c-color chaining problem in $O(1)$ time whenever $\sum_{i=1}^{c} |S_i| < n/(\lg n)^6$. (The induction step cannot be made to work because at the end of step 3, we will have to choose representatives from each segment *for each color*, and thus the set of representatives may not be small enough for the recursive call to work.) However, by a simple modification, we can improve this slightly:

Theorem 16 *The c-color chaining problem can be solved in $\tilde{O}(1)$ time with using n* COLLISION *processors whenever $\sum_{i=1}^{c} |S_i| < n/(\lg n)^{1+\epsilon}$ for any prespecified number $\epsilon > 0$.*

PROOF. As before, we combine processors into groups of size $\lg n$ each. If each $p \in NZ$ attempts to grab one of these groups at random, then the probability of failure will be at most $(\lg n)^{-\epsilon}$. This means that the number of non-allocated elements will be attenuated by a factor of $O((\lg n)^{-\epsilon})$, and it is easy to see that after d/ϵ stages, for some sufficiently large d, the number of unallocated non-zero elements will be less than $n/(\lg n)^6$ with very high probability, and the processor allocation algorithm of theorem 14 can be applied. □

Remarks: Theorem 14 implies that ordered chaining can be done with high probability in $O(\lg^* n)$ time using $O(n)$ processors for all values of m, which is inferior to Ragde's result, and thus it is still an open question whether the chaining problem can be solved in constant time for all values of m. Also, since our algorithms are randomized, they cannot easily determine when an unexpectedly high number of non-zero elements appear in the input, since an aborted computation could also be the result of an unfavorable sequence of coin tosses.

Also, the probability that the chaining algorithm terminates within the stated time bounds can be improved to $1 - 2^{-n^\beta}$ for any constant $\beta < 1/4 - \epsilon$. This can be done as follows: all except the "base case" algorithm actually have success probability of the required order of magnitude. To improve the base case, after step 2, we observe that at most n^β elements will remain with probability $1 - 2^{-n^\beta}$, and we allocate processors to these by compressing the remaining non-zero elements into the first $n/\lg n$ locations of the array.

5 Conclusions and Open Problems

To conclude, we state our main results once again. We have a randomized algorithm that sorts n numbers in the range $\{0, \ldots, m-1\}$ that runs in time $O(\lg n/\lg\lg n + \lg\lg m)$ time with high probability, using $O(n)$ space and $O(n \lg\lg m)$ work. The model of computation is the CRCW (COLLISION) PRAM. This algorithm runs as fast as the best currently known algorithm [2] and uses no more processors, while using only linear space and running on a weaker model of parallel computation. This paper does not resolve the main open problem of sorting n integers in a range polynomial in n optimally in polylogarithmic time, though like the algorithm of [2] it achieves optimal speedup for certain ranges of m. It would be interesting to see if a deterministic algorithm with the same time complexity can be constructed for the COLLISION model. It appears difficult to weaken the model of computation any further, and in particular to achieve $O(n \lg\lg n)$ processor-time product and $O(\lg n)$ running time on the COMMON model of computation.

In the case of the chaining problem, we have addressed the same open question that Ragde [15] posed, namely whether or not chaining can be done in constant time with a linear number of processors. Ragde gave a partial answer to this question: our paper gives a much improved, but still partial, answer to it. In addition, our algorithms are easily modified to solve a generalized version of the chaining problem. Ragde's original open problem still stands, however.

6 Acknowlegdements

We would like to thank Paul Dietz for the explanation of the version of the EKZ data structure used in this paper and Sanjay Jain for his proof of lemma 7. Danny Krizanc was a very accessible storehouse of information on parallel computation. We would also like to thank Paul Dietz, Sanjay Jain, Danny Krizanc, Lata Narayanan and Joel Seiferas for helpful discussions.

References

[1] D. Angluin and L. Valiant. Fast probabilistic algorithms for Hamiltonian circuits and matchings. *Journal of Computer and System Science*, 18, 1979.

[2] P. Bhatt, K. Diks, T. Hagerup, V. Prasad, T. Razdik, and S. Saxena. Improved deterministic parallel integer sorting. Technical Report TR 15/89, Fachbereich Informatik, Universitat des Saarlandes, November 1989.

[3] B. Chlebus, K. Diks, T. Hagerup, and T. Radzik. New simulations between CRCW PRAMs. In *Fundamentals of Computation Theory*, 1989.

[4] R. Cole. Parallel merge sort. In *Proc. 27th IEEE FOCS*, 1986.

[5] R. Cole and U. Vishkin. Faster optimal parallel prefix sums and list ranking. *Information and Control*, 81:334–352, 1989.

[6] M. Dietzfelbinger, A. Karlin, K. Mehlhorn, F. Meyer auf der Heide, H. Rohnhert, and R. Tarjan. Dynamic perfect hashing: upper and lower bounds. In *Proc. 29th IEEE FOCS*, pages 524–531, 1988.

[7] F. Fich, P. Radge, and A. Wigderson. Relations among concurrent write models of parallel computation. *SIAM Journal of Computing*, 17, 1988.

[8] F. Fich, P. Ragde, and A. Wigderson. Relations between concurrent-write models of parallel computation. In *Proc. 3rd. Annual ACM PODC*, pages 179–189, 1984.

[9] M. Fredman, J. Komlós, and E. Szemerédi. Storing a sparse table with $O(1)$ worst case access time. *Journal of the ACM*, 31(3):538–544, 1984.

[10] T. Hagerup. Towards optimal parallel integer sorting. *Information and Computation*, 75:39–51, 1987.

[11] T. Hagerup and M. Nowak. Parallel retreival of scattered information. In *Proc. 16th Annual ICALP*, 1989.

[12] D. Kirkpatrick and S. Reisch. Upper bounds for sorting intgers on a random access machine. *Theoretical Computer Science*, 28:263–276, 1984.

[13] D. E. Knuth. *The Art of Computer Programming, Vol. 3: Sorting and Searching.* Addison-Wesley, 1973.

[14] Y. Matias and U. Vishkin. On parallel hashing and integer sorting. Technical Report CS-TR-2935, University of Maryland, January 1990. To appear, *ICALP '90.*

[15] P. Ragde. The parallel simplicity of compaction and chaining. In *Proceedings 17th Annual ICALP*, 1990. To appear.

[16] S. Rajasekaran and J. Reif. Optimal and sublogarithmic time randomized parallel sorting algorithms. *SIAM Journal of Computing*, 18(3):594–607, 1989.

[17] P. van Emde Boas, R. Kaas, and E. Ziljstra. Design and implementation of an efficient priority queue. *Math. Sys: Theory*, 10:99–127, 1977.

[18] U. Vishkin. Implementation of simultaneous memory address access in models that forbid *Journal of Algorithms*, 1983.

A General Sort on Collision

We now prove lemma 2. All the steps in the original algorithm can be trivially modified to work on Collision except the algorithm for the following 'estimation' problem:

Lemma 17 *Let $S = \{0, \ldots, n-1\}$ be a set of indices and let each element of S belong to exactly one of $\sqrt{n}$ groups $G_0, \ldots, G_{\sqrt{n}-1}$, such that $\max_i\{|G_i|\} \leq \sqrt{n}\lg n$, and such that in constant time, for each index in S we can determine the group it belongs to. Then we can compute numbers $N_1, \ldots, N_{\sqrt{n}}$ such that $\sum_{i=0}^{\sqrt{n}-1} N_i = O(n)$, and such that with probability $1-n^{-\beta}$, $N_i \geq |G_i|$ for each $i \in \{0, \ldots, \sqrt{n}-1\}$, in $\tilde{O}(\lg n/\lg\lg n)$ time using $n(\lg n)^\epsilon$ Collision processors, for any constants $\epsilon, \beta > 0$*

Proof. The algorithm is a modification of the original one. We use a common array B of size $n/\lg n$, partitioned into $\sqrt{n}$ contiguous groups $B_0, \ldots, B_{\sqrt{n}}$ of size $\sqrt{n}/\lg n$ each. For each location $l \in B$, we also have an array A_l of size $(\lg n)^{1+\epsilon}$.

Step 1: $n/\lg^2 n$ processors in parallel each choose a random index from $\{0, \ldots, n-1\}$.

Step 2: For each index i so chosen, let $g(i)$ be such that $i \in G_{g(i)}$. The processors compute, for each i, L_i which is the number of elements from G_i which are chosen in step 1. In [16] it is shown that setting $N_i = d_2 \lg^2 n \max(1, L_i)$ for some sufficiently large constant d_2 suffices. This is done in the following manner: each of the $n/\lg^2 n$ processors with index i chooses a random location within $B_{g(i)}$. Let S_j be the set of processors that chooses location j in the array B. Clearly, $L_j = \sum_{k \in B_j} |S_k|$. In [16] the $|S_j$s are computed by showing that, with high probability, $\max_i\{|S_j|\} = O(\lg n/\lg\lg n)$, and then by sequentially computing, using the properties of Arbitrary, the exact value of $|S_j|$. An alternative method is for each of the processors in S_j allocate itself a unique location the array A_j, and then using $(\lg n)^{1+\epsilon}$ processors, one for each location in A_j, to compute the numbers $|S_j|$ in $O(\lg\lg n)$ further time. The allocation of indices can be done in the following way: each processor in S_j chooses a location at random in A_j. Processors that succeed in choosing a location not chosen by any other, allocate that location to themselves. Similarly, for s more stages, each 'unallocated' processor attempts to randomly choose a location that has neither been previously allocated nor has been chosen by some other processor in the same stage: if it succeeds, it allocates that location to itself and does nothing for the remainder of the stages. The probability of failure of any processor in any stage is at most $(\lg n)^{-\epsilon}$, which implies that if $s = d_1 \lg n / \lg\lg n$, for some sufficiently large constant d_1, then with sufficiently high probability all the elements of S_j will have succeeded in finding assignments.

Step 3: A parallel prefix computation on the values $|S_j|$ is then performed to compute the quantities L_i, and N_i is set to $d_2 \lg^2 n \max(1, L_i)$.

The analysis is as in [16] and will not be repeated here. □

Fast Parallel Algorithms for Cographs

R. Lin
Department of Computer Science
SUNY at Geneseo
Geneseo, NY 14454

S. Olariu†
Department of Computer Science
Old Dominion University
Norfolk, VA 23529-0162

Abstract *In this paper we propose a new way of looking at cographs and show how it affords us a fast parallel recognition algorithm. Additionally, should the graph under investigation be a cograph, our algorithm constructs its unique tree representation. Next, given a cograph along with its tree representation we obtain a fast parallel coloring algorithm. Specifically, for a graph G with n vertices and m edges as input, our parallel recognition algorithm runs in* $O(\log n)$ *EREW time using* $O(\frac{n^2+mn}{\log n})$ *processors. Once the cotree of a cograph is available, our coloring algorithm runs in* $O(\log n)$ *EREW time using* $O(\frac{n}{\log n})$ *processors.*

1. Introduction

A well-known class of graphs arising in a wide spectrum of practical applications is the class of cographs, or complement-reducible graphs. The cographs have been studied extensively from both the theoretical and algorithmic points of view [1,2,5-13]. In particular, Corneil et al [7] have obtained a linear time incremental recognition algorithm for cographs. An early result of Lerchs [9], asserts that the cographs admit a unique tree representation up to isomorphism. An interesting feature of the algorithm in [7] is that it constructs the tree representation of the cograph as well. This representation has been exploited for the purpose of obtaining fast solutions to a number of optimization problems that are hard for general graphs [6,7].

We assume the Parallel Random Access Machine model which consists of autonomous processors, each having access to a common memory. At each step, every processor performs the same instruction, with a number of processors masked out. In the Concurrent Read Concurrent Write PRAM (CRCW) model, several processors may simultaneously read from and/or write to the same memory location; in the Concurrent Read Exclusive Write PRAM (CREW) model, several processors may simultaneously read the same memory location, but exclusive access is used for writing; in the Exclusive Read Exclusive Write PRAM (EREW) model, a memory location cannot be simultaneously accessed by more than one processor. The interested reader is referred to [14] for a competent discussion on the PRAM family. Several authors argue that EREW is the only model that is reasonably close to real machines, making it of a particular practical interest. With this observation in mind, we shall adopt the EREW as our model of computation.

Recently, several parallel recognition algorithms for cographs have been proposed: in particular, the algorithm of Adhar and Peng [2] runs in $O(\log^2 n)$ CRCW time using mn processors; the algorithm of Kirkpatrick and Przytycka [8] takes $O(\log^2 n)$ CREW time using

† This work was supported by the National Science Foundation under grant CCR-8909996.

$O(\frac{n^3}{\log^2 n})$ processors; the algorithm of Novick [10] runs in O(log n) CRCW time using n^3 processors; finally, Shyu [12] proposed an algorithm that takes O(log n) CRCW time using n^3 processors.

Very recently, Abrahamson et al [1] have shown that the tree contraction technique can be used to devise optimal parallel algorithms for the following problems on cographs: computing the size of the largest clique, number of cliques, number of maximal independent sets, number of cliques of the largest size, number of independent sets of largest size, and the problem of identifying a clique of maximum size. All these problems can be solved in O(log n) EREW time using $O(\frac{n}{\log n})$ processors by solving a corresponding tree contraction problem.

The purpose of this paper is to propose a new way of looking at cographs and to show how it can be used to obtain a fast parallel recognition algorithm for cographs. More precisely, with an arbitrary graph G with n vertices and m edges as input, our algorithm runs in O(log n) time using $O(\frac{n^2+mn}{\log n})$ processors in the EREW model. At the same time, in case G is a cograph, our algorithm constructs the corresponding cotree T(G).

Once the unique tree repesentation of the cograph is available, we show that the tree contraction technique can be used to obtain an optimal coloring algorithm for cographs running in O(log n) time using $O(\frac{n}{\log n})$ processors in the EREW-PRAM model.

Our first result, Theorem 1, is of an independent interest: it provides a new characterization of the class of cographs, in terms of a certain decomposition of their vertex-set. The key to our fast parallel recognition algorithm is provided by Theorem 2 which reveals an intimate connection between our decomposition and the cotree associated with a cograph.

The paper is organized as follows: Section 2 gives the theoretical results in the form of new characterizations for cographs; Section 3 is devoted to the recognition and tree construction algorithm; Section 4 discusses an optimal parallel coloring algorithm for cographs.

2. A new way of looking at cographs

A graph is termed a *cograph* if it contains no chordless path with four vertices and three edges. Lerchs [9] showed how to associate with every cograph G a unique rooted tree T(G) called the *cotree* of G, and defined as follows.

• every internal node, except possibly for the root, has at least two children; furthermore, the root has only one child if, and only if, the underlying graph G is disconnected.

• the internal nodes are labeled by either 0 (0-nodes) or 1 (1-nodes) in such a way that the root is always a 1-node, and such that 1-nodes and 0-nodes alternate along every path in T(G) starting at the root;

• the leaves of T(G) are precisely the vertices of G, such that vertices x and y are adjacent in G if, and only if, the lowest common ancestor of x and y in T(G) is a 1-node.

Let G=(V,E) be a finite graph with no loops and multiple edges. We let N(x) denote the set of vertices of G which are adjacent to x; we let N[x] stand for the *closed* neighborhood of x, defined as $N(x)\cup\{x\}$. N'(x) denotes the set of vertices adjacent to x in the complement $\overline{G}$ of G. As usual, d(w) stands for $|N(w)|$.

Call a graph G *partitionable* if for every vertex x of G, there exists a partition $F_1(x), F_2(x), \ldots, F_{p_x}(x)$ of N(x) satisfying the conditions (1.1) and (1.2) below.

$$\text{for every } i\ (1\le i\le p_x) \text{ and for every } y, z \text{ in } F_i(x),\ N[y]-N[x]=N[z]-N[x]; \qquad (1.1)$$

$$\text{for every } y, z \text{ in } N(x),\ N[z]-N[x]\subset N[y]-N[x] \text{ iff } y\in F_i(x) \text{ and } z\in F_j(x)\ (1\le i<j\le p_x). \qquad (1.2)$$

The sets $F_1(x), F_2(x), \ldots, F_{p_x}(x)$ determine a partition $H_0(x), H_1(x), \ldots, H_{p_x}(x)$ of N'(x) defined as follows

(2.1) $H_i(x)=(N[y]-N[x])-(N[z]-N[x])$, with $y\in F_i(x)$, $z\in F_{i+1}(x)$ $(1\le i\le p_x-1)$;

(2.2) $H_{p_x}(x)=N[y]-N[x]$, with $y\in F_{p_x}(x)$; $H_0(x)=N'(x)-\bigcup^{p_x} H_i(x)$.

By (1.1) and (1.2), the sets $H_i(x)$, $(1 \le i \le p_x)$ are well defined; to see that $H_0(x), H_1(x), ..., H_{p_x}(x)$ determines a partition of $N'(x)$, note that for every i with $1 \le i \le p_x-1$, (1.2) and (2.1) imply that all the $H_i(x)$'s are pairwise disjoint and nonempty. Furthermore, by (2.2) all the $H_i(x)$'s are disjoint, with $H_0(x)$ and $H_{p_x}(x)$ possibly empty.

It is easy to see that every cograph is partitionable. Our plan is to obtain a characterization of the cographs by further restricting the class of partitionable graphs. The following simple observations follow directly from the definition.

Observation 1. *Let G be a partitionable graph, and let x be an arbitrary vertex of G. Then the sets* $F_1(x), F_2(x), ..., F_{p_x}(x)$ *and* $H_0(x), H_1(x), ..., H_{p_x}(x)$ *are unique; furthermore* $\{x\} \cup \bigcup_{i=1}^{p_x} (F_i(x) \cup H_i(x))$ *induces a connected subgraph of G.* □

Observation 2. *No vertex in* $H_0(x)$ *is adjacent to a vertex in* $N(x)$. □

Observation 3. *Every vertex in* $H_i(x)$ $(1 \le i \le p_x)$ *is adjacent to all the vertices in* $\bigcup_{j=1}^{i} F_j(x)$ *and non-adjacent to all the vertices in* $N(x) - \bigcup_{j=1}^{i} F_j(x)$. □

Observation 4. *Every vertex in* $F_i(x)$ $(1 \le i \le p_x)$ *is adjacent to all the vertices in* $\bigcup_{j=i}^{p_x} H_j(x)$ *and nonadjacent to all the vertices in* $\bigcup_{j=0}^{i-1} H_j(x)$. □

A partitionable graph is said to be *well partitioned* if for every vertex x of G, and for every i with $0 \le i \le p_x$,

$$\text{no vertex in } H_i(x) \text{ is adjacent to a vertex in } \bigcup_{j \ne i} H_j(x). \qquad (4)$$

Lemma 1. *Let G=(V,E) be a well partitioned graph and let x be an arbitrary vertex in G. Every vertex in* $F_i(x)$ *is adjacent to all the vertices in* $\bigcup_{j \ne i} F_j(x)$.

Proof. Suppose not; we find nonadjacent vertices $y \in F_i(x)$ and $z \in F_j(x)$ with $i<j$. By Observation 3 we find a vertex u in $H_i(x)$ with $yu \in E$ and $zu \notin E$. Let t be the subscript for which $y \in F_t(u)$. Since $ux, uz \notin E$, it follows that $x, z \in N'(u)$; since $xy \in E$, $yz \notin E$, (2) guarantees that x, z are in distinct sets $H_r(u)$ and $H_s(u)$, contradicting (4). □

Lemma 2. *A graph G is a cograph if and only if G is well partitioned.*

Proof. First, if G is well-partitioned then (4) and Lemma 1 imply that G is a cograph. Conversely, assume that G=(V,E) is a cograph, x an arbitrary vertex in G, and y, z are arbitrary vertices in N(x). It is easy to conform that precisely one of the conditions $N[y]-N[x]=N[z]-N[x]$, $N[y]-N[x] \subset N[z]-N[x]$, or $N[z]-N[x] \subset N[y]-N[x]$ is satisfied. Consequently, we partition N(x) into $F_1(x), F_2(x), ..., F_{p_x}(x)$ satisfying (1.1) and (1.2). It is immediate that this partition of N(x) induces a partition $H_0(x), H_1(x), ..., H_{p_x}(x)$ satisfying (2.1)-(2.2). Finally, to see that (4) is satisfied, consider adjacent vertices $u \in H_i(x)$ and $v \in H_j(x)$ with $i<j$. By Observation 3 we find a vertex y in $F_j(x)$ with $yv \in E$, $uy \notin E$. But now, {x,y,v,u} induces a P_4, a contradiction. □

Lemma 2 motivates a further investigation of the properties of the sets $F_1(x), F_2(x), ..., F_{p_x}(x)$ and $H_0(x), H_1(x), ..., H_{p_x}(x)$ in a well partitioned graph.

Lemma 3. *Let G be a well partitioned graph. For every pair x, y of vertices of G with* $y \in F_i(x)$ *or* $y \in H_i(x)$ *the following four conditions are satisfied:*

(3.1) For all j=1,...,i-1, $F_j(x)=F_j(y)$ *and* $H_j(x)=H_j(y)$;

(3.2) $F_i(y) \supseteq \{x\} \cup \bigcup_{j=i+1}^{p_x} (F_j(x) \cup H_j(x)) \cup H_i(x)$, *in case* $y \in F_i(x)$;

(3.3) $F_i(x)=F_i(y)$ *and* $H_i(y) \supseteq \{x\} \cup \bigcup_{j=i+1}^{p_x} (F_j(x) \cup H_j(x))$, *in case* $y \in H_i(x)$;

(3.4) For all $j=i+1,\dots,\min\{p_x,p_y\}$, $F_j(x)\cap F_j(y)=\emptyset$ and $H_j(x)\cap H_j(y)=\emptyset$.

Sketch of proof. Let $G=(V,E)$ be well-partitioned, and let x, y be distinct vertices of G. For convenience write $Z=\{x\}\cup\bigcup_{j=i+1}^{p_x}(F_j(x)\cup H_j(x))$, and $T=\bigcup_{j=1}^{i-1}F_j(x)$.

First, let $y\in F_i(x)$. To settle (3.1), note that Observation 4 and Lemma 1 allow us to write $N(y)=A\cup T\cup Z\cup H_i(x)$, with $A=\{w\in F_i(x)\mid yw\in E\}$.

By Observation 3, Lemma 1, (1.2) and (4), $N[u]-N[y]\subset N[v]-N[y]$, for every choice of vertices u, v in $A\cup Z\cup H_i(x)$ and T, respectively. Consequently, in this case, $F_j(y)=F_j(x)$ and $H_j(y)=H_j(x)$ for all $j=1,2,\dots,i-1$.

To settle (3.2), observe that by Observation 3, Lemma 1, (1.2) and (4) combined, for every vertex z in $Z\cup H_i(x)$ $N[x]-N[y]=N[z]-N[y]$, implying that $Z\cup H_i(x)\subseteq F_i(y)$.

Finally, settle (3.4) in case $y\in F_i(x)$, note that the previous observation guarantees that for all $j=i+1,\dots,p_x$, $F_j(y)\subseteq A$ and $H_j(y)\subseteq F_i(x)-(\{y\}\cup A)$, and so $F_j(x)\cap F_j(y)=H_j(x)\cap H_j(y)=\emptyset$, for all $j=i+1,\dots,\min\{p_x,p_y\}$.

The case $y\in H_i(x)$ is similar and left to the reader. □

Let $G=(V,E)$ be a partitionable graph and let x be an arbitrary vertex of G. It is helpful to define the following sequence of sets.

(5.1) $U_0(x)=V$;

(5.2) for every i $(1\le i\le 2p_x)$ $U_i(x)=U_{i-1}(x)-\begin{cases}F_t(x) & i=2t\\ H_t(x) & i=2t+1.\end{cases}$

(5.3) $U_{2p_x+1}(x)=\begin{cases}\{x\} & \text{if } H_{p_x}(x)\neq\emptyset\\ \emptyset & \text{otherwise}\end{cases}$

Note that (5.1)-(5.3) imply the following intermediate results whose justification is immediate.

Observation 5. *$U_j(x)\subset U_i(x)$ whenever $0\le i<j\le 2p_x+1$.*

Observation 6. *For all i $(0\le i\le 2p_x)$*

$$U_i(x)=\{x\}\cup\bigcup_{j=t+1}^{p_x}(F_j(x)\cup H_j(x))\cup\begin{cases}H_t(x) & i=2t\\ \emptyset & \text{otherwise}\end{cases}$$

Observation 7. *For every k with $1\le k\le p_x$ there exists a subscript α with $3\le\alpha\le 2p_x+1$, such that*

$$U_\alpha(x)=U_1(x)-\bigcup_{j=1}^{k}(F_j(x)\cup H_j(x)).\ \square$$

We are now in a position to state our main result in the form of a new structure theorem for cographs. As we shall see later, this new characterization has several interesting implications, leading to our parallel recognition algorithm for cographs.

Theorem 1. *A graph $G=(V,E)$ is a cograph if and only if G is partitionable and for every pair of vertices x, y in G, and for every subscript i with $0\le i\le\min\{2p_x,2p_y\}$, either $U_i(x)=U_i(y)$ or else $U_i(x)\cap U_i(y)=\emptyset$.*

Sketch of proof. To prove the if part assume that G is partitionable, but not a cograph; we only need exhibit vertices x and y and a subscript i $(1\le i\le\min\{2p_x,2p_y\})$ such that $U_i(x)\cap U_i(y)\neq\emptyset$ and yet $U_i(x)\neq U_i(y)$. For this purpose, note that since G is not a cograph, some set {a, b, c, d} induce a P_4 in G with edges ab, bc, cd.

We note that $H_0(a)=H_0(c)$: since b is adjacent to both a and c, we have $b\notin H_0(a)$ and $b\notin H_0(c)$, implying $b\in U_1(a)$ and $b\in U_1(c)$. On the other hand, if $H_0(a)\neq H_0(c)$ then $U_1(a)\neq U_1(c)$, and we are done.

We may assume, without loss of generality, that $b\in F_j(a)$, $c\in H_k(a)$, and $d\in H_i(a)$, for some i, j, k with $1\le i\neq j\neq k\le p_a$, and that $a\in H_r(c)$, $b\in F_q(c)$, $d\in F_s(c)$, for some q, r, s with $1\le q\neq r\neq s\le p_c$.

Note that by Observation 3, $i<j\underset{i}{\le}k$ and $q\le r<s$. Further, by Observation 7 there exists a subscript α such that $U_\alpha(a)=U_1(a)-(\bigcup_{t=1}^{i}F_t(a)\cup H_t(a))$. Similarly, we find a subscript β such that $U_\beta(c)=U_1(c)-(\bigcup_{t=1}^{s-1}F_t(c)\cup H_t(c))$.

Consequently, we have b, $c\in U_\alpha(a)$ and $d\notin U_\alpha(a)$, and c, $d\in U_\beta(c)$ and $b\notin U_\beta(c)$.

To obtained the desired contradiction, we only need show that with $\gamma=\alpha$ or $\gamma=\beta$ $U_\gamma(a)\cap U_\gamma(c)\neq\emptyset$, and $U_\gamma(a)\neq U_\gamma(c)$.

First, if $\alpha\leq\beta$ then, $U_\beta(c)\subseteq U_\alpha(c)$ and c, $d\in U_\alpha(c)$. But now, clearly, $U_\alpha(a)\cap U_\alpha(c)\neq\emptyset$, and yet $d\in U_\alpha(c)-U_\alpha(a)\neq\emptyset$.

Next, if $\beta<\alpha$, then $U_\alpha(a)\subset U_\beta(a)$ and b, $c\in U_\beta(a)$. However, now $U_\beta(a)\cap U_\beta(c)\neq\emptyset$, and $b\in U_\beta(a)-U_\beta(c)\neq\emptyset$. The conclusion follows.

To prove the only if part assume that G is a cograph; by Lemma 2 G is well partitioned. Consider distinct vertices x, y in components X, Y of G. First, if X and Y are distinct then, trivially, $H_0(x)=G-X$ and $H_0(y)=G-Y$, and so $U_1(x)$ and $U_1(y)$ are disjoint. By (5.1), and (5.2) combined, $U_i(x)$ and $U_i(y)$ are disjoint for all i with $1\leq i\leq\min\{2p_x,2p_y\}$.

Now X and Y coincide, and so we have $H_0(x)=H_0(y)$. Write, as usual, $y\in F_i(x)$ or $y\in H_i(x)$.

By (3.1) we have $F_j(x)=F_j(y)$ and $H_j(x)=H_j(y)$, for j=1,2,...i-1, and so, by (5.1) and (5.2) $U_j(x)=U_j(y)$ for j=1,2,...,2i-1.

We distinguish between the following two cases.

Case 1. $y\in F_i(x)$.

We propose to show that $U_j(x)\cap U_j(y)=\emptyset$, for all $j=2i,\dots,\min\{p_x,p_y\}$. First, we note that $U_j(x)=U_j(y)$, together with Observation 6, (3.2), and (5.2) guarantees that $U_{2i}(y)\subseteq F_i(x)$.

By Observation 6, $U_{2i}(x)=\{x\}\cup\bigcup_{j=i+1}^{p_x}(F_j(x)\cup H_j(x))\cup H_i(x)$ implying that $U_{2i}(y)\cap U_{2i}(x)=\emptyset$.

Now the conclusion follows by (12), and Case 1 is settled.

Case 2. $y\in H_i(x)$.

The proof follows in essence that of Case 1 and is, therefore, omitted. □

3. A recognition algorithm

Before we show how the characterization provided by Theorem 1 can be exploited to obtain an NC recognition algorithm for cographs, it is instructive to get a handle on the sets $F_1(x)$, $F_2(x)$, ..., $F_{p_x}(x)$, $H_0(x)$, $H_1(x)$, ..., $H_{p_x}(x)$, and $U_0(x)$, $U_1(x)$, ..., $U_{2p_x+1}(x)$ defined in the previous section. A nice interpretation of these sets can be given in terms of the cotree associated with a cograph G.

Note that Lerch's definition of the cotree [9] implies that the root is always a 1-node. Let G be a cograph and let T(G) stand for the unique cotree corresponding to G. For an arbitrary node w of T(G), we let L(w) stand for the set of all the leaves in the subtree of T(G) rooted at w. Given an arbitrary vertex x of G, we shall let the *unique* path in T(G) joining x and R be described by:

$$(\Pi)\quad x=u_{q_x}(x),\ u_{q-1}(x),\ \dots,\ u_0(x)=R \text{ with } q_x\geq 0.$$

For every subscript i ($0\leq i\leq q_x$) define

$$\Delta_i(x)=\begin{cases} L(u_i(x))-L(u_{i+1}(x)) & 0\leq i<q_x \\ \{x\} & i=q_x \end{cases}$$

Note that every internal node of T(G) has degree at least two, whenever G has at least two vertices and, therefore, $\Delta_i(x)\neq\emptyset$ for all $i=0,1,\dots,q_x$. By the definition of the cotree we can write:

$$N(x)=\bigcup_{\substack{0\leq j<q_x\\ u_j(x)\text{ a 1-node}}}\Delta_j(x) \text{ and } N'(x)=\bigcup_{\substack{0\leq j<q_x\\ u_j(x)\text{ a 0-node}}}\Delta_j(x).$$

The following simple observations follow directly from definitions.

Observation 8. *Let* $u_i(x)$ *be an arbitrary 1-node on the path* (Π). *For every choice of the vertex y in* $\Delta_i(x)$, $N[y]-N[x]=N'(x)-\bigcup_{\substack{0\leq j\leq i-1\\ u_j(x)\text{ a 0-node}}}\Delta_j(x)$.

Observation 8 implies that N[y]−N[x]=N[z]−N[x], for every choice of vertices y, z in

$\Delta_i(x)$ with $u_i(x)$ a 1-node.

Observation 9. *Let* $u_i(x)$ *and* $u_j(x)$ *be distinct 1-nodes belonging to* (Π), *with* $i<j$. *Then,* $N[y]-N[x] \supset N[z]-N[x]$, *for every choice of vertices y, z in* $\Delta_i(x)$ *and* $\Delta_j(x)$, *respectively.* □

Observation 10. *Let* $u_i(x)$, $u_{i+2}(x)$ *be consecutive 1-nodes with* $0 \le i < q_x-2$. *Then, for every choice of vertices y, z in* $\Delta_i(x)$ *and* $\Delta_{i+2}(x)$, *respectively,* $\Delta_{i+1}(x) = (N[y]-N[x])-(N[z]-N[x])$. □

We are now in a position to summarize our theoretical results concerning the cographs. More precisely, we have

Theorem 2. *For every vertex x of a cograph G=(V,E),* $q_x=2p_x$ *or else* $q_x=2p_x+1$. *Furthermore, for every subscript i with* $0 \le i \le q_x-1$, *the following statements are satisfied:*

(ι) $\Delta_i(x)=\begin{cases} H_t(x) & i=2t \\ F_t(x) & i=2t+1. \end{cases}$

(ιι) $L(u_i(x))=U_i(x)$.

Proof of Theorem 2. By Observation 9 the sets $\Delta_i(x)$ with $u_i(x)$ *a 1-node* satisfy the conditions (1.1) and (1.2) in the definition of the sets $F_i(x)$. The uniqueness implied by Observation 1, guarantees that q_x-1 equals either $2p_x-1$ or $2p_x$, as claimed. Furthermore, $\Delta_i(x) = F_t(x)$, whenever $u_i(x)$ is a 1-node ($0 \le i \le q_x-1$).

By Observation 10, (0.2), (2.1), and (2.2), $\Delta_i(x) = H_t(x)$, whenever $u_i(x)$ is a 1-node ($0 \le i \le q_x-1$). Note that if $H_{p_x}(x)$ is empty, then $q_x=2p_x$, otherwise $q_x=2p_x+1$, and $\Delta_{2p_x}=H_{p_x}(x)$.

To prove (ιι), note that by definition, for $i=1,\dots,q_x-1$, $L(u_{i-1}(x))=L(u_i(x))\cup\Delta_{i-1}(x)$.

By (ι), for $i=1,\dots,q_x-1$,

$$\Delta_{i-1}(x)=\begin{cases} F_t(x) & i=2t \\ H_t(x) & i=2t+1. \end{cases}$$

and so,

$$L(u_i(x))=L(u_{i-1}(x))-\begin{cases} F_t(x) & i=2t \\ H_t(x) & i=2t+1. \end{cases}$$

Letting $L(u_1(x))=V$ and $L(u_{q_x})=\{x\}$, (5.1)-(5.3) together with the uniqueness implied by Observation 1 imply that for $i=0,2,\dots,q_x$, $L(u_i(x))=U_i(x)$, as claimed. This completes the proof of Theorem 2. □

A representation scheme for the cotree T(G) of a cograph G involves associating with every node w of T(G) the label L(w). It is immediate that in this scheme, distinct nodes of T(G) always receive distinct labels. The following result is directly implied by Theorem 2.

Corollary 2.a. *For every vertex x of a cograph G, the sets* $U_{q_x}=\{x\}$, $U_{q_x-1}(x)$, ..., $U_0(x)$ *represent the labels of the unique path* (Π) *joining x to the root of T(G).* □

We are now in a position to propose a parallel recognition algorithm for cographs whose idea is motivated by the characterization contained in Theorem 1. With an arbitrary graph G=(V,E) with $|V| = n$ and $|E| = m$ as input, the algorithm constructs, for every vertex x of G, the sets $F_1(x)$, $F_2(x)$, ..., $F_{p_x}(x)$, and then tests whether or not G is partitionable. If G is not partitionable, then G cannot be a cograph and, consequently, G is rejected. Otherwise, the algorithm proceeds to construct the sets $H_0(x)$, $H_1(x)$, ..., $H_{p_x}(x)$ and $U_0(x)$, $U_1(x)$, ..., $U_{2p_x+1}(x)$. By Theorem 1, G is a cograph if, and only if, the $U_i(x)$'s satisfy a certain property.

Furthermore, it it worth noting that by Corollary 2.a, the sets $U_i(x)$ characterize the unique path from x to the root of T(G), whenever G is a cograph. To obtain the cotree T(G) of G, we only need merge all these paths.

As we are about to explain, our algorithm can be implemented in such a way that the running time of the recognition algorithm and the construction of the cotree is bounded by O(log n) using a number of processors bounded by $O(\frac{n^2+mn}{\log n})$ in the EREW model. For this purpose, the graph G is assumed to be represented by its adjacency lists. For every vertex x of G, we assign a processor to every entry on the adjacency list of x.

For convenience, the vertices of G are enumerated as v_1, v_2, ..., v_n in a way that will be explained later. A set S of vertices will be represented by its characteristic vector $(b_1,b_2,\dots b_n)$

such that, for all i= 1,2,...,n, b_i=1 if $v_i \in S$, and 0 otherwise. Assuming that with every set S we associate $O(\frac{n}{\log n})$ processors, it is easy to see that

- the cardinality $|S|$ of S can be computed in O(log n) time using the $O(\frac{n}{\log n})$ processors associated with S;
- given sets S, S' of vertices of G, computing $S-S'$, $S \cup S'$, $S \cap S'$, as well as testing $S=S'$, $S=\emptyset$, $S \subseteq S'$, $S \subset S'$ take O(log n) time using $O(\frac{n}{\log n})$ processors.

We further note that, for every vertex x of G, computing N[x] (resp. N'(x)) takes O(log n) time using $O(\frac{n}{\log n})$ processors. Specifically, the computation is carried out in the following two steps: first, in O(log n) time, the $O(\frac{n}{\log n})$ processors associated with N[x] (resp. N'(x)) initialize N[x] (resp. N'(x)) to $\emptyset$ (resp. all 1's). Next, the d(x) processors associated with the entries on x's adjacency list write a 1 (resp. 0) into the corresponding bit of N[x] (resp. N'(x)).

Hence, to compute all the sets N[x] and N'(x) we spend O(log n) time, using $O(\frac{n^2}{\log n}+m)$ processors.

Our first algorithm determines whether or not an arbitrary graph G is partitionable. For this purpose, with every i ($1 \le i \le n$) and every j such that $v_j \in N(v_i)$ we associate a set D(i,j) to stand for $N[v_j]-N[v_i]$. For later reference, we note that for every i ($1 \le i \le n$) there are exactly $d(v_i)$ sets D(i,j) having i as the first parameter, and there are $d(v_i)$ sets D(k,i) having i as the second parameter. Since no read conflicts are allowed, $N[v_i]$ will have to be broadcast to the sets D(i,j) that need it.

To restrict the running time to O(log n) we use $\lceil \frac{d(v_i)}{\log n} \rceil$ "superprocessors" for every value of i ($1 \le i \le n$). Each of these "superprocessors" can be thought of as a set of n hidden processors which will be used to transfer an n-bit vector in O(1) time. With this trick, to broadcast $N[v_i]$ to the $d(v_i)$ sets D(i,j) that need it we do the following:

- in $O(\log \lceil \frac{d(v_i)}{\log n} \rceil) \subseteq O(\log n)$ time $N[v_i]$ will be broadcast to the $\lceil \frac{d(v_i)}{\log n} \rceil$ "superprocessors" (equivalently, to $\lceil \frac{d(v_i)}{\log n} \rceil$ sets D(i,j));
- each of the $\lceil \frac{d((v_i)}{\log n} \rceil$ "superprocessors" will broadcast the value of $N[v_i]$, sequentially, to log n sets D(i,j) in O(log n) time.

Visibly, the broadcast operation takes O(log n) time altogether using $O(\frac{n}{\log n}\sum_{i=1}^{n} d(v_i))=O(\frac{mn}{\log n})$ processors.

After the broadcast step is over, each set D(i,j) inherits $O(\frac{n}{\log n})$ processors described above: since there are $O(\sum_{i=1}^{n} d(v_i))=O(m)$ sets D(i,j) we can reuse the $O(\frac{mn}{\log n})$ processors that performed the broadcasting. More specifically, with every set D(i,j) we associate $1+\lceil \frac{n}{\log n} \rceil$ processors. One of these processors, that we call P(i,j,0) remembers in its own memory the values of i, j, $d(i,j)=|D(i,j)|$, along with a pointer to D(i,j). The remaining $\lceil \frac{n}{\log n} \rceil$ processors associated with D(i,j) are used for computational purposes only.

The details of the algorithm are spelled as follows.

```
Procedure Test_Partitionable(G);
0. begin
1.    for every vertex v_i of G do in parallel
2.         begin
3.              for every vertex v_j in N(v_i) do in parallel
4.                  begin
5.                       D(i,j) ← N[v_j]−N[v_i];
6.                       d(i,j) ← | D(i,j) |
7.                  end;
8.              let D(i,j_1),...,D(i,j_d(v_i)) be a permutation of
                the D(i,j)'s in non-increasing order of d(i,j);
9.              for k=1 to d(v_i) do in parallel
10.                 if D(i,j_{k+1})−D(i,j_k)≠∅ then
11.                           processor P(i,j_k,0) writes a 1 in its own memory;
12.             if at least a 1 was written then return("no")
13.        end
14. end;
```

Lemma 4. *With an arbitrary graph $G=(V,E)$ with $|V|=n$ and $|E|=m$ as input, the procedure Test_Partitionable correctly determines whether G is partitionable. Furthermore, its running time is bounded by $O(\log n)$ using $O(\frac{nm}{\log n})$ processors in the EREW model.* □

Note that procedure Test_Partitionable determines whether a graph G is partitionable without actually computing, for a vertex x of G, the sets $F_1(x)$, $F_2(x)$, ..., $F_{p_x}(x)$. However, since the these sets play a crucial role in determining whether G is a *cograph*, we now present a procedure that, for every vertex x of G determines $F_1(x)$, $F_2(x)$, ..., $F_{p_x}(x)$. In this context, it is convenient to inherit all the data structures produced by Test_Partitionable. For the purpose of computing the sets $F_j(v_i)$ for every vertex v_i, we use a vector F^i with subscripts running from $d(i,j_{d(v_i)})$ to $d(i,j_1)$ and whose elements are n-bit vectors themselves. The intention here is that, for every $d(i,j_k)$ with $k=1,2,...,d(v_i)$, $F^i(d(i,j_k))$ contains the characteristic vector of some $F_j(x)$. The details are spelled out as follows.

```
Procedure Find_F;
0. begin
1.     for every vertex v_i of G do in parallel
2.         for every vertex v_j in N(v_i) do in parallel
3.                processor P(i,j,0) does the following
4.                  - sets the j-th bit of F^i(d(i,j));
5.                  - remembers that it has written into F^i(d(i,j));
6.         let F_{i_1}, F_{i_2}, ..., F_{i_{p_i}} be the entries of F^i that have been written into in line 4;
7.         for t=1 to p_i do in parallel
8.             F_t(v_i)←F_{i_t}
9. end;
```

Lemma 5. *Procedure Find_F correctly computes the sets $F_1(v_i)$, $F_2(v_i)$, ..., $F_{p_i}(v_i)$ for every $i=1,2,...,n$. Furthermore, its running time is bounded by $O(\log n)$ using $O(\frac{mn}{\log n})$ processors in the EREW model.* □

It is convenient to have, for every vertex x of G, $1+\lceil\frac{n}{\log n}\rceil$ processors assigned to each of the sets $F_j(x)$ $(1\leq j\leq p_x)$. The total number of processors assigned in this way is bounded by $\sum_{x\in V} d(x)(1+\lceil\frac{n}{\log n}\rceil)=m(1+\lceil\frac{n}{\log n}\rceil)\leq m(2+\frac{n}{\log n})=2m+\frac{mn}{\log n}$.

Computing the sets $H_0(x)$, $H_1(x)$, ..., $H_{p_x}(x)$ for every vertex $x(=v_i)$ of G is now straightforward: by (2.1), for $1\leq i\leq p_x-1$, $H_i(x)$ is precisely $D(i,j_r)-D(i,j_s)$ with v_{j_r} and v_{j_s} in $F_i(x)$ and

$F_{i+1}(x)$, respectively. Similarly, by (2.2), $H_{p_x}(x)$ is precisely $D(i,j_t)$ for some v_{j_t} in $F_{p_x}(x)$. By (1) the choice of the vertices v_{j_r} and v_{j_s} in $F_i(x)$ and $F_{i+1}(x)$, is arbitrary. Hence, we can pick the vertex corresponding to the first 1 bit in the characteristic vector of $F_i(x)$ and $F_{i+1}(x)$ respectively. This can be conveniently done using a function First which, for a set S of vertices of G returns the position of the leftmost 1 in the characteristic-vector representation of S. (If S is empty, First(S) returns 0.) Clearly, with our processor allocation scheme, the $O(\frac{n}{\log n})$ processors allocated to the sets $F_j(x)$ $(1 \le j \le p_x)$ compute $\text{First}(F_j(x))$ in $O(\log n)$ time.

It is interesting to note that we can think of every $H_j(v_i)$ as "inheriting" the processors previously owned by $D(i,j)$. This is justified by the fact that the sets $D(i,j)$ are no longer needed in our algorithm. The details are spelled out by the following procedure.

Procedure Find_H;

begin
    for all v_i in G **do in parallel**
        begin
            let $F_1(v_i), F_2(v_i), \ldots, F_{p_i}(v_i)$ be computed in line 8 of Find_F;
            $H_0(v_i) \leftarrow N'(v_i) - D(i,\text{First}(F_1(v_i)))$;
            for $j=1$ **to** p_i-1 **do in parallel**
                $H_j(v_i) \leftarrow D(i,\text{First}(F_j(v_i))) - D(i,\text{First}(F_{j+1}(v_i)))$;
            $H_{p_i}(v_i) \leftarrow D(i,\text{First}(F_{p_i}(v_i)))$
        end {for}
end; {Find_H}

Lemma 6. *Procedure Find_H correctly computes the sets* $H_1(v_i), H_2(v_i), \ldots, H_{p_i}(v_i)$ *for every* $i=1,2,\ldots,n$. *Furthermore, its running time is bounded by O(log n) using O(mn) processors in the EREW model.* □

Next, for the purpose of computing the sets $U_0(x), U_1(x), \ldots, U_{q_x}(x)$ for a vertex $x(=v_i)$ of G, we shall proceed in the following two stages.

Stage 1. For every vertex x of G we initialize the sets $U_0(x), U_1(x), \ldots, U_{q_x}(x)$ by the following procedure.

Procedure Initialize_U(x);

begin
    for $i \leftarrow 1$ **to** $2p_x$-1 **do in parallel**

$$U_i(x) \leftarrow \begin{cases} F_t(x) & i=2t-1; \\ H_t(x) & i=2t; \end{cases}$$

    $q_x \leftarrow 2p_x$;
    if $H_{p_x}(x) \neq \varnothing$ **then begin**
        $U_{q_x}(x) \leftarrow H_{p_x}(x)$;
        $q_x \leftarrow q_x+1$
    end; {if}
    $U_{q_x}(x) \leftarrow \{x\}$
end; {Initialize_U}

Stage 2. Using a variant of the well-known binary prefix technique, that we are about to explain, we compute for every vertex x of G, the final value of each $U_i(x)$.

The outcome of Stage 1 can be viewed as a set of "lists" of the type $U_0(x), U_1(x), \ldots, U_{q_x}(x)$, for every vertex x of G. A natural question to ask is whether there is a natural upper bound on the total length of these lists. As we shall see, this is, indeed, the case. As it turns out, for every vertex x of G, q_x is bounded by a small multiple of d(x). More precisely, we have the following result.

Lemma 7. *For every vertex x of a partitionable graph G,* q_x *is bounded by O(d(x)).* □

Lemma 7 has the following surprising corollary.

Corollary 16.a. *In a partitionable graph G=(V,E) with n vertices and m edges,* $\sum_{x\in V} q_x$ *is bounded by 2m+n.* □

For later reference, we note that as a byproduct of procedure Initialize_U, we can tacitely assume that, in line 2, every $U_i(x)$ inherits the processors assigned to $F_t(x)$ or $H_t(x)$, and that $U_{q_x}(x)$ in line 8 receives $1+\lceil\frac{n}{\log n}\rceil$ processors. Consequently, for every i ($1\le i\le n$) and for every j ($1\le j\le p_i$), $U_j(v_i)$ has $1+\lceil\frac{n}{\log n}\rceil$ processors assigned to it. One of these is referred to as p(i,j,0) and will be used for housekeeping tasks (as explained below), while the remaining $\lceil\frac{n}{\log n}\rceil$ processors are anonymous, serving for computational purposes only. By lemma 7, the total number of processors assigned to sets $U_j(v_i)$ ($1\le j\le p_i$), ($1\le i\le n$) is $O(\frac{n^2+mn}{\log n})$.

We are now ready to make the enumeration $v_1, v_2, ..., v_n$ precise. We insist on having:

$$q_{v_i}\ge q_{v_j}, \text{ whenever } v_i < v_j.$$

[Note that this amounts to sorting the sequence of q_x's for $x\in V$ in non-increasing order. By Lemma 7, the q_x's are numbers in the range from 1 to 2n-1, and so, using the algorithm in [3], this enumeration can be performed in O(log n) time using O(n) processors.]

For the sake of simplicity, we assume that for all x in G, the sets $U_{q_x}(x)$, $U_{q_x-1}(x)$, ..., $U_0(x)$ computed in Stage 1 are stored in an array A whose elements are n-bit vectors themselves. By Lemma 7, the entries in A are subscripted from 1 to $\sum_{x\in V}(q_x+1)\le 2(m+n)$. We further assume that within A, the sets $U_j(v_1)$ are stored from A[1] through $A[q_1+1]$, the sets $U_j(v_2)$ are stored from $A[q_1+2]$ through $A[q_1+q_2+1]$, and so on. In addition, with every entry A[i] of A, we associate the "label" j, whenever A[i] contains some set $U_k(v_j)$. Computing the starting address of every "list" can be done in O(log n) time using $O(\frac{n}{\log n})$ processors by binary fan-in.

We now describe how Stage 2 works. To begin, it is well-known that given N real numbers $x_1, x_2, ..., x_N$, the "prefix" sums $\sum_{j=1}^{i} x_j$, for all i=1,2,...,N can be computed in O(log N) time using $O(\frac{N}{\log N})$ processors. As we are about to explain, this technique can be extended in two distinct ways:

- first, we can compute a "selective" prefix sum in the following sense: instead of performing $x_{i+1}\leftarrow x_{i+1}+x_i$ we perform

if $p(x_{i+1},x_i)$ **then**
$x_{i+1}\leftarrow x_{i+1}+x_i$

Here, $p(x_{i+1},x_i)$ is a predicate involving the reals x_{i+1} and x_i. Trivially, if for every pair x_{i+1} and x_i, the predicate $p(x_{i+1},x_i)$ can be evaluated in constant time, then the "selective" prefix can be computed in O(log N) time using $O(\frac{N}{\log N})$ processors.

- second, we can let $x_1, x_2, ..., x_N$ stand for n-bit characteristic vectors and perform a "selective" union of these vectors as above. However, to keep the running time bounded by O(log N) we need to associate n processors with every set x_i, for a total of $O(\frac{nN}{\log N})$ processors. (Of course, as before, we assume that every predicate $p(x_{i+1},x_i)$ can be evaluated in constant time.)

We plan to apply the previous ideas for the purpose of computing the "selective" prefix of A, in the form of $\bigcup_{j=1}^{i} A[j]$ for i=1,2,..., $\sum_{x\in V}(q_x+1)$, with the predicate p(A[j],A[j+1]) **true** if, and only if, A[j] and A[j+1] have the same label (i.e. the sets stored in A[j] and A[j+1] belong to the "list" of the same vertex v_k). Trivially, p(A[j],A[j+1]) can be evaluated in constant time by one of the processors associated with A[j].

Stage 1 and Stage 2 mentioned above can be combined in the form of the following procedure.

Procedure Find_U;

0. **begin**
1.   **for** every vertex x of G **do in parallel**
2.   Initialize_U(x);
3.   compute the "selective" prefix of A;
4.   return(A)
5. **end**; {Find_U}

We can summarize our previous discussion by the following result.

Lemma 8. *Procedure Find_U correctly computes the sets* $U_0(v_i)$, $U_1(v_i)$, ..., $U_{q_i}(v_i)$ *for every* $i=1,2,\ldots,n$. *Furthermore, its running time is bounded by* $O(\log n)$ *using* $O(\frac{mn}{\log n})$ *processors in the EREW model.* □

In the remainder of this work we assume that for every j ($1 \le j \le q_i$) and for every i ($1 \le i \le n$), processor p(i,j,0) remembers the values of i, j, as well as the index of $U_j(v_i)$ in A. In addition, processor p(i,j,0) maintains two pointers which will be used for the purpose of constructing the corresponding cotree, should the graph turn out to be a cograph. For $i \ge 1$, the first pointer, h(p(i,j,0)) points to p(i-1,j,0), while the second pointer v(p(i,j,0)) is set to **nil** initially, for all $i \ge 0$.

Recall that by Theorem 2, a partitionable graph G is a cograph if, and only if, for every i and for every j, k, $U_i(v_j)$ and $U_i(v_k)$ coincide whenever they intersect.

To make the presentation of the following algorithms easier to understand, we assume that there are n_i processors p(i,j,0) whose first component is i, namely p(i,1,0), p(i,2,0),...,p(i,n_i,0). The following procedure tests a partitionable graph for being a cograph. More precisely we have:

Procedure Check_Cograph;

0. **begin**
1.   **for** $i \leftarrow 1$ **to** q_1 **do in parallel**
2.   **for** $j \leftarrow 1$ **to** n_i **do in parallel**
3. $f(i,j) \leftarrow First(U_i(v_j))$;
4.   sort the $U_i(v_j)$'s in non-decreasing order of the corresponding f(i,j);
      {let $U_i(j_1), U_i(j_2), \ldots, U_i(j_{n_i})$ be this order}
5.   processor $p(i,j_1,0)$ marks itself;
6.   **for** t=2 **to** n_i **do in parallel**
7.   **if** $U_i(v_{j_t}) \cap U_i(v_{j_{t-1}}) \neq \emptyset$ **then**
8.   **if** $(U_i(v_{j_t}) = U_i(v_{j_{t-1}}))$ **then**
9. $v(p(i,j_t,0)) \leftarrow p(i,j_{t-1},0)$
10.   **else**
11.   processor $p(i,j_t,0)$ writes a "1" in its own memory
12.   **else**
13.   processor $p(i,j_t,0)$ marks itself;
14.   **if** a "1" was written in line 11 **then** return("no");
15.   **for** all marked processors $p(i,j_t,0)$ **do in parallel**
16.   **for** k=1 **to** n **do in parallel**
17.   compute s(i,k), the arithmetic sum of all the bits
            of rank k in the corresponding U_i;
18.   **if** any of the s(i,k)'s is distinct from 1 **then**
19.   return("no");
20.   return("yes")
21. **end**;

Lemma 9. *Procedure Check_Cograph correctly tests whether a partitionable graph G is a cograph. Furthermore, its running time is bounded by* $O(\log n)$ *using* $O(\frac{n^2+mn}{\log n})$ *processors in* *the EREW model.* □

Finally, we turn our attention to the construction of the cotree T(G) corresponding to a cograph G. For this purpose, we shall find it useful to inherit all the data structures of procedure Check_Cograph. In this context, it is useful to note that for every i with $1 \le i \le q_1$, some of the processors p(i,j,0) are marked during the execution of Check_Cograph. To anticipate, these marked processors correspond, in a very strong sense, to the nodes of the cotree T(G). In addition, the processors p(i,j,0) that are not marked are linked in a list pointing to the corresponding marked processor: see line 9 in Check_Cograph

The procedure Construct_Cotree that we are about to present starts by collapsing each such linked list in such a way that every element in the list will point directly to the head of the list (the marked processor). This process is reminiscent of the procedure used by Cole and Vishkin [4]. Furthermore, since every list contains at most O(n) elements, the collapsing takes at most O(log n) time using O(n) processors in the EREW model (for the technical details, the reader is referred to [4]).

Now constructing the cotree T(G) corresponding to a cograph G is easy: the nodes of the cotree are precisely the marked processors. All we need do is set the corresponding parent pointers (these are the h pointers). The details are spelled out by the following procedure.

```
Procedure Construct_Cotree;
begin
   for i=1 to q1 do in parallel
      for j=1 to ni do in parallel
         begin
            collapse_list;
            if p(i,j,0) is marked then
               if h(p(i,j,0)) is not marked then
                  h(p(i,j,0))←v(h(p(i,j,0)))
         end;
   if U0(v1)=U1(v1) then
      Root←U1(v1)
   else
      Root←U0(v1)
end;
```

Lemma 10. *Procedure Construct_Cotree correctly constructs the cotree corresponding to a cograph G with n vertices and m edges in O(log n) time using* $O(\frac{n^2+mn}{\log n})$ *processors in the EREW model.* □

Finally, combining Lemmas 4-10, we obtain the following result.

Theorem 3. *For an arbitrary graph G=(V,E) with* $|V|=n$ *and* $|E|=m$ *as input, membership in the class of cographs can be detected in O(log n) time using* $O(\frac{n^2+mn}{\log n})$ *processors in the EREW model.* □

4. An optimal coloring algorithm for cographs

We shall adopt the terminolgy of [1]. We assume the trees represented by an unordered array with every node in the tree featuring a parent pointer along with a doubly linked list of children. Next, it turns out that we can restrict ourselves to binary trees. To see this, note that every ordered rooted tree T can be transformed into a regular binary tree BT as follows: referring to Figure 1, note that if a node x has degree k in T then, in BT we add k-2 identical copies of x, namely $x_1, x_2, ..., x_{k-2}$ in such a way that, with x_0 standing for x,

- the parent of x_i is x_{i-1} whenever $i \ge 1$;
- the left child of x_i is the (i+1)st child of x in T;
- the right child of x_i is x_{i+1} in case $i \le k-3$, and the k-th child of x in T otherwise.

As pointed out in [1], there is no cost associated with the construction of BT, since all we need do is to reinterpret the existing pointers in T.

Given a binary tree T, a *tree contraction sequence* is a sequence of trees $T=T_1, T_2, ..., T_m$ such that T_i is obtained for T_{i-1} by one of the following basic operations:

- prune(v) - leaf v of T_{i-1} is removed;
- bypass(v) - a node v having exactly one child is removed from T_{i-1}, with the unique child of v replacing v.

Abrahamson et al [1] show that every binary tree has an optimal contraction sequence of length O(log n), and that this sequence can be obtained in O(log n) time using $O(\frac{n}{\log n})$ processors in the EREW-PRAM model.

We are now in a position to show how the tree contraction technique can be used to obtain an optimal parallel coloring algorithm for cographs. For this purpose, consider an n-vertex cograph G represented by its parse tree T(G). We may assume that T(G) is a binary tree, otherwise we proceed to *binarize* T(G) as before.

Our algorithm proceeds in the following three stages. In the first stage, we invoke the tree contraction algorithm in [1] to construct an optimal contraction sequence $T_1, T_2, ..., T_m$ for T(G). This sequence will be used explicitely in the next stages.

In the second stage, using the contraction sequence obtained before, we compute for every node x in T(G) the largest size $\omega(x)$ of a clique in the subgraph G_x of G corresponding to the subtree of T(G) rooted at x. At the end of the second stage, every node x in T(G) contains the following information:

- $\omega(x)$ - the largest size of a clique in G_x;
- with y, z standing for the children of x, $\omega(y)$ and $\omega(z)$.

Since every cographs is *perfect* (see [13]), $\omega(x)$ must equal the number of colors needed in an optimal coloring of G_x. Put differently, at the end of the second stage of our algorithm, every node x in the tree knows the number of colors to be used in an optimal coloring of G_x, along with the number of colors to be used in G_y and G_z. In particular, the root R of T knows the total number ω of colors to be used in an optimal coloring of G itself.

The third stage of the algorithm is the actual color assigning stage. Specifically, we traverse the sequence $T_1, ..., T_m$ *backwards* allocating colors to the subtrees in the following recursive way: with the root R of T(G) we assign the colors 1, 2, ..., ω represented by the *color interval* $[1..\omega]$. In general, if a node x receives a color interval $[a_x,b_x]$, it will transmit color intervals to its children y and z according to the following rule:

- if x is a 1-node then y receives the color interval $[a_x,a_x+\omega(y)]$ and z receives the color interval $[a_x+\omega(y)+1,b_x]$;
- if x is a 0-node then y receives the color interval $[a_x,a_x+\omega(y)]$ and z receives the color interval $[a_x+\omega(z)]$

Note that by (1) this is a correct color assignment. Furthermore, it is easy to confirm that when this stage ends, every leaf receives a color interval containing a *unique* color. We should note that the third stage of our algorithm mimics the second stage only in reverse. The details are spelled out by the following procedure.

Procedure Color(G);
{Input: a cograph G represented by T(G);
Output: an optimal coloring of the vertices of G}

```
begin
    find an optimal contraction sequence T1, ..., Tm for T(G);
    for all nodes x of T(G) do in parallel
        find the size ω(x) of the largest clique in Gx;
    let ω stand for the size of the largest clique in G;
    assign the color interval [1..ω] to the root of T(G);
    for all nodes x of T(G) do in parallel
        let x have children y and z and let x have received the color interval [ax,bx];
        if x is a 1-node then begin
            assign color interval [ax,ax+ω(y)] to y;
```

```
10.            assign color interval [ax+ω(y)+1,bx] to z
11.            end
12.        else begin
13.            assign color interval [ax,ax+ω(y)] to y;
14.            assign color interval [ax,ax+ω(z)] to z
15.            end
16.        end {for}
17. end
```

Theorem 3. Procedure Color correctly colors an n-vertex cograph represented by its parse tree in O(log n) time using $O(\frac{n}{\log n})$ processors in the EREW-PRAM model.

Proof. The correctness follows trivially by the previous discussion. To address the complexity, consider an arbitrary n-vertex cograph G represented by its parse tree T(G). As mentioned previously, we assume without loss of generality that T(G) is a binary tree.

To obtain the optimal contraction sequence $T_1, \ldots, T_m$ in line 1 we use the tree contraction algorithm in [1]. Next, lines 2 and 3 take, O(log n) time using $O(\frac{n}{\log n})$ processors by using the maximum clique algorithm for cographs developed in [1].

The for loop in lines 6-16 amounts to traversing the tree sequence in reverse order. It is easy to confirm that the color interval for every node in T_{i-1} is obtained in O(1) time once we know the color interval for every node in T_i. Consequently, when the execution of the loop terminates (in O(log n) steps), all the leaves of T(G) and, therefore, all vertices of G have received a unique color. □

References

1. K. Abrahamson, N. Dadoun, D. G. Kirkpatrick, and T. Przytycka, A simple parallel tree contraction algorithm, *Journal of Algorithms* 10 (1989) 287-302.

2. G. Adhar, S. Peng, Parallel Algorithms for Cograph Recognition and Applications, *Proc. of 1989 Workshop on Algorithms and data Structures*, August 1989, Ottawa, pp. 335-351.

3. R. Cole, Parallel Merge Sort, *SIAM Journal on Computing*, 17, (1988), 770-785.

4. R. Cole and U. Vishkin, Approximate Parallel Scheduling, Part I: The basic techniques with applications to optimal parallel list ranking in logarithmic time, *SIAM Journal on Computing*, 17, (1988) 128-142.

5. D. G. Corneil and D. G. Kirkpatrick, Families of recursively defined perfect graphs, *Congressus Numerantium*, 39 (1983), 237-246.

6. D. G. Corneil, H. Lerchs, and L. Stewart Burlingham, Complement Reducible Graphs, *Discrete Applied Mathematics*, 3, (1981), 163-174.

7. D. G. Corneil, Y. Perl, and L. K. Stewart, A linear recognition algorithm for cographs, *SIAM J. on Computing*, 14 (1985), 926-934.

8. D. G. Kirkpatrick, T. Przytycka, Parallel recognition of cographs and cotree construction, The University of British Columbia, Tech. Report 1-88, to appear in Discrete Applied Math.

9. H. Lerchs, On the clique-kernel structure of graphs, Dept. of Computer Science, University of Toronto, October 1972.

10. M. Novick, Fast Parallel Algorithms for Modular Decomposition, Cornell University, Tech. Report TR 89-1016.

11. D. Seinsche, On a property of the class of n-colorable graphs, *J. Comb. Theory (B)*, 16, (1974), 191-193.

12. C. H. Shyu, A fast algorithm for cographs, *French-Israeli Conference on Comb. and Algorithms*, Jerusalem, Israel, November 1988.

13. L. Stewart, Cographs, a class of tree representable graphs, M. Sc. Thesis, dept. of Computer Science, University of Toronto, 1978, TR 126/78.

14. U. Vishkin, Synchronous parallel Computation - a Survey, TR 71, Dept. of Computer Science, Courant Institute, NYU, 1983.

Optimally Representing Euclidean Space Discretely for Analogically Simulating Physical Phenomena

John Case Dayanand S. Rajan Anil M. Shende*

Department of Computer and Information Sciences

103 Smith Hall, University of Delaware, Newark, DE 19716, USA

1 Introduction

Existing applications for the prediction of the qualitative behavior of a physical phenomenon use analytical models of the phenomenon in computing the state of the phenomenon after a pre-determined time interval. These models involve sets of equations. (See [AG89].) The attributes of the objects involved (location in space, mass, velocity, acceleration, etc.) are the parameter values for the set of equations in an analytic model for the phenomenon and the methods for solving this set of equations are the procedures. Most *parallel* computer approaches concentrate on ingeniously parallelizing, in a manner suited to particular parallel architectures, the methods for solving the set of equations, and, then distributing data amongst the processors. Most often, this widens the gap between the problem being solved and its representation. In the case of physical phenomena, such approaches also neglect to use the inherent parallelism in the phenomenon (As a real object moves in real space, its component particles move in *parallel.* It is just this *natural* parallelism our approach, which we sketch in the next paragraph, exploits.). In particular, in these cases, the simulations do *not* unfold linear in the real-time for the corresponding phenomena to unfold.

We are interested in the *literal, analogical* simulation of physical phenomena using a mesh connected computer. We would like to model physical spaces discretely by mesh(-like) massively parallel computers (with local connectivity only). Here's the point of that. Each processor in such a mesh represents a point in space and each path built of a succession of immediate connections in the mesh represents a path in the space. Physical motion of tangible or intangible "objects" can be simulated by algorithmically passing, in the mesh, *fragments* of the objects from simulated point to adjacent simulated point in much the same way as the actual fragments of objects passing from point to point in real spaces constitutes the real motion of those objects. In a mesh those fragments could/would just be the algorithms governing how they are to be passed around. We require, of course, that our individual processors be synchronized. Clearly, then, our simulations can possibly be linear in real-time. In [CRS90] we present one of our algorithms showing how we can achieve uniform motion in spite of the anisotropies *inherent* in any mesh-like representation of space.

Our approach is similar, but *not equivalent to*, computational models of physics based on cellular automata

*Research supported in part by NSF Grant CCR 8713846 at the University of Delaware. The email address for communication regarding this paper is 'case@cis.udel.edu'.

[Fey82, Min82, FT82, Tof84, TM87, Sny47, Ung58, Mar84, SW86, Mac86, Tof77b, Tof77a, Vic84, Wol83, Zus69, Hil55, Svo86]. Lattice Gas models [Has87] are often studied using cellular automata to simulate complex physical phenomena. In a cellular automaton implementation of a Lattice Gas model, emphasis is placed on the simplicity of the local transition rule for the cellular automaton [FHP86]. Results are computed by the statistical averaging of the states over cells in a pre-determined "neighborhoods" in the cellular automaton [Has87]. Our methodology differs from Lattice Gas models in both these regards. We do not restrict ourselves to overly simple cellular automaton-like rules. Unlike individual cells in a cellular automaton, the individual processors in our meshes are assumed to be computationally more powerful than finite state automata. Averaging over the states of individual processors in our mesh is just irrelevant to our approach of literally simulating physical phenomena.

Clearly, the accuracy of our approach depends on (i) the choice of a discrete representation of physical space, and (ii) the timing of each of the algorithms representing the local behavior of the "objects" in the phenomenon being simulated. Of course, since the algorithms must be "spatial" in nature, they will depend on the particular choice of a discrete representation of physical space.

In *this* paper, we deal only with the issue of discretely representing euclidean space *well*. Researchers in discrete physics who use cellular automata have noticed that some problems in physics need the dimension of the cellular automaton to be greater than 3 [Hil55, Tof77b, Svo86, Fey82]. Furthermore, [Tof77b] shows that every cellular automaton, C, can be made reversible by embedding C in a cellular space that has dimension one more than that of C. This is useful in modeling macroscopic phenomena [Tof77b]. So, we will deal with the general issue of discretely representing euclidean n-space and not restrict ourselves to euclidean 3-space.

Let $\mathbf{N} = \{0, 1, 2, \ldots\}$, the set of natural numbers. We consider interconnection schemes, for each dimension $n \in \mathbf{N}$, suitable for a mesh designed especially to simulate phenomena in euclidean n-space. We present a particular family, $\{\mathcal{M}(\mathbf{A}_n)\}_{n\in\mathbf{N}}$, of interconnection schemes and *prove that this family is optimal* for our purpose, under some reasonable, practical assumptions which we detail. Our assumptions on the interconnection schemes nicely combine criteria that the lattice–works resulting from the interconnection schemes model euclidean spaces well, and that the most basic, relevant operations can be carried out efficiently and cleanly. Interestingly, the family of underlying sets of points (defined in Section 3) $\{\mathbf{A}_n\}_{n\in\mathbf{N}}$ is well known, but, except for $\mathcal{M}(\mathbf{A}_2)$, no member of $\{\mathcal{M}(\mathbf{A}_n)\}_{n\in\mathbf{N}}$ has (to our knowledge) been used as the interconnection scheme for a mesh computer.

2 Euclidean n-Space and Literal Simulations

In this paper, $\mathbf{N}$, $\mathbf{Z}$, $\mathbf{Q}$, and $\mathbf{R}$ will denote the sets of natural numbers, integers, rationals, and reals, respectively. For $n \in \mathbf{N}$ and $R \in \{\mathbf{N}, \mathbf{Z}, \mathbf{Q}, \mathbf{R}\}$, R^n is the n-fold cartesian product $R \times \cdots \times R$. The (standard) orthonormal basis (see, e.g., [Her64]) for $\mathbf{R}^n$ is denoted by $\{\vec{e}_1, \ldots, \vec{e}_n\}$.

n-dimensional Euclidean space ($\mathbf{R}^n$) is continuous and infinite, and any (buildable) mesh (whose processors represent points in space) approximates at best only a bounded subset of it, by a *finite* number of "chosen" points. In order to consider possible candidates for a mesh that will be most suitable, it is best to remove the constraint of finiteness in the beginning and consider a countable (infinite) subset of $\mathbf{R}^n$ which approximates it and then intersect this approximation with a bounded subset of $\mathbf{R}^n$ in order to get one of our meshes. The rule for interconnecting processors (points) is that each processor is connected to all and only its nearest (measured by euclidean distance in $\mathbf{R}^n$) neighbors.

Each processor contains information regarding what kind of point it represents, e.g., whether the point is part of space occupied by an object or not. For instance, if a point is part of space that an object occupies, the corresponding processor will have information about the local properties of that object. This suggests that we will need a large number of processors in our mesh, *but* that each processor needs to be capable of storing only limited information and have limited computing ability. As pointed out earlier, we will, nonetheless, not restrict ourselves to the simplicity of the local transition rules of cellular automata.

The way we simulate motion, collision, forces etc. in our mesh is by propagating messages. Each processor will need to compute what its next state should be and then do accordingly. This can be done without a global monitor or controller provided each processor can store *small* programs which tell the processor what to do *in its present state*; then after computing its next state, the processor receives all relevant information (perhaps including programs) stored in a neighboring processor. This way, a point that "belonged" to an object in space can pass on relevant information to one of its neighbors and the object can "move" through the mesh. The object could be intangible, e.g., a wavefront, force, etc. In effect, the mesh as a whole, "pictures" the movement of the object.

Since motion is simulated by passing messages between processors, and all messages must be passed simultaneously, it is important (in the idealized, infinite case) that the local environment of each processor be pictorially similar to that of any other processor in the mesh. Hence, the relative locations of processors, as seen from any processor in the mesh, would be the same. This, in turn, implies that the *length* of each connection must be representative of the actual distance between processors, i.e., the time taken to transfer the same message across any connection in the mesh should be a constant.

In the next section, we formally describe the desirable properties mentioned in this section. We also show that there is an essentially unique approximation of euclidean n-space, which approximation is optimal for our purposes.

3 A_n: An Optimal Approximation of Euclidean n-Space

Let D be a set of points in Euclidean n-space. We are interested in the possibility that points in D could correspond to processors in some *idealized* mesh computer (an infinite network of processors). Such an idealized mesh computer will be denoted by $\mathcal{M}(D)$, and will be referred to as the *idealized mesh computer based on D*. D is called the *underlying set* of $\mathcal{M}(D)$. More generally, given any subset X of D, $\mathcal{M}(X)$ will denote the sub-mesh of $\mathcal{M}(D)$ consisting of all those processors of $\mathcal{M}(D)$ corresponding to points in X, together with all possible interconnections which exist in $\mathcal{M}(D)$, between these processors. X is then the underlying set of $\mathcal{M}(X)$. In this paper, we will not make any distinction between the interconnection scheme for $\mathcal{M}(D)$ and $\mathcal{M}(D)$ itself. We introduce desirable properties (1 through 5) for D to have, in sequence.

Property 1 ALL OF EUCLIDEAN SPACE IS WELL REPRESENTED BY D; that is, we want D to be an "approximation" in the sense defined below.

Definition 1 *An* approximation *of* $\mathbf{R}^n$ *is a countable subset,* D*, of* $\mathbf{R}^n$ *so that there is a* $\mu = \mu(D) \geq 0$ *so that every open ball, in* $\mathbf{R}^n$*, with radius greater than* μ *contains at least one point of* D*.* μ *is then the* measure of proximity of D.

Informally, every point in Euclidean n-space is "not very far away" from D.

The sets $\mathbf{Q}^n$, $\mathbf{Z}^n$, $D_1 = \mathbf{Z}^n \setminus (2\mathbf{Z})^n$ and $D_2 = \mathbf{Z}^n \cup \{(x_1, \ldots, x_n) \mid x_j = (2k + 1/i), k, i \in \mathbf{Z}, i > 0\}$ are all approximations of $\mathbf{R}^n$, while $\{(\pm 2^{i_1}, \ldots, \pm 2^{i_n}) \mid i_1, \ldots, i_n \in \mathbf{Z}\}$ is not.

Definition 2 *An approximation* D *of* $\mathbf{R}^n$ *is* equivalent *to an approximation* D' *of* $\mathbf{R}^n$*, denoted by* $D \cong D'$*, iff there is a positive real number* m*, and an isometry (i.e., an isomorphism which preserves actual euclidean distances between corresponding points,)* $T : \mathbf{R}^n \to \mathbf{R}^n$ *so that* $m \cdot T(D) = D'$.

Note that $\cong$ is in fact an equivalence. Approximations belonging to the same equivalence class are similar in their "layout". For example, $\mathbf{Z}^2$ and $2\mathbf{Z}^2$ are equivalent.

Property 2 NO BOUNDED REGION OF $\mathbf{R}^n$ CONTAINS AN INFINITE SUBSET OF D.

We require this property because any one of our actual (buildable) meshes will be an intersection of a suitable bounded region of $\mathbf{R}^n$ with D. This is equivalent to the requirement that D be a "discretization":

Definition 3 *An approximation* D *of* $\mathbf{R}^n$ *is a* discretization *iff each point of* D *can be contained in an open ball, of* $\mathbf{R}^n$*, containing no other point of* D.

Of the four approximations in the examples above, $\mathbf{Q}^n$ and D_2 are not discretizations, while $\mathbf{Z}^n$ and D_1 are.

Physical connections between processors in the mesh cannot be of arbitrarily small length. So we require D to have the following property.

Property 3 POINTS IN D DO NOT CLUSTER TOO CLOSELY; that is, there is a real number, $\delta > 0$, so that the distance between any two points in D is at least δ. If there are two points in D so that the distance between these two points *is* δ, then we say D *has minimal distance* δ (or that the *minimal distance of* D *is* δ).

Obviously, if D has Property 3, then D has Property 2. The converse is not true, since, for example, the discretization $D = \mathbf{Z} \cup \{i + (1/i) \mid i \in \mathbf{Z}, i \neq 0\}$, of $\mathbf{R}$, has Property 2, but does not have Property 3.

Property 4 Euclidean n-space is represented "similarly", by D, "everywhere". Even more informally, if one were to stand at *any* point in D and "look around", the n-dimensional picture, including actual depth of points, would be the same. Formally, D IS INVARIANT UNDER TRANSLATIONS.

The following theorem is a combination of theorems 1 and 2 proved in [GL87][pp. 18–19]. An *n-dimensional lattice* is an abelian subgroup (i.e., a $\mathbf{Z}$-submodule), of rank n, of $\mathbf{R}^n$. Intuitively, an n-dimensional lattice is a subset of Euclidean n-space, which subset is just like an n-dimensional vector-space, except that the scalar multipliers of vectors are restricted to be integers (For a precise treatment of lattices and their properties, again see [GL87].). The notions of vector, origin, basis, linear independence, linear transformation, isomorphism, etc., are all similar to those in Euclidean space (considered as a vector-space over the field of real numbers). The length of a vector in a lattice is the same as the length of that vector in Euclidean space.

Theorem 1 *A subset D of $\mathbf{R}^n$ is an n-dimensional lattice iff D has properties 1, 3 and 4.* □

Note that a translation invariant subset of $\mathbf{R}^n$, has property 2 iff it has property 3, so we have not lost property 2.

Convention: From now on we will assume (without loss of generality) that, unless we explicitly say otherwise, *every lattice we mention has minimal distance 1.* Further, *D will always denote an n-dimensional lattice with minimal distance 1.*

The distance between points, P and Q, in a lattice is the length of the vector $(Q - P)$, from P to Q. So the minimal length of vectors in a lattice is exactly the minimal distance of that lattice considered as an approximation of euclidean space (of appropriate dimension). In this paper, we will never make this distinction, between the points in a lattice and the corresponding vectors, again.

Definition 4 *The* set of directions *in D, denoted $Dir(D)$, is the set of all vectors, in D, of length 1.*

Lattices exist in abundance, and are quite varied in their properties [GL87, CN88]. Although the study of lattices is quite incomplete [GL87, CN88], it is known that a lot of facts, intuitively clear about $\mathbf{R}^n$, are not true in all lattices [GL87, CN88]. In fact, there is *only one* (upto isometry) n-dimensional lattice, $\mathbf{Z}^n$, with an orthonormal basis. The presence of an orthonormal basis facilitates clean computation within $\mathbf{Z}^n$. Cleanness in computation is crucial for the efficient realization of our methodology in a mesh. Yet, considering the way we expect to use a mesh to simulate physical phenomena, it would be to our advantage if there were "many connections per processor". The reason is that we wish to represent as many local angles exactly as possible.

$\mathbf{Z}^n$ does not have the maximum number of direction vectors (among lattices with minimal distance 1). Hence, we will drop the requirement of having an orthonormal basis in the hope that we will find a lattice with more direction vectors, and in which computations are nearly as clean. To this end, we characterize $\mathbf{Z}^n$ using the property of regularity:

Definition 5 *A basis, $B = \{\vec{b}_1, \ldots, \vec{b}_n\}$, for D, is* regular *iff there is a constant, $K(D, B)$, so that the inner product*

$$(\vec{b}_i, \vec{b}_j) = \begin{cases} K(D,B), & \text{if } i \neq j, \\ 1, & \text{if } i = j. \end{cases}$$

If D has a regular basis, we say that D is regular.

Having a regular basis is important for both computational cleanness and having a lattice that *nicely* represents the corresponding euclidean space of the same dimension. Our methodology dictates that our algorithms be local and independent of any fixed co-ordinatization of euclidean space. Vector inner product is an *extremely* basic operation in our algorithms; having its calculation simplified is guaranteed by the existence of a regular basis. This makes computations more efficient. The following characterization of $\mathbf{Z}^n$ shows that it is regular in the strongest possible sense.

Proposition 1 *$\mathbf{Z}^n$ is the unique (up to isometry) regular lattice, D, in which every basis contained in $Dir(D)$ is regular.* □

On the other hand, there are numerous lattices, D, satisfying:

Property 5 D IS REGULAR.

The best we can hope for is that there is a unique (up to isometry) regular n-dimensional lattice (on which to base an idealized mesh) for which the number of direction vectors is maximum. We now state and prove a theorem (Theorem 2) which, by explicitly giving expressions for the number of direction vectors in regular lattices, shows us that our hope can be fulfilled (see Theorem 3). The corollaries that follow isolate some other useful consequences.

The following lemma is easy to prove, and shows that Theorem 2, in fact, covers all regular lattices.

Lemma 1 *In a lattice, D, with minimal distance 1, the inner product of any two non-collinear vectors $\vec{d}_1, \vec{d}_2$ in $Dir(D)$ lies in the interval $[-1/2, 1/2] \subset \mathbf{R}$.* □

Theorem 2 *Let $n > 1$, and let D be regular with regular basis B, and, let $k = K(D, B)$. Then,*

$$card(Dir(D)) = \begin{cases} 2n, & \text{if } 0 \leq k < \frac{1}{2}; \\ n(n+1), & \text{if } k = \frac{1}{2}; \\ 2(n+1), & \text{if } -\frac{1}{2} \leq k < 0. \end{cases}$$

PROOF. Let $\vec{d} = \sum_{i=1}^n p_i \vec{b}_i \in Dir(D)$, $\vec{b}_i \in B, p_i \in \mathbf{Z}$. Then $1 = \| \vec{d} \|^2 = \sum_{i=1}^n p_i^2 + 2k \sum_{j>i=1}^n p_i p_j$.
CASE 0: $2k \sum_{j>i=1}^n p_i p_j = 0$. Then $1 = \sum_{i=1}^n p_i^2$. So $\vec{d} = \pm \vec{b}_i$ for some $\vec{b}_i$, giving us $card(Dir(D)) = 2n$ in this case.

CASE 1: $0 \leq k < 1/2$.

This case reduces to Case 0: If $k = 0$, this is obvious, so suppose $k > 0$. Then, $\sum_{i=1}^n p_i^2 + 2k \sum_{j>i=1}^n p_i p_j = 1$, so, $\sum_{j>i=1}^{n} p_i p_j \leq 0$. If $\sum_{j>i=1}^n p_i p_j \neq 0$, then,

$$1 > \sum_{i=1}^{n} p_i^2 + \sum_{j>i=1}^{n} p_i p_j > \sum_{i=1}^{n} p_i^2 + 2 \sum_{j>i=1}^{n} p_i p_j \geq 0.$$

Since each p_i is an integer, $\sum_{i=1}^n p_i^2 + 2 \sum_{j>i=1}^n p_i p_j = 0$, and, $\sum_{i=1}^n p_i^2 + \sum_{j>i=1}^n p_i p_j = -\sum_{j>i=1}^n p_i p_j = 0$, giving us a contradiction. Therefore, $card(Dir(D)) = 2n$ in this case.

CASE 2: $k = 1/2$. Then, $1 = \sum_{i=1}^{n} p_i^2 + \sum_{j>i=1}^{n} p_i p_j$. Therefore, $0 \geq \sum_{j>i=1}^{n} p_i p_j$, which gives

$$1 \geq 1 + \sum_{j>i=1}^{n} p_i p_j = \sum_{i=1}^{n} p_i^2 + 2 \sum_{j>i=1}^{n} p_i p_j = \left(\sum_{i=1}^{n} p_i \right)^2 \geq 0.$$

So, $\sum_{j>i=1}^{n} p_i p_j = 0$ *or* -1.

If $\sum_{j>i=1}^{n} p_i p_j = 0$ then Case 0 applies, and we have the $2n$ possibilities: $\vec{d} = \pm \vec{b}_i$. Otherwise, $\sum_{j>i=1}^{n} p_i p_j = -1$, and $\sum_{i=1}^{n} p_i^2 = 2$ and so, $\sum_{i=1}^{n} p_i = 0$. Thus, exactly two of the p_i's are non-zero; one of the non-zero p_i's is a 1 and the other is a -1. This gives us $n(n-1)$ choices for $\vec{d}$. So, in all we have $n(n-1) + 2n = n(n+1)$ choices for $\vec{d}$ in this case, i.e., $card(Dir(D)) = n(n+1)$.

CASE 3; $-1/2 \leq k < 0$.

Claim 1: For each $i, p_i \geq 0$ or for each $i, p_i \leq 0$.

Let $p_{i_0} \neq 0$, $1 \leq i_0 \leq n$. Then, $1 = \sum_{i=1}^{n} p_i^2 + 2k \sum_{j>i=1}^{n} p_i p_j = \| \vec{d} - p_{i_0} \vec{b_{i_0}} \|^2 + p_{i_0}^2 + 2k p_{i_0} (\sum_{i=1,\ i \neq i_0}^{n} p_i)$. Therefore, $-2k p_{i_0} (\sum_{i=1,\ i \neq i_0}^{n} p_i) = \| \vec{d} - p_{i_0} \vec{b_{i_0}} \|^2 + p_{i_0}^2 - 1$. Since, $-2k > 0$, we add $p_{i_0}^2$ to both sides above to get $p_{i_0} (\sum_{i=1}^{n} p_i) \geq p_{i_0}^2 > 0$, thus showing that Claim 1 is true.

Claim 2: $k = -1/n$.

To show that $k \leq -1/n$, it is enough to prove that $n(\sum_{i=1}^{n} p_i^2 - 1) - 2\sum_{i,j=1}^{n} p_i p_j \geq 0$, because, $k = -(\sum_{i=1}^{n} p_i^2 - 1)/(2\sum_{i,j=1}^{n} p_i p_j)$ and $\sum_{i,j=1}^{n} p_i p_j > 0$. But,

$$n(\sum_{i=1}^{n} p_i^2 - 1) - 2 \sum_{i,j=1}^{n} p_i p_j = \sum_{j>i=1}^{n} (p_i^2 - 2p_i p_j + p_j^2) + \sum_{i=1}^{n} p_i^2 - n = \sum_{j>i=1}^{n} (p_i - p_j)^2 + \sum_{i=1}^{n} p_i^2 - n.$$

Now, if $s \geq 1$ of these p_i's are non-zero, then $\sum_{i=1}^{n} p_i^2 \geq s$ and $\sum_{j>i=1}^{n} (p_i - p_j)^2 \geq (n-s)s$. So,

$$\sum_{j>i=1}^{n} (p_i - p_j)^2 + \sum_{i=1}^{n} p_i^2 - n \geq s + (n-s)s - n = (n-s)(s-1) \geq 0.$$

Thus, we have $k \leq -1/n$. To prove that $n - 1 \geq -kn(n-1)$, let $\vec{v}$ be the vector $\sum_{i=1}^{n} \vec{b}_i$. Then,

$$\| \vec{v} \|^2 = \sum_{i=1}^{n} 1^2 + 2k \sum_{j>i=1}^{n} 1 \cdot 1 = n + 2k \frac{n(n-1)}{2} = n + kn(n-1) \geq 1.$$

So, $k \geq -1/n$, and Claim 2 is proved.

Claim 3: Let, without loss of generality, $p_i > 0$ for $1 \leq i \leq m \leq n$ and $p_i = 0$ otherwise. Then, $m = n$ or $m = 1$ and $p_i = 1$ for $i \leq m$.

Let $p_i = 1 + q_i$, $q_i \geq 0$ for $1 \leq i \leq m$ and let $\vec{w} = \sum_{i=1}^{m} q_i \vec{b}_i$. Then,

$$\begin{aligned} \| \vec{d} \| &= \sum_{i=1}^{m} p_i^2 - \frac{2}{n} \sum_{j>i=1}^{m} p_i p_j = \sum_{i=1}^{m} (1 + q_i)^2 - \frac{2}{n} \sum_{j>i=1}^{m} (1 + q_i)(1 + q_j) \\ &= m - \frac{m(m-1)}{n} + \| \vec{w} \|^2 + (2 - \frac{2(m-1)}{n})(\sum_{i=1}^{m} q_i). \end{aligned}$$

Now, $m - (m(m-1)/n) \geq 1$ for $1 \leq m \leq n$, and equality holds iff $m = 1$ or $m = n$. Also, the last two terms are positive unless every q_i is 0, i.e., unless every $p_i = 1$. Thus, Claim 3 is true.

Thus, in the case $-1/2 \leq k < 0$, we get, $\| \vec{d} \| = 1$ iff $\vec{d} = \pm \vec{b}_i$ or $\vec{d} = \pm \sum_{i=1}^{n} \vec{b}_i$. Therefore, $card(Dir(D)) = 2n + 2 = 2(n+1)$. □

The following three corollaries follow from the proof of the above theorem.

Corollary 1 *For a n-dimensional regular lattice, D, with regular basis, B, either $0 \leq K(D,B) \leq 1/2$, or $K(D,B) = -1/n$.*

PROOF. Claim 2 in Case 3 in the proof of the theorem above asserts that if $K(D,B) < 0$, then $K(D,B) = -1/n$. □

Corollary 2 *Let D be a n-dimensional regular lattice with regular basis, B. Then, $Dir(D) = P(B) \cup Q(B)$, where,*

$$
\begin{aligned}
P(B) &= \{ \pm\vec{b} \mid \vec{b} \in B \} \quad \textit{and} \\
Q(B) &= \begin{cases} \emptyset & \textit{if } 0 \leq K(D,B) < 1/2; \\ \{ (\vec{b} - \vec{b}') \mid \vec{b}, \vec{b}' \in B,\ \vec{b} \neq \vec{b}' \} & \textit{if } K(D,B) = 1/2; \\ \{ \pm(\sum_{\vec{b} \in B} \vec{b}) \} & \textit{if } K(D,B) = -1/n. \end{cases}
\end{aligned}
$$

PROOF. The proof of this corollary follows from the last few lines of the proofs of each of the Cases 0, 1 and 3 in the proof of the theorem above. □

Corollary 3 *For a n-dimensional, $n \geq 2$, regular lattice, D, with regular bases B, C,*

$$
K(D,C) = \begin{cases} \pm K(D,B) & \textit{if } n = 2 \textit{ and } K(D,B) = \pm\frac{1}{2} \\ K(D,B) & \textit{otherwise.} \end{cases}
$$

PROOF. We first show that (i) $K(D,C) = \pm K(D,B)$ for every n, and then that (ii) $K(D,C) \neq -K(D,B)$ if $n > 2$.

To prove (i), it is enough to show that for some $\vec{c}_1, \vec{c}_2 \in C$, $\vec{c}_1 \neq \vec{c}_2$, $(\vec{c}_1, \vec{c}_2) = \pm K(D,B)$. $B, C \subset Dir(D)$. The previous corollary provides us with explicit descriptions of the possible forms for $\vec{c}_1$ and $\vec{c}_2$ in each of the three cases for $K(D,B)$.

CASE 1: $0 \leq K(D,B) < 1/2$. $C \subset P(B)$ (in the notation of the previous corollary). So, $\vec{c}_1 = \pm\vec{b}_1$ and $\vec{c}_2 = \pm\vec{b}_2$, for some $\vec{b}_1, \vec{b}_2 \in B$, and hence $(\vec{c}_1, \vec{c}_2) = \pm K(D,B)$.

CASE 2: $K(D,B) = 1/2$. $card(Dir(D)) = n(n+1)$ in this case. Suppose $K(D,C) \neq 1/2$. Then, $-1/2 \leq K(D,C) < 1/2$. If $0 \leq K(D,C) < 1/2$, then, $card(Dir(D)) = 2n \neq n(n+1)$ giving us a contradiction. If $K(D,C) < 0$, then, $card(Dir(D)) = 2n+2$, which is equal to $n(n+1)$ iff $n = 2$. Then, $K(D,C) = -1/n = -1/2 = -K(D,B)$.

CASE 3: $K(D,B) = -1/n$. If $C \subset P(B)$, then the proof is identical to the proof of Case 1. If $\vec{c}_1 = \pm\vec{b}_1 \in P(B)$ and $\vec{c}_2 \in Q(B)$, then, $(\vec{c}_1, \vec{c}_2) = (\pm\vec{b}_1, \pm(\sum_{\vec{b} \in B} \vec{b})) = \pm(1 - (n-1)/n) = \pm 1/n = K(D,B)$. The case $\vec{c}_1, \vec{c}_2 \in Q(B)$ cannot arise since each element in $Q(B)$ is the additive inverse of the other, and hence $Q(B)$ is not a linearly independent set.

To prove (ii), notice that if D has bases B and C with $K(D,B) > 0$ and $K(D,C) < 0$, then $card(Dir(D))$ can be expressed simultaneously as $2n+2$ and also as $2n$ or $n(n+1)$. This is possible iff $n = 2$ and $card(Dir(D)) = n(n+1)$. □

As mentioned earlier, our algorithms sometimes depend on calculations using $K(D,B)$, for different regular bases B. By the last corollary, the quantity $K(D,B)$ does not depend on the choice of B, except possibly in dimension 2. This is good, computationally, for our purposes, as we will see in Section 4.1. This motivates the following definition.

Definition 6 *The* regular inner product *of a n-dimensional regular lattice, D, denoted K(D), is defined by*

$$K(D) = \begin{cases} \frac{1}{2} & \text{if } n = 2 \text{ and } K(D,B) = \pm\frac{1}{2} \\ K(D,B) & \text{otherwise.} \end{cases}$$

for some regular basis B for D.

It is not difficult to construct, for each positive integer, n, and for each k in the interval $[0, 1/2]$ the unique (upto isometry) n-dimensional regular lattice with regular inner product equal to k. We denote by $\mathbf{A}_n$, the n-dimensional regular lattice whose regular inner product is $1/2$.

$\mathbf{A}_n$ is equivalent to the well known (see [CN88, GL87]) lattice, A_n, defined in Section4.1. For each $n > 1$, the dual lattice, A_n^* (see [CN88, GL87]), of A_n, is equivalent to the unique (upto isometry) n-dimensional regular lattice with regular inner product equal to $-1/n$.

We conclude this section with the following important theorem (a direct consequence of Theorem 2) which asserts the existence and uniqueness of a mesh computer, whose underlying set satisfies Properties 1 through 5 (i.e., is a regular lattice), and which has maximum connectivity.

Theorem 3 *The (unique) idealized mesh computer, $\mathcal{M}(\mathbf{A}_n)$, has maximum connectivity among all idealized meshes based on n-dimensional regular lattices.* □

4 Some Additional Merits of $\mathbf{A}_n$

As stated above, the lattice A_n, which is equivalent to $\mathbf{A}_n$, is well known and a substantial number of its properties have been tabulated [CN88, GL87]. This is useful because $\mathcal{M}(A_n)$ has the same (network) topology as $\mathcal{M}(\mathbf{A}_n)$, and so, every property of A_n contributes to some property of $\mathcal{M}(\mathbf{A}_n)$. In the following sections (Sections 4.1 through 4.3), we state some of the elementary properties of $\mathbf{A}_n$, and mention their relevance to our approach of literally simulating physical phenomena in $\mathcal{M}(\mathbf{A}_n)$. Finally, in Section 4.4, we discuss why we do not choose to base our meshes on lattices that are denser than $\mathbf{A}_n$.

4.1 Properties of $\mathbf{A}_n$ Related to Computational Cleanness

One of the main reasons for using square meshes, is that a lot of the commonly used quantities, such as inner product, are easy to compute in the lattice $\mathbf{Z}^n$. The properties of $\mathbf{A}_n$ described in this section indicate that some of these computations are almost as easy in $\mathbf{A}_n$.

Ease of representation: The set $A_n = \{ (x_0, \ldots, x_n) \in \mathbf{Z}^{n+1} \mid \sum x_i = 0 \}$ is a faithful representation of $\mathbf{A}_n$ in $\mathbf{R}^{n+1}$.

This means that there is an additive group isomorphism, from $\mathbf{A}_n$ to A_n, which isomorphism scales distances by a constant factor. A_n is necessarily an n-dimensional lattice contained in $\mathbf{R}^{n+1}$. In this representation of $\mathbf{A}_n$ (by A_n), the constant scaling factor, and hence the minimal distance of A_n, is $\sqrt{2}$. This is a good representation for $\mathbf{A}_n$ as is indicated by the following features.

1. All points in A_n have integer co-ordinates, thus aiding in restricting ourselves to integer computations only (in fact, accurately representing the co-ordinates of points in $\mathbf{A}_n$, in terms of the standard basis for $\mathbf{R}^n$, is not possible without symbolic computation, due to the presence of irrationals).

2. Each direction vector in $\mathbf{A}_n$ is represented easily in A_n as the difference, $(\vec{e}_i - \vec{e}_j)$, of two distinct standard basis vectors of $\mathbf{Z}^{n+1}$.

3. An important [CRS90] consequence of 1 above is that the usual inner product of any pair of vectors in A_n is an integer. Thus, although the euclidean distances between points in A_n need not be integral, the squares of these distances are.

4. The hardware implementation of the computation of the usual inner product of two vectors in A_n can be easily parallelized.

5. The test for membership in A_n, of a point in $\mathbf{Z}^{n+1}$, is computationally very easy.

6. The path length, in A_n, between points P and Q in A_n is the sum of all the positive co-ordinates in the vector $(P - Q)$. This facilitates estimating the minimum time required for the propagation of a message from the processor at P to the processor at Q in $\mathcal{M}(\mathbf{A}_n)$.

7. Using this representation (of $\mathbf{A}_n$ by A_n), it is easy to derive expressions for certain relevant quantities. For example, it is easy to derive (and compute) the expression $\sum_{r=0}^{R}\sum_{i=0}^{n+1}(-1)^i\binom{n+1}{i}\binom{n+r-i}{n}^2$ for the number of processors at most R connections away from a given processor in $\mathcal{M}(\mathbf{A}_n)$.

Predecessor containment: *Every* $k < n$ dimensional sublattice of $\mathbf{A}_n$, spanned by k vectors from a regular basis B for $\mathbf{A}_n$, is isometric with $\mathbf{A}_k$.

A similar property is true for $\mathbf{Z}^n$. $\mathcal{M}(\mathbf{A}_n)$ contains several copies of every predecessor, $\mathcal{M}(\mathbf{A}_k), k < n$, of $\mathcal{M}(\mathbf{A}_n)$ in the family of idealized meshes $\mathcal{M}(\mathbf{A}_n)$. This allows our algorithms to be independent of dimension.

Spanning set: *Every* set of n linearly independent, minimal length vectors in $\mathbf{A}_n$ generates (spans) $\mathbf{A}_n$.

There are lattices not having this property [GL87]. Suppose B is a set of n linearly independent, minimal length vectors, in such a lattice, such that B does not span that lattice. Intuitively, if one tries to walk about in that lattice using *only* the vectors in B as basic steps, there are points, actually in the lattice, that one will not be able to reach. Of course the lattice that *is* spanned by B will be n-dimensional too. Such lattices (not having the spanning set property) are *very* unlike n-dimensional euclidean space. If one were to use a mesh based on such an "unnatural" lattice, one would expect the task of designing new algorithms (for the literal simulation of physical phenomena) to be more complicated.

4.2 Comparison of $\mathbf{A}_n$ with $\mathbf{Z}^n$

Currently, most meshes in use [TM87, PD84, Uhr72, Dye, AS84, PF+85, Lev85, DL81, PU82] are essentially (though, some of these meshes make toroidal connections,) two-dimensional square meshes, i.e., essentially meshes based on $\mathbf{Z}^2$. $\mathcal{M}(\mathbf{A}_n)$ is preferable over $\mathcal{M}(\mathbf{Z}^n)$ for several reasons:

Embedding: $\mathbf{Z}^n$ is *isometrically* embeddable in $\mathbf{A}_{2n-1}$, but $\mathbf{A}_n$ is not embeddable in $\mathbf{Z}^m$ for any m.

Density of points: For each n, $\mathcal{M}(\mathbf{A}_n)$ offers far better resolution, in the number of points of euclidean space approximated by the underlying set, than does $\mathcal{M}(\mathbf{Z}^n)$. In fact, we can show that given an n-dimensional ball, $\mathcal{B}_r$, of euclidean radius $r \in \mathbf{R}$, the ratio of the number of points of $\mathbf{A}_n$ in $\mathcal{B}_r$ to the number of points of $\mathbf{Z}^n$ in $\mathcal{B}_r$ is exponential in the dimension n.

Well covering of $\mathbf{R}^n$: Suppose δ is the length of minimal length vectors in D. For each d in D, informally we define the *sphere of influence* of d as the set of all points in euclidean n-space of distance $< \delta$ from d. It is clearly desirable that each point in euclidean n-space reside in the sphere of influence of some point in D, because, then, in a sense, euclidean n-space is *well-covered* by the points in D. Consider the measure of proximity μ, for D. We have that D well-covers euclidean n-space iff $\delta > \mu$. For $\mathbf{A}_n$, the lattice corresponding to our idealized n-dimensional mesh, the maximum dimension for which $\delta > \mu$ is 6, but for $\mathbf{Z}^n$, the lattice corresponding to the idealized n-dimensional square mesh, this maximum dimension is only 3. Further, for each n, $\mu(\mathbf{A}_n) < \mu(\mathbf{Z}^n)$. Therefore, the family $\{ \mathcal{M}(\mathbf{A}_n) \}$ is superior to the family, $\{ \mathcal{M}(\mathbf{Z}^n) \}$ of square meshes also in regard to well-covering.

Proximity of processors: The number of processors at most R connections away from a given processor in $\mathcal{M}(\mathbf{Z}^n)$ is given by $\sum_{r=0}^{R} \sum_{i=0}^{n} (-1)^i \binom{n}{i} \binom{n+r-i-1}{n-1}$. Comparing this with the corresponding expression for $\mathcal{M}(\mathbf{A}_n)$ from feature 7 in Section 4.1, we find that the number of processors at most R connections away is less in $\mathcal{M}(\mathbf{Z}^n)$ than in $\mathcal{M}(\mathbf{A}_n)$, for each $n > 1$. In particular, the number of near neighbor connections for $\mathcal{M}(\mathbf{A}_n)$ is $n(n+1)$, a feasible quadratic in n, *but*, for $\mathcal{M}(\mathbf{Z}^n)$, the number is only $2n$, a small linear expression in n.

Interconnection bandwidth across partitions: The predecessor containment property of $\mathbf{A}_n$ (see Section 4.1 above) ensures that $\mathbf{A}_n$ can be partitioned cleanly and naturally.

If $B = \{ \vec{b}_1, \ldots, \vec{b}_n \}$ is a regular basis for D, $P_D(t_1, \ldots t_n) = \sum_{i=1}^{n} p_i \vec{b}_i$, $p_i \in \mathbf{Z}$, $0 \leq p_i < t_i$ is a *standard n-dimensional parallelopiped*, in D, with thickness t_i in direction $\vec{b}_i$. The sub-mesh, $\mathcal{M}(P_D(t_1, \ldots t_n))$, of $\mathcal{M}(D)$ is called a *parallelopiped mesh (with thickness t_i in direction $\vec{b}_i$)*. The predecessor containment property of D ensures that each face of a standard n-dimensional parallelopiped is the translate of a *standard* $(n-1)$ dimensional parallelopiped.

Let t be a positive integer, and let $P_D = P_D(t \ldots t) \subset D$. An $(n-1)$-dimensional plane, C, parallel to one of the $(n-1)$-dimensional faces of P_D, which plane does not pass through any processors of $\mathcal{M}(P_D)$, partitions $\mathcal{M}(P_D)$ into two components, each of which is (a translate of) a parallelopiped mesh.

The number, $B_D(t)$, of processor *interconnections*, of $\mathcal{M}(P_D)$, that pass through C is the *bandwidth of the partition (by C of $\mathcal{M}(P_D)$)*. We can show that $B_{\mathbf{A}_n}(t) = t^{n-2}(nt - n + 1)$ and $B_{\mathbf{Z}^n}(t) = t^{n-1}$, so that $\lim_{t \to \infty} B_{\mathbf{A}_n}(t)/B_{\mathbf{Z}^n}(t) = n$. Hence, in general, our reasonably thick parallelopiped meshes of dimension n will have about n times as many "parallel communication channels" from one partition to the other compared to an analogous n-dimensional square mesh. For our philosophy/methodology of computing, this is a good thing.

Automorphism groups: The order of the automorphism group of $\mathbf{A}_n$ is $2 \cdot (n+1)!$ while that of $\mathbf{Z}^n$ is $2^n \cdot n!$ [CN88]. The automorphism group is an important consideration for Lattice Gas theorists because of the simplicity of their local transition rules [Has87, FHP86]. It is not as important a consideration for us, although we note that the automorphism group of $\mathbf{A}_n$ is not of extremely low order.

Tessellating euclidean space: One common reason for using $\mathcal{M}(\mathbf{Z}^n)$ is that n-dimensional cubes are the only regular bodies that tessellate euclidean n-space, for $n > 2$ [CN88]. We do not wish to tessellate space with copies of a single regular body; ***having a low measure of proximity for the underlying set is sufficient for our purposes.*** As seen in Section 4.2, by this criterion, $\mathcal{M}(\mathbf{A}_n)$ is superior to $\mathcal{M}(\mathbf{Z}^n)$. Further, we would like to point out that the set of standard n-dimensional parallelopipeds, each with thickness 2 in each direction (in a regular basis) in $\mathbf{A}_n$, does, in fact, tessellate euclidean n-space. Of course, these parallelopipeds are not as symmetric as n-dimensional cubes.

4.3 Embedding $\mathcal{M}(\mathbf{A}_n)$ In Physical 3-Space

For ***actually building*** any finite sub-mesh of $\mathcal{M}(\mathbf{A}_n)$, of possibly high dimension, we are constrained by physical reality—a ***physical instance*** of any one of these finite sub-meshes, ostensibly, must be ***physically embeddable*** in euclidean 3-space. Furthermore, for our approach, the embedding in euclidean 3-space must be such that the physical length of the connection between adjacent processors is a *feasible constant*. Constant length interconnections are clearly important to help achieve ***synchronous*** motion of the "particles" making up a simulated object. For a given size of processor (of course > 0), we *can* embed $\mathcal{M}(\mathbf{A}_n)$ in physical 3-space with constant length interconnections. ***In our embedding***, the minimal (constant) length of the interconnection between immediately connected processors does depend, but only ***sub***polynomially, on the dimension of the mesh; furthermore, for each fixed dimension, it does ***not*** depend on the number of processors in the mesh. We will report elsewhere on the details of our physical embedding schemes.

4.4 Why Not Meshes Based on Denser Lattices?

Consider the classical problems of packing unit sized n-spheres into euclidean n-space (i) as densely as possible and (ii) so that each sphere touches the maximum number of neighbors [CN88, GL87]. Consider a solution to one (or both) of these problems. One could define a corresponding mesh (for approximating euclidean n-space) with processors at the centers of each sphere and its near neighbor connections to all and only those processors at the center of the spheres touching it. In general, the set D of points corresponding to the centers of the spheres need not even be a lattice [CN88, GL87]. Hence, such D would be too hard to deal with computationally and fail to have very important properties in common with euclidean n-space. A more severe consideration is that, for most cases of interest, the solutions to problems (i) and (ii) above are just unknown.

While more is known about problems (i) and (ii) ***modified*** to further require the solutions to be lattices, only a few cases of interest are solved [CN88], and the solutions, for dimensions ≥ 4, all ***must*** fail to be regular. Also, the (few) known solutions apparently come from totally different *families* of lattices [CN88], and, hence, it would be hard to design and *prove* algorithms for use in meshes based on such lattices.

References

[AG89] George S. Almasi and Allan Gottlieb. *Highly Parallel Computing*. Benjamin/Cummings Publishing Company, Inc., 1989.

[AS84] N. Ahuja and S. Swamy. Multiprocessor pyramid architecture for bottom-up image analysis. *IEEE Trans. on PAMI*, PAMI-6:463–474, 1984.

[CN88] J. H. Conway and N. J. A. Sloane. *Sphere Packings, Lattices and Groups*. Springer Verlag, 1988.

[CRS90] John Case, Dayanand S. Rajan, and Anil M. Shende. Avoiding anisotropy in mesh computer representation of physical space. 1990. Unpublished manuscript.

[DL81] M. J. B. Duff and S. Levialdi, editors. *Languages and Architectures for Image Processing*. Academic Press, 1981.

[Dye] C. R. Dyer. A quadtree machine for parallel image processing. Technical Report KSL 51, Univ. of Illinois at Chicago Circle.

[Fey82] Richard P. Feynman. Simulating physics with computers. *International Journal of Theoretical Physics*, 21(6/7), 1982.

[FHP86] U. Frisch, B. Hasslacher, and Y. Pomeau. Lattice-gas automata for the navier stokes equation. *Physical Review Letters*, 56(14):1505–1508, April 1986.

[FT82] Edward Fredkin and Tommaso Toffoli. Conservative logic. *International Journal of Theoretical Physics*, 21(3/4), 1982.

[GL87] Peter M. Gruber and Gerrit Lekkerkerker. *Geometry of Numbers*. North-Holland Mathematical Library, 1987.

[Has87] Brosl Hasslacher. Discrete fluids. *Los Alamos Science*, (15):175–217, 1987. Special Issue.

[Her64] I. N. Herstein. *Topics in Algebra*. Blaisdell Publishing Co., 1964.

[Hil55] E. L. Hill. Relativistic theory of discrete momentum space and discrete space–time. *Physical Review*, 100(6), December 1955.

[Lev85] S. Levialdi, editor. *Integrated Technology for Parallel Image Processing*. Academic Press, Inc., 1985.

[Mac86] Thinking Machines. Introduction to data level parallelism. Technical Report 86.14, Thinking Machines, April 1986.

[Mar84] Norman Margolus. Physics–like models of computation. *Physica 10D*, pages 81–95, 1984.

[Min82] Marvin Minsky. Cellular vacuum. *International Journal of Theoretical Physics*, 21(6/7), 1982.

[PD84] Kendall Preston and M. J. B. Duff. *Modern Cellular Automata: Theory and Applications*. Plenum Publishers, 1984.

[PF+85] John Poulton, Henry Fuchs, et al. PIXEL–PLANES: Building a VLSI–based graphic system. In *Chapel Hill Conference on VLSI*, 1985.

[PU82] Kendall Preston and Leonard Uhr, editors. *Multicomputers and Image Processing: Algorithms and Programs*. Academic Press, 1982.

[Sny47] Hartland S. Snyder. Quantized space–time. *Physical Review*, 71(1):38–41, 1947.

[Svo86] Karl Svozil. Are quantum fields cellular automata? *Physics Letters A*, 119(4), December 1986.

[SW86] James B. Salem and S. Wolfram. Thermodynamics and hydrodynamics with cellular automata. In S. Wolfram, editor, *Theory and Applications of Cellular Automata*. World Scientific, 1986.

[TM87] Tommaso Toffoli and Norman Margolus. *Cellular Automata Machines*. MIT Press, 1987.

[Tof77a] Tommaso Toffoli. Cellular automata machines. Technical Report 208, Comp. Comm. Sci. Dept., University of Michigan, 1977.

[Tof77b] Tommaso Toffoli. Computation and construction universality of reversible cellular automata. *Journal of Computer and System Sciences*, 15:213–231, 1977.

[Tof84] Tommaso Toffoli. CAM: A high-performance cellular-automaton machine. *Physica 10D*, pages 195–204, 1984.

[Uhr72] L. Uhr. Layered 'recognition cone' networks that preprocess, classify, and describe. *IEEE Trans. on Computers*, C-21:758–768, 1972.

[Ung58] S. H. Unger. A computer oriented towards spatial problems. In *Proceedings of the IRE*, volume 46, pages 1744–1750, 1958.

[Vic84] Gérard Y. Vichniac. Simulating physics with cellular automata. *Physica 10D*, pages 96–116, 1984.

[Wol83] Stephen Wolfram. Statistical mechanics of cellular automata. *Reviews of Modern Physics*, 55(3):601–644, July 1983.

[Zus69] K. Zuse. *Rechnender Raum*. Vieweg, Braunschweig, 1969. Translated as Calculating Space, Tech. Transl. AZT-70-164-GEMIT, MIT Project MAC, 1970.

Optimal parallel algorithms for testing isomorphism of trees and outerplanar graphs

Christos Levcopoulos Andrzej Lingas Ola Petersson
Lund University, Dept. of Computer Science
Box 118, S-221 00 Lund, Sweden

Wojciech Rytter
Warsaw University, Institute of Informatics
PKiN, 00-901 Warsaw, Poland

Abstract: We show that isomorphism of trees and outerplanar graphs can be tested in O(log n) time with n/log(n) processors on a CRCW PRAM and in $O(\log^2 n)$ time with $n/\log^2 n$ processors on an EREW PRAM. This gives the first optimal parallel algorithm for the isomorphism testing for a nontrivial class of graphs . We give also an optimal parallel algorithm for the equivalence of expressions.
A related result is a general optimal and very simple parallel method of tree compression which can be applied for other problems.

1. Introduction

The isomorphism problem for graphs is a hard combinatorial problem. It is obvi ously in NP, however it is not known if it is NP-complete for general graphs. There are many subclasses of graphs for which the isomorphism problem is in P, e.g. planar, partial k-trees (Bo 88) and graphs of bounded valence (Lu 80). In particular, the isomorphism problem for trees is solvable in linear time (AHU 74).

Miller and Reif (MR 85) gave NC algorithms for isomorphisms of planar graphs and trees. Their algorithm for tree isomorphism uses $n^2 \log n$ processors, being far from optimal. Previously an NC algorithm was claimed in (Ru 81), where it was noticed that for a class of trees the sub-isomorphism problem can be solved by a polynomial time pushdown machine with small auxiliary memory. Recently, Gazit and Reif have presented a randomized algorithm for isomorphism of planar graphs running in logarithmic time and using a subquadratic number of processors (GR 90).

An efficient parallel algorithm for tree isomorphism was given in (CDR 88). It is optimal to within a logarithmic factor. We show that given two trees T1 and T2 we can compress them to the tree T1' and T2' by a factor log(n). The compression will preserve the isomorphism. The CDR algorithm (CDR 88) can then be applied on the compressed trees which will give an optimal parallel algorithm for tree isomorphism. Then we extend this result to outerplanar graphs.

A given planar graph is outerplanar iff it can be embedded in the plane in such a way that all nodes lie on an external infinite face. Each such graph consists of a set of partially triangulated polygons connected in a tree-like manner. The embedding of such graphs can be done by an optimal parallel algorithm, see (DHR 89). Then each polygon (biconnected component) can be suitably encoded, see (CDR 88). The polygons can be compressed to single labelled vertices and then the isomorphism problem for outerplanar graphs is reduced to isomorphism of labelled trees. Such a compression can also be done by an optimal parallel algorithm. Hence the optimality of tree isomorphism implies the optimality of parallel isomorphism of outerplanar graphs. This result is due to the tree structure of outerplanar graphs and it is the main result of the paper.

Our basic procedure is the compression of trees. We believe that the presented method of tree compression can be useful in other problems related to isomorphisms, e.g. optimal parallel isomorphism testing for general planar graphs or for some classes of tree-structured graphs (partial k-trees, for some small k's).

Our model of computation is the parallel random access machine (PRAM), see for example (GR 88). Two types of PRAM's are considered, ARBITRARY CRCW PRAMS (read and write conflicts are allowed, however we do not know which processor succeeds to write in a given location), and EREW PRAM (no read or write conflicts are allowed). The basic tools in the tree compression are Euler tour technique, see (TV 85), on trees and efficient sorting of small integers. A basic operation is a coding and decoding of binary strings of logarithmic size by integers. We assume that the cost of such an operation is proportional to the number of bits of the coded string. This is a realistic assumption in an EREW PRAM model. It resembles the "four Russians" trick, see (AHU 74). However in our case the encoding of small binary strings by small integers has to be done carefully to preserve the isomorphism. The encoding will be mixed with some sorting phases. Also we cannot partition the sequence of leaves roughly into groups of logarithmic size, as it was done for example, in optimal evaluation of expression trees, see (GR 89) and (ADKP 89). The reason is that the final compression will depend on the sequencing we choose and this will not always preserve the isomorphism between trees.

2. The tree compression method

Assume T is a rooted unlabelled tree with n vertices. We describe how to construct a tree T' =COMPRESS(T) in such a way that the function COMPRESS satisfies:

(a) size(T') ≤ n/log(n),

(b) for any two trees T1 and T2:

T1 is isomorphic to T2 iff COMPRESS(T1) is isomorphic to COMPRESS(T2).

(c) the transformation COMPRESS can be computed in O(log n) time using n/log(n) processors on an EREW PRAM.

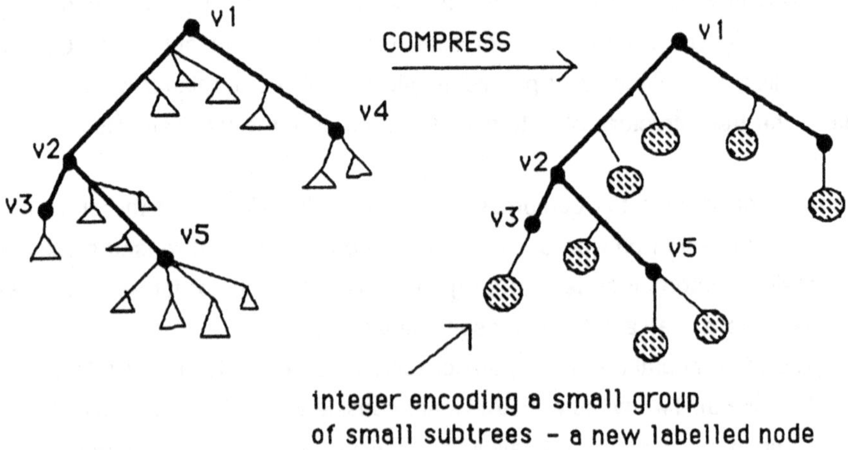

Fig.1. Big nodes (of at least log(n) weight) are marked. Each big node of total weight m is replaced by a tree with labelled nodes and of total size m/log(m). Each big subchain between big nodes is replaced by a chain of smaller weight. The small nodes disappear.

A root of a subtree is said to be big if the subtree contains more than log(n) nodes and each subtree of the subtree contains no more than log(n) nodes. Moreover, a root of a subtree is said to be big if it has two sons that are ancestors of big nodes. Also, the root of the tree is always big. A node of the tree which is not big is called small. In the above definition and throughout the paper a subtree means always a full subtree.

Assume we are given a tree T of size n and let us examine the structure of the tree T" which results from T after the removal of all small nodes. Examine also the structure of another tree T′ which encodes T. T' includes all nodes of T", which are labelled as big. Let $T_{v,v'}$ be a subtree of T consisting of all nodes between v and v' together with subtrees rooted at these nodes, except node v'. Replace each minimal chain between big nodes v, v' in the tree by a subtree $F1(T_{v,v'})$. Then replace each big node v by a tree $F2(T_v)$. Preserve the labels of big nodes. The resulting tree is denoted by T'. It is easy to see that the trees T', T" satisfy the following lemma:

Lemma 1 (key lemma):

(i) T" has at most n/log(n) leaves;

(ii) T" has at most n/log(n) internal nodes with at least two sons;

(iii) if the functions F1, F2 preserve the isomorphism of trees then (T1 isomorphic to T2) implies (T1' isomorphic to T2').

Sketch: The first two points are obvious. The third point follows from the fact that the big nodes in T have special labels in T′. The isomorphism between T1 and T2 is a two-stage isomorphism: first between trees T1" and T2" of big nodes, and then between the corresponding subtrees hanging at the big leaf nodes or between the subtrees of the form $T_{v,v'}$. ■

The transformation F2 deals with subtrees such that only the root is a big node. The transformation F1 deals with chains. It is enough to implement these transformations in such a way that the ratio of compression is logarithmic and the work to do it is small.

First we define an operation lowcompress(T) of compressing "low" trees.
A tree T is said to be low iff for each son v of the root r of T we have:
size(T_v) is small, where T_v is the tree rooted at v.
For low trees we define COMPRESS(T) = lowcompress(T). For other trees the operation COMPRESS will be constructed using lowcompress locally.

For a small tree K denote by int(K) a binary number which encodes the tree K uniquely (up to isomorphism). We require that int(K) has O(size(K)) bits and we can construct it in time O(size(K)) with a single RAM processor.
We can construct Int(K) by using the standard linear-time algorithm for tree isomorphism (see (AHU 74)). The algorithm assigns ordered tuples of integers to each node v of the

tree. The integers in the tuple assigned to v correspond to the rank of the tuples assigned to the sons of v in nondecreasing order on the level below. Now, using the correspondances we can substitute the tuples for the ranks ascending level by level to obtain a bracket representation of the root and hence the whole tree. The representation has O(size(K)), it can be build in time O(size(K)), and it is unique up to isomorphism. Thus, its straightforward bit encoding satsifies the requirements on Int(K).
Now, we can prove the following, using technique similar to that from (Re 85):

Lemma 2: Let X be a sequence of k, $k \leq n$, integers consisting of s bits each, $s < \log n$. X can be sorted in O(log n) time using an EREW PRAM with ks/log n processors.

Proof: We hash the elements in X into an array Y of length $k2^s$ by an order preserving function and then compress them, as follows:

Step 1. For all i set Y(j) to x_i iff $j = kx_i + i - 1$
Step 2. For all j such that Y(j) contains an element x_i, find the closest following position in Y containing an element from X.
(The x_i in Y are now connected in a linked list of length k).
Step 3. Perform list ranking.
Step 4. Put the elements in their correct positions in an output array.

The only non-trivial step is the second one, which requires some carefulness in avoiding concurrent reads.■

Note that the sorting algorithm requires $O(n^2)$ space, which due to its stableness can be reduced to $O(n^{1+\varepsilon})$ by standard techniques. Moreover, if the algorithm is slightly modified it can be shown to sort k binary integers of total length n lexicographically in O(log n) time using n/log n processors. That is, all integers need not have the same number of bits.
Using Lemma 2, we can derive the following technical one on tree compression.

Lemma 3: We can construct a transformation lowcompress working for low trees T and satisfying conditions (a), (b) and (c) in the definition of the function COMPRESS.
Sketch: Assume that $T_1, T_2, ..., T_k$ are subtrees rooted at the sons of the root r of T. The size of the tree is the sum of sizes of these subtrees plus one (the root). There are at most log(n) different sizes of T_j. It is an easy matter to sort the sequence of trees according to their sizes by an optimal parallel algorithm. It can be reduced to a prefix

sums computation and list ranking. The sequence can be partitioned into subsegments of logarithmic weight and in each such subsegment one processor can construct in logarithmic time lists of elements of the same size j, for j =1..log(n). Then these lists can be linked between subsegments.

Later on we can assume that each subtree T_i is of the same size s. Observe that s≤log(n). We can apply Lemma 2 to sort the sequence of integers x_i = int(T_i). According to this lemma the time is logarithmic and the number of processors is optimal. Let log(n) = ps. Then we partition the sequence $x_1, x_2, ..., x_k$ into subsequences of length p of consecutive integers. Each such sequence is encoded uniquely by a single integer with a logarithmic number of bits. We obtain a sequence $y_1, y_2, ..., y_t$ of integers, where t=k/p.

Each y_i encodes a group of subtrees of logarithmic total size. Let T' be a tree with t sons. The i-th son has the label y_i. Define T' = lowcompress(T).

We can easily drop the assumption about equal sizes of subtrees since they were sorted with respect to their sizes. The compression can be done inside each subsequence of subtrees of the same size. We omit the détails. The described operation lowcompress satisfies conditions (a), (b) and (c). This completes the proof. ■

We define yet another encoding of small trees. Assume that T is a small tree with a distinguished path $\pi=v_1, v_2, ..., v_t$ from the root to a leaf v_t. Let x_i be an integer coding uniquely (up to isomorphism) all subtrees rooted at sons of v_i for i=1..t-1. Let x be the integer whose binary representation is (bin(x_1) bin(x_2) ...), where bin(z) is the binary representation of the integer z. Then define pathcompress(T,π)=T', where T' is the tree with root r and two leaves v_t and v'. The vertex v' is a newly created vertex with the label x. Obviously the transformation pathcompress can be computed by one processor in logarithmic time if the tree T is small (is of logarithmic size).

Theorem 1: We can construct a transformation COMPRESS satisfying conditions (a), (b) and (c), and working for all trees T whose vertices are unlabelled or labelled with O(1) types of labels.

Proof. The set of big nodes and the tree T" can be computed in log(n) time with n/log(n) processors of an EREW PRAM (using Euler tour technique, see (TV 85)). Then each chain of nodes of T between two consecutive big nodes v,v′ can be partitioned into subchains which have at most size($T_{v,v'}$)/log(n) nodes, see Figure 2. In one subchain we can independently apply pathcompress (if the size of the subtree to be compressed is small) or lowcompress (if the subtree is low but contains many small subtrees rooted at the root). In the same time we can apply the operation lowcompress to all subtrees rooted at the leaf big nodes. This completes the proof. ■

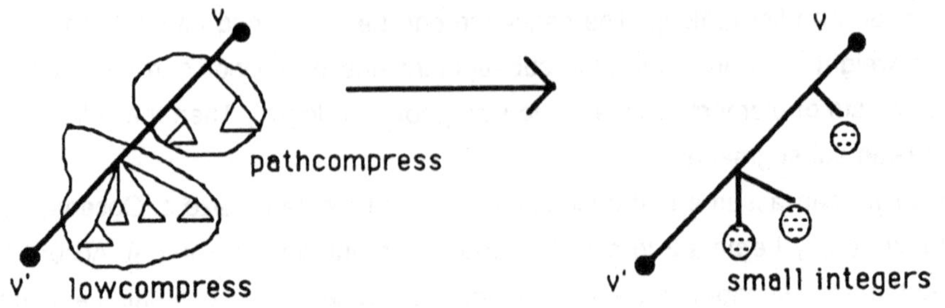

Fig. 2. The subtree $T_{v,v'}$ of size r is compressed to a subtree of size r/log(n) with nodes v, v' labelled as distinguished big nodes and other nodes labelled by small integers.

3. Testing isomorphism of trees, outerplanar graphs and expressions

Combining the results from the previous section, we obtain our first main result:

Theorem 2: The tree isomorphism problem can be solved in O(log n) time by a CRCW PRAM with n/log(n) processors and in $O(\log^2 n)$ time by an EREW PRAM with $n/\log^2 n$ processors.

Sketch: The algorithm of (CDR 88) for isomorphism of labelled trees works on a CRCW PRAM in O(log n) time with n processors. Hence we can compress the unlabelled rooted tree and then apply that algorithm. The root can be chosen to be the center of the tree (at most two possibilities). The only write conflicts in the algorithm of (CDR 88) are in comparing two strings of length $m \leq n$ in constant time. We can make it on an EREW PRAM in O(log n) time with m/log(n) processors. We omit the details of the whole construction. ■

Assume that we are given two rooted expression-trees T1 and T2 with operations + and *. The leaves correspond to pairwise distinct input variables. Expressions represented by T1, T2 are equivalent if T1 can be transformed into T2 by making a local redirection of edges. We can change the order of the sons of a single vertex (due to the commutativity) or the structure of a tree of height two rooted at a given vertex due to the associativity. If we deal with arithmetics of integers then both operations are commutative. However, when we deal with matrix arithmetics they are no longer commutative.

Theorem 3: The equivalence of two expressions can be tested in O(log n) time by a CRCW PRAM with n/log(n) processors and in $O(\log^2 n)$ time by an EREW PRAM with $n/\log^2 n$ processors.

Sketch: The proof is essentially the same as of the preceding theorem. Initially some local reconstructions can be done to reflect associativity. In the algorithm of (CDR 88) one is sorting codes of sons only if the operation is commutative. We omit details. ■

The outerplanar graph G can be viewed as a two-level tree, or as a tree-like collection of trees of faces. Let $B_1,\ldots,B_k$ be biconnected components of G. Then G is a (first-level) tree of biconnected components. Each of B_i is a partially triangulated polygon which can be decomposed into a (second-level) tree of its faces.

Theorem 4: The isomorphism problem for outerplanar graphs can be solved in O(log n) time by a CRCW PRAM with n/log(n) processors and in $O(\log^2 n)$ time by an EREW PRAM with $n/\log^2 n$ processors.

Sketch: We could make a suitable compression of a given outerplanar graph G in two stages: first the removal of small objects (biconnected components) in the first tree, then in each of the remaining objects examine its structure.The tree of biconnected components and trees of faces can be computed by an optimal algorithm due to (DHR 89). Each biconnected component consists of a tree of subobjects of the second level (faces) and small subobjects can be removed. Hence we could apply first the removal of small biconnected components and then inside each component the removal of small faces. "Small" means here of logarithmic size. However such an approach encounters difficulties. After reducing small biconnected components we are left with a smaller outerplanar graph . Unfortunately it might be not small enough. Hence we have to apply the compression at the second-level: within the tree of faces of an individual biconnected component. We cannot apply Theorem 1 here since after the first-level compression the remaining nodes could get labels of non-constant size.

We apply two-level tree structure of G to get in a simple way a representation of G as one big tree T(G) with some of the vertices newly created. The newly created vertices will be labelled with the same special label. We will have only O(1) types of labels and

Theorem 1 can be applied. First we can transform the graph G into graph G' such that all connected components will be simple cycles (without diagonals). This can be done by inserting in each cycle several copies of the old vertices in such a way that two faces adjacent to this cycle have no common vertex, see Figure 3.a. New vertices will have a special label of the same type. Because of the tree structure of the biconnected outerplanar graph it can be computed optimally how many vertices are to be added and how the new edges have to be linked.

Then for each edge (v,w) joining two cycles we make these cycles disjoint. We will have two copies of the same edge (v,w) in each of the cycles. Let us label both copies of v with the same letter 'a' and both copies of w with the same letter 'b'. We have free choice to give labels to v,w (could be 'a' for w and 'b' for v), and we fix a chosen choice. Then, we create a special middle vertex inside both copies of edge (v,w) and join these middle vertices, see Fig.3.b.

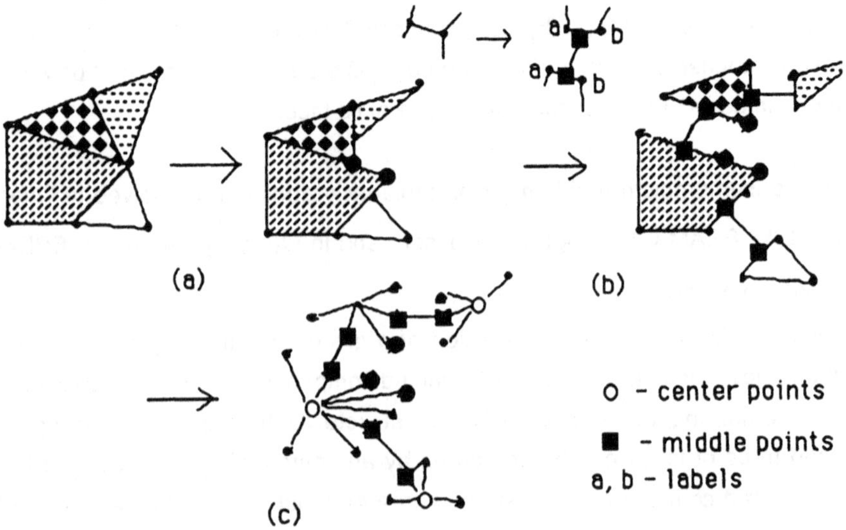

Fig. 3.

At this moment we can remove the boundary edges of each cycle by connecting all nodes of the cycle to a specially created center vertex (with the label 'center'), see Fig.3.c. For such a center vertex the cyclic order of its sons has to be preserved in the transformation. In this way we obtain a tree with O(1) types of labels of the vertices and with fixed cyclic order of sons of some special vertices. The transformation preserves the isomorphism. Now, in the isomorphism, we have to take care of the labels and also the cyclic order of sons for some vertices . Theorem 1 cannot be directly applied, because of such orders.

However Theorem 1 still holds for this type of trees. The proof is essentially the same. The main point is that the number of types of labels is O(1). The cyclic orientations pose only a technical difficulty. We can find a center of the tree of faces of each biconnected component in the initial graph. Then it will be a master face, it can have two orientations. Note that a given orientation in a master face of one original connected componenet (in the initial graph) determines the orientation of edges of all faces in this (original) componenet. This removes the danger of the blow up of the number of possible orientations. In fact in each original component there are essentially two orientations. The code can be chosen as a smallest with respect to these two orientations. The ideas from (CDR 88) can be also used here. We omit the tedious details. This completes the proof. ∎

4. Final remarks

Is it possible to obtain an optimal parallel time algorithm for the subtree isomorphism problem for trees of constant bounded valence ? NC algorithms for this problem were given in (GKMS 88, LK 89). In fact the subtree isomorphism problem for general trees is probably not in NC, since it is NC-equivalent to the bipartitie matching problem, see (LK 89). Anyway we think that our tree compression method could be useful in obtaining an optimal parallel algorithm for the subisomorphism problem for restricted classes of trees.

References

(ADKP 89) K.Abrahamson, N.Dadoun, D.Kirkpatrick, T.Przytycka, "A simple tree contraction method", Journal of Algorithms 10, 1989, 287-302

(AHU 74) A.Aho, J.Hopcroft, J.Ullman, "The design and analysis of computer algorithms", Addison-Weley, Reading, 1984

(Bo 88) H.Bodlaender, "Polynomial algorithms for graph isomorphism and chromatic index on partial k-trees", in SWAT'88, Lect.Notes in Com.Science 318, 223-232, 1988

(CDR 88) B.Chlebus, K.Diks, T.Radzik, "Testing isomorphism of outerplanar graphs in parallel", in MFCS'88, Lect.Notes in Comp.Science, 1988

(GR 90) H.Gazit, J.Reif, "A randomized parallel algorithm for planar graph isomorphism", SPAA'90,210-219.

(GR 88) A.Gibbons, W.Rytter, "Efficient parallel algorithms", Cambridge University Press

(GR 89) A.Gibbons, W.Rytter, "Optimal parallel evaluation of expressions and applications to context-free recognition", Information and Computation, 1989

(GKMS 88) P.Gibbons, R.Karp, G.Miller, D.Soroker, "Subtree isomorphism is in random NC", AWOC'88, 43-52

(DHR 89) K.Diks, T.Hagerup, W.Rytter, "Optimal parallel recognition and colouring of outerplanar graphs", MFCS'89, Lect.Notes in Comp.Science, 1989

(LK 89) A.Lingas, M.Karpinski, "Subtree isomorphism is NC reducible to bipartite perfect matching", IPL 30, 1989, 27-32

(Lu 80) E.M. Luks,."Isomorphism of bounded valence can be tested in polynomial time", in Proc. 21st Ann. Symp. of Foundations of Computer Science (IEEE, New York, 1980).

(MR 85) G.Miller, J.Reif, "Parallel tree contraction and its application", FOCS, 1985

(Re 85) J H Reif, "An optimal parallel algorithm for integer sorting", Proc. 26th Ann. Symp. on Foundations of Computer Science, 1985.

(Ru 81) W.L.Ruzzo, "On uniform circuit complexity", JCSS 22, 1981

(TV 85) R.Tarjan, U.Vishkin, "An efficient parallel biconnectivity algorithm", SIAM J.Comp. 14, 1985, 862-874

Randomized Parallel Selection

(Extended Abstract)

Sanguthevar Rajasekaran
Department of Computer and Information Sciences
University of Pennsylvania
Philadelphia, PA 19104

ABSTRACT

We show that selection on an input of size N can be performed on a P-node hypercube ($P = N/(\log N)$) in time $O(N/P)$ with high probability, provided each node can process all the incident edges in one unit of time (this model is called the *parallel model* and has been assumed by previous researchers (e.g., [17])). This result is important in view of a lower bound of Plaxton that implies selection takes $\Omega((N/P) \log\log P + \log P)$ time on a P-node hypercube if each node can process only one edge at a time (this model is referred to as the *sequential model*).

1 Introduction

Given a set of N keys, and an integer k ($1 \leq k \leq N$), the problem of selection is to find the kth smallest key in the set. This important comparison problem has an elegant linear time sequential algorithm [1]. Optimal algorithms also exist for certain parallel models like the CRCW PRAM, the comparison tree model etc.

We are interested in solving the selection problem on the hypercube interconnection network. On any parallel model that uses P processors, one would like to know if there exists a selection algorithm that runs in time $O(N/P)$. Plaxton has proved a lowerbound of $\Omega((N/P) \log\log P + \log P)$ for the hypercube (under the assumption that each processor can process at most one incident edge per time step). An interesting open question was: 'Is there an $O(N/P)$ selection algorithm for the hypercube if each processor can handle all its incident edges in a single time step?' (The routing algorithm proposed originally by Valiant and Brebner [17] runs on the hypercube under this assumption).

We give a randomized selection algorithm in this paper that acheives this $O(N/P)$ time bound (for the worst case input with overwhelming probability).

1.1 Model Definition

Any fixed connection network can be represented as a graph $G(V, E)$ where the vertices correspond to processing elements and the edges correspond to communication links. Examples of fixed connection networks include the hypercube, the butterfly, the shuffle exchange etc. Real computers have been built based on fixed connection models.

A hypercube of dimension n consists of $N = 2^n$ nodes (or vertices) and $n2^n$ edges. Thus each node in the hypercube can be named with an n-bit binary number. If x is any node in V, then there is a bidirectional link from x to a node y if and only if x and y (considered as binary numbers) differ in one bit position (i.e., the hamming distance between x and y is 1.) Therefore, there are exactly n edges going out of (and coming into) any vertex.

If a hypercube processor can handle only one edge at any time step, this version of the hypercube will be called the *sequential model*. Handling (or processing) an edge here means either sending or receiving a key along that edge. A hypercube model where each processor can process all its incoming and outgoing edges in a unit step is called the *parallel model* [9].

In this paper we assume the parallel version of the hypercube.

1.2 Previous Results

Plaxton [10] has presented an algorithm that runs on the sequential hypercube in time $O((N/P)\log\log P + (T_1 + T_2 \log P)\log(N/P))$ using P processors, where T_1 is the time needed for sorting N keys (located one per processor) on an N-processor hypercube, and T_2 is the time needed for broadcasting and summing on an N-node hypercube. He [11] has also proved a lowerbound of $\Omega((N/P)\log\log P + \log P)$ for selection. For $N \geq P\log^2 P$ the lowerbound matches the upperbound (to within a multiplicative constant). The only operations allowed on the keys are copying and comparison (for both the upperbound and the lowerbound).

Several results are known regarding selection on PRAM models. Vishkin's [18] algorithm is optimal with a time bound of $O(\log n \log\log n)$. Cole [3] has given an $N/\log N$

processor, $O(\log N)$ time CREW PRAM algorithm. His algorithm also runs in time $O((N/P)\log\log P + \log P \log^* P)$ on the EREW PRAM. It is optimal for $N = \Omega(P \log P \log^* P)$.

Selection has also been well studied on the parallel comparison tree model. Ajtai, Kómlos, Steiger, and Szemeredi's [2] $O(n)$ processor, $O(\log\log n)$ time algorithm, Cole and Yap's [4] $O((\log\log n)^2)$ and $O(n)$ processor algorithm are some of the well known algorithms.

Randomization has been used to solve selection on a wide variety of parallel models. Meggido's [7] algorithm does maximal and median selection in constant time using a linear number of processors on the comparison tree model. Reischuk's [15] selection algorithm runs in $O(1)$ time using N comparison tree processors. Floyd and Rivest's [5] sequential algorithm takes $N+\min(k, N-k)+o(N)$ time. Rajasekaran and Sen [13] give an $O(\log N)$ time $N/\log N$ processor maximal selection algorithm for the CRCW PRAM model. All these results hold for the worst case input with high probability. The underlying idea behind all these algorithms is to sample $o(N)$ keys at random, and to eliminate keys (from future consideration) in stages.

For an extensive survey of randomized selection algorithms, see [12]. In this paper we present a randomized algorithm for selection (on an input of N keys) on the parallel hypercube model that uses $N/\log N$ processors (with $\log N$ keys initially residing at each processor) and runs in $O(\log N)$ time on the worst case input with high probability. We also assume that the only operations allowed on the keys are copying and comparison.

2 Preliminary Facts

The following results related to packet routing and sorting on the hypercube will be used in our algorithm.

The problem of *routing* is this: Given a network and a set of packets of information, a packet being an <origin,destination> pair. To start with the packets are placed in their origins. Only one packet can be sent along any edge at any time. The problem is to send all the packets to their correct destinations as quickly as possible. The restriction of this problem where exactly one packet originates from any node and exactly one packet is destined for any node is called *permutation routing*. A routing algorithm is given by specifying a path that each packet should take, together with a *queueing discpline*, i.e., a rule for resolving contentions for the same edge. The *run time* of a routing algorithm is the time needed for the last packet to reach its destination, and the *queue size* is defined to be the maximum number of packets that any node will have to store during the entire algorithm.

Valiant and Brebner gave a randomized permutation routing algorithm for the parallel hypercube that runs in $O(\log N)$ time on an N-node network, the queue size being $O(\log N)$. Their algorithm also works for *partial permutations*, i.e., routing with at the most one packet originating at any node and at the most one packet destined for any node.

Upfal [16] calls a routing problem to be a *q-bounded communication request* if intially at most q packets are located at any node, and no more than q packets will have to be sent to any node.

The following theorem is due to Ranade [14]

Theorem 2.1 *There exists a randomized algorithm for routing partial permutations on an N-node butterfly that runs in time $O(\log N)$ and needs only $O(1)$ sized queues.*

As a consequence of the above theorem, we can prove the following

Lemma 2.1 *Any $O(\log N)$-bounded communication request can be routed on an N-node parallel hypercube in $O(\log N)$ time, with a queue size of $O(\log N)$.*

Proof. We can trivially embed an $N \log N$-node butterfly on an N-node parallel hypercube [6]. Each node in the hypercube will correspond to $\log N$ butterfly nodes.

Also, Ranade's algorithm runs in the same time bound even for an $O(1)$-bounded communication request. These two facts imply the lemma.

This proof assumes that the $O(\log N)$ packets that are destined for any hypercube node are distinct, i.e., they have addresses of the corresponding butterfly nodes ($O(1)$ packets destined for each butterfly node). This assumption can be eliminated for the following special case.

Lemma 2.2 *If no more than $O(\log N)$ packets originate from any node and no more than $O(1)$ packets are destined for any node, routing can be done in $O(\log N)$ time on an N-node hypercube. The queue size will not exceed $O(\log N)$ at any node.*

The following theorem has been proved by Palis, Rajasekaran, and Wei [9]:

Theorem 2.2 *Any partial permutation on an N-node sequential hypercube can be routed in $O(\log N)$ steps using a randomized algorithm.*

We also use the following sorting algorithms on the hypercube.

Theorem 2.3 *(Nassimi and Sahni [8]) [Sparse Enumeration Sort] Sorting of n keys can be performed in $k \log n$ time on a hypercube using $n^{1+1/k}$ processors. (Initially the keys are located in a subcube of size n, one key per processor).*

Broadcasting is the operation of a single processor sending some information to all the other processors. The *summing* problem is this. Each processor in a hypercube has an integer. We need to obtain the sum of all these integers at some designated processor (say $00\ldots0$). Given two sorted sequences, the problem of *merging* is to obtain a sorted list of elements from both the lists.

Lemma 2.3 *Both broadcasting and summing can be completed in $O(\log P)$ steps on a P-node hypercube. Also, two sorted sequences of length P each can be merged in $O(\log P)$ time, given P hypercube processors.*

Definitions. Let $B(n,p)$ stand for a binomial random variable with parameters n and p. By *high probability* we mean a probability $\geq (1 - N^{-\alpha})$ for any $\alpha \geq 1$ (N being the input size). We let 'w.h.p.' stand for 'with high probability'.

3 The Selection Algorithm

3.1 Summary

The algorithm we present can be thought of as an extension of existing randomized selection algorithms (in particular Floyd and Rivest's [5]) to the hypercube. Given a set X of N keys and an integer k, $1 \leq k \leq N$. Assume the keys are distinct (without loss of generality). We need to identify the kth smallest key. Like in previous randomized selection algorithms we sample a set S of $o(n)$ keys at random. Sort the set S. Let l be the key in S with rank $m = \lceil k(|S|/N) \rceil$. We will expect the rank of l in X to be roughly k. We identify two keys l_1 and l_2 whose ranks are $m - \delta$ and $m + \delta$ respectively, δ being a 'small' integer, such that the rank of l_1 in X is $< k$, and the rank of l_2 in X is $> k$, with high probability.

Next we eliminate all the keys in X which are either $< l_1$ or $> l_2$. The remaining keys are sorted and the key that we are looking for will be one such with high probability. We do a trivial selection on the remaining keys to identify the right key.

3.2 Detailed Algorithm

Assume that the hypercube has $P = N/\log N$ processors. At the beginning each processor has $\log N$ keys. There is a queue associated with each edge incident on any node. There are 8 simple steps in the algorithm:

step1

Each processor flips an $N^{1/3}$-sided coin (for each of its $\log N$ keys) to decide if the key is in the 'random sample' with probability $N^{-1/3}$. This step takes $\log N$ time and with high probability $O(N^{2/3})$ keys (from among all the processors) will be selected to be in the random sample. Also no more than $O(1)$ packets will be selected from any node.

step2

P processors perform a prefix operation to compute the number of keys that succeeded in step 1. Let l be this number.

step3

Concentrate the keys that survived in step 2 in a subcube (call it C) of size $N^{3/4}$. This is done as follows. Each surviving key chooses a random node in the subcube. No more than $O(1)$ keys will choose any node of C w.h.p. Packets are routed to these destinations using Ranade's algorithm (see lemma 2.2).

step4

Sort the subcube C using sparse enumeration sort. Pick keys k_1 and k_2 from C with ranks $\lceil \frac{kl}{N} \rceil - \sqrt{N^{2/3}\log N}$ and $\lceil \frac{kl}{N} \rceil + \sqrt{N^{2/3}\log N}$ respectively.

step5

Broadcast k_1 and k_2 to all the processors in C.

step6

All the keys with a value $< k_1$ or $> k_2$ drop out. The kth smallest key of the original input will be located in this range w.h.p. Count the number of surviving keys and call it m. Also count the number of keys $< k_1$. Let it be s.

step7

Concentrate the surviving keys in a subcube (say C') of size $N^{3/4}$ (similar to step 3).

step8

Sort C' using sparse enumeration sort. Find the key in C' with rank $k - s$ and output.

Analysis.

step1. Number of keys succeeding in step 1 is $B(N, N^{-1/3})$. Using Chernoff bounds, this number is $\leq c\alpha N^{2/3}$ with probability $\geq (1 - N^{-\alpha})$, for some constant c. Also, since there are $\log N$ keys per node at the beginning, the number of keys suceeding at any node is $B(\log N, N^{-1/3})$. Using Chernoff bounds again, this number is $O(1)$ w.h.p.

step2. This step takes $O(\log N)$ time since each node has $O(1)$ packets w.h.p.

step3. Given that the number of keys succeeding in step 1, l is $O(N^{2/3})$, probability that more than e keys will choose the same node in C is $O\left(\frac{N^{2/3}}{N^{3/4}}\right)^e \leq N^{-\alpha}$ for any $\alpha \geq 1$ and some appropriate constant e. The routing step takes $O(\log N)$ steps according to lemma 2.2.

step4. Sparse enumeration sort takes $O(\log N)$ steps (since there are $O(1)$ packets per node w.h.p.) This can be done in $O(1)$ stages each taking $O(\log N)$ steps. In each stage pick one key per node and sort the whole cube. Finally, merge these $O(1)$ sorted lists. (Nodes which do not have any key generate a dummy key with value ∞).

Once the sorting is done, k_1 and k_2 can be picked in $O(1)$ time.

step5. Broadcasting takes $O(\log N)$ steps (see lemma 2.3).

step6. If k_1 and k_2 are chosen as in step 4, the kth smallest key will be in the range $[k_1, k_2]$ and also the value of m will be $O(N^{2/3}\sqrt{\log N})$ w.h.p. This can be proved using the sampling lemma given in [12].

step7. Similar to step 3, this step can also be performed in $O(\log N)$ time.

step8. Sorting C' and the final selection can also be completed in $O(\log N)$ steps (similar to step 4).

Thus we have the following

Theorem 3.1 *Selection on an input of size N can be performed on a $P = N/(\log N)$-node parallel hypercube network in time $O(N/P)$.*

4 Expected Behavior on the Sequential Model

In this section we show that the above algorithm has an expected run time of $O(\log N)$ even on the sequential model of the hypercube (under the assumption that each input permutation is equally likely to be the input). Notice that Plaxton's lower bound proof rules out a worst case $O(\log N)$ time deterministic algorithm.

In the algorithm given in section 3, at the end of step 6, some nodes of the hypercube can still have $\log N$ keys each. This is the reason why we need the parallel model to perform routing (in step 7). Also, step 7 is the only step in the entire algorithm where the stronger model is needed. In every other step, a sequential model will do. In particular, step 3 can be completed on the sequential model in $O(\log N)$ steps (see theorem 2.2).

Under the assumption that each input permutation is equally likely to be the input, the number of keys surviving at any given node (after step 6) is $B(\log N, N^{-1/3})$. This number is $O(1)$ w.h.p. Thus step 7 can be performed on the sequential model in $O(\log N)$ steps w.h.p. (this probability is over the input space).

This means that the algorithm of section 3 runs for a large fraction ($\geq 1 - N^{-\beta}, \beta \geq 1$) of all possible inputs, and on each such input the algorithm terminates in $O(\log N)$ steps w.h.p. (this probability being over the space of coin flips).

Acknowledgement. The author thanks Michael Palis, Sandeep Sen, Sunil Shende, Hui Wang, and David Wei for many stimulating discussions.

References

[1] Aho, Hopcroft, and Ullman, *The Design and Analysis of Computer Algorithms*, Addison-Wesley, 1974.

[2] Ajtai, M., K'omlos, J., Steiger, W.L., and Szemeredi, E., 'Deterministic Selection in $O(\log\log n)$ Parallel Time,' Proc. ACM Symposium on the Theory of Computing, 1986, pp. 188-195.

[3] Cole, R., 'An Optimally Efficient Selection Algorithm,' Information Processing Letters 26, Jan. 1988, pp. 295-299.

[4] Cole, R., and Yap, C., 'A Parallel Median Algorithm,' Information Processing Letters 20(3), 1985, pp. 137-139.

[5] Floyd, R.W., and Rivest, R.L., 'Expected Time Bounds for Selection,' Communications of the ACM, vol. 18, no.3, 1975, pp. 165-172.

[6] Leighton, T., Lecture Notes on Parallel Algorithms, MIT, 1988.

[7] Meggido, 'Parallel Algorithms for Finding the Maximum and the Median Almost Surely in Constant Time', Preliminary Report, CS Department, Carnegie-Mellon University, Pittsburg, PA, Oct. 1982.

[8] Nassimi, D., and Sahni, S., 'Data Broadcasting in SIMD Computers,' IEEE Transactions on Computers, vol. c30, n0.2, 1981.

[9] Palis, M., Rajasekaran, S., and Wei,D., 'General Routing Algorithms for Star Graphs,' Technical Report, Department of Computer and Information Science, Univ. of Pennsylvania, 1989.

[10] Plaxton, C.G., 'Load Balancing, Selection and Sorting on the Hypercube,' Proc. First Annual ACM Symposium on Parallel Algorithms and Architectures, 1989, pp. 64-73.

[11] Plaxton, C.G., 'On the Network Complexity of Selection,' Proc. IEEE Symposium on Foundations Of Computer Science, 1989, pp. 396-401.

[12] Rajasekaran, S., and Reif, J.H., 'Derivation of Randomized Algorithms,' Technical Report, Aiken Computing Lab., Harvard University, March 1987.

[13] Rajasekaran, S., and Sen, S., 'Random Sampling Techniques and Parallel Algorithms Design,' to appear in *Synthesis of Parallel Algorithms*, Editor: Reif, J.H., 1990.

[14] Ranade, A., 'How to Emulate Shared Memory,' Proc. IEEE Symposium on Foundations Of Computer Science, 1987, pp. 185-194.

[15] Reischuk, R., 'Probabilistic Parallel Algorithms for Sorting and Selection,' SIAM Journal of Computing, vol. 14, no. 2, 1985, pp. 396-409.

[16] Upfal, E., 'Efficient Schemes for Parallel Communication,' Journal of the ACM, vol. 31, no. 3, July 1984, pp. 507-517.

[17] Valiant, L.G., and Brebner, G.J., 'Universal Schemes for Parallel Communication,' Proc. ACM Symposium on Theory Of Computing, 1981, pp. 263-277.

[18] Vishkin, U., 'An Optimal Parallel Algorithm for Selection,' Unpublished Manuscript, 1983.

APPENDIX A: Chernoff Bounds

Lemma A.1 *If X is binomial with parameters (n,p), and $m > np$ is an integer, then*

$$Probability(X \geq m) \;\leq\; \left(\frac{np}{m}\right)^m e^{m-np}. \tag{1}$$

Also,

$$Probability(X \leq \lfloor(1-\epsilon)pn\rfloor) \;\leq\; exp(-\epsilon^2 np/2) \tag{2}$$

and

$$Probability(X \geq \lceil(1+\epsilon)np\rceil) \;\leq\; exp(-\epsilon^2 np/3) \tag{3}$$

for all $0 < \epsilon < 1$.

A Fast Parallel Algorithm for Finding a Maximal Bipartite Set

David Pearson* Vijay Vazirani†
Computer Science Department
Cornell University
Ithaca, NY 14853

1 Introduction

In the last few years several efficient parallel algorithms have appeared for the maximal independent set (MIS) problem [KW, Luby, GS]. This may be thought of as the problem of finding a maximal 1-colorable set in a given graph. In this paper we consider the natural extension to finding a maximal 2-colorable set.

A maximal bipartite set (MBS) in an undirected graph $G = (V, E)$ is a maximal collection of vertices B such that the subgraph induced on B is bipartite. A MBS can be constructed by an obvious sequential algorithm, adding each vertex in turn whenever this does not introduce an odd-length cycle. There appears to be no way to parallelize this algorithm, however. We will present a fast parallel algorithm for computing a MBS that uses an entirely different method, using the MIS algorithm as a subroutine.

The extension to maximal k-colorable subgraphs, $k \geq 3$, is NP-hard since the problem of deciding whether a graph is k-colorable is NP-complete for $k \geq 3$ [GJ].

Let I_1 be a MIS in $G = (V, E)$ and I_2 be a MIS in the graph induced on $V - I_1$. The graph induced on $I_1 \cup I_2$ is bipartite; however, it may not be maximal, since a recoloring of $I_1 \cup I_2$ may allow us to include additional vertices. This is where the difficulty of our problem arises.

---

*Supported by a General Electric Foundation Graduate Fellowship

†Supported by NSF Grant DCR 85-52938 and PYI matching funds from AT&T Bell Laboratories and Sun Microsystems Inc.

2 The MBS algorithm

This algorithm proceeds in stages, maintaining a bipartite set which is extended incrementally until it cannot be extended any further. Let $G = (V, E)$ be the original graph, and let $B \subseteq V$ be the current bipartite set. Initially, let B be the null set.

For each bipartite set B, we will define an incompatibility relation R_B on the vertices of $V - B$. Two vertices v_1 and v_2 are *incompatible* if there is an odd-length path from v_1 to v_2 whose intermediate vertices, if any, come from B. (The length of a path is the number of edges it traverses.) Any two vertices which share an edge in the original graph will always be incompatible, so R_B may be considered as an extension of the original edge set. Intuitively, two vertices are compatible if they can both be added to B and given the same color.

At each iteration, perform the following steps:

1. Set $U = V - B$.

2. Compute the incompatibility relation R_B on vertices in U.

3. Let I be a MIS of the graph with vertices U and edges R_B. If $I = \phi$ then stop and output B.

4. Set $B = B \cup I$.

Note that the incompatibility relation computed in step 2 may be reflexive, i.e. a vertex v may be incompatible with itself. If this happens, $\{v\}$ is a dependent set. We assume the MIS procedure will never include such a vertex in any independent set. This is why the MIS I may be empty, even if $B \neq V$. Alternatively, it is simple to remove any such vertices with self-loops before invoking the MIS subroutine.

3 Correctness and running time

A well-known theorem of König states that a graph is bipartite if and only if it contains no odd-length cycles [Harary]. It will be convenient to use this characterization in proving the correctness of the algorithm.

Lemma 1 *At each iteration, the set B is a bipartite set.*

Proof. By induction. At the start of the algorithm, $B = \phi$, which is trivially bipartite. At each iteration, assume that the original B is bipartite. We wish to establish that $B \cup I$ is also bipartite. Consider any cycle in $B \cup I$. If the cycle contains no vertices from I, it lies entirely within B, and since B is bipartite the cycle must have even length. Otherwise we may write the cycle as $i_1, \overline{b_1}, i_2, \overline{b_2}, \ldots, i_n, \overline{b_n}, i_1$ where $i_j \in I$ and $\overline{b_j}$ is a sequence of elements of B. Since all the elements of I are compatible, the path length from i_j to i_{j+1} (or i_n to i_1) must be even, so the entire cycle must also have even length. Since every cycle has even length, $B \cup I$ is a bipartite set. □

Lemma 2 *If at some iteration $I = \phi$, then B is a maximal bipartite set.*

Proof. Suppose $I = \phi$, but B is not maximal. Then there is a bipartite set B', such that $B \subset B'$. Choose $v \in B' - B$. There can be no odd-length path from v to itself using intermediate vertices in B, since any such path would be an odd-length cycle in B'. So v is compatible with itself, and the set $\{v\}$ is therefore an independent set on (U, R_B). This contradicts the fact that the maximal independent set I was null. □

Step 3 of the algorithm can be performed using Luby's MIS algorithm in time $O(\log^2 n)$ on an EREW P-RAM using $O(n^4)$ processors deterministically, or $O(n^2)$ processors using randomization [Luby]. Step 2, forming the incompatibility relation, can also be implemented in $O(\log^2 n)$ time on n^3 processors using matrix multiplication and matrix powers. We will establish in lemma 3 that the number of iterations is $O(\log n)$, making the total running time of the MBS algorithm $O(\log^3 n)$. This establishes that the MBS problem is in NC^3 (see [Cook] for a discussion of the class NC).

Lemma 3 *The number of iterations required by the MBS algorithm is $O(\log n)$.*

Proof. To see why $O(\log n)$ iterations are sufficient, it is convenient to start from the end and work backward to the beginning. Let k be the total number of iterations performed, and let I_j and B_j be the sets I and B computed in stage $j \geq 1$.

Suppose a new vertex v is introduced at step $j > 2$. Since I_{j-1} was a maximal independent set, we know that v must have been incompatible with some vertex $u \in I_{j-1}$, relative to B_{j-1}. By the same argument, v must have been incompatible with some vertex $t \in I_{j-2}$, and u must have been incompatible with some vertex $s \in I_{j-2}$. Leaving aside the question of whether these vertices are all distinct, we can apply the same argument to s and t and construct the binary tree in Figure 1.

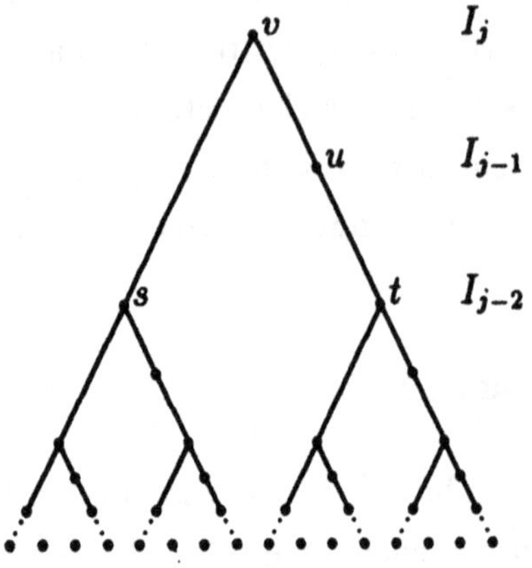

Figure 1

We must now establish that all the vertices in this tree are distinct. Clearly the vertices on different levels are distinct, since they were added to B at different iterations. But what about vertices on the same level? Suppose that two of these are actually the same vertex. Let a be such a vertex, occurring at the highest level containing any shared vertices. Let $b \in I_j$ be the lowest common ancestor of the two tree positions where a occurs, and let c and d be the vertices two levels below b, as in Figure 2. Then we know that there is a path from c to d in B_{j-2}, through the shared vertex (in fact, it may be that $c = d = a$, which we will consider to be a zero-length path). Since c and d both belong to I_{j-2}, we know that there is no

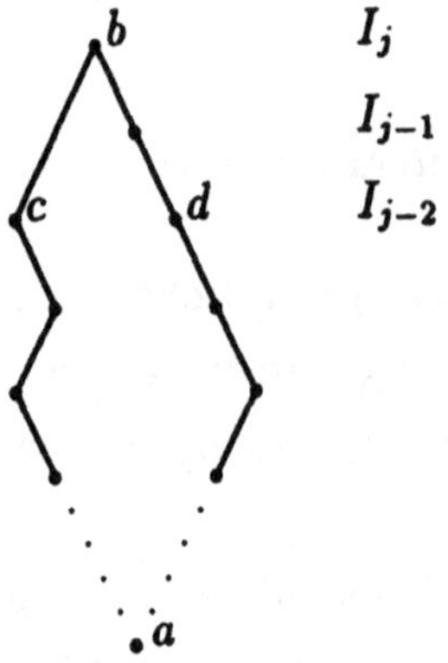

Figure 2

odd-length path between them in B_{j-2}, so the path must have even length. But this would give us an odd-length cycle in B_j, by combining the three odd-length paths connecting c to d through b, then returning by the even-length path from d to c through a. This contradicts the fact that B_j is bipartite, so there can be no such shared vertex a.

Since all the vertices in the tree in Figure 1 are distinct, this tree contains at least $\Omega(2^{k/2})$ vertices, and so the total height k can only be $O(\log n)$ where n is the number of vertices in the original graph. □

The following theorem summarizes the results above.

Theorem 1 *There is a parallel algorithm that solves the MBS problem in $O(\log^3 n)$ time using $O(n^4)$ processors.*

4 A lower bound

We have established that the MBS algorithm will never take more than $O(\log n)$ phases. Now we consider the question of whether it will ever actually require that many. We can show that the bound is tight, in the following sense.

Theorem 2 *An adversary that may choose the initial graph and the MIS obtained at each phase can force the MBS algorithm to use $\Omega(\log n)$ phases.*

Proof. By construction. We will define a class of graphs G_k as follows. Each G_k will be a forest of k trees, and will contain $2^k - 1$ vertices. G_1 is just a single vertex. G_{k+1} consists of two copies of G_k with one new root vertex, and edges from the new vertex to all the root vertices of one copy of G_k. Figure 3 shows G_5.

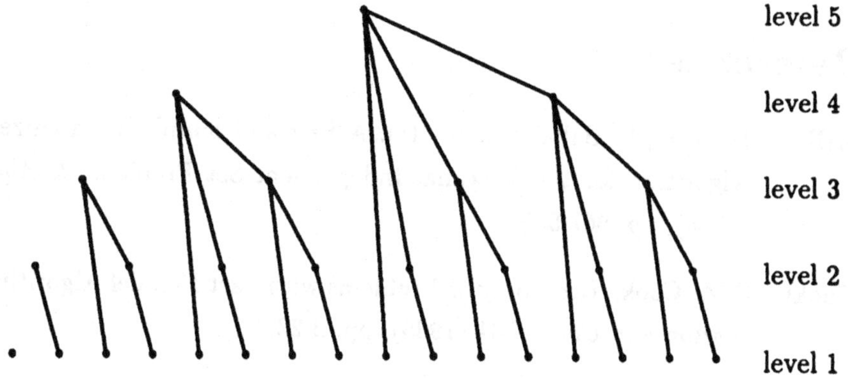

Figure 3

G_k contains no cycles, so the entire graph is clearly bipartite. Note also that every non-leaf vertex has an edge to some vertex at *each* lower level.

To force the MBS algorithm to use k phases, we will give it the graph G_k. At each iteration i our adversary MIS routine will return the vertices at level i. At this point, the bipartite set (B in the algorithm) will consist of levels 1 through $i-1$, and the remaining vertices (U) will contain levels i through k. Because every connected component of B has an edge to at most one vertex outside B, the only incompatible vertices in U will be those that share an edge—the incompatibility relation will add no new edges. The vertices at level i are therefore an independent set, and since every vertex at a higher level has a neighbor at level i, this set will also be maximal.

Let $n = 2^k - 1$, the number of vertices in G_k. Then the number of phases required, k, is $\Omega(\log n)$. □

To establish this result we treated the MIS subroutine as a black box, that might make the worst possible choice of independent set each time it is called. We would like something stronger—a lower bound on the total running time, given a *specific* MIS algorithm. To obtain such a bound would require a precise analysis of the independent sets actually constructed by the various MIS algorithms (or for random algorithms, of the distribution of the sets). We would also need a lower bound for the time required by the MIS algorithms. These are still open problems.

5 Acknowledgements

We wish to thank Steve Mitchell, Samir Khuller, and Alessandro Panconesi for valuable discussions about this problem.

References

[ABI] N. Alon, L. Babai and A. Itai. A Fast and Simple Randomized Parallel Algorithm for the Maximal Independent Set Problem. *J. Algorithms* 7 (1986), pp. 567-583.

[Cook] S. A. Cook. Taxonomy of Problems with Fast Parallel Algorithms. *Information and Control* 64 (1985), pp. 2-22.

[GJ] M. R. Garey and D. S. Johnson. *Computers and Intractability: A Guide to the Theory of NP-Completeness.* W. H. Freeman, New York (1979).

[GS] M. Goldberg and T. Spencer. A New Parallel Algorithm for the Maximal Independent Set Problem. *SIAM J. Computing* 18 (1989), pp. 419-427.

[Harary] F. Harary, *Graph Theory.* Addison-Wesley, Reading, Mass. (1969).

[KW] R. M. Karp and A. Wigderson. A Fast Parallel Algorithm for the Maximal Independent Set Problem. In *Proc. 16th Annual ACM Symposium on Theory of Computing* (1984), pp. 266-272.

[Luby] M. Luby. A Simple Parallel Algorithm for the Maximal Independent Set Problem. *SIAM J. Computing* 15 (1986), pp. 1036-1053.

On the Parallel Evaluation of Classes of Circuits [1]

S. Rao Kosaraju
Department of Computer Science
The Johns Hopkins University
Baltimore, Maryland 21218

Abstract

We treat the problem of parallel evaluation of two important classes of circuits: polynomial degree circuits, and leveled monotone planar circuits. We show that if the operators form a non-commutative semi-ring, then there exists a circuit of degree $0(n)$ and size $0(n)$ for which the minimum depth after any restructuring is n . We also establish that any leveled monotone planar boolean circuit of size n can be evaluated by $poly(n)$ processors in $0(log^3 n)$ parallel time.

I. Introduction

The general circuit value problem (CVP) is believed to be hard in the sense that there might not exist a parallel evaluation strategy for all circuits of size n making use of a polynomial of n, $poly(n)$, of processors and computing in parallel time $poly(log(n))$, $polylog(n)$. Valiant, et al [6] and Miller, et al [5] introduced the notion of the degree of a circuit and established that when the circuit is composed of operators forming a commutative semi-ring and is of degree $poly(n)$, it can be evaluated by $poly(n)$ processors in $polylog(n)$ steps. Here we prove that if the multiplication operator is non-commutative, then there exists a $2n$ degree, $9n + 1$ size circuit which cannot be evaluated in time less than n, irrespective of the number of processors. This partially answers a problem posed in [5]. Even though [5] poses the problem when the operators form a ring, our result is significant since the constructions in [5,6] don't exploit the existence of additive inverses.

Goldschlager [2] first established that a special case of leveled monotone planar CVP (L-CVP) is in $0(log^2 n)$ Turing space complexity. Subsequently, Dymond and Cook [1] refined the argument and proved that the same class can be evaluated by $poly(n)$ processors in $0(log^2 n)$ time. We prove that the general L-CVP can also be evaluated by $poly(n)$ processors in $0(log^3 n)$ time.

II. Degree-bounded Circuits

The circuits are directed acyclic graphs (dags) composed of constants and binary operators '+' and '$\times$', satisfying properties:

$+$ is associative and commutative,
$\times$ is associative, and
$\times$ distributes over $+$.

The additive identity '0' and multiplicative identity '1' exist.

---

[1]Supported by NSF Grant #CCR-8804284 and NSF DARPA Grant #CCR-8908092

The **degree** of a circuit is defined as follows:

degree (constant) = 1
degree ($c_1 + c_2$) = $max\{degree(c_1), degree(c_2)\}$
degree ($c_1 \times c_2$) = $degree(c_1) + degree(c_2)$

The **size** of a circuit is the number of nodes in it. The **delay** of a node u, denoted *delay* (u), is the length of the longest path from any node to u. (If the circuit is a tree, then $delay(u)$ is the height of u). The delay of the circuit is the delay of its output node.

Theorem 1: There exists a degree $2n$, size $9n + 1$ circuit which cannot be parallelized into a circuit of delay less than n.

Proof: Consider the Circuit A of Figure 1.

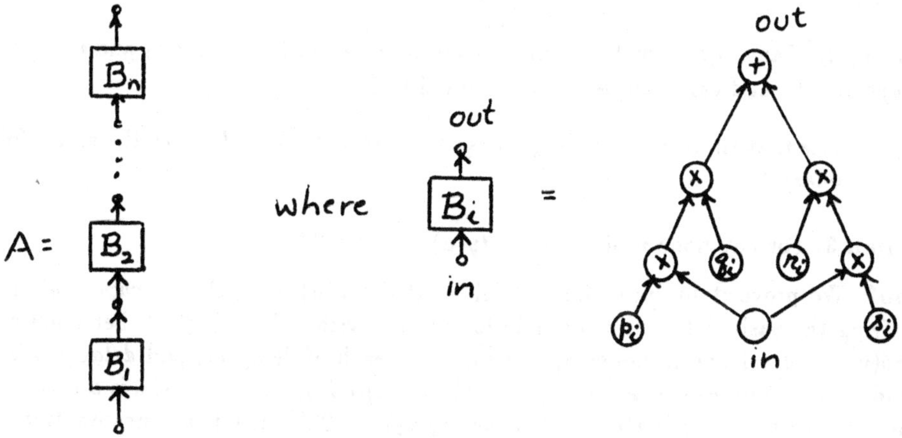

Figure 1

Since each B_i increases the degree by 2 and the size by 9 , the degree and the size of A are $2n$ and $9n + 1$, respectively.

We assign the following language interpretation to the constants and the operators. The alphabet is $\{a, b, c\}$. Constant c is interpreted as the language $\{c\}$; each constant p_i, q_i, r_i, and s_i is interpreted as $\{a\}, \{a\}, \{b\}$, and $\{b\}$, respectively. The operators + and $\times$ are replaced by union, $\cup$, and concatenation, $\hat{}$, respectively. Note that $\cup$ is associative and commutative, and $\hat{}$ is associative and distributes over $\cup$. Note also that the output of the circuit is the language,

$$L = \{\alpha \, c \, \alpha^R | \alpha \in \{a, b\}\dagger \text{ and } |\alpha| = n\}.$$

Before completing the proof of the theorem, we first establish three lemmas.

Lemma 1: There cannot exist $x_1, x_2, y_1, y_2 \in \{a, b, c\} *$ *s.t.* $x_1 \neq x_2, y_1 \neq y_2$, *and* $\{x_1, x_2\} \hat{} \{y_1, y_2\} \subseteq L$.

Proof: Let $x_1 y_1 \in L$ and $|x_1| > |y_1|$. Then x_1 must be of the form $a_1 a_2 ... a_n \, c \, a_n a_{n-1} ... a_k$ in which each $a_i \in \{a, b\}$ and $k \leq n$. If $x_1 y_2$ is also in L, we must have $y_1 = y_2 = a_{k-1} ... a_2 a_1$.

The case $|y_1| < |x_1|$, can be handled analogously by proving $x_1 = x_2$. In addition, $|x_1| \neq |y_1|$ since every string in L is of odd length.

Corollary 1: There cannot exist $x, x_1, x_2, y_1, y_2, y \in \{a,b,c\}^*$ s.t. $x_1 \neq x_2$, $y_1 \neq y_2$ and $\{x\}\{x_1, x_2\}\{y_1, y_2\}\{y\} \subseteq L$.

Proof: If not, $\{xx_1, xx_2\}\{y_1y, y_2y\} \subseteq L$ - contradicting the above lemma.

In the following lemma, without loss of generality, we consider only circuits from each node of which there is at least one path to the output node. Let $L(u)$ be the language realized by any node u.

Let a circuit P realize L. For any node u in P, let $capacity(u)$ be the number of strings in $L(u)$.

Lemma 2: If any node v of P is a concatenation node, with in-nodes v_1 and v_2, then one of $capacity(v_1)$ and $capacity(v_2)$ must be equal to 1.

Proof: Note that there exist x and y s.t. $\{x\}L(v_1)L(v_2)\{y\} \subseteq L$. Now the result follows from Corollary 1.

Lemma 3: For any node u of P, $capacity(u) \leq 2^{delay(u)}$.

Proof: We prove it by induction on delay. If $delay(u) = 0$, clearly $capacity(u) = 1$, satisfying the basis. let the lemma hold for every u with $delay(u) \leq d$. Let node v have $delay(v) = d+1$ and in-nodes v_1 and v_2. Since each of $delay(v_1)$ and $delay(v_2)$ is $\leq d$, by inductive hypothesis, $capacity(v_1) \leq 2^d$ and $capacity(v_2) \leq 2^d$. If v is a union node, then $capacity(v) \leq capacity(v_1) + capacity(v_2) \leq 2^{d+1}$. If v is a concatenation node, then by lemma 2, $capacity(v) = max\{capacity(v_1), capacity(v_2)\} \leq 2^d$.
Hence in either case the inductive step holds.

Now we complete the proof of theorem 1. Let r be the output node of P. Since the number of strings in L is 2^n, we have $2^{delay(r)} \geq 2^n$. Thus in any parallel realization of circuit A, the delay is at least n.

III. Leveled Monotone Planar Circuit Value Problem (L-CVP)

The circuit is a planar dag, and is leveled in the sense that every node has a (level) label ≥ 1 such that all the in-nodes of each label i node, $i \geq 1$, are labeled $i+1$. In addition, the planar embedding satisfies the constraint that each level i node, $i \geq 1$, is above (by the y coordinate value) each level $i+1$ node, and each edge is a straight line segment. Each node can be an AND, '$\wedge$', node, an OR, 'v', node, a '0' node, a '1' node, or an identity, id, node. An AND and an OR node has each in-degree two and computes the corresponding boolean function. A '0' and a '1' node has each in-degree zero, and outputs the corresponding value. An id node has in-degree one and transmits its input value to its out-nodes. The output consists of computing the value of each node (its output value). The size of the circuit is its number of nodes. Thus the L-CVP of Figure 2 is of size 14, and for each node its label and its output value are shown on its left and right, respectively.

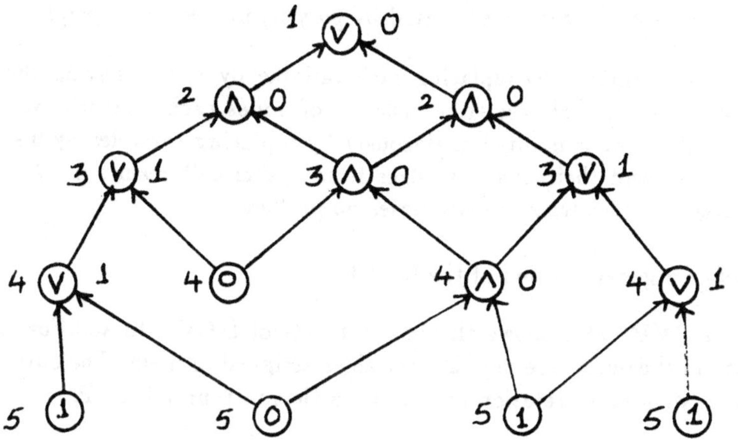

Figure 2

The special case considered in [1,2] assumes that 0 and 1 nodes are on the outer face only. The example of Figure 2 is not in this class since a 0 node is in an internal face.

We first consider a generalization of the special case of [1,2].

Type 1 L-CVP: All the 0, and 1 nodes are on the outer face, and some zero in-degree nodes on the outer face can have variables assigned to them. Variable nodes don't contribute to the size of the circuit.

The required output consists of $< S_0, S_1, G >$, where S_0 (respectively, S_1) is the set of nodes each of which evaluates to 0 (respectively, 1) irrespective of the values of the variables. G consists of the circuit obtained by deleting nodes $S_0 \cup S_1$, and their incident edges.

An example of a type 1 L-CVP is shown in Figure 3 on the left, and the corresponding output is shown on the right.

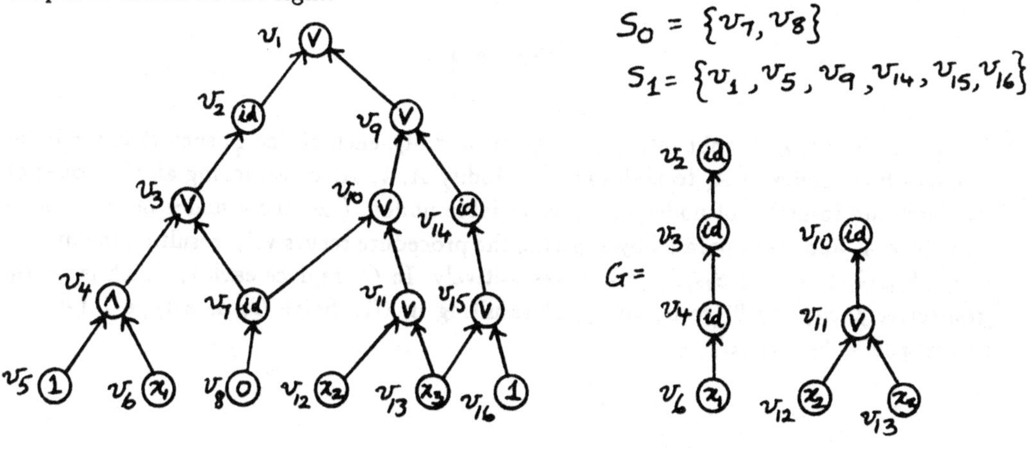

Figure 3

Lemma 4: Type 1 L-CVP can be evaluated by $poly(n)$ processors in $polylog(n)$ time.

Proof: S_0 can be computed by replacing each variable by 1, and solving the resulting problem as the known special case [1,2]. The set of nodes each of which evaluates to 0 constitutes S_0. S_1 can be computed analogously by replacing variables by $0's$. Removal of S_0 and S_1 nodes and their incident edges from the circuit results in G. Note that exclusion of variable nodes from the size poses no problem.

Now we define a generalization of the L-CVP.

Generalized L-CVP: This allows all the constructs of L-CVP. In addition, some zero in-degree nodes on the outer face can have variables assigned to them. The output consists of $< S_0, S_1, G >$, with interpretation analogous to that in type 1 L-CVP.

Theorem 2: Generalized L-CVP can be evaluated by $poly(n)$ processors in $0(log^3 n)$ time.

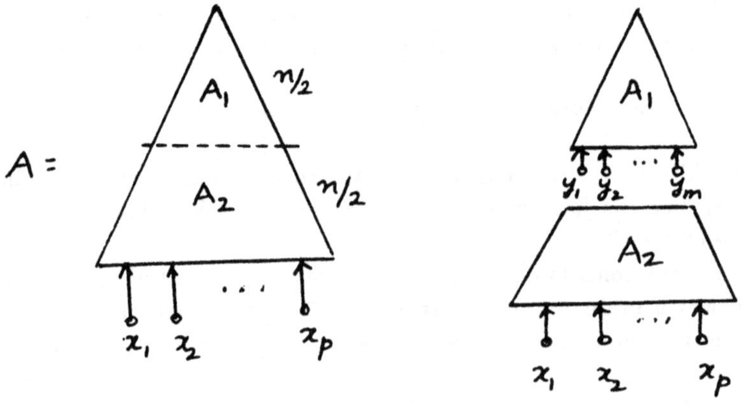

Figure 4

The given circuit, A, is split into 2 circuits, A_1 and A_2, each of size $\frac{n}{2}$, such that there are no edges from nodes in A_1 to nodes in A_2. Modify A_1 to A_1' by attaching all the nodes of A_2 which are in-nodes of nodes in A_1 as variable nodes. (Let these nodes be $y_1, ..., y_m$.) Now solve A_1' and A_2 in parallel by applying the procedure recursively, resulting in outputs $< S_{10}, S_{11}, G_1 >$ and $< S_{20}, S_{21}, G_2 >$, respectively. In G_1 replace each y_i which is in S_{20} (respectively, S_{21}) by 0 (respectively, 1) resulting in G_1'. Solve G_1' as a type 1 L-CVP, resulting in $< S_{30}, S_{31}, G_3 >$.

The output, $< S_0, S_1, G >$, for the original circuit A is given by:

$$\begin{aligned} S_0 &= S_{10} \cup S_{20} \cup S_{30}, \\ S_1 &= S_{11} \cup S_{21} \cup S_{31}, \text{ and} \\ G &= G_2 \text{ and } G_3 \text{ properly attached.} \end{aligned}$$

If we denote the time needed for solving a problem of size n by $t(n)$, we have

$$\begin{aligned} t(n) &\leq t(\tfrac{n}{2}) + clog^2 n, \text{ for some constant } c, \text{ and} \\ t(1) &= 0(1). \end{aligned}$$

In the recurrence, the first term is for the recursive call, and the second term is for solving a type 1 L-CVP (all other steps of the algorithm can be easily executed within $log^2 n$ steps). Hence $t(n) = 0(log^3 n)$.

Clearly, the number of processors needed is $poly(n)$.

References

1. P. W. Dymond, and S. A. Cook: Hardware Complexity and Parallel Computation, Proceedings of the 21st Annual Symp. on Foundations of Computer Science, 1980, 360-372.

2. L. M. Goldschlager: A Space Efficient Algorithm for the Monotone Planar Circuit Value Problem, IPL, 1980, 25-27.

3. L. M. Goldschlager, and I. Parberry: On the Construction of Parallel Computers from Various Bases of Boolean Functions, Theoretical Computer Science, 1986, 43-58.

4. R. E. Ladner: The Circuit Value Problem is log space complete for P, SIGACT News 7, 1975, 18-20.

5. G. L. Miller, V. Ramachandran, and E. Kaltofen: Efficient Parallel Evaluation of Straight-line Code and Arithmetic Circuits, Lecture Notes in Computer Science 227, VLSI Algorithms and Architectures, 1986, 236-245.

6. L. G. Valiant, S. Skyum, S. Berkowitz, and C. Rackoff: Fast Parallel Computation of Polynomials Using Few Processors, SIAM J. on Computing, 1983, 641-644.

VORONOI DIAGRAMS OF MOVING POINTS IN THE PLANE

Jyh–Jong Fu R. C. T. Lee

Institute of Computer Science, National Tsing Hua University

Hsinchu, Taiwan 30043, R. O. C.

ABSTRACT

In this paper, we consider the dynamic Voronoi diagram problem. In this problem, a given set of planar points are moving and our objective is to find the Voronoi diagram of these moving points at any time t. A preprocessing algorithm and a query processing algorithm are presented in this paper. Assume that the points are in k–motion, and it takes $O(k)$ time to find the roots of a polynomial with degree $O(k)$. The preprocessing algorithm uses $O(k^2n^3 logn \bullet 2^{O(\alpha(n)^{5k+1})})$ time to process moving functions of given points, and uses $O(k^2n^3 \bullet 2^{O(\alpha(n)^{5k+1})})$ space to store the preprocessing result where $\alpha(n)$ is the functional inverse of Ackermann's function. The query processing algorithm is designed to report the Voronoi diagram of these points for a query time t. It takes $O(n)$ time which is optimal.

SECTION 1. INTRODUCTION

Given a point set $S=\{p_i \mid 1 \leq i \leq n\}$ in the plane, the set of points closer to a point p_i of S than to any other point of S defines a convex polygonal region V(i). V(i) is called the **Voronoi polygon** associated with p_i. V(i)'s for $1 \leq i \leq n$ partition the plane into a convex net which we may call as the **Voronoi diagram**, denoted as Vor(S). The vertices of the diagram are **Voronoi vertices**, and its line segments (or rays) are **Voronoi edges**. The Voronoi diagram of a point set in the plane has been studied for years [VORO08, ROGE64, BENT80a, KIRK79, LEE80, SHAM75, SHAM78]. Figure 1.1 shows an example of the Voronoi diagram of four points in the plane.

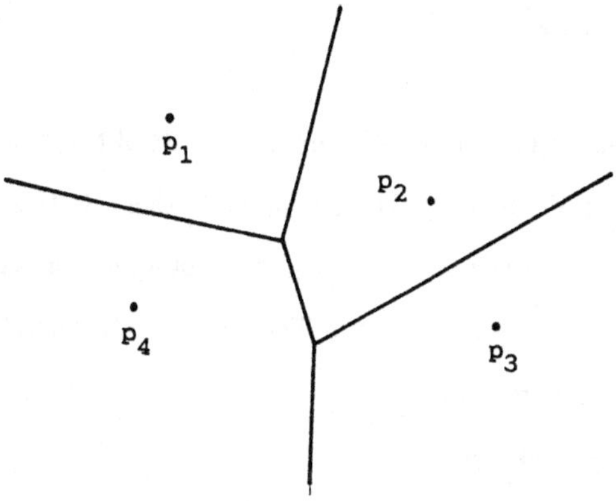

Figure 1.1

In this paper, we consider the problem of constructing Voronoi diagrams of dynamic points in the plane where the points are moving. In our discussion, we follow the definition of k–motion defined by Atallah [ATAL83]. If the given points are in k–motion, it means that x and y coordinates of every point are polynomial functions of time with degree$\leq k$. Thus each point p_i can be described by $(x_i(t),y_i(t))$, where

$$x_i(t)=a_{i,k}t^k+a_{i,k-1}t^{k-1}+...+a_{i,0}$$
$$y_i(t)=b_{i,k}t^k+b_{i,k-1}t^{k-1}+...+b_{i,0}$$

and $a_{i,\ell}$'s and $b_{i,\ell}$'s $(0\leq\ell\leq k)$ are constant coefficients of polynomial functions $x_i(t)$ and $y_i(t)$ respectively. Atallah [ATAL83] has solved some dynamic computational geometry problems, such as dynamic closest pair problem, dynamic convex hull problem, and etc.

In this paper, we present a preprocessing algorithm to process n moving points in the plane. It takes $O(k^2n^3 logn \bullet 2^{O(\alpha(n)^{5k+1})})$ time and uses $O(k^2n^3 \bullet 2^{O(\alpha(n)^{5k+1})})$ space to store the preprocessing result if the points are in k–motion. And a query processing algorithm is proposed to find the Voronoi diagram of these points for a query time t. The query time is O(n) which is optimal since the reporting size of the Voronoi diagram is O(n).

SECTION 2. PRELIMINARIES

We understand that each Voronoi edge exists because of two points, say p_i and p_j. Yet, not every two points will have a Voronoi edge corresponding to them. In this section, we shall try to answer the following question: Given two points p_i and p_j of a set S of static points, will there be a Voronoi edge corresponding to these two points? The answer to this question will be useful to solve the dynamic Voronoi diagram problem.

Let us define some notations.

- $S=\{p_i \mid 1 \le i \le n\}$: A set of distinct points in the plane. The x–y coordinates of p_i are represented by (x_i,y_i). If the given points are static, x_i and y_i are constants. If they are dynamic, x_i and y_i are polynomial functions of time and denoted as $x_i(t)$ and $y_i(t)$.
- Vor(S): The Voronoi diagram of S.
- $\overline{p_i p_j}$: The line segment connecting points p_i and p_j.
- $\overleftrightarrow{p_i p_j}$: The line passing through p_i and p_j.
- e_{ij}: The perpendicular bisector of $\overline{p_i p_j}$.
- m_{ij}: The midpoint of line segment $\overline{p_i p_j}$.
- length(u,v): The Euclidean distance between two points u and v in the plane.
- A point (x,y) is on the **right** hand side of $\overline{p_i p_j}$ if and only if $(y_j-y_i)x-(x_j-x_i)y+(x_jy_i-x_iy_j)>0$
- A point (x,y) is on the **left** hand side of $\overline{p_i p_j}$ if and only if $(y_j-y_i)x-(x_j-x_i)y+(x_jy_i-x_iy_j)<0$
- Each e_{ij} can be treated as a real line with m_{ij} as the point of origin. For a point v on e_{ij}, it has a measure d. d is positive if v is on the right hand side of $\overline{p_i p_j}$, that is d=length(v,m_{ij}). Whereas it is negative if v is on the left hand side of $\overline{p_i p_j}$, that is d=–length(v,m_{ij}).
- For two points on e_{ij}, say v_1 and v_2, let their measures on e_{ij} be d_1 and d_2 respectively, and $d_1<d_2$. $[d_1,d_2]$ can be used to denote line segment $\overline{v_1 v_2}$ on e_{ij}. If it does not include left (or right) end–point, the bracket '[' (or ']') is replaced by parenthesis '(' (or ')'). For example, (d_1,d_2) represents line segment $\overline{v_1 v_2}$ excluding two end–points v_1 and v_2.
- c_{ijk}: The circumcenter of $\Delta p_ip_jp_k$.
- d_{ijk}: The measure of c_{ijk} on e_{ij}.
- r_{ijk} and r'_{ijk}: e_{ij} is partitioned by c_{ijk} into two rays, where ray $[d_{ijk},\infty]$ on e_{ij} is denoted by r_{ijk}, and ray $[-\infty,d_{ijk}]$ on e_{ij} is denoted by r'_{ijk}.

The above notations can be explained by considering Figure 2.1. In Figure 2.1, where c_{123}

is the circumcenter of $\Delta p_1p_2p_3$. Three rays starting from c_{123} constitute the Voronoi diagram of p_1, p_2 and p_3. The line segment connecting p_1 and p_2 is $\overline{p_1p_2}$. m_{12} is the midpoint of $\overline{p_1p_2}$, e_{12} is the perpendicular bisector of $\overline{p_1p_2}$, c_{123} is on the left hand side of $\overline{p_1p_2}$, and d_{123}=–length(c_{123},m_{12}).

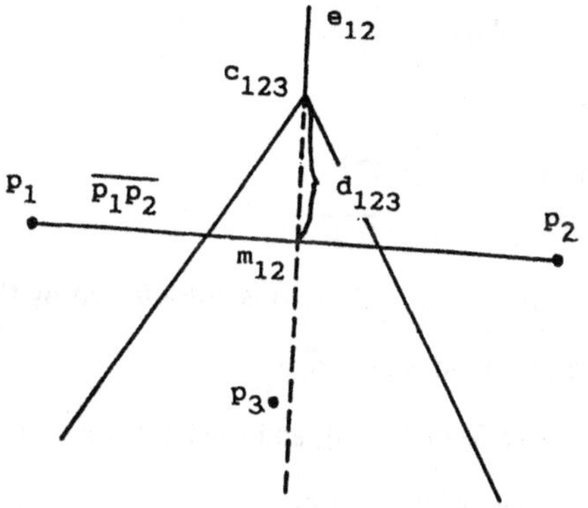

Figure 2.1

The following description in this section is based on that S contains static points.

Assumption 2.1

No four points of S are cocircular.

The following are three basic properties of Vor(S) [PREP85].

Property 1

For any point v in the plane, it is a Voronoi vertex of Vor(S) if and only if

(a) there exist three points, say p_i, p_j, p_k, of S, such that v is the circumcenter of p_i, p_j and p_k, and

(b) for any point p_ℓ of S other than p_i, p_j and p_k, length(v,p_i) = length(v,p_j) =length(v,p_k) <length(v,p_ℓ).

Property 2

For any point v in the plane, v is on a Voronoi edge of Vor(S), but not a Voronoi vertex if and only if

(a) there exist two points, say p_i and p_j, of S, such that v is on e_{ij}, and

(b) for any point p_k of S other than p_i and p_j, length(v,p_i)= length(v,p_j)< length(v,p_k).

Property 3

There exists a Voronoi edge of Vor(S) which is a part of e_{ij} if and only if $\overline{p_ip_j}$ is an edge of the Delaunay triangulation of S.

According to these properties, we use the following theorems to answer the question stated before.

<u>Lemma 2.1</u>

For a point pair p_i and p_j of S, the existence of a third point p_k of S affects the appearance of e_{ij} in Vor(S) according to the following rules:

Case 1. p_k is on $\overline{p_i p_j}$.

e_{ij} disappears from Vor(S).

Case 2. p_k is on $\overleftrightarrow{p_i p_j}$, but not on $\overline{p_i p_j}$.

The appearance of e_{ij} in Vor(S) is not affected by the existence of p_k.

Case 3. p_k is on the right hand side of $\overline{p_i p_j}$.

r_{ijk} disappears from Vor(S), and the appearance of r'_{ijk} in Vor(S) is not affected by the existence of p_k.

Case 4. p_k is on the left hand side of $\overline{p_i p_j}$.

r'_{ijk} disappears from Vor(s), and the appearance of r_{ijk} in Vor(S) is not affected by the existence of p_k.

Proof.

Case 1 and Case 2 are obvious.

Case 3: Since p_i, p_j, and p_k are not collinear, there must exist a circumcenter c_{ijk} of $\Delta p_i p_j p_k$. e_{ij} is partitioned into r_{ijk} and r'_{ijk} by c_{ijk}. Let ℓ be any part of r_{ijk}. For any point, say v, on ℓ, since p_k is on the right hand side of $\overline{p_i p_j}$, length(v,p_i) = length(v,p_j) > length(v,p_k). According to Property 2 listed above, no part of r_{ijk} can be a Voronoi edge of Vor(S). And for any point, say u, on r'_{ijk}, length(u,p_i)=length(u,p_j)<length(u,p_k). Thus the appearance of r'_{ijk} in Vor(S) is not affected by the existence of p_k.

Case 4 can be proved similarly.

Q. E. D.

In the above, we showed how part of e_{ij} may disappear from Vor(S). In the following, we shall show how the entire e_{ij} may disappear. This is always due to the presence of some other point of S located in $\overline{p_i p_j}$, or some other two points of S located on opposite sides of $\overline{p_i p_j}$ that cause the entire e_{ij} to disappear.

Consider Figure 2.2. There are four points. r'_{123} will disappear because of the presence of p_3 and r_{124} will disappear because of the presence of p_4. Since r'_{123} and r_{124} overlap, e_{12} disappears entirely.

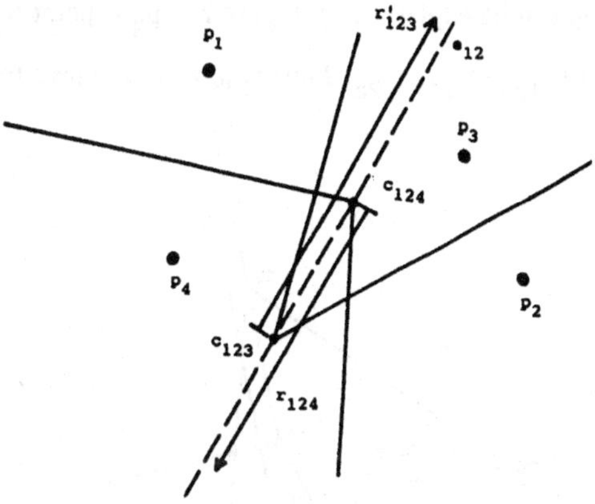

Figure 2.2

Consider Figure 2.3. Again, there are four points. In this case, r'_{123} and r_{124} do not overlap and consequently, part of e_{12} remains in Vor(S).

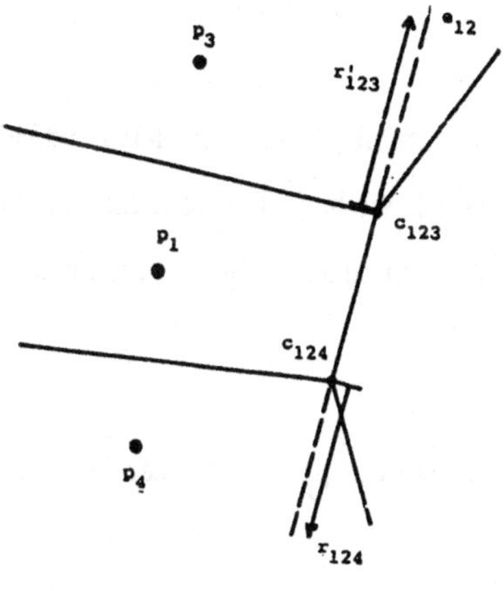

Figure 2.3

So far as p_i and p_j are concerned, assume there is no other point of S located on $\overleftrightarrow{p_i p_j}$, we may divide all other points of S into two sets: those on the right hand side of $\overline{p_i p_j}$ and those on the left hand side of $\overline{p_i p_j}$. Consider the set of points on the right hand side of $\overline{p_i p_j}$. For each point p_k, there is a corresponding c_{ijk} on e_{ij}. Thus there is a sequence of c_{ijk}'s on e_{ij}. Among all of those c_{ijk}'s, let p_α be the point whose corresponding $c_{ij\alpha}$ is the leftmost point. p_α defines the part of e_{ij} which will disappear due to all points on the right hand side of $\overline{p_i p_j}$. That is, ray $r_{ij\alpha}$ will disappear from Vor(S).

The above discussion can be explained by Figure 2.4. p_3 is point p_α because c_{123} is the leftmost point of the sequence c_{123}, c_{124}, c_{125}. Thus r_{123} will disappear from Vor(S) entirely.

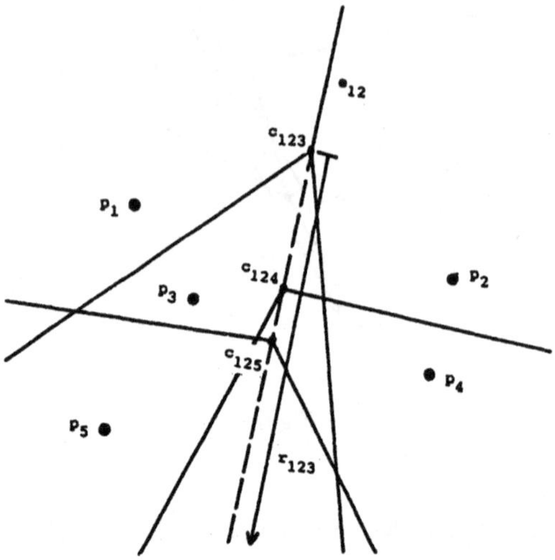

Figure 2.4

The same reasoning also applies to all points to the left hand side of $\overline{p_i p_j}$.

Based on the result of Lemma 2.1, we have Theorem 2.2 and Corollary 2.3 that can be used to determine whether there exists a Voronoi edge in Vor(S) which is part of e_{ij} for points p_i and p_j of S.

<u>Theorem 2.2</u>

For a point pair p_i and p_j of S, besides p_i and p_j, S can be partitioned into four subsets, A, B, C, and D, where

$A=\{p_k | p_k \in S, p_i \neq p_k \neq p_j, p_k$ is on $\overline{p_i p_j}\}$,

$B=\{p_k | p_k \in S, p_i \neq p_k \neq p_j, p_k$ is on $\overleftrightarrow{p_i p_j}$, but not on $\overline{p_i p_j}\}$,

$C=\{p_k | p_k \in S, p_i \neq p_k \neq p_j, p_k$ is on the right hand side of $\overline{p_i p_j}\}$,

$D=\{p_k | p_k \in S, p_i \neq p_k \neq p_j, p_k$ is on the left hand side of $\overline{p_i p_j}\}$.

Let $d_{ij\alpha}=\text{MIN}\{\infty, d_{ijk} | \text{for all } p_k \in C\}$ and $d_{ij\beta}=\text{MAX}\{-\infty, d_{ijk} | \text{for all } p_k \in D\}$.

There is no Voronoi edge of Vor(S) that is part of e_{ij} if and only if any one of the following conditions occurs:

Condition 1: $A \neq \phi$.

Condition 2: $d_{ij\alpha} < d_{ij\beta}$

Proof. **if part.**

According to Case 1 of Lemma 2.1, if Condition 1 is held, obviously e_{ij} will disappear. Assume that Condition 2 is satisfied. By the definitions of $d_{ij\alpha}$ and $d_{ij\beta}$, for any point $p_k \in C$, $r_{ijk}=[d_{ijk},\infty] \subseteq [d_{ij\alpha},\infty]=r_{ij\alpha}$, and according to Case 3 of Lemma 2.1, $r_{ij\alpha}$ will disappear from Vor(S). Similarly, for any point $p_k \in D$, $r'_{ijk}=[-\infty,d_{ijk}] \subseteq [-\infty,d_{ij\beta}]=r'_{ij\beta}$, and according to Case 4 of Lemma 2.1, $r'_{ij\beta}$ will also disappear from Vor(S). Since $d_{ij\alpha}<d_{ij\beta}$, $r_{ij\alpha}$ overlaps with $r'_{ij\beta}$. Hence there is no Voronoi edge of Vor(S) that is part of e_{ij}.

only if part.

Assume that Condition 1 and Condition 2 are not satisfied. *A* is an empty set and $d_{ij\alpha} \geq d_{ij\beta}$. The points of *B* do not affect the appearence of e_{ij} on Vor(S) (Case 2 of Lemma 2.1). The points that will affect the appearance of e_{ij} are in *C* or *D*. And $d_{ij\alpha} \neq d_{ij\beta}$ because four points p_i, p_j, p_α, and p_β cannot be cocircular (Assumption 2.1). Thus $d_{ij\alpha}>d_{ij\beta}$. Let v be any point on $(d_{ij\beta},d_{ij\alpha})$. For every $p_k \in S$ other than p_i and p_j, length(v,p_i)= length(v,p_j)< length(v,p_k). Hence line segment $[d_{ij\beta},d_{ij\alpha}]$ of e_{ij} must be a Voronoi edge of Vor(S).

Q. E. D.

Corollary 2.3

Let $d_{ij\alpha}$ and $d_{ij\beta}$ be defined as in Theorem 2.2. For a point pair p_i and p_j of S, there exists a Voronoi edge of Vor(S) that is part of e_{ij} if and only if there is no other point of S located on $\overline{p_i p_j}$ and $d_{ij\alpha}>d_{ij\beta}$. The Voronoi edge is line segment $[d_{ij\beta},d_{ij\alpha}]$ of e_{ij}.

SECTION 3. DYNAMIC VORONOI DIAGRAMS

In this section, we investigate the problem that for a point pair p_i and p_j of S, when Vor(S) contains a Voronoi edge that is part of e_{ij}. According to Corollary 2.3, this is equivalent to determining when $d_{ij\alpha}>d_{ij\beta}$. Thus, in the following, we concentrate on deriving functions $d_{ij\alpha}$ and $d_{ij\beta}$, and then finding time–intervals during which $d_{ij\alpha}>d_{ij\beta}$. Firstly, for any point $p_k \in S$ other than p_i and p_j, its corresponding d_{ijk} function is derived as follows.

For simplicity, we eliminate "(t)" from the notations used in the following formulas or equations. For instance, x_i represents $x_i(t)$, etc.

e_{ij} can be formulated as equation (3.1).

$$e_{ij} : 2(x_j-x_i)x+2(y_j-y_i)y+(x_i^2+y_i^2-x_j^2-y_j^2)=0 \tag{3.1}$$

The midpoint m_{ij} of $\overline{p_i p_j}$ can be described as (3.2).

$$m_{ij} : (\frac{x_i+x_j}{2}, \frac{y_i+y_j}{2}) \tag{3.2}$$

The circumcenter c_{ijk} can be derived by calculating the intersection of two perpendicular bisectors e_{ij} and e_{jk}.

$c_{ijk} : (x_o,y_o)$, where

$$x_o=\frac{(y_j-y_i)(x_i^2+y_i^2-x_k^2-y_k^2)-(y_k-y_i)(x_i^2+y_i^2-x_j^2-y_j^2)}{2(x_j-x_i)(y_k-y_i)-2(x_k-x_i)(y_j-y_i)}$$

$$y_o=\frac{(x_k-x_i)(x_i^2+y_i^2-x_j^2-y_j^2)-(x_j-x_i)(x_i^2+y_i^2-x_k^2-y_k^2)}{2(x_j-x_i)(y_k-y_i)-2(x_k-x_i)(y_j-y_i)}$$

Thus d_{ijk} can be derived by computing

$\pm[(x_o-\frac{x_i+x_j}{2})^2+(y_o-\frac{y_i+y_j}{2})^2]^{1/2}$, that is

$$d_{ijk}=\pm\left[\frac{((x_k-x_j)(x_k-x_i)+(y_k-y_j)(y_k-y_i))^2((y_j-y_i)^2+(x_j-x_i)^2)}{4((x_j-x_i)(y_k-y_i)-(x_k-x_i)(y_j-y_i))^2}\right]^{1/2} \tag{3.3}$$

Note that the sign of d_{ijk} can be determined by that c_{ijk} is on the right hand side or on the left hand side of $\overline{p_i p_j}$. We have the following lemma to determine the sign of d_{ijk}.

Lemma 3.1

The sign of d_{ijk} can be determined by the following table.

Which side of $\overline{p_i p_j}$ that p_k is on	$\angle p_i p_k p_j$ is	Sign of d_{ijk}
right	acute	plus
right	obtuse	minus
left	acute	minus
left	obtuse	plus

Proof.

If $\angle p_i p_k p_j$ is an acute angle, draw a circle circumscribing $\Delta p_i p_k p_j$. The circumcenter c_{ijk} and p_k must be on the same side of $\overline{p_i p_j}$ (refer to Figure 3.1(a)). When p_k is on the right hand side of $\overline{p_i p_j}$, c_{ijk} is on the right hand side of $\overline{p_i p_j}$. Hence d_{ijk} is positive. And when p_k is on the left hand side of $\overline{p_i p_j}$, c_{ijk} is on the left hand side of $\overline{p_i p_j}$. Hence d_{ijk} is negative. Whereas if $\angle p_i p_k p_j$ is an obtuse angle, the proof can be derived similarly (refer to Figure 3.1(b)).

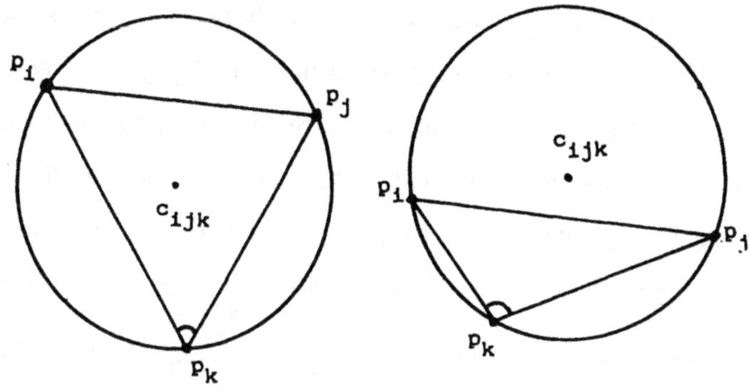

(a) (b)

Figure 3.1

By the definitions listed in Section 2, it is easy to determine when p_k is on the right hand side (or the left hand side) of $\overline{p_i p_j}$ by solving

$(y_j(t)-y_i(t))x_k(t)-(x_j(t)-x_i(t))y_k(t)+(x_j(t)y_i(t)-x_i(t)y_j(t))>0$

(or$(y_j(t)-y_i(t))x_k(t)-(x_j(t)-x_i(t))y_k(t)+(x_j(t)y_i(t)-x_i(t)y_j(t))<0$). And to determine when $\angle p_ip_kp_j$ is an acute or obtuse angle can be done by comparing the values of $\text{length}^2(p_i,p_k)+\text{length}^2(p_k,p_j)$ and $\text{length}^2(p_i,p_j)$. When $\text{length}^2(p_i,p_k)+\text{length}^2(p_k,p_j)> \text{length}^2(p_i,p_j)$, $\angle p_ip_kp_j$ is an acute angle. And when $\text{length}^2(p_i,p_k) +\text{length}^2(p_k,p_j) < \text{length}^2(p_i,p_j)$, $\angle p_ip_kp_j$ is an obtuse angle.

For a pair of points p_i and p_j, once all d_{ijk}'s ($1\leq k\leq n$, $i\neq k\neq j$) are derived and for every p_k, ($1\leq k\leq n$, $i\neq k\neq j$), we can determine time–intervals during which p_k is on the right (or left) hand side of $\overline{p_i p_j}$. This information can then be used to derive functions $d_{ij\alpha}$ and $d_{ij\beta}$. For each point p_k ($1\leq k\leq n$, $i\neq k\neq j$), partition the time from 0 to ∞ into time–intervals such that during each time–interval I, if p_k is on the right hand side of $\overline{p_i p_j}$, put $<d_{ijk},I>$ into a set $\mathscr{R}$, and if p_k is on the left hand side of $\overline{p_i p_j}$, put $<d_{ijk},I>$ into another set $\mathscr{L}$ where $<d_{ijk},I>$ denotes that d_{ijk} is defined during I, and undefined at other times. In order to make $d_{ij\alpha}$ and $d_{ij\beta}$ be defined from t=0 to t=∞, sets $\mathscr{R}$ and $\mathscr{L}$ are initialized to be $\{<\infty,[0,\infty]>\}$ and $\{<-\infty,[0,\infty]>\}$ respectively.

Based on Theorem 2.2, $d_{ij\alpha}=$ MIN $\{<d_{ijk},I>|\text{For all } <d_{ijk},I>\in\mathscr{R}\}$, where MIN is defined to find the minimum function among all defined functions in $\mathscr{R}$. And $d_{ij\beta}=$ MAX $\{<d_{ijk},I>|\text{For all } <d_{ijk},I>\in\mathscr{L}\}$, where MAX is defined to find the maximum function among all defined functions in

For each p_i, p_j pair, its $d_{ij\alpha}$ and $d_{ij\beta}$ functions can be found by a divide–and–conquer algorithm developed by Atallah [ATAL83]. Atallah assumed that $g_1, g_2, \dots, g_n$ are real–valued functions of time such that (i) every g_i is continuous except for at most k_1 jumps and k_2 transitions, has an O(1) storage description and can be evaluated at any t in O(1) time, and (ii) for any two distinct functions g_i and g_j, the (at most k_3) real solutions to the equation $g_i(t)=g_j(t)$ can be computed in O(1) time. The algorithm to compute $h(t)=\min_{1\le i\le n}\{g_i(t)\}$ partitions $\{g_1, g_2, \dots, g_n\}$ into two parts, $\{g_1, g_2, \dots, g_{\lceil n/2\rceil}\}$ and $\{g_{\lceil n/2\rceil+1}, g_{\lceil n/2\rceil+2}, \dots, g_n\}$, computes $\mathrm{MIN}\{g_1, g_2, \dots, g_{\lceil n/2\rceil}\}$ and $\mathrm{MIN}\{g_{\lceil n/2\rceil+1}, g_{\lceil n/2\rceil+2}, \dots, g_n\}$ recursively, and merges them together to obtain h(t). Therefore the time needed is $T(n)\le 2T(n)+c\lambda(n,2k_1+2k_2+k_3)$, where $\lambda(n,s)$ is the Davenport–Schinzel sequence [AGAR87, HART86, SHAR87]. The assumption (ii) listed above was not made appropriate if the degree of $g_i(t)$'s is much higher. So we change assumption (ii) of Atallah to (ii) for any two distinct functions g_i and g_j with degree $O(k)$, the (at most k_3) real solutions to the equation $g_i(t)=g_j(t)$ can be computed in $O(k)$ time. The time needed to find h(t) is thus $T(n)\le 2T(n/2)+ck\lambda(n,2k_1+2k_2+k_3)$. The best bound (almost linear) of $\lambda(n,s)$ found to be $O(n\bullet 2^{O(\alpha(n)^{(s-2)/2})})$ when s is even, where $\alpha(n)$ is Ackermann's function and grow extremely slowly. Finding $d_{ij\alpha}$ or $d_{ij\beta}$ is equivalent to finding h(t). Since $k_1=0$, $k_2=2$, and $k_{23}=10k$, the time needed to find $d_{ij\alpha}$ or $d_{ij\beta}$ is $T(n)\le 2T(n/2)+ckn\bullet 2^{O(\alpha(n)^{5k+1})}$. Thus $T(n)=O(kn\log n\bullet 2^{O(\alpha(n)^{5k+1})})$.

We have the following statement to describe the time needed to find $d_{ij\alpha}$ and $d_{ij\beta}$ for a pair of points p_i and p_j of S.

For a pair of points p_i and p_j of S, if each point of S is in k–motion, then $d_{ij\alpha}$ and $d_{ij\beta}$ can be found in $O(kn\log n\bullet 2^{O(\alpha(n)^{5k+1})})$ time, and $d_{ij\alpha}$ or $d_{ij\beta}$ is composed of $O(kn\bullet 2^{O(\alpha(n)^{5k+1})})$ pieces of functions.

To find when $d_{ij\alpha}>d_{ij\beta}$ can be done by comparing $d_{ij\alpha}$ and $d_{ij\beta}$ piece by piece. For any time–interval I during which $d_{ij\alpha}>d_{ij\beta}$, there must exist a Voronoi edge of Vor(S) that is a part of e_{ij} during I. To compare $d_{ij\alpha}$ and $d_{ij\beta}$ is just to scan two sequences of function pieces. Each comparison of two function pieces of $d_{ij\alpha}$ and $d_{ij\beta}$ takes $O(k)$ time. The total number of pieces of $d_{ij\alpha}$ and $d_{ij\beta}$ is $O(kn\bullet 2^{O(\alpha(n)^{5k+1})})$. Therefore finding time–intervals during which $d_{ij\alpha}>d_{ij\beta}$

needs $O(k^2 n \bullet 2^{O(\alpha(n)^{5k+1})})$ time, and the total number of time–intervals during which $d_{ij\alpha} > d_{ij\beta}$ is $O(k^2 n \bullet 2^{O(\alpha(n)^{5k+1})})$. We summarize as follows.

For a point pair p_i and p_j of S, if each point of S is in k–motion, the number of time–intervals during which there exists a Voronoi edge of Vor(S) that is a part of e_{ij} is $O(k^2 n \bullet 2^{O(\alpha(n)^{5k+1})})$. And these time–intervals can be found in $O(kn\log n \bullet 2^{O(\alpha(n)^{5k+1})})$ time if $n >> k$.

SECTION 4. PREPROCESSING AND QUERY PROCESSING ALGORITHMS

For each pair of points p_i and p_j of S, by applying the method described in Section 3, we can obtain a set of time–intervals, say T_{ij}, such that during any time–interval of T_{ij}, there exists a Voronoi edge of Vor(S) that is part of e_{ij}. Figure 4.1 shows all T_{ij} for the points defined in Example 1.1. For simplicity, the scale of Figure 4.1 is not shown precisely. It is illustrated only for the explanation of the following idea.

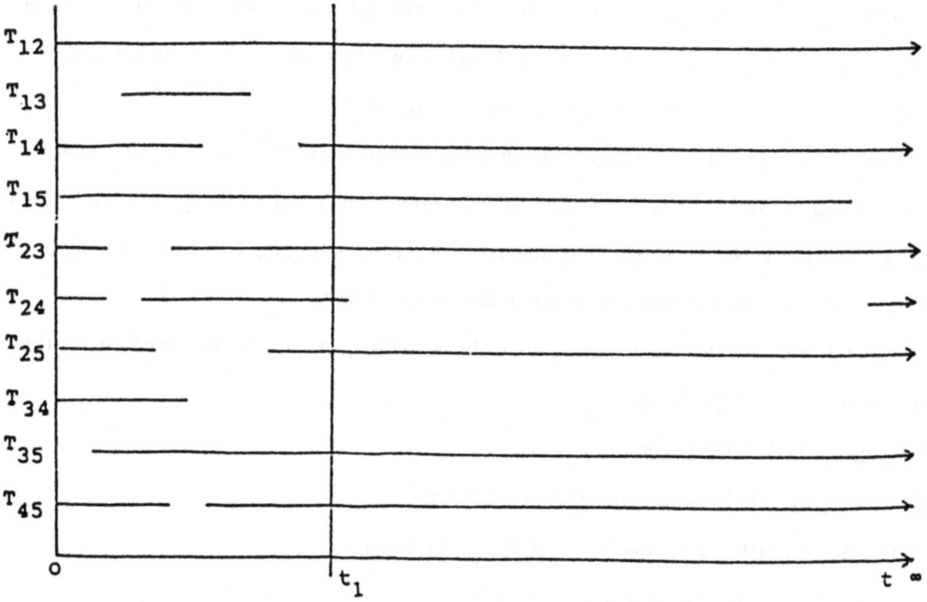

Figure 4.1

In Figure 4.1, if we draw a vertical line along a time t_1, it intersects with a set of time–intervals. Each T_{ij} that contains a time–interval intersected with the vertical line tells us that there exists a Voronoi edge of Vor(S) that is part of e_{ij} at time t_1. For example, from Figure 4.1, we note that Vor(S) contains eight Voronoi edges at time t_1. These Voronoi edges are part of e_{12}, e_{14}, e_{15}, e_{23}, e_{24}, e_{25}, e_{35}, and e_{45}. Hence our preprocessing algorithm is first to find T_{ij}'s for all point pairs of S, and then use an efficient data structure to store all T_{ij}'s. Our query processing algorithm is designed to search the data structure to find Vor(S) at t. The problem to store all T_{ij}'s and to process queries is equivalent to the so called "one–dimensional point enclosure problem" [BENT80b, EDEL80, MCCR80, MCCR85, and CHAZ86] which is defined as: Preprocess a given set T of time–intervals. Then for a query time t, report time–intervals in T that enclose t. There are many optimal results proposed in their previous works. The simplest, but also optimal, method is the "filtering searching" technique proposed by Chazelle [CHAZ86]. In the filtering search technique, the time–interval set $T=\{ [a_1,b_1], ..., [a_N,b_N] \}$ is preprocessed and a "window–list" W(T) is constructed. W(T) is an ordered sequence of linear list (or windows), w_1, $w_2, ..., w_p$, each containing a number of time–intervals from T, and $p \leq 2N$. Let $T^* = \{[a_i,b_i] \in T \mid a_i \leq t \leq b_i\}$. The key idea of this method is to ensure that the window enclosing the query time t contains a superset of T^*, but this superset contains at most $\delta|T^*|$ time–intervals where δ can be set to any integer constant>1. It has been proved that the window–list can be constructed in $O(N \log N)$ time and the storage required for the window–list is O(N).

Once the window–list is constructed, when we want to report T^* of a query time t, a simple binary search can be performed to find the window w_j which enclose the query time t. Then the time–intervals in w_j are checked one by one to report those containing t. If t falls exactly on the boundary between two windows, we check both of the windows.

The following are the preprocessing algorithm and the query processing algorithm for the dynamic Voronoi diagram problem.

PREPROCESSING ALGORITHM

INPUT: $S=\{p_i \mid 1 \leq i \leq n\}$. Each point p_i is in *k*–motion.

OUTPUT: Window list of all time–intervals of T_{ij}'s $(1 \leq i < j \leq n)$.

Step 1. For each point pair p_i and $p_j (1 \leq i < j \leq n)$,

begin

Step 2. Set $\mathcal{R} := \{<\infty,[0,\infty]>\}$, $\mathcal{L} = \{<-\infty,[0,\infty]>\}$;

Step 3. For each point p_k ($1 \le k \le n$, $i \ne k \ne j$),

begin

Step 4. Find function d_{ijk};

Step 5. Determine time–intervals during which p_k is on the right hand side of $\overline{p_i p_j}$, and time–intervals during which p_k is on the left hand side of $\overline{p_i p_j}$;

Step 6. For each time–interval I during which p_k is on the right hand side of $\overline{p_i p_j}$, put $<d_{ijk}, I>$ into $\mathcal{R}$;

Step 7. For each time–interval I during which p_k is on the left hand side of $\overline{p_i p_j}$, put $<d_{ijk}, I>$ into $\mathcal{L}$

end;

Step 8. Find function $d_{ij\alpha} = \text{MIN}\{<d_{ijk}, I> \mid \text{For all } <d_{ijk}, I> \in \mathcal{R}\}$ by the algorithm proposed by Atallah;

Step 9. Find function $d_{ij\beta} = \text{MAX}\{<d_{ijk}, I> \mid \text{For all } <d_{ijk}, I> \in \mathcal{L}\}$ by the algorithm proposed by Atallah;

Step 10. Compare functions $d_{ij\alpha}$ and $d_{ij\beta}$ piece by piece to obtain time–intervals during which $d_{ij\alpha} > d_{ij\beta}$. Let the set of these time–intervals be T_{ij}.

end;

Step 11. Let the union of all T_{ij} ($1 \le i < j \le n$) be T. Construct the window–list of T by the filtering search technique.

<u>QUERY PROCESSING ALGORITHM</u>

INPUT: The window–list constructed in the preprocessing algorithm and a query time t

OUTPUT: Vor(S) at time t.

Step 1. Perform a binary search on the window–list to find the window enclosing the query time t. Let it be w_j.

If t falls exactly on the boundary between two windows, let them be w_j and $w_{j'}$;

Step 2. Determine those time–intervals in w_j (and $w_{j'}$ if it exists) which contains t. Let the set of these time–intervals be T^*;

Step 3. For each time–interval of T^*,

If it belongs to time–interval set T_{gh},

begin

Step 4. Compute the positions of p_g and p_h at time t;

Step 5. Set line–segment $\overline{p_g p_h}$ as an edge of the Delaunay triangulation of S at time t;

end;

Step 6. Compute the straight–line dual of the Delaunay triangulation of S found in Step 3. That is Vor(S) at time t.

Step 2 to Step 10 of the preprocessing algorithm is used to compute T_{ij} for a point pair p_i and p_j. We have shown that it takes $O(kn\,logn \bullet 2^{O(\alpha(n)^{5k+1})})$ time to compute each T_{ij}, and the number of time–intervals in T_{ij} is $O(k^2 n \bullet 2^{O(\alpha(n)^{5k+1})})$. Since there are $O(n^2)$ point pairs, it takes $O(kn^3 logn \bullet 2^{O(\alpha(n)^{5k+1})})$ time to compute out all T_{ij}'s ($1 \leq i < j \leq n$), and the total number of time–intervals in T is $O(k^2 n^3 \bullet 2^{O(\alpha(n)^{5k+1})})$. To construct the window–list in Step 11 of the preprocessing algorithm needs $O(N\,logN)$ time if there are N time–intervals, and the space needed is O(N) [CHAZ86]. In this case, $N = O(k^2 n^3 \bullet 2^{O(\alpha(n)^{5k+1})})$. Thus the window–list can be constructed in $O(k^2 n^3 logn \bullet 2^{O(\alpha(n)^{5k+1})})$ time and the space needed to store the result is $O(k^2 n^3 \bullet 2^{O(\alpha(n)^{5k+1})})$. Hence the total time needed for the preprocessing algorithm is $O(k^2 n^3 logn \bullet 2^{O(\alpha(n)^{5k+1})})$, and it takes $O(k^2 n^3 \bullet 2^{O(\alpha(n)^{5k+1})})$ space to store the result. We summarize as follows:

The preprocessing algorithm of the dynamic Voronoi diagram problem takes $O(k^2 n^3 logn \bullet 2^{O(\alpha(n)^{5k+1})})$ time and uses $O(k^2 n^3 \bullet 2^{O(\alpha(n)^{5k+1})})$ space to store the result.

Step 1 and Step 2 of the query processing algorithm can be run in $O(\delta|T^*|+logN)$ time, where δ is a constant>1, and $|T^*|$ is the number of time–intervals enclosing the query time t. $|T^*|$ is also the number of Voronoi edge of Vor(S) at time t. Since the Voronoi diagram of a point set is planar, $|T^*|=O(n)$, which dominates $logN$. Thus Step 1 and Step 2 in the query processing algorithm takes O(n) time. Since the Delaunay triangulation of a point set is also planar, it contains only O(n) edges. Thus Step 3, Step 4, and Step 5 of the query processing algorithm take O(n) time to set the edges of the Delaunay triangulation of S at time t. And to construct the straight–line dual of the Delaunay triangulation also takes O(n) time. Hence the query processing algorithm can be run in optimal O(n) time. We have the following statement.

The query processing algorithm of the dynamic Voronoi diagram takes O(n) time, which is optimal.

SECTION 5. CONCLUDING REMARKS

In this paper, a preprocessing and a query processing algorithms are proposed to solve the dynamic Voronoi diagram problem, where the points considered are moving in the plane. In our result, given n moving points in k–motion, the preprocessing algorithm can be run in $O(k^2 n^3 \log n \cdot 2^{O(\alpha(n)^{5k+1})})$ time, and the space needed to store the preprocessing result is $O(k^2 n^3 \cdot 2^{O(\alpha(n)^{5k+1})})$. After the preprocessing step, if we want to know the Voronoi diagram of these points at a query time t, the query processing algorithm can be used to find the result in O(n) time which is optimal because the reporting size of a Voronoi diagram is also O(n).

REFERENCES

[AGAR87] P. Agarwal, M. Sharir, and P. Shor, "Sharp upper and lower bounds on the length of general Davenport–Schinzel sequences," *Technical Report 332. Computer Science Department*, New York University, New York, 1987.

[ATAL83] M. J. Atallah, "Dynamic computational geometry," in *Proceeding of 24th IEEE Annual Symposium on Foundations of Computer Science*, Nov. 1983, pp. 92–99.

[BENT80a] J. L. Bently, B. Weide and A. C. Yao, "Optimal expected time algorithms for closest–point problems," *ACM Transactions on Mathematical Software*, Vol. 6, 1980, pp. 563–580.

[BENT80b] J. L. Bentley and D. Wood, "An optimal worst–case algorithm for reporting intersections of rectangles," *IEEE Transactions on Computers*, Vol. C–29, July 1980, pp. 571–577.

[CHAZ86] B. Chazelle, "Filtering search: a new approach to query–answering," *SIAM Journal on Computing*, Vol. 15. No. 4, Aug. 1986, pp.703–724.

[EDEL80] H. Edelsbrunner, "A time– and space–optimal solution for the planar all–intersecting–rectangles problem," *Technical Report 50*, IIG Technische University Graz, Austria, April 1980.

[HART86] S. Hart and M. Sharir, "Nonlinearity of Davenport–Schinzel sequences and of generalized path compression schemes," *Combinatorica*, No. 6, 1986, pp.151–177.

[KIRK79] D. G. Kirkpatrick, "Efficient computation of continuous skeletons," in *Proceeding of 20th IEEE Symposium on Fundation of Computer Science*, October 1979, pp. 18–27

[LEE80] D. T. Lee, "Two dimensional Voronoi diagrams in the L_p–metric," *Journal of Association on Computing Machinery*, October 1980, pp. 604–618.

[MCCR80] E. M. McCreight, "Efficient algorithms for enumerating intersecting intervals and rectangles," *Technical Report*, Xerox PARC, CLS–80–9, 1980.

[MCCR85] E. M. McCreight, "Priority search trees," *SIAM Journal on Computing*, Vol. 14, 1985, pp. 257–276.

[PREP85] F. P. Preparata and M. I. Shamos, *Computational Geometry*, New York: Springer–Verlag, 1985.

[ROGE64] C. A. Rogers, "Packing and covering," *Combridge University Press*, Cambridge, England, 1964.

[SHAM75] M. I. Shamos and D. Hoey, "Closest–point problems," in *Proceeding of 16th IEEE Symposium on Foundation of Computer Science*, October 1975, pp. 151–162.

[SHAM78] M. I. Shamos, "Computational geometry," *Ph.D. Thesis*, Department of Computer science, Yale University, 1978.

[SHAR87] M. Sharir, "Almost linear upper bounds on the length of general Davenport–Schinzel sequences," *Combinatorica*, No. 7, 1987, pp.131–143.

[VORO08] G. Voronoi,"Nouvelles applications des parametres continus à la theorie des formes quadratiques. Deuxième Mémorie: Recherches sur les paralleloedres primitifs," *Journal of reine angew. Math.*, No. 134, 1908, pp. 198–287.

EFFICIENT ALGORITHMS FOR IDENTIFYING ALL MAXIMAL ISOTHETIC EMPTY RECTANGLES IN VLSI LAYOUT DESIGN

Subhas C Nandy, Bhargab B Bhattacharya and Sibabrata Ray *
Electronics Unit
Indian Statistical Institute, Calcutta - 700 035, India

Abstract: In this paper, we consider the following problem of computational geometry which has direct applications to VLSI layout design: given a set of n isothetic solid rectangles on a rectangular floor, identify all maximal-empty-rectangles (MER's). A tighter upper bound on the number of MER's is derived. A new algorithm based on interval trees for identifying all MER's is then presented which runs in $O(n\log n+R)$ time in the worst case and in $O(n\log n)$ time in the average case, where R denotes the number of MER's. The space complexity of the algorithm is $O(n)$. Finally, we explore the problem of recognizing the *maximum* (area)- empty- rectangle without explicitly generating all MER's. Our analysis shows that, on an average, around 70% of MER's need not be examined in order to locate the maximum. The proposed algorithm can readily be tailored to solve the MER problem in an ensemble of points as well as within an isothetic polygon.

Keywords: Computational geometry, VLSI layout, placement, geometric algorithms, complexity, interval trees.

1. INTRODUCTION

Computational geometry [1] involving isothetic polygons, particularly the geometric intersection problem [7-9], plays a significant role in VLSI, e.g., layout design [2, 10], design rule checking, circuit extraction [3], resizing [2], routing and testing [6] and also in image processing and pattern recognition. An *isothetic* polygon is a polygon which is formed by isothetic(straight) lines parallel to X or Y axis [6]. The layout pattern in VLSI reflects the manhattan geometry [3] and thus its relation to isothetic polygons is immediate.

Given an isothetic rectangular floor containing a set of isothetic non-overlapping solid rectangles, an important problem that arises in VLSI layout design is to identify a suitable empty rectangular space where a solid rectangle with a given area and aspect ratio is to be placed. This problem arises in VLSI placement [12] where some rectangular components are already placed on a chip, and a new component is to be placed; the objective is to search for a region where the new module can be accommodated without any overlap with the existing solid rectangles. This calls for an algorithm to identify the maximum empty rectangle in the layout area. This is a generalization of the problem discussed by Naamad et.al [11], where the goal was to find the maximum empty rectangle on a cartesian plane amidst a set of randomly placed points, for which an $O(\min(n^2, R\log n))$ algorithm was described, where n is the number of points on the floorplan and R is the total number of maximal-empty-rectangles(MER) present on the floor. The complexity was later improved to $O(n\log^2 n + R)$ in [14] and then to $O(n\log n + R)$ in [16,17,18]. The algorithms given in [13], [15] locate the maximum-area-rectangle in a point set, without inspecting all MER's in time $O(n\log^3 n)$ and $O(n\log^2 n)$ respectively. The algorithm developed in [11] was used in [12] to find an efficient strategy of automatic/interactive general block placement. A related problem is to locate a largest rectangle contained in an isothetic polygon [6] for which an $O(n^2)$ time and $O(n\log n)$ space algorithm is known. Here, our motivation is to develop a unified algorithm applicable to the MER problem for the following three cases: (i) in a collection of solid rectangles, (ii) in an ensemble of points and (iii) within an isothetic polygon. In this paper, a new algorithm for generating all MER's is suggested which runs in $O(n\log n + R)$ time and consumes $O(n)$ space. The algorithm is simple and is based on the well-known concept of interval trees [4]. We also provide a tighter upper bound on the number of MER's. Finally, we describe a technique for finding the largest-empty-rectangle without generating all MER's.

---

* Present Address: Department of Computer Science, University of Nebraska, Lincoln, NE - 68588, USA

2. CLASSIFICATION AND ENUMERATION OF MER's

Consider a rectangular floor on which n isothetic non-overlapping solid rectangles(blocks) are placed. We will represent an isothetic rectangle by an ordered tuple. The upper left corner of the rectangular floorplan is assumed to be the *origin* of our co-ordinate system with X and Y axes running towards the *right* and the *bottom* respectively.

Definition : A blank isothetic rectangle R in a given layout is called a *maximal empty rectangle* (MER) if

(a) R does not intersect any other solid block in the given layout and

(b) any other empty rectangle with property (a) does not contain R.

Two solid blocks P and Q are said to be *rectilinearly visible* if there exists an isothetic line which intersects P and Q and does not intersect any other solid block in between.

Now we classify MER's in two groups: namely *type-A* and *type-B* as follows.

An MER R is said to be of *type-A* if

(a) R does not touch any boundary of the chip floor and (b) no two solid blocks, one touching the north(east) side and other touching the south(west) boundary of R, have rectilinear-visibility.

An MER is of *type-B* if it is not of *type-A*.

Examples of such MER's are shown in Fig. 1. An isothetic rectangle (solid or blank) with upper left corner at (a_1,b_1) and lower right corner at (a_2,b_2) is *represented by* $[(a_1,b_1),(a_2,b_2)]$.

Here, we present an exact upper bound on the number of type-B MER's and a tighter upper bound for type-A MER's in contrast to that in [11,12].

To enumerate type-B MER's, we use the concept of maximal horizontal strips [19] for describing a floorplan layout using corner stitching data structure. In this data structure the entire blank area in a floorplan is represented by a set of disjoint isothetic rectangular space blocks or tiles called *maximal horizontal strips*. One can easily find such a partition by drawing lines parallel to X-axis that touch the top and bottom of every solid rectangle. For an example, see Fig. 2. Similarly, one can think of *maximal vertical strip* representation of the blank area.

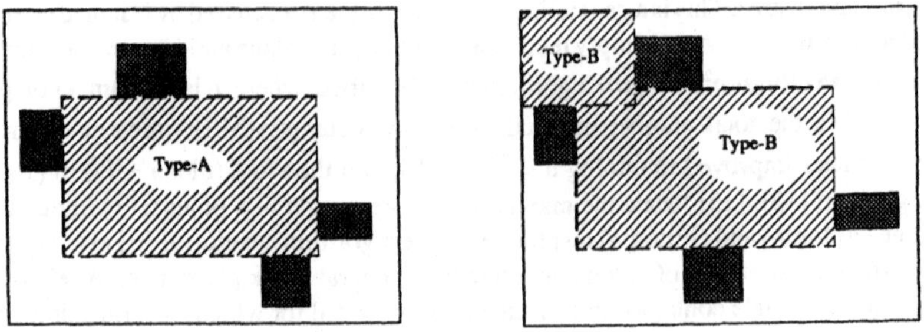

Fig. 1 : Examples of type-A and type-B MER's

Lemma 1: An MER is of type-B iff it completely contains at least one maximal horizontal or vertical strip.

Theorem 1: The number of type-B MER's in a layout with n solid rectangles, n >= 4, is less than or equal to 6n-6.

Proof : In [19] it has been shown that the maximum number of maximal (blank) horizontal strips in a floorplan with n solid rectangles is 3n+1. By a similar argument it follows that the number of maximal vertical strips is also <= 3n+1. Thus the total number of maximal vertical and horizontal strips is always less than or equal to 6n+2. From Lemma 1, each type-B MER must contain at least one maximal vertical or one maximal horizontal strip. Again, no maximal vertical or horizontal strip can be contained in two distinct MER's. The rest of the proof follows from counting the minimum number of peripheral MER's containing both maximal horizontal and vertical strips.

This bound is exact as depicted in the example of Fig.3 where the maximum number of type-B MER's is attained.

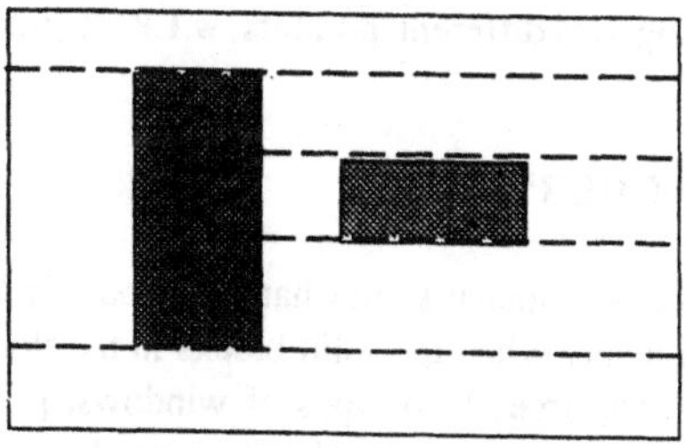

Fig. 2 : Maximal horizontal strips

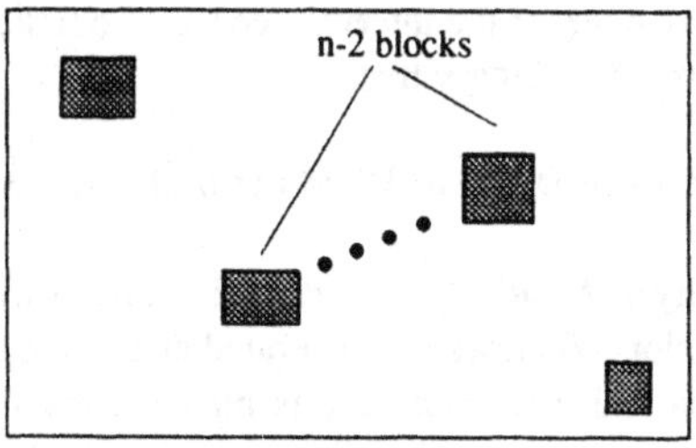

Fig. 3 : Layout with 6n-6 type-B MER's

Theorem 2: The number of type-A MER's in a given layout with n solid rectangles is less than or equal to $\lfloor 3n^2/8 \rfloor$, where $\lfloor x \rfloor$ denotes the greatest integer smaller than x.

Proof: Notice that any two solid rectangles can touch the north and south boundary of at most one type-A MER. Moreover, there must exist at least two solid blocks one touching the top and other touching the bottom of every type-A MER.

Consider now an undirected graph G(V,E) where each solid rectangle is represented as a node (i.e., $|V| = n$). An edge $e_{ij} \in E$, if the corresponding rectangles i and j define the top and bottom of an MER. One can now easily verify that G does not contain any K_5 (a complete graph of 5 nodes) as a subgraph. From an elementary theorem in extremal graph theory [21, p.18], it now follows that the number of edges, a graph with n nodes can have without containing a forbidden subgraph K_5 is less than or equal to $\lfloor 3n^2/8 \rfloor$. Since every type-A MER has a representative edge in G and no edge corresponds to more than one type-A MER, the claim follows.

Conjecture : The maximum number of type-A MER that can be present in any arbitrary layout having n solid blocks is equal to $\lfloor (n/2-1)^2 \rfloor$.

Fig.9a depicts an example where this bound on the number of type-A MER's is attained.

3. IDENTIFICATION OF MER's : CONCEPTS AND TECHNIQUES

Let $\mathcal{R}$ denote the number of all MER's in a given layout. In Section 2, we found that in the worst case $\mathcal{R}$ may be $O(n^2)$. In this section, we introduce the concept of a window and formulate a new algorithm for identifying all MER's with worst case time complexity $O(n\log n + \mathcal{R})$ and space complexity $O(n)$. The average case time complexity turns out to be $O(n\log n)$. Before describing our technique, we summarize some attributes of an interval tree which is used here as a vehicle to guide our search. For details, the reader is referred to [4], [5]. Here, we use a slightly different version of a static interval tree suited to our purpose.

An *interval tree* (T) is a leaf-oriented balanced binary search tree where the leaf nodes from left to right hold distinct X-co-ordinates of the left and the right side of solid blocks (whose extremes are in the set $\{x_1, x_2, ..., x_{2n}\}$) sorted in ascending order. Each internal node w will have the following information:

(i) a discriminant value $d(w)=(d(w_1)+d(w_2))/2$, where w_1 and w_2 are the left and the right child of w respectively. The discriminant value of a leaf node is the X-co-ordinate attached to it.

(ii) a secondary list (w.L) of nodes with three fields L.l, L.r and L.h, sorted in increasing order with respect to L.h, is attached to each node w of T in the form of a doubly-linked list with an additional direct forward link from w to the last node in the list.

A node in T is *active* if it contains non-empty secondary lists or it has active nodes in both of its subtrees. The active nodes in the interval tree are also linked using two different pointers, w.LPTR and w.RPTR, in the form of a binary tree.

3.1. Birth and Death of Windows and Generation of MER's

To identify all MER's, we introduce the concept of a *window*, which is somewhat analogous to a horizontal peeping slot. Windows are generated and killed dynamically when the solid blocks in the floorplan are processed and their data base is managed by the interval tree. Two types of windows, primary and secondary, are generated while processing the bottom and top of solid blocks respectively.

3.1.1. Processing the bottom of a solid block

Consider a solid block whose south side(bottom) s lies at height(Y-co-ordinate) h. Consider a point p on s and draw a line from p to the left, parallel to X-axis, till it hits the east side of a solid block or the west boundary of the floor. Similarly, extend the line from p to the right. Let l and r denote the X-co-ordinates of the above hit-points. A *primary window* is said to be generated in this event and is represented by an ordered tuple ([l,r],h), where [l,r] is a horizontal interval and h denotes the height where it was originated (see Fig. 4). The roof (north boundary) of the floorplan is treated as the south side of a dummy solid block.

Insertion of a window S([l,r],h) in the interval tree is solely dictated by the interval [l,r]. When an interval [l,r] is to be inserted in T, a top-down scan is made starting from the root of T till it finds a node w when the condition $l<=d(w)<=r$ is satisfied for the first time. Window S is then attached to node w, i.e., l, r and h are inserted into the appropriate *node of the linked list* w.L, if it is not already there. Similarly, the corresponding node in the list w.L is removed while deleting a window. Notice that the number of nodes (leaves plus internal) in T *remains invariant when windows are inserted or deleted from T*.

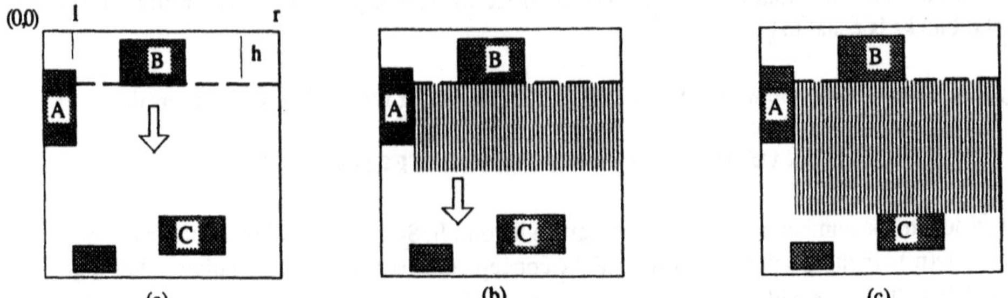

(a) (b) (c)

(a) : Generation of a new window ([l,r],h) while processing the bottom of a solid block B at height h.
(b) : A curtain coinciding with the interval [l,r] continues to fall from height h.
(c) : The window remains live till the falling curtain first hits a solid block C. The corresponding MER is identified.

Fig. 4 : Processing the bottom of a solid block B

Life-span of windows

Assume that a window ([l,r],h) has been generated by the above process. Consider a curtain coinciding with the interval [l,r] at height h and let it fall down as shown in Fig. 4. The window remains active until the falling curtain first hits the top of some solid block or the bottom of the floor and then becomes inactive. All active windows are kept in the interval tree and the inactive ones are deleted.

3.1.2. Processing the top of a solid block

Consider a window S([l,r],h) which remains active till it strikes the top of a solid block $C[(a_1,b_1),(a_2,b_2)]$, as in Fig. 5. Before it dies down, it returns an $MER[(l,h),(r,b_1)]$ and splits itself to give birth to either zero or one or two new windows whose intervals are subsumed by the interval [l,r] of the parent window S and whose heights are inherited. These windows are called *secondary windows*, which in turn, may give birth to other secondary windows. The following cases may now arise :

(i) If $l >= a_1$ and $r <= a_2$, then S dies leaving no offspring.
(ii) If $l >= a_1$ and $r > a_2$, then S dies and a secondary window $([a_2,r],h)$ is generated.
(iii) If $l < a_1$ and $r <= a_2$, then S dies and window $([l,a_1],h)$ is generated.
(iv) If $l < a_1$ and $r > a_2$, then two windows $([l,a_1],h)$ and $([a_2,r],h)$ are generated while S disappears.

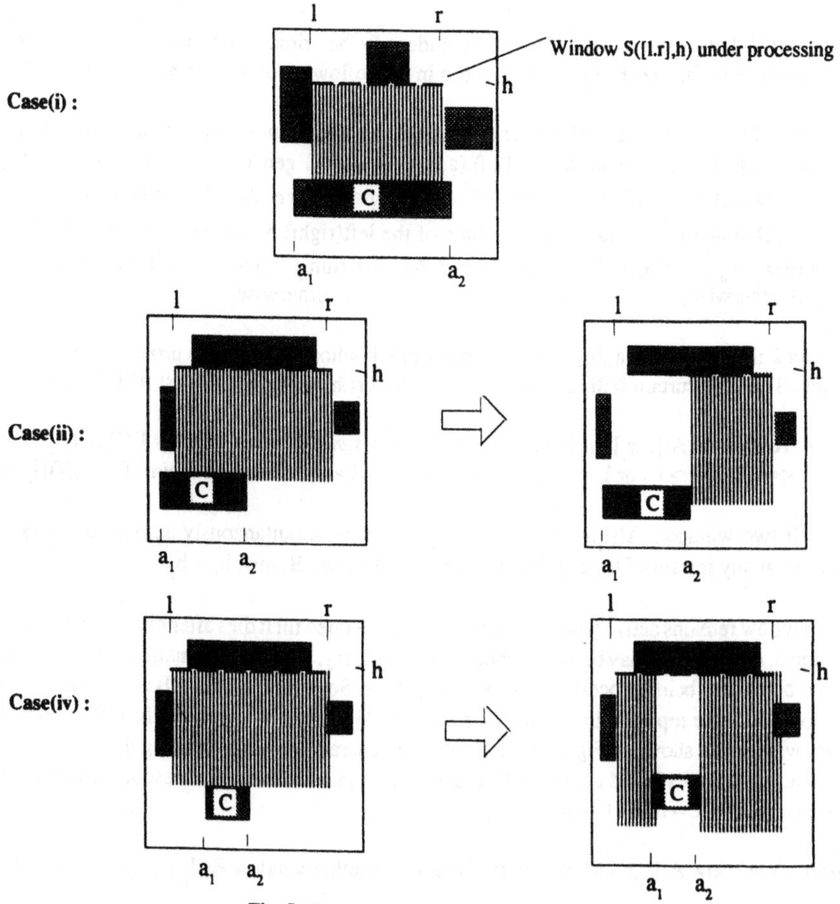

Fig. 5 : Processing the top of a solid block C

If an active window strikes *more than one solid block whose tops lie at the same height*, a slight modification is required. For the first solid block from the left, the MER is generated and splitting of parent window takes place as usual. For the remaining solid blocks which are hit by the window, only splitting of the current window takes place. Similarly, *if the bottom boundaries of several solid blocks are aligned* and they qualify for the same primary window, only one window is generated instead of many.

3.2. Processing of Window and Related Properties

Since windows are generated and killed dynamically, the set of active windows present in the interval tree at any instant of time and their interrelationship heavily depend on the sequence how the top and bottom boundaries of different solid blocks are processed. Given a floorplan with solid blocks, we first create an empty interval tree T. Then we process the roof of the floorplan. The top and bottom boundaries of all solid blocks are then processed one by one such that their Y-co-ordinates are sorted in non-decreasing order. Such a sequence of processing of solid blocks is called a *proper sequence*. Furthermore, when the top of a solid block P is processed, several active windows may be found to be falling on P. The top of P is said to be *completely processed* when *all these windows* are processed with respect to P, i.e., the corresponding MER's and secondary windows are generated. The process terminates when every solid block is processed and all active windows hit the south boundary of the floorplan. Henceforth we will assume that solid blocks are always properly sequenced and the tops so far considered are completely processed. We now observe the following properties.

Processing of solid blocks in proper sequence help identify the primary windows conveniently and nicely simulates the *curtain-fall* mechanism, as captured in the following observations.

Observation 1: Let $C[(a_1,b_1),(a_2,b_2)]$ denote a solid block whose bottom is to be currently processed per proper sequencing on a rectangular floor $[(0,0),(a,b)]$. Assume C generates a primary window $S([l,r],b_2]$. Let $\mathcal{H}$ denote the set of all blocks excluding C *whose tops are already processed but bottoms are yet to be processed.* Denote by h_{il} (h_{ir}) the X co-ordinate of the left(right) boundary of block $H_i \in \mathcal{H}$. Then,

$$l = \max_i (h_{ir} \mid h_{ir} < a_1), \text{ if } \{h_{ir} \mid h_{ir} < a_2\} \neq \phi; \quad r = \min_i (h_{il} \mid h_{il} > a_2) \text{ if } \{h_{il} \mid h_{il} > a_2\} \neq \phi$$
$$= 0, \text{ otherwise}; \qquad\qquad = a, \text{ otherwise}.$$

Observation 2 :Let $C[(a_1,b_1),(a_2,b_2)]$ denote a solid block whose top is to be processed now, per proper sequencing. Then the curtain falling from a window $S([l,r],h)$ will strike C first iff $[l,r] \cap [a_1,a_2] \neq \phi$.

Definition : A window $A([l_1,r_1],h_1)$ is said to *properly subsume* another window $B([l_2,r_2],h_2)$ denoted by $A \supset B$, if $l_1 <= l_2$ and $r_1 > r_2$, or $l_1 < l_2$ and $r_1 >= r_2$. A and B are said to be *disjoint* if $[l_1,r_1] \cap [l_2,r_2] = \phi$.

Lemma 2: If two windows $A([l_1,r_1],h_1)$ and $B([l_2,r_2],h_2)$ are simultaneously active (i.e., present in the interval tree) at any instant of time and if A properly subsumes B, then $h_1 > h_2$.

Proof: A window remains active from the moment it is generated till it dies after hitting a solid block. Now let $A \supset B$ and $h_1 < h_2$. Now, B may be either primary or secondary. The former situation is depicted in Fig.6a. Recall that blocks are being processed in proper sequence. So, before window B is generated, A must hit a solid block P whose top has already been processed. Therefore, A is dead before B is born. If B is a secondary window, as shown in Fig.6b, then B must be generated while processing the top of a solid block say Q. Since A subsumes B and the top of Q must have been completely processed, A should already die out. The case where $h_1 = h_2$, is trivial.

Definition : A window $A([l_1,r_1],h_1)$ is said to *dominate* another window $B([l_2,r_2],h_2)$ if $l_1 = l_2$, $r_1 = r_2$ and $h_1 < h_2$.

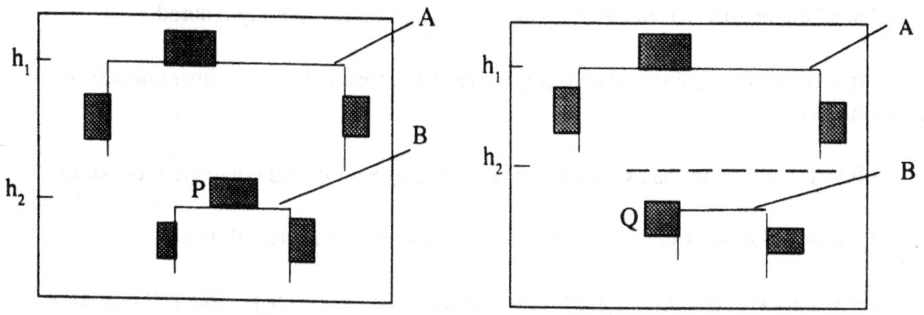

(a) (b)

Fig. 6 : Proof of lemma 2

An example of dominance is shown in Fig.7a. Dominance can manifest in the following way : let A'([l,r],h) and B'([l',r'],h') be two windows such that, A' properly subsumes B' and r = r' or l = l'. By Lemma 2, h > h'. Let r = r' (see Fig.7b) and assume A' and B' hit the top of a solid block C, the X-co-ordinate of the right side of which is c. If c >= l', A' and B' will generate two secondary windows ([c,r],h) and ([c,r],h') respectively. Notice that the latter dominates the former. A similar case arises when l = l'. It is easy to verify that dominance can occur in no other way.

(a)

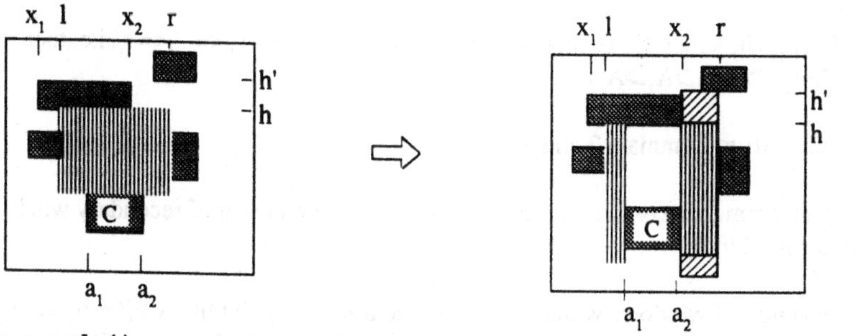

$x_1 < a_1$, and $x_2 <= a_2$; In this case, only one new window ([l, a_1],h) is inserted in the interval tree. The other window ([a_2,r],h) is dominated by an existing window ([a_2,r],h'), h'<h.

(b)

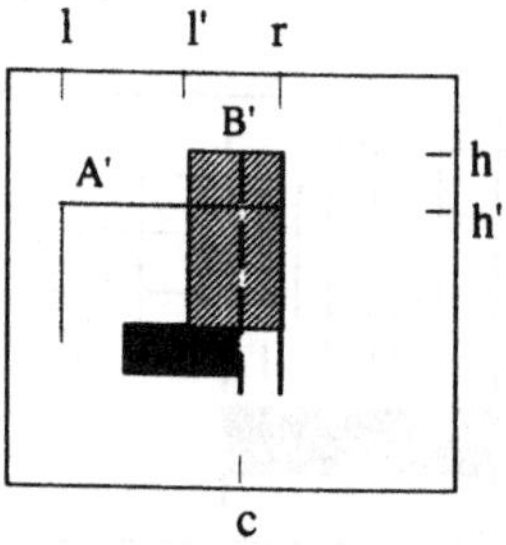

Fig. 7 : Example illustrating dominance.

Remark 1: Let W_p and W_s denote the set of all primary and secondary windows respectively, which are present in the interval tree at any instant of time. Then, no member of W_p can either be properly subsumed or dominated by any member of W_s and by any other member of W_p.

Remark 2: If a window B is dominated by another window, then B can never return an MER.

The concept of dominance thus suggests the following strategy: the secondary windows which are dominated need not be inserted in the interval tree and can be completely ignored.

Lemma 3 : If two windows are simultaneously active at any instant of time, either one subsumes the other or they are disjoint.

Proof : Follows easily from the assumption of proper sequencing and complete processing.

The following observation is immediate from the properties of an interval tree.

Observation 3: Let window $A([l_1,r_1],h_1)$ subsume window $B([l_2,r_2],h_2)$. Now if B is attached to node p in the interval tree, then A will be attached to a node q where either p and q are identical or q is an ancestor of p.

Lemma 4 :If two windows $A([l_1,r_1],h_1)$ and $B([l_2,r_2],h_2)$ are attached to a node w in the interval tree T at any instant of time, either $A \supset B$ or $B \supset A$.
Proof: Assume the contrary. Then by Lemma 3, A and B must be disjoint. Since both the windows are attached to w, we have : $l_1 <= d(w) <= r_1$ and $l_2 <= d(w) <= r_2$, implying that A and B are not disjoint.

Let $A_1([l_1,r_1],h_1)$, $A_2([l_2,r_2],h_2)$,...,$A_k([l_k,r_k],h_k)$ denote all the windows attached to any node w in T. Clearly, $h_1, h_2,...,h_k$ are all distinct.

Theorem 3 : Let $h_1 < h_2 < .... < h_k$. Then, $l_1 >= l_2 >= ..... >= l_k$ and $r_1 <= r_2 <= .... <= r_k$, i.e.,there exists a linear ordering : $A_k \supset A_{k-1} \supset ..... \supset A_2 \supset A_1$.

Proof : Immediate from Lemmata 2 and 4.

The following theorem reflects an important correlation among the set of secondary windows generated by the top of a solid block.

Consider a collection of windows which are hitting the top t of a solid block $P[(a_1,b_1),(a_2,b_2)]$. When t is completely processed, a set of secondary windows is generated and let this set be C. Clearly, C contains two disjoint sets C_1 and C_2 such that all windows in C_1 (C_2) have the same right(left) boundary a_1 (a_2). See Fig. 8.

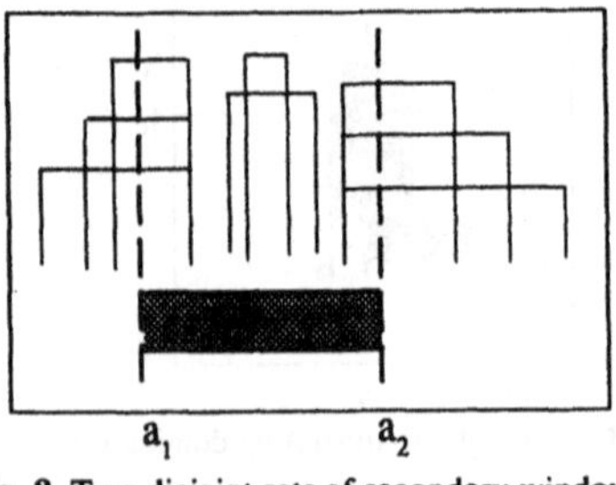

Fig. 8. Two disjoint sets of secondary windows

Theorem 4 : The windows in C_1 (C_2) are linearly ordered with respect to subsumption relation.
Proof : Clear.

Theorem 5 : Every window generated during the process returns exactly one MER and every existing MER is generated by at least one window.

Proof: Immediate from the growth and decay process of windows, the concepts of dominance, proper sequencing and complete processing, as described earlier.

Theorem 6 : The number of active windows that can be present in the interval tree at any instant of time is at most $O(n)$.

Proof : Every solid block generates exactly one primary window, so this number is $O(n)$. The set of secondary windows created while processing the top of a solid block consists of two disjoint sets, the members of which share a common left or right extremity. By Lemma 3, no two active windows can intersect at any instant of time. Furthermore, no active window present in the interval tree is dominated by any other active window. Therefore, either the left or the right extreme of every active window must be unique. Since there can be at most 2(n+1) such X co-ordinates, the claim follows.

4. DATA STRUCTURE AND ALGORITHM

To find all MER's, our algorithm also needs the following data structures:

(a) A list Y, whose elements have three fields as follows :
   (i) Y(i).val : containing the Y co-ordinate of the top or bottom of a solid block;
   (ii) Y(i).solid: containing the dimension of the corresponding solid block;
   (iii) Y(i).ind: having an indicator 't' or 'b' to indicate whether it is top or bottom boundary of the associated solid block.

(b) Two height-balanced [20] binary search trees : TEMP_TREE_L and TEMP_TREE_R.

List Y is *sorted in non-decreasing order* with respect to Y(i).val. If two or more blocks have same value of Y(i).val,then they are kept in Y in increasing order with respect to the X co-ordinates of their left boundaries.

When the top of a solid block is processed, the X-co-ordinates of its left and right boundaries are kept in TEMP_TREE_L and TEMP_TREE_R respectively until its bottom boundary is processed. During the generation of a primary window, the left and right extemities of its interval can easily be obtained by searching these two trees as indicated in Observation 1.

4.1. Scheme of the Algorithm

Initially an empty interval tree T is prepared with the left and right boundaries of solid blocks in sorted order. A window ([0,a],0) corresponding to the roof of the floorplan[(0,0),(a,b)], is inserted in the interval tree. We then start processing solid blocks in proper sequence. Let $P[(a_1,b_1),(a_2,b_2)]$ be the current solid block whose top is to be processed.

Search the interval tree from the root to get a node w* such that $a_1 <= d(w^*) <= a_2$. Let P_{IN} be the set of nodes traversed from the root to w* (excluding w*). From w* scan upto leaf level to get a_1 and a_2. Let P_L and P_R be the set of nodes along these two paths. It is obvious [4] that all active windows in T which intersect the interval $[a_1,a_2]$, will appear with the nodes in P_{IN}, P_L and P_R. As a matter of fact all windows associated with w* will intersect $[a_1,a_2]$.The windows associated with nodes in P_{IN}, P_L and P_R other than w* may or may not intersect $[a_1,a_2]$. The search for such nodes can be efficiently accomplished using pointers w.LPTR and w.RPTR. All the windows intersecting the interval $[a_1,a_2]$ will generate corresponding MER's and can be found in time proportional to $O(n\log n)$ plus the number of reported intersections with no additional search overhead [4].

While processing the top of a solid block $P[(a_1,b_1),(a_2,b_2)]$ two pointers, POINTER_L and POINTER_R are maintained. Initially, these pointers point to the root of T. Later, POINTER_L points the current node of the interval tree which contains the last inserted secondary window with right extremity at a_1 and POINTER_R points the current node containing the last inserted secondary window with left extremity at a_2.

Let w be a node whose associated windows may return MER. The list of windows in w.L are processed from the *end of the list* (i.e., the window with the largest interval first and then in decreasing order) until a window non-intersecting with the interval $[a_1,a_2]$ is found. By Theorem 4, the secondary windows generated at this moment consist of two disjoint linearly ordered sets. From Observation 3, it follows that each time a new secondary window needs to be inserted in T, the search for its position is to be initiated from the node currently pointed by either POINTER_L or POINTER_R, down the tree. Thus all windows generated by the top of a solid block can be inserted in T including the check for dominance by traversing *exactly two paths* in T and can be effected in time $O(\log n)$ plus the number of such windows. These two pointers are inilialized to the root of T when the top of the current solid block is completely processed.

4.2. ALGORITHM MER

Input: A rectangular floor [(0,0),(a,b)] with n solid blocks
Output: All MER's
Method :

Begin
1. create an interval tree T with the left and right boundary co-ordinates of all solid blocks;
2. insert a window ([0,a],0) corresponding to the roof of the floorplan.
3. create the sorted list Y , i.e.,arrange the top and bottom boundaries of solid blocks in *proper sequence* . /* This gives the sequence of processing */
4. insert a in TEMP_TREE_L and 0 in TEMP_TREE_R (which were initially empty)
5. repeat
   let $P[(a_1,b_1),(a_2,b_2)]$ be the current solid block
   if the top boundary of P is to be processed perform steps 5.1 through 5.4 else perform step 5.5
   5.1. scan T from the root to find the first node w* in T such that $a_1 <= d(w^*) <= a_2$ form three sets of nodes P_{IN}, P_L, P_R of the interval tree.
   5.2. find all windows attached to w* and to nodes in P_{IN}, P_L, P_R whose intervals intersect $[a_1,a_2]$. Let this set of windows be $\mathcal{A}$.
   5.3. for each member $A \in \mathcal{A}$,
      (a) return the corresponding MER and generate the secondary windows;
      (b) delete A from T and insert the secondary windows found in 5.3(a) using POINTER_L and POINTER_R as described earlier after checking dominance.
   5.4 . insert $a_1(a_2)$ in TEMP_TREE_R (TEMP_TREE_L);
   5.5 . (a) find the left(right) extremity of the primary window associated to the bottom of the current solid block from TEMP_TREE_R(TEMP_TREE_L) and generate the corrosponding window.
      (b) insert the window found in 5.5(a) in T and delete $a_1(a_2)$ from TEMP_TREE_R(TEMP_TREE_L).
   until (top and bottom boundaries of all solid blocks are processed).
6. process the bottom of the floorplan as the top boundary of a dummy solid block.

end.

4.3. Complexity Analysis

The number of nodes in the interval tree T is 4n-1[4]. From Theorem 6, the number of active windows present in T at any instant of time is at most $O(n)$. Thus the lists w.L for all nodes in T consume O(n) space. TEMP_TREE_L and TEMP_TREE_R and list Y need $O(n)$ and POINTER_L and POINTER_R take $O(1)$ space. Therefore, in total, the data stucture requires $O(n)$ space.

The construction of the interval tree including the sorting of abscissae can be effected in $O(n\log n)$ time[4]. Each insertion(deletion) of an window takes $O(\log n)$ time. Thus steps 1 to 4 take $O(n\log n)$ time.

Step 5 is iterated n times. In each iteration, steps 5.1 and 5.2 takes time proportional to the number of intersecting windows $|A|$ plus $O(\log n)$. From Observation 2 and Theorem 5, the number of MER's generated in the current iteration is $|A|$. For step 5.3(a), notice that the number of secondary windows (including the dominated ones) generated from the entire set A is at most 2 $|A|$. Since all members of A are associated to nodes in P_{IN}, P_L, P_R, deletion of all $A \in A$ in step 5.3(b) can be effected in $O(\log n + |A|)$ time. By virtue of Theorem 4, all secondary windows generated from set A can be inserted in T after checking dominance in $O(\log n + |A|)$ time by properly using POINTER_L and POINTER_R as explained in Section 4.1. Steps 5.4 and 5.5 need $O(\log n)$ time in each iteration. Step 6 is clearly similar to step 5.1 to 5.3 and iterated only once. Thus the total time complexity of Algorithm MER is $O(n\log n + R)$. The correctness of the algorithm is guaranteed by Theorem 5. It can easily be shown that the expected number of MER's in a floorplan is $O(n\log n)$ by following an argument similar to that in [11]. Thus the avearge-case complexity is $O(n\log n)$.

5. LOCATION OF THE MAXIMUM MER

If only an MER with the largest area is required, our earlier algorithm generates all possible MER's and then finds one with the largest area. Similar approaches were reported in [11], [14], [16] for finding the maximum MER amidst a set of points. Algorithms presented in [13], [15] solve the same problem without inspecting all MER's. None of these existing algorithms fits directly when solid rectangles are present instead of points. Here we devise some criteria which can accelerate the search for the maximum without making an exhaustive computation. Recall that only the number of type-A MER can increase quadratically with n. This can happen if there exists a pair of stairs of solid rectangles as in Fig. 9a. For such configurations we propose the following technique which may considerably speed up the search.

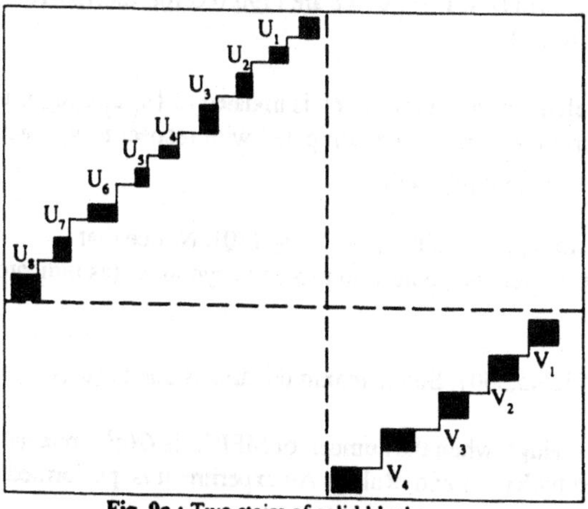

Fig. 9a : Two stairs of solid blocks.

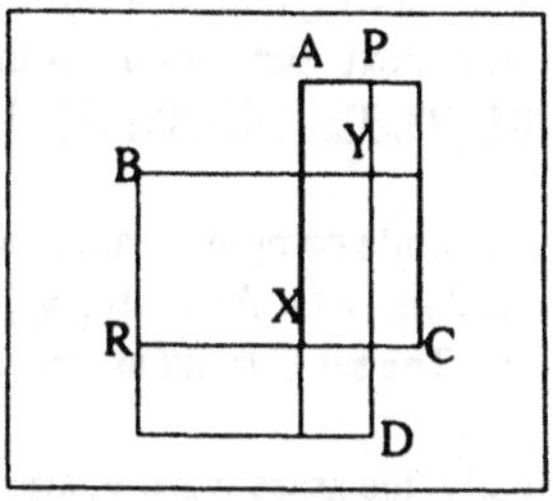

Fig. 9b : Proof of theorem 7.

Let us consider a configuration as in Fig. 9a ,with two stairs of rectangles such that none of the pairs has rectilinear visibility. Let $U = \{u_i (x^1_i, y^1_i), i=1,...,n_1\}$ denote the set of north-west corner points and $V = \{v_i(x^2_i, y^2_i), i=1,...,n_2\}$ be the set of south-east corner points of the possible MER's. Clearly, the following relations will hold among the points in U and V.

i) $x^1_1 > x^1_2 >...> x^1_{n1}, y^1_1 < y^1_2 <...< y^1_{n1}$, ii) $x^2_1 > x^2_2 >...> x^2_{n2}, y^2_1 < y^2_2 <...< y^2_{n2}$,
iii) $x^1_1 < x^2_{n2}$ and $y^1_{n1} < y^2_1$. ...(1)

Each $u_i \in U$ produces an MER with every $v_j \in V$. Thus in total, there will be $(n_1.n_2)$ MER's. Let AREA$[u_i,v_j]$ denote the area of rectangle$[u_i(x^1_i,y^1_i),v_j(x^2_j,y^2_j)]$.

Theorem 7: Consider two points $A(x^1_i,y^1_i)$, $B(x^1_{i+k},y^1_{i+k})$ from U and two points $C(x^2_j,y^2_j)$, $D(x^2_{j+1},y^2_{j+1})$ from V, $1 <= k <= n_1$, $1 <= j <= n_2$ as in Fig.9b. Then,

(a) if AREA[A,C] <= AREA[B,C] then AREA[A,D] < AREA[B,D]
and (b) if AREA[B,D] <= AREA[B,C] then AREA[A,D] < AREA[A,C].

Proof: Follows from geometry of rectangles.

The above theorem suggests that it is unnecessary to generate all MER's in order to recognize the maximum. We thus introduce the following notion of *marking* in Rule 1 to reflect the impact of Theorem 7(a). Similarly we phrase Rule 2 for part(b).

Rule 1: Initially, mark u_j for the highest value of j (assuming an instance as in Fig. 9a). Mark point $u_j \in U$ with respect to v_i if AREA$[u_j,v_i]$ > AREA$[u_k,v_i]$,for all k > j and update U keeping only the marked points. In the next pass, calculate the areas of those MER's whose south-east corner is v_{i+1} in V and the other diagonally opposite corners are those in U which were marked in the earlier pass.

Rule 2: In the current pass, for the next point v_{i+1} in V, start calculating area from the right end of the updated list U. If for some point u_k, AREA(u_k,v_{i+1}) < AREA(u_k,v_i), there is no need to consider points u_j for j < k, by part(b) of the theorem.

Example: For illustration consider the example in Fig. 9a. Let
$U = \{u_1,u_2,u_3,u_4,u_5,u_6,u_7,u_8\}$ = {(21,1),(20,3),(16,4),(15,5),(9,6),(4,8),(3,9),(1,10)}
and $V = \{v_1,v_2,v_3,v_4\}$ = {(40,11),(38,13),(27,15),(26,24)}.
In the first pass, areas are calculated for all points in U w.r.t. v_1 which are {<u>190</u>,160,<u>168</u>,150,<u>155</u>,<u>108</u>,<u>74</u>,<u>39</u>}. Marking is initiated from the right end per Rule 1.

The u_i's corresponding to the underscored elements are marked . U is updated to $\{u_1,u_2,u_3,u_4,u_6,u_8\}$. In the next step, for all points in the current U , areas are computed with respect to v_2 which are {<u>204</u>,198,<u>203</u>,<u>170</u>,<u>140</u>,<u>111</u>}. The updated U is $\{u_1,u_2,u_3,u_4,u_8\}$.

Next, while computing areas with respect to v_3, we find {*,*,<u>161</u>,<u>144</u>,<u>130</u>}. Notice that AREA$[u_3,v_3]$ < AREA$[u_3,v_2]$. So by Rule 2, there is no need to proceed beyond v_3 (as indicated by *). The set U remains unchanged.

Finally, the areas w.r.t. v_4 are {115,306,352,345,350}. So the maximum area is due to $[u_3,v_4]$.

Experiment: To estimate the amount of savings when the number of MER's is $O(n^2)$, one has to find the expected number of rectangles rejected by Rule 1 and Rule 2. An experiment is performed by simulating a floorplan containing two stairs of randomly selected points U and V satisfying (1). Notice that the set of points satisfying (1) in a stair is random, implies that the differences in abscissae and in the ordinates of two consecutive points in any stair are randomly distributed. We partition the floorplan into four quadrants. The dimensions of quadrants are inputs to our experiment. The stairs are formed by generating random points satisfying (1).

Table 1 shows the experimental result with different sets of parameters describing the layout structure and the number of points in each stair. The result for each experimental set is averaged over 100 random instances.

While calculating areas of rectangles for all points in U with respect to the first point in V, we notice that around 50% points in U are marked by Rule 1. Thus the rest was not considered for the remaining points in V. It is also observed that Rule 1 is not so much beneficial after the first pass due to the fact that from the second pass onwards, the remaining points in the list U are not randomly distributed. Rule 2 is found to give around 10% savings on the average. The results also depend on the layout configuration and distribution of points in two stairs. Our experimental results suggest that on an average almost 70% savings in calculation can be achieved by applying these two rules of acceleration.

Table 1

Experiment number (100samples each)	No. of points in stair		Total number of MER's	Pass 1 number of MER's		Total number of MER's rejected			% savings
	U	V		present	rejected by Rule 1	by Rule 1	by Rule 2	Total	
1	100	20	2000	100	47	1001	430	1431	71.55
2	100	20	2000	100	53	1157	225	1382	69.10
3	100	20	2000	100	58	1273	102	1375	68.75
4	100	20	2000	100	50	1030	407	1437	71.85
5	100	30	3000	100	47	1410	1094	2504	83.47
6	1000	50	50000	1000	306	30732	7564	38296	76.59
7	1000	50	50000	1000	464	25111	13754	38865	77.73
8	10000	20	200000	10000	5829	123196	16337	139533	69.77

6. CONCLUSION

In this paper, we investigate the problem of finding maximal-empty-rectangles(MER's) in a rectangular floorplan containing a set of non-overlapping isothetic rectangles. A tighter quadratic upper bound on the number of MER's is derived. Then an $O(n\log n + R)$ worst-case time and $O(n)$ space algorithm is developed for identifying all MER's, where R is the number of MER's in a given floorplan with n solid rectangles. The algorithm runs in $O(n\log n)$ time in the average case. The corresponding MER problem in a point set follows as a special case . This compares favorably well with the best existing algorithms. The proposed method along with the contour-detection algorithm [4,5], can be used for finding MER's in a floorplan with or without overlapping isothetic solid polygons. Our algorithm can also be adopted without any degradation of complexity, to locate a largest-area-rectangle contained in an isothetic polygon with n vertices, for which an $O(n^2)$ algorithm is currently known [6]. This is accomplished by constructing the minimum rectangle enclosing the given polygon and then filling the additional region with solid blocks as shown in Fig. 10. Lastly, few guidelines are suggested to speed up the search for identifying the MER with maximum area without generating all MER's. But this technique of acceleration is yet to be implemented in our present data structure.

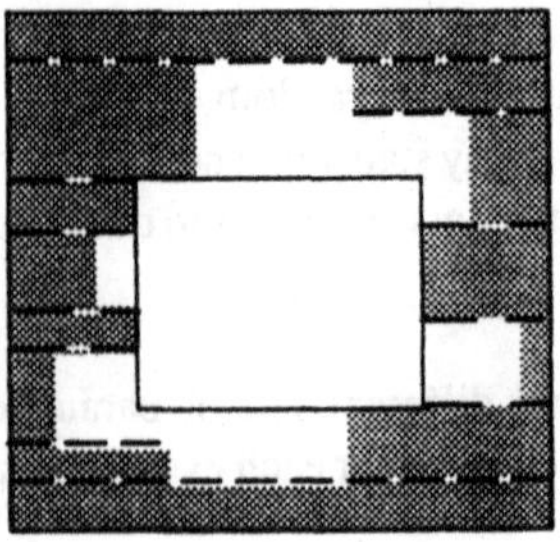

Fig .10 : Largest rectangle contained in a polygon

REFERENCES

1. D. T. Lee and F. P. Preparata, "Computational geometry - a survey", *IEEE Trans. on Computers,* Vol C-33, pp. 1072-1101, Dec. 1984.

2. A. Asano, M. Sato and T. Ohtsuki, "Computational geometry algorithms", in Layout Design & Verification, *Advances in CAD for VLSI,* Vol-4, (Ed. T. Ohtsuki), pp. 295-347, North Holland, 1986.

3. T. G. Szymanski and C. J. Van Wyk, "Layout analysis and verification", in *Physical Design Automation of VLSI Systems,* Ed. B. T. Preas and M. J. Lorenzette, Benjamin Cummings Publishing Company, Inc., 1988.

4. F. P. Preparata, and M. L. Shamos, Computational Geometry : An Introduction, *Springer Verlag,* NY, 1985.

5. Kurt Mehlhorn, Multidimensional Searching and Computational Geometry, *Springer Verlag,* NY, 1984.

6. D. Wood, "An isothetic view of computational geometry", in *Computational Geometry* (G. T. Toussaint, Edited), North Holland, 1985.

7. J. L. Bentley and D. Wood, "An optimal worst case algorithm for reporting intersection of rectangles", *IEEE Trans. on Computers,* Vol C-29, pp. 571-577, July 1980.

8. J. L. Bentley and T. A. Ottman, "Algorithms for reporting and counting geometric intersections", *IEEE Trans. on Computers,* Vol C-28, pp. 643-647, Sept. 1979.

9. M. I. Shamos and D. Hoey, "Geometric intersection problems", Proc. 17th Annual *IEEE Symp. on Foundations of Computer Science,* pp. 208-215, Oct. 1976.

10. K. Yoshida, "Layout verification", in *Layout Design and Verification,* Ed. T. Ohtsuki, Elsevier Science Publication B.V.(North Holland), 1986.

11. A. Naamad, D. T. Lee and W. L. Hsu, "On the maximum empty rectangle problem", *Discrete Appl. Math.,*8,1984, pp. 267-277.

12. S. Wimer and I. Koren, "Analysis of strategies for constructive general block placement", *IEEE Trans on CAD,* Vol CAD-7, No. 3, pp. 371-377, 1988.

13. B. Chazelle, R. L. Drysdale and D. T. Lee, "Computing the largest empty rectangle", *SIAM J. Comput.,* Vol. 15, No. 1, pp. 300-315, February 1986.

14. M. J. Atallah and G. N. Frederickson, "A note on finding a maximum empty rectangle ", *Discrete Applied Math.,* Vol. 13, pp. 87-91, 1986.

15. A. Aggarwal and S. Suri, "Fast algorithms for computing the largest empty rectangle", Proc. 3rd Annual *ACM Symp. on Computational Geometry,* pp. 278-290, 1987.

16. M. Orlowski, "A new algorithm for the largest empty rectangle problem ", *Algorithmica,* Vol. 5, pp. 65-73, 1990.

17. T. Dey, "Two problems in computational geometry", *M.E. Thesis*, Indian Institute of Science, Bangalore, India, 1987.

18. M.J. Atallah and S.R. Kosaraju, "An efficient algorithm for maxdominance, with applications", *Algorithmica,* Vol. 4, pp. 221-236, 1989.

19. J. K. Ousterhout, "Corner stitching : data structuring technique for VLSI layout tools",*IEEE Trans. on CAD,* Vol CAD-3No. 1, 1984, pp. 87-100.

20. D. E. Knuth, The Art of Computer Programming, Vol. 3, Sorting and Searching, *Addison Wesley,* 1973.

21. F. Harary, Graph Theory, *Addison Wesley,* 1972.

ON SOME LARGEST EMPTY ORTHOCONVEX POLYGONS IN A POINT SET

Amitava Datta G.D.S. Ramkumar
Department of Computer Science and Engineering
Indian Institute of Technology, Madras 600 036, INDIA

ABSTRACT

Efficient algorithms for finding some largest empty ortho convex polygons in a point set are presented in this paper. This class of problems are generalizations of the maximum empty rectangle problem. We present simple and efficient algorithms for finding the largest empty ortho convex polygons of the following classes. The algorithm for the L (which is the simplest isothetic polygon after a rectangle) runs in $O(n^2 \log n)$ time in the expected case and $O(n^3)$ time in worst case. The algorithms for the cross shaped polygon, the point visible ortho convex polygon and line visible ortho convex polygon run in $O(n^3)$ time. Finally, the algorithm for the edge visible ortho convex polygon runs in $O(n^2)$ time.

1. INTRODUCTION

In this paper, we present efficient algorithms for some geometric optimization problems in the plane. The problem of finding largest convex k-gons in a simple polygon (the 'potato peeling' problem and its variants) has been studied in [5]. Boyce *et al*[4] have studied the problem of finding the maximum area and perimeter convex k-gons in a point set. Such a convex k-gon may contain points from the set inside it. Their results have been subsequently improved in [3]. The maximum empty rectangle problem is the following. Given an isothetic rectangle R and a point set P inside it, the problem is to find out the largest area or perimeter isothetic rectangle which does not contain any point from P and is contained completely in R. This problem has been studied extensively in recent years [1,2,6,7]. The fastest existing algorithm to solve the maximum empty rectangle problem runs in $O(n \log^2 n)$ time for the area problem and in $O(n \log n)$ time for the perimeter problem [1,2]. In case of isothetic polygons, the only convex polygon is a rectangle. So, for isothetic polygons the largest convex polygon problem reduces to the maximum empty rectangle problem.

In this paper, we study some largest empty ortho-convex isothetic polygon problems in a point set enclosed in an isothetic rectangle BR. An isothetic ortho-convex polygon [11] has either zero or two intersections with any line parallel to either the x- or the y-axis. A similar problem of finding the largest ortho-convex polygon in a simple isothetic polygon was studied in [13]. In this paper, we provide four algorithms for four different classes of ortho-convex polygons. We define these classes of orthoconvex polygons in section 2. First, we give an algorithm for finding the largest empty L in the presence of a point set. Our algorithm for this problem runs in $O(n^3)$ time in the worst case and $O(n^2 \log n)$ time in the expected case, where n is the number of points in the set. The next algorithm is for finding the largest empty ortho-convex polygon which we call an ortho convex cross shaped polygon. The running time of this algorithm is $O(n^3)$. The next problem we study is a simpler version of the problem of finding the largest empty ortho-convex polygon in a point set. Instead, we find the largest empty point visible ortho-convex (PVOC) polygon in the presence of a point set . This algorithm also runs in $O(n^3)$ time. Next, we modify this algorithm to detect the largest empty line visible ortho-convex (LVOC) polygon. The last problem we study is the largest empty edge visible ortho-convex (EVOC) polygon in the presence of a point set. This algorithm runs in $O(n^2)$ time.

This paper is organized as follows. In section two, we give some definitions and notations. In sections three, four, five and six, we discuss algorithms for largest L, largest cross-shaped polygon, largest PVOC (and LVOC) polygon and largest EVOC polygons respectively. We conclude with some remarks and open problems in section seven.

2. DEFINITIONS AND NOTATION

The bounding rectangle is denoted by *BR*. The four sides of BR are *BR.top*, *BR.right*, *BR.bottom* and *BR.left*. The point set inside BR is represented as $P=\{p_1,p_2,\ldots,p_n\}$. or $\{q_1,q_2,\ldots,q_n\}$ alternately. The x and y coordinates of point p_i are represented as $p_i.x$ and $p_i.y$ respectively.

We define some terms related to isothetic polygons as in [12]. An isothetic *straight line* (*line segment*) is a straight line (line segment) that is parallel to either the x-axis or y-axis. A polygon P is an *isothetic polygon* if all its edges are parallel either to the x-axis or to the y-axis. A simple polygon P is a convex polygon if any straight line L intersects at most two edges of P. A variation of the above definition is used in defining ortho-convex polygons. An isothetic polygon P is called an *ortho-convex* polygon if any vertical or horizontal line intersects atmost two edges of P. A non-closed isothetic curve is a *staircase* if either for all points p_i and p_j on the curve, with p_i to the left of p_j, p_i is not above p_j, or for all points p_i and p_j on the curve, with p_i to the left of p_j, p_i is not below p_j. Suppose, p_i is the top-most and p_j is the bottom-most point of a staircase. If the staircase is monotonically decreasing in the south and west direction from p_i to p_j, it is called a *north-west* (NW) staircase. We draw a vertical line L_1 and a horizontal line L_2 through the top most and bottom most points of the staircase respectively (Figure 9). The north-west staircase divide the rectangle formed by BR.left, BR.top, L_1 and L_2 in two parts. The part bounded by BR.left, BR.top and the staircase is called the *external part* of the north-west staircase (marked II in Figure 9). The other part is called the *internal part* (marked I in Figure 9). A north-west staircase is *minimal* if it does not contain any point from the set P in its internal part. A point p_i is said to be *included* in the NW staircase, if it is on or in the external part of the NW staircase. Similarly, the *north-east*, *south-east* and *south-west* staircases and their internal and external parts are defined. If a side S of an empty ortho convex polygon passes through a point p_i, we call p_i a *support* of S. If S overlaps a side of BR, e.g., BR.left, we say that S is *flush* with BR.left. For all the largest empty polygons of this paper, the sides are either supported by points from P or flush with some side of BR.

An *L* is a polygon with six sides and one reflex angle (Figure 1a). A *cross-shaped ortho convex* polygon has twelve sides and four reflex angles (Figure 1b). A *point visible ortho convex* (PVOC) polygon has at least one point p inside it such that the whole polygon is visible from p (Figure 1c). A *line visible ortho convex* (LVOC) polygon is such that we can place either a vertical or a horizontal line LL inside it and the polygon is weakly visible from LL,i.e., any point of the polygon is visible from at least one point on LL. An *edge visible ortho convex* (EVOC) polygon has at least one edge e such that the polygon is weakly visible from e (Figure 1d). In fact, for EVOC polygons, there is at least one point p on the edge e such that the entire polygon is visible from p. The relation between these classes of polygons is that EVOC is a subclass of PVOC, PVOC is a subclass of LVOC and finally, LVOC is a subclass of general ortho convex polygons. In other words, all EVOC polygons are PVOC(but the converse is not true) and so on. For general visibility problems, see [8].

3. LARGEST EMPTY L-SHAPED POLYGON IN A POINT SET

3.1. CHARACTERIZATION

An L is composed of two rectangles joined together at the ends. We divide the Ls in four classes depending on the position of the rectangles. We only show the first kind of L in Figure 1a. We discuss an algorithm for recognising the largest area L of the first kind, algorithms for the other three being similar. The six sides of the L are called the *top*, *mid-right*, *mid-top*, *right*, *bottom* and *left*. The vertex at the junction of the mid-right and mid-top is called the *ankle* of the L (Figure 2a).

Lemma 3.1. *In the worst case, the total number of Ls is $O(n^3)$.*

Proof. (*sketch*) It can be shown that an L is completely fixed by fixing the top, left and right supports. Since, there are $O(n^3)$ such triplets, the lemma follows. Q.E.D.

Remark. The bound in lemma 3.1 is rather loose, because many of the Ls will be non empty. Currently, we do not have an example of a point set where this bound can be achieved.

Lemma 3.2. *If the points in the set $S=\{p_1,p_2,\ldots,p_n\}$ are drawn randomly and independently from a rectangle BR, the expected number of Ls is* $O(n^2 \log n)$.

Proof. (*sketch*) The proof is similar to that in [7]. We consider the Ls whose sides are supported by the points from the set. When we fix the mid_top support of the L, the expected number of points which can act as the bottom support for an empty L is $O(\log n)$ The expected number of pairs of points which can act as top and mid_top supports of an empty L are $O(n^2)$. So, total expected number of Ls is $O(n^2 \log n)$. Q.E.D.

3.2. BACKGROUND TO THE ALGORITHM

We solve this problem by a line sweep approach. During the line sweep, an L can exist in two stages. In the first stage, only the left side exists and the L is denoted by the y interval of its left side [I_L.up,I_L.down] and the left support p_L. In the second stage along with the above information, the coordinates of the ankle are also stored. The top, right, bottom and left supports can be points from the set P or sides of the bounding rectangle BR. But the mid-top and mid-right supports are points from the set P. For an L L_i, the interval between the current position of the ankle to the bottom support is called the *gap* G_i of L_i (Figure 2b). The point which determines the position of the ankle is called the *support* of the gap. For an L in the first stage, the gap is the interval between the top and bottom supports and the support of the gap is the same as the top support. It is easy to see that a point p_k can modify L_i during the line sweep if the y coordinate of p_k lies within the gap G_i (Figure 2b). We represent the interval of the gap G_i as [G_i.up,G_i.down]. The modifications when a point p_i meets the gap of an L are the following. M_1 to M_3 give the modifications for Ls in the first stage (Figure 3).

M_1 : An ankle is introduced in the old L at the point p_i, the gap becomes [p_i.y,I_L.down]. The left side of the old L remains the same.

M_2 : If p_i.y>p_L.y, a new L is introduced. The left side and hence the gap of the new L is [p_i.y,I_L.down] and the left support is p_L.

M_3 : If p_i.y<p_L.y, a new L is introduced with the left side [I_L.up,p_i.y] and p_L as left support.

If L_i is in the second stage, an L is reported with p_i as the right support. The modifications made are the following.

M_4 : The ankle of the old L is modified and the new position of the ankle becomes p_i. So the gap is [p_i.y,I_L.down].

M_5 : If p_i.y>p_L.y, a new L in the first stage is introduced with [p_i.y,I_L.down] as the left side and gap and p_L as the left support.

M_6 : If p_i.y<p_L.y, a new L in the second stage is introduced with left side as [I_L.up,p_i] and left support as p_L. The gap is [G_i.up,p_i].

We first discuss some useful properties of the gaps. Consider two gaps G_i,G_j of the Ls L_i and L_j.

Lemma 3.3. *Either the gaps G_i and G_j are disjoint or they are nested (i.e., one contains the other).*

Proof : Suppose G_i and G_j overlap but they are not nested. The interval G_i is represented as [G_i.up,G_i.down]. Similarly for G_j. Suppose, the supports of G_i and G_j are the points p_i and p_j. We assume without loss of generality p_i.x<p_j.x,i.e., p_j is to the right of p_i. So, p_j will encounter G_i and modify it in either of two ways. In the first case, the support of G_i will be p_j and the gap G_i will be changed to [G_j.up,G_i.bottom]. This happens due to the modifications M_1 and M_4. (Figure 4a). In the second case, the bottom support of the L corresponding to G_i will be raised to G_j.up (due to M_6) (Figure 4b). In the first case the two gaps are nested and in the second case they are disjoint. So, we have a contradiction. The other cases are similar. Q.E.D.

Lemma 3.4. *If two Ls, L_i and L_j have the same left and bottom supports, they have the same gap.*

Proof : Suppose L_i and L_j have same left and bottom supports but their gaps G_i and G_j are different. Since the bottom support of an L is the same as the bottom of its gap, the top of the gaps,i.e., the supports of G_i and G_j will differ. Suppose p_i and p_j are the supports of G_i and G_j and we assume without loss of generality, $p_i.y>p_j.y$. Two cases may arise. Either $p_i.x>p_j.x$ (Figure 5a) or $p_i.x<p_j.x$ (Figure 5b). In the first case, L_i contains p_j and hence not empty. In the second case, p_j will modify the support of G_i to p_j. So, we have a contradiction. Q.E.D.

So, fixing the left and bottom supports of two Ls is equivalent to fixing their gaps. We divide the Ls in different groups depending on the gaps they share. Since there are $O(n^2)$ pair of left and bottom supports, there may be $O(n^2)$ such groups.

3.3. THE ALGORITHM

We use the line sweep method. The supporting data structures are the following. An interval tree T is used to store the gaps of the Ls. The group of Ls GR_i having the same gap G_i will be represented by a unique interval in T. All the Ls in the ith group GR_i are kept in a list and a pointer PT_i to this list is stored along with G_i.

Step 1. Sort the points according to increasing x coordinate and keep them in a list. These are the event points. Construct a skeletal interval tree as in [10]. The algorithm starts by inserting the gap [BR.top,BR.bottom] due to the left side of the bounding rectangle. When the next point in the event point schedule is reached, the steps 2 to 4 are executed.

Step 2. We search in the interval tree T with p_i. During the search, if an interval I_j contains p_i, we go to the corresponding list GR_j of Ls pointed by PT_j. All the Ls in this group will be modified. Notice that an L in the first stage will be modified in either of the two ways ,i.e, either M_1 and M_2 (we call it M_{12}) or M_1 and M_3 (M_{13}). Similarly, an L in the second stage will be modified either according to M_4 and M_5 (M_{45}) or M_4 and M_6 (M_{46}). Since, initially the Ls in group GR_j had the same gap (Lemma 3.4), we have some relationships between these modifications.The modifications in M_{12} and M_{45} are due to the fact that $p_i.y>p_L.y$, where p_L is the left support of the Ls which p_i modify. So, the new gaps after modifications due to M_{12} and M_{45} will be same. Similarly, the gaps due to the modifications M_{13} and M_{46} are same. While modifying the Ls in group GR_j, we keep two lists S_1 and S_2 which contain the new Ls after the modifications M_{12} and M_{45} and those due to M_{13} and M_{46} respectively. If we denote the interval due to the original gap I_j as $[I_j.up, I_j.down]$, the gaps of the Ls in S_1 and S_2 will be respectively $[p_i, I_j.down]$ and $[I_j.up, p_i]$. During this modification process, we compute the area of all Ls in the second stage with p_i as the right support and update the variable containing the maximum area L if necessary.

Step 3. The interval I_j has been split into two intervals. One of these two intervals will remain at the same node n_i of T, and the other has to be reinserted at the left or right subtree of n_i depending on the search path taken by p_i. This can be done simultaneously during the execution of step 2 as in [9]. From lemma 3.3, we know that the gaps in node n_i are nested. So, the modified gaps which are to be reinserted will also be nested. We initially keep the gaps at n_i in a list with the largest gap at n_i as the first element of this list. When p_i modifies this list, the gaps which are displaced from n_i are also kept in a list LL with the largest element as the first. We assume that during the search with p_i, p_i goes to the left subtree of n_i, the other case being similar. In its search path, suppose p_i comes to a node n_j such that discriminant(n_j)>p_i.y,i.e., p_i goes right at n_j. p_i will modify the gaps at n_j according to step 2 and the new gaps to be displaced from n_j are added at the bottom of LL. All the intervals in LL will be nested. This is due to the fact that the intervals at n_i (which is an ancestor of n_j) contains the intervals at n_j due to lemma 3.3. If discriminant(n_j)<p_i.y,i.e., p_i turns left from n_j, the intervals in LL has to be inserted at n_j. Since the intervals at both n_j and LL are nested, we do the following. While executing step 2 for the gaps in the list of n_j, we walk along the list LL and insert them at appropriate places in the list of n_j. Again the modified gaps to be displaced from n_j are added at the bottom of LL and we repeat the process down the tree while searching with p_i (Figure 6). When this search is done with the right side of BR,i.e., [BR.top,BR.bottom], all the intervals at T will be affected and the algorithm stops after this.

Step 4. When steps 2 and 3 are over, we insert a new L with left side [BR.top,BR.bottom] and left support p_i as the first element of the list of gaps at root(T).

Theorem 3.1. *The time complexity of the algorithm is O(nlogn+K), where K is the number of Ls of the first kind.*

Proof : The sorting and construction of the skeletal interval tree takes *O(nlogn)* time. In step 2, only time spent is due to the Ls which are affected by the point p_i. So, step 2 takes $O(\log n+k_1)$ time, where k_1 is the number of Ls affected by p_i. Reinsertion of the intervals modified by p_i (step 3) can be done simultaneously with step 2 as described above. For each L we spent three units of time. The insertion of the left side, the insertion of the ankle and final reporting. So, the total time spent is *O(nlogn+ #Ls of the first kind)*. So, from lemma 3.1 and lemma 3.2, the algorithm runs in $O(n^2\log n)$ time in the expected case and in $O(n^3)$ time in worst case. Q.E.D.

4. LARGEST EMPTY CROSS-SHAPED POLYGON IN A POINT SET

4.1. CHARACTERIZATION

A cross-shaped polygon is illustrated in Figure 1b. It has twelve sides and four reflex angles. Our main motivation for studying this problem is its similarity to the other problems we study in this paper. Each edge of this polygon has a point as its support, as indicated. There are four outer supports q_1, q_2, q_3 and q_4 and eight inner supports, as shown in Figure 1b. Without loss of generality, we assume that $q_2.y <= q_3.y$.

We observe that supports q_1 and q_2 determine the two inner supports r and r' between them. Similarly, each of the eight inner supports are determined by the four outer supports q_1, q_2, q_3 and q_4.

Lemma 4.1. *Consider the horizontal band between q_2 and q_3. In this band, let p be the first point to the left of q_1 and let p' be the first point to the right of q_1 (Figure 7). We claim that $p.x < q_4.x < p'.x$.*

Proof: The proof is by contradiction. We prove that the following two conditions are impossible $q_4.x < p.x$ and $p'.x < q_4.x$.

First, let $q_4.x < p.x$. This means that p is included both in the quadrant formed by q_1,q_2 and by q_3,q_4. This means that the two quadrants intersect causing the polygon to be non-simple, which is not permissible.

Let $p'.x < q_4.x$. It is clear that in this case, p' is included in none of the quadrants. This implies that the polygon has p' inside it and hence is non-empty. Since the polygon is assumed to be empty, this leads to a contradiction. Q.E.D.

4.2 ALGORITHM

By lemma 4.1, we observe that for a particular choice of q_1, q_4 is such that $q_4.x$ is between $q_2.x$ and $q_3.x$. Also, $q_4.y < q_2.y$. It is clear that all points which satisfy these two conditions can play the role of q_4. Our method to find the largest cross-shaped polygon is as follows.

We perform two passes simultaneously. One is the varying of q_1 in increasing order of x-coordinate between q_2 and q_3 and above q_3. The other is the varying of q_4 in increasing order of x-coordinate between q_2 and q_3 and below q_2.

As a preprocessing, for all points q_i, we prepare the following arrays. The array ABOVE stores all the points above q_i sorted according to increasing x coordinate. Similarly, the array BELOW stores all the points below q_i and sorted according to increasing x coordinate. In actual implementation, if we have all the points sorted according to increasing x coordinate in an array, we can reconstruct the arrays ABOVE and BELOW in the following way. When we want the elements of ABOVE while traversing this array, we ignore the points below q_i and vice versa. So, this preprocessing step can be avoided. For ease of exposition we will assume the existence of these arrays for each point. We first describe how to find the two inner supports r and r' between q_1 and q_2 (Figure 1b). r is the point with minimum y coordinate, such that, $q_1.x < r.x < q_2.x$, $q_2.y > r.y > q_1.y$. So, it is easy to keep track of such a point during our left to right sweep. For each q_1, the support r' can be found in the following way. Suppose, we have all the points $q_1,\ldots,q_i$ in a stack. Moreover, q_i and q_{i-1} are two consecutive candidates for q_1. If $q_{i-1}.y > q_i.y$, q_i becomes the support r' for q_{i-1}. If $q_{i-1}.y < q_i.y$, we pop the points from the stack until we reach a point q_a such that $q_a.y < q_{i-1}.y$. The points between $q_{a-1},\ldots,q_i$ cannot be the support r' in future. This follows from the emptiness property of such polygons. So, omitting the details, in one pass we can find the support r' for all points which are candidates for q_1. The two internal supports between q_1 and q_3 and the supports between (q_2,q_4) and (q_3,q_4) can be found similarly. When we vary q_1, we keep track of p and p', the first points to the left and the right of q_1 in between q_2 and q_3. This can be done by using the array ABOVE for q_2. When q_1 moves to the right, points p and p' will either be stationary or will move to the right. For a particular q_1, we vary q_4 until $q_4.x$ reaches p'.x and we maintain the largest cross-shaped polygon for choices of q_4 between p.x and p'.x. For each choice of q_4, the area of the cross shaped polygon can be found in constant time.

The above pass takes O(n) time and finds the largest cross-shaped polygon given points q_2 and q_3. Hence, by repeating for every pair of points p_2 and p_3, we find the overall largest cross-shaped polygon in $O(n^3)$ time.

5.LARGEST EMPTY POINT-VISIBLE ORTHO-CONVEX (PVOC) POLYGON IN A POINT SET

5.1. PREPROCESSING

We require information about staircases consisting of points $p_1,p_2,\dots,p_n$. Let p_i and p_j be two points such that p_j is above and to the right of p_i, as shown in Figure 8. Consider the staircase within the quadrant formed by the pair of points p_i and p_j. The points $p_{k1},p_{k2},\dots$ are chosen in such a way that the isothetic polygon $p_ip_{k1}p_{k2}\dots p_jp_i$ is empty. For a particular choice of points p_i and p_j, there exists only one such staircase. Varying p_i and p_j, we find the areas (of external parts) and the perimeters of all such staircases. We provide an algorithm which, given a p_i, finds the areas (of external parts) and perimeters of staircases corresponding to all pairs of points p_i and p_j, $1<=j<=n$.

We make a left to right pass through the points above and to the right of p_i. Let p_j be the point presently under consideration (Figure 8). The points of the staircase $p_i,p_{k1},\dots,p_j$ are held in a stack. Let the contents of the stack from the bottom to the top be $p_i,p_{k1},p_{k2},p_{k3},\dots,p_{km}p_j$. To obtain the new staircase for the pair of points p_i and p_{j+1}, we pop off points from the stack until the top of the stack p_{kl} has a lesser y-coordinate than p_{j+1}. At the same time, we easily keep track of the new area and perimeter. Notice that, when $p_j.x>p_i.x$ and $p_j.y>p_i.y$, the staircase may act as a NW or a SE staircase. The above algorithm works when we are finding the NW minimal staircase with p_j as top and p_i as bottom support. The minimal SE staircase with the same top and bottom supports can be found by a right to left pass. Similarly, for a pair of points (p_i,p_j), such that, $p_i.x>p_j.x$ and $p_j.y>p_i.y$, the staircase between them may act as a SW or NE staircase. In this case, the minimal SW staircase can be found by a bottom to top pass and the minimal NE staircase by a top to bottom pass. In practice, we find all minimal NW staircases with p_i as the bottom point in a single left to right pass. So, for all NW staircases, we have to make n such left to right passes each taking *O(n)* time,i.e., overall *O(n²)* time. Similarly, we can find the other three minimal staircases. These staircases are stored (we describe for the area of the external parts) in a two dimensional array *AREA*. This array is indexed by the bottom and top points of the staircases. We store in each array location, both the areas and indicate the corresponding staircase. For example, for the location AREA[i,j], such that, $p_i.x<p_j.x$ and $p_i.y<p_j.y$, two external areas are stored. One is for the minimal NW staircase and the other for the minimal SE staircase. The above preprocessing takes $O(n^2)$ time using $O(n^2)$ space. In our subsequent algorithms in this paper, we assume that the above preprocessing has been performed.

5.2. CHARACTERIZATION

We refer to (Figure 9) for our algorithm. The polygon is bound by four minimal staircases. The top and bottom points of the north west (NW) staircase is q_1 and q_3, for the south west (SW) staircase these are q_5 and q_7, for south east (SE) staircase q_6 and q_8 and for the north east (NE) staircase q_2 and q_4. We assume without loss of generality $q_4.y>q_3.y$.

Lemma 5.1. *The four extreme edges of the largest empty PVOC polygon touch the sides of the bounding rectangle BR.*

Proof : Otherwise we can extend some of the sides and increase area and perimeter without destroying the emptiness and ortho convexity. Q.E.D.

Lemma 5.2. *The ortho convex polygon is a PVOC polygon if and only if the four bands i.e., the two vertical bands between the pairs (q_1,q_2) and (q_7,q_8) and the two horizontal bands between the pairs (q_3,q_5) and (q_4,q_6) have a common region of intersection.*

Proof : It can easily be shown that this common region of intersection is the kernel of the polygon. The lemma follows from the fact that a polygon is point visible if and only if it has a non empty kernel. Q.E.D.

Corollary : i) *$q_7.x<q_2.x$, ii) $q_8.x>q_1.x$ and iii). $q_3.y>q_6.y$.*

We draw horizontal lines through q_3 and q_4. Consider the rectangular band between these two lines. We call this the *mid_band.*

Lemma 5.3. *If there are points in the mid_band, they should be included in the NW staircase.*

Proof : These points cannot be included in the SW staircase or NE staircase because, their y coordinate is greater than q_3 and less than q_4 respectively. If we include them in the SE staircase, the top point of the SE staircase will have higher y coordinate than q_3 which violates the point visibility condition of lemma 5.2, corollary iii. Q.E.D.

Corollary : *If there are points in the mid_band with x coordinate greater than q_4, we cannot have a point visible polygon with q_3 and q_4 as the bottom of NW and NE staircases respectively.*

Now, we explore the possible choices of q_1 and q_2 with q_3 and q_4 fixed. Both q_1 and q_2 should have y coordinate greater than q_4. We sort all the points above q_4 according to increasing x coordinate and store them in an array *Up_band.* The first point in Up_band which can play the role of q_1 is the first point to the right of the rightmost point of the mid_band (due to lemma 5.3). Similarly, the last point for q_1 is the rightmost point in Up_band which is left of q_4. We call these two points as Up_band[start] and Up_band[end]. Two consecutive points always play the role of q_1 and q_2 in this sequence. For the last point, q_4 plays the role of q_2. We draw two vertical lines L_1 and L_2 through a pair of possible choices of q_1 and q_2 e.g., Up_band[i] and Up_band[i+1], start<=i<=end. We sort all the points below q_3 according to increasing x coordinate and store in an array *Down_band.* Suppose, the elements of Down_band are Down_band[j] to Down_band[j+k] between the vertical lines through Up_band[i] and Up_band[i+1].

Lemma 5.4. *The possible candidates for q_7 are the points from Down_band[j-1] to*

Down_band[j+k] with Up_band[i] and Up_band[i+1] fixed as a choice of q_1 and q_2. Furthermore, the possible choices of q_8 are from Down_band[j] to Down_band[j+k+1]. If a point Down_band[p] plays the role of q_7, the next point in the sequence i.e, Down_band[p+1] plays the role of q_8.

Proof : The first part can be proved from the visibility conditions of lemma 5.2. The second part follows from the fact that if there is another point in between q_7 and q_8 in the Down_band, it will be inside the polygon. **Q.E.D.**

Corollary 1. *If there is no point of Down_band in the vertical band formed by L_1 and L_2, the only possible choice for q_7 is the rightmost point in Down_band to the left of L_1 and the only choice for q_8 is the leftmost point to the right of L_2.*

Corollary 2. *Suppose, Up_band[i], Up_band[i+1] and Up_band[i+2] are two consecutive pair of positions for q_1 and q_2 and L_1, L_2 and L_3 are the three vertical lines through them. There is at most one point which plays the role of q_7 for both the pairs.*

Proof : The rightmost point left of L_2 in Down_band is the only such point. **Q.E.D.**

When q_1 and q_2 are moved from Up_band[start] to Up_band[end], q_7 and q_8 moves towards right in the array Down_band. This causes change in q_5 and q_6.

Lemma 5.5. *If Down_band[j] and Down_band[j+1] are a pair of positions for q_7 and q_8, the point Down_band[i] with highest y coordinate in Down_band[1] to Down_band[j] plays the role of q_5.*

Proof: Follows from the emptiness of the polygon. **Q.E.D.**

Suppose, two positions for q_7 and q_8 are Down_band[k] and Down_band[k+1] such that k>j.

Lemma 5.6. *The new q_5 will be either Down_band[i] or the point Down_band[p] which has the highest y coordinate in the subarray Down_band[j+1] to Down_band[k], such that Down_band[p] has a higher y coordinate than Down_band[i].*

Proof : No point to the left of Down_band[i] can become q_7, because such a polygon will have Down_band[i] inside it. Similar argument applies for points from Down_band[i] to Down_band[j]. If there is a point Down_band[p] higher than Down_band[i] between Down_band[j+1] to Down_band[k], it will become the new q_5 to keep the polygon empty. **Q.E.D.**

We can characterize the point q_6 in an almost similar fashion. We store the points below q_3 in decreasing order of y coordinates in an array called *Below*. Suppose, Down_band[j] and Down_band[j+1] are a pair of positions for q_7 and q_8 and the corresponding point for q_6 is Below[m]. Consider another pair of positions for q_7 and q_8, e.g., Down_band[k] and Down_band[k+1] such that k>j. The following lemma characterizes the new q_6.

Lemma 5.7. *If the x coordinate of Down_band[k+1] is less than or equal to that of Below[m], Below[m] remains q_6. If Down_band[k+1] has a greater x coordinate than Below[m], the new q_6 is a point Below[n] such that, n>m (i.e., Below[n] has a lower y coordinate than Below[m]) and Below[n] is the highest such point having a greater x coordinate than Down_band[k+1].*

Proof : Follows from the emptiness of the polygon. **Q.E.D.**

The characterization of the top and bottom points of the staircases is similar when $q_3.y>q_4.y$.

5.3. ALGORITHM PVOC

We will describe the algorithm for the case when $q_3.y<q_4.y$, the other case being similar. Initially, we have all the points sorted according to decreasing y coordinate. We maintain the index used during the preprocessing step in section 5.1 along with each point.

Step 1. For each point, form the arrays Up_band, Down_band and Below. We also keep an array *Above*, of points sorted according to increasing y coordinate above each point. In actual implementation, this preprocessing step can be avoided in the following way. While scanning the array which stores all the points in increasing order of x coordinate, we can get the elements of Up_band for q_i by ignoring the points below q_i and so on. But, for ease of exposition, we will assume this preprocessing step.

Step 2. For each pair of points (q_i,q_j) such that $q_j.x>q_i.x$, (q_i and q_j plays the role of q_3 and q_4 in our previous discussion) do the following steps :

a) We walk along the array Above of q_i to find the rightmost point q_{ext} in the mid_band of (q_i,q_j). If this point has x cordinate greater than q_j, reject this pair and goto step 2. Otherwise, continue.

b) We walk along the array Up_band for q_j to reach the point Up_band[start] which is leftmost point right of q_{ext}. From now on, for each consecutive pair of points in Up_band until Up_band[end], we do the following :

i) We walk along the array Down_band of q_i to find the first point which can play the role of q_7. The next point will play the role of q_8. For each such pair of points (q_7,q_8), we keep a pointer PT_1 in the array Down_band indicating the position of q_5. Similarly we keep a pointer PT_2 in the array Below of q_i to indicate the current position of q_6. For each pair Up_band[k], Up_band[k+1] we keep the pair (q_7,q_8) and the corresponding q_5 and q_6 which minimizes the combined external area of the SW staircase formed by (q_5,q_7) and the SE staircase formed by (q_6,q_8). This can be done in constant time for each pair (q_5,q_7) by consulting the array *AREA* constructed during the preprocessing step of section 5.1. This area is added to the combined external area of the NW staircase formed by (Up_band[k],q_i) and the NE staircase formed by (Up_band[k+1],q_j). Update the variable which keeps the supports of the maximum empty PVOC if necessary. By slight modification, we can avoid the recomputation mentioned in lemma 5.4, corollary 2. At the end of the algorithm, we will have the top and bottom supports of all four staircases of the maximum empty PVOC. From this information, the actual polygon can be constructed in $O(n)$ time.

Theorem 5.1. The above algorithm works in $O(n^3)$ time and $O(n^2)$ space.

Proof : The correctness of the algorithm follows from the discussion before. The preprocessing takes $O(n^2)$ time, step 1 takes $O(n^2 \log n)$ time. The dominant step is step 2. We claim that for each pair of points (q_i,q_j) as the bottom points of the NW and NE staircase, we spend $O(n)$ time. This is because in all the arrays Up_band, Down_band and Below, we always walk forward. This is due to lemmas 5.4, 5.6 and 5.7. So, for each pair the time spent is $O(n)$. The time complexity follows from the fact that there are $O(n^2)$ such pairs. For each point we use $O(n)$ space for storing the arrays. Also the preprocessing takes $O(n^2)$ space. Q.E.D.

Now we show how to change this algorithm to detect the largest empty line visible ortho convex polygon (LVOC). We consider the case when we can place a vertical line L inside the polygon P such that every point in P is visible from at least one point on L. The case of the horizontal line being similar. So, in lemma 5.2, the horizontal bands between the pairs (q_3,q_5) and (q_4,q_6) may not intersect, but the vertical bands between the pairs (q_1,q_2) and (q_7,q_8) should intersect. We can place the line L in this common vertical band. In this case, we modify lemma 5.3 in the following way.

Lemma 5.8. *If there are points in mid_band with x coordinate between q_3 and q_4, they can be included either in NW or SE staircase. But the points in mid_band towards right of q_4 should be included in the SE staircase.*

We modify our algorithm in the following way. Again we assume that $q_3.y<q_4.y$, the other case being similar. The arrays Up_band, Down_band and Below are constructed as in step 1 of algorithm PVOC. In step 2, we walk along the array UP_band of q_3 for the pairs of points which play the roles of q_1 and q_2. These points for q_1 may range from q_3 to the rightmost point left of q_4 in the Up_band of q_3. Again we call these Up_band[start] and Up_band[end] and for the pairs (q_1,q_2), we walk from Up_band[start] to Up_band[end]. For each pair (q_1,q_2), we find the possible points for (q_7,q_8) and q_5 as before. The only change comes for q_6. For q_6, we walk down the Below array of q_4. During this walk, if we come across a point q_j such that $q_j.x>q_4.x$ and q_j is the highest such point, q_j becomes the permanent top point of the SE staircase. The other parts of the algorithm are also similar. So, we state the following.

Theorem 5.2. *The largest empty LVOC polygon can be found in $O(n^3)$ time using $O(n^2)$ space.*

6. LARGEST EMPTY EDGE VISIBLE ORTHO-CONVEX (EVOC) POLYGON IN A POINT SET

6.1. CHARACTERIZATION

As the name implies, an EVOC polygon is an ortho-convex polygon which is weakly visible from one of its edges. The edge from which the EVOC polygon is visible is called its special edge. An EVOC polygon can be in four different orientations. The EVOC polygon shown in (Figure 1d) is oriented such that its special edge is parallel to the bottom edge of BR. For the other three orientations of the EVOC polygon, the special edge is parallel to the left edge, the top edge or the right edge of BR, respectively.

Without loss of generality, we consider an EVOC polygon P with the orientation shown in (Figure 1d). We observe that EVOC polygons have two staircases shown as $q_1,\ldots,q_3$ and $q_2,\ldots,q_4$ in (Figure 1d). We denote the point q_5 on the special edge of P as the bottom support of P.

6.2. ALGORITHM EVOC

Given a point q_5, we provide an algorithm to find the largest EVOC polygon with q_5 as the bottom support. This algorithm does not require any preprocessing.

We notice that q_2 is the first point to the right of q_1 and above q_5. Hence, q_2 is determined immediately by q_1 and q_5. For each choice of q_5, there are clearly O(n) choices of pairs q_1 and q_2 and these are consecutive pairs of points above q_5. We informally describe the algorithm for the maximum empty EVOC.

Initially, we make a pass from left to right through the points above q_5. We do not need the points above q_5 sorted according to increasing x coordinate. Instead, we have the whole point set sorted according to increasing x coordinate. While making the pass, we simply ignore the points below q_5. We find the areas (of the external parts) of the minimal NW staircases, i.e., staircases of the form $q_3,\ldots,q_1$ by the algorithm in section 5.1. We store the top points of all such staircases along with their area in an array *AREA*. AREA[i] stores the area of the NW staircase with q_i as the top point. Then we compute the area of the external parts of the NE staircases by a right to left pass by the algorithm in section 5.1. We simultaneously walk along the array AREA from higher index to lower index. For each top point q_j of the NE staircases, we find out the previous point (the point immediately to the left of p_j) in x sorted order above q_5 and the corresponding entry in AREA. By knowing the external areas of both the staircases, we can find the area of the EVOC and the maximum area empty EVOC can be found after this right to left pass is over. These two passes clearly take $O(n)$ time. The emptiness of the polygon is assured from the fact that both the staircases are minimal and q_1 and q_2 are always two consecutive points above q_5.

This algorithm is used for every different choice of point q_5, giving a time complexity of $O(n^2)$. The space complexity is $O(n)$, because we can reuse the space taken by the array AREA.

7. CONCLUSION

For five different classes of ortho-convex polygons, we studied the problem of finding the largest (in terms of area/ perimeter) empty polygon of that kind in the presence of a point set in a bounding rectangle. However, we have not solved the general problem of finding the largest empty ortho-convex polygon. It appears that our methods are not directly applicable for this problem. We briefly describe this difficulty. Suppose, two opposite staircases (e.g.,NW and SE) have overlapping quadrants,i.e., there are points which can be included in either of the staircases. For PVOC polygons, this condition is avoided due to lemma 5.2. For LVOC polygons, this case may occur (lemma 5.8), but the staircases are uniquely determined due to the fact that the vertical bands between (q_1,q_2) and (q_7,q_8) should intersect. If we drop both the visibility conditions, a point which is common to both the quadrants, may or may not be included in a particular staircase. We do not have any characterization for the largest empty ortho convex polygons to prevent this exponential number of possibilities. Notice that, in case of ortho convex cross shaped polygon, this condition does not occur and so we could find the largest such polygon without any visibility constraint. Several other open problems remain. It will be better if the complexity of our algorithms are improved. In [2], an $\Omega(n\log n)$ lower bound in the algebraic decision tree model of computation has been given for the maximum empty rectangle problem. No lower bound is currently available for the problems studied in this paper.

ACKNOWLEDGEMENTS

The authors would like to thank Kamala Krithivasan for many helpful discussions, Meena Mahajan for suggesting the proof of lemma 3.2 and the referees for their comments which improved the presentation of this paper considerably.

REFERENCES

[1] Aggarwal,A. and Suri,S., "Fast Algorithms for Computing the Largest Empty Rectangle", *Proc. of the Third Annual ACM Symposium on Computational Geometry*, pp.278-290, 1987.

[2] Aggarwal,A. and Suri,S., "Fast Algorithms for Computing Largest Empty Rectangles", *Manuscript*, 1989.

[3] Aggarwal,A., Klawe,M., Moran,S., Shor,P., and Wilber,R., "Geometric Applications of a Matrix-Searching Algorithm", *Algorithmica*,2, pp.195-208,1987.

[4] Boyce,J.E., Dobkin,D.P., Drysdale,R.L., and Guibas,L.J., "Finding extremal polygons," *SIAM J. on Comput.*,Vol.14,pp.134-147,1985.

[5] Chang,J.S., and Yap,C.K., "A polynomial solution to potato-peeling and other polygon inclusion and enclosure problems," *Proc. 25th IEEE Symp. on Foundations of Computer Science*, 1984.

[6] Chazelle,B.M., Drysdale,R.L., and Lee,D.T., "Computing the Largest Empty Rectangle", *SIAM J. Computing*,Vol.15,No.1,pp.300-315, 1986.

[7] Naamad,A., Lee,D.T., and Hsu,W.L., "On the Maximum Empty Rectangle Problem", *Discrete Applied Mathematics*,Vol.8,pp.267-277,1984.

[8] O'Rourke,J., "Art Gallery Theorems and Algorithms", Oxford University Press, 1987.

[9] Overmars,M.H., and Wood,D., "On Rectangular Visibility", *Journal of Algorithms*,Vol.9, pp.372-390, 1988.

[10] Preparata,F.P., and Shamos,M.I., "Computational Geometry : an Introduction", Springer, New York, 1985.

[11] Rawlins,G.J.E., and Wood,D., "Ortho-Convexity and its Generalizations", *in Computational Morphology*, G.T.Toussaint (Ed.), North-Holland, pp.137-152, 1988.

[12] Wood,D., "An Isothetic View of Computational Geometry", *in Computational Geometry*, G.T.Toussaint(Ed.), North-Holland,pp.429-459,1985.

[13] Wood,D., and Yap,C.K., "The rectilinear convex skull problem," *Technical Report 132*, Courant Institute of Mathematical Sciences, 1984.

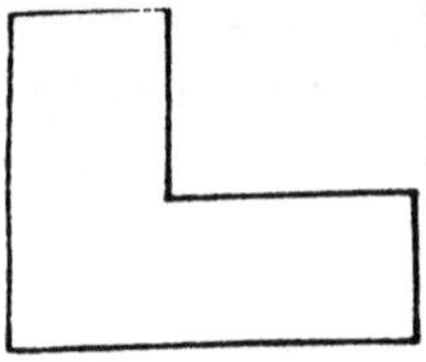

FIG.1.(a)

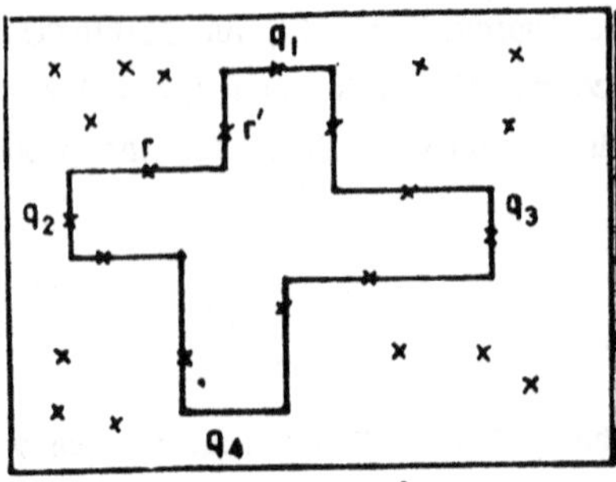

FIG.1.(b)

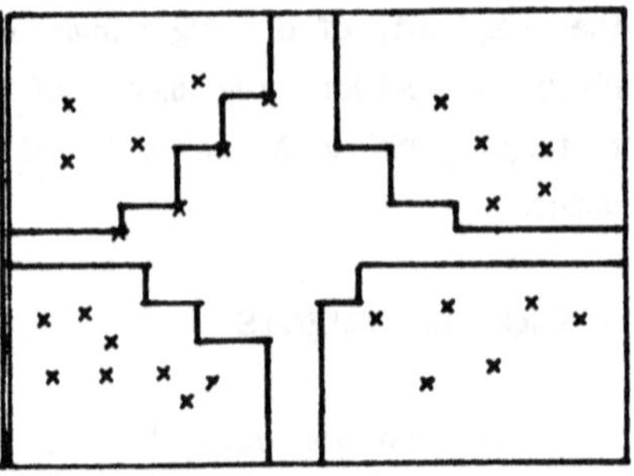

FIG. 1.(c)

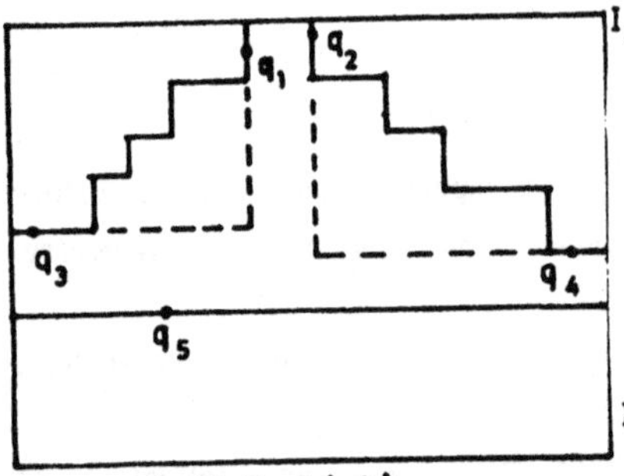

FIG.1.(d)

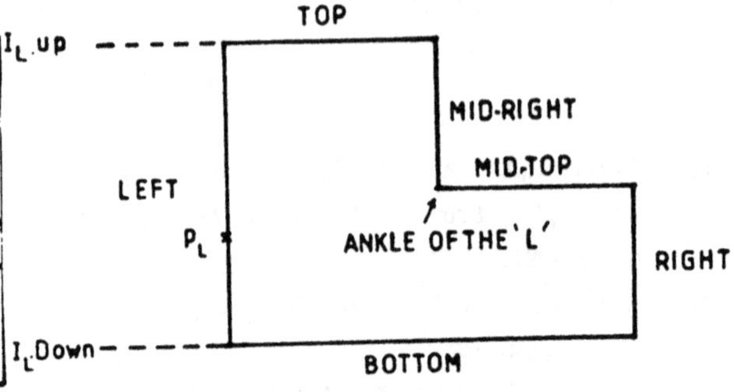

FIG 2 (a)

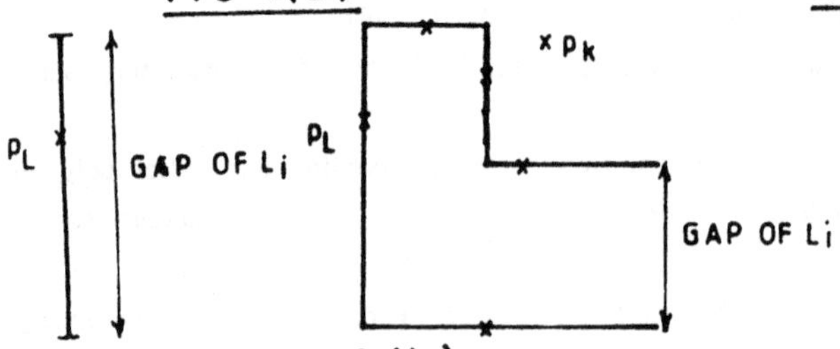

FIG. 2.(b)

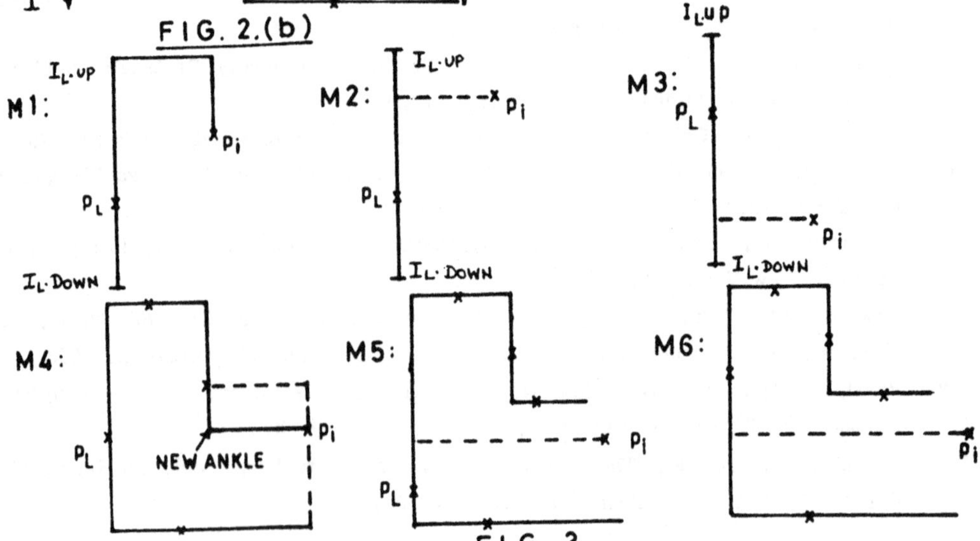

FIG. 3

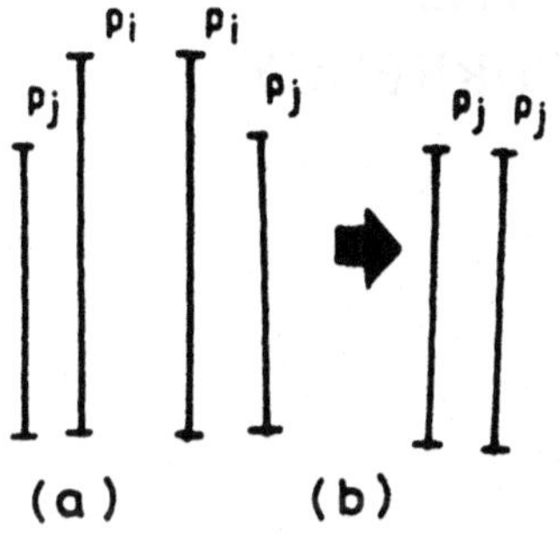

FIG. 5.

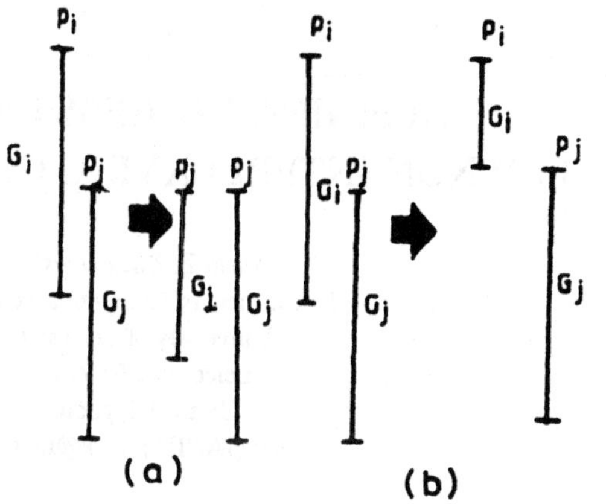

FIG. 4

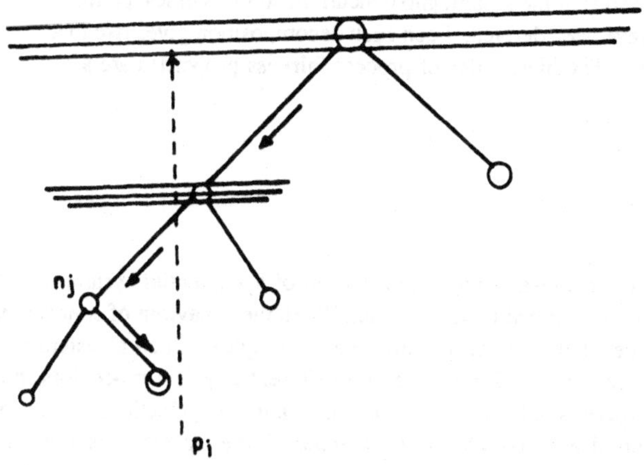

FIG. 6

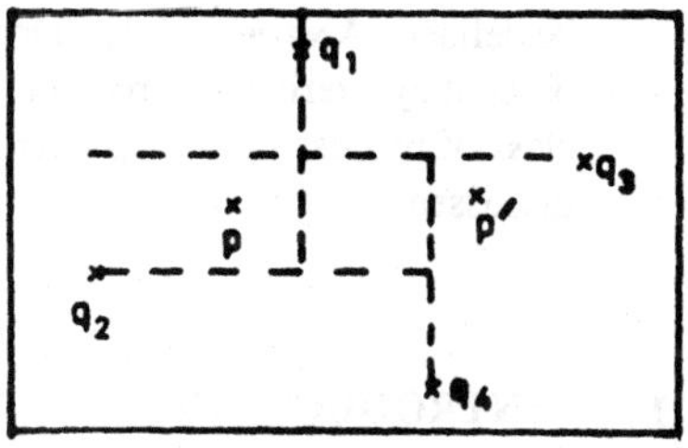

FIG_7

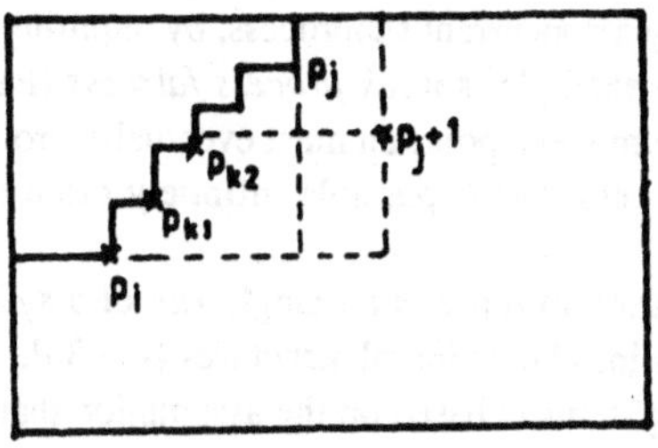

FIG_8

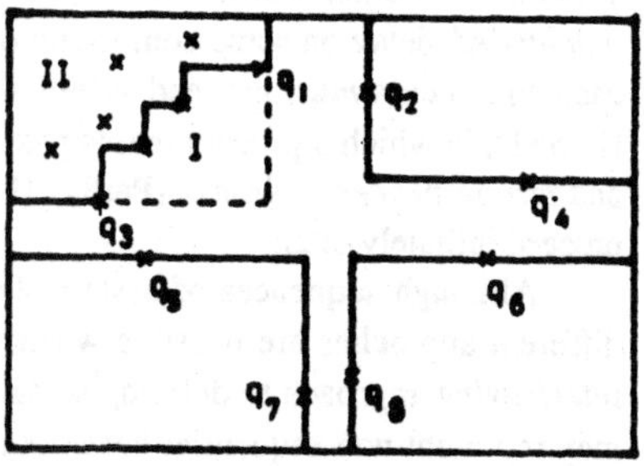

FIG_9

DEFINING PROCESS FAIRNESS FOR NON-INTERLEAVING CONCURRENCY

Marta Z. Kwiatkowska
Department of Computing Studies
University of Leicester
Leicester LE1 7RH
United Kingdom
e-mail (JANET): mzk@uk.ac.le

Abstract

Process fairness properties are semantically characterized in a non-interleaving model for concurrency, which allows a causality-based representation of finite and infinite concurrent behaviours. The model has been extended with additional structure so that process fairness can be defined. A variety of decompositions of the system into concurrent sub-processes, partially ordered by a refinement relation, have been derived. Each such decomposition gives rise to a class of process fairness properties. The hierarchies of process fairness properties are also discussed.

1. INTRODUCTION

A sequence of states models a complete, or *non-extendable*, execution of a sequential system if it is infinite, or if it is finite but no action could be applied in its last state. When the behaviour of *concurrent* systems is modelled using state sequences, the situation becomes more complex. Such a system is a collection of asynchronous processes (agents), possibly running on different physical processors in a distributed environment. Every agent proceeds in (atomic) steps by engaging in *local* actions as well as *communication* actions that require synchronization possibly with a number of other agents. It is desirable that whenever an agent can proceed, it is only *finitely* delayed. Thus, for a state sequence to be a complete execution of a *concurrent* system, it is necessary to exclude not only the sequences that are extendable in the sequential sense, but also those sequences that indefinitely delay some concurrent agent within a system, or, in other words, do not satisfy *fairness* constraints. Fairness essentially imposes *finite*, but *unbounded*, delay on some component of the system, usually a concurrent subprocess, by requiring that each subprocess *must* proceed sufficiently often. A typical example is *weak process fairness* [Par81] [LPS81], in which a process that is possible continuously from some point on must eventually proceed, and *strong process fairness* [Par81] [LPS81], where a process that is possible infinitely often must proceed infinitely often.

Although sequences of system states are commonly used to represent a single *run* of a system, different approches are possible when grouping these runs into behavioural structures [Pnu86]. The *interleaving* approach to defining semantics of concurrent systems is based on the assumption that one may represent non-sequential behaviour by a choice between the possible interleavings of activities of concurrent processes. The behavioural structure used in the interleaving models is essentially a *set* of runs. The main attraction of the interleaving models is that they are highly abstract and compositional; however, fairness must be introduced as an *external* constraint, see e.g. [Pnu86].

An alternative semantic approach, often called *non-interleaving*, originates from net theory and includes e.g. trace languages [Maz89] [Kwi89b], behavioural presentations [Shi88] and event structures [Win86]. The behavioural structure used in this approach is usually a *partially ordered set* of events. Such a behavioural structure has been criticised for being more complex than its interleaving counter-part, but, on the other hand, the notion of *maximality* with respect to the partial order not only guarantees non-extendability in the sense explained above, but also coincides with a certain notion of fairness [Kwi89a].

The issue of fairness has caused some confusion recently because of its sensitivity to the granularity level and strength, the behavioural structure used, and the decomposition into concurrent subprocesses. Also, contrary to common expectations, fairness does not manifest itself as a coherent notion, but rather as a loose collection of properties. The interested reader may find surveys of fairness in [Fra86] [Kwi89d].

The purpose of the paper is to formally define an *abstract* notion of a process fairness property in a non-interleaving model for concurrency. Several authors have drawn attention to the fact that the choice between interleaving and non-interleaving affects properties such as liveness and fairness, see e.g. [Rei84] [Kwi89b] [Kwi89a] [MOP89]; this statement is further supported here, and the advantages of using the non-interleaving, as opposed to the interleaving, approach are discussed. Asynchronous transition systems with trace language semantics, also dealt with in [Bed87] [Shi89] [Kwi89a], are used as the basic model. The work draws on the topological characterization of safety and liveness properties presented in [Kwi89b] [Kwi90]. This paper enhances asynchronous transition systems with additional structure so that process fairness may be introduced, and then investigates the classes of weak, strong and unconditional process fairness. A preliminary discussion of fairness issues in asynchronous transition systems, restricted to event fairness only, appeared in [Kwi89a]. It should be stressed that fairness is viewed as an issue to do with *concurrent processes* [Pnu86] [CoS87], rather than *non-deterministic choice* [Fra86].

2. CONCURRENT SYSTEMS & BEHAVIOUR

2.1. Notation & Basic Definitions

This section introduces the notation and recalls standard definitions, which may be found in e.g. [Kur66] [GHK80] [Law88].

Let A denote a (finite) set of symbols. A^* denotes the set of all finite *strings* (sequences) of symbols in A, A^ω denotes the set of all infinite strings, and A^∞ is the union of A^* and A^ω. The notation of regular expressions extended with ω-iteration will be used to describe infinitary string languages.

A *topology* on a set S is a collection of subsets of S that contains $\emptyset$ and S, and is closed under finite intersection and arbitrary union. A set S together with a topology $\mathcal{T}$ on S is called a *topological space*; the elements of $\mathcal{T}$ are the *open sets* of the space. Equivalently, a topological space is a set S and a function called *closure* assigning to each set $X \subseteq S$ a set Cl(X) satisfying the following four axioms:

(i) $Cl(X \cup Y) = Cl(X) \cup CL(Y)$
(ii) $X \subseteq Cl(X)$
(iii) $Cl(\emptyset) = \emptyset$
(iv) $Cl(Cl(X)) = Cl(X)$.

A *base* of the topology is a subset $\mathfrak{B} \subseteq \mathcal{T}$ such that every open set is the union of elements of $\mathfrak{B}$. A *subbase* of the topology $\mathcal{T}$ is a family of open sets such that the family of all finite intersections of elements of the subbase is a base of $\mathcal{T}$. A set X is *closed* iff its complement S\X is open. A set is *dense* iff its closure is the set S. Equivalently, a set is dense iff its complement contains no non-empty open sets. A G_δ*-set* is a countable (finite or infinite) intersection of a family of open sets. For a subset T of S, we say $X \subseteq T$ is *open (closed) relative to* T iff X is an intersection of T and some open (closed) set. $X \subseteq T$ is *dense relative to* T iff $Cl(X) \cap T = T$.

Let (P, ⊑) be a partially ordered set *(poset)*. If it exists, the *least upper bound* (also called *supremum* or *sup*) wrt ⊑ of a subset $X \subseteq P$ will be denoted by $\bigsqcup X$; similarly, the *greatest lower bound* (the *infimum* or *inf*) is denoted by $\sqcap X$. For x, y ∈ P it is customary to write $x \sqcup y$ for $\bigsqcup\{x,y\}$ and $x \sqcap y$ for $\sqcap\{x,y\}$.

Let (P, ⊑) be a poset. Elements x, y ∈ P are *comparable* iff either $x \sqsubseteq y$ or $y \sqsubseteq x$, and *incomparable* otherwise. $X \subseteq P$ is *totally ordered*, or a *chain*, iff every x, y ∈ X are comparable. $X \subseteq P$ is a *directed set* iff it is non-empty and every pair x, y ∈ X has a bound z ∈ X.

Let (P, ⊑) be a poset. For $X \subseteq P$ and x ∈ P write: $\downarrow X = \{y \in P \mid y \sqsubseteq x \text{ for some } x \in X\}$, $\uparrow X = \{y \in P \mid x \sqsubseteq y \text{ for some } x \in X\}$, $\downarrow x = \downarrow\{x\}$, $\uparrow x = \uparrow\{x\}$. $X \subseteq P$ is a *lower set* (also *prefix-* or *downward-closed*) iff $X = \downarrow X$. $X \subseteq P$ is an *upper set* (or *upward-closed*) iff $X = \uparrow X$. $X \subseteq P$ is an *ideal* iff it is a directed lower set.

Let (P, ⊑) be a poset. P is a *lattice* iff every pair of elements x, y ∈ P has a least upper bound $x \sqcup y$ and a greatest lower bound $x \sqcap y$. P is a *complete lattice* iff every $X \subseteq P$ has a least upper bound and a greatest lower bound.

(P, ⊑) is a *complete partial order* (cpo) iff P has a least element and every directed subset $X \subseteq P$ has a least upper bound $\bigsqcup X$ in P. Let (P, ⊑) be a poset, and let Id(P) denote the set of ideals of P ordered by inclusion. Then (Id(P), ⊆) is a cpo, often called the *ideal completion* (or the *order completion*) of P.

Let (D, ⊑) be a cpo and x, y ∈ D. We say x is *essentially below* (or *way below*) y, denoted $x \sqsubseteq^{fin} y$, iff given a directed set $M \subseteq D$ such that $y \sqsubseteq \bigsqcup M$ there exists z ∈ M such that $x \sqsubseteq z$. Intuitively, x is essentially below y if x is some finite approximation of y. For $X \subseteq D$ and x ∈ D write: $\downarrow^{fin} X = \{y \in D \mid y \sqsubseteq^{fin} x \text{ for some } x \in X\}$, $\uparrow^{fin} X = \{y \in D \mid x \sqsubseteq^{fin} y \text{ for some } x \in X\}$, $\downarrow^{fin} x = \downarrow^{fin}\{x\}$, $\uparrow^{fin} x = \uparrow^{fin}\{x\}$.

Let (D, ⊑) be a cpo. x ∈ D is a *finite element* (also called *compact*) iff $x \sqsubseteq^{fin} x$. The set of all finite elements of D is denoted B_D. D is *algebraic* iff, for every x ∈ D, the set $M = \{y \in B_D \mid y \sqsubseteq x\} = \downarrow^{fin} x$ is directed and $\bigsqcup M = x$. D is *consistently complete* iff every $X \subseteq D$ with an upper bound has a least upper bound. D is a (Scott) *domain* iff D is algebraic, consistently complete and B_D is countable. The set of all finite elements B_D of an algebraic cpo D is often called the *finitary basis* in the case of B_D countable.

Let (D, ⊑) be a Scott domain. The *Scott* topology is the topology consisting of all the sets U such that U is upward-closed and, for every directed set $M \subseteq D$, if $\bigsqcup M \in U$ then some element of M is in U. The basis of the Scott topology is the family of the sets $\uparrow x$, where $x \in B_D$. A set L is *Scott-closed* iff it is a lower set closed under suprema of directed subsets. The *Lawson* topology of a domain is defined as the topology generated by a sub-basis containing all Scott-open sets, together with the sets $D \setminus \uparrow x$, for $x \in B_D$.

For example, in the domain $(A^\infty, \leq)$ of strings, the family of sets $\uparrow x$, where x is a finite string, forms the basis of the Scott topology. The family of Scott open sets in this domain, together with the family of complements of the basic Scott open sets, forms a subbasis of the Lawson topology.

2.2 Traces as a Representation of Concurrent Behaviour

Let A be a finite alphabet of symbols, and let $\iota \subseteq A \times A$ be a symmetric and irreflexive relation (called *the independency*). Intuitively, two actions are *independent* if they can happen concurrently, and *dependent* otherwise. $\iota = \emptyset$ corresponds to behaviours that are sequential, but possibly non-deterministic, whereas ι

$\neq \emptyset$ permits concurrency. Define *trace equivalence* $\equiv$ [Maz89] as the least congruence in the monoid of finite strings $S = (A^*, ., \varepsilon)$ such that:

$$a \iota b \Rightarrow ab \equiv ba. \tag{2.2.1}$$

The pair (A, ι) is called a *concurrent alphabet*. We shall refer to the set-theoretic complement of the independency ι as the *dependency* δ.

The quotient algebra $T = (A^*, ., \varepsilon)/_{\equiv}$ of *traces* (i.e. equivalence classes of strings) is a cancellative monoid. Denote $A^*/_{\equiv}$ by Θ^*. Traces are sets of possible *sequentializations* of a non-sequential computation. Define *trace prefix ordering* $\sqsubseteq$ in the monoid of finite traces by:

$$\sigma \sqsubseteq \tau \Leftrightarrow \exists \gamma \in \Theta^*: \sigma\gamma = \tau \tag{2.2.2}$$

for all $\sigma, \tau \in \Theta^*$. $(\Theta^*, \sqsubseteq)$ is a poset [Maz89]. Let $Id(\Theta^*)$ denote the set of ideals of the poset $(\Theta^*, \sqsubseteq)$. Then $Id(\Theta^*)$ ordered by inclusion can be identified with all finite and infinite traces [Kwi89c]. It can be shown that $(Id(\Theta^*), \subseteq)$ is a domain in the sense of Scott, Θ^* constitute the (countable) finitary basis, and the inherited order agrees with the new order on Θ^* [Kwi89c]. Denote the ideal completion of $(\Theta^*, \sqsubseteq)$ by $(\Theta^\infty, \sqsubseteq)$. A subset T of Θ^∞ is called an *infinitary trace language*.

Traces can be viewed as generalizations of strings to form non-sequential computations. It can be shown [Kwi89b] [Kwi89c] that if $\iota = \emptyset$ then $(\Theta^\infty, \sqsubseteq)$ is isomorphic to the domain $(A^\infty, \leq)$ of strings with the usual string prefix ordering of [BoN79].

Example 1. Let $A = \{a, b, c\}$ with $a \iota b$. Then $abc \equiv bac$ (both abc and bac are sequentializations of the trace [abc]), whereas $abc \not\equiv acb$. Also, $[b] \sqsubseteq [ab] \sqsubseteq [abc]$, $[c] \not\sqsubseteq [abc]$. $[b^\omega] \sqsubseteq [ab^\omega]$, but $[b^\omega] \not\sqsubseteq [cb^\omega]$. $[a^*] \cup [a^\omega]$ is a Scott-closed and Lawson-closed infinitary trace language; $[a^*]$ is neither Scott- nor Lawson-closed because it does not contain its least upper bound $[a^\omega]$.

There exists an equivalent definition of trace equivalence, originating from Shields, which is based on string projections. This formulation is sometimes easier to use than the definition in terms of permutations. For a relation $R \subseteq A \times A$ define a non-empty subset B of A to be a *clique* of R iff, for all a, $b \in A$, a R b. Let (A, ι) be a concurrent alphabet, $\alpha = \{\alpha_1, ..., \alpha_n\}$ be a set of cliques of the dependency δ such that $a \delta b \Rightarrow \exists \alpha_i \in \alpha: \{a,b\} \subseteq \alpha_i$. We use $\pi_i(x)$ to denote the projection of the string $x \in A^\infty$ onto the set α_i. Then the following holds:

Lemma 2.2.1. ([Kwi89b]) $\forall x, y \in A^\infty: x \equiv y \Leftrightarrow (\forall \alpha_i \in \alpha: \pi_i(x) = \pi_i(y))$.

By the above lemma, the definition of projection π_i may be extended onto traces.

In the remainder of the paper we shall also refer to an extension of the concatenation of traces onto the whole of the domain Θ^∞. It can be shown [Kwi89c] that one can extend the concatenation to a (non-associative) total operation on Θ^∞. Let $\sigma, \tau \in \Theta^\infty$ and define:

$$\sigma\tau = \bigsqcup\{\sigma'\tau' \mid \sigma' \sqsubseteq^{fin} \sigma \wedge \tau' \sqsubseteq^{fin} \tau \wedge \tau' \text{ is tail-independent with } \sigma \text{ after } \sigma'\} \tag{2.2.3}$$

where τ' is *tail-independent with* σ *after* σ', for $\sigma' \sqsubseteq^{fin} \sigma$, is defined to be:

$$\forall \sigma'': \sigma'\sigma'' \sqsubseteq^{fin} \sigma \Rightarrow \sigma'' \text{ and } \tau \text{ are independent.} \tag{2.2.4}$$

Although associativity fails, the following important result may be shown (note that in general β is not unique):

Theorem 2.2.2. ([Kwi89c]) *For all* $\sigma, \tau \in \Theta^\infty$:

$$\sigma \sqsubseteq \tau \Leftrightarrow \exists \beta \in \Theta^\infty \text{ s.t. } \sigma\beta = \tau.$$

Example 2. Let A = {a, b, c} with a ι b. Then:

$$[a^\omega][b] = [ba^\omega]$$
$$[a^\omega][b^\omega] = [(ab)^\omega]$$
$$[a^\omega][c] = [a^\omega]$$
$$(([a^\omega][c])[b]) = [a^\omega][b] = [ba^\omega] \neq [a^\omega] = [a^\omega][cb] = (([a^\omega]([c][b])).$$

2.3 Asynchronous Systems and Non-Interleaving Semantics

Recall that an *asynchronous transition system* (ATS) [Bed87, Kwi89e, Shi89] is a quadruple $(Q, A, \rightarrow, \iota)$ such that Q is a non-empty, countable set of *states*, A is a non-empty, finite set of *action labels*, $\rightarrow \subseteq Q\times A\times Q$ is a *transition relation*, $\iota \subseteq A\times A$ is an *independency* relation, and:

$$\forall q, q', q'' \in Q, \forall a, b \in A: \quad (q \rightarrow^a q' \rightarrow^b q'' \wedge a \,\iota\, b) \Rightarrow \exists q''': q \rightarrow^b q''' \rightarrow^a q'' \tag{2.3.1}$$

An asynchronous transition system is called *forward stable* [Bed87] iff, in addition, the following holds:

$$\forall q, q', q'' \in Q, \forall a, b \in A: \quad (q \rightarrow^a q' \wedge q \rightarrow^b q'' \wedge a \,\iota\, b) \Rightarrow \exists q''': (q' \rightarrow^b q''' \wedge q'' \rightarrow^a q'''). \tag{2.3.2}$$

We shall only consider forward stable and unambiguous systems systems. A system is said to be *unambiguous* iff $\rightarrow^a$ is a (partial) function for every $a \in A$. Conditions (2.3.1) and (2.3.2) are independent and reduce concurrency to *commutativity*.

It should be pointed out that the independency relation is *global*, which may be viewed as a restriction. However, global independency is adequate to express Condition-Event nets (see Example 3 below) as well as a subset of CCS-like expressions [Kwi90]. To allow *dynamic* independency it may be necessary to use techniques of [KaP90].

Let $S = (Q, A, \rightarrow, \iota)$ be an ATS. A *rooted* asynchronous transition system is an ordered pair $\Sigma = (S, q_0)$, where $q_0 \in Q$.

Example 3. Let N = (B, E; F) be a Condition/Event net. Then $S_N = (Q, A, \rightarrow, \iota)$ is a forward stable unambiguous ATS where $Q = \wp(B)$, $A = E$, $\rightarrow = Q\times A\times Q \cap \_[\_>\_$, and:

$$e_1 \,\iota\, e_2 \Leftrightarrow (\bullet e_1 \cup e_1\bullet) \cap (\bullet e_2 \cup e_2\bullet) = \varnothing, \text{ for } e_1, e_2 \in E.$$

Let $S = (Q, A, \rightarrow, \iota)$ be an unambiguous ATS, $\Sigma = (S, q_0)$, $q_0 \in Q$, be a rooted ATS. We say that $u \in A^\infty$ is a *derivation* of Σ iff $u = \varepsilon$ or there exists a sequence of states (q_i), $i \in \{0,1,..\mathrm{len}(u)\}$, such that:

$$q_0 \rightarrow^{u_1} q_1 \rightarrow^{u_2} \ldots q_{i-1} \rightarrow^{u_i} q_i \ldots.$$

The set of all (finite or infinite) derivations of Σ is denoted by $D^\infty(\Sigma)$; we refer to $D^\infty(\Sigma)$ as the *interleaving semantics* of Σ. The *non-interleaving semantics* of Σ is defined as the set $T^\infty(\Sigma) = [D^\infty(\Sigma)]$ of traces determined by the derivations of Σ.

By definition, every derivation of Σ belongs to some trace of Σ. It can be shown [Kwi89c] that every representant of a trace of Σ is a derivation of Σ; in other words, taking a quotient wrt trace equivalence does not add sequentializations which the system cannot already exhibit. Also, we can write $q \rightarrow^{\sigma} q'$ whenever $q \rightarrow^{x} q'$ for some finite derivation x. Thus, traces correspond to *events* (and uniquely determine states of Σ), and trace prefix ordering may be viewed as a *causality* order on events that occur during system execution.

The following states the relationship between infinitary trace languages and asynchronous transition systems.

Proposition 2.3.1. ([Kwi89c])
(i) *$T^{\infty}(\Sigma)$ is a Scott-closed infinitary trace language.*
(ii) *If $T \subseteq \Theta^{\infty}$ is a Scott-closed infinitary trace language then there exists a rooted ATS Σ such that $T^{\infty}(\Sigma) = T$.*

Corollary 2.3.2. *$T^{\infty}(\Sigma)$ is a prefix-closed and Lawson-closed infinitary trace language.*

One advantage of using trace languages, rather than string languages, to represent behaviours of systems is apparent in the way *confusion*, a phenomenon originating from net theory, is dealt with. Let $S = (Q, A, \rightarrow, \iota)$ be an ATS, and let $q \in Q$, $a, b \in A$ such that $a \iota b$, $q \rightarrow^{a} q'$ and $q \rightarrow^{b} q''$. The ordered triple (q, a, b) is a *confusion* (at q) iff the set of actions at conflict with a in the state q differs from the set of actions at conflict with a in the state q". Confusion creates difficulty because sequentializations of the same behaviour can differ radically in terms of non-deterministic choices available at each step. For example, it is possible to construct a system, in which there are two equivalent derivations x, y such that some action is enabled infinitely often in x, but is is *never* enabled in y. Now, x and y are two different sequentializations of the same concurrent behaviour, and thus one would expect both to be be fair, or both unfair, at the same time. Since fairness usually enforces that actions which become infinitely often enabled are taken sufficiently often, confusion is likely to create problems by giving rise to fairness notions that are not closed under trace equivalence. Trace semantics, in contrast to the interleaving semantics in terms of strings, overcomes this problem, as will be shown later.

2.4 Maximality and Fairness

We say a trace $\tau \in T^{\infty}(\Sigma)$ is *maximal in* Σ if it is maximal in $T^{\infty}(\Sigma)$ wrt trace prefix ordering; the set of all maximal traces of Σ is denoted $Max(\Sigma)$. A derivation of Σ is *maximal* iff it is a representant of a maximal trace of Σ. Maximal traces correspond to *complete*, that is non-extendable, computations of the system. This notion of extendability carries the same meaning as the extendability of runs of sequential systems represented by sequences of system states, in the sense of a run being infinite or no action being applicable in its *last* state. A trace, however, may be extended by applying an action in some *intermediate* state. The consequence of this may seem somewhat counter-intuitive: some *infinite* traces may be extendable, that is *not yet complete.*

Example 4. Let A = {a, b, c} with $a \iota b$. Then $[b^{\omega}] \sqsubseteq [ab^{\omega}] \sqsubseteq [(ab)^{\omega}]$; $[(ab)^{\omega}]$ is maximal, but $[b^{\omega}]$ and $[ab^{\omega}]$ are not. $[c^{\omega}]$ and $[ac^{\omega}]$ are also maximal.

The main advantage of using the non-interleaving, as opposed to the interleaving, approach is that the notion of maximality allows not only to filter out those traces that are extendable, but also serves as a certain fairness notion [Kwi89a]. We shall illustrate it on the following example informally using a CCS-like notation to represent systems of processes. Consider the following (unambiguous) system:

$$p = (\text{fix } X.aX) \parallel (\text{fix } X.bX)$$

where $a \, \iota \, b$. The infinite derivation $p \to^{a} p \to^{a} p \ldots$ is not maximal; in fact, the only maximal derivations are those that allow an *infinite* number of both a- and b-moves. On the other hand, *any* infinite derivation is maximal for the system $q = \text{fix } X.(aX + bX)$, where a and b are dependent, including the one consisting solely of an infinite number of a-moves. This agrees with our intuition about fairness - in both cases maximality corresponds to a fairness notion in the sense that no concurrent subprocess may be indefinitely delayed (p has two concurrent sub-processes, while q only itself).

However, in formalisms that allow inter-process communication or synchronization, fairness notions *stronger* than maximality are desirable. This is because a process may be prevented from proceeding by a *refusal* of its partner to synchronise. Consider the system:

$$r = (\text{fix } X.(aX + bX) \parallel \overline{b}NIL)\backslash b$$

where a and τ_b are dependent (r may choose to make an a-move or synchronise giving rise to a τ_b-move, which is *not* considered silent). It is easy to see that r determines the domain of traces isomorphic (up to labelling) to the one arising from the system q in the previous section. However, the infinite derivation $\underline{p} \to^{a} p \to^{a} p \ldots$, which disallows the τ_b-move, is *unfair* in the above sense wrt to the subprocess $\overline{b}$NIL. Thus, a process fairness property *excluding* this (maximal) derivation would be required.

Note that asynchronous transition systems are low-level, and hence are incapable of making distinctions between local and communication actions. An additional structure has to be added to asynchronous transition systems to record *agents* or *processes*. We achieve this by decomposing the system into subprocesses.

2.5 Decomposition into Concurrent Subprocesses

To distinguish between communicating and local actions of processes, it is proposed to introduce a decomposition of an asynchronous transition system into (concurrent) subprocesses. Let (A, ι) be a concurrent alphabet. $\beta \subseteq A$ is a *process alphabet* iff all elements of β are pairwise dependent (i.e. β is a clique of the dependency δ). An *alphabet structure* over (A, ι) is a subset α of the powerset $\wp(A)$ of the set of action symbols A that satisfies the following conditions:

(i) $\forall \alpha_i \in \alpha$: α_i is an alphabet (2.5.1)
(ii) $\forall \beta \subseteq A$: β alphabet $\Rightarrow$ $(\exists \alpha_i \in \alpha: \beta \subseteq \alpha_i)$
(iii) $\forall \alpha_i \in \alpha, \forall \beta \subseteq A, \beta$ alphabet: $(\alpha_i \subseteq \beta) \Rightarrow (\beta \in \alpha)$.

Condition (i) ensures that each subprocess is sequential, but possibly non-deterministic. Conditions (ii) and (iii) require that each decomposition is 'complete'. Note that each α is a cover of A.

A *process structure* over S is any ordered pair $\Pi = (\alpha, p)$ where α is an alphabet structure over (A, ι) and $p: Q \to \wp(\alpha)$ is a labelling function defined by $p(q) = \{\alpha_i \in \alpha \mid \exists a \in \alpha_i : q \to^{a}\}$. Let $\Sigma = (S, q_0)$ be a rooted ATS. $\Pi = (\alpha, p)$ is a process structure over Σ if it is a process structure over S. Thus, concurrent subprocesses are *static*, and are identified with their alphabets.

Let (A, ι) be a concurrent alphabet, α and α' be alphabet structures over (A, ι). It is easy to see that $\alpha \cup \alpha'$ and $\alpha \cap \alpha'$ are also alphabet structures. We say that α' is *a refinement of* α iff $\alpha \subseteq \alpha'$; process refinement relation is a partial order. For a given concurrent alphabet (A, ι) there exist unique *minimal* and *maximal* alphabet structures (denoted α^{min}, α^{max} respectively) with respect to the inclusion ordering.

Proposition 2.5.1.
The class of all alphabet structures over a concurrent alphabet (A, ι) *forms a complete lattice with inclusion ordering.*

Example 5. Let A = {a, b, c} with b ι c. {{a,b}, {a,c}, {a}} is a refinement of α^{min} = {{a,b}, {a,c}}. α^{max} = {{a,b}, {a,c}, {a}, {b}, {c}}. Fig. 1 shows the lattice of alphabet structures for this case.

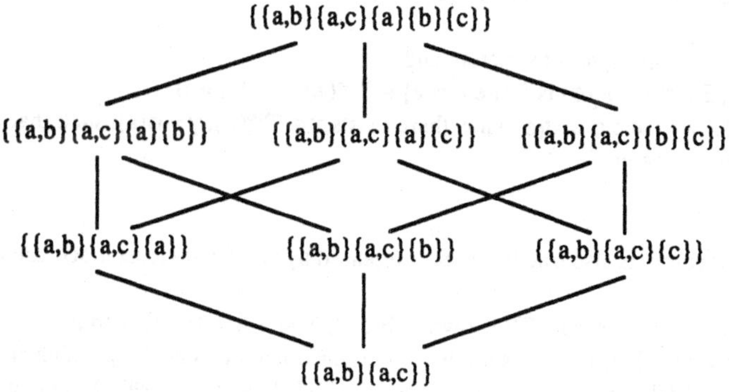

Fig. 1. The lattice of alphabet structures over A = {a,b,c} with b ι c.

2.6 Process Decomposition and Maximality

The following characterization theorem relates process decomposition and maximality. It states that a non-maximal trace, whether finite or infinite, is a trace which is *not yet complete*, that is, there exists a process which has proceeded only *finitely often* and can extend it non-trivially. It follows that, in a maximal computation, each process proceeds an infinite number of times *unless* it has terminated or it is prevented from proceeding (by a refusal of its synchronisation partner).

Theorem 2.6.1. *For every alphabet structure* α, *the following statements are equivalent.*

(i) $\sigma \in T^{\infty}(\Sigma)$ *is* not *maximal in* Σ

(ii) $\exists\, \alpha_i \in \alpha, \exists\, a \in \alpha_i$:

$$\pi_i(\sigma) \text{ is finite } \wedge\ \sigma[a] \in T^{\infty}(\Sigma)\ \wedge\ \sigma[a] \neq \sigma$$

where $\sigma[a]$ *denotes the concatenation of the traces* σ *and* [a].

Proof.
(i) ⇒ (ii) Suppose $\sigma \in T^{\infty}(\Sigma)$ is *not* maximal in Σ. Then by definition of a maximal trace:

(*) $\exists\, \gamma \in T^{\infty}(\Sigma)$: $\sigma \sqsubseteq \gamma \wedge \sigma \neq \gamma \Rightarrow$

$\exists\, \gamma \in T^{\infty}(\Sigma), \exists\, \beta$: $\sigma\beta = \gamma \wedge \sigma\beta \neq \sigma$ (by Theorem 2.2.2) $\Rightarrow$

$\exists\, \gamma \in T^{\infty}(\Sigma), \exists\, a \in A$: $\sigma[a] \sqsubseteq \gamma \wedge \sigma[a] \neq \sigma \Rightarrow$

(**) $\exists\, a \in A : \sigma[a] \in T^{\infty}(\Sigma) \wedge \sigma[a] \neq \sigma$ (because $\sigma[a] \sqsubseteq \gamma, \gamma \in T^{\infty}(\Sigma)$ and Proposition 2.3.1(i))

The final step of this part of the proof is by contradiction. Let α be an arbitrary alphabet structure over (A, ι). Suppose (**) holds and:

(***) $\forall\, \alpha_i \in \alpha, \forall\, b \in \alpha_i$:

$$\pi_i(\sigma) \text{ is infinite } \vee\ \sigma[b] \notin T^{\infty}(\Sigma)\ \vee\ \sigma[b] = \sigma.$$

Since α is a cover of A, it follows from (**) that $\exists\ \alpha_i \in \alpha$ such that $a \in \alpha_i$. By (**) in conjunction with (***), $\pi_i(\sigma)$ is infinite for all $\alpha_i \in \alpha$ such that $a \in \alpha_i$. As $\sigma \sqsubseteq \sigma[a]$, $\pi_i(\sigma[a])$ is also infinite by monotonicity of π_i. Hence:

$$\pi_i(\sigma) = \pi_i(\sigma[a]) \text{ for all } \alpha_i \in \alpha \text{ such that } a \in \alpha_i.$$

Also, $\pi_k(\sigma) = \pi_k(\sigma[a])$ for all $\alpha_k \in \alpha$ such that $a \notin \alpha_k$ (by definition of projection π_k). Thus, for all $\alpha_i \in \alpha$ we have shown $\pi_i(\sigma) = \pi_i(\sigma[a])$, and hence, by Lemma 2.2.1, $\sigma = \sigma[a]$, which contradicts (**). Thus:

$$\exists\ \alpha_i \in \alpha, \exists\ a \in \alpha_i :$$
$$\pi_i(\sigma) \text{ is finite } \wedge\ \sigma[a] \in T^{\infty}(\Sigma)\ \wedge\ \sigma[a] \neq \sigma.$$

(ii) $\Rightarrow$ (i) Suppose α is an alphabet structure and:

$$\exists\ \alpha_i \in \alpha, \exists\ a \in \alpha_i: \pi_i(\sigma) \text{ is finite} \wedge \sigma[a] \in T^{\infty}(\Sigma)\ \wedge\ \sigma[a] \neq \sigma.$$

By Theorem 2.2.2 we have $\sigma \sqsubseteq \sigma[a]$.Thus there exists $\gamma \in T^{\infty}(\Sigma)$, $\gamma = \sigma[a]$, such that $\sigma \sqsubseteq \gamma\ \wedge\ \sigma \neq \gamma$. Clearly, σ is not maximal in Σ.

□

The above theorem is also true if $T^{\infty}(\Sigma)$ is replaced by any Scott-closed trace language.

Example 6. Let us consider the ATS shown in Fig. 2, where A = {a, b} with a ι b. The only alphabet structure in this case is {{a}, {b}}. Examples of non-maximal traces are [a^*], which can be concatenated with [a] or [b], and [a^ω], which can be concatenated with [b] yielding [ba^ω]. Note that $\pi_2([a^\omega])$ is finite. The only maximal trace is [ba^ω].
On the other hand, let us consider the ATS in Fig. 3, where A = {a, τ_b} with a δ τ_b. There are four alphabet structures in this case, for example {{a,τ_b}} and {{a,τ_b}, {τ_b}}. Non-maximal traces are [a^*]. Maximal traces are [$a^*\tau_b$] and [a^ω]. When [a^ω] is concatenated with [a] or [τ_b] the resulting trace is [a^ω].

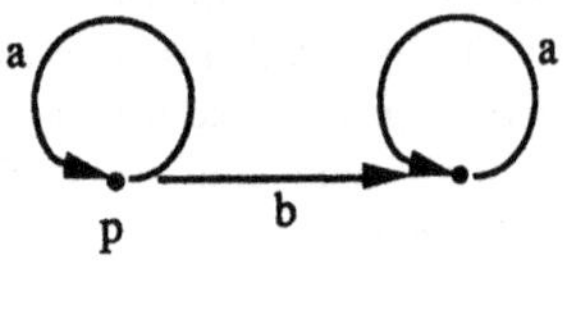

Fig. 2. ATS determined by p = (fix X.aX) || bNIL.

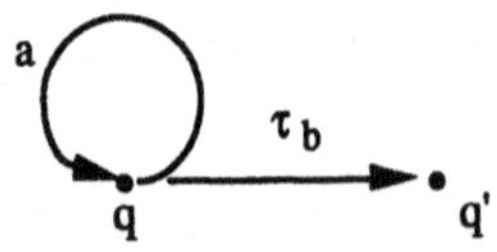

Fig. 3. ATS determined by q = (fix X.(aX+bNIL) || $\bar{b}$NIL)\b.

3. FAIRNESS FOR NON-INTERLEAVING CONCURRENCY

3.1 Behavioural Properties

Fairness properties form a subclass of a larger class of properties called behavioural properties. A topological characterization of behavioural properties in a non-interleaving semantic model can be found in [Kwi90]; here, we shall recall a few definitions.

Let (A, ι) be a concurrent alphabet, $T \subseteq \Theta^\infty$ be a Scott-closed infinitary trace language. By Proposition 2.3.1, every rooted ATS can be identified with a Scott-closed infinitary trace language. Hence, it is sufficient to characterize properties of asynchronous transition systems relative to Scott-closed trace languages.

Let $T^{fin} = T \cap \Theta^*$ and $T^{inf} = T \cap \Theta^\omega$. A *property* is a subset Ψ of T. A property $\Psi \subseteq T$ is a *finitary* property iff:

$$\sigma \in \Psi \cap T^{inf} \Leftrightarrow (\exists \tau \in \Psi \cap T^{fin}: \tau \sqsubseteq \sigma) \qquad (3.1.1)$$

and *infinitary* otherwise.

A trace $\sigma \in \Theta^\infty$ *has the property* Ψ if σ is contained in Ψ. Let $S = (Q, A, \rightarrow, \iota)$ be an ATS, $\Sigma = (S, q_0)$ be a rooted ATS over S. Σ is said to *satisfy* property Ψ iff $Max(\Sigma) \subseteq \Psi$.

A property $\Psi \subseteq T$ is a *safety property* in T iff Ψ is Scott-closed. A property $\Psi \subseteq T$ is a *liveness property* in T iff Ψ is a Scott-dense G_δ-set. Liveness properties state that some action *must* happen, while safety properties state that it *must not* happen.

Any liveness property $\Phi \subseteq Max(T)$ in T is a *fairness property* in T. This states that, unless the system terminates, some action must happen *infinitely often*. Fairness properties have *infinitary* character in the sense described above. By denseness, every *partial* computation may be extended to a (possibly infinite) complete *fair* computation, but some infinite computations may be excluded. It is clear that Max(T) is also a fairness property. Fairness properties are closed under countable intersection and finite union [Kwi90].

3.2 Unconditional Process Fairness Properties

First, let us consider the class of asynchronous transition systems with *non-terminating* processes. Process fairness properties are a subclass of fairness properties determined by alphabet structures. Informally, we say an infinite trace is *unconditionally process fair* (impartial) [LPS81] [Pnu86] iff every process proceeds infinitely often (irrespective of it being enabled).

Let (A, ι) be a concurrent alphabet and $\alpha \subseteq \wp(A)$ be an alphabet structure over (A, ι). Formally, a property $\Phi_u(\alpha) \subseteq \Theta^\omega$ is the *unconditional process fairness property with respect to* α iff:

$$\Phi_u(\alpha) = \{\sigma \in \Theta^\omega \mid \forall \alpha_i \in \alpha: \pi_i(\sigma) \text{ is infinite}\}$$

It is not difficult to see that this definition is consistent with the definition in the previous section, i.e. $\Phi_u(\alpha)$ is a dense subset of $Max(\Theta^\omega)$ which is also a Scott-G_δ-set (the Scott-open sets whose intersection $\Phi_u(\alpha)$ is are $\{\sigma \in \Theta^\infty \mid \forall \alpha_i \in \alpha: \pi_i(\sigma)$ contains at least k symbols$\}$). The following result concerning process fairness properties may be shown.

Theorem 3.2.1. (Refinement Hierarchy of Unconditional Process Fairness)
Let (A, ι) *be a concurrent alphabet,* $\alpha, \alpha' \subseteq \wp(A)$ *be alphabet structures over* (A, ι).

(i) *If* α' *is a refinement of* α *then* $\Phi_u(\alpha') \subseteq \Phi_u(\alpha)$.

(ii) $\Phi_u(\alpha) \cap \Phi_u(\alpha') = \Phi_u(\alpha \cup \alpha')$.

(iii) $\Phi_u(\alpha) \cup \Phi_u(\alpha') = \Phi_u(\alpha \cap \alpha')$.

Proof.
(i) Let $\sigma \in \Phi_u(\alpha')$; then, by definition of unconditional process fairness, for all $\alpha_i \in \alpha'$: $\pi_i(\sigma)$ is infinite. Suppose $\alpha_k \in \alpha$, then $\alpha_k \in \alpha'$ (because α' is a refinement of α, and hence $\alpha \subseteq \alpha'$). Thus, $\pi_k(\sigma)$ is also infinite, and hence $\sigma \in \Phi_u(\alpha)$.
(ii) $\sigma \in \Phi_u(\alpha) \cap \Phi_u(\alpha') \Leftrightarrow \forall \alpha_i \in \alpha$: $\pi_i(\sigma)$ is infinite and $\forall \alpha_k \in \alpha'$: $\pi_k(\sigma)$ is infinite $\Leftrightarrow$
$\forall \alpha_m \in \alpha \cup \alpha'$: $\pi_m(\sigma)$ is infinite $\Leftrightarrow \sigma \in \Phi_u(\alpha \cup \alpha')$.
(iii) Similarly. □

Corollary 3.2.2.

(i) $\Phi_u(\alpha) \subseteq \Phi_u(\alpha^{min})$ *for any alphabet structure* α.

(ii) $\Phi_u(\alpha^{max}) \subseteq \Phi_u(\alpha)$ *for any alphabet structure* α.

(iii) *Unconditional process fairness properties form a complete lattice with inclusion.*

Thus, the lattice structure of process alphabets induces a lattice structure on unconditional process fairness notions.

Example 7. Let $A = \{a, b\}$ with $a \iota b$; $[(ab)^\omega]$ is the only unconditional process fairness property in Θ^∞. Fig. 4 shows the lattice of unconditional process fairness properties for $A = \{a, b\}$ with a and b dependent.

$[(aa^*bb^*)^\omega]$

/ \

$[(aa^*b^*)^\omega]$ $[(a^*bb^*)^\omega]$

\ /

$[(a^*b^*)^\omega]$

Fig. 4. The lattice of unconditional fairness properties for $A = \{a, b\}$ with a, b dependent.

3.3 Weak and Strong Process Fairness

The unconditional process fairness properties require that each process proceeds infinitely often independent of (i) whether it has terminated or not (ii) whether it can proceed or not. This is undesirable, and usually leads to weaker formulations of fairness, so called *weak* and *strong* fairness, which allow to incorporate (i) and (ii).

Informally, a computation is said to be weakly process fair wrt to the process p iff p enabled continuously from some point onwards implies p proceeds infinitely often. A computation is strongly process fair wrt the process p iff p enabled infinitely often implies p proceeds infinitely often.

Let $S = (Q, A, \rightarrow, \iota)$ be an ATS, $\Sigma = (S, q_0)$, where $q_0 \in Q$, a rooted ATS, and α an alphabet structure over (A, ι). Define $\sigma \in T^\infty(\Sigma)$ to be *weakly process fair* iff:

$\forall\, \alpha_i \in \alpha :$ (3.3.1)

α_i continuously enabled in $\sigma \Rightarrow \alpha_i$ proceeds infinitely often in σ.

Define $\sigma \in T^{\infty}(\Sigma)$ to be *strongly process fair* iff:

$\forall\, \alpha_i \in \alpha :$ (3.3.2)

α_i infinitely often enabled in $\sigma \Rightarrow \alpha_i$ proceeds infinitely often in σ.

Finally, the meaning of *continuously enabled, infinitely often enabled* and *proceeds infinitely often* is:

(i) α_i *continuously enabled in* σ $\Leftrightarrow$ (3.3.3)

$\exists\, \tau \sqsubseteq^{fin} \sigma, \exists\, a \in \alpha_i : \forall\, \gamma\!: \tau\gamma \sqsubseteq^{fin} \sigma \Rightarrow \tau\gamma[a] \in T^{\infty}(\Sigma)$

(ii) α_i *infinitely often enabled in* σ $\Leftrightarrow$

$\exists$ infinitely many $\tau \sqsubseteq^{fin} \sigma : \exists\, a \in \alpha_i : \tau[a] \in T^{\infty}(\Sigma)$

(iii) α_i *proceeds infinitely often in* σ $\Leftrightarrow$

$\pi_i(\sigma)$ is infinite.

Given a rooted ATS Σ and an alphabet structure α, denote the weak process fairness by $\Phi_w(\alpha)$ and strong process fairness $\Phi_s(\alpha)$. Then the following may be shown.

Proposition 3.3.1. (Strength Hierarchy of Process Fairness)
Let $\Phi_u(\alpha)$, $\Phi_s(\alpha)$, $\Phi_w(\alpha)$ denote the sets of all traces of an ATS Σ that are respectively unconditionally, strongly and weakly process fair. Then:

$$\Phi_u(\alpha) \subseteq \Phi_s(\alpha) \subseteq \Phi_w(\alpha)$$

and the inclusion is strict.

Proof. Straightforward. □

Example 8. Consider the CCS process p = fix X.a(bNIL + cX). The concurrent alphabet is {a, b, c} with empty independency. If we take α = {{a,b,c}, {a,b}, {b,c}, {b}} as the alphabet structure then the trace $[(ac)^{\omega}]$ is weakly process fair (because b is not enabled continuously), but it is *not* strongly process fair (because b is enabled infinitely often and not taken infinitely often). $[(ac)^{\omega}]$ is not unconditionally process fair either. Unconditional process fairness makes sense only in the context of non-terminating processes - note that the (terminating and maximal) trace $[(ac)^{*}b]$, although both strongly and weakly fair, is not unconditionally process fair because the process with the alphabet {b} does not proceed infinitely often!

Proposition 3.3.2. (Refinement Hierarchy of Weak and Strong Process Fairness)

(i) *If α' is a refinement of α then $\Phi_w(\alpha') \subseteq \Phi_w(\alpha)$.*

(ii) $\Phi_w(\alpha) \cap \Phi_w(\alpha') = \Phi_w(\alpha \cup \alpha')$.

(iii) $\Phi_w(\alpha) \cup \Phi_w(\alpha') = \Phi_w(\alpha \cap \alpha')$.

(iv) *If α' is a refinement of α then $\Phi_s(\alpha') \subseteq \Phi_s(\alpha)$.*

(v) $\Phi_s(\alpha) \cap \Phi_s(\alpha') = \Phi_s(\alpha \cup \alpha')$.

(vi) $\Phi_s(\alpha) \cup \Phi_s(\alpha') = \Phi_s(\alpha \cap \alpha')$.

Proof.

(i) Let $\sigma \in \Phi_w(\alpha')$; then, by definition of weak process fairness:

(*) $\forall \alpha_i \in \alpha'$:

α_i continuously enabled in $\sigma \Rightarrow \alpha_i$ proceeds infinitely often in σ.

Suppose $\alpha_k \in \alpha$, then $\alpha_k \in \alpha'$ (because α' is a refinement of α, and hence $\alpha \subseteq \alpha'$). Thus, (*) also holds for α_k, and thus $\sigma \in \Phi_w(\alpha)$.

(ii) $\Phi_w(\alpha \cup \alpha') \subseteq \Phi_w(\alpha) \cap \Phi_w(\alpha')$ is clear because $\alpha \cup \alpha'$ is a refinement of α and α'.

Let $\sigma \in \Phi_w(\alpha) \cap \Phi_w(\alpha')$; then, by definition of weak process fairness:

(*) $\forall \alpha_i \in \alpha$:

α_i continuously enabled in $\sigma \Rightarrow \alpha_i$ proceeds infinitely often in σ

(**) $\forall \alpha_k \in \alpha'$:

α_k continuously enabled in $\sigma \Rightarrow \alpha_k$ proceeds infinitely often in σ.

Let $\alpha_m \in \alpha \cup \alpha'$, and suppose α_m is continuously enabled in σ. There are two cases:

(1) $\alpha_m \in \alpha \Rightarrow \alpha_m$ proceeds infinitely often in σ

(2) $\alpha_m \in \alpha' \Rightarrow \alpha_m$ proceeds infinitely often in σ

from which it follows $\sigma \in \Phi_w(\alpha \cup \alpha')$.

(iii) - (vi) Similarly.

□

4. CONCLUSION

An abstract, uniform characterization of process fairness properties has been presented. Since the topological characterization relies solely on the space of behaviours forming a Scott domain with the causality ordering, the results presented here are largely model-independent. Other fairness properties such as event fairness, equifairness and state fairness [Fra86] are also expressible within this framework. The latter may be achieved by introducing strength predicates similar to *continuously enabled* and *infinitely often enabled.* A topological characterization of safety and liveness in an interleaving model (domain of sequences) also appeared in [MaP89]. As the domain of sequences is a special case of the domain of traces, it would be interesting to relate these two characterizations.

What are the main conclusions regarding the non-interleaving approach to concurrency? Considering the approach to modelling concurrency taken in this paper does not, on the face of it, seem substantially different from the interleaving approach (i.e. sets of equivalent sequences are considered instead of just the set of sequences, with branching structure ignored), one would expect that by taking the interleaving approach and deriving fairness following, say, the ideas of [LPS81], a compatible result can be achieved. What we mean by this is that, given a system, the set of all derivations (sequences) that are, for example, strongly process fair in the sense of [LPS81] coincides with the union of all traces that are strongly process fair in the sense of Section 3.3. Unfortunately, this is *not* the case, which we shall illustrate by means of the following example. Let p = fix X.a(cX + bNIL), q = fix X.d(eX + $\bar{b}$NIL), and r = (p || q)\b. Let us view r as consisting of three concurrent processes, p, q and τ_bNIL, with their respective alphabets $\{a, c, \tau_b\}$, $\{d, e, \tau_b\}$ and $\{\tau_b\}$. The derivation $(acde)^\omega$ is weakly process fair in the sense of [LPS81] because τ_b is *never* enabled, while the derivation $(adce)^\omega$ is not because τ_b is enabled infinitely often but never taken. Thus, the set of all derivations that are fair in the sense of [LPS81] would *exclude* $(adce)^\omega$. On the other hand, $(adce)^\omega$ would be *included* in the union of all traces fair in the sense of Section 3.3 because it is trace equivalent to $(acde)^\omega$. This phenomenon is caused by the presence of confusion; the precise relationship of fairness and confusion will be investigated separately.

We can thus conclude that non-interleaving semantics, by viewing system execution as a partial order rather than a set of total orders, helps overcome problems with confusion. It also provides a fairness notion 'for free' - maximality with respect to the partial order.

The work presented here is by no means complete. An investigation of metric-space and topological properties of the domain of traces is under way. Further research would also include a proof system interpreted over a partial order that enables the verification of properties under fairness constraints.

ACKNOWLEDGEMENTS

The help of Mike Shields, Mike Smyth, Colin Stirling, Amir Pnueli and Paul Warren is gratefully acknowledged.

REFERENCES

[Bed87] M. Bednarczyk, Categories of Asynchronous Systems, PhD Thesis, University of Sussex, 1987.

[BoN79] L. Boasson, M. Nivat, Adherences of Languages, *Journal of Computer and System Sciences* **20** (1980) 285-309.

[CoS87] G.Costa, C. Stirling, Weak and Strong Fairness in CCS, *Information and Computation* **73** (1987) 207-244.

[Fra86] N. Francez, *Fairness* (Springer-Verlag, New York, 1986).

[GHK80] G. Gierz, K.H. Hofmann, K. Keimel, J.D. Lawson, M. Mislove, D. Scott, *A Compendium of Continuous Lattices* (Springer-Verlag, 1980).

[KaP90] S. Katz and D. Peled, Defining Conditional Independence Using Collapses, in: M.Z. Kwiatkowska *et al*, eds., *Semantics for Concurrency* (Springer-Verlag, 1990) 262-280.

[Kur66] K. Kuratowski, *Topology* (Academic Press, 1966).

[Kwi89a] M.Z. Kwiatkowska, Event Fairness and Non-Interleaving Concurrency, *Formal Aspects of Computing* **1** 3 (1989)

[Kwi89b] M.Z. Kwiatkowska, Fairness for Non-Interleaving Concurrency, PhD Thesis, University of Leicester, 1989. Also available as Technical Report 22, Department of Computing Studies, University of Leicester, 1989.

[Kwi89c] M.Z. Kwiatkowska, On Infinitary Trace Languages, Technical Report 31, Department of Computing Studies, University of Leicester, 1989.

[Kwi89d] M.Z. Kwiatkowska, Survey of Fairness Notions, *Information and Software Technology* **31** 7 (1989).

[Kwi90] M.Z. Kwiatkowska, On Topological Characterization of Behavioural Properties, to appear in: G.M. Reed and A.W. Roscoe, eds., *Topology in Computer Science* (Oxford University Press, 1990).

[Law88] J.D. Lawson, The Versatile Continuous Order, in: M. Main *et al*, eds., *Mathematical Foundations of Programming Language Semantics, 3rd Workshop*, Lecture Notes in Computer Science **298** (Springer-Verlag, 1988).

[LPS81] D. Lehman, A. Pnueli, J. Stavi, Impartiality, Justice and Fairness: The Ethics of Concurrent Termination, in: S.Even, O.Kariv, eds., *Automata, Languages and Programming*, Lecture Notes in Computer Science **115** (Springer-Verlag, 1981).

[MaP89] Z. Manna, A. Pnueli, The anchored version of the temporal framework, in: J.W. de Bakker, W.-P. de Roever, G. Rozenberg, eds., *Linear Time, Branching time and Partial*

Order in Logics and Models for Concurrency, Lecture Notes in Computer Science **354** (Springer-Verlag, 1989) 201-284.

[Maz89] A. Mazurkiewicz, Basic Notions of Trace Theory, in: J.W. de Bakker, W.-P. de Roever, G. Rozenberg, eds., *Linear Time, Branching time and Partial Order in Logics and Models for Concurrency*, Lecture Notes in Computer Science **354** (Springer-Verlag, 1989) 285-263.

[MOP88] A. Mazurkiewicz, E. Ochmanski, W. Penczek, Concurrent Systems and Inevitability, *Theoretical Computer Science* **64** (1989) 281-304.

[Par81] D. Park, Concurrency and Automata on Infinite Sequences, in: P. Deussen, ed., *Proceedings of the 5th GI Conference on Theoretical Computer Science*, Lecture Notes in Computer Science **104** (Springer-Verlag, 1981).

[Pnu86] A. Pnueli, Applications of temporal logic to the specification and verification of reactive systems: a survey of current trends, in: J.W. de Bakker, W.-P. de Roever, G. Rozenberg, eds., *Current Trends in Concurrency*, Lecture Notes in Computer Science **224** (Springer-Vrlag, 1986).

[Rei84] W. Reisig, Partial Order Semantics versus Interleaving Semantics for CSP-like Languages and its Impact on Fairness, in: J. Paradaens, ed., *Automata, Languages and Programming*, Lecture Notes in Computer Science **172**, Springer-Verlag (1984) 403-413.

[Shi88] M.W. Shields, Behavioural Presentations, in: in: J.W. de Bakker, W.-P. de Roever, G. Rozenberg, eds., *Linear Time, Branching time and Partial Order in Logics and Models for Concurrency*, Lecture Notes in Computer Science **354** (Springer-Verlag, 1989).

[Shi89] M.W. Shields, Elements of a Theory of Parallelism, to be published.

[Win86] G. Winskel, Event Structures, Technical Report No.95, Computer Laboratory, Cambridge University, 1986.

OBSERVATIONAL LOGICS AND CONCURRENCY MODELS

Rocco De Nicola
IEI - CNR
Via S. Maria, 46 I-56125 Pisa - ITALY
E_mail: denicola@icnucevm.cnuce.cnr.it

Gian Luigi Ferrari
Dipartimento di Informatica
Corso Italia, 40 I-56126, Pisa - ITALY
E_mail: giangi@dipisa.di.unipi.it

Abstract

The aim of this paper is to examine some basic topics of true concurrency from the viewpoint of program logics. In particular, logical characterizations of observational (bisimulation) equivalences based on partial ordering observations are studied. To date, in contrast with the interleaving approach, such equivalences have been almost exclusively studied from the operational standpoint. We shall show that they can be defined in a logical setting and that standard modal and temporal techniques can also be applied to true concurrency models. As a result, the interleaving and the partial ordering views of concurrency are reconciled within a logical setting.

Introduction

As it has been developed, the semantic theory of concurrent and distributed systems is mainly a theory of *observation*; the crucial point is to identify the "important" aspects of concurrent and distributed computations, and thus what should be observed of them. Indeed, the main division between the different models of concurrency concerns assumptions about the power of the observers, and leads to the division between *interleaving* models and *true concurrency* models.

Interleaving models (see, for example, [Hoa85, Mil89]) assume sequential observers, and express concurrency among events by saying that they may occur in any order. In this class of models, concurrency cannot be directly observed; it is not a primitive concept as it is simulated in terms of non-deterministic interleaving of events. True concurrency models (see, for example, [BC88, DM87, NPW81, Rei85, Pra86]) assume instead powerful observers, which are able to determine causal dependencies between subsystems. Within these models concurrency is a primitive concept; system behaviours are described by means of partial ordering of events and concurrency is determined by the absence of ordering.

Observations can be used to define notions of behavioural equivalence among systems: two systems are equivalent whenever no sequence of observations can distinguish between them. Many different equivalences have been proposed especially for interleaving models (see [DeN87] for a comparative presentation). In the last years, some equivalence notions which preserve concurrency have also been proposed (see [vGG89] for an account of many of them).

Together with the definition of equivalences, different attempts have been made towards defining logics which permit specifying and proving correctness of concurrent and distributed systems; in particular, temporal logic has been seen as a promising approach (see [REX89]). To date, there is no general

Research partially supported by Esprit Basic Research Action Program, Project 3011 CEDISYS, and by Progetto Finalizzato Sistemi Informatici e Calcolo Parallelo, Project LAMBRUSCO.

agreement on the type of temporal logic to be used, and often the logics proposed have been compared with the operational equivalences to gain a better insight. The classic result is that of Hennessy and Milner [HM85] for the (modal) logical characterization of *observational (bisimulation) equivalence* [Par81]. More recently, it has been proved that observational equivalence coincides with that induced by CTL* [BCG88].

There have also been attempts at defining temporal logics tailored towards true concurrency models [KP87, LT87, LRT89, Pen88, Rei89]. For these new logics too, a key point is to define formal criteria to determine their expressive power, the properties that can be naturally expressed by them and, once again, their relationships with operational models.

The aim of this paper is to tackle some basic topics of the true concurrency approach from the standpoint of modal and temporal logics. We show that bisimulation equivalences based on partial ordering observations can be characterized in a logical setting, and that existing models of true concurrency can be analyzed and better understood by means of standard logical techniques. To this purpose, we introduce a general framework for interpreting modal and temporal logics on both interleaving and truly concurrency models. The main feature of the framework is that the observation function plays a crucial role as a semantic entity; the validity of the logic formulae is explicitly based on the outcome of computation observations.

Within our framework, modal logics with modalities like $<t>\varphi$, where t is a term describing an observation, can be interpreted. These modalities reflects the observable behaviour of computations. In this perspective, Hennessy-Milner Logic (HML) is characterized by a simple notion of observation: the observation function yields sequences of actions. Building on this, we will show that a simple extension of HML, named L_{PO}, whose modalities are paremeterized with partial orders, characterizes the partial ordering equivalence (sometimes called *pomset bisimulation*) introduced in [DDM88] and in [BC88].

Pomset bisimulation equivalence naturally discriminates between parallelism and its simulation via nondeterministic interleaving. However, there are also grounds under which it may be considered not completely satisfactory. Indeed, it has been argued [RT88, DDM89, vGG89] that it cannot take fully into account the branching structure of computations: it cannot capture the interplay between concurrency and nondeterminism. This limitation is overcome by considering other behavioural equivalences which identify only systems with the same actual history and equivalent possible futures [DDM87-89, RT88, vGG89].

In this paper, we characterize some of these history-based equivalences within a temporal logic framework which permits reasoning about computation histories in two alternatives ways. First, a temporal language, the logic of tree-like frame L_T, whose atomic formulae corresponds to partial ordering observations is proposed; the atomic formulae are used to explicitly take histories into account. Then, the temporal logic L_P, whose distinctive feature is the presence of a relativized past operator and the absence of atomic formulae is introduced., It is the relativized past operator which permits recovering computation histories. We prove that L_T and L_P both characterize the bisimulation equivalence introduced in [DDM87] which is known as NMS-partial ordering equivalence. The correspondence between L_T and L_P throws light on the duality between the structure of the modalities and the validity of the atomic formulae.

1. Modal and Temporal Logics with Interleaving Models

In this section, we briefly recall some basic notions for describing the semantics of concurrent languages and systems, and we review some results on the logical characterization of behavioural equivalence.

Definition 1.1 (*Labelled Transition Systems*)
A Labelled Transition System T is a triple $T = (S, A, \rightarrow)$ where:

- S is a non empty set of states;
- A is a non empty set of action labels;
- $\rightarrow$ is a family of indexed relations $\xrightarrow{a}$, where $\xrightarrow{a} \subseteq S \times A \times S$. ♦

The transition relation $\xrightarrow{a}$ describes the effect of executing the action a. The transition $s \xrightarrow{a} s'$ indicates that state s may evolve to state s' by performing action a. Interleaving operational semantics of concurrent languages and systems have often been defined in terms of labelled transition systems. However, these description are often too concrete: the addition of a *behavioural equivalence* identifying those states which cannot be distinguished by external observations yields more abstract models. A notable example of behavioural equivalences is provided by the observational (bisimulation) equivalence [Par81, Mil89].

Definition 1.2 (*Observational Equivalence*)
Let $T = (S, A, \rightarrow)$ be a labelled transition system. A relation $R \subseteq S \times S$ is called *bisimulation* if it is symmetric and satisfies the following property:

$$\text{if } s\,R\,q \text{ and } s \xrightarrow{a} s', \text{ then } \exists\, q' \text{ such that } q \xrightarrow{a} q' \text{ and } s'\,R\,q'$$

Two states s and q of S are *observational equivalent*, $s \sim q$, if there exists a bisimulation relating them. ♦

The arbitrary union of bisimulation is again a bisimulation and it is an equivalence relation [Par81].

Labelled transition systems have also been used to define the semantics of propositional modal languages.

Definition 1.3 (*Hennessy-Milner Logic*)
The syntax of Hennessy-Milner Logic is defined by the following grammar where φ denotes a generic formula of the language:

$$\varphi ::= \text{true} \mid \neg\varphi \mid \varphi_1 \vee \varphi_2 \mid [a]\,\varphi.$$

Given a labelled transition system T, the satisfaction relation is inductively defined as follows :

$s \models \text{true}$ for every $s \in S$;
$s \models \neg\varphi$ if and only if *not* $s \models \varphi$;
$s \models \varphi_1 \vee \varphi_2$ if and only if $s \models \varphi_1$ *or* $s \models \varphi_2$;
$s \models [a]\,\varphi$ if and only if $s' \models \varphi$ for all $s' \in S$ such that $s \xrightarrow{a} s'$. ♦

Hennessy and Milner have shown [HM85] for *image-finite* labelled transition systems, i.e. for transition systems where for any state s, the set $\{s' \mid s\,R\,s'\}$ is finite, two states are bisimilar if and only if they satisfy the same HML formulae, i.e. the same modal properties.

Theorem 1.4 (*Modal Characterization Theorem*)
$s \sim q$ if and only if $s \models \varphi \Leftrightarrow q \models \varphi$, for each φ in HML. ♦

On many occasions, it is useful to describe properties of computations, not just of states. For this purpose, temporal logics which explicitly refer to computations are introduced. Hennessy and Stirling [HS85] have defined a temporal version of HML named L_T'. The main feature of this logic is the presence of modalities of the form [u], where u belongs to the set of the finite and infinite strings over an alphabet A. They proved that the equivalence induced by L_T' coincides with the equivalence induced by HML when Generalized Transition Systems are image finite and *standard* (the infinite computations are the limit of sequences of finite computations).

The main contributions of the paper are three characterization theorems which extends the classical results of Hennessy and Milner to truly concurrent semantics. The relationships between the equivalences induced by three observational logics and two partial ordering observational equivalences are clearly established.

2. Parameterized Hennessy-Milner Logics

In this section, we introduce a new class of modalities, their meaning strictly depends on a notion of observability of computations. The idea is that of defining modalities like [t], where t is a term describing an observation. Intuitively, these modalities emphasize the structure of the observation of those computations that cause a state change within systems. Clearly, the type of observation allowed greatly influences the expressive power of the logic.

Definition 2.1 (*Generalized Labelled Transition Systems*)
Let T = (S, A, →) be a labelled transition system.

A computation of T is a sequence

$$s_1 (s_1 \xrightarrow{a_1} s_2)\ s_2 (s_2 \xrightarrow{a_2} s_3) \ldots s_n (s_n \xrightarrow{a_n} s_{n+1}) \ldots, \quad \text{where } s_i \xrightarrow{a_i} s_{i+1} \in R, \text{ for } i \geq 1;$$

A *generalized labeled transition system* is a pair G = (T, Σ), where Σ is a non empty set of computations. ♦

Definition 2.2 (*Observation Frames*)
Let G = (T, Σ) be a generalized labelled transition system. Let D be the domain of observations, and let obs be the observation function of the computations of G, obs : Σ → D. An *observation frame* on D is a pair F = (G, obs). ♦

We now introduce the observational logic L_D together with its semantics. L_D is an extension of L'_T of [HS85]: it is obtained by parameterizing modalities with respect to a domain D of observations.

Definition 2.3 (*The Observational Logic L_D*)
Let d be an observation (d ∈ D), and φ be a formula, the language L_D is defined as follows:

$$\varphi ::= \text{true} \mid \neg\varphi \mid \vee \{ \varphi_i \mid i \in I \} \mid [d]\, \varphi \mid \langle d\rangle\varphi$$

where I is a (possibly infinite) non empty set of indices ♦

The semantics of L_D is defined by considering observation frames. First, we introduce a few notational conventions which will be adopted from now onwards in the paper

Notation 2.4
Let σ be a computation, then:

- init(σ) denotes the initial state of the computation σ;
- term(σ) denotes the final state of the computation σ, if any;
- $s \rightarrow_\sigma s'$ indicates that there is a (finite) computation σ such that s = init(σ) and s' = term(σ). ♦

Definition 2.5 (*The satisfaction relation for L_D*)

$s \models$ true for every $s \in S$;
$s \models \neg\varphi$ if and only if *not* $s \models \varphi$;
$s \models \bigvee\{\varphi_i \mid i \in I\}$ if and only if $s \models \varphi_j$ for some $j \in I$;
$s \models [d]\varphi$ if and only if $\forall\, \sigma \in \Sigma$, $((s \rightarrow_\sigma s')$ and $(obs(\sigma) = d) \Rightarrow s' \models \varphi)$;
$s \models \langle d\rangle\varphi$ if and only if $\exists\, \sigma \in \Sigma$, $((s \rightarrow_\sigma s')$ and $(obs(\sigma) = d)$ and $s' \models \varphi)$. ♦

As usual, <d> and [d] are duals of each other, i.e. $\langle d\rangle \equiv \neg[d]\neg$. Clearly, L_D stands for a family of observational logics. To obtain a specific logic in this family, the domain D of observations has to be fixed. Each observational logic induces an equivalence over the states of the observation frame. We will study the relationships between the equivalence induced by L_D, denoted by $\equiv_{L_D}$, and an equivalence explicitly defined over observation frames. The behavioural equivalence we will consider is a bisimulation relation which, like $\equiv_{L_D}$, is parameterized with respect to the observation mechanism. In the following, obs will indicate a generic observation mechanism, and equality will be assumed up to isomorphism.

Definition 2.6 (*Logical Observational Equivalence*)
Let s and s' be two states of an observation frame F, we have

$$s \equiv_{L_D} s' \text{ if and only if } s \models \varphi \Leftrightarrow s' \models \varphi, \text{ for each } \varphi \text{ in } L_D.$$ ♦

Definition 2.7 (*Relativized Observational Equivalence*)
Let F = (G, obs) be an observation frame. A relation R_{obs} between the states of F is called *relativized bisimulation* if it is symmetric and satisfies the following property:

$$\text{if } s\ R_{obs}\ q \text{ and } s \to_\sigma s', \text{ then } \exists\, q' \text{ such that } q \to_{\sigma'} q',\ obs(\sigma) = obs(\sigma') \text{ and } s'\ R_{obs}\ q'$$

We say that $s \approx_{obs} q$ if there exists a relativized bisimulation R_{obs} such that $s\ R_{obs}\ q$. ♦

The arbitrary union of relativized bisimulation is again a bisimulation and it is an equivalence relation [DDM87]. The next theorem is a generalization of Theorem 2.2 of [HM85]. Indeed, we can retrieve the expressiveness results previously obtained for interleaving models simply by considering interleaving observation functions.

Theorem 2.8 (*Logical Equivalence and Relativized Observational Equivalence Coincide*)

$$s_1 \approx_{obs} s_2 \text{ if and only if } s_1 \equiv_{LD} s_2.$$

Proof.
⇒) We have to prove that $s_1 \approx_{obs} s_2$ implies $s_1 \models \varphi \Leftrightarrow s_2 \models \varphi$. We will prove that $s_1 \approx_{obs} s_2$ implies $s_1 \models \varphi$ implies $s_2 \models \varphi$ by induction on the structure of φ. We show the non trivial case only.

Assume $\varphi = \langle d\rangle\varphi'$ then $s_1 \models \langle d\rangle\varphi$ if and only if $s' \models \varphi'$ for some computation $\sigma \in \Sigma$, with $obs(\sigma) = d$ and $s_1 \to_\sigma s'$. By hypothesis $s_1 \approx_{obs} s_2$, there exists then a computation σ', $s_1 \to_{\sigma'} s''$, such that $obs(\sigma')$ = d and $s' \approx_{obs} s''$. Applying the inductive hypothesis we get $s'' \models \varphi'$ and thus, by definition, $s_2 \models \langle d\rangle\varphi'$.

⇐) We show that $\equiv_{LD}$ is a relativized bisimulation. Suppose $\equiv_{LD}$ is not a relativized bisimulation. Thus, there exist states s_1, s_2 such that $s_1 \equiv_{LD} s_2$ but for some computation σ with observation d and $s_1 \to_\sigma s'$, we have that either for no computations σ' $s_2 \to_{\sigma'} s''$ we have $obs(\sigma') = d$ or for every s" which can be reached via a computation from s_2 whose observation is d it does not hold that $s' \equiv_{LD} s''$. If there exists no computation with a d-observation, we have $s_2 \models [d]$ false, and $s_1 \models \langle d\rangle$ true.

If the set of states reachable from s_2 via computations with a d-observation is not empty (possibly denumerable infinite) and say equal to $After(s_2, d) = \{p_1, p_2, p_3, \ldots, p_i, \ldots\}$. To prove the claim, we can make use of the set of formulae $F = \{\varphi_i \mid p_i \in After(s_2, d), p_i \models \varphi_i, \textit{not } s' \models \varphi_i\}$. Since $s' \not\equiv_{LD} s''$ we can always find an appropriate φ_i for each i. We have that $s_2 \models [d] \bigvee F$ while s_1 does not satisfy $[d] \bigvee F$. ♦

3. A Logic for Partial Ordering Observational Equivalence

In this section, we provide a concrete model for the logics introduced in the previous section by taking advantage of the generalization of Plotkin's SOS approach to semantics proposed by Degano, De Nicola and Montanari (see e.g. [DDM88, DDM89]). They have shown that it is possible to equip concurrent languages and systems with operational definitions which take causal dependencies fully into account. We introduce a variant of the model of Distributed Transition Systems (DTS), originally described in [DM87], and show that it naturally leads to a uniform framework for interpreting Observational Logics.

Definition 3.1 (*Distributed Transition System*)
A Distributed Transition System D_T is a triple, $D_T = (P, A, r)$, where

- P is a set of *process names*,
- A is a set of actions,
- r is a set of *indexed rewrite rules*, $r \subseteq Fin(P) \times A \times Fin(P)$, where Fin(P) is the set of the finite subsets of P. ♦

Distributed Transition System are nothing but a generalization of transition systems where the (global) state of the system is broken into a set of local states and where a rewrite rule applies only to a subpart of the global state. A subset of P represents part of the state of a system, and each indexed rewrite rule describes the synchronous evolution of a finite set of processes. We write X – a –> Y to denote a rewrite rule indexed by the action "a", and say that the set of processes X becomes the set Y through action "a".

It is worth noting that Distributed Transition Systems can be easily related with a special class of Petri nets called Place/Transition Petri Nets [Rei85]. Here, we have considered the basic model of Distributed Transition Systems rather than nets because our main aim is introducing a computational model, which emphasizes the role of the observation mechanism of computations in the definition of behavioural equivalences. To this purpose, the simple model of Distributed Transition Systems summarizes the main features of many of the proposed true concurrency models.

Definition 3.2 (*Distributed Computations*)
A computation of a distributed transition system is a sequence

$$\sigma = (S_1\ X_1 - a_1 \rightarrow Y_1\ S_2 \ldots S_{n-1}\ X_{n-1} - a_n \rightarrow Y_{n-1}\ S_n)$$

where:

- $S_i \subseteq P$ for every i, $1 \leq i \leq n$; and
- $X_i \subseteq S_i$, $Y_i \subseteq S_{i+1}$, and $S_{i+1} = S_i - X_i \cup Y_i$ for every elementary step $S_i\ X_i - a_i \rightarrow Y_i\ S_{i+1}$, $1 \leq i < n$. ♦

The elementary steps provide full information to single out active and idle part of the rewriting. Indeed, on one hand the rule, $X_i - a_i \rightarrow Y_i$, specifies the active processes involved in the change of the state (together with its effect); on the other hand $S_i - X_i$ gives the processes which are not involved in the actual change: they are idles. In order to complete the construction of the model, we have to define the *observation mechanism* for the computations of DTS.

The interleaving observation of a computation is just the sequence of the labels of its rewrite rules. The partial ordering observations are obtained in two steps: first an event is associated to each indexed rewrite rule of the computation and the obvious causal dependencies between events and processes are established; all processes are then discarded.

Definition 3.3 (*Labelled Partial Orderings*)
A *labelled partial ordering* is a triple $h = (E, \lambda, \leq)$, where

i) E is a finite set of events
ii) λ: $E \rightarrow A$ is a *labelling function*
iii) $\leq$ is a partial ordering relation on E, called *causal relation*. ♦

Definition 3.4 (*Partial Ordering Observations*)
Given a computation $\sigma = (S_1\ X_1 - a_1 \rightarrow Y_1\ S_2 \ldots S_{n-1}\ X_{n-1} - a_{n-1} \rightarrow Y_{n-1}\ S_n)$, the partial ordering observation function **po** detects the labelled partial ordering $h = (E, \lambda, \leq)$, where

i) $E = \{e_1, \ldots, e_{n-1}\}$,
ii) $\lambda(e_i) = a_i$,
iii) The partial order $\leq$ is obtained by taking the restriction to the set E of the transitive and reflexive closure of relation F over the set $S_1 \times \{1\} \cup S_2 \times \{2\} \ldots \cup S_n \times \{n\} \cup E$ defined as follows:

$$\frac{p \in S_i - X_i}{\langle p; i \rangle\ F\ \langle p; i+1 \rangle} \qquad \frac{p \in X_i}{\langle p; i \rangle\ F\ e_i} \qquad \frac{p \in Y_i}{e_i\ F\ \langle p; i+1 \rangle}$$ ♦

Example 3.5
The next figure shows a computation and its partial ordering observation of the distributed transition system having the following indexed rewrite rules:

$$\{p\} - \alpha \rightarrow \{p\}, \qquad \{p, q\} - \beta \rightarrow \{p, q\}, \qquad \{q\} - \alpha \rightarrow \{q\}.$$

In the figure the thick arrows represent the rewritings. Notice that the interleaving observation of this computation is simply the sequence $\alpha \cdot \alpha \cdot \beta \cdot \alpha$. ♦

Distributed Transition Systems are the basis for introducing the distributed observational frames which provide a class of models for the family of parameterized logics introduced in the previous section.

Definition 3.6 (*Distributed Observational Frame*)
Given a Distributed Transition System D_T a *distributed observational frame* is the triple F = (W, Σ, obs) where:

- W = Fin(P), the set of the finite subsets of P;
- Σ is the set of the computations of D_T;
- obs is the observation function of Σ. ♦

In the case of partial ordering observations, the modalities of the observational logic L_{PO} have the form [h] where h is a labelled partial ordering. The operator [h] emphasizes the causal structure of the events in the computation.

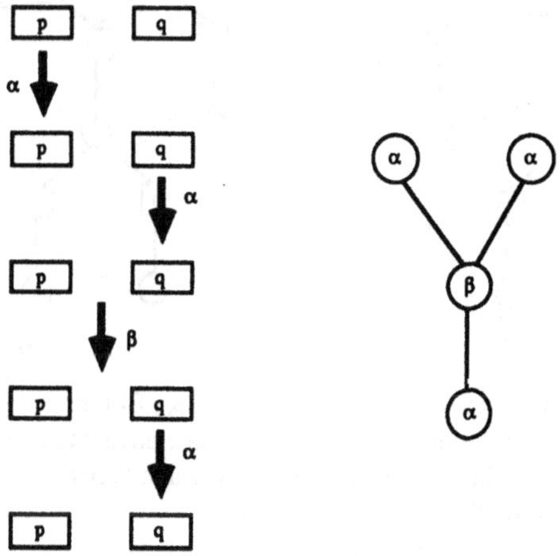

We can extend the notion of relativized bisimulation to distributed observational frames and prove the correspondence theorem between logical and behavioural equivalence by resorting to techniques similar to that for Theorem 2.8. An immediate consequence of this instantiation is that the observational logic L_{PO} characterizes the behavioural equivalence called pomset bisimulation [vGG89] which is based on transition, i.e. the relation $\rightarrow_\sigma$, labelled by partial orders (pomsets in the Pratt's terminology [Pra86]).

Theorem 3.7 (*Logical Characterization of Pomset Equivalence*)

$s_1 \equiv_{L_{PO}} s_2$ if and only if $s_1 \approx_{\mathbf{po}} s_2$. ♦

The observational logic L_{PO} captures the notion of parallelism, and indeed discriminates between parallel systems and their simulation via nondeterministic interleaving. This fact and the above theorem provide sufficient motivations for studying the logic L_{PO}. However, there are also grounds under which it may be considered not completely satisfactory. The last example of this section shows that L_{PO} cannot take fully into account the branching structure of computations and in particular the interplay between concurrency and nondeterminism. In the examples, we will resort to a linear representation of partial orders: ";"will indicate causal dependence, while "||" will indicate independence of events.

Example 3.8 (*Concurrency ≠ Interleaving*)
Let us consider the distributed transition system determined by the two rewrite rules below:

$$\{p\} - \alpha \rightarrow \{stop\},\ \{q\} - \beta \rightarrow \{stop\}.$$

We can easily see that $\{p, q\} \models \langle\alpha \parallel \beta\rangle$ true $\wedge$ $[\alpha;\beta]$ false $\wedge$ $[\beta;\alpha]$ false. ♦

Example 3.9 (*Weakness of L_{PO}*)
Let D_T be the distributed transition system determined by the rewriting rules below:

i) $\{p\}-\alpha\rightarrow\{stop\}$, $\{q\}-\beta\rightarrow\{stop\}$,

ii) $\{p, q\}-\alpha\rightarrow\{p'\}$, $\{p'\}-\beta\rightarrow\{stop\}$, $\{p'\}-\gamma\rightarrow\{stop\}$

and let $D_{T'}$ be the distributed transition system obtained by adding the following rules to those of D_T:

iii) $\{p, q\}-\alpha\rightarrow\{p''\}$, $\{p''\}-\beta\rightarrow\{stop\}$.

Roughly speaking, D_T and $D_{T'}$ correspond to the two Petri nets below

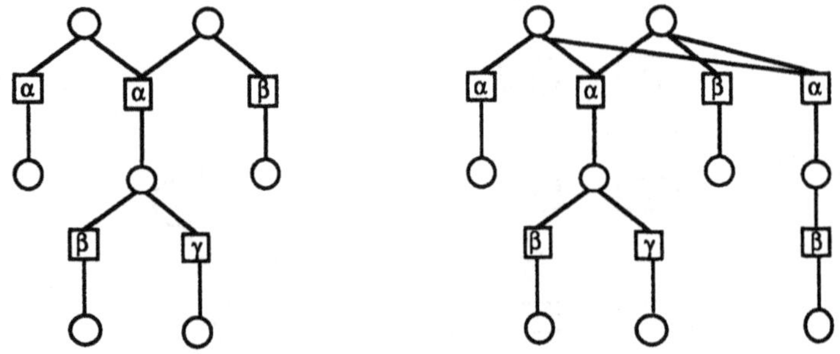

a) b)

In both systems, the state $\{p, q\}$ satisfies the same set of L_{PO} formulae. The only difference may arise because of the rewrite rules iii); but, it is not possible to take advantage within L_{PO} of the fact that $D_{T'}$, starting from $\{p, q\}$ may reach, via an α action, a state in which either both β and γ are possible or just β is, while D_T after α does not offer this choice. ♦

4. History Preserving Observational Logics

Branching structures play a pivotal role in the semantics of concurrent systems and the fact that L_{PO} does not completely capture the interplay between nondeterminism and concurrency is not irrelevant. Indeed, several models for concurrency describe the behaviour of a concurrent system by means of tree-like structures, see e.g. Synchronization Trees [Mil89], Nondeterministic Measurement Systems [DDM87], Causal Trees [DD89], Behaviour Structure [RT88]. In this section, we propose two new logics which are interpreted over tree-like frames and permit taking full into account the branching structure of systems by recording the whole history of each of their states. We follow the approach of [DDM87] and unfold the computations of Distributed Transition Systems to obtain a tree-like partial order where the elements of the partial order are computations.

Within these new logics, we make use of two alternatives ways of representing the past (history) of computations. The first temporal language has atomic formulae corresponding to partial ordering observations of computations which are used to explicitly take histories into account. The second temporal language is equipped with a relativized past operator which is used to recover the observations of the computation which has lead to the present state. We will show that the logical equivalences induced by both temporal languages coincide with the concurrency preserving equivalence introduced in [DDM87], which is similar to the history preserving equivalence of [RT88], and has been further investigated in [vGG89] under the name of weak history preserving bisimulation equivalence.

Definition 4.1 (*Tree-like Frames*)
A tree-like frame T is a triple T = (T, ≤, V) where:

- (T, ≤) is a non empty partially ordered set where

  i) T has minimum element denoted by r_T,
  ii) the ordering satisfies: $t_1 \leq t$ and $t_2 \leq t$ implies $t_1 = t_2$ or $t_1 \leq t_2$ or $t_2 \leq t_1$,
  iii) V is the evaluation function associating a subset of T to any atomic formula. ♦

A sub-tree of a tree-like frame T is a tree-like frame T' which consists of a node of T (the minimum of the sub-tree), together with all its descendents in the partial order. In the following, we will identify the sub-tree with its minimum element. The literature shows several types of tree-like frames. A special kind of tree-like frames have been introduced in [DDM87], and called Nondeterministic Measurement Systems.

Definition 4.2 (*Nondeterministic Measurement Systems*)
Given a domain of observations D, a *Nondeterministic Measurement System* is a triple <N, ≤, obs> where:

- <N, ≤> is a tree-like partial order,
- obs : N → D is a monotone function, called observation function. ♦

Nondeterministic measurement systems are obtained by means of the prefix ordering of the computations and by labelling each node with the observation of the corresponding computation. In order to build a nondeterministic measurament system, from a state X of a distributed transition system D_T = (P, A, r), and we consider all the computations of D_T, which have X as initial state. The observation function of the nondeterministic measurament system is just the same of the distributed transition system, The identity computation performed by the state X (consisting just of X) is the minimum of the partial order, and the associated observation is the empty observation ε.

Example 4.3 (*Two Nondeterministic Measurement Systems*)
The figure below shows the NMS derived by the two DTS of the Example 3.9.

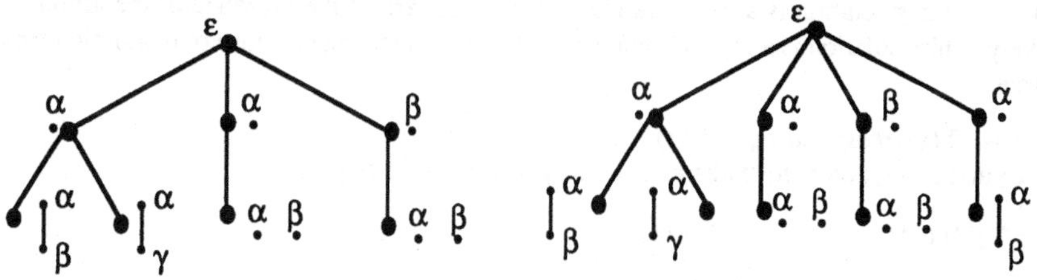

♦

Definition 4.4 (*Paths of Tree-Like Frames and Coverings*)
Let t, t_1 and t_2 be elements of the tree-like frame (T, ≤, V).

- A path through t is a maximal linearly ordered subset of T which includes t.
- Path(t) will be used to denote the set of all the paths through t.
- t_1 *is covered by* t_2, $t_1 \langle t_2$, if and only if $t_1 \leq t_2$, $t_1 \neq t_2$ and for every t, $t_1 \leq t \leq t_2$ implies $t_1 = t$ or $t_2 = t$. ♦

We now introduce the temporal logic L_T which is essentially CTL* of [CES86]. The satisfaction relation differs from the standard presentation of CTL*; since we will not introduce the subset CTL, we will not adopt the distinction between state formula and path formulae and we will follows instead [Sti90].

Definition 4.5 (*L_T Syntax*)
Let φ denote a formula of the language, q, q_1, …, q_n … be atomic formulae and I be a non empty, possibly infinite, set of indices. The syntax of L_T is defined as follows:

$$\varphi ::= q \mid \neg\varphi \mid \vee\{\ \varphi_i \mid i \in I\ \} \mid \forall\varphi \mid X\ \varphi.$$ ♦

Definition 4.6 (*The Satisfaction Relation of L_T*)
Let $\mathbf{T} = (T, \leq, V)$ be a tree-like frame. The satisfaction relation $\models$ is defined as follows:

$\langle\pi, t\rangle \models q$ if and only if $t \in V(q)$ for any atomic formula q;
$\langle\pi, t\rangle \models \neg\varphi$ if and only if $\langle\pi, t\rangle \not\models \varphi$;
$\langle\pi, t\rangle \models \bigvee\{\varphi_i \mid i \in I\}$ if and only if $\langle\pi, t\rangle \models \varphi_k$ for some $k \in I$;
$\langle\pi, t\rangle \models \forall\varphi$ if and only if $\langle\pi', t\rangle \models \varphi$ for every $\pi' \in Path(t)$;
$\langle\pi, t\rangle \models X\varphi$ if and only if there exists $t' \in \pi$ such that $t \langle t'$ and $\langle\pi, t'\rangle \models \varphi$. ♦

It is possible to define within L_T the other classical temporal operators. For instance, the "until" operator U can be defined in terms of the infinitary disjunction and the next operator. Similarly, we can derive the existential path quantifier $\exists$ in terms of the universal path quantifier: $\exists \equiv \neg\forall\neg$.

Definition 4.7 (*Satisfiability*)
Let t be an element of the tree-like frame **T**, and φ a formula of L_T. Then t satisfies φ, $t \models_{\mathbf{T}} \varphi$, if and only if for every $\pi \in Path(t)$ $\langle\pi, t\rangle \models \varphi$. ♦

Definition 4.8 (*L_T Equivalence*)
Let $\mathbf{T}_1$ and $\mathbf{T}_2$ tree-like frames. Then, $r_{T_1} \equiv_{L_T} r_{T_2}$ if and only if $r_{T_1} \models_{\mathbf{T}_1} \varphi \Leftrightarrow r_{T_2} \models_{\mathbf{T}_2} \varphi$. ♦

Definition 4.9 (*Zig-zag and Tree-like Frames*)
Let $\mathbf{T}_1 = (T_1, \leq_1, V_1)$ and $\mathbf{T}_2 = (T_2, \leq_2, V_2)$ be tree-like frames. Let Φ a function from relations to relations on tree-like frames defined as follows:

- $\Phi(Z) = \{<\mathbf{T}_1, \mathbf{T}_2> \mid$
  - i) $r_{T_1} \in V_1(q)$ if and only if $r_{T_2} \in V_2(q)$ for any atomic formula q;
  - ii) $r_{T_1} \langle_1 t_1$ implies that there exists t_2, $r_{T_2} \langle_2 t_2$, such that $<t_1, t_2> \in Z$
  - iii) $r_{T_2} \langle_2 t_2$ implies that there exists t_1, $r_{T_1} \langle_1 t_1$, such that $<t_1, t_2> \in Z\}$
- $\approx = \cup\{ Z \mid Z \subseteq \Phi(Z)\}$ is called *zig-zag* equivalence. ♦

Intuitively, a zig-zag relation is a bisimulation which takes care of the presence of the atomic formulae. Alternatively, a bisimulation is a zig-zag relation for temporal languages whose only atomic formula is the formula true.

Definition 4.10 (*Corresponding Paths*)
Let $\mathbf{T}_1 \approx \mathbf{T}_2$ and $t_1 \approx t_2$; then the paths $\pi_1 \in Path(t_1)$ and $\pi_2 \in Path(t_2)$

$$\pi_1 = r_{T_1};\ t_{1,0};\ t_{1,1};\ \ldots,\ t_{1,p};\ t_1;\ t_{1,p+1};\ \ldots$$

$$\pi_2 = r_{T_2};\ t_{2,0};\ t_{2,1};\ \ldots,\ t_{2,p};\ t_2,\ t_{2,p+1},\ \ldots$$

are called *corresponding paths* if for every $i \geq 1$ $t_{1,p+i} \approx t_{2,p+i}$. ♦

Lemma 4.11
Let $\mathbf{T}_1 \approx \mathbf{T}_2$ and $t_1 \in T_1$, $t_2 \in T_2$, then $t_1 \approx t_2$ implies

(a) For every path $\pi_1 \in Path(t_1)$ there exists a corresponding path $\pi_2 \in Path(t_2)$;
(b) For every path $\pi_2 \in Path(t_2)$ there exists a corresponding path $\pi_1 \in Path(t_1)$. ♦

Theorem 4.12 (*Logical and Zig-Zag Equivalences Coincide*)

$$\mathbf{T}_1 \approx \mathbf{T}_2 \text{ if and only if } r_{T_1} \equiv_{L_T} r_{T_2}$$

Proof.
$\Rightarrow$) Assuming $\mathbf{T}_1 \approx \mathbf{T}_2$, we prove that for any pair of elements t_1 and t_2 of $\mathbf{T}_1$ and $\mathbf{T}_2$ such that $t_1 \approx t_2$, we have $\langle\pi_1, t_1\rangle \models \varphi$ if and only if $\langle\pi_2, t_2\rangle \models \varphi$ where π_1 and π_2 are corresponding paths. The proof is by induction of the structure of the formula φ.

• $\varphi = q$ where q is an atomic formula. We have that $\langle\pi_1, t_1\rangle \models q$ if and only if $t_1 \in V(q)$. By definition of zig-zag equivalence we have that $t_1 \in V_1(q)$ if and only if $t_2 \in V_2(q)$ for any atomic formula q, and therefore $\langle\pi_2, t_2\rangle \models q$.

Inductive step (we only consider non-trivial cases).

• $\varphi = \forall\varphi'$. Let us suppose that $\langle\pi_1, t_1\rangle \models \forall\varphi'$ but $\langle\pi_2, t_2\rangle \not\models \forall\varphi'$. By definition $\langle\pi_2, t_2\rangle \not\models \forall\varphi'$ if and only if there exists, at least, a path $\pi'_2 \in \text{Path}(t_2)$ such that $\langle\pi'_2, t_2\rangle \not\models \varphi'$. Therefore, by Lemma 4.11, given a path $\pi'_2 \in \text{Path}(t_2)$ such that $\langle\pi'_2, t_2\rangle \models \varphi'$, there exists a corresponding path $\pi'_1 \in \text{Path}(t_1)$.

By the induction hypothesis, $\langle\pi'_1, t_1\rangle \models \varphi'$ if and only if $\langle\pi'_2, t_2\rangle \models \varphi'$. We have a contradiction because there exists, a path $\pi'_1 \in \text{Path}(t_1)$ such that $\langle\pi'_1, t_1\rangle \not\models \varphi'$. We can use the same argument to prove the other direction of the implication.

• $\varphi = X\,\varphi'$. By definition, we have $\langle\pi_1, t_1\rangle \models X\,\varphi'$ if and only if there exists exists $t' \in \pi_1$, $t_1 \langle t'$ and $\langle\pi_1, t'\rangle \models \varphi'$. Now, because π_1 and π_2 are corresponding paths we can apply the inductive hypothesis and therefore we have that there exists t", $t'' \in \pi_2$, $t_2 \langle t''$, such that $\langle\pi_2, t''\rangle \models \varphi'$, and therefore $\langle\pi_2, t_2\rangle \models X\,\varphi'$.

$\Leftarrow$) In order to prove this direction, we show that $\equiv_{Lp}$ is a zig-zag between tree-like frames. The proof goes by reduction ad absurdum. Suppose $\equiv_{Lp}$ is not a zig-zag. By definition this may arise in two cases:

a) There exists an atomic formula q such that $r_{T1} \in V_1(q)$ and $r_{T2} \notin V_2(q)$. We have $r_{T1} \models q$ while $r_{T2} \not\models q$ and this fact contradicts the hypothesis that $r_{T1} \equiv_{Lp} r_{T2}$.

b) There exists an element t of T_1, $r_{T1} \langle_1 t$, such that for every element t' of T_2, $r_{T2} \langle_2 t'$ it does not hold that $t \equiv_{Lp} t'$. Let $\{t' | r_{T2} \langle_2 t'\} = \{t_1, t_2, \ldots, t_i, \ldots\}$ be the set of such elements. Thus, we have that for each index i there exists a formula φ_i such that $t \not\models \varphi_i$ and $t_i \models \varphi_i$. Because of this, we have that $r_{T2} \models \forall X \bigvee_i \varphi_i$. On the other hand, $r_{T1} \not\models \forall X \bigvee_i \varphi_i$. We have thus found two formulas that can distinguish between r_{T1} and r_{T2} and the claim follows. ♦

The above theorem shows that, like L_{PO}, the equivalence induced by L_T has a direct correspondence with an operational model. Indeed, L_T completely characterizes the concurrency preserving equivalence which relies on Nondeterministic Measurement Systems. The two examples below express that, in the case of partial ordering observations, the equivalences induced by L_T and L_{PO} are incomparable. Moreover, when interleaving observations are assumed, the two logics are equivalent, i.e. the two equivalences collapse.

Example 4.13 (*Comparing L_{PO} and L_T: L_{PO} does not imply L_T*)
L_T is able to characterize the interplay between nondeterminism and concurrency. Let us consider the nondeterministic measurement systems of Example 4.3. Since the atomic formulae are indeed the observations, we will write $\vartheta(d)$ to indicate the atomic formula interpreted by the observation of d. Therefore, we can see that the following formula

$$\varphi = \exists(X\,\vartheta(\alpha) \wedge \forall X\,\vartheta(\alpha;\beta))$$

is able to differentiate the process the two NMS. Formula φ expresses that there exists a path π and a (future) state s in the path π, where an α-action can be observed, from the state s only a β-action is possible ($\langle\pi, s\rangle \models \forall X\,\vartheta(\alpha;\beta)$). Clearly, the nondeterministic measurement systems on the right hand side of the figure above satisfies the formula φ, while the one on the left cannot. ♦

Example 4.14 (*Comparing L_{PO} and L_T: L_T does not imply L_{PO}*)
It can be shown that, in the case of partial ordering observations there exist systems which are not equivalent according to pomset bisimulation but are equivalent according to history preserving bisimulation. The two nets below, inspired by a counterexample of Alex Rabinovich which has been reported in [vGG89], can be used to prove the claim.

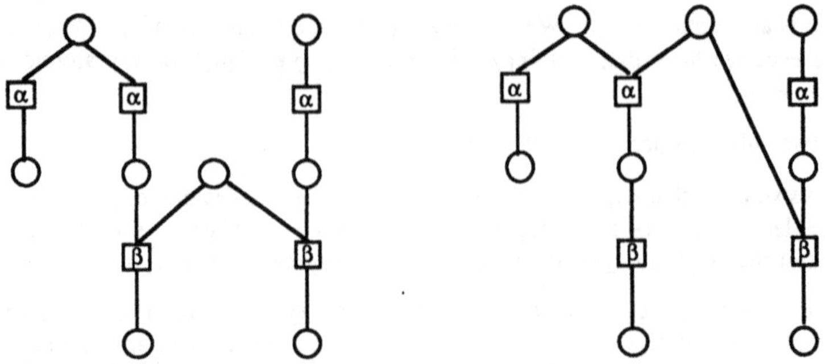

The formula of L_{PO},

$$\varphi_1 = \langle\alpha\rangle\, (\langle\alpha\, ;\, \beta\rangle \text{ true} \vee \langle\alpha \parallel \beta\rangle \text{ true}),$$

is satisfied by the net on the left, and not by that on the right.

Similarly, the formula of L_{PO},

$$\varphi_2 = \langle\alpha\rangle\, [\alpha\, ;\, \beta] \text{ false}$$

is satisfied by the net on the right, but not by that on the left.

Moreover, there does not exist any formula of L_T which is is able to distinguish between (the NMS derived by) the two nets above. The reason of the problem is that within a partial order identity of events (partial orders are defined up to isomorphism) is lost, and therefore different histories may lead to isomorphic partial orders, i.e. to satisfaction of the same atomic formula.

We have already remarked that atomic formulae of L_T have the role of recording computation histories. This corresponds to considering an *integral description* of computations. In this perspective, one can only observe the global outcome of a computation, and not what is left at each stage. The latter view, i.e. the observation of gradual advances of computations, underlies the structure of the modalities of L_{PO}. This is why L_{PO} can distinguish between two computations which have the same global observation while L_T cannot. Indeed, the requirement that only the whole history of a state has to be considered hinders the different choices which had to be taken while progressing within the computation.

We now provide an alternative logical characterization of history bisimulation equivalence. We will now introduce a logic which will be interpreted over tree-like frames, and explicitly assume that the element of tree-like frames are computations. The distinguishing feature of this new logic is the presence of the relativized past operator $S(\mathrm{d})\, \varphi$ expressing that φ is a property of an intermediate stage of the computation.

In the following we will use U(X) to indicate the nondeterministic measurement system derived from X which consists of all the computation of a distributed transition system having X as initial states. Moreover, the improper (identity) computation consisting of just the state X we will denoted by idle(X).

Definition 4.15 (*The Observational Logic L_P*)
Let φ denote any formula of the language, and let d any element of the domain of observations.

The syntax of the observational logic L_P is defined as follows.

$$\varphi ::= \text{true} \mid \neg\varphi \mid \bigvee\{\, \varphi_i \mid i \in I \,\} \mid \forall\varphi \mid X\varphi \mid S(\mathrm{d})\, \varphi$$

where I is a non empty, possibly infinite, set of indices. ♦

Definition 4.16 (*The Satisfaction Relation*)
The satisfaction relation is defined as follows

    $\langle \pi, \sigma \rangle \vDash$ true for any computation σ;

    $\langle \pi, \sigma \rangle \vDash \neg\varphi$ if and only if not $\langle \pi, \sigma \rangle \vDash \varphi$;

    $\langle \pi, \sigma \rangle \vDash \bigvee \{ \varphi_i \mid i \in I \}$ if and only if $\langle \pi, \sigma \rangle \vDash \varphi_k$ for some $k \in I$;

    $\langle \pi, \sigma \rangle \vDash \forall\varphi$ if and only if $\langle \pi', \sigma \rangle \vDash \varphi$ for every $\pi' \in Path(\sigma)$;

    $\langle \pi, \sigma \rangle \vDash X\varphi$ if and only if there exists $\sigma' \in \pi$, $\sigma \langle \sigma'$, and $\langle \pi, \sigma' \rangle \vDash \varphi$;

    $\langle \pi, \sigma \rangle \vDash S(d)\,\varphi$ if and only if there exists $\sigma' \in \pi$, $\sigma = \sigma'\sigma''$, for some computation σ''
        such that $init(\sigma'') = term(\sigma')$, $term(\sigma'') = term(\sigma)$, $obs(\sigma'') = d$, and $\langle \pi, \sigma' \rangle \vDash \varphi$.   ◆

We can define within Lp a relativized next operator $X(\alpha)$, which holds if we the next step is an action labelled by α: $X(\alpha) \equiv XS(\alpha)X$. It is easy to prove that

$$\langle \pi, \sigma \rangle \vDash X(\alpha)\varphi \text{ if and only if } \exists\, \sigma', \sigma' = \sigma\, Z\text{—}\alpha\text{—}{>}WY, \text{ and } \langle \pi, \sigma' \rangle \vDash \varphi.$$

Definition 4.17 (*Satisfiability*)
We say that σ satisfies the formula φ, $\sigma \vDash_U \varphi$, if and only if $\langle \pi, \sigma \rangle \vDash \varphi$ for every $\pi \in Path(\sigma)$.   ◆

Definition 4.18 (*Lp Equivalence*)
$U(X_1) \equiv_{Lp} U(X_2)$ if and only if, for every φ of L_T, $idle(X_1) \vDash_U \varphi \Leftrightarrow idle(X_2) \vDash_U \varphi$.   ◆

The logic Lp is able to correctly capture the interplay between nondeterminism and concurrency. If we consider the distributed transition systems of the Example 3.9 and their state $\{p, q\}$, we have:

$$idle(\{p, q\}) \vDash_{U2(\{p,q\})} \exists\, X(\alpha)\, X(\beta)\, S(\alpha\,;\,\beta)\,(X(\alpha) \,\forall\, (X(\alpha) \text{ true} \wedge \neg X(\gamma) \text{ false})$$

$$idle(\{p, q\}) \nvDash_{U1(\{p,q\})} \exists\, X(\alpha)\, X(\beta)\, S(\alpha\,;\,\beta)\,(X(\alpha) \,\forall\, (X(\alpha) \text{ true} \wedge \neg X(\gamma) \text{ false}).$$

Theorem 4.19
The equivalence $\equiv_{LT}$ coincides with the equivalence $\equiv_{Lp}$
Proof(outline).
Let us assume that $U(X_1) \equiv_{Lp} U(X_2)$. The proof is by induction on the structure of the formula φ of Lp. The two logical languages differ because of the presence of the past operator in Lp (and because of the presence of sophisticated atomic formulae in L_T), the key point of the proof is to show that the past operator $S(d)$ takes care of the observations of the computations. We have that $\langle \pi, \sigma \rangle \vDash S(d)$true if and only if $obs(\sigma) = d$, but, in the case of the logic L_T this means that the atomic formula $\vartheta(d) \in V(\sigma)$, and this implies that $\langle \pi, \sigma \rangle \vDash \vartheta(d)$.   ◆

The next theorem shows role of the relativized past operator in the case of interleaving observations.

Theorem 4.20
Let φ be any formula of Lp where the since operator is relativized only with atomic actions and let $U(X_1)$ and $U(X_2)$ be non deterministic measurament systems with an interleaving observation function.

$$U(X_1) \equiv_{Lp} U(X_2) \text{ if and only if } idle(X_1) \vDash_U \varphi \text{ if and only if } idle(X_2) \vDash_U \varphi$$

Proof.
The key idea is to show that, in the case of interleaving observations, the full expressive power of the past operator can be simulated in terms of sequence of relativized next. Now, by hypothesis we we have that

$$\langle \pi_1, \sigma_1 \rangle \vDash \varphi \text{ if and only if } \langle \pi_2, \sigma_2 \rangle \vDash \varphi, \text{ for any formula } \varphi$$

where π_1 and π_2 are corresponding paths in $U(X_1)$ and $U(X_2)$, respectively. We have that

$$\langle \pi_1, \sigma_1 \rangle \vDash S(d)\varphi \text{ if and only if } \langle \pi_2, \sigma_2 \rangle \vDash S(d)\varphi.$$

Therefore, $\langle \pi_1, \sigma_1 \rangle \vDash S(d)\varphi$ if and only if there exists $\sigma' \in \pi$, $\sigma_1 = \sigma\sigma_i$, $obs(\sigma_i) = d$, and $\langle \pi, \sigma' \rangle \vDash \varphi$, this holds if and only if $\langle \pi_2, \sigma_2 \rangle \models S(d)\varphi$ if and only if there exists $\sigma'' \in \pi$, $\sigma_2 = \sigma'\sigma_j$, $obs(\sigma_j) = d$, and $\langle \pi, \sigma'' \rangle \models \varphi$. But, in the case of interleaving observations, the observation d corresponds to the sequence of actions of the rewrite rule of the computation, i.e. $d = \alpha_1 \alpha_2 \dots \alpha_n$, thus

$\langle \pi_1, \sigma_1 \rangle \models S(d)\varphi$ if and only if $\langle \pi_1, \sigma' \rangle \models X(\alpha_1) X(\alpha_2) \dots X(\alpha_n) \wedge \varphi$ and this holds if and only if

$\langle \pi_2, \sigma'' \rangle \models X(\alpha_1) X(\alpha_2) \dots X(\alpha_n) \wedge \varphi$. From this observation the theorem follows. ♦

It is worth remarking that the crucial point of the proof of the above theorem is that the a relativized next operator is sufficient to get interleaving observations, i.e. sequences of actions. Indeed, it is easy to see that $\forall X(\alpha)$ is equivalent to $[\alpha]$, i.e. the modality of the Hennessy-Milner Logic [HM85]. This should suggest that the same construction cannot be immediately generalized when partial ordering observations are assumed. Indeed, while the string concatenation is a uniquely defined function, it is difficult to devise a function for uniquely composing two partial orders; it is not at all evident whether the final and initial elements of the first and second partial ordering respectively have to be considered as causally related or as concurrent.

Conclusions

In this paper, we have introduced a general framework for interpreting logics which permit reasoning about observable properties of computations. We have shown that known operational models for true concurrency fit naturally into this framework, and that bisimulation equivalences via partial orders can be elegantly characterized in a logical setting. These results vindicate the operational models for true concurrency based on rewriting systems and the associated equivalences. An additional contribution of our investigation is that we reconcile the interleaving and the true concurrency views into a uniform logical framework.

We have focussed on a class of observation functions which does not assume that computations contain unobservable actions. In other words, we do not take into account actions which has the special status of being invisible (like Milner's τ-action). Thus, the characterization results of the true concurrency equivalences holds in the so-called strong version. We can easily generalize the characterization theorem of the pomset bisimulation to cope with unobservable actions and obtain τ-forgetful (weak) partial ordering bisimulation; it is sufficient to add a further step to the observation function which forgets invisible actions. The operational counterpart of L_P and L_T with weak observations is not immediate, this investigation will be the subject of future works. We conjecture that the generalization of the equivalence induced by the logic L_T via τ-forgetful partial ordering observations leads to a partial ordering version of branching bisimulation equivalence [vGW89]. Indeed, the interleaving branching bisimulation has been proved to be in full agreement with an extension of HML with past operators [DV90].

Finally, the logical framework will be used to give an axiomatic account of true concurrency. In this respect, the axiomatization of the logic L_D requires defining composition operations for labelled partial orders, which as mentioned above is not immediate. However, it is worth noting that the idea of considering observations as atomic formulae makes the search for an axiomatic base easier.

Other logics for truly concurrent distributed systems have been proposed by a number of researchers, see [KP87, LT87, Pen88] for some examples. In those papers, the stress is more concentrated on capturing distributed aspects of systems, on obtaining compositional logical specifications and on equipping the logics with complete proof systems.

Acknowledgements

We wish to thank the referees for detailed comments and helpful suggestions.

References

[BC88] Boudol,G. and Castellani,I. Concurrency and Atomicity. *Theoret. Comput. Sci.*, **59**, 1988, pp. 25-84

[BCG88] Browne,M.C., Clarke,E.M.and Grümberg,O. Characterizing Finite Kripke Structure in Propositional Temporal Logic, *Theoret. Comput. Sci.*, **59**, 1988, pp. 115-131

[CES86] Clarke,E., Emerson,A., Sistla,P. Automatic Verifications of Finite State Concurrent Systems using Temporal Logic Specifications, *ACM TOPLAS*, **8**, 1986, pp. 244-263.

[DD89] Darondeau,P. and Degano,P. Causal Trees, in proceedings ICALP '89, LNCS, **372**, pp.234-248, 1989.

[DDM87] Degano,P., De Nicola,R. and Montanari,U. Observational Equivalences for Concurrency Models, in *Formal Description of Programming Concepts III*, M. Wirsing, ed., North Holland,1987, pp. 105-132.

[DDM88] Degano,P., De Nicola,R. and Montanari,U. A Partial Ordering Semantics for CCS, Technical Report, Dipartmento di Informatica, Università di Pisa, 1988, To appear in *Theoret. Comput. Sci.*.

[DDM89] Degano,P., De Nicola,R. and Montanari,U. Partial Ordering Descriptions and Observations of Nondeterministic Concurrent Processes, in [REX89].

[DeN87] De Nicola,R. Extensional Equivalences for Transition Systems, *Acta Informatica*, **24**, 1987, pp. 211-237.

[DM87] Degano,P. and Montanari,U. Concurrent Histories: A Basis for Observing Distributed Systems, *Journal of Computer and System Sciences*, **34**, 1987, pp. 442-461.

[DV90] De Nicola,R. and Vaandrager,F. Three Logics for Branching Bisimulations, IEEE LICS Conference, 1990

[vGG89] van Glabbeek,R. and Goltz,U. Equivalence Notions for Concurrent Systems and Refinement of Actions, in proceeding MFCS '89, LNCS, **379**, 1989.

[vGW89] van Glabbeek,R. and Weijland,P. Branching Time and Abstraction in Bisimulation Semantics, in Information Processing 89, (Ritter ed.) North Holland, 1989.

[Hoa85] Hoaare,C.A.R. Communicating Sequential Processes, Prentice Hall, 1985

[HM85] Hennessy,M. and Milner,R. Algebraic Laws for Nondeterminism and Concurrency, *Journal of ACM*, **32**, 1985.

[HS85] Hennessy, M. and Stirling,C. The Power of Future Perfect in Program Logics, *Info and Co.*, 1985, pp. 23-52.

[KP87] Katz,S. and Peled,D. Interleaving set Temporal Logic, in 6th ACM Symp. on Distributed Computing, 1987.

[Kel76] Keller, R., *Formal Verification of Parallel Programs*, Com. ACM, 7, 1976,

[LT87] Lodaya,K and Thiagarajan,P.S. A Modal Logic for a Subclass of Event Structures, CALP '87, LNCS, **267**, pp.290-303, 1987.

[LRT89] Lodaya,K, Ramanujam, R. and Thiagarajan,P.S. A Logic for Distributed Systems, in [REX89].

[Mil89] Milner,R. Communication and Concurrency, Prentice Hall 1989.

[NPW81] Nielsen,M., Plotkin,G.and Winskel,G. Petri Nets, Event Structures and Domains, Part 1, *Theoret. Comput. Sci.*, **13**, 1981, pp.85-108.

[Par81] Park,D. Concurrency and Automata on Infinite Sequences, in Proc. *GI*, LNCS, **104**, 1981, pp. 167-183.

[Pen88] Penczek,W. A Temporal Logic for Event Structures, *Fundamenta Informaticae*, **11**, 1988, pp. 297-326.

[Pra86] Pratt,V. Modelling Concurrency with Partial Orders, *International Journal of Parallel Programming*, **15**, 1986, pp. 33-71.

[Rei85] Reisig,W. Petri Nets, An Introduction. EATCS Monographs in Computer Science, Springer Verlag, 1985.

[Rei89] Reisig,W. Towards a Temporal Logic of Causality and Choice in Distributed Systems in [REX89].

[REX89] Linear Time, Branching Time and Partial Order in Logics and Models for Concurrency, deBakker, deRoever and Rozenberg eds., LNCS, **354**, 1988.

[RT88] Rabinovich,A. and Trakhtembrot,B. Behaviour Structures and Nets, *Fundamenta Informaticae* , 1988.

[Sti90] Stirling,C. Modal and Temporal Logics, In Handbook of Logic in Computer Science, Vol I, Abramsky ed., to appear, 1989.

Distributed Reset

(Extended Abstract)

Anish ARORA *Mohamed GOUDA*

Department of Computer Sciences, The University of Texas at Austin†

Microelectronics and Computer Technology Corporation, Austin, TX, USA

Abstract

We describe a reset subsystem that can be embedded in an arbitrary distributed system in order to allow the system processes to reset the system when necessary. The effect of each reset is to start the system in a global state that is reachable from a predefined state. Our reset subsystem has a number of nice features: it is modular, layered, self-stabilizing and can tolerate the failures and subsequent repairs of processes and channels. There are three main components in our design of the reset subsystem: a leader election, a spanning tree construction, and a diffusing computation. Each of these components is both self-stabilizing and tolerant of process and channel failures and repairs; thus, our design of each component is more robust than earlier designs of similar components.

Categories and Subject Descriptors: C.2.4 [Computer Communication Systems]: Distributed Systems–*distributed applications, network operating systems;* D.1.3 [Programming Techniques]: Concurrent Programming; D.4.5 [Operating Systems]: Reliability–*fault-tolerance, verification;* G.2.2 [Discrete Mathematics]: Graph theory–*trees, graph algorithms.*

General Terms: Algorithms, Reliability.

Additional Key Words and Phrases: Self-stabilization, spanning trees, diffusing computations.

†Email Address: anish@cs.utexas.edu, gouda@cs.utexas.edu

1 Introduction

We describe in this paper how to "augment" an arbitrary distributed system so that each of its processes can, when deemed necessary, reset the system to a predefined global state. The augmentation does not introduce new processes or new communication channels to the system. It merely introduces additional modules to the existing processes. The added modules, communicating with one another over existing channels, comprise what we call the reset subsystem.

Ideally, resetting a distributed system to a given global state implies resuming the execution of the system starting from the given state. With this characterization, however, each reset of a distributed system can be achieved only by a "global freeze" of the system. This seems rather limiting and, in many applications, more strict than needed. Therefore, we adopt the following, more lax, characterization: resetting a distributed system to a given global state implies resuming the execution of the system from a global state that is reachable, by some system computation, from the given global state.

There are many occasions in which it is desirable for some processes in a distributed system to initiate resets; for example,

- *Reconfiguration*: When the system is reconfigured, for instance, by adding processes or channels to it, some process in the system can be signaled to initiate a reset of the system to an appropriate "initial state".
- *Mode Change*: The system can be designed to execute in different modes or phases. If this is the case, then changing the current mode of execution can be achieved by resetting the system to an appropriate global state of the next mode.
- *Coordination Loss*: When a process observes unexpected behavior from other processes, it recognizes that the coordination between the processes in the system has been lost. In such a situation, coordination can be regained by a reset.
- *Periodic Maintenance*: The system can be designed such that a designated process periodically initiates a reset as a precaution, in case the current global state of the system has deviated from the global system invariant.

In many of these reset applications, the distributed system in question is subject to failures during system execution. For instance, memory may be lost, transient failures may occur, processes may fail or channels may break down. As these failures can occur while a reset is in progress, we are led to designing a reset subsystem that is fault-tolerant; in particular, it can tolerate the loss of coordination between different processes in the system (which may be caused by transient failures or memory loss) and, also, can tolerate the fail-stop failures and subsequent repairs of processes and channels.

The ability to regain coordination when lost is achieved by making the reset subsystem *self-stabilizing* in the following sense. If the reset subsystem is at a global state in which coordination between processes is lost, then the reset subsystem is guaranteed to reach, within a finite number of steps, a global state in which coordination is restored. Once coordination is restored, it is maintained unless a later failure causes it to be lost again, and the cycle repeats [BGW89,BP89,BGM88]. The ability to tolerate fail-stop failures and subsequent repairs of processes and channels is achieved by allowing each process and channel in the system to be either "up" or "down" and by ensuring that the ability of the system to self-stabilize is not affected by which processes or channels are "up" or "down".

Our reset subsystem is designed in a simple, modular, and layered manner. The design consists of three major components: a leader election, a spanning tree construction, and a diffusing computation. Each of these components is self-stabilizing and can tolerate process and channel failures and repairs. These features distinguish our design of these components from earlier designs [DS80,SG87,YK88,DIM89,T89].

The rest of the paper is organized as follows. In the next section, we describe the layered structure of our reset subsystem. This structure consists of three layers: a (spanning) tree correction layer, a wave correction layer, and an application layer. These three layers are discussed in Sections 3, 4, and 5 respectively. In Section 6, we discuss implementation issues; in particular, we exhibit bounded, low atomicity implementations of each layer. Finally, we make concluding remarks in Section 7.

2 Layers of the Reset Subsystem

We make the following assumptions concerning the distributed system to be augmented by our reset subsystem. The system consists of K processes named $P.1$, ... , $P.K$. At each instant, each process is either *up* or *down*, and there is a binary, non-reflexive, and symmetric relation defined over the up processes. We call this relation the *adjacency relation*. Only adjacent processes can communicate with one another.

The set of up processes and the adjacency relation defined over them can change with time. For simplicity, however, we assume that the adjacency relation never partitions the up processes in the system. (Clearly, if partitioning does occur, then any reset request initiated in a partition will result in resetting the global state of only that partition.)

Each process $P.i$ in the system consists of two modules *adj.i* and *appl.i*; see Figure 0a. The task of module *adj.i* is to maintain a set $N.i$ of the indices of all processes adjacent to $P.i$. The specific details of implementing *adj.i* are outside the scope of this paper. (One possibility, though, is that each *adj.i* periodically checks every potentially adjacent process *P.j* and uses a timeout to determine whether or not *P.j* should be in *N.i*.) The other module, *appl.i*, is application specific; it communicates only with the processes whose indices are in *N.i*.

Augmenting such a distributed system with a reset subsystem consists of adding two modules, *tree.i* and *wave.i*, to each process *P.i* in the system; see Figure 0b. The *tree.i* modules of adjacent processes communicate in order to maintain a rooted spanning tree that involves all the up processes in the system. Henceforth, the two terms "process" and "up process" are used interchangeably. The constructed tree is maintained to be consistent with the current adjacency relation of the system; thus, any changes in the adjacency relation are eventually followed by corresponding changes in the spanning tree. Each *tree.i* module keeps the index of its "father" process, *f.i*, in the tree; this information is used by the local *wave.i* module in executing a distributed reset.

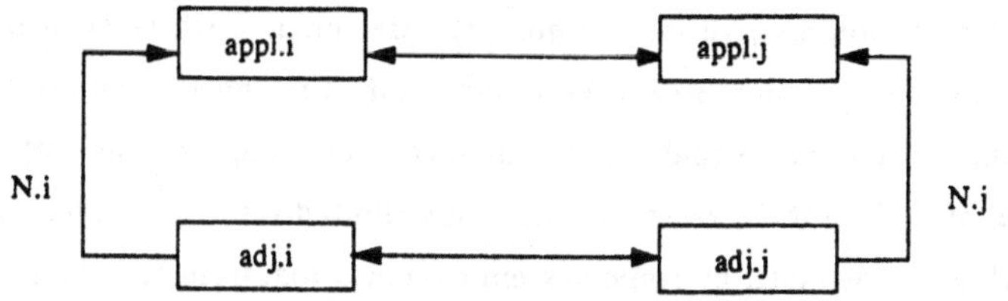

a. The given system.

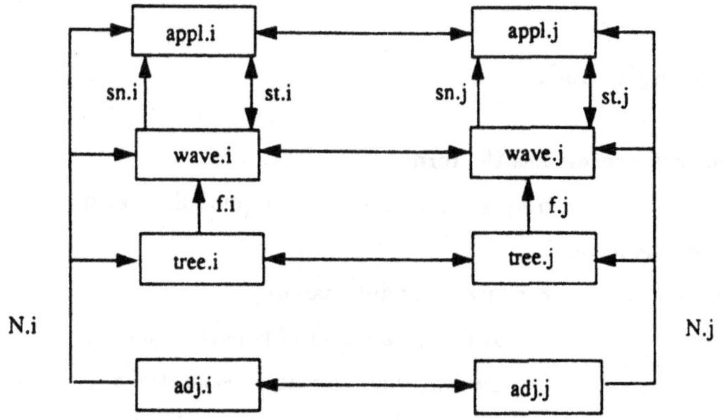

b. The augmented system.

Figure 0.

A distributed reset is executed by the *wave.i* modules in three phases or "waves". In the first phase, some *appl.i* requests a system reset from its local *wave.i* which forwards the request to the root of the spanning tree. If other reset requests are made at other processes, then these requests are also forwarded to the root process, and it is convenient to think of all these requests as forming one "request wave". In the second phase, module *wave.i* in the root process receives the request wave, resets the state of its local *appl.i*, and initiates a "reset wave" that travels down the spanning tree and causes the *wave.j* module of each encountered process to reset the state of its local *appl.j*. When the reset wave reaches a leaf process it is reflected as a "completion wave" that travels back to the root process; this wave comprises the third phase. Finally, when the completion wave reaches the root, the reset is complete, and a new request wave can be started whenever some *appl.i* deems necessary.

From the above description, it follows that the states of different *appl.i* modules are reset at different times within the same distributed reset. This can cause a problem if some *appl.i* whose state has been reset communicates with an adjacent *appl.j* whose state has not yet been reset. To avoid this problem, we provide a session number *sn.i* in each *appl.i*. In a global state, where no distributed reset is in progress, all session numbers are equal. Each reset of the state of *appl.i* is accompanied by incrementing *sn.i*. We then require that no two adjacent *appl.i* modules communicate unless they have equal session numbers. This requirement suffices to ensure our characterization of a distributed reset; that is, a distributed reset to a given global state yields a global state that is reachable, by some system computation, from the given global state.

The *tree.i* modules in different processes constitute the tree correction layer discussed in Section 3. The *wave.i* modules constitute the wave correction layer discussed in Section 4. The *appl.i* modules constitute the application layer discussed in Section 5.

2.1 Programming Notation

The program of each process has the form

begin ⟨module⟩ ▯ ... ▯ ⟨module⟩ **end**

Each module is of the form

module ⟨module name⟩
    shared var ⟨variable declarations⟩ ;
    owned var ⟨variable declarations⟩ ;
    parameter ⟨parameter declarations⟩ ;
    begin
        ⟨action⟩ ▯ ... ▯ ⟨action⟩
    end

Thus, a module is defined by a set of variables, shared or owned, a set of parameters, and a set of actions. Each of these is defined in some detail next.

Each variable in the variable set of a module is either *owned* or *shared*. An owned variable is one that can be updated (i.e., written) by only one module in the process. A shared variable is one that can be updated by two or more modules in the process. All variables can be read by each module in the process and by each module in adjacent processes.

Each parameter in the parameter set of a module ranges over a finite domain. The function of a parameter is to define a set of actions as one parameterized action. For example, let j be a parameter whose value is 0, 1 or 2; then the parameterized action $act.j$ in the action set of a module abbreviates the following set of three actions.

$$act.(j := 0) \;[]\; act.(j := 1) \;[]\; act.(j := 2)$$

Each action in the action set of a module has the form

$$\langle \text{guard} \rangle \quad \longrightarrow \quad \langle \text{assignment statement} \rangle$$

A guard is a boolean expression over the variables and parameters in the module, and the variables of one adjacent process. An assignment statement updates one or more variables in the module.

The operational semantics for a system of such processes is as follows. A *state* of the system is defined by a value for every variable in the up processes of the system. An action whose guard is true at some state is said to be *enabled* at that state. We assume fair, nondeterministic interleaving semantics: a computation of the system is a fair sequence of system steps. In each step, some action that is enabled at the current state is executed, thereby yielding the next state. The fairness of a computation means that each continuously enabled action is eventually executed in the computation [F86].

3 The Tree Correction Layer

The task of the tree correction layer is to continually maintain a rooted spanning tree. Recall that this task is complicated by the fact that the system is subject to changes in the set of up processes and the adjacency relation. In the solution described next, we account for this fact by ensuring that the tree correction layer can meet its task irrespective of the initial state of the layer.

We represent the rooted spanning tree by associating a father process with each up process in the system. The index of the father of each process $P.i$ is maintained in a variable $f.i$. Since the initial state of the layer is arbitrary, the following two scenarios of the father relation between processes can exist in the initial state. For one, more than one process may be its own father. And two, the initial father relation between processes may include cycles. To rectify such scenarios, we introduce two variables *root.i* and *d.i* in each process *P.i*. Variable *root.i* contains the index of the process that *P.i* considers to be the root, and *d.i* contains the current distance between *P.i* and its root via the father process.

To take care of the first scenario, we choose to give priority to processes with higher root values. This is achieved as follows. If *root.i* in a process *P.i* is higher than *root.j* in an adjacent process *P.j*, then module *tree.i* assigns the value of *root.j* to *root.i*, and makes process *P.j* the father of *P.i*. Also, if the index i of a process *P.i* exceeds *root.i*, then module *tree.i* assigns the value i to *root.i* and makes process *P.i* its own father. The net effect of these actions is that eventually the value of *root.i* in each process *P.i* is the maximum of process indices of all up processes.

To take care of the second scenario, we note that the length of each path in the adjacency graph is bounded by $K - 1$, where K is the maximum possible number of up processes in the system. Based on this observation, we require that each process *P.i* whose father is $P.j, j \neq i$, maintain *d.i*, the distance from *P.i* to the root, to be one more than the distance from the father process to the root (i.e., *d.j*). Now, if the father relationship between processes includes a cycle then, due to the preceding requirement, the *d.i* values of the processes along the cycle get bumped up repeatedly. Eventually, some *d.i* value exceeds $K - 1$ and a cycle is detected. The cycle is then broken by making the detecting process its own father.

An informal description of the program for module *tree.i* in each process *P.i* now follows. Module *tree.i* has three actions. The first action corrects the state of the module upon detecting an inconsistency in its local state. This can happen in four situations. Variable *root.i* may be less than i or a cycle may be detected ($d.i \geq K$)or the father of *P.i* may be inconsistent ($f.i \notin (N.i \cup \{i\})$) or, finally, *P.i* may be its own father but either *d.i* or *root.i* may be incorrect. In each of these situations, *P.i* is established as its own father, *root.i* is set to i, and *d.i* is set to 0.

The second action is used to correct the state of the module based on the state of its father process *P.j*, provided *P.j* is adjacent to *P.i*. In this case, the root value of *P.j* is assigned to *P.i* and, due to the method of cycle detection, *d.i* is set to $d.j + 1$.

Finally, the last action is used to change the father of *P.i*. If there is an adjacent process *P.j* such that $root.i < root.j$, then priority is given to *P.j*; i.e., *root.i* is set to *root.j*. Also, *P.j* is made the father of *P.i* and *d.i* is set to $d.j + 1$.

Module *tree.i* is given in Figure 1.

module $tree.i\ (i : 1 \,..\, K)$
owned var $root.i, f.i : 1 \,..\, K;$
$d.i$: **integer**;
parameter $j : 1 \,..\, K;$

begin

$$(root.i < i) \lor (f.i = i \land (root.i \neq i \lor d.i \neq 0)) \lor (f.i \notin (N.i \cup \{i\}) \lor d.i \geq K) \longrightarrow root.i, f.i, d.i := i, i, 0$$

$[\!]$

$$f.i = j \land j \in N.i \land d.j < K \land (root.i \neq root.j \lor d.i \neq d.j+1) \longrightarrow root.i, d.i := root.j, d.j+1$$

$[\!]$

$$(root.i < root.j \land j \in N.i \land d.j < K) \lor (root.i = root.j \land j \in N.i \land d.j+1 < d.i) \longrightarrow root.i, f.i, d.i := root.j, j, d.j+1$$

end

Figure 1: Module *tree.i*

The correctness proof of the tree correction layer involves showing that upon starting at an arbitrary state, the tree correction layer is guaranteed to eventually reach a state in which a rooted spanning tree is correctly established. In this state, for each process $P.i$, the $root.i$ variable equals the highest index among all up processes, $f.i$ is such that some minimal length path between the process and the root in the adjacency graph passes through the father, and $d.i$ equals length of this path. The correctness proof is relegated to the full paper [AG90].

To conclude this section, we remark that the problems of leader election and spanning tree construction, have received considerable attention in the literature (see, for example, [FLP85], [SG87] ,[T89], [YK88]). Most of these algorithms, however, are based on the assumption that all processes start execution in some designated initial state. This restriction is severe for our purpose, and we have lifted it by designing the tree correction layer to be self-stabilizing; i.e., insensitive to the initial state. We note that, a self-stabilizing spanning tree algorithm has been recently described in [DIM89]. However, the algorithm in [DIM89] is based on the simplifying assumption that, at all times, there exists a special process which knows that it is the root. We have not make this assumption: if a root process fails, then the remaining up process of highest index among all up processes is eventually elected to be the new root.

4 The Wave Correction Layer

As outlined in Section 2, the task of the wave correction layer is to perform a diffusing computation in order to reset the state of each *appl.i* module in the system. The diffusing computation uses the spanning tree maintained by the tree correction layer and consists of three phases. In the first phase, some *appl.i* module requests its local *wave.i* to initiate a global reset; the request is propagated by the wave modules along the spanning tree path from process *P.i* to the tree root *P.j*. In the second phase, module *wave.j* in the tree root resets the state of its local *appl.j* and initiates a reset wave that propagates along the tree towards the leaves; whenever the reset wave reaches a process *P.k* the local *wave.k* module resets the state of its local *appl.k*. In the third phase, after the reset wave reaches the tree leaves it is reflected as a completion wave that is propagated along the tree to the root; the diffusing computation is complete when the completion wave reaches the root,

The interface between each *wave.i* module and its local *appl.i* consists of two variables *sn.i* and *st.i*. Variable *sn.i* is an integer that defines the current session number for *appl.i*; it is incremented by module *wave.i* each time *wave.i* resets the state of *appl.i*, and is read by module *appl.i*. Variable *st.i* has three possible values: *normal*, *initiate*, and *reset*. When *st.i* = *normal*, module *wave.i* has completed the last diffusing computation and is ready for the next one. When *st.i* = *initiate*, module *wave.i* is propagating the request wave in the ongoing diffusing computation. When *st.i* = *reset*, module *wave.i* is propagating the reset wave in the ongoing diffusing computation.

The steady states of the system, which are reached between successive diffusing computations, are characterized by:

all the *sn.i* values are equal and each *st.i* has the value *normal*.

Starting from a steady state, the next diffusing computation is initiated when some *appl.i* assigns the value *initiate* to variable *st.j*. (Note that it is possible that before the completion wave of the a diffusing computation has reached the root, the request wave of the next diffusing computation may start. In this case, there is no steady state.)

The request wave is propagated from *P.j* to its father *P.i* in the spanning tree by the following action in the *wave.i* module:

$$st.i = normal \wedge f.j = i \wedge j \in N.i \wedge st.j = initiate \longrightarrow st.i := initiate$$

When the request wave reaches the root process, say *P.i*, a reset wave is started by the following action in the *wave.i* module:

$$st.i = initiate \wedge f.i = i \longrightarrow st.i, sn.i := reset, sn.i+1; \{\text{reset } appl.i \text{ state}\}$$

The reset wave is propagated from a process *P.j* to each *P.i* such that *P.j* is the father of *P.i* in the spanning tree. The propagation is performed by the following action in the *wave.i* module:

$$st.i \neq reset \wedge f.i = j \wedge st.j = reset \wedge sn.i \neq sn.j \longrightarrow st.i, sn.i := reset, sn.j; \{\text{reset } appl.i \text{ state}\}$$

When the reset wave reaches the tree leaves, it is reflected as a completion wave that is propagated from the children processes to the father process. The propagation is performed by the following action in the *wave.i* module:

$$\begin{array}{l} st.i = reset \wedge \\ (\forall j \in N.i : (f.j = i) \Rightarrow (st.j \neq reset \wedge sn.i = sn.j)) \longrightarrow st.i := normal \end{array}$$

In order to make our design of the module *wave.i* self-stabilizing; that is, make its correctness insensitive to the initial state of the system, we add the following action to module *wave.i*:

$$st.i = st.j \wedge f.i = j \wedge sn.i \neq sn.j \longrightarrow sn.i := sn.j$$

Module *wave.i* is given in Figure 2. The proof of correctness for the wave correction layer is relegated to the full paper.

```
module        wave.i (i : 1 .. K)
owned var     sn.i : integer;
shared var    st.i : {normal , initiate , reset};
parameter     j : 1 .. K;

begin

       st.i = normal ∧ f.j = i ∧ j ∈ N.i ∧ st.j = initiate      ⟶  st.i := initiate
  ▯
       st.i = initiate ∧ f.i = i                                ⟶  st.i, sn.i := reset, sn.i+1; {reset appl.i st
  ▯
       st.i ≠ reset ∧ f.i = j ∧ st.j = reset ∧ sn.i ≠ sn.j      ⟶  st.i, sn.i := reset, sn.j; {reset appl.i state}
  ▯
       st.i = reset ∧
       (∀j ∈ N.i : (f.j = i) ⇒ (st.j ≠ reset ∧ sn.i = sn.j))    ⟶  st.i := normal
  ▯
       st.i = st.j ∧ f.i = j ∧ sn.i ≠ sn.j                      ⟶  sn.i := sn.j

end
```

Figure 2: Module *wave.i*

5 The Application Layer

The application layer in a given distributed system is composed of the *appl.i* modules as shown in Figure 0. In this section, we discuss how to modify the application layer so that our reset subsystem can be correctly added to the given system. As discussed in Section 2, it is required that the *appl* modules communicate only when they have the same session number (sn) values. In our programming notation, this requirement is achieved by transforming each action in each *appl.i* module as follows: if a variable that can be updated by *appl.j*, $i \neq j$, is accessed in the action then the expression ($sn.i = sn.j$) is conjoined to the guard of the action. With this modification, the *appl.i* modules can continue to execute while a distributed reset is in progress. Note that the sn variables are maintained to have identical value when no reset is in progress.

Each *appl.i* module should be also modified to allow it to request a distributed reset when it deems necessary. The modification consists of adding one action to *appl.i* that assigns the value *initiate* to variable *st.i*, provided $st.i = normal$.

6 Implementation Issues

Bounded Construction

Module *wave.i* uses an unbounded session number variable. A bounded construction is also possible. The present module can be transformed by making *sn.i* of type $\{0..N-1\}$, where N is an arbitrary natural constant greater than 1, and replacing the increment operation in the first action by an increment in *modulo* N arithmetic. The correctness of this transformation is relegated to the full paper.

Transformation to Read/Write Atomicity

Our design of the reset subsystem is based on stepwise refinement methodology. As a first step, we have presented the *tree.i* and *wave.i* modules without considering atomicity constraints. Some actions in these modules are of high atomicity; these actions read variables updated by other processes and instantaneously write other variables. We now refine our design so as to implement these modules using low atomicity actions only.

Consider the following transformation. For each variable $x.i$ updated by process $P.i$, introduce a local variable $x.j.i$ in each process $P.j, j \neq i$, that reads $x.i$. Replace every occurrence of $x.i$ in the actions of $P.j$ with $x.j.i$, and add the read action $x.j.i := x.i$ to the actions of $P.j$. Based on this transformation, read/write atomicity modules for *tree.i* and *wave.i* are presented next. These modules can be implemented using single-writer, multiple-reader atomic registers.

The code for read/write atomicity implementation of module *tree.i* is shown in Figure 3. The code for read/write atomicity implementation of module *wave.i* is shown in Figure 4. The proof of correctness for the read/write atomicity implementations is relegated to the full paper.

7 Conclusions

We have presented algorithms for leader election, spanning tree construction, and maintenance of diffusing computations. These algorithms are novel in that they are self-stabilizing and can tolerate the fail-stop failures and repairs of arbitrary processes and channels. We have shown how these algorithms can be used to perform distributed resets for arbitrary distributed systems.

Among other applications, distributed resets provide a paradigm for achieving the self-stabilization of the application layer and, thus, of the given (arbitrary) distributed system. For instance, application layer modules can perform a global state detection periodically, and can request a distributed reset upon detecting an erroneous global states. This will ensure that the application layer is self-stabilizing. (A self-stabilizing global snapshot algorithm for message passing systems is in [KP89].)

It should also be noted that it is possible to implement a self-stabilizing global state "snapshot" algorithm and a self-stabilizing termination detection algorithm for distributed systems with minor modifications to the reset algorithm.

Areas of interest for future research include replacing the single-writer multiple-reader atomic registers (which correspond to channels with a capacity of one message) by channels of unbounded lengths. Towards this end, we are currently investigating conditions under which low atomicity shared variable systems can be transformed to message passing systems while preserving self-stabilization.

References

[AG90] A. Arora and M.G. Gouda, "Distributed Reset," 1990, in preparation.

[BGM88] J.E. Burns, M.G. Gouda, and R.E. Miller, "On relaxing interleaving assumptions," Technical Report GIT-ICS-88/29, School of ICS, Georgia Institute of Technology, 1988; also submitted for journal publication.

[BGW89] G.M. Brown, M.G. Gouda, and C.-L. Wu, "Token systems that self-stabilize," *IEEE Transactions on Computers*, Vol. 38, No. 6 (1989), pp. 845-852.

[BP89] J.E. Burns and J. Pachl, "Uniform self-stabilizing rings," *ACM Transactions on Programming Languages and Systems*, Vol. 11, No. 2 (1989), pp. 330-344.

[DIM89] S. Dolev, A. Israeli, and S. Moran, "Self-stabilization of dynamic systems," *Proceedings of the MCC Workshop on Self-Stabilizing Systems* , MCC Technical Report Number STP-379-89.

[DS80] E.W. Dijkstra, and C.S. Scholten, "Termination detection for diffusing computations," *Information Processing Letters* , Vol. 11, No. 1 (1980), pp. 1-4.

[KP89] S. Katz and K. Perry, "Self-stabilizing extensions for message-passing systems," *Proceedings of the MCC Workshop on Self-Stabilizing Systems* , MCC Technical Report Number STP-379-89.

[FLP85] M. Fischer, N. Lynch, and M. Paterson, "Impossibility of distributed consensus with one faulty process," *Journal of the ACM*, Vol. 32, No. 2 (1985), pp. 374-382.

[F86] N. Francez, *Fairness*, Springer-Verlag, 1986.

[SG87] L. Shrira and O. Goldreich, "Electing a leader in the presence of faults: A ring as a special case," *Acta Informatica*, Vol. 24 (1987), pp. 79-91.

[T89] G. Taubenfeld, "Leader election in the presence of $n-1$ initial failures", *Information Processing Letters*, Vol. 33 (1989), pp. 25-28.

[YK88] R.B. Yehuda and S. Kutten, "Fault tolerant distributed majority commitment", *Journal of Algorithms*, Vol. 9 (1988), pp. 568-582.

```
module      tree.i (i : 1 .. K)
owned var root.i, f.i : 1 .. K;
            d.i : integer;
            root.i.j : 1 .. K;
            d.i.j : integer;
parameter j : 1 .. K , j ≠ i;

begin

      (root.i<i) ∨
      (f.i = i ∧ (root.i≠i ∨ d.i≠0)) ∨
      (f.i ∉ (N.i ∪ {i}) ∨ d.i ≥ K)                       ⟶ root.i, f.i, d.i := i, i, 0
   ▯
      f.i = j ∧ j∈N.i ∧ d.i.j<K ∧
      (root.i≠root.i.j ∨ d.i≠d.i.j+1)                     ⟶ root.i, d.i := root.i.j, d.i.j+1
   ▯
      (root.i<root.i.j ∧ j∈N.i ∧ d.i.j<K) ∨
      (root.i=root.i.j ∧ j∈N.i ∧ d.i.j+1<d.i)             ⟶ root.i, f.i, d.i := root.i.j, j, d.i.j+1
   ▯
      j∈N.i ∧ (root.j≠root.i.j ∨ f.j≠f.i.j ∨ d.j≠d.i.j) ⟶ root.i.j, f.i.j, d.i.j := root.j, f.j, d.j

end
```

Figure 3: Implementation of *tree.i* using Read/Write Atomicity

module $wave.i\ (i : 1 .. K)$
shared var $st.i : \{normal\ ,\ initiate\ ,\ reset\}$;
owned var $sn.i$: **integer**;
$sn.i.j$: **integer**;
$st.i.j : \{normal\ ,\ initiate\ ,\ reset\}$;
parameter $j : (1 .. K)\ ,\ j \neq i$;

begin

$st.i = normal \wedge f.i.j = i \wedge st.i.j = initiate \longrightarrow st.i := initiate$

$[\!]$

$st.i = initiate \wedge f.i = i \longrightarrow st.i, sn.i := reset, sn.i + 1$; {reset *appl.i* st

$[\!]$

$st.i \neq reset \wedge f.i = j \wedge st.i.j = reset \wedge sn.i \neq sn.i.j \longrightarrow st.i, sn.i := reset, sn.i.j$; {reset *appl.i* state

$[\!]$

$st.i = reset\ \wedge$
$(\forall j \in N.i\ , (f.i.j = i) \Rightarrow (st.i.j \neq reset \wedge sn.i = sn.i.j)) \longrightarrow st.i := normal$

$[\!]$

$st.i = st.i.j \wedge f.i = j \wedge sn.i \neq sn.i.j \longrightarrow sn.i := sn.i.j$

$[\!]$

$(f.i.j = i \vee f.i = j) \wedge (st.j \neq st.i.j \vee sn.j \neq sn.i.j) \longrightarrow st.i.j, sn.i.j := st.j, sn.j$

end

Figure 4: Implementation of *wave.i* using Read/Write Atomicity

Refinement and Composition of Transition-based Rely-Guarantee Specifications with Auxiliary Variables

Peter Grønning *Thomas Qvist Nielsen*
Hans Henrik Løvengreen

Department of Computer Science
Building 344, Technical University of Denmark
DK-2800 Lyngby, Denmark

Keywords: Rely-guarantee specification, compositional verification, safety properties, shared variables, transition systems.

Abstract

We combine two ideas for specification and verification of concurrent systems: The rely-guarantee paradigm and transition-based specification. We consider specification of safety properties of shared variable systems. A component is specified by stating which transitions its environment is allowed to make to the interface variables and which changes the component then guarantees to stay within. Auxiliary variables are used to carry history information. For such specifications, we present proof rules for verifying that one specification refines another and that parallel composition of components implements a given specification. Application of the rules is illustrated by small examples.

1 Introduction

Many languages and techniques have been proposed for specifying and verifying concurrent and distributed systems. In this paper, we combine two promising ideas for making such techniques applicable in practice, viz. the rely-guarantee paradigm[1] and specification by transition systems.

[1]The rely-guarantee paradigm is also known as *assumption-commitment* and many variations hereof.

Our work is motivated by practical examples in which components take different rôles in a common protocol, relying on the other components to confine to their rôles. This gives rise to specifications which are mutually dependent.

A *rely-guarantee* (r-g) specification for a component C could look like:

$$(\mathsf{R}, \mathsf{G}) : C$$

meaning that *provided* the environment of C behaves according to the *rely-condition* R, the component will guarantee to behave according to the *guarantee-condition* G. This r-g paradigm is widely recognized as useful for hierarchical system development where it may be used to impose mutually dependent r-g conditions between components.

An early work by Misra and Chandy [17] considered r-g specification in the context of CSP-communication while at the same time work by Jones [7] dealt with shared variables. Our approach extends Jones' work by inclusion of auxiliary variables.

Many approaches based on e.g. temporal logic express the r-g idea by the implication $\mathsf{R} \Rightarrow \mathsf{G}$, e.g. [20]. In this case, however, mutually dependent properties become hard to verify since they require an inductive proof. If the rely and guarantee-conditions are clearly separated, the induction can be built into the proof rules such that the proof rule for parallel composition becomes:

$$\frac{\begin{array}{l}(\mathsf{R}_i,\mathsf{G}_i) : C_i, \;\; i = 1,2 \\ \mathsf{R} \wedge \mathsf{G}_1 \Rightarrow \mathsf{R}_2 \\ \mathsf{R} \wedge \mathsf{G}_2 \Rightarrow \mathsf{R}_1 \\ \mathsf{G}_1 \wedge \mathsf{G}_2 \Rightarrow \mathsf{G}\end{array}}{(\mathsf{R},\mathsf{G}) : C_1 \parallel C_2} \qquad (*)$$

In the important case where the conditions are mutually dependent, i.e. $\mathsf{G}_1 \Rightarrow \mathsf{R}_2$ and $\mathsf{G}_2 \Rightarrow \mathsf{R}_1$, we may conclude that $\mathsf{G}_1 \wedge \mathsf{G}_2$ holds for $C_1 \parallel C_2$. For a further discussion, see [19].

In specification techniques based on logic, the idea is to specify a component by predicates expressing whether an execution is legal or not. An alternative to this, introduced by Lamport [12], is to state the admissible transitions of the component as a kind of state-machine. This specifies the possible executions of the component as those that may be generated by the state-machine. The machine may include *auxiliary variables* that are not part of the observable interface but serve to record history information that may influence transition possibilities.

The transition-based approach has been used for specifying especially asynchronously communicating systems [8, 14]. To verify that one specification implements another, various *simulation techniques* have been devised, including complete ones [1, 9, 10]. In all of these approaches, however, a specification does not put any constraints on the behaviour of the environment and may therefore be seen as a "pure" guarantee specification.

The purpose of our work is to develop a theory of transition-based specifications which includes a *rely-condition*. The theory includes the proof rules necessary to prove correctness of refinement steps between r-g specifications on different abstraction levels and a proof rule for composition similar to (*) above. In both cases, the rules exploit the well-known simulation technique which ties together the states on different abstraction levels by a simulation relation, but extended to deal also with rely-conditions. The soundness of the rules is proven.

A major obstacle in the theory is the presence of auxiliary variables. Even defining the semantics of r-g specifications becomes non-trivial. In the case of the refinement rules, we have to restrict ourselves to so-called separable or deterministic auxiliary variables.

Our approach is largely semantic, seeing specifications as sets of transitions. However, in the examples we express transitions by the simple syntactic form of conditional assignments as in e.g. UNITY [4].

Our theory has been especially developed for shared variable systems with VLSI applications in mind [22]. It is not directly applicable in the realm of synchronously communicating processes [6, 16].

The paper is organized as follows. In section 2, we introduce a model of shared variable systems including operations for hiding and parallel composition. In section 3, we define the form and semantics of r-g specifications and give specification examples with and without auxiliary variables. Section 4 presents the proof rule for refinement and proves its soundness. Application of the rules is illustrated. In section 5, the rule for composition is given and illustrated. Finally, in section 6, the approach is discussed and related to other work.

2 The Behaviour Model

In this section, we define a model of the behaviour of our system components. First, however, we have to introduce some basic transition notions.

Definition 1 (Transition relation)

Let V be a set of variables and Λ a set of labels. We define a labelled transition relation $\mathcal{R}$ to be a relation $\mathcal{R} \subseteq \Sigma(V) \times \Lambda \times \Sigma(V)$, where $\Sigma(V)$ denotes the set of states over V. A state $\sigma \in \Sigma(V)$ is a mapping from V into some set of values. We write $\sigma \xrightarrow{\lambda} \sigma' \in \mathcal{R}$ instead of $(\sigma, \lambda, \sigma') \in \mathcal{R}$.

The set of transitions over V, $\Sigma(V) \times \Lambda \times \Sigma(V)$, will be denoted by $\mathsf{Trans}(V, \Lambda)$. Usually, $\Lambda = \{\mathsf{e}, \mathsf{i}\}$ representing respectively *external* and *internal transitions*.

We shall also need the simpler notion of *unlabelled transitions* defined in the obvious way. The set of unlabelled transitions over V is denoted by $\mathsf{Trans}(V)$.

A transition in which the state does not change is called a *silent transition*.

We define the restriction-operator $\lceil$ by :

$$\begin{array}{ll}\sigma \lceil V' & \stackrel{\text{def}}{=} [v \mapsto \sigma(v) \mid v \in V'] \\ (\sigma \xrightarrow{\lambda} \sigma') \lceil V' & \stackrel{\text{def}}{=} \sigma \lceil V' \xrightarrow{\lambda} \sigma' \lceil V'\end{array}$$

$$\mathcal{R} \lceil V' \stackrel{\text{def}}{=} \{t \lceil V' \mid t \in \mathcal{R}\}$$

where V' is a subset of V.

■

Definition 2 (Computation)

Given a set of variables V and a set of labels Λ, we define a *computation* ρ *over* V, Λ to be a finite or infinite sequence of transitions from $\mathsf{Trans}(V, \Lambda)$:

$$\sigma^0 \xrightarrow{\lambda^0} \sigma^1 \xrightarrow{\lambda^1} \sigma^2 \rightarrow \ldots$$

- By $\rho[i]$ we denote the transition $\sigma^i \xrightarrow{\lambda^i} \sigma^{i+1}$ of ρ.
- By $t \in \rho$ we understand $\exists i : t = \rho[i]$.
- $|\rho|$ gives the length of a given computation ρ, i.e. the number of transitions. If ρ is infinite $|\rho|$ is infinite too.
- By $\rho[i..j]$ where $i \le j \le |\rho|$, we denote the sequence of transitions:

$$\sigma^i \xrightarrow{\lambda^i} \sigma^{i+1} \xrightarrow{\lambda^{i+1}} \sigma^{i+2} \rightarrow \ldots \rightarrow \sigma^{j-1} \xrightarrow{\lambda^{j-1}} \sigma^j$$

The set of infinite and finite computations over V, Λ will be denoted by $\mathsf{Comp}(V, \Lambda)$. The set of computations of $\mathsf{Comp}(V, \Lambda)$ with initial state $\sigma^I \lceil V$ will be denoted by $\mathsf{Comp}(V, \Lambda, \sigma^I)$.

If V' is a subset of V, we define the restriction on a computation $\rho \lceil V'$ to be the restriction by V' on every transition in the sequence.

We define a label renaming operator $\rho[\lambda_2/\lambda_1]$ which changes all occurrences of the label λ_1 to λ_2 in the computation ρ. The operator can be generalized to lists of labels as usual.

■

Behaviour

Each component of our system will interact with its environment through a set of shared *interface variables*. By an *observable computation* of such a component we think of a recording of all the changes made to these interface variables. The recording should for each change note whether the change was made by the component or by the environment, cf. [3]. The behaviour of the component is then given by the set of all possible observable computations.

Definition 3 (Observable Behaviour)

An *observable behaviour* over a set of interface variables V is a non-empty set of computations $\mathcal{B} \subseteq \mathsf{Comp}(V, \{\mathrm{i}, \mathrm{e}\})$, such that :

- The initial state of all computations in $\mathcal{B}$ is the same.
- The environment may make arbitrary changes at any time, i.e. for any state σ, if p is a prefix of some computation $\rho \in \mathcal{B}$ then $p \xrightarrow{\mathrm{e}} \sigma \in \mathcal{B}$ must be a prefix of some computation $\rho' \in \mathcal{B}$.[2]

■

In the following, we shall often identify a component with its observable behaviour.

Composition

A number of components may be put together in parallel (if they agree on the initial values of their common interface variables). The components may then interact with each other through the common interface variables. Together, they may be considered a single component whose interface variables are the union of all the interface variables of the individual components. A computation of the composed system will be an interleaving of the (atomic) transitions of the components. We here consider the behaviour of the composed system in the case of two components.

Definition 4 (Composition)

Let V_1, V_2 be two sets of variables and $\mathcal{B}_i$ be observable behaviours over V_i. We define the *composed observable behaviour* $\mathcal{B} = \mathcal{B}_1 \parallel \mathcal{B}_2$ over $V = V_1 \cup V_2$ by

$$\begin{aligned}\mathcal{B} = \{\rho[\mathrm{i},\mathrm{i}/\mathrm{i}_1,\mathrm{i}_2] \mid \\ & \rho \in \mathsf{Comp}(V, \{\mathrm{e}, \mathrm{i}_1, \mathrm{i}_2\}) \wedge \\ & ((\rho \lceil V_1)[\mathrm{e},\mathrm{i}/\mathrm{i}_2,\mathrm{i}_1]) \in \mathcal{B}_1 \wedge \\ & ((\rho \lceil V_2)[\mathrm{e},\mathrm{i}/\mathrm{i}_1,\mathrm{i}_2]) \in \mathcal{B}_2 \wedge \\ & \forall \sigma \xrightarrow{\mathrm{i}_1} \sigma' \in \rho : \sigma \lceil V_{21} = \sigma' \lceil V_{21} \wedge \\ & \forall \sigma \xrightarrow{\mathrm{i}_2} \sigma' \in \rho : \sigma \lceil V_{12} = \sigma' \lceil V_{12} \ \}\end{aligned}$$

where $V_{12} = V_1 \setminus V_2$ and $V_{21} = V_2 \setminus V_1$.

■

[2] To allow behaviour refinement in general, we could also require a behaviour to be closed wrt. *insertion* of internal and external silent transitions but this is not relevant for this presentation. Our semantics of an r-g specification, however, has this property.

Thus, an observable computation of the composed system is derived from a (virtual) computation ρ over V where we record which component carries out each internal transition. From the point of view of component 1, internal transitions in component 2 are external, so ρ changed according to this must be a possible observable computation of $\mathcal{B}_1$. Furthermore, variables not in V_1 must not change during a transition in component 1. Correspondingly for component 2.

The composed observable behaviour is then given by the set of computations ρ satisfying the above constraints, forgetting about the origin of internal transitions.

Hiding

Given a component, we may conceal or *hide* some of its interface variables from the environment meaning that they can be changed only by the component.

Definition 5 (Hiding)

Let $\mathcal{B}$ be an observable behaviour over a set of interface variables V, and let V' be a subset of V. Then the behaviour of $\mathcal{B}$ *with V' hidden* denoted by $\mathcal{B} \setminus V'$ is the behaviour over $V \setminus V'$ given by:

$$\mathcal{B} \setminus V' \stackrel{\text{def}}{=} \{\rho \lceil (V \setminus V') \mid \rho \in \mathcal{B} \wedge \forall \sigma \stackrel{e}{\rightarrow} \sigma' \in (\rho \lceil V') : \sigma = \sigma'\}$$

■

That is, we consider the computations in which the environment does not (cannot) change the variables in V' and then forget about these variables.

Refinement

Finally we shall define when a behaviour $\mathcal{B}_1$ implements/entails/refines another behaviour $\mathcal{B}_2$ denoted by $\mathcal{B}_1 \models \mathcal{B}_2$. Intuitively, this will be the case if $\mathcal{B}_1$ can be substituted for $\mathcal{B}_2$ in all contexts. As in [1, 8] we define this to mean that any computation possible for $\mathcal{B}_1$ is also possible for $\mathcal{B}_2$. In general, we allow $\mathcal{B}_1$ to have more interface variables than $\mathcal{B}_2$ in which case the superfluous variables are implicitly hidden.

Definition 6 (Refinement)

Given two observable behaviours $\mathcal{B}_1$ and $\mathcal{B}_2$ over two sets of variables V_1 and V_2 where $V_2 \subseteq V_1$, we define that $\mathcal{B}_1$ *refines* $\mathcal{B}_2$ by

$$\mathcal{B}_1 \models \mathcal{B}_2 \stackrel{\text{def}}{=} \mathcal{B}_1 \setminus (V_1 \setminus V_2) \subseteq \mathcal{B}_2$$

■

Transition schemes

In order to define concrete behaviours, we introduce the notion of transition schemes as a convenient way of describing sets of unlabelled transitions. A *transition scheme* has the form $\langle p \rightarrow a \rangle$ where p is a state-predicate and a is a (multiple) assignment statement. The set of transitions defined by the transition scheme is the set of unlabelled transitions $\sigma \rightarrow \sigma'$ where the precondition p holds in state σ and σ' equals σ changed according to the assignment. We say that a transition scheme is *enabled* in a state σ if $p(\sigma)$ holds.

3 Rely-Guarantee Specifications

An r-g specification of a component defines the possible course of events on the interface variables of the component. This is done by two sets of transitions – the transitions that the environment is allowed to make (the *rely*-set) and the transitions that the component *guarantees* to stay within.

But we also want to let the possible transitions be influenced by the history of the interface variables (i.e. the previous course of events). This is done by introducing a set of auxiliary (history) variables[3]. Thereby the *rely* and *guarantee* transitions must be over both the interface and the auxiliary variables.

Definition 7 (Specification)

A *rely-guarantee specification* is a tuple $\mathsf{S} = \langle \mathsf{A}, \mathsf{O}, \mathsf{I}, \mathsf{R}, \mathsf{G} \rangle$, where

- A is a set of auxiliary variables
- O is a set of interface variables disjoint from A
- I is the initial state. $\mathsf{I} \in \Sigma(\mathsf{A} \cup \mathsf{O})$
- R, G are sets of unlabelled transitions over $\mathsf{A} \cup \mathsf{O}$, i.e. $\mathsf{R}, \mathsf{G} \subseteq \Sigma(\mathsf{A} \cup \mathsf{O}) \times \Sigma(\mathsf{A} \cup \mathsf{O})$. R,G must contain the identity relation on $\Sigma(\mathsf{A} \cup \mathsf{O})$ (i.e. all silent transitions).

■

Given these definitions we can define the notion of *legal transitions* of an r-g specification.

[3] Our notion of auxiliary variables corresponds to the notion of internal variables in [2].

Definition 8 (Legal transitions)

Let $S = \langle A, O, I, R, G \rangle$ be an r-g specification. Then we define a transition to be *legal wrt.* S by

$$Legal(\sigma \xrightarrow{\lambda} \sigma', S) \Leftrightarrow (\sigma \rightarrow \sigma' \in G \wedge \lambda = i) \vee (\sigma \rightarrow \sigma' \in R \wedge \lambda = e)$$

i.e. a transition is legal wrt. S if:

- it is an internal transition from the *guarantee*-set
- or an external transition from the *rely*-set.

Given a computation, we say that the *computation is legal* iff it contains only legal transitions.

■

Explanations

Although an r-g specification describes how the environment is supposed to behave there is no certainty that it will do so. We can, however, express that the environment has behaved in a legal manner until a certain point; viz. when the behaviour on the interface variables can be explained by legal transitions until this point. The sequence of legal transitions restricted to the auxiliary variables is called an *explanation* of the behaviour on the interface variables.

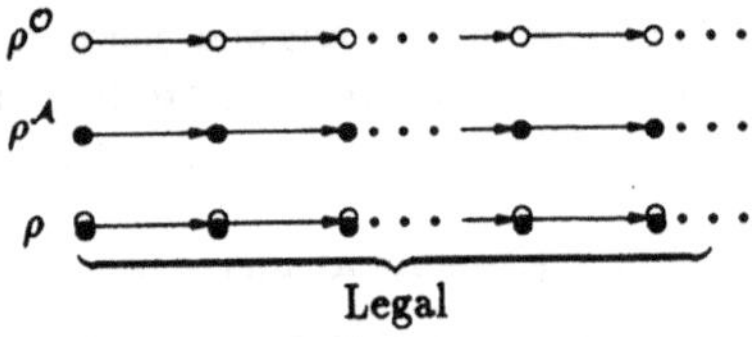

Figure 1

Given an observable computation ρ^O, an explanation ρ^A is a computation over the auxiliary variables, such that the joined computation ρ is a legal computation.

Definition 9 (Explanation)

Let there be given an r-g specification $S = \langle A, O, I, R, G \rangle$ and a computation ρ^O over the interface variables, i.e. $\rho^O \in \mathrm{Comp}(O, \{e, i\}, I)$.

We then say that $\rho^A \in \mathrm{Comp}(A, \{e, i\}, I)$ *is an explanation of* ρ^O *wrt.* S iff there exists a legal computation $\rho \in \mathrm{Comp}(A \cup O, \{e, i\}, I)$ of S which contains both ρ^O and ρ^A (i.e. both computations can be found as a restriction of ρ). We use the predicate $Explain(\rho^A, \rho^O, S)$ to denote that ρ^A is an explanation of ρ^O wrt. S:

$$\begin{aligned} & Explain(\rho^A, \rho^O, S) \Leftrightarrow \\ & \quad \exists \rho \in \mathrm{Comp}(A \cup O, \{e, i\}, I) : \\ & \quad\quad \forall t \in \rho : Legal(t, S) \wedge \\ & \quad\quad (\rho \lceil O = \rho^O) \wedge (\rho \lceil A = \rho^A) \end{aligned}$$

■

Notice that if ρ exists, it is uniquely given by ρ^O and ρ^A.

Semantics

Having defined formally what it means to explain an observable computation, we are able to give semantics to an r-g specification. We require that as long as the computation on the interface variables can be explained as an interleaving of legal transitions, the computation extended with an *internal* transition can be explained as an interleaving of legal transitions too. The semantics is defined as the set of observable computations satisfying this constraint.

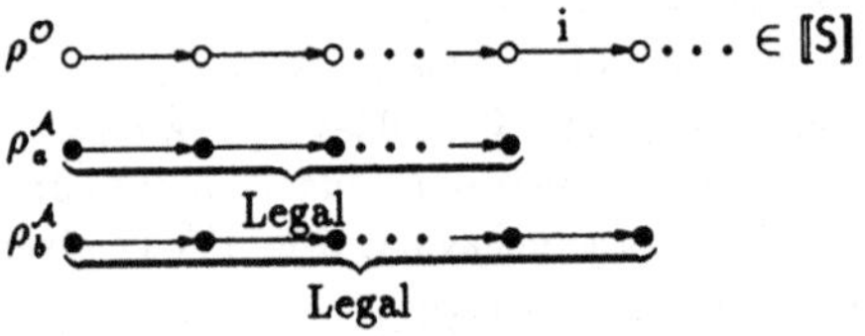

Figure 2

Given an observable computation ρ^O, if there exists an explanation ρ_a^A of a prefix of ρ^O and the next transition is internal then there exists an explanation ρ_b^A of the extended prefix too

Definition 10 (Semantics)

Let $S = \langle A, O, I, R, G \rangle$ be an r-g specification. We define the *semantics of* S, written $[\![S]\!]$ to be the set of computations ρ^O over O which satisfy:

$$\begin{aligned} & \forall i \in \{0..\left|\rho^O\right| - 1\} : \\ & \quad [\exists \rho_a^A \in \mathrm{Comp}(A, \{e, i\}, I) : \\ & \quad\quad Explain(\rho_a^A, \rho^O[0..i], S) \wedge \\ & \quad \rho^O[i] = \sigma \xrightarrow{i} \sigma'] \Rightarrow \\ & \quad\quad \exists \rho_b^A \in \mathrm{Comp}(A, \{e, i\}, I) : \\ & \quad\quad\quad Explain(\rho_b^A, \rho^O[0..i+1], S) \end{aligned}$$

■

This definition corresponds very closely to the trace based semantics given by Misra and Chandy in [17] (although their work is based on a model with communication).

Example: The four-phase protocol

The four-phase protocol is frequently used when there exists a request-grant communication between a server (issuing the grants) and a client (issuing the requests). For instance, it can be used for synchronization in asynchronous circuits design [15]. The idea of the protocol is very simple:

- There are two shared variables between the server and the client: *in* and *out* which may take the values true ($\mathtt{t}$) or false ($\mathtt{f}$).
- The server is allowed to write only to *out*, and the client only to *in*.
- The server is a slave – whenever the client (master) writes a value to *in*, the only action the server may take is to copy the value to *out*.

The four-phase protocol is visualized in figure 3.

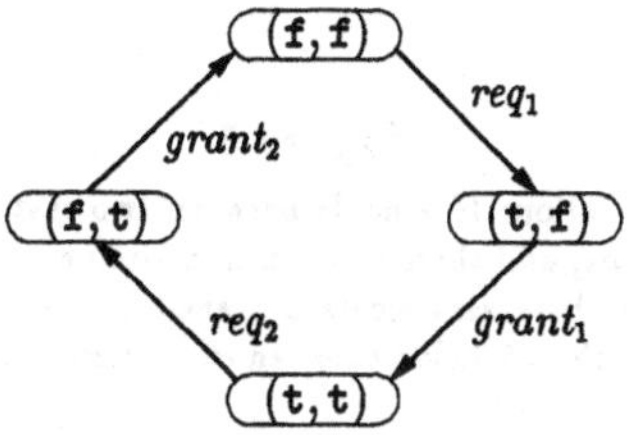

Figure 3

The actions in a four-phase protocol

An r-g specification of a server which uses the four-phase protocol for communication with a client is given by:

$$
\begin{aligned}
&\mathit{Server}(in, out) \stackrel{\text{def}}{=}\\
&\quad \mathsf{A} = \{\}\\
&\quad \mathsf{O} = \{in, out\}\\
&\quad \mathsf{I} = [in \mapsto \mathtt{f}, out \mapsto \mathtt{f}]\\
&\quad \mathsf{R} = req_1 : \langle \neg in \wedge \neg out \rightarrow in := \mathtt{t} \rangle,\\
&\qquad\quad req_2 : \langle in \wedge out \rightarrow in := \mathtt{f} \rangle\\
&\quad \mathsf{G} = grant_1 : \langle in \wedge \neg out \rightarrow out := \mathtt{t} \rangle,\\
&\qquad\quad grant_2 : \langle \neg in \wedge out \rightarrow out := \mathtt{f} \rangle
\end{aligned}
$$

R is defined as the union of the transitions defined by each of the transition schemes labelled req_1 and req_2 implicitly extended with all silent transitions. Likewise, G is defined by the transitions schemes labelled $grant_1$ and $grant_2$.

Example: A two-element split-node

A two-element split-node [9] receives messages through *in* and nondeterministically transmits these messages through either out_1 or out_2. Received but not yet transmitted messages are kept in an internal two-element buffer. Ignoring the contents of the messages sent, the buffer can be modelled as a counter c.

The specification should express that the node is assumed to be able to contain only two messages, i.e. that the environment must not insert more than two elements without removing any elements through either out_1 or out_2. To do this we introduce an external counter n modelling the environment's information on how many elements have been inserted and not yet removed.

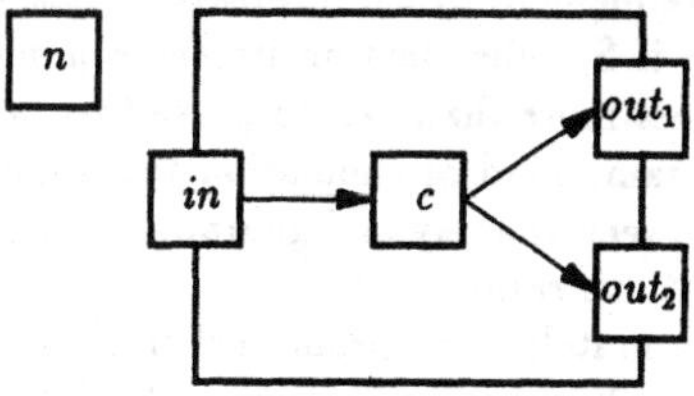

Figure 4

A two-element split-node

The buffer can be formally specified by the r-g specification:

$$
\begin{aligned}
&\mathit{Split} \stackrel{\text{def}}{=}\\
&\quad \mathsf{A} = \{c, n\}\\
&\quad \mathsf{O} = \{in, out_1, out_2\}\\
&\quad \mathsf{I} = [in \mapsto \mathtt{f}, out_1 \mapsto \mathtt{f}, out_2 \mapsto \mathtt{f},\\
&\qquad\quad c \mapsto 0, n \mapsto 0]\\
&\quad \mathsf{R} = \langle n < 2 \wedge \neg in \rightarrow n, in := n+1, \mathtt{t} \rangle,\\
&\qquad\quad \langle out_1 \rightarrow out_1, n := \mathtt{f}, n-1 \rangle,\\
&\qquad\quad \langle out_2 \rightarrow out_2, n := \mathtt{f}, n-1 \rangle\\
&\quad \mathsf{G} = \langle in \rightarrow c, in := c+1, \mathtt{f} \rangle,\\
&\qquad\quad \langle \neg out_1 \wedge c > 0 \rightarrow c, out_1 := c-1, \mathtt{t} \rangle,\\
&\qquad\quad \langle \neg out_2 \wedge c > 0 \rightarrow c, out_2 := c-1, \mathtt{t} \rangle
\end{aligned}
$$

4 Refinement

In this section we establish two proof rules to show that one r-g specification implements or refines another. We naturally define the refinement relation between specifications on basis of the observable behaviour they determine.

Definition 11 ($S_1 \models S_2$)

Given two r-g specifications S_1 and S_2, we define that S_1 *refines* S_2 written $S_1 \models S_2$ iff the observable behaviour of S_1 refines the observable behaviour of S_2:

$$S_1 \models S_2 \text{ iff } [S_1] \models [S_2]$$

■

If the interface variables of S_2 form a proper subset of those of S_1 we may add the missing variables to S_2 while further relying on the environment not to access them (see theorem 17). We therefore consider the case $O_1 = O_2$ where the refinement condition becomes $[S_1] \subseteq [S_2]$.

Given a concrete r-g specification S_1 and an abstract one S_2 with the same interface variables, we would like to have a method for verifying that S_1 is a refinement of S_2. Intuitively, this will be the case if S_1 relies less on its environment but guarantees more than S_2. To prove this, we shall use the same kind of simulation technique as in [1, 8] between the rely and guarantee parts of the specifications respectively.

Unfortunately, our proof technique does not work for all r-g specifications. Luckily, there are certain useful classes of r-g specifications for which the technique does work: specifications with deterministic or separable auxiliary variables. In this paper we consider only separable auxiliary variables.

Simulation

The r-g specifications we want to compare will usually contain auxiliary variables to collect history information. The information can be collected in many ways using different auxiliary variables. To be able to compare the transition-sets of different r-g specifications we need to establish a connection between these variables.

Definition 12 (State relation)

Let V_1 and V_2 be two sets of variables which may be overlapping.

- A *state relation* $\mathcal{S}$ is a subset of the state-space over both V_1 and V_2 (i.e. $\mathcal{S} \subseteq \Sigma(V_1 \cup V_2)$).
- Given two states $\sigma_1 \in \Sigma(V_1), \sigma_2 \in \Sigma(V_2)$ we say that the state relation holds between the states (often written $\mathcal{S}(\sigma_1, \sigma_2)$), if $\mathcal{S}$ contains a state which corresponds to σ_1 and σ_2:

$$\mathcal{S}(\sigma_1, \sigma_2) \Leftrightarrow (\exists \sigma \in \mathcal{S} : \sigma \lceil V_1 = \sigma_1 \wedge \sigma \lceil V_2 = \sigma_2)$$

■

Note that this definition always requires the value of common variables to be the same in both states when the state relation holds.

Definition 13 (Simulation)

Let T_1, T_2 be sets of unlabelled transitions and σ_1^I, σ_2^I initial states over two sets of variables V_1 and V_2, i.e. $T_i \subseteq \mathsf{Trans}(V_i)$ and $\sigma_i^I \in \Sigma(V_i)$. Let $\mathcal{S}$ be a state relation between the states of V_1 and V_2, i.e. $\mathcal{S} \subseteq \Sigma(V_1 \cup V_2)$.

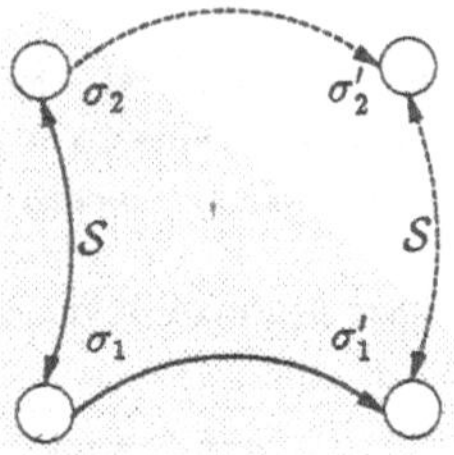

Figure 5

Simulation: If $\mathcal{S}$ holds between two states σ_1 and σ_2, and there exists a transition $\sigma_1 \to \sigma_1'$, then there also exists a transition $\sigma_2 \to \sigma_2'$ such that $\mathcal{S}$ holds between σ_1' and σ_2'

Given the state relation $\mathcal{S}$ we define that T_1 and T_2 *simulate wrt.* $\mathcal{S}$ written $T_1 \subseteq_{\mathcal{S}} T_2$ iff:

1. $\mathcal{S}(\sigma_1^I, \sigma_2^I)$: The relation holds between the initial states.
2. $\forall \sigma_2 \in \Sigma(V_2) : \forall \sigma_1 \to \sigma_1' \in T_1 :$
   $\mathcal{S}(\sigma_1, \sigma_2) \Rightarrow \exists \sigma_2 \to \sigma_2' \in T_2 : \mathcal{S}(\sigma_1', \sigma_2')$

   See figure 5.

We say that $\mathcal{S}$ is a *simulation relation* between T_1 and T_2 if $\mathcal{S}$ is a state relation between V_1 and V_2 and T_1 and T_2 simulate wrt. $\mathcal{S}$.

■

Separable Auxiliary Variables

In many cases the environment's use of auxiliary variables does not affect the component's use of auxiliary variables. In this section we will introduce the notion *separable auxiliary variables* to denote this property of the auxiliary variables.

Semantically this enables us to talk separately about internal and external explanations. These do not depend on each other, in the sense that any internal explanation can be combined with any external explanation to form a total explanation. This property becomes a central condition for the proof rules to hold.

To be able to formalize the notion of separable auxiliary variables we introduce two operations extending the state-space of transition sets: $\uplus$ and $\boxplus$ which allow no changes respectively any changes on the introduced variables. Let A be a set of variables such that $V \subseteq A$ and $\mathcal{R}$ be an unlabelled transition relation over V. We define $\mathcal{R} \uplus A$ by

$$\mathcal{R} \uplus A \stackrel{\text{def}}{=} \{\sigma \to \sigma' \in \mathsf{Trans}(A) \mid (\sigma \to \sigma') \lceil V \in \mathcal{R} \wedge \sigma \lceil (A \setminus V) = \sigma' \lceil (A \setminus V)\}$$

and $\mathcal{R} \boxplus A$ by

$$\mathcal{R} \boxplus A \stackrel{\text{def}}{=} \{t \in \mathsf{Trans}(A) \mid (t \lceil V) \in \mathcal{R}\}$$

We say that a set A of auxiliary variables is separable wrt. R and G if there exists two disjoint subsets $\mathsf{A_e}$ and $\mathsf{A_i}$ of A such that $\mathsf{A_e} \cup \mathsf{A_i} = \mathsf{A}$, and such that the transitions from R:

1. do not *change* variables from $\mathsf{A_i}$ and
2. do not *depend* on variables from $\mathsf{A_i}$, i.e.:

   For all variables v of $\mathsf{A_i}$ *and all transitions in* R *with a given value of v there must exist corresponding transitions in* R *for all possible values of v.*

and similarly wrt. G and $\mathsf{A_e}$.

Definition 14 (Separability)

Let A be a set of auxiliary variables, O a set of interface variables and T_1, T_2 sets of transitions over $\mathsf{A} \cup \mathsf{O}$.

We say that T_1 and T_2 have *separate auxiliary variables* iff:

$$\exists \mathsf{A_1}, \mathsf{A_2} \subseteq \mathsf{A} : (\mathsf{A_1} \cap \mathsf{A_2} = \{\}) \wedge (\mathsf{A_1} \cup \mathsf{A_2} = \mathsf{A}) \wedge (T_1 \lceil (\mathsf{A_1} \cup \mathsf{O}) \uplus (\mathsf{A} \cup \mathsf{O}) = T_1) \wedge (T_2 \lceil (\mathsf{A_2} \cup \mathsf{O}) \uplus (\mathsf{A} \cup \mathsf{O}) = T_2)$$

We will say that the auxiliary variables are separable into $\mathsf{A_1}$ and $\mathsf{A_2}$ wrt. T_1 and T_2. Given an r-g specification $\mathsf{S} = \langle \mathsf{A}, \mathsf{O}, \mathsf{I}, \mathsf{R}, \mathsf{G} \rangle$, we say that S has *separable auxiliary variables* iff A is separable into $\mathsf{A_e}$ and $\mathsf{A_i}$ wrt. R and G. In this case we call $\mathsf{A_i}$ the *internal auxiliary variables* and $\mathsf{A_e}$ the *external auxiliary variables*.

■

In the sequel, a specification S is often understood to have separated auxiliary variables.

Internal and external explanation

Given an r-g specification with separable auxiliary variables S, we are able to define when a transition is an *externally* respectively an *internally legal transition*.

$$\mathit{ExtLegal}(\sigma \xrightarrow{\lambda} \sigma', \mathsf{S}) \Leftrightarrow (\sigma \to \sigma' \in \mathsf{R} \wedge \lambda = \mathsf{e}) \vee (\sigma \lceil \mathsf{A_e} = \sigma' \lceil \mathsf{A_e} \wedge \lambda = \mathsf{i})$$

Dually we define *IntLegal* as internal transitions from G or external transitions not changing the internal auxiliary variables.

Definition 15

Let $\rho^{\mathcal{O}}$ be an observable computation of a specification S. We define an *external explanation* $\rho_e^{\mathcal{A}}$ of $\rho^{\mathcal{O}}$ to be a computation over $\mathsf{A_e}, \{\mathsf{i}, \mathsf{e}\}$ such that there exists a computation ρ over $\mathsf{A} \cup \mathsf{O}, \{\mathsf{e}, \mathsf{i}\}$ where all transitions in ρ are externally legal transitions and ρ restricted to $\mathsf{O}, \mathsf{A_e}$ gives $\rho^{\mathcal{O}}, \rho_e^{\mathcal{A}}$ respectively, i.e.

$$\mathit{ExtExplain}(\rho_e^{\mathcal{A}}, \rho^{\mathcal{O}}, \mathsf{S}) \Leftrightarrow \exists \rho \in \mathsf{Comp}(\mathsf{A} \cup \mathsf{O}, \{\mathsf{i}, \mathsf{e}\}, \mathsf{I}) : \forall t \in \rho : \mathit{ExtLegal}(t, \mathsf{S}) \wedge (\rho \lceil \mathsf{O} = \rho^{\mathcal{O}}) \wedge (\rho \lceil \mathsf{A_e} = \rho_e^{\mathcal{A}})$$

likewise we define an *internal explanation* and *IntExplain*.

■

Joining internal and external explanations

As one would expect, it is possible to combine/join an internal and an external explanation of an observable computation, and get an explanation of the observable computation. The reason is the independence between the internal and the external auxiliary variables and by that between the internal and the external explanation. A lemma expressing this formally and a proof hereof can be found in the appendix (lemma 19).

Proof Rule for Refinement

A final implementation does not rely on the environment at all. Therefore a refinement of an r-g specification should rely less on the environment so that we move towards the final implementation.

On the other hand, the refinement should preserve the properties of the more abstract specification, i.e. when placed in an environment satisfying the abstract rely conditions, the refinement should guarantee at least the abstract guarantee conditions.

Formally this intuitive condition can be expressed, using a simulation relation $\mathcal{S}$, by:

$$\mathcal{S}(\mathsf{I}_1, \mathsf{I}_2) \wedge \mathsf{R}_2 \subseteq_{\mathcal{S}} \mathsf{R}_1 \wedge \mathsf{G}_1 \subseteq_{\mathcal{S}} \mathsf{G}_2$$

Here, $\mathsf{R}_2 \subseteq_{\mathcal{S}} \mathsf{R}_1$ expresses that the refinement S_1 of S_2 rely less on the environment. Likewise, $\mathsf{G}_1 \subseteq_{\mathcal{S}} \mathsf{G}_2$ expresses that S_1 guarantees at least the same as S_2, but only for the transitions preserving the simulation relation. In this way the simulation relation transfers the rely information from S_2 to S_1, which in return through the simulation relation guarantees to stay within the guarantee part of S_2.

Notice that the concrete specification might guarantee less than the abstract specification, but when placed in an environment satisfying the abstract rely-part, the concrete specification guarantees at least as much as the abstract one.

Obviously it would be nice if we could prove that the above condition formally ensures refinement of r-g specifications. According to definition 6, this means that we need to prove that every observable computation $\rho^{\mathcal{O}}$ included in the semantics of S_1 is included in the semantics of S_2 too.

From the definition of the semantics for an r-g specification (definition 10) we extract the following proof obligation:

> For any prefix p of $\rho^{\mathcal{O}}$, if there exists an explanation $\rho_2^{\mathcal{A}}$ of p in S_2 and the next transition in $\rho^{\mathcal{O}}$ is internal then there must exist an explanation of p extended with this transition in S_2.

With reference to figure 6, we proceed as follows:

1. Assume we have an explanation $\rho_2^{\mathcal{A}}$ of p in S_2.

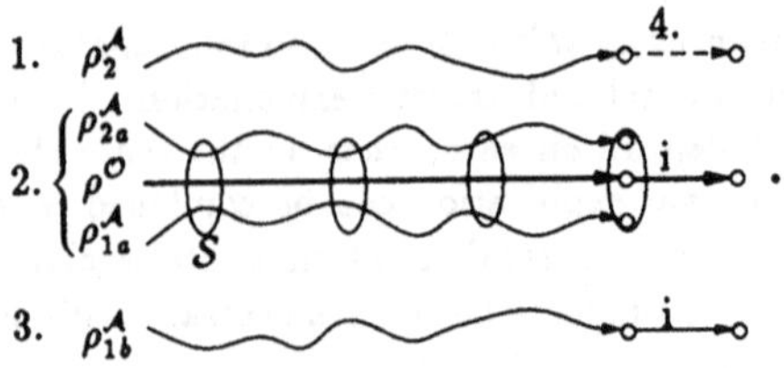

Figure 6

2. By induction, we can find an explanation $\rho_{1a}^{\mathcal{A}}$ of p in S_1 and an explanation $\rho_{2a}^{\mathcal{A}}$ in S_2 (which might be equal to $\rho_2^{\mathcal{A}}$) such that the simulation relation holds between the states of $\rho^{\mathcal{O}}, \rho_{1a}^{\mathcal{A}}, \rho_{2a}^{\mathcal{A}}$ (lemma 21 in appendix).

3. Since $\rho^{\mathcal{O}} \in [\mathsf{S}_1]$ and $\rho_{1a}^{\mathcal{A}}$ explains p then according to definition 10 we can find an explanation $\rho_{1b}^{\mathcal{A}}$ of p extended with the internal transition.

4. As the step is internal, the external part of $\rho_2^{\mathcal{A}}$ can be extended with a silent transition to give an external explanation $\rho_{2b,e}^{\mathcal{A}}$ of the extended p.

5. From $\rho_{2b,e}^{\mathcal{A}}$ and the internal explanation of $\rho_{1b}^{\mathcal{A}}$ we can construct an explanation of the extended p in S_2, due to the separability of the auxiliary variables (lemma 20 in appendix).

Since we now have found an explanation in S_2 of p extended with the internal transition, we have proved:

Theorem 16 (Refinement)

Let S_1 and S_2 be two r-g specifications, where $\mathsf{S}_i = \langle \mathsf{A}_i, \mathsf{O}_i, \mathsf{I}_i, \mathsf{R}_i, \mathsf{G}_i \rangle$, and $\mathsf{O}_1 = \mathsf{O}_2$ and the auxiliary variables are separable.

If there exists a simulation relation $\mathcal{S} \subseteq \Sigma(\mathsf{A}_1 \cup \mathsf{O}_1 \cup \mathsf{A}_2 \cup \mathsf{O}_2)$ such that:

$$\mathcal{S}(\mathsf{I}_1, \mathsf{I}_2) \wedge \mathsf{R}_2 \subseteq_{\mathcal{S}} \mathsf{R}_1 \wedge \mathsf{G}_1 \subseteq_{\mathcal{S}} \mathsf{G}_2$$

then

$$\mathsf{S}_1 \models \mathsf{S}_2$$

■

Proof Rule for Hiding

So far we have shown how to verify refinement between specifications with equal sets of interface variables. Sometimes we do, however, want to verify that a specification S_1 with interface variables O_1 refines a specification S_2 with interface variables O_2, where $O_2 \subseteq O_1$, i.e. S_1 has more interface variables than S_2.

Instead of hiding the extra interface variables in S_1, we show that they can be added to S_2 without changing the behaviour on the original interface variables of S_2.

Theorem 17 (Hiding)

Let S_1 and S_2, $S_i = \langle A_i, O_i, I_i, R_i, G_i \rangle$, be r-g specifications where $O_2 \subseteq O_1$. Then

$$S_1 \models S_2' \;\Rightarrow\; S_1 \models S_2$$

where $S_2' = \langle A_2', O_2', I_2', R_2', G_2' \rangle$ is given by:

- $A_2' = A_2$: the auxiliary variables are unchanged.
- $O_2' = O_1$: the interface variables are extended to the larger set O_1.
- $I_2' = I_2 \cup I_1(O_1 \setminus O_2)$: The initial state is the initial state of S_2 extended with the initial values of the variables that the state-space is extended with.
- $R_2' = R_2 \uplus (O_1 \cup A_2)$: The rely-set is R_2 extended to the new state-space by transitions which leave the new variables unchanged.
- $G_2' = G_2 \boxplus (O_1 \cup A_2)$: The guarantee-set is G_2 extended to the new state-space by transitions which may change the new variables arbitrarily.

Proof: Left out – follows the scheme of the previous proof.

■

Note that S_1 and S_2' have the same interface variables. Therefore we can use this theorem in conjunction with theorem 16 to verify that S_1 refines S_2 when $O_2 \subset O_1$.

Example: Refinement of the two-element split-node

The two-element split-node *Split* introduced previously can be refined into a more implementation-oriented specification *Split'*. The counter c is replaced by two boolean elements a, b and the transitions only shift boolean values from one element to another. The simplicity of the transitions makes e.g. a VLSI-implementation of the split-node easy.

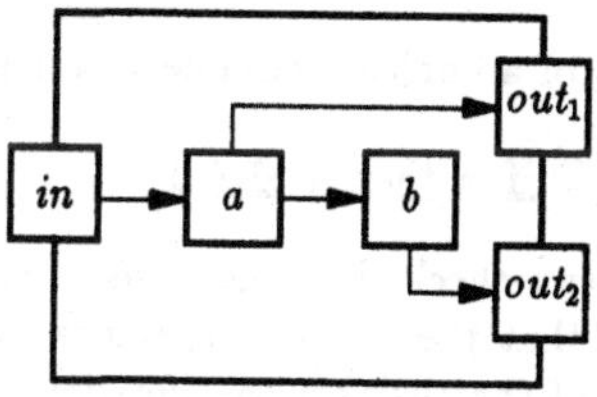

Figure 7

Refinement of the two-element split-node

$$
\begin{aligned}
\mathit{Split}' \stackrel{\text{def}}{=}\; & \\
& A = \{a, b\} \\
& O = \{in, out_1, out_2\} \\
& I = [in \mapsto \mathtt{f}, out_1 \mapsto \mathtt{f}, out_2 \mapsto \mathtt{f}, \\
& \qquad a \mapsto \mathtt{f}, b \mapsto \mathtt{f}] \\
& R = \langle \neg in \rightarrow in := \mathtt{t} \rangle, \\
& \qquad \langle out_1 \rightarrow out_1 := \mathtt{f} \rangle, \\
& \qquad \langle out_2 \rightarrow out_2 := \mathtt{f} \rangle \\
& G = \langle in \wedge a \rightarrow in, a, b := \mathtt{f}, in, a \rangle, \\
& \qquad \langle in \wedge \neg a \rightarrow in, a := \mathtt{f}, \mathtt{t} \rangle, \\
& \qquad \langle a \wedge \neg b \rightarrow a, b := \mathtt{f}, \mathtt{t} \rangle, \\
& \qquad \langle \neg out_1 \wedge a \rightarrow out_1, a := \mathtt{t}, \mathtt{f} \rangle, \\
& \qquad \langle \neg out_2 \wedge b \rightarrow out_2, b := \mathtt{t}, \mathtt{f} \rangle
\end{aligned}
$$

Note that *Split'* does not put any limits on how many elements the environment may insert. The first transition scheme in G, however, is an optimization that shifts two values at a time. Therefore, if more than two elements are inserted an element may be lost. On the other hand – if at most two elements are in the node at a time, *Split'* should behave like *Split*. To verify this we apply theorem 16.

Thus, in the following the concrete specification S_1 and the abstract specification S_2 of theorem 16 will be referring to *Split'* and *Split* respectively.

First of all we must make sure that the auxiliary variables are separable in both S_1 and S_2. In S_2

the auxiliary variables n and c occur only in the transition schemes for R and G respectively so they are obviously separable. Likewise in S_1 the auxiliary variables occur only in the transitions schemes for G.

The next step is to find a simulation-relation $\mathcal{S} \subseteq \Sigma(\{in, out_1, out_2, n, c, a, b\})$. The simulation-relation is defined by the predicate:

$$n = c + |in| + |out_1| + |out_2| \wedge$$
$$c = |a| + |b| \wedge$$
$$n \leq 2,$$

where $|x|$ of a boolean variable x is defined by:

$$|x| \stackrel{\text{def}}{=} \underline{\text{if}}\ x\ \underline{\text{then}}\ 1\ \underline{\text{else}}\ 0$$

Now we can check the conditions of theorem 16 to verify that the concrete specification is a refinement of the abstract specification:

1. $\mathcal{S}(\mathsf{I}_1, \mathsf{I}_2)$: We can directly verify that the simulation relation holds between the initial states.

2. $\mathsf{R}_2 \subseteq_{\mathcal{S}} \mathsf{R}_1$: For each transition-scheme T_2 of R_2, we can find a corresponding transition-scheme T_1 of R_1, such that $T_2 \subseteq_{\mathcal{S}} T_1$. This implies that $\mathsf{R}_2 \subseteq_{\mathcal{S}} \mathsf{R}_1$.

3. $\mathsf{G}_1 \subseteq_{\mathcal{S}} \mathsf{G}_2$: As above we are able to pair the transition-schemes.

To prove that $T_1 \subseteq_{\mathcal{S}} T_2$ we use the following more syntactic proof condition: $T_1 \subseteq_{\mathcal{S}} T_2$ iff:

> For all states where $\mathcal{S}$ holds: if T_1 is enabled, then T_2 is enabled too, and the simulation relation holds after the assignments.

We will now sketch the proof for two pairs of corresponding transition schemes. For the rely-part we e.g. have to prove $T_2 \subseteq_{\mathcal{S}} T_1$ where

$$T_2 : \langle\, n < 2 \wedge \neg in \rightarrow n, in := n + 1, \mathtt{t} \,\rangle$$
$$T_1 : \langle\, \neg in \rightarrow in := \mathtt{t} \,\rangle$$

It is obvious that if T_2 is enabled in the pre-state then T_1 is enabled too. Furthermore it can be verified that the simulation relation holds in the post-state (if it held in the pre-state) by checking each line of the predicate defining $\mathcal{S}$.

For the guarantee-part we must e.g. prove that $T_1 \subseteq_{\mathcal{S}} T_2$ where

$$T_1 : \langle\, in \wedge a \rightarrow in, a, b := \mathtt{f}, in, a \,\rangle$$
$$T_2 : \langle\, in \rightarrow c, in := c + 1, \mathtt{f} \,\rangle$$

It is easy to see that if T_1 is enabled then T_2 is enabled too. We now want to prove that if $\mathcal{S}$ holds in the pre-state then $\mathcal{S}$ will also hold in the post-state. The only state-change that could violate the simulation relation is the case where b is true in the pre-state. This would mean that T_1 shifts a new value into b, and thus looses one value.

This cannot be the case. If b is true in the pre-state, this state cannot be in $\mathcal{S}$. This is so because all of a, b and in would be true in the pre-state, causing n to exceed its allowed bounds (cf. the definition of $\mathcal{S}$).

Note the strength of the simulation relation: To verify that the guarantee-condition of the concrete specification simulates the guarantee-condition of the abstract specification (i.e. the node correctly splits the message read at in between out_1 and out_2 without losing any elements) we need the rely-condition of the abstract specification (R_2), i.e. that no more than two elements are inserted by the environment.

Instead of using a proof condition like: $\mathsf{R}_2 \wedge \mathsf{G}_1 \Rightarrow \mathsf{G}_2$, the simulation relation holds the necessary information about R_2, such that the proof-obligation becomes $\mathsf{G}_1 \subseteq_{\mathcal{S}} \mathsf{G}_2$.

5 Composition

In this section we will investigate the conditions for decomposing an abstract r-g specification S, into two concrete r-g specifications S_1, S_2, such that the composition of S_1 and S_2 is a refinement of S. By the phrase "composition of r-g specifications" we mean composition of the observable behaviours they denote, i.e. $[\![S_1]\!] \parallel [\![S_2]\!]$.

To be able to describe these conditions we introduce two operations on transition relations: $\sqcap$ and $\sqcup$.

Let V_1 and V_2 be two possibly overlapping sets of variables and $\mathcal{R}_1$ and $\mathcal{R}_2$ be two transition relations where $\mathcal{R}_1 \subseteq \mathsf{Trans}(V_1)$ and $\mathcal{R}_2 \subseteq \mathsf{Trans}(V_2)$. We define $\mathcal{R}_1 \sqcap \mathcal{R}_2$ by

$$\mathcal{R}_1 \sqcap \mathcal{R}_2 \stackrel{\text{def}}{=} (\mathcal{R}_1 \uplus (V_1 \cup V_2)) \cap (\mathcal{R}_2 \uplus (V_1 \cup V_2))$$

and $\mathcal{R}_1 \sqcup \mathcal{R}_2$ by

$$\mathcal{R}_1 \sqcup \mathcal{R}_2 \stackrel{\text{def}}{=} (\mathcal{R}_1 \sqcap \mathcal{R}_2) \cup (\mathcal{R}_1 \uplus (V_1 \cup V_2)) \cup (\mathcal{R}_2 \uplus (V_1 \cup V_2))$$

The operation $\mathcal{R}_1 \sqcap \mathcal{R}_2$ can be seen as what $\mathcal{R}_1$ and $\mathcal{R}_2$ could agree upon, and $\mathcal{R}_1 \sqcup \mathcal{R}_2$ as what they can do altogether. Notice that if $V_1 = V_2$ then $\sqcap$ and $\sqcup$ become normal intersection and union respectively.

Intuitively, the conditions for composition should express the same as for normal refinement, i.e. that the two concrete specifications together rely less on the environment than the abstract specification, and when placed in an environment satisfying the abstract rely-condition, each of the concrete specifications should guarantee at least the same as the abstract guarantee-part. Beside this, the two concrete specifications should mutually satisfy the rely-condition of the other concrete specification. These conditions can formally be expressed, using a simulation relation $\mathcal{S}$, by:

- $\mathcal{S}(\mathsf{I}_1, \mathsf{I}_2, \mathsf{I})$ – the initial condition.
- $\mathsf{R} \subseteq_{\mathcal{S}} \mathsf{R}_1 \sqcup \mathsf{R}_2$ – the two specifications together rely less on the environment than the abstract specification.
- $\mathsf{G}_1 \subseteq_{\mathcal{S}} \mathsf{G} \sqcup \mathsf{R}_2$ – given the abstract rely-condition (imposed through the simulation relation) the guarantee-part of the first concrete specification should stay within the abstract guarantee-condition and satisfy the rely-condition of the second concrete specification.
- $\mathsf{G}_2 \subseteq_{\mathcal{S}} \mathsf{G} \sqcup \mathsf{R}_1$ – similar to the above.

The result is expressed in the following theorem.

Theorem 18 (Composition)

Let there be given three r-g specifications $\mathsf{S}_1, \mathsf{S}_2$ and S, where $\mathsf{S}_i = \langle \mathsf{A}_i, \mathsf{O}_i, \mathsf{I}_i, \mathsf{R}_i, \mathsf{G}_i \rangle$ and

1. $\mathsf{O}_1 \cup \mathsf{O}_2 = \mathsf{O}$
2. $\mathsf{A}_1 \cap \mathsf{A}_2 = \mathsf{A}_1 \cap \mathsf{A} = \mathsf{A}_2 \cap \mathsf{A} = \{\}$, i.e. the auxiliary variables are *not* shared.
3. The auxiliary variables are separable in $\mathsf{S}_1, \mathsf{S}_2$ and S.

If there exists a simulation relation $\mathcal{S} \subseteq \Sigma(\mathsf{A}_1 \cup \mathsf{O}_1 \cup \mathsf{A}_2 \cup \mathsf{O}_2 \cup \mathsf{A})$ such that:

- $\mathcal{S}(\mathsf{I}_1, \mathsf{I}_2, \mathsf{I})$
- $\mathsf{R} \subseteq_{\mathcal{S}} \mathsf{R}_1 \sqcup \mathsf{R}_2$
- $\mathsf{G}_1 \subseteq_{\mathcal{S}} \mathsf{G} \sqcup \mathsf{R}_2$
- $\mathsf{G}_2 \subseteq_{\mathcal{S}} \mathsf{G} \sqcup \mathsf{R}_1$

then

$$[\![\mathsf{S}_1]\!] \parallel [\![\mathsf{S}_2]\!] \models [\![\mathsf{S}]\!]$$

Proof: left out – the proof is a generalization (with three specifications instead of two) of the proof of theorem 16 and is proved by introducing the corresponding generalized lemmas.

■

Example: Composition of servers

Let in the following

$$\mathsf{S}_1 = \mathit{Server}(\mathit{in}, \mathit{inout})$$

$$\mathsf{S}_2 = \mathit{Server}(\mathit{inout}, \mathit{out})$$

$$\mathsf{S} = \mathit{Server}(\mathit{in}, \mathit{out})$$

We now want to prove that the composition of S_1 and S_2 refines the server-specification S:

$$([\![\mathsf{S}_1]\!] \parallel [\![\mathsf{S}_2]\!]) \setminus \{\mathit{inout}\} \subseteq [\![\mathsf{S}]\!] \qquad (**)$$

i.e. "piping" the output of S_1 to the input of S_2 through the shared variable *inout* behaves as a server when *inout* is hidden.

We start by using the hiding theorem (theorem 17 on page 10). This enables us to extend S with a "dummy" variable *inout*, so that we get a new specification S' with $\mathsf{R}' = \mathsf{R} \uplus \{\mathit{in}, \mathit{out}, \mathit{inout}\}$ and $\mathsf{G}' = \mathsf{G} \uplus \{\mathit{in}, \mathit{out}, \mathit{inout}\}$, and $\mathsf{I}' = \mathsf{I} \cup [\mathit{inout} \mapsto \mathbf{f}]$. Theorem 17 says that it is sufficient to prove that $[\![\mathsf{S}_1]\!] \parallel [\![\mathsf{S}_2]\!] \models [\![\mathsf{S}']\!]$ holds to ensure (**).

The next step is to use theorem 18. It is obvious that the auxiliary variables are separable – there is *no* auxiliary variables.

Since the two specifications have exactly the same variables, and thereby the same state-space, it might seem obvious to include every state over the variables in the simulation-relation. However, that relation would not be strong enough to prove the above constraints. When looking at the composition of two servers, it becomes clear that there exists an invariant, which secures that *inout* equals either *in* or *out*. Therefore we define $\mathcal{S}$ to be the set of states satisfying the predicate:

$$\mathit{in} = \mathit{inout} \vee \mathit{out} = \mathit{inout}$$

We now have to prove that

$$\mathcal{S}(\mathsf{I}',\mathsf{I}_1,\mathsf{I}_2) \wedge \mathsf{R}' \subseteq_{\mathcal{S}} \mathsf{R}_1 \sqcup \mathsf{R}_2 \wedge \mathsf{G}_1 \subseteq_{\mathcal{S}} \mathsf{G}' \sqcup \mathsf{R}_1 \wedge \mathsf{G}_2 \subseteq_{\mathcal{S}} \mathsf{G}' \sqcup \mathsf{R}_2$$

• $\mathcal{S}(\mathsf{I}',\mathsf{I}_1,\mathsf{I}_2)$: The simulation relation holds in the initial state, where $in = \mathtt{f}$, $out = \mathtt{f}$ and $inout = \mathtt{f}$.

• $\mathsf{R}' \subseteq_{\mathcal{S}} \mathsf{R}_1 \sqcup \mathsf{R}_2$. Recall that R is given by:[4]

$$\mathsf{R}(in, out) = \{\mathtt{ff} \rightarrow \mathtt{tf}, \mathtt{tt} \rightarrow \mathtt{ft}\}$$

To ease the reading we do not write the silent transitions explicitly. The set of transitions given by $\mathsf{R}' = \mathsf{R} \uplus \{in, inout, out\}$ is :

$$\mathsf{R}'(in, inout, out) = \{\mathtt{fff} \rightarrow \mathtt{tff}, \mathtt{ftf} \rightarrow \mathtt{ttf}, \mathtt{tft} \rightarrow \mathtt{fft}, \mathtt{ttt} \rightarrow \mathtt{ftt}\}$$

$\mathsf{R}_1 \sqcup \mathsf{R}_2$ is given by:

$$\mathsf{R}_1 \sqcup \mathsf{R}_2(in, inout, out) = \{\mathtt{fff} \rightarrow \mathtt{tff}, \mathtt{fff} \rightarrow \mathtt{ftf}, \mathtt{fft} \rightarrow \mathtt{tft}, \mathtt{ftt} \rightarrow \mathtt{fft}, \mathtt{tff} \rightarrow \mathtt{ttf}, \mathtt{ttf} \rightarrow \mathtt{ftf}, \mathtt{ttt} \rightarrow \mathtt{ftt}, \mathtt{ttt} \rightarrow \mathtt{tft}\}$$

The reason for including the invariant in the simulation-relation is that $\mathtt{ftf} \rightarrow \mathtt{ttf}$ and $\mathtt{tft} \rightarrow \mathtt{fft}$ both are in R', but not in $\mathsf{R}_1 \sqcup \mathsf{R}_2$. We see that $\mathcal{S}$ does not hold in the pre-state of these transitions, therefore they need not be present in $\mathsf{R}_1 \sqcup \mathsf{R}_2$.

• $\mathsf{G}_1 \subseteq_{\mathcal{S}} \mathsf{G}' \sqcup \mathsf{R}_2$.

G_1 is given by:

$$\mathsf{G}_1(in, inout) = \{\mathtt{tf} \rightarrow \mathtt{tt}, \mathtt{ft} \rightarrow \mathtt{ff}\}$$

$\mathsf{G}' = \mathsf{G} \uplus \{in, inout, out\}$ is given by:

$$\mathsf{G}'(in, inout, out) = \{\mathtt{tff} \rightarrow \mathtt{tft}, \mathtt{tff} \rightarrow \mathtt{ttt}, \mathtt{ttf} \rightarrow \mathtt{tft}, \mathtt{ttf} \rightarrow \mathtt{ttt}, \mathtt{fft} \rightarrow \mathtt{fff}, \mathtt{fft} \rightarrow \mathtt{ftf}, \mathtt{ftt} \rightarrow \mathtt{fff}, \mathtt{ftt} \rightarrow \mathtt{ftf}\}$$

$\mathsf{G}' \sqcup \mathsf{R}_2$ is given by:

$$\mathsf{G}' \sqcup \mathsf{R}_2(in, inout, out) = \{\mathtt{tff} \rightarrow \mathtt{tft}, \mathtt{tff} \rightarrow \mathtt{ttt}, \mathtt{ttf} \rightarrow \mathtt{tft}, \mathtt{ttf} \rightarrow \mathtt{ttt}, \mathtt{fft} \rightarrow \mathtt{fff}, \mathtt{fft} \rightarrow \mathtt{ftf}, \mathtt{ftt} \rightarrow \mathtt{fff}, \mathtt{ftt} \rightarrow \mathtt{ftf}, \mathtt{fff} \rightarrow \mathtt{ftf}, \mathtt{tff} \rightarrow \mathtt{ttf}, \mathtt{ftt} \rightarrow \mathtt{fft}, \mathtt{ttt} \rightarrow \mathtt{tft}\}$$

[4]We write xy instead of $[in \mapsto x, out \mapsto y]$

We see directly that $\mathsf{G}_1 \subseteq_{\mathcal{S}} \mathsf{G}' \sqcup \mathsf{R}_2$.

• $\mathsf{G}_2 \subseteq_{\mathcal{S}} \mathsf{G}' \sqcup \mathsf{R}_1$: This proof is similar to the proof above and is therefore left out.

Beside the compositionality of servers this example again shows the strength of the simulation relation. The simulation relation does not only express the relation between the different state-spaces, *it is also able to describe invariants of the variables on both abstraction levels.*

6 Discussion

In this paper we have introduced transition-based *rely-guarantee* specifications as a method for describing individual components of a concurrent system. To talk about a previous course of events we use auxiliary variables. Since the rôle of auxiliary variables is not quite clear in r-g specifications we have worked with two restricted classes of auxiliary variables:

- *Deterministic*: The auxiliary variables are said to be deterministic if their value is uniquely given by the changes made to the interface variables.
- *Separable*: The auxiliary variables are separable if they can be split in two parts, such that one part can affect and is affected only by the *rely* transitions and the other part only by the *guarantee* transitions. The auxiliary variables need not be deterministic.

In this paper we have only considered separable auxiliary variables, but in [5] the proof rules are shown to be valid for any combination of these classes. On the other hand, we have examples showing that our refinement rule does not hold for arbitrary forms of auxiliary variables.

The proof rules we have presented allow us to verify:

1. That one specification S_1 *refines* another specification S_2.
2. That the *composition* of two specifications refines a specification of the composed system. Especially, we can handle mutually dependent safety properties.

In order to utilize any relation between specifications at different abstraction levels we use the notion of a *simulation relation* which ties together the states on both abstraction levels. An important purpose of the relation is to express invariants which ensure that a component — when placed in an environment satisfying the *rely* condition of an abstract specification — will actually behave in such a restricted way that it conforms to the abstract *guarantee* condition.

As shown in the work of Abadi and Lamport [1] on pure guarantee specification we cannot achieve completeness with just a normal "forward" simulation relation in the case where a specification takes a non-deterministic choice before the implementation does. Abadi and Lamport introduce special *prophecy variables* in the implementation to "align" the non-determinism. Using these prophecy variables, or the similar notion of "backward" simulation by Jonsson [9], the method becomes complete for pure *guarantee* specifications.

Related work

Our work is, on one hand an extension of transition-based proof techniques [1, 8, 12, 13, 14, 21] to incorporate the pragmatically useful r-g concept and, on the other hand, a restriction of more general r-g languages [18] towards practical verification techniques.

The work by Jones [7] combined pre/post and r-g specifications, but did not consider auxiliary variables which add considerably to the complexity of the theory.

For UNITY, [4] Chandy and Misra use *conditional specifications*, but their proof system is not able to cope with mutually dependent specifications.

After the completion of our work, a very similar work by Abadi and Lamport has been reported [2]. They too present rules for refinement and composition of shared variable systems specified by a *environment part* and a *system part*. Some minor differences are: Their approach is more semantic, using sets of executions rather than the single transitions. They separate simulation and composition where we have a combined rule. They do not allow an implementation to rely *more* on the environment than the specification does. We allow this case which can be of practical interest, e.g. when one wants to apply a standard component. Finally, we define the semantics for common auxiliary variables, where they only treat the case of separable auxiliary variables. A more significant difference is that Abadi and Lamport incorporate certain liveness properties in the specifications. These cannot be mutually dependent, however.

Another closely related approach is presented in [11]. Here the environment part of a specification is not as much seen as a description of how the environment is *supposed* to behave but rather how it *actually* behaves. The implementation relation seems defined only for unchanged environment assumptions.

Future work

Although we have indications that our approach is useful, there are still a number of problems to be addressed.

Obviously, complete simulation techniques like backward simulation could be taken into account to make our proof rules complete.

A theoretic problem would be to characterize the properties of auxiliary variables necessary to ensure the validity of our refinement rule. Whereas others have confined themselves to separable auxiliary variables [2, 11] we believe that sharing of history information can be useful in practical specification. On the other hand, our general semantics adds considerably to the complexity of our theory.

The current theory only deals with safety properties. Liveness properties can be added as various fairness properties of the transition systems [8] or separately by temporal formulas [21]. In any case, liveness properties cannot be mutually dependent and therefore they must either be restricted [2] or special techniques such as "cut sets" [20] must be incorporated in the rules.

The shared variable concept allows for handling asynchronous communication [4]. To deal with synchronous communication we would have to extend the theory considerably by including a notion of *common events* at the interface.

The presentation given is based on sets of transitions. As shown by the examples, however, the connection with transition schemes or pre/post specifications is immediate. In [5] we show how the simulation conditions can be syntactically verified.

Finally, it should be noted that r-g specifications are not the goal but rather a foundation for specifications based on a *protocol* concept. E.g., if we have a protocol describing the behaviour of a buffer, a single buffer element may be indirectly specified by:

> *If one part of the environment behaves like an n-buffer, the component will behave like an $n+1$-buffer to the other part of the environment.*

Each rôle in the protocol will generate rely and guarantee conditions which are mutually dependent with the conditions of the other rôles. In [5] we have shown how the r-g theory can be used to establish the soundness of simple composition rules for protocol based specifications.

In general we see the rely-guarantee paradigms as a foundation for the *compositional* methods that are necessary for verification of larger concurrent systems.

Acknowledgements

We would like to thank Pierre Colette for many good suggestions for this and future work.

References

[1] Martin Abadi & Leslie Lamport: *The Existence of Refinement Mappings.* Digital Equipment Corporation 1988. Shortened version in *Proceedings of the LICS Conference*, Edinburgh, Scotland. July 1988.

[2] Martin Abadi & Leslie Lamport: *Composing Specifications.* In proc. of REX workshop on stepwise refinement of distributed systems, LNCS 430, Springer-Verlag 1990, pages 1–41.

[3] Howard Barringer, Ruurd Kuiper & Amir Pnueli: *Now You May Compose Temporal Logic Specifications* Proceedings of the 16th ACM SOTCS, Washington 1984, pages 57–63.

[4] Mani Chandy & Jajadev Misra: *Parallel Program Design – A Foundation.* Addison-Wesley Publishing Company Inc. 1988.

[5] P. Grønning & T. Qvist Nielsen: *Compositional Specification and Verification of Concurrent Systems.* Master's Thesis, Department of Computer Science, Technical University of Denmark, January 1990.

[6] C.A.R Hoare: *Communicating Sequential Processes*, Prentice Hall, 1985.

[7] Cliff B. Jones: *Specification and Design of (Parallel) Programs.* Proceedings of IFIP 83, pages 321–332.

[8] Bengt Jonsson: *Compositional Verification of Distributed Systems.* Ph.D. Thesis. Uppsala DoCS 87/09 1987.

[9] Bengt Jonsson: *On Decomposing and Refining Specifications of Distributed Systems.* In proc. of REX workshop on stepwise refinement of distributed systems, LNCS 430, Springer-Verlag 1990, pages 361–385

[10] N. Klarlund & F.B. Schneider: *Verifying Safety Properties Using Infinite-State Automata.* Technical Report, No. TR 89–1036, Cornell University, 1989.

[11] Reino Kurki-Suonio: *Operational Specification with Joint Actions: Serializable Databases.* To appear in Distributed Computing.

[12] Leslie Lamport: *Specifying Concurrent Program Modules.* ACM Transactions on Programming Languages and Systems, Vol. 5, No. 2, April 1983, pages 190–222.

[13] S.S. Lam & A.U. Shankar: *Protocol verification via projections.* IEEE Transactions on Software Engineering, Vol. SE–10, No. 4, July 1984, pages 325–342.

[14] Nancy A. Lynch & Mark R. Tuttle: *Hierachical Correctness Proofs for Distributed Algorithms.* In proc. of the Sixth Symposium on the Principles of Distributed Computing, ACM, August 1987, pages 137–151.

[15] Alain J. Martin: *Compiling communicating processes into delay-insensitive VLSI circuits*, Distributed Computing, Vol. 1 1986, pages 226–234.

[16] Robin Milner: *Communication and Concurrency*, Prentice Hall, 1989.

[17] Jayadev Misra & K. Mani Chandy: *Proofs of Networks of Processes.* IEEE Transactions of Software Engineering, Vol. SE-7. No. 4, July 1981, pages 417-426.

[18] P. Pandya: *Compositional Verification of Distributed Programs*. Ph.D. Thesis. University of Bombay, 1988.

[19] Amir Pnueli: *In Transition From Global to Modular Temporal Reasoning about Programs*. NATO ASI Series, Vol. F13, Logics and Models of Concurrent Systems, Springer-Verlag 1985, pages 123–144.

[20] Eugene W. Stark: *A Proof Technique for Rely/Guarantee Properties*. Foundations of Software Technology and Theoretical Computer Science, LNCS 206, Springer-Verlag, 1985, pages 369–391.

[21] Eugene W. Stark: *Proving Entailment Between Conceptual State Specifications*. European Symposium on Programming, Saarbrücken, LNCS 213, Springer-Verlag, 1986, pages 197–209.

[22] Jørgen Staunstrup & Mark Greenstreet: *Synchronized Transitions*. In Jørgen Staunstrup (ed) Formal Methods for VLSI Design, North-Holland, 1990.

A Lemmas for the Refinement Theorem

Lemma 19 (Joining explanations)

Let $\mathsf{S} = \langle \mathsf{A}, \mathsf{O}, \mathsf{I}, \mathsf{R}, \mathsf{G} \rangle$ be an r-g specification with the auxiliary variables separated into A_i and A_e.

Given an observable computation $\rho^{\mathcal{O}}$ of S, let $\rho_i^{\mathcal{A}}$ be any internal explanation of $\rho^{\mathcal{O}}$ and let $\rho_e^{\mathcal{A}}$ be any external explanation of $\rho^{\mathcal{O}}$. Then the computation $\rho^{\mathcal{A}}$ which results from pointwise union of the states of the two explanations

$$\rho^{\mathcal{A}} = \rho_i^{\mathcal{A}} \ \cup \ \rho_e^{\mathcal{A}}$$

is an explanation of $\rho^{\mathcal{O}}$.

Proof: We must prove that there exists a computation $\rho \in \mathsf{Comp}(\mathsf{A} \cup \mathsf{O}, \{i, e\}, \mathsf{I})$ such that

$$\forall t \in \rho : \mathit{Legal}(t, \mathsf{S}) \wedge$$
$$(\rho \lceil \mathsf{O} = \rho^{\mathcal{O}}) \wedge (\rho \lceil \mathsf{A} = \rho_i^{\mathcal{A}} \cup \rho_e^{\mathcal{A}})$$

For ρ we take $\rho^{\mathcal{O}} \cup \rho_i^{\mathcal{A}} \cup \rho_e^{\mathcal{A}}$ which obviously satisfies the projection properties. Since $\rho_i^{\mathcal{A}}$ is an internal explanation there exists an $\rho_{\bullet}^{\mathcal{A}}$ over A_e such that for $\rho_i = \rho^{\mathcal{O}} \cup \rho_i^{\mathcal{A}} \cup \rho_{\bullet}^{\mathcal{A}}$, all transitions in ρ_i are internally legal. Due to the independence of the two sets of auxiliary variables, $\rho_{\bullet}^{\mathcal{A}}$ can be exchanged with $\rho_e^{\mathcal{A}}$ without violating the internal legacy. Thus in the resulting ρ, all transitions are internally legal. Symmetrically, we can conclude that all transitions of ρ are externally legal.

Given that the auxiliary variables are separable it follows directly from the definitions that

$$\mathit{Legal}(t, \mathsf{S}) \Leftrightarrow \mathit{ExtLegal}(t, \mathsf{S}) \wedge \mathit{IntLegal}(t, \mathsf{S})$$

Thus, all transitions of ρ are legal such that $\rho_i^{\mathcal{A}} \cup \rho_e^{\mathcal{A}}$is an explanation of $\rho^{\mathcal{O}}$

■

Lemma 20 (Constructing explanations)

Let S_1 and S_2, $\mathsf{S}_i = \langle \mathsf{A}_i, \mathsf{O}_i, \mathsf{I}_i, \mathsf{R}_i, \mathsf{G}_i \rangle$, be two r-g specifications such that $\mathsf{O}_1 = \mathsf{O}_2$, the auxiliary variables are separable, and there exists a simulation relation $\mathcal{S} \subseteq \Sigma(\mathsf{A}_1 \cup \mathsf{O}_1 \cup \mathsf{A}_2 \cup \mathsf{O}_2)$ satisfying:

$$\mathcal{S}(\mathsf{I}_1, \mathsf{I}_2) \wedge \mathsf{R}_2 \subseteq_{\mathcal{S}} \mathsf{R}_1 \wedge \mathsf{G}_1 \subseteq_{\mathcal{S}} \mathsf{G}_2$$

Let $\rho^{\mathcal{O}}$ be an observable computation.

For any *external* explanation $\rho_{2,e}^{\mathcal{A}}$ of $\rho^{\mathcal{O}}$ in S_2 and any *internal* explanation $\rho_{1,i}^{\mathcal{A}}$ of $\rho^{\mathcal{O}}$ in S_1 there exists an explanation $\rho_2^{\mathcal{A}}$ of $\rho^{\mathcal{O}}$ in S_2 and an explanation $\rho_1^{\mathcal{A}}$ of $\rho^{\mathcal{O}}$ in S_1 such that the simulation relation $\mathcal{S}$ holds between the states of $\rho_1^{\mathcal{A}}, \rho_2^{\mathcal{A}}$ and $\rho^{\mathcal{O}}$.

Proof: We prove the existence of the explanations by generating them. By lemma 19, this can be done by constructing an internal explanation $\rho_{2,i}^{\mathcal{A}}$ of $\rho^{\mathcal{O}}$ in S_2, and an external explanation $\rho_{1,e}^{\mathcal{A}}$ of $\rho^{\mathcal{O}}$ in S_1, such that the simulation relation $\mathcal{S}$ holds between the states of $\rho_{1,i}^{\mathcal{A}}, \rho_{1,e}^{\mathcal{A}}, \rho_{2,i}^{\mathcal{A}}, \rho_{2,e}^{\mathcal{A}}$ and $\rho^{\mathcal{O}}$.

The proof is by induction over the length of a prefix p of $\rho^{\mathcal{O}}$:

Initially: The initial states of S_1 and S_2 restricted to respectively $\mathsf{A}_{1,e}$ and $\mathsf{A}_{2,i}$ serve as the initial states of $\rho_{1,e}^{\mathcal{A}}$ and $\rho_{2,i}^{\mathcal{A}}$. The fact that $\mathcal{S}(\mathsf{I}_1, \mathsf{I}_2)$ secures that $\mathcal{S}$ holds between the joined explanations and the empty prefix.

Inductive step: Given a prefix p of length i for which there exist $\rho_{2,i}^{\mathcal{A}}$ and $\rho_{1,e}^{\mathcal{A}}$ such that $\mathcal{S}$ holds between the states of these and $\rho_{1,i}^{\mathcal{A}}[0..i]$, $\rho_{2,e}^{\mathcal{A}}[0..i]$, we must show that $\rho_{2,i}^{\mathcal{A}}$ and $\rho_{1,e}^{\mathcal{A}}$ can be extended such that $\mathcal{S}$ holds between the states of these,

$\rho^{\mathcal{A}}_{1,i}[0..i+1]$, $\rho^{\mathcal{A}}_{2,e}[0..i+1]$, and p extended with the next transition of $\rho^{\mathcal{O}}$.

The next transition of $\rho^{\mathcal{O}}$ can be either internal or external:

internal step:

- $\rho^{\mathcal{A}}_{1,e}$: The internal transitions cannot change the external auxiliary variables $\mathsf{A}_{1,e}$ of $\rho^{\mathcal{A}}_{1,e}$, thus $\rho^{\mathcal{A}}_{1,e}$ can be extended by a silent transition.
- $\rho^{\mathcal{A}}_{2,i}$: By joining the extended external explanation $\rho^{\mathcal{A}}_{1,e}$ and the internal explanation $\rho^{\mathcal{A}}_{1,i}$ of $\rho^{\mathcal{O}}$ the explanation $\rho^{\mathcal{A}}_{1}$ is extended by one step.

  Since $\mathcal{S}$ holds before the step and $\mathsf{G}_1 \subseteq_{\mathcal{S}} \mathsf{G}_2$, there also exists an extension of $\rho^{\mathcal{A}}_{2}$ which maintains $\mathcal{S}$. From this extension we can extract the internal explanation and get the extension of $\rho^{\mathcal{A}}_{2,i}$.

Hereby we have extended the two explanations and preserved the simulation relation.

external step: This case is symmetric to the internal step described above.

■

Lemma 21 (Prefix-explanation)

Let S_1 and S_2, $\mathsf{S}_i = \langle \mathsf{A}_i, \mathsf{O}_i, \mathsf{I}_i, \mathsf{R}_i, \mathsf{G}_i \rangle$, be two r-g specifications such that $\mathsf{O}_1 = \mathsf{O}_2$, the auxiliary variables are separable, and there exists a simulation relation $\mathcal{S} \subseteq \Sigma(\mathsf{A}_1 \cup \mathsf{O}_1 \cup \mathsf{A}_2 \cup \mathsf{O}_2)$ satisfying:

$$\mathcal{S}(\mathsf{I}_1, \mathsf{I}_2) \wedge \mathsf{R}_2 \subseteq_{\mathcal{S}} \mathsf{R}_1 \wedge \mathsf{G}_1 \subseteq_{\mathcal{S}} \mathsf{G}_2$$

Then, for every prefix p of an observable computation $\rho^{\mathcal{O}} \in [\![\mathsf{S}_1]\!]$, if $\rho^{\mathcal{A}}_{2}$ is an explanation of p in S_2 there exist explanations $\rho^{\mathcal{A}}_{1a}$ of p in S_1 and $\rho^{\mathcal{A}}_{2a}$ of p in S_2 such that $\mathcal{S}$ holds between the states of $\rho^{\mathcal{A}}_{1a}$,$\rho^{\mathcal{A}}_{2a}$ and p.

Proof: The proof is by induction over the length of p:

Initially: Initially the initial state of $\rho^{\mathcal{A}}_{2}$ ($\mathsf{I}_2 \lceil \mathsf{A}_2$) is an explanation of the initial state of $\rho^{\mathcal{O}}$. Likewise $\mathsf{I}_1 \lceil \mathsf{A}_1$ explains the initial state of $\rho^{\mathcal{O}}$. Since $\mathcal{S}(\mathsf{I}_1, \mathsf{I}_2)$ holds, the simulation relation holds for the empty prefix.

Inductive step: Given a prefix p of length i, an explanation $\rho^{\mathcal{A}}_{1a}$ of p in S_1, and an explanation $\rho^{\mathcal{A}}_{2a}$ of p in S_2 such that the simulation relation holds between the states of $\rho^{\mathcal{A}}_{1a}$, $\rho^{\mathcal{A}}_{2a}$ and p, we must show the existence of similarly related explanations of p extended with the next transition of p.

The prefix p can be extended by either internal or external transitions.

- **internal**: If the next transition t of $\rho^{\mathcal{O}}$ is internal, we know that there exists an explanation $\rho^{\mathcal{A}}_{1b}$ of p_a extended with t in S_1, because we know that $\rho^{\mathcal{O}} \in [\![\mathsf{S}_1]\!]$.

  From this explanation we extract the *internal* explanation $\rho^{\mathcal{A}}_{1b,i}$. From $\rho^{\mathcal{A}}_{2}$ we extract an external explanation with length $i+1$.
- **external**: The internal explanation of $\rho^{\mathcal{A}}_{1a}$ can be extended by a silent transition, and from the explanation $\rho^{\mathcal{A}}_{2}$ we can extract an external explanation with length $i+1$.

In both cases we now have an internal explanation in S_1 and an external explanation in S_2, both of length $i+1$. From lemma 20 we get that there exist an explanation of p extended with t, such that the simulation relation holds.

■

EFFICIENT ALGORITHMS FOR CRASH RECOVERY IN DISTRIBUTED SYSTEMS

Tony T-Y. Juang *S. Venkatesan*

Computer Science Program, MP 31
University of Texas at Dallas
Richardson, TX 75083-0688

ABSTRACT

We consider the problem of recovering from processor failures efficiently in distributed systems. Each message received is logged in volatile storage when it is processed. At irregular intervals, each processor independently saves the contents of its volatile storage in stable storage. By appending only O(1) extra information to each message, we show that for recovery in general networks $O(n^2)$ messages are sufficient and in ring networks $\Theta(n)$ messages are necessary and sufficient when an arbitrary number of processors fail. By appending $O(n)$ extra information to each message that is sent, we show that $O(kn)$ messages are sufficient for rollingback all of the processors to the maximum consistent states when there are k failures.

1. INTRODUCTION

Distributed systems are replacing centralized systems as a result of increasing demand for high system performance, high availability and high reliability. Since the failure of processors causes the loss of the contents in its volatile storage, it is important to cope with failures in order to achieve these advantages. In order to cope with the failure of processors in many critical situation, the distributed systems must provide some recovery mechanism, and checkpointing is a technique frequently used in recovery. This paper presents three recovery algorithms which are based on asynchronous message logging to cope with arbitrary processor failures. We consider distributed systems where the underlying network may be represented by general graphs. We also consider ring networks for which we present a recovery algorithm which is asymptotically message-optimal and time-optimal.

Checkpointing is an effective method for maintaining consistency of distributed systems. The goal of checkpointing is to log a snapshot of previous state of the processors in stable storage. In case of a failure, the stored data can be used to restore the system to a *consistent* state. In a consistent system state, each pair of processor states agree on the sending and the receiving of messages between each other -- in no way there would be a processor state that reflects the receipt of a message when there is no processor state that corresponds to sending of the same message. Checkpointing has been widely used and studied by many researchers [2, 5-7, 10-13].

Some recovery algorithms were presented in [5, 10, 12]. The algorithm in [12] causes a process to rollback $O(2^n)$ times for the worst case where n is the total number of processors in the system. It also needs an exponential number of message exchanges to recover from the failure of one processor. The algorithm in [5] is a centralized one. In [10], algorithms are presented that require $O(n^2)$ message exchanges when $O(n)$ information is appended to each application message and $O(n^3)$ message exchanges when $O(1)$ extra information is appended to each message.

We present several recovery algorithms in this paper when faced with k simultaneous processor failures. Our first algorithm deals with distributed systems where the underlying network can be represented by a general graph network. In such networks, only $O(n^2)$ message exchanges are needed when only)(1) extra information is appended to each message. This scheme requires appending extra information of size $O(n)$ to each application message. The second recovery algorithm is for the ring networks which requires that $O(1)$ extra information be added to on each application message and it uses $O(n)$ messages to recover from multiple processor failures. The third algorithm appends only $O(n)$ addition information appended to each message and requires $O(kn)$ message exchanges for the general graph network when there are k faulty processors. The algorithms are shown to be correct as long as no further failures occur during the run of the recovery procedure.

The paper is organized as follows. Section 2 describes the model of distributed systems. In section 3, we present the first recovery algorithm with no transitive dependency. In section 4, the recovery algorithm for ring networks is described. In section 5, we give a recovery algorithm with transitive dependency. Finally, section 6 concludes the paper.

2. SYSTEM MODEL

A distributed system consists of a collection of distinct processors which are spatially separated, without shared memory or clock, and which communicate with each other by exchanging messages through reliable first-in-first-out (FIFO) channels with finite transmission time. In addition, the distributed system is assumed to be connected. When a processor fails, all other processors are informed of the failures in finite time and each processor p knows the identities of the failed processors before the recovery algorithm begins at p.

As defined in [12], a set of process states in which each pair of processes agrees on communication between them has taken place is called a set of consistent states. If the state of a process that has sent a message is ever lost, then in order for the system state to be consistent, the state change resulting from the receipt of that message in the receiving process must be undone; that is, the process must be *rollbacked.* We say that the system is in a *maximum consistent state* if every processor rollbacks to its "most recent" state and never needs to rollback again. For example, the time cuts c and c' in Figure 2.1 are consistent and inconsistent cuts respectively.

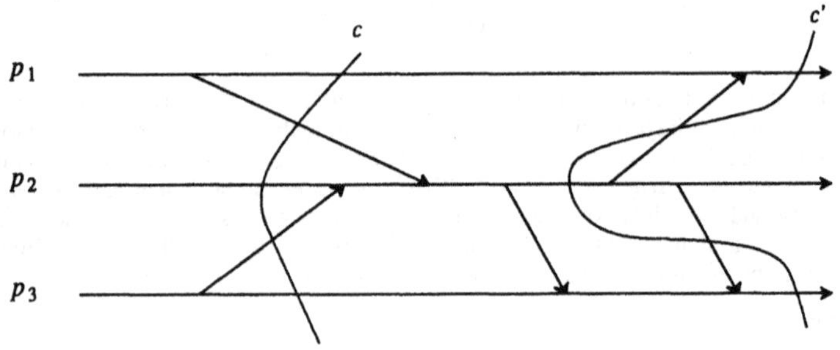

Figure 2.1

To recover from processor crashes to a consistent state, we use two types of logs - volatile log and stable log [4,9]. We assume that the underlying computation or the application program is event-driven where a processor p waits until a message m is received, processes the message m, changes its state from s to s', and sends a (possible empty) set of messages to some of its neighbors. The new state s' and the contents of the messages transmitted depend on its state s when m was received, the state of the sender and the contents of the message m. For example, in Figure 2.2, processor p_2 changes its state from s_{21} to s_{22} when it processes message m sent by p_3.

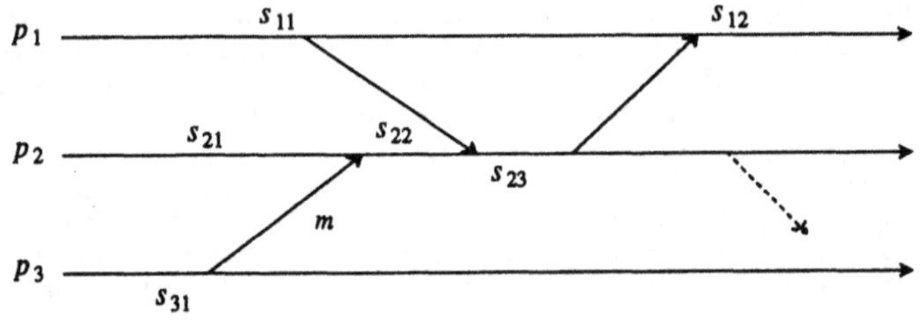

Figure 2.2

Each time a processor receives a message, it begins a new *State Transition Interval* (or STI) which is the interval of time between a processor receiving a message and the time it completes all of the actions associated with processing the message received (including sending messages to its neighbors). Each STI is identified by a unique sequential number called *interval index*, which is simply a count of the number of messages that the processor has received and processed.

The resulting state of the receiver of a message depends on the state of the sender and a *dependency* is created by each message. For example, in Figure 2.2, state s_{22} depends on state s_{31} and s_{21}. Note that this dependency relation is transitive. In our example, state s_{23} depends on state s_{11} and s_{22}, and state s_{12} depends on state s_{23} and s_{11}. As a result, state s_{12} transitively depends on state s_{31}. If the sender of a message fails after sending the message but before logging the message in stable storage, the message becomes an *orphan message* and the receiver of that message becomes an *orphan processor.*

At irregular intervals, each processor (independently) saves the contents of the volatile log in a stable storage. More frequent checkpoints may cause more disk activity and hence may delay the application program; less frequent checkpoints may result in recovery taking a longer time.

3. RECOVERY WITH NO TRANSITIVE DEPENDENCY

We now consider the problem of recovering from failures when messages sent do not contain additional information about *transitive dependencies*. We allow only O(1) additional information to be appended to each message. Thus, the length of the messages is not increased by large amounts.

The interval of time between a node receiving a message and the time it completes all of the actions associated with processing the message received (including sending messages to its neighbors) is called a State Transition Interval (or STI). The state of processor p immediately after completing STI i is denoted by $PS_p(i)$. A unique time stamp TS_p(STI) is associated with each STI within a processor p. A message m that is sent by processor p is time stamped with the time stamp of the STI in p during which m was generated. Thus, if m was sent by p during the STI i, then $TS_p(i)$ is appended to m. Let m.TS be the corresponding time stamp. The time stamps of the successive STI's are monotonically increasing within each processor. Let i be an STI of processor p and let i+1 be the STI immediately following i. Let m be the message sent by q that triggered the STI i+1. The time stamp of STI i+1 is set to a value that is greater than $TS_p(i)$ and m.TS. Processor p sets $TS_p(i+1)$ to $\max\{TS_p(i)+1, m.TS+1\}$. Now, $TS_p(i+1)$ is appended to each message generated by p in STI i+1. The time stamps are similar to the logical clocks of [8].

After the end of STI i but before the beginning of STI i+1 at p, processor p stores the triple $\{PS_p(i), TS_p(i), m\}$ in its volatile storage where m is the message which triggered the STI i. Each processor, from time to time, independently saves its volatile log in its stable storage and clears the volatile log.

Now consider the case when a set of processors fail. The recovery procedure at each processor is started when it learns about the processor crash(es). We assume that there exists a spanning tree of the underlying network, a predetermined node r acts as a coordinator or root (several algorithms for leader election exist. For example, see [3]) , no further failures occur when the recovery procedure is in progress (when there is another processor failure before the recovery procedure ends, the recovery procedure can be initialized at each processor; the results of [1] can be used for resetting), and each failed processor, when it restarts after failures, knows the fact that it has failed.

The recovery procedure consists of n iterations. At the end of n iterations, we ensure that all of the processors rollback to their correct recovery point. Initially, each processor p (including the root r) sets its (temporary) recovery point RP(p) and time-stamp of the recovery point TRP(p) as follows: If p is one of the failed processors, then it sets RP(p) to i and TRP(p) to $TS_p(i)$ where i is the last STI found in the stable log. On the other hand, if p is one of the non-faulty processors (it is taking part in the recovery procedure because of the failure of other processors), then it sets RP(p) to j and TRP(p) to $TS_p(j)$ where j is the last STI found in the volatile log. Thus, based on the local information alone, each processor decides on a temporary recovery point. The processors communicate with each other and find the final recovery point as one processor's recovery point may force other processors to rollback further.

Each iteration consists of two phases. The root starts the first phase of each iteration of the recovery procedure by broadcasting a *compute_min* message using the spanning tree. Each processor now has a value (time-stamp of the temporary recovery point or TRP), and all of the processors compute the minimum value using the following well-known convergecast procedure: A leaf processor sends its value to its parent; an interior processor waits for a message containing a value from each of its children, finds the minimum value using its own value and the values it received from its children, and sends the minimum value to its parent; the root behaves like an interior processor, computes the minimum value and broadcasts the message *min_value(x)* where x is the result of the *min* function. This concludes the first phase.

During the second phase, any processor q such that TRP(q) = x marks itself as an eligible processor. An eligible processor q infers that it has the minimum value of TRP and has determined the correct recovery point (TR(q)). Thus, it broadcasts a message *rollback_point(q,TRP(q))* to all of the processors and sets TRP(q) to ∞ as q need not take part in the subsequent iterations but must participate in the process of computing the min function. Any processor r such that TRP(r) $\neq \infty$, on receipt of a *rollback_point(q,y)* message, scans its (volatile and stable) storage backwards starting from the latest logged STI and finds the triple $\{PS, TS, m\}$ representing the STI i of processor r such that

1. m was received from q
2. m.TS > y
3. i is the smallest STI among those satisfying the above two conditions.

If no such STI exists (that is r does not depend on a message sent by q after RP(q)), then i is set to ∞ (where $TS_r(\infty) = \infty$). In any case, RP(r) is set to min{RP(r),i-1} and TRP(r) is set to min{TRP(r),$TS_r(i-1)$}. After all eligible processors broadcast *rollback_point* messages, second phase of the iteration ends and the root starts the next iteration. The end of the second phase can be detected using the convergecast procedure. The recovery procedure ends when all of the processors in the system broadcast a *rollback_point* message. A formal description of the recovery procedure can be found in Figure 3.1

3.1. Example

Consider a distributed computer system consisting of five processors. Figure 3.2 shows the complete run of the system when an application program is run. In that figure each message is numbered by its time-stamp, and for each STI of a processor, the STI and the time-stamp of the STI are shown (numbers in parenthesis represent the time-stamp of the STI and numbers outside the parenthesis denote STI).

Assume that processor p_5 fails and the first two STI's of p_5 are logged in stable storage. For convenience, let RP(*) represent a vector of RP values of all of the processors where the ith component of RP(*) = RP(p_i). Similarly, TRP(*) represents the TRP values of all of the processors. When the recovery procedure is started, RP(*) = [7,11,4,7,2] and TRP(*) = [15,12,12,8,2[1]]. Processor p_5 has the minimum value of TRP and broadcasts the message *rollback_point(p_5,2)*. Processor p_1 sets RP(p_1) to 6 and TRP(p_1) to 14 as it received a message time-stamped 7 sent by p_5 in an STI after RP(p_5) and that message triggered STI 7 of p_1. Processor p_4 sets RP(p_4) to 5 as STI 6 of p_4 was triggered by a message time-stamped 3 that was sent by p_5. Similarly, processors p_2 and p_3 also rollback, and at the end of the first iteration, RP(*) = [6,10,3,5,2] and TRP(*) = [14,11,11,5[2],∞]. In the second iteration, p_4 has the minimum value of TRP, and broadcasts the message *rollback_point(p_4,5)*. At the end of the second iteration, RP(*) = [5,9,1,5,2] and TRP(*) = [13,10,8,∞,∞]. During the third iteration, p_3 has the minimum value of TRP and broadcasts the message *rollback_point(p_3,8)*. Processors p_1 and p_2 rollback on receipt of such a message, and RP(*) = [4,8,1,5,2] and TRP(*) = [12,9,∞,∞,∞]. Now processor p_2 broadcasts the message *rollback_point(p_2,9)*. On receipt of such a message, p_1 rollbacks to STI 3, RP(*) = [3,8,1,5,2] and TRP(*) = [10,∞,∞,∞,∞]. During the fifth iteration, p_1 has the minimum value of TRP and broadcasts the message *rollback_point(p_1,10)*. After five processors broadcast *rollback_point* messages, the recovery procedure terminates and RP(*) = [3,8,1,5,2]. In the next section, we present the proof of correctness of the recovery procedure.

3.2. Correctness

We now show that the algorithm of section 3.2 is correct. For each failed processor p, let LS_p be the last STI found on the stable log.

Lemma 3.1: At the end of k iterations, the rollback points of at least k processors are consistent.

Proof: The proof is by induction on k. For each k, let Pr_k be the processor that has the minimum value of *TRP* among all of the processors at the end of the kth iteration. Consider the case when $k = 1$. Assume for contradiction that STI RP(Pr_1) is not consistent. This implies that there exits a failed processor p such that the message m that started STI RP(Pr_1) was sent by p after STI LS_p of p. From the rules for assigning time stamps, it is clear that TS_p(RP(p)) < TS_{Pr_1}(RP(Pr_1)), a contradiction as Pr_1 has the minimum value of *TRP* 's of all of the processors during the beginning.

Assume that the result holds for some k. We now show that the result is true for k+1. Let C_k be the set of processors that have minimum values of *TRP* during the first k iterations ($C_k = \{Pr_1, Pr_2, ..., Pr_k\}$). Assume for contradiction that STI RP(Pr_{k+1}) is not consistent. Thus, the STI RP(Pr_{k+1}) transitively depends on an unlogged STI i_0 of a failed processor q_0. There exists a series of STI's i_1, ..., i_s on processors q_1, ..., q_s respectively such that $s \geq 0$, m_0 was sent by q_0 to q_1 during an unlogged STI i_0 of q_0, m_0 triggered STI i_1 on q_1 and m_1 was sent in STI i_1 by q_1 to q_2, ..., STI RP(Pr_{k+1}) was triggered by message m_s sent by q_s in STI i_s. The situation is as shown in Figure 3.3. There are totally two cases to consider. In both cases, we arrive at a contradiction.

Case 1: q_0 is not a processor in C_k. Since q_0 is a failed processor, at the end of the $k+1^{st}$ iteration, we can establish the following inequalities:

---

[1] We assume that $TS_5(2) = 2$.

[2] We assume that $TS_4(4) = 4$.

```
/* procedure executed by processor p that is not the root   */
/* root behaves like other processors; in addition, it coordinates
   the computation of min function and broadcasts the result   */
begin
      if p is a failed processor then
            i ← latest STI found in the stable storage
      else
            i ← latest STI found in the volatile storage
      RP(p) ← i;
      TRP(p) ← TS_p(i);
      terminated_processors ← 0;
      while terminated_processors < n do begin
            wait for a message;
            m ← message received;
            case m of
                  compute_min:
                        wait for a value from each children (if any);
                        compute minimum value among values received and TRP(p);
                        send the result to parent;
                  min_value(x):
                        if TRP(p) = x then begin
                              broadcast rollback_point(p,TRP(p))
                              TRP(p) ← ∞;
                              end;
                  rollback_point(q,y):
                        terminated_processors ← terminated_processors+1;
                        if (p ≠ q) and (TRP(p) ≠ ∞) then begin
                              find smallest STI i such that i was triggered by a
                              message m sent by q and m.TS > y (set i to ∞ if no such STI exists);
                              RP(p) ← min{RP(p),i-1};
                              TRP(p) ← min{TRP(p), TS_p(i-1)};
                              end;
                  end /* end case */
            end /* end while */
end;
```

Figure 3.1: Recovery procedure

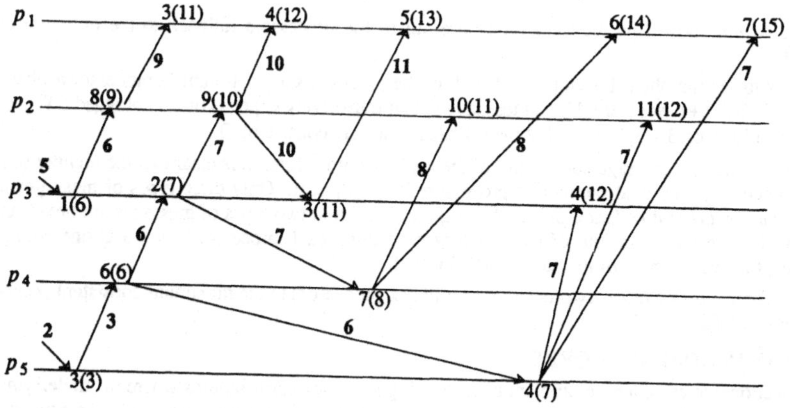

Figure 3.2

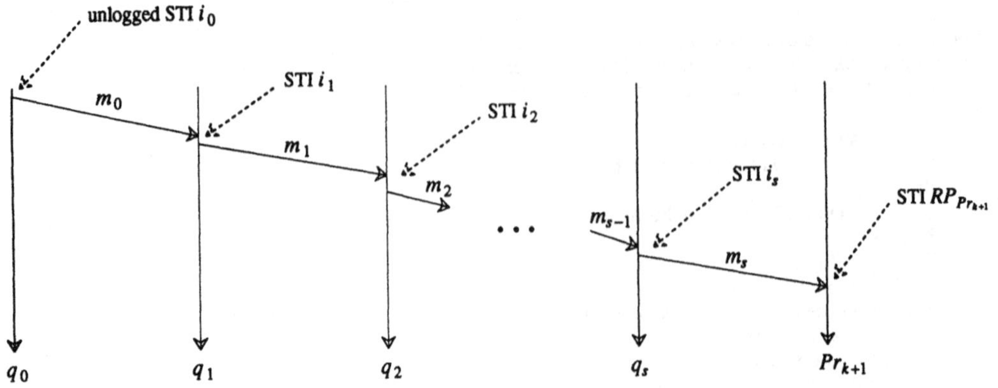

Figure 3.3

0. TRP(q_0)< $TS_{q_0}(i_0)$ because i_0 is an unlogged STI, a failed processor r initializes TRP(r) to $TS_r(j)$ where $j = LS_r$, and as the recovery procedure executes, the value of *TRP* can never increase for any processor as long as it is not in C_k.
1. $TS_{q_0}(i_0) < TS_{q_1}(i_1)$ because of the way in which each STI is time-stamped.

--

s. $TS_{q_{s-1}}(i_{s-1}) < TS_{q_s}(i_s)$.

$s+1$. $TS_{q_s}(i_s) < TS_{Pr_{k+1}}(\mathrm{RP}(Pr_{k+1}))$.

From the above relationships and from the fact that < is a transitive relation, it is clear that at the end of the $k+1^{st}$ iteration TRP(q_0) < TRP(Pr_{k+1}), a contradiction since we assumed that Pr_{k+1} has the minimum *TRP* value among the processors at the end of the $k+1^{st}$ iteration.

case 2: $q_0 \in C_k$. Let d = TRP(Pr_{k+1}). Let $m \leq k$ be an integer such that $Pr_m = q_0$. At the end of the mth iteration, q_0 has the minimum value of *TRP*, and it broadcasts the message *rollback_point*(q_0,TRP(q_0)). Every processor in the system receives the message containing TR_{q_0}. Specifically, q_1 receives this message and it sets RP(q_1) such that RP(q_1) ≤ STI i_1-1. By following the < relationships in case 1, it is easy to see that TRP(q_1) < $TS_{q_1}(i_1)$ < d. Since Pr_{k+1} has the minimum value of *TRP* during the $k+1^{st}$ iteration, it is clear that $q_1 \in C_k$. Similarly, it can be proved that $q_l \in C_k$ for all $0 \leq l < s$. When q_s has the minimum value of *TRP*, it broadcasts a message containing TRP(q_s), Pr_{k+1} receives it and sets TRP(Pr_{k+1}) such that TRP(Pr_{k+1}) < d. During the beginning of the $k+1^{st}$ iteration, $d < d$, a contradiction.□

Theorem 3.2: At the end of the recovery procedure, all of the processors rollback to the optimum consistent recovery point.

Proof: It is easy to see that the rollback points for all of the processors are optimum (a processor rollbacks to STI i only because its STI $i+1$ was started by a message m_1 that transitively depends on an unlogged STI j of a failed processor). From Lemma 3.1, it is clear that the rollback states are consistent.□

We now consider the message complexity of the recovery procedure. It is clear that the number of iterations is at most n where n is the total number of processors in the system. Only three types of messages are sent - *compute_min*, *min_value* and *rollback_point*. Among these, the first two types of messages are broadcast once in each iteration. During the entire run of the recovery procedure, each processor broadcasts one *rollback_point* message. Thus, the total number of messages used is O(n^2).

Theorem 3.3: There exists a recovery procedure to rollback processors to the maximum consistent points using at most O(n^2) messages□

4. RECOVERY IN RING NETWORKS

In this section, we consider the problem of recovering from processor failures where the underlying network is a ring. There are exactly two simple paths from any processor i to a different processor j in a ring network. So, it is not necessary to keep dependency and version vectors for processors and messages. In addition, each processor does not have to know the identities of the failed processors before the recovery algorithm begins. Instead, each processor p only numbers its STIs using consecutive numbers. At the start of the distributed system, STI is initialized to zero for all of the processors.

When a processor p sends a message m to processor q, p appends the STI number to message m before sending. When q receives a message m from processor p, q increments its STI number and logs the information {STI number of q, q, m} in volatile storage.

As in section 3, we assume that there exists a leader, and the *leader* processor *Lp* starts the recovery algorithm. Before describing the recovery algorithm, we define the term *critical processor*. A *critical processor* is a failed processor that can locally determine its checkpoint and does not have to rollback again. If a processor has received an orphan message and it is not a critical processor, it should rollback to some earlier state because a critical processor rollbacks.

The idea of the algorithm is as follows. When a processor p fails and then restarts, it sends a *start_recovery* message to *Lp*. Then, *Lp* starts the recovery algorithm and sends *recovery* message to its right and left neighbors. When a processor receives a recovery message from its right(left) neighbor, it processes it and sends a recovery message to its left(right) neighbor. After the *recovery* message passes around the ring twice in both clockwise and counterclockwise direction, the recovery procedure ends and the system rollbacks to a consistent state.

The recovery algorithm is correct as long as no further failures occur between the failed processor receives any recovery message and the recovery procedure completes.

4.1. RECOVERY ALGORITHM

Before we describe the algorithm, some parameters and messages are defined first. Parameter *left(right)_Lp* counts the number of left(right) recovery messages which have passed. Message *start_recovery* is used to inform the leader processor *Lp* processor to start the recovery algorithm. The recovery messages, which contain the STI number or null symbol, are sent by *Lp* initially and passes around the ring network. There are two kinds of recovery messages, one is *left recovery* message which passes around the ring network in clockwise direction and the other is the *right_recovery* message which passes in counter_clockwise direction.

When a failed processor r restarts from the latest checkpoint, r first sends the *start_recovery* message to its neighbors and waits for the recovery message from *Lp*. Processor r ignores the *start_recovery* message from other processor before p completes the recovery procedure.

After receiving the left(right)_recovery message from the right (left) neighbor, r increments the value of *left(right)_Lp* and checks whether the message is null or not. If it is null, r send a left(right)_recovery message with current STI to its right(left) neighbor. Otherwise, r scans its stable storage backwards starting from the latest logged STI and find the triple {STI number, processor id, m} representing the STI i of processor r such that

1. m was received from the right(left) neighbor processor.
2. STI of m is greater than STI of the recovery message.
3. i is the smallest STI among those satisfying the above two conditions.

If no such STI exists (that is r does not depend on a message sent by right(left) neighbor processor after STI of the recovery message), r sends a left(right)_recovery message with current STI to the left(right) neighbor.

Processor r repeats the above procedure until *left_Lp* and *right_Lp* both equal two. Then, r starts its normal operation.

A non-failed processor p receives a *start_recovery* message, it stops its normal operation and waits for the recovery message from *Lp*. Processor p ignores the *start_recovery* message from other processor before p completes the recovery procedure.

After receiving the left(right)_recovery message from the right (left) neighbor, p increments the value of *left(right)_Lp* and checks whether the message is null or not. If it is null, r sends a null left(right)_recovery message to its right(left) neighbor, or sends a left(right)_recovery message with the STI number of roll_back state if p rollbacks to some roll_back state. Otherwise, scans its (volatile and stable) storage backwards starting from the latest logged STI and find the triple {STI number, processor id, m} representing the STI i of processor p such that

1. m was received from the right(left) neighbor processor.
2. STI of m is greater than STI of the recovery message.
3. i is the smallest STI among those satisfying the above two conditions.

If no such STI exists (that is p does not depend on a message sent by right(left) neighbor processor after STI of the recovery message), then p sends a null left(right)_recovery message to the left(right) neighbor. Processor p repeats the above procedure until *left_Lp* and *right_Lp* both equal two. Then, p starts its normal operation.

As for the leader processor *Lp*, if it receives the *start_recovery* message or it restarts from the processor crash, *Lp* starts the recovery algorithm and sends out *left(right)_recovery* messages to its left (right) neighbor. If *Lp* is a failed processor, then *left(right)_recovery* is appended the current STI value. Otherwise, *left(right)_recovery* is a null message. Then, *Lp* executes the same steps as the failed/non_fail processor does, depending on the status of *Lp*. A formal description of the recovery procedure can be found in Figure 4.1.

Example

Consider a ring network consisting of five processors. Figure 4.2 shows the complete run of the system when an application program is run. Each message is appended with a STI number of the sender. The STI for each processor and the STI of each received message are shown (numbers in parenthesis represent the STI number appended with the received messages and numbers outside the parenthesis denote the STI for the processor).

Assume that processor p_3 fails and sends a start_recovery message to the leader processor L_p (i.e. p_2). Moreover, for the time being, we assume the time for the recovery message to pass between any two processors is the same, i.e. the left_recovery and right_recovery messages sent by L_p will go around the ring and come back to L_p at the same time. For convenience, let Lrm(*) represent a vector of the values in the left_recovery message from L_p to p_1, p_1 to p_5, p_5 to p_4, p_4 to p_3 and p_3 to L_p, Rrm(*) represent the one in the right_recovery message in the opposite direction and RP(*) represents a vector of STI value of the recovery point for all processors. After the first round, i.e., after the left_recovery and right_recovery messages coming back to L_p the first time, according to the recovery procedure, Lrm(*)=[null,null,null,3,3], Rrm(*)=[null,3,3,3,3,3] and the temporary recovery point RP(*)=[4,2,3,4,4]. After the second round, the recovery algorithm terminates and Lrm(*)=[1,2,2,2,3], Rrm(*)=[1,3,3,2,2] and RP(*)=[2,1,3,2,2].

```
/* procedure executed by processor p */
begin
    left_Lp ← 0;
    right_Lp ← 0;
    if p is a failed processor then
            send the start_recovery message to its neighbors.
    wait for the recovery message m from Lp; /* ignore other start_recovery message*/
    repeat
        if m came from right neighbor then
            left_Lp ← left_Lp + 1;
        else
            right_Lp ← right_Lp + 1;
        end
        find smallest STI i such that i was triggered by a message me
        sent by q and STI of me > STI of m;
        if i exists then
        /* m is a message from right(or left) neighbor*/
            p rollbacks to STI i and sends a left(or right)_recovery message with
            value i to its right(or left) neighbors;
        else
          begin
            if p is a failed processor then
                p sends a left(or right)_recovery message with current STI index
                to the left(or right) neighbor;
            else
                p sends a null left(or right)_recovery message to its left(or right) neighbor;
          end
    until (left_Lp =2) and (right_Lp =2) /* end of repeat*/
end.
```

Figure 4.1 Recovery procedure

Lemma 4.1: There is only one critical processor which determines the final recovery point of processor p which needs to rollback to, if p has received an orphan message from the failed processor.

Theorem 4.1: After completing the recovery algorithm, the system is restored to a maximum consistent states.

Proof: From Lemma 4.1, for processor p, lets CP(p) be the critical processor of p. Processor p will rollback to the correct recovery point if the recovery message first visits CP(p) and then p (in clockwise and counterclockwise direction) call such a processor p a safe processor. Since the recovery message goes around the ring twice in each direction, it is clear that each processor in the ring is safe.□

Theorem 4.2: There exists a recovery procedure to rollback processors to the maximum consistent points using at most $O(n)$ messages.□

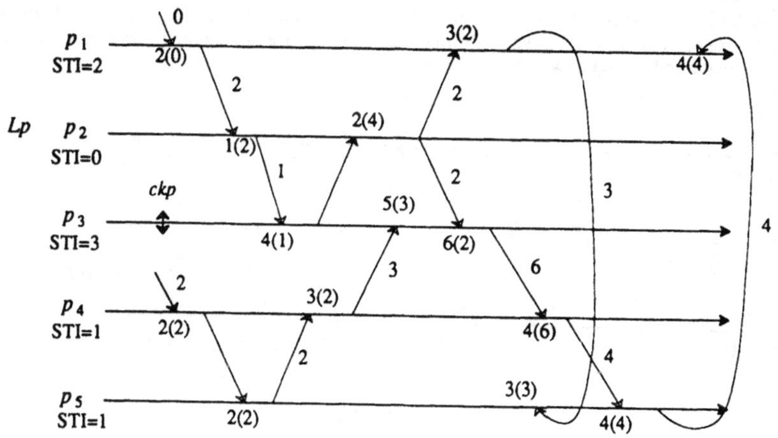

Figure 4.2

5. RECOVERY WITH TRANSITIVE DEPENDENCY

In this section, each message is appended $O(n)$ additional information to infer transitive dependencies. The dependency of a processor p on some processor q can be encoded as the latest interval index of any STI of processor q on which the state of processor p depends. Assume that the processors are numbered from the set $\{1,2,...,n\}$, where n is the number of processors in the system. Each processor p keeps a *global dependency vector*

$$GDV_j=[\delta_1,...,\delta_n]$$

where $\delta_i \geq 0$ is the dependency of processor p on processor i and $GDV_p[i]=\delta_i$, $1 \leq i \leq n$. Thus, $GDV_p[i]$ at any time gives the largest index of the STI of processor i on which the current state of p transitively depends.

To distinguish between messages sent by a processor before its failure and after failure, we keep a variable *version* in each processor. The version of a processor p is the number of times that p has crashed. It is used to clear the messages in the channel when a processor crashs. In other words, it prevents any processor from receiving messages in the channel which were sent before some processor crashs and received after the recipient completes the crash recovery procedure. Each processor j keeps a *global version vector*

$$GVV_j=[\alpha_1,...,\alpha_n]$$

where $\alpha_i \geq 0$ is the version of processor i and $GVV_j[i]=\alpha_i$, $1 \leq i \leq n$.

For example, in Figure 5.1 message m was sent by p_1 with version vector GVV_1=[1,0,2] before p_2 failed. After p_2 crashed, m becomes an orphan message (assume when time reached the cut c, all the three processors have already updated their version vectors [1,1,2]). When p_3 receives m, it discovers that m has an old version vector and discards it.

At the start of the distributed system, both vectors are initialized to zero for all of the processors.

When a processor p sends a message m to q, p appends the current vector GDV_p and the current GVV_p to m and sends it to q. Then, q sends back an acknowledgement *receive_no* where *receive_no* $= GDV_q[q]$ when the message is being processed, to inform p that q has already received the message m, and m is the $(GDV_q[q])$th message received by q. Processor p logs the information $\{GDV_q[q], q, m\_send\}$ in volatile storage.

When messages are received by q, they are put into q's *processing queue*. For each queued message, say message m from processor p, q first checks whether the version of m is the same as GVV_q or not. If they are the same, q increments the value of $GDV_q[q]$ and sends an acknowledgement *receive_no* to p and replaces GDV_q by the union of GDV_q and GDV_p of m where the union of two dependency vectors A=$[\alpha_1..\alpha_n]$ and B=$[\beta_1..\beta_n]$ is defined as

$$i \ \gamma_i = \begin{cases} \alpha_i & \textit{iff } \alpha_i \geq \beta_i \\ \beta_i & \textit{otherwise} \end{cases}$$

Then, q starts a new STI and logs the information $\{GDV_q, p, m, receive\}$ in volatile storage. Otherwise, message m should have been sent by some failed processor with old version. Thus, q discards the message m. Figure 5.2 is an example to show the relationship between each processor sending and receiving messages with the dependency vector and the acknowledgement *receive_no*.

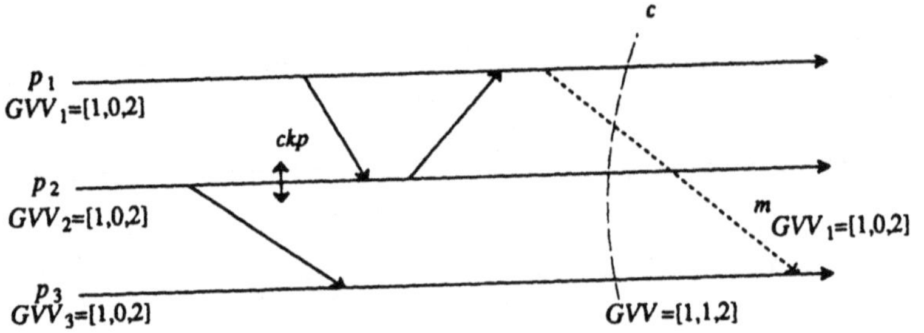

Figure 5.1

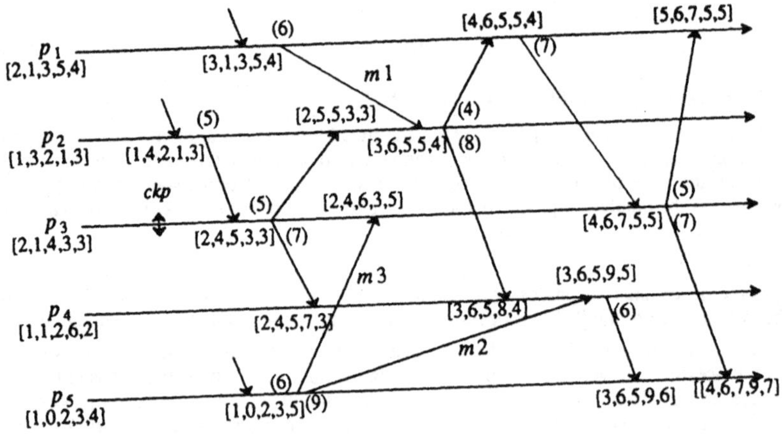

Figure 5.2

5.1. Recovery algorithm

Without loss of generality, we assume that processors 1 to k failed. When a processor q $(1 \leq q \leq k)$ restarts after its failure, it sets its recovery point to the latest checkpoint (i.e. *recovery checkpoint*) available in the stable storage and increments $GVV_q[q]$ by 1. It, then, sends a recovery message which contains the largest value of the STI which is available in the checkpoint, $GDV_q[q]$ and the new version (i.e. $GVV_q[q]$) to its children using the existed spanning tree.

Every processor may need to rollback to some point which depending on the recovery messages. Specifically speaking, upon receiving the recovery message sent by q, a processor p first sends the recovery message to its children, updates its $GVV_p[q]$ to new version and stores the new GVV_p in the stable log. In the meanwhile, p scans its (volatile and stable) storage backwards starting from the latest logged STI and finds the quadruple $\{GDV_p, q, m, receive\}$ representing the STI i of processor p such that

1. $GDV_p[q]$ of m is greater than $GDV_q[q]$ of the recovery message.
2. STI i is the smallest among those satisfying the first condition.

If no such STI exists (that is p does not depend on a message sent by q after recovery checkpoin of q), then i is set to ∞. After that, p finds all of the *pre-sent messages*. A pre-sent message m is defined to be a message which has been sent to q satisfying the following conditions:

a) The *receive_no* value of m is greater than the $GDV_q[q]$ of recovery message from q.

b) m is not an orphan message (i.e. $GDV_p[q] < GDV_q[q]$).

If a pre-sent message is found, then p needs to resend this message with new version vector to the original receiver. The receiver puts these messages into its processing queue in ascending order according to the *receive_no* value. If i is not equal to ∞, processor p needs to find its *pre-received messages*. A pre-received message is a message of which $GDV_p[p]$ are greater than $GDV_p[p]$ of i, and which has already been processed but not an orphan message of some failed processor. Processor p must modify every found pre-received message m by updating its version in GVV_p and then puts it into the processing queue in the received order. Finally, p finds whether there are any messages sent out before the recovery point if p needs to rollback and have not yet received the corresponding acknowledgement. There are three subcases for this kind of messages.

a). The message is still in the channel.

b). The message is in the processing queue.

c). The message has been processed and acknowledgement is in the channel.

If there is any such message, p needs to resend this message to its destination. Subcases (a) and (b) do not pose any problems, since the messages should be discarded. In order to prevent subcase(c) from happening, p needs to add a special marker on these messages. When a processor q receives a message with this kind of special marker, q checks whether there is any such message which has already been processed. A formal description of the recovery procedure can be found in Figure 5.3.

5.2. Example

Consider a distributed computer system consisting of five processors. In Figure 5.2, each message is appended by its global dependency vector and each message sent to other processor keeps a *receive_no* value. In addition, the $GDV_i[i]$ value is the index of each state transition interval for processor i. For example, the global vector [3,1,3,5,4] is appended to message $m1$, the first value 3 is the STI for p_1 and p_1 keeps a *receive_no* value, 6 in the parenthesis, which is sent back from processor p_2 after receiving $m1$. When processor p_3 failed and restarted from its latest checkpoint (i.e. *ckp* in the figure), it sends $GDV_3[3]$ value, 4, to all other processors. As the conclusion of the recovery algorithm, RP(*)=[3,1,2,2,1], message $m1$ and $m2$ are the pre-received messages which need to update their version vector and put into the processing queue by p_2 and p_4 and message $m3$ is a pre-sent message which needs to be resent by p_5 to p_3.

Theorem 5.1: After completing the above algorithm, the system is restored to a maximum consistent states.

Proof: The proof is by contradiction. Suppose that the system was not in a maximum consistent states after completing the recovery algorithm. Then, there must exist a processor p and a failed processor q such that the STI index of q's checkpoint is greater than the STI index of p's final recovery point. But in step 1 of the recovery algorithm, we know that every processor needs to rollback to some earliest state where $GDV_p[q]$ is greater than $GDV_q[q]$, which is a contradiction.□

Theorem 5.2: There exists a recovery procedure to rollback processors to the maximum consistent points using at most $O(kn)$ messages where k is the number of failed processors.□

```
/* procedure executed by the failed processor q after q restarts from
  its latest checkpoint */
begin
      GVV_q[q] ← GVV_q[q] + 1;
      Send the recovery message which conatins the largest value of GDV_q[q] available and
      GVV_q[q] to its children;
end.
```

```
/* procedure executed by processor p which receive a recovery message from
  the failed processor q */
begin
      Send the recovery message to its children;
      find smallest STI i such that the GDV_p[q] of i is greater than GDV_q[q]
      of recovery message (set i to ∞ if no such STI exists);
        GVV_p[q] ← GVV_q[q];
        Restore GVV_p in the stable log;
        Find pre-sent message m which satisfies the following conditions:
           1. The receive_no value of m is greater than GDV_q[q];
           2. GDV_p[q] of m is smaller than GDV_q[q];
      if pre-sent message m exist then
           send m with new version to q;
      end
      if i ≠ ∞ then
             find the pre-received message ms which satisfies the following conditions:
           1. GDV_p[p] is greater than GDV_p[p] of i;
           2. ms is not an orphan message;
             if message ms exists then
                    update their version of the message and put them into
                    the processing queue in received order;
      if there are any messages sent to other processors and the GDV_p[p] of
             these messages is not greater than GDV_p[p] of i and have not yet
             received the corresponding acknowledgement then
              resend the messages to its destination;
end
```

Figure 5.3 Recovery procedure

6. CONCLUSIONS

In this paper, we considered three algorithms for recovering from processor failures and rollbacking the processors to the maximum consistent processor states in distributed systems. When only O(1) extra information is added to each application message, we present an algorithm for recovery that uses $O(n^2)$ messages in arbitrary networks. This algorithm is an improvement over the algorithm of Sistla and Welch [10] which uses $O(n^3)$ messages for recovery. For the case of ring networks, our algorithm uses $O(n)$ messages (and $O(n)$ time) when only O(1) extra information is appended to each application message. It is easy to see that the algorithm is message-optimal (and time-optimal) since in the worst case all of the processors may need to be informed of processor failure. When $O(n)$ information is added to each message, $O(kn)$ messages are sufficient for recovery.

There are several questions that arise from our paper. Efficient algorithms for committing outputs, establishing lower bounds on message complexity, determining exactly what kind of information need to be added to minimize messages or time, etc. We are currently investigating these and related problems.

References

1. Afek, Y., Awerbuch, B., and Gafni, E., ''Applying static network protocols to dynamic networks,'' *Proceedings of the twenty eighth Annual Symposium on Foundations of Computer Science*, pp. 358-370, 1987.
2. Chandy, K.M. and Lamport, L., ''Distributed snapshots: Determining global states of distributed systems,'' *ACM Transactions on Computer Systems*, vol. 3, no. 1, pp. 63-75, 1985.
3. Gallager, R. G., Humblet, P.A., and Spira, P.M., ''A distributed algorithm for minimum weight spanning trees,'' *ACM Transactions on Programming Languages and Systems*, vol. 5, no. 1, pp. 66-77, 1983.
4. Gray, J., ''Notes on database operating systems: Operating Systems: An advanced course:,'' *Lecture notes in computer science, 60, Springer-Verlag*, pp. 393-481, 1978.
5. Johnson, D. and Zwaenepoel, W., ''Recovery in distributed systems using optimistic message logging and checkpointing,'' *Proceedings of ACM Symposium on Principles of Distributed Computing*, pp. 171-180, 1988.
6. Koo, R. and Toueg, S., ''Checkpointing and Rollback-Recovery for Distributed Systems,'' *IEEE Transactions on Software Engineering*, vol. SE-13, no. 1, pp. 23-31, 1987.
7. L'Ecuyer, P and Malenfant, J., ''Computing Optimal Checkpointing Strategies for Rollback and Recovery Systems,'' *IEEE Transactions on Computers*, vol. 37, no. 4, pp. 491-496, 1988.
8. Lamport, L., ''Time, clocks, and the ordering of events in a distributed system,'' *Communication of the Association for Computing Machinery*, vol. 21, no. 7, pp. 558-565, 1978.
9. Powell, M. and Presotto, D., ''Publishing: a reliable broadcast communication mechanism,'' *Proceedings of the ninth ACM Symposium on Operating System Principles*, pp. 100-109, 1983.
10. Sistla, A.P. and Welch, J., ''Efficient distributed recovery using message logging,'' *Proceedings of Principles of Distributed Computing*, 1989.
11. Son, S.H. and Agrawala, A.K., ''Distributed Checkpointing for Globally Consistent States of Databases,'' *IEEE Transactions on Software Engineering*, vol. 15, no. 10, pp. 1157-1167, 1989.
12. Strom, R.E. and Yemini, S., ''Optimistic recovery in distributed systems,'' *ACM Transactions on Computer Systems*, vol. 3, no. 3, pp. 204-226, 1985.
13. Venkatesan, K., Radhakrishnan, T., and Li, H., ''Optimal Checkpointing and Local Recording for Domino-Free Rollback Recovery,'' *Information Processing Letters*, vol. 25, no. 5, pp. 295-304, 1987.

A Non-Standard Inductive Semantics

Gianna Reggio

Dipartimento di Matematica – Università di Genova

Via L.B. Alberti 4 – 16132 Genova (ITALY)

Introduction

Structural Operational Semantics (SOS in what follows), as introduced and developed by G.Plotkin in his landmark papers [P1, P2], is well known and has been successfully applied in several cases. While, in the traditional approach, operational semantics is essentially a description of a program execution by an abstract machine, SOS consists in an inductive definition, through a logical deduction system guided by the abstract syntactic structure of the language. Not only the semantic definition is more abstract; but it also benefits of an associated proof technique.

Noticing that SOS is more than a method for giving an operational semantics, various authors have revisited it from different viewpoints and adopting different names. The "natural semantics" of G. Kahn and his group (see [K]) emphasizes the natural deduction aspects of the SOS systems giving new applications. E. Astesiano in [A] focuses on the foundational aspects of Plotkin's approach showing that the underlying definition method, far from being operational in nature, is a unifying framework for expressing semantics at different levels of abstraction (from the standard denotational semantics to detailed structural operational semantics). He uses the name "inductive semantics", in order to emphasize that the various semantic definitions are all inductive definitions of families of sets associated with inductive systems (see [Ac]). Correspondingly there is an associated principle of (proof by) induction, which is more general than the well-known principle of structural induction. The same emphasis on the use of various forms of induction is in many papers from the "Edinburgh school" (see eg [MT], where they use the name "relational semantics"). Here we adopt the name "inductive semantics" as in [A] to stress that we are interested in relating the inductive SOS aspects with the denotational approach.

It is not difficult to show that, at least for the case of Pascal-like languages, any denotational semantics has a corresponding, and isomorphic, inductive semantics (see [A]). This is true in particular of standard denotational semantics which uses environments and stores (see eg, [S]); let us call standard inductive semantics its inductive counterpart. These semantics are quite easy to understand, but can be criticized because they have a somewhat implementative flavour. In this paper we propose an inductive non-standard semantics which is in some sense more abstract and avoids the explicit use of environments and store. We also show how to derive from it a non-standard denotational semantics. The method is presented by applying it to a small Pascal-like language, called WHILE.

Our definition consists in a logical deductive system which associates with each pair <program, input> the corresponding result, if any. In order to obtain a compositional semantics, the system must define

---

Work partially supported by COMPASS-Esprit-BRA-W.G. n 3264, by MPI-40% and by CNR-PF-Sistemi Informatici e Calcolo Parallelo.

(equivalently, prove) various "natural properties" of the components of the language; these properties are the "natural" ones for defining all and only the dynamic features of the language. The formulas of the system have the form $h \vdash \phi$, where h is a history, ie a syntactic term corresponding to the execution path of a program up to a certain point, and ϕ is a formula expressing a natural property holding at that point. Histories are defined inductively, by enlarging the syntax of the language, and the clauses of the logical system are given by structural induction.

This approach applies to static semantics as well.

In the standard approach one defines "a priori" the various semantic domains (as environments, states, locations and so on). Here the properties which we need to take into account arise naturally when writing down the inductive system. However in the end we can derive from the logical system a compositional (denotational) semantics for the language and define appropriate semantic domains (roughly corresponding to the sets of natural properties holding for the various constructs). We think that those domains are "the most abstract" possible, because the properties defining them seem to correspond to the exact amount of information required to attach a meaning to each construct of the language. It is worthwhile to note that the resulting semantics is fully abstract.

In [BH] the authors present another non-standard semantics without explicit environment and store based on a particular substitution rule. There are some similarities with the approach presented here; the main point of contact is the use of a transformed syntax as the inductive basis for the clauses. However the emphasis is on different issues and the resulting systems are quite different; in particular here we deduce the semantic domains for an associated denotational semantics, while they are interested in seeing their inductive systems as a part of a more general logical framework (ELF, Edinburgh Logical Framework). We think that it would be worthwhile to compare and fully assess the two approaches.

The WHILE language is briefly introduced in section 1; in section 2 we formally define the histories; the static and the dynamic semantics of WHILE are given in section 3 and 4 respectively; finally in section 5 we show how to derive the associated compositional semantics. The proofs will be found in the full version of the paper.

1 The WHILE Language

The concrete syntax of WHILE is given by the following BNF like rules (more precisely called *pattern rules* in [A], where their use for defining syntax in an inductive framework is explored); n and id are the non-terminal symbols for integer constants and variable identifiers, which are not further specified here.

e	::=	n ∣ **tt** ∣ **ff** ∣ $(e_1\ op\ e_2)$ ∣ $\neg e$ ∣ id
op	::=	+ ∣ * ∣ - ∣ > ∣ < ∣ = ∣ ∧ ∣ ∨
d	::=	t **var** $id = e$ ∣ t **const** $id = e$ ∣ $d_1 ; d_2$
t	::=	bool ∣ int
c	::=	$id := e$ ∣ **if** e **then** c_1 **else** c_2 **fi** ∣ **while** e **do** c **od** ∣
		with d **begin** c **end** ∣ **read** id ∣ **write** e ∣ $c_1 ; c_2$
p	::=	**program** c

In the following we use Num, Id, Exp, Dec, Type, Com and Prog to denote the sets of the elements of the language derived from the non-terminals n, id, e, d, t, c and p respectively.

The **read** and **write** commands introduce a rudimentary facility for reading and writing; we assume that two files, one for input and one for output, simply modelled by sequences of values, are coexisting with the execution of the program: the execution of **read** *id* associates with *id* and erases the first value on the current content of the input file; the execution of **write** e adds the value of e to the current content of the output file.

Notice that because of the associativity of the concatenation of strings, a command like

$$x := e_1 \,;\, y := e_2 \,;\, z := e_3$$

can be generated and parsed in two different ways; in other words the above definition of the language is ambiguous. Of course the semantics for WHILE is given respecting this associativity law.

2 Histories

Histories are syntactic elements intended to represent the various program execution stages which are distinguished with respect to some of the natural properties used either to check the static correctness or to obtain the final result of a program; so the histories for WHILE must include elements for representing:

- the stages after the execution of a command;
- the stages after the elaboration of a declaration;
- the stages after the evaluation of an expression;
- some initial stage for representing the information known before a program execution start (just the content of the input file in the case of dynamic semantics and nothing in the case of static semantics).

The histories for WHILE are defined by the following pattern rules.

$$h \quad ::= \quad \textit{init-h} \mid h \,;\, c \mid h \,;\, d \mid h \,;\, e$$

The non-terminal *init-h* defines the initial histories; in the case of static semantics we have

$$\textit{init-h} \quad ::= \quad \Lambda$$

while for the dynamic semantics we have

$$\begin{array}{lll} \textit{init-h} & ::= & \textbf{input}(vls) \\ vls & ::= & \Lambda \mid v \bullet vls \\ v & ::= & \textit{int} \mid \textit{bool} \end{array}$$

where the non-terminals *int* and *bool*, not further defined here, correspond to representations of integer and boolean values respectively. In the following we use History, Val^* and Val to denote the sets of the elements corresponding to the non-terminals h, vls and v respectively.

Before the start of the execution of a WHILE program we only know what is the input and so the initial histories have form

$$\textbf{input}(vls).$$

A history having form

$$\textbf{input}(vls) \,;\, c$$

represents the stage after the execution of the command c; a history having form

$$\textbf{input}(vls) \,;\, c \,;\, d$$

represents the stage after the execution of the command c and the elaboration of the declaration d; and one having form

$$\textbf{input}(vls) \,;\, c \,;\, e$$

represents the stage after the execution of the command c and the evaluation of the expression e.

Notice that the above definition of histories is ambiguous, but here, as in section 1, we consider ";" to be associative and coinciding with the semicolon operators on WHILE commands and declarations; thus "$h ; (c_1 ; c_2)$" is identified with "$(h ; c_1) ; c_2$" and "$h ; (d_1 ; d_2)$" with "$(h ; d_1) ; d_2$".

3 Context Constraints (Static Semantics)

Clearly the definition of the syntax of WHILE in section 1 generates many syntactic objects that we consider "illegal". For example a well-formed syntactic object is illegal when the informal type discipline is violated (eg, by writing (tt + $\underline{5}$)); moreover we can add the restriction that in a legal program every occurrence of an identifier in an expression has to be preceded by a declaration to which that occurrence is bound. We give here the definition of legal constructs and hence of the context constraints following our non-standard style.

The overall aim is to define the legal (correct) programs; so we define an inductive system STAT such that a program p is *statically correct* iff in STAT we can prove $p \vdash$ok. In order to do this in an inductive way our system checks also the static correctness of histories, ie individuates the histories which are possible partial execution paths of statically correct programs. Thus we check also the static correctness of commands, expressions and declarations.

In this case we need to know:
- the type of a declared identifier,
- if an identifier represents either a variable or a constant,
- which is the type of an expression.

So the formulas representing the WHILE natural properties needed for checking static correctness are:

- ok and ok: t where $t \in$ Type;
  $h \vdash$ ok and $h \vdash$ ok: t mean that the partial execution represented by h consists of executions of statically correct constructs, the second form says also that the partial execution represented by h was terminated with the evaluation of a correct expression of type t ($\mathcal{Ok}$-formulas);

- id: t and id: t var, where $id \in$ Id and $t \in$ Type;
  $h \vdash id$: t (var) means that after the partial execution represented by h, id identifies a constant (variable) of type t ($\mathcal{T}$-formulas);

The clauses of the inductive system STAT are reported in the following, where
$n \in$ Num; $bc \in$ { tt, ff }; $iop \in$ { +, *, - }; $rop \in$ { >, <, = }; $bop \in$ { $\wedge$, $\vee$ }; $e, e_1, e_2 \in$ Exp; $id \in$ Id; $t \in$ Type; $c, c_1, c_2 \in$ Com; $d \in$ Dec; $h \in$ History.
Notice that because of the associativity assumption on the syntax of the histories we do not need to give particular clauses for the histories having form $h ; (c_1 ; c_2)$ and $h ; (d_1 ; d_2)$.

Program

$$\frac{\Lambda ; c \vdash \text{ok}}{\textbf{program } c \vdash \text{ok}}$$

Initial history

$$\Lambda \vdash \text{ok}$$

Command

$$\frac{h\,;e \vdash \mathrm{ok}{:}\ t \qquad h \vdash id{:}\ t\ \mathrm{var}}{h\ ;\ id := e \vdash\ \mathrm{ok}} \qquad\qquad \frac{h \vdash \phi \qquad h\ ;c \vdash \mathrm{ok}}{h\ ;c \vdash\ \phi} \quad \text{for all } \mathcal{T}\text{-formulas } \phi$$

$$\frac{h\,;e \vdash \mathrm{ok}{:}\ \mathtt{bool} \qquad h\ ;c_1 \vdash \mathrm{ok} \qquad h\ ;c_2 \vdash \mathrm{ok}}{h\ ;\mathbf{if}\ e\ \mathbf{then}\ c_1\ \mathbf{else}\ c_2\ \mathbf{fi} \vdash\ \mathrm{ok}} \qquad\qquad \frac{h\,;e \vdash \mathrm{ok}{:}\ \mathtt{bool} \qquad h\ ;c \vdash \mathrm{ok}}{h\ ;\mathbf{while}\ e\ \mathbf{do}\ c\ \mathbf{od} \vdash \mathrm{ok}}$$

$$\frac{h\ ;d\ ;c \vdash \mathrm{ok}}{h\ ;\mathbf{with}\ d\ \mathbf{begin}\ c\ \mathbf{end} \vdash \mathrm{ok}}$$

$$\frac{h \vdash id{:}\ t\ \mathrm{var}}{h\ ;\mathbf{read}\ id \vdash \mathrm{ok}} \qquad\qquad \frac{h\ ;e \vdash \mathrm{ok}{:}\ t}{h\ ;\mathbf{write}\ e \vdash \mathrm{ok}}$$

Declaration

$$\frac{h\ ;e \vdash \mathrm{ok}{:}\ t}{h\ ;t\ \mathbf{var}\ id = e \vdash id{:}\ t\ \mathrm{var} \qquad\qquad h\ ;t\ \mathbf{var}\ id = e \vdash \mathrm{ok}}$$

$$\frac{h\ ;e \vdash \mathrm{ok}{:}\ t}{h\ ;t\ \mathbf{const}\ id = e \vdash id{:}\ t \qquad\qquad h\ ;t\ \mathbf{const}\ id = e \vdash \mathrm{ok}}$$

$$\frac{h \vdash \phi \qquad h\ ;e \vdash \mathrm{ok}{:}\ t}{h\ ;t\ \mathbf{const}\ id = e \vdash \phi \qquad\qquad h\ ;t\ \mathbf{var}\ id = e \vdash \phi}$$

for all $\phi \in \{\ \phi' \mid \phi'$ is a $\mathcal{T}$-formula and $\phi' \neq id{:}\ t', id{:}\ t'\ \mathrm{var}$ for $t' \in \mathrm{Type}\ \}$

Expression

$$\frac{h \vdash \mathrm{ok}}{h\ ;n \vdash \mathrm{ok}{:}\ \mathtt{int}} \qquad\qquad \frac{h \vdash \mathrm{ok}}{h\ ;bc \vdash \mathrm{ok}{:}\ \mathtt{bool}}$$

$$\frac{h\ ;e_1 \vdash \mathrm{ok}{:}\ \mathtt{int} \qquad h\ ;e_2 \vdash \mathrm{ok}{:}\ \mathtt{int}}{h\ ;(e_1\ iop\ e_2) \vdash \mathrm{ok}{:}\ \mathtt{int}} \qquad\qquad \frac{h\ ;e_1 \vdash \mathrm{ok}{:}\ \mathtt{int} \qquad h\ ;e_2 \vdash \mathrm{ok}{:}\ \mathtt{int}}{h\ ;(e_1\ rop\ e_2) \vdash \mathrm{ok}{:}\ \mathtt{bool}}$$

$$\frac{h\ ;e_1 \vdash \mathrm{ok}{:}\ \mathtt{bool} \qquad h\ ;e_2 \vdash \mathrm{ok}{:}\ \mathtt{bool}}{h\ ;(e_1\ bop\ e_2) \vdash \mathrm{ok}{:}\ \mathtt{bool}} \qquad\qquad \frac{h\ ;e \vdash \mathrm{ok}{:}\ \mathtt{bool}}{h\ ;\neg\ e \vdash \mathrm{ok}{:}\ \mathtt{bool}}$$

$$\frac{h \vdash id{:}\ t}{h\ ;id \vdash \mathrm{ok}{:}\ t} \qquad\qquad \frac{h \vdash id{:}\ t\ \mathrm{var}}{h\ ;id \vdash \mathrm{ok}{:}\ t}$$

Proposition 1 gives some soundness properties of the inductive system defined above.

Prop. 1 Assume that $h \in$ History.

- For all $id \in$ Id there exists at most one $t \in$ Type s.t. either $h \vdash id{:}\ t$ or $h \vdash id{:}\ t$ var; moreover $h \vdash id{:}\ t$ and $h \vdash id{:}\ t$ var cannot hold both.
- For all $e \in$ Exp there exists at most one $t \in$ Type s.t. $h\ ;e \vdash \mathrm{ok}{:}\ t$.
- If $h \vdash \mathrm{ok}{:}\ t$, then there exists $e \in$ Exp, $h' \in$ History s.t. $h = h'\ ;e$.
- If $h \vdash \mathrm{ok}$, then $h \neq h'\ ;e$ for all $e \in$ Exp and $h' \in$ History. □

To show how the inductive system STAT works we report here the proof that the WHILE program

program with int **var** $x = \underline{2}$ **begin** $x := x + \underline{1}$; **write** x **end**

is statically correct (α and β indicate partial deductions).

$$\alpha)\qquad \dfrac{\dfrac{\Lambda \vdash \text{ok}}{\Lambda ; \underline{2} \vdash \text{ok: int}}}{\Lambda ; \text{int } \mathbf{var}\ x = \underline{2} \vdash x\text{: int var}}$$

$$\beta)\qquad \dfrac{\dfrac{\alpha}{\Lambda ; \text{int } \mathbf{var}\ x = \underline{2} ; x \vdash \text{ok: int}} \qquad \dfrac{\dfrac{\dfrac{\Lambda \vdash \text{ok}}{\Lambda ; \underline{2} \vdash \text{ok: int}}}{\Lambda ; \text{int } \mathbf{var}\ x = \underline{2} \vdash \text{ok}}}{\Lambda ; \text{int } \mathbf{var}\ x = \underline{2} ; \underline{1} \vdash \text{ok: int}}}{\Lambda ; \text{int } \mathbf{var}\ x = \underline{2} ; x + \underline{1} \vdash \text{ok: int}}$$

$$\dfrac{\dfrac{\dfrac{\dfrac{\beta \quad \alpha}{\Lambda ; \text{int } \mathbf{var}\ x = \underline{2} ; x := x + \underline{1} \vdash \text{ok}} \qquad \dfrac{\dfrac{\alpha}{\Lambda ; \text{int } \mathbf{var}\ x = \underline{2} ; x := x + \underline{1} \vdash x\text{: int var}}}{\Lambda ; \text{int } \mathbf{var}\ x = \underline{2} ; x := x + \underline{1} ; x \vdash \text{ok: int}}}{\Lambda ; \text{int } \mathbf{var}\ x = \underline{2} ; x := x + \underline{1} ; \mathbf{write}\ x \vdash \text{ok}}}{\Lambda ; \mathbf{with}\ \text{int } \mathbf{var}\ x = \underline{2} ; \mathbf{begin}\ x := x + \underline{1} ; \mathbf{write}\ x\ \mathbf{end} \vdash \text{ok}}}{\mathbf{program\ with}\ \text{int } \mathbf{var}\ x = \underline{2}\ \mathbf{begin}\ x := x + \underline{1} ; \mathbf{write}\ x\ \mathbf{end} \vdash \text{ok}}$$

4 Dynamic Semantics

In this section we consider only statically correct programs and histories.

For giving the dynamic semantics of WHILE we define an inductive system SEM such that a program p returns a result r starting from an input i iff in SEM we can prove $p \vdash i, r$. In order to do that SEM must be able to prove the following formulas representing natural properties of the language constructs (Val and Val* have been defined in section 3).

- $id = v$, where $id \in$ Id and $v \in$ Val;
  $h \vdash id = v$ means that after the partial execution represented by h, the value either of the variable or of the constant identified by id is v (*Id*-formulas);

- v where $v \in$ Val;
  $h \vdash v$ means that the partial execution represented by h has terminated with the evaluation of an expression whose value is v ($\mathcal{V}$-formulas);

- $\text{i} = vls$, where $vls \in$ Val*;
  $h \vdash \text{i} = vls$ means that after the partial execution represented by h, the content of the input file is vls (*I*-formulas);

- $o = vls$, where $vls \in \mathrm{Val}^*$;
  $h \vdash o = vls$ means that after the partial execution represented by h, the content of the output file is vls (O-formulas).

The clauses of the system SEM defining the WHILE semantics are reported in the following, where we use the following notations and definitions.

- The function Bound from Dec into finite parts of Id is defined by

  $\mathrm{Bound}(t\ \mathbf{var}\ id = e) = \{\ id\ \}$, $\mathrm{Bound}(t\ \mathbf{const}\ id = e) = \{\ id\ \}$,
  $\mathrm{Bound}(d_1\ ;\ d_2) = \mathrm{Bound}(d_1) \cup \mathrm{Bound}(d_2)$.

- The predicate Sametype on pairs of values is defined by

  $\mathrm{Sametype}(v, v') = (v, v' \in \mathrm{Bool}$ or $v, v' \in \mathrm{Int})$.

- For any operation symbol op, $\widetilde{op}$ denotes the corresponding interpretation over Int and Bool; in particular: for any $n \in \mathrm{Num}$, $\tilde{n}$ denotes the corresponding value in Int and *true*, *false* denote truth and falsity in Bool.

- Also in this case (because of the associativity assumption on the syntax of the histories) we do not give particular clauses for the histories having form $h ; (c_1 ; c_2)$ and $h ; (d_1 ; d_2)$.

- $v, v_1, v_2 \in \mathrm{Val}$; $vls, vls' \in \mathrm{Val}^*$, $c, c_1, c_2 \in \mathrm{Com}$; $d \in \mathrm{Dec}$; $id \in \mathrm{Id}$; $t \in \mathrm{Type}$; $e, e_1, e_2 \in \mathrm{Exp}$; $zop \in \mathrm{Num} \cup \{\ \mathbf{tt}, \mathbf{ff}\ \}$; $op \in \{\ +, *, -, >, <, =, \wedge, \vee\ \}$; $h \in \mathrm{History}$.

Program

$$\frac{\mathbf{input}(vls)\ ;\ c \vdash o = vls'}{\mathbf{program}\ c \vdash vls, vls'}$$

Initial history

$$\mathbf{input}(vls) \vdash i = vls \qquad\qquad \mathbf{input}(vls) \vdash o = \Lambda$$

Command

$$\frac{h\ ;\ e \vdash v}{h\ ;\ id{=}e \vdash id = v}$$

$$\frac{h \vdash \phi}{h\ ;\ id{=}e \vdash \phi} \qquad \text{for all } \phi \in \{\ \phi' \mid \phi' \text{ is an } I, O, Id\text{-formula and } \phi' \neq id = v' \text{ for } v' \in \mathrm{Val}\}$$

$$\frac{h\ ;\ e \vdash true \quad h\ ;\ c_1 \vdash \phi}{h\ ;\ \mathbf{if}\ e\ \mathbf{then}\ c_1\ \mathbf{else}\ c_2\ \mathbf{fi} \vdash \phi} \qquad \frac{h\ ;\ e \vdash false \quad h\ ;\ c_2 \vdash \phi}{h\ ;\ \mathbf{if}\ e\ \mathbf{then}\ c_1\ \mathbf{else}\ c_2\ \mathbf{fi} \vdash \phi} \qquad \text{for all } \phi$$

$$\frac{h\ ;\ e \vdash false \quad h \vdash \phi}{h\ ;\ \mathbf{while}\ e\ \mathbf{do}\ c\ \mathbf{od} \vdash \phi} \qquad \frac{h\ ;\ e \vdash true \quad h\ ;\ c\ ;\ \mathbf{while}\ e\ \mathbf{do}\ c\ \mathbf{od} \vdash \phi}{h\ ;\ \mathbf{while}\ e\ \mathbf{do}\ c\ \mathbf{od} \vdash \phi} \qquad \text{for all } \phi$$

$$\frac{h \vdash i = v \cdot vls \qquad h \vdash id = v'}{h\ ;\ \mathbf{read}\ id \vdash i = vls \qquad h\ ;\ \mathbf{read}\ id \vdash id = v} \qquad \mathrm{Sametype}(v, v')$$

$$\frac{h \vdash \mathrm{i} = v \bullet vls \qquad h \vdash id = v' \qquad h \vdash \phi}{h\ ;\ \mathbf{read}\ id \vdash \phi} \qquad \text{Sametype}(v, v')$$

for all $\phi \in \{ \phi' \mid \phi'$ is an O, Id-formula and $\phi' \neq id = v'$ for $v' \in \text{Val}\}$

Notice in the above two clauses how the premises $h \vdash \mathrm{i} = v \bullet vls$, $h \vdash id = v'$ and the side condition Sametype(v, v') allow to individuate the dynamic errors (for the WHILE language just reading an empty file or reading a value of the wrong type).

$$\frac{h \vdash \mathrm{o} = vls \quad h\ ;\ e \vdash v}{h\ ;\ \mathbf{write}\ e \vdash \mathrm{o} = v \bullet vls} \qquad \frac{h \vdash \phi}{h\ ;\ \mathbf{write}\ e \vdash \phi} \quad \text{for all } I, Id\text{-formulas } \phi$$

$$\frac{h\ ;\ d\ ;\ c \vdash \phi}{h\ ;\ \mathbf{with}\ d\ \mathbf{begin}\ c\ \mathbf{end} \vdash \phi}$$

for all $\phi \in \{ \phi' \mid \phi'$ is an I, O, Id-formula and $\phi' \neq id = v$, for $v \in \text{Val}$ $id \in \text{Bound}(d)$ $\}$

$$\frac{h \vdash id = v}{h\ ;\ \mathbf{with}\ d\ \mathbf{begin}\ c\ \mathbf{end} \vdash id = v} \qquad id \in \text{Bound}(d)$$

Expression

$$h\ ;\ zop \vdash \widetilde{zop} \qquad \frac{h\ ;\ e \vdash v}{h\ ;\ \neg\ e \vdash \widetilde{\neg}\, v}$$

$$\frac{h\ ;\ e_1 \vdash v_1 \quad h\ ;\ e_2 \vdash v_2}{h\ ;\ (e_1\ op\ e_2) \vdash v_1\ \widetilde{op}\ v_2} \qquad \frac{h \vdash id = v}{h\ ;\ id \vdash v}$$

Declaration

$$\frac{h\ ;\ e \vdash v}{h\ ;\ t\ \mathbf{var}\ id = e \vdash id = v \qquad h\ ;\ t\ \mathbf{const}\ id = e \vdash id = v}$$

$$\frac{h \vdash \phi}{h\ ;\ t\ \mathbf{var}\ id = e \vdash \phi \qquad h\ ;\ t\ \mathbf{const}\ id = e \vdash \phi}$$

for all $\phi \in \{ \phi' \mid \phi'$ is an I, O, Id-formula and $\phi' \neq id = v'$ for $v' \in \text{Val}\}$

Proposition 2 gives some soundness properties of the inductive system SEM; the last point shows that the histories for which no O-formula holds represent dynamic error situations.

Prop. 2 Assume that $h \in$ History.

- For all $id \in$ Id there exists at most one $v \in$ Val s.t. $h \vdash id = v$.
- For all $e \in$ Exp there exists at most one $v \in$ Val s.t. $h\ ;\ e \vdash v$.
- There exists at most one $vls \in \text{Val}^*$ s.t. $h \vdash \mathrm{o} = vls$.
- There exists at most one $vls \in \text{Val}^*$ s.t. $h \vdash \mathrm{i} = vls$.

- Assume that h is a command or declaration history (ie, $h = h'; c$ or $h = h'; d$),
  [$h \nvdash \phi$ for all O-formulas ϕ] iff
  [$h = h'$; **read** id ; x and either ($h' \vdash \mathrm{i} = \Lambda$) or
  ($h' \vdash \mathrm{i} = v \bullet vls,\ h' \vdash id = v'$ and not Sametype(v, v'))]. □

To show how the inductive system SEM works we report here the proof that the result of the WHILE program

program with int **var** $x = \underline{2}$ **begin** $x := x + \underline{1}$; **write** x **end**

with empty input is $3 \bullet \Lambda$.

$$
\dfrac{\dfrac{\dfrac{
\dfrac{\dfrac{\mathbf{input}(\Lambda)\vdash \mathrm{o}=\Lambda}{\mathbf{input}(\Lambda);\ \text{int }\mathbf{var}\ x=2\vdash \mathrm{o}=\Lambda}}{\mathbf{input}(\Lambda);\ \text{int }\mathbf{var}\ x=\underline{2};\ x:=x+\underline{1}\vdash \mathrm{o}=\Lambda}
\quad
\dfrac{\dfrac{\dfrac{\mathbf{input}(\Lambda);\ \text{int }\mathbf{var}\ x=2;\ \underline{1}\vdash 1 \quad \dfrac{\dfrac{\mathbf{input}(\Lambda);\ \underline{2}\vdash 2}{\mathbf{input}(\Lambda);\ \text{int }\mathbf{var}\ x=\underline{2}\vdash x=2}}{\mathbf{input}(\Lambda);\ \text{int }\mathbf{var}\ x=\underline{2};\ x\vdash 2}}{\mathbf{input}(\Lambda);\ \text{int }\mathbf{var}\ x=\underline{2};\ x+\underline{1}\vdash 3}}{\mathbf{input}(\Lambda);\ \text{int }\mathbf{var}\ x=\underline{2};\ x:=x+\underline{1}\vdash x=3}}{\mathbf{input}(\Lambda);\ \text{int }\mathbf{var}\ x=\underline{2};\ x:=x+\underline{1};\ x\vdash 3}
}{\mathbf{input}(\Lambda);\ \text{int }\mathbf{var}\ x=\underline{2};\ x:=x+\underline{1};\ \mathbf{write}\ x\vdash \mathrm{o}=3\bullet\Lambda}}{\mathbf{input}(\Lambda);\ \mathbf{with}\ \text{int }\mathbf{var}\ x=\underline{2};\ \mathbf{begin}\ x:=x+\underline{1};\ \mathbf{write}\ x\ \ \mathbf{end}\vdash \mathrm{o}=3\bullet\Lambda}}{\mathbf{program\ with}\ \text{int }\mathbf{var}\ x=\underline{2}\ \mathbf{begin}\ x:=x+\underline{1};\ \mathbf{write}\ x\ \ \mathbf{end}\vdash \Lambda,\ 3\bullet\Lambda}
$$

5 Associated Compositional Semantics

From the deductive system SEM used for defining the dynamic semantics it is possible to derive naturally a compositional (denotational) semantics for the language in the following way:

> the semantic value of a construct of the language is an object in some domain corresponding to the variations of the validity of the formulas (which represent the natural properties) caused by the execution of that construct.

For the WHILE language we have that

- the command semantic values are functions from Id, I and O-formulas into Id, I and O-formulas;
- the declaration semantic values are functions from Id-formulas into themselves;
- the expression semantic values are functions from Id-formulas into $\mathcal{V}$-formulas;
- the program semantic values are as usual functions from inputs into results ($\mathrm{Val}^* \to \mathrm{Val}^*$).

The following definition shows how to define domains representing the formulas of some kinds valid at a certain point in the execution of a program; then those domains will be used for giving the compositional semantics to WHILE.

Def. 3 For all $\mathcal{F}_1, \ldots, \mathcal{F}_n \in \{ \mathcal{V}, \mathit{Id}, I, O \}$,

- $\sim\mathcal{F}_1 \ldots \mathcal{F}_n$ indicates the equivalence relation on History defined by:
  $h \sim\mathcal{F}_1 \ldots \mathcal{F}_n h'$ iff [for all formulas ϕ of type either $\mathcal{F}_1$ or ... or $\mathcal{F}_n$ $h \vdash \phi$ iff $h' \vdash \phi$];
- $H(\mathcal{F}_1 \ldots \mathcal{F}_n)$ indicates the quotient History/$\sim\mathcal{F}_1 \ldots \mathcal{F}_n$ (in the following we write $\bar{h}$ to indicate the equivalence class of h). □

The following proposition is a soundness result, preliminary to the definition of the compositional semantics.

Prop. 4 Assume $h, h' \in$ History.

- For all $c \in$ Com,
  $h \sim_{\mathit{Id}\, I\, O} h'$ implies $h\,; c \sim_{\mathit{Id}\, I\, O} h'\,; c$.
- For all $d \in$ Dec,
  $h \sim_{\mathit{Id}} h'$ implies $h; d \sim_{\mathit{Id}} h'\,; d$.
- For all $e \in$ Exp,
  $h \sim_{\mathit{Id}} h'$ implies $h\,; e \sim_{\mathcal{V}} h'; e$. □

Def. 5 (Compositional semantics)

- P: Prog $\rightarrow$ (Val* $\rightarrow$ Val*)
  $\mathsf{P}[p]vls = vls'$ iff $\mathrm{p} \vdash vls, vls'$.
- C: Com $\rightarrow$ (H($\mathit{Id}\, I\, O$) $\rightarrow$ H($\mathit{Id}\, I\, O$))
  $\mathsf{C}[c]\bar{h} = \overline{h\,;\,c}$
  (by prop. 4 we have that $\mathsf{C}[c]$ is a function from H($\mathit{Id}\, I\, O$) into H($\mathit{Id}\, I\, O$)).
- D: Dec $\rightarrow$ (H(Id) $\rightarrow$ H(Id))
  $\mathsf{D}[d]\bar{h} = \overline{h\,;\,d}$
  (by prop. 4 we have that $\mathsf{D}[d]$ is a function from H(Id) into H(Id)).
- E: Exp $\rightarrow$ (H(Id) $\rightarrow$ H($\mathcal{V}$))
  $\mathsf{E}[e]\bar{h} = \overline{h\,;\,e}$
  (by prop. 4 we have that $\mathsf{E}[e]$ is a function from H(Id) into H($\mathcal{V}$)). □

In the following propositions, if s indicates a type of constructs of WHILE, then S indicates the semantic function for the constructs of type s.

Prop. 6 P, C, D and E give for programs, commands, declarations and expressions respectively, a compositional semantics, ie:

- for any σ constructor of WHILE which takes n constructs of types $s_1, \ldots, s_n$ respectively and returns a construct of type s_{n+1},
- for all $c_1, c_1', \ldots, c_n, c_1'$ constructs of WHILE of appropriate type
  if for $i = 1, \ldots, n$ $\mathsf{S}_i[c_i] = \mathsf{S}_i[c_i']$
  then $\mathsf{S}_{n+1}[\sigma(c_1, \ldots, c_n)] = \mathsf{S}_{n+1}[\sigma(c_1', \ldots, c_n')]$. □

Prop. 7 P, C, D and E give for programs, commands, declarations and expressions respectively, a fully abstract semantics, ie:

- for s = command, declaration and expression
- for all c, c' constructs of WHILE of type s
  if (for any context of type program in WHILE $p[x]$ with a hole of the type s
  $P[p(c)] = P[p(c')]$)
  then $S[c] = S[c']$. □

Acknowledgements. I thank E. Astesiano for introducing myself to the niceties of the inductive semantics and for useful discussions on the subject.

References

[A] Astesiano E. "Inductive Semantics", to appear in *Formal Descriptions of Programming Concepts* (Neuhold E.J.; Paul M. eds.), Springer Verlag, 1990.

[Ac] Aczel, P. "An introduction to inductive definitions", (J. Barwise ed.) *Handbook of Mathematical Logic*, Amsterdam, North-Holland, 1977.

[BH] Burstall R.; Honsell F. "A natural Deduction Treatment of Operational Semantics", *Proc. 8th Conf. on Foundations of Software Technology and Theoretical Computer Science*, Berlin, Springer Verlag, (Lecture Notes in Computer Science n. 287), 1987.

[K] Kahn G. "Natural Semantics", *Proc. of STACS'87*, Berlin, Springer Verlag, 1987 (Lecture Notes in Computer Science n. 247), pp. 22-39.

[MT] Milner R.; Tofte M. "Co-induction in Relational Semantics", LFCS report Series, ECS-LFCS-88-65, University of Edinburgh, 1988.

[P1] Plotkin, G. "A structural approach to operational semantics", Lecture notes, AArhus University, 1981.

[P2] Plotkin, G. "An operational Semantics for CSP", (Bjørner, D. ed.), *Proc. IFIP TC 2-Working Conference: Formal Description of Programming Concepts II, Garmisch-Partenkirchen, June 1982* Amsterdam, North-Holland, 1983, pp. 199-223.

[S] Stoy, J.E. *Denotational semantics: the Scott-Strachey approach to programming language theory*, London, The MIT Press, 1977.

Relating Full Abstraction Results for Different Programming Languages

Kurt Sieber*
FB 14 Informatik
Universität des Saarlandes
66 Saarbrücken
West Germany
e-mail: sieber@cs.uni-sb.de

Abstract. We prove that Plotkin's model of bottomless cpos and partial continuous functions [19] is fully abstract for PCF_v, a call-by-value version of the language PCF [17]. This settles a 'folk theorem' which has occasionally been misunderstood. We then show that the (known) full abstraction results for *lazy* PCF [2] and PCF with *control* [22] can be derived as corollaries from this theorem. Such a connection is particularly surprising, because observational congruence—the central notion in the definition of full abstraction—is usually not preserved by many known translations between different programming languages. We expect that *new* full abstraction theorems for some extensions of PCF_v can be derived in the same way.

1 Introduction

The semantics of a programming language is usually specified by an *operational* description [10], i.e. by a mathematically precise definition of its interpreter. On the other hand a *denotational* description of the same language allows us to reason about programs on a more abstract mathematical level, which—in particular—can be useful as the basis for a formal proof system [4,21]. Hence the question arises, how closely both descriptions are related.

The minimum expectation is that the denotational semantics correctly explains the 'observable behavior of programs'; more precisely: The (operational) definition of a programming language comes with a set O of *observations*; certain expressions of the language are called *programs*; and the *behavior* of each program P is defined as a set $beh(P) \subseteq O$. A denotational semantics is called **computationally adequate** if $[\![P]\!] = [\![Q]\!]$ implies $beh(P) = beh(Q)$ for all programs P, Q, i.e. if the denotational meaning of a program uniquely determines its behavior.

The strength of the denotational method is of course, that it assigns meanings not only to programs, but to *arbitrary* expressions. The question is then, whether semantic equality between expressions has some operational meaning. Two expressions M, N are called **observationally**

*The author is supported by DFG Research Fellowship Si 373/2-1.

congruent ($M \approx N$), if $beh(C[M]) = beh(C[N])$ for every program context $C[\ ]$ (a program context is a 'term with a hole' such that $C[M]$ and $C[N]$ are programs). If a denotational semantics is computationally adequate and the meaning $[\![M]\!]$ is defined by induction on the structure of M, then $[\![M]\!] = [\![N]\!]$ implies $M \approx N$. If also the converse holds, i.e. if semantic equality coincides with observational congruence, then the denotational semantics is called **fully abstract**.

The classical study of computational adequacy and full abstraction is contained in Plotkin's paper "LCF considered as a programming language" [17]. His example language, PCF, is a simply typed functional language with call-by-name interpreter. Its only programs are the closed expressions of ground type ι (integer), and the only possible observation for a program is the integer which it produces (provided that it terminates). Plotkin shows that the standard Scott model is computationally adequate for PCF and—if a parallel conditional operator is added to the language—even fully abstract.

In the first part of this paper we prove the analogue of Plotkin's full abstraction theorem for a call-by-value version of PCF, which we call PCF_v. As the underlying model we use (our own variant of) Plotkin's 'bottomless' cpos and partial continuous functions [19]. We can largely imitate Plotkin's full abstraction proof for PCF; the additional complications which are caused by value parameters will be pointed out in section 3.

It should be mentioned that this result—which we announced in the `types@theory.lcs.mit.edu` electronic forum in 1989—has already been cited in [21] and [22]. Moreover a slightly different model is claimed fully abstract in [22]. But actually full abstraction fails for that model, because observationally congruent *open* terms are not always assigned the same meaning. We will discuss this error briefly in section 2.

In the second part of this paper we show that full abstraction theorems for two other languages can be obtained as 'corollaries' of our result. These languages are *lazy* PCF [2,4] and PCF with *control* facilities [22]; henceforth called PCF_l and PCF_c. Both theorems are already known, but were proved from scratch by imitating Plotkin's proof [2,22]. This can be particularly tedious if the language is sufficiently complex like PCF_c. Our method avoids a good deal of these technical difficulties.

We briefly introduce PCF_l and PCF_c.

PCF_l is a call-by-name language, which has the same syntax and interpreter as PCF, but comes with more programs and observations. Its additional programs are the closed expressions of function type, the only possible observation for such a program is its termination. In this new setting the Scott model is no longer adequate, because it identifies a diverging expression Ω of function type with the terminating expression $\lambda x.\Omega x$. This was the motivation to introduce the *lazy*[1] or *lifted* model in [2] (and similar models for untyped and recursively typed languages in [9,14] and [3,10]). The lazy model is computationally adequate for the new set of observations, and full abstraction is obtained by adding (besides parallel conditional) a 'convergence test' operator $up?_\tau : \tau \to \iota$ for each type τ. This operator forces its argument to be evaluated and returns some ground type value, say 1, if the evaluation terminates. Note that—as soon as the *up?*-operators are added to the language—the new observations are no longer necessary, because $up?_\tau$ transforms a (non)terminating expression of type τ to a (non)terminating expression of ground type ι. Hence we may assume that PCF_l—like the other two languages—only allows ground type observations.

PCF_c is an extension of PCF_v which has a sophisticated control structure. In particular it

[1] "Lazy" does *not* refer to infinite lists here. It only means that the 'laziness' of the interpreter, i.e. its immediate termination on arbitrary λ-abstractions, is captured in the model.

contains typed versions of the function call/cc (call-with-current-continuation) of the programming language SCHEME [20,7]. The underlying denotational model is the CPS (continuation passing style) model of [22]. This model is computationally adequate, and full abstraction is obtained by adding first class prompts [6] (besides parallel conditional).

How can full abstraction theorems for different programming languages follow from each other? Note that this is not at all obvious. Although various semantics preserving translations between different languages are known, such translations usually do not preserve observational congruence [15]. Indeed our method is not so much based on a syntactic translation, but more on semantic connections between models. We briefly explain how full abstraction for $\mathrm{PCF_l}$ follows from full abstraction for $\mathrm{PCF_v}$. A detailed proof is presented in section 4.

The starting point is to consider name parameters as value parameters of function type, so-called *thunks*. This defines a (semantic !) embedding of the lazy model into the call-by-value model, which maps lazy elements of type τ to call-by-value elements of some higher type τ^* (e.g. each v of ground type ι is mapped to the constant function $\underline{\lambda} u.v$ of type $\iota \to \iota$.)[2] The important observation is that these embedding functions φ^τ can be simulated in $\mathrm{PCF_l}$ by closed expressions $I^\tau : \tau \to \tau^*$. The *up?*-operators play a prominent role at this point, because they allow us to simulate all the juggling with thunks, which is contained in the definition of the functions φ^τ.

Now full abstraction is inherited as follows. If $M_1, M_2 : \tau$ are $\mathrm{PCF_l}$-expressions with different semantics, then $\varphi^\tau [M_1] \neq \varphi^\tau [\![M_2]\!]$ in the call-by-value model, hence some closed $\mathrm{PCF_v}$-expression $M : \tau^* \to \iota$ exists which maps these elements to different ground type values. (This is actually a slightly stronger assumption than full abstraction for $\mathrm{PCF_v}$, but it comes for free with our proof in section 3.) A simple translation of M then delivers a closed $\mathrm{PCF_l}$-expression $\bar{M} : \tau^* \to \iota$ such that $[\![\bar{M}(I^\tau M_1)]\!] \neq [\![\bar{M}(I^\tau M_2)]\!]$. By computational adequacy this means $beh(\bar{M}(I^\tau M_1)) \neq beh(\bar{M}(I^\tau M_2))$, hence $M_1 \not\approx M_2$, and we are done.

The proof for $\mathrm{PCF_c}$ follows the same lines. Each function in the CPS model has a continuation as an implicit second parameter. In order to obtain a corresponding function in the call-by-value model, we must only make this continuation parameter visible, i.e. we replace it by an explicit parameter of function type. This defines an embedding of the CPS model into the call-by-value model, and now we can play the same game as for $\mathrm{PCF_l}$. The central role is played here by the call/cc operators, because they allow us to compute with continuations as if they were parameters of function type.

The paper is structured as follows. In section 2 we introduce the language $\mathrm{PCF_v}$ and define some general concepts which allow a uniform approach to all three languages. Section 3 contains a sketch of our full abstraction proof for $\mathrm{PCF_v}$. In section 4 and 5 we define the two other languages and obtain their full abstraction as corollaries of the full abstraction for $\mathrm{PCF_v}$. In the conclusion we discuss further applications of our method.

2 PCF and Call-by-Value

$\mathrm{PCF_v}$ is essentially a simply typed λ-value-calculus [15] with conditional and fixed-point operators and some first order arithmetic functions; more precisely:

The *types* $\sigma, \tau, \ldots$ of $\mathrm{PCF_v}$ are defined by

$$\sigma ::= \iota \mid \sigma \to \sigma;$$

[2] We use $\underline{\lambda}$ as the meta symbol for functional abstraction.

the constants and their types are

$$\begin{array}{rll} \underline{n}: & \iota & \text{for each } n \in \omega = \{0,1,\ldots\}, \\ succ, pred: & \iota \to \iota, & \\ \mathrm{Y}_{\sigma\to\tau}: & ((\sigma \to \tau) \to (\sigma \to \tau)) \to \sigma \to \tau & \text{for each pair of types } \sigma, \tau. \end{array}$$

We use superscripts to indicate the types of constants c and variables x. With this convention, *expressions* $M, N, \ldots$ and their types are defined by:

$$\begin{array}{rlll} c^\tau: & \tau & & \text{(constant)}, \\ x^\tau: & \tau & & \text{(variable)}, \\ (\lambda x^\sigma.M): & \sigma \to \tau & \text{if } M:\tau & \text{(abstraction)}, \\ (MN): & \tau & \text{if } M:\sigma\to\tau \text{ and } N:\sigma & \text{(application)}, \\ (\mathbf{if}_\tau MNP): & \tau & \text{if } M:\iota \text{ and } N,P:\tau & \text{(conditional)}, \\ (\mathbf{pif}\, MNP): & \iota & \text{if } M,N,P:\iota & \text{(parallel conditional)}. \end{array}$$

In favor of a simple presentation we have restricted ourselves to the single ground type ι of integers, hence integers serve as truth values in conditional expressions. Instead of the constructs $\mathbf{if}_\tau$ and **pif** we could have used constants $cond_\tau$ and *pcond* to define conditional expressions (cf. [22]). But note that—because of call-by-value—such constants need parameters of function type (*thunks*) in order to avoid evaluation of the wrong branch of a condition, e. g. $cond_\tau : \iota \to (\iota \to \tau) \to (\iota \to \tau) \to \tau$.

The set $FV(M)$ of *free* variables of an expression M is defined as usual; M is *closed* if $FV(M)$ is empty. $M[x := N]$ denotes the expression obtained from M by substituting N for all free occurences of x. By a *program* we mean a closed expression of ground type ι. Constants, variables and abstractions are called *value expressions*; we use meta variables $U, V, \ldots$ for them (usually they are called *values*, but we want to reserve this word for semantic objects). Ω_τ (or just Ω) stands for some closed diverging expression of type τ, say $\Omega_\tau \equiv \mathrm{Y}_{\iota\to\tau}(\lambda x^{\iota\to\tau}.x)\underline{0}$.

A structured operational semantics [18] for PCF_v is specified in the Appendix. Note that—in contrast to call-by-name—an argument must first be reduced to a value expression before it can be passed as a parameter (rules (APPL 2) and (BETA-V)). As a consequence, $\mathrm{Y}_{\sigma\to\tau}V$ must be reduced to $\lambda x^\sigma.V(\mathrm{Y}_{\sigma\to\tau}V)x$ and not to $V(\mathrm{Y}_{\sigma\to\tau}V)$, because the latter reduction would always lead to divergence.

The behavior of a program P can now be formally defined by

$$beh(P) = \{n \in \omega \mid P \xrightarrow{*} \underline{n}\},$$

where $\xrightarrow{*}$ denotes the reflexive transitive closure of the transition relation $\to$. It is easy to see that $\xrightarrow{*}$ has the Church-Rosser property and hence $beh(P)$ contains at most one element, but this will also follow from computational adequacy of our denotational model.

For defining the denotational semantics we follow [19]. By a *cpo* (complete partial order) we simply mean a partial order in which every nonempty directed set has a lub (least upper bound). We do not insist that a cpo must have a least element; if it has one, then it is called a *pointed* cpo. (This terminology was proposed in [19].) We use the notation *Nat* for the cpo of natural numbers $0, 1, \ldots$ with the *discrete* order, $D \to E$ for the cpo of *continuous* functions from D to E, and $D_\perp$ for the *lifted* cpo obtained from D. D is considered as a subset of $D_\perp$, i.e. the lifting operator will not always be explicitly mentioned.

In order to obtain a uniform approach to all three languages, we will always distinguish between a cpo V^τ of *values* and a cpo C^τ of *computations* of type τ. These cpo's will come equipped with functions

$$\eta^\tau : V^\tau \to C^\tau,$$
$$app^{\sigma,\tau} : C^{\sigma\to\tau} \times C^\sigma \to C^\tau.$$

Instead of $app^{\sigma,\tau}(d,e)$ we also use the notation $d \bullet e$.

The distinction between values and computations is in the spirit of Moggi's *computational λ-calculus* [12]. Values are those semantic objects which are bound to variables (by the current environment) and serve as interpretations of constants, while computations serve as meanings of expressions (in a given environment). η^τ maps a value v to the 'trivial computation with result v', and $app^{\sigma,\tau}$ will always be tailored to define the meaning of an application MN. (In Moggi's approach $app^{\sigma,\tau}$ is composed from more elementary combinators, which we don't need for our purposes.)

For PCF$_v$ we define

$$\begin{aligned} V^\iota &= Nat, \\ V^{\sigma\to\tau} &= V^\sigma \to C^\tau, \\ C^\tau &= V^\tau_\bot; \end{aligned}$$

η^τ is simply the lifting function, and $app^{\sigma,\tau}$ is defined by

$$app^{\sigma,\tau}(d,e) = \begin{cases} \bot & \text{if } d = \bot \text{ or } e = \bot, \\ de & \text{otherwise.} \end{cases}$$

Note that—for each type τ—the cpo C^τ contains an element $\bot \notin V^\tau$. This situation, characterized by the slogan 'bottom is not a value', is typical for a call-by-value language. As $\bot$ stands for the meaning of a diverging expression, and each expression must be evaluated *before* it can be passed as a parameter, there is no need to bind $\bot$ to a variable. Instead, the definition of $app^{\sigma,\tau}$ takes care of diverging arguments. For the same reason the functions in $V^{\sigma\to\tau} = V^\sigma \to V^\tau_\bot$ have $\bot$ only in their codomain and not in their domain. If we consider $\bot$ as a notation for 'undefined', then these are just the *partial continuous* functions from V^σ to V^τ as defined in [19].

At this point a warning seems appropiate: One might be tempted to add $\bot$ to the cpo of values and to compensate this by using *strict* functions. This was done in [22], but actually leads to a model which is *not* fully abstract. Namely, if x is of type $\sigma \to \tau$ and $\rho x = \bot$, then (in the semantics of [22])

$$[\![x]\!]\,\rho = \bot \neq \underline{\lambda} v.\bot = [\![\lambda y^\sigma.xy]\!]\,\rho,$$

although x and $\lambda y^\sigma.xy$ are observationally congruent.

We return to our approach. The *interpretation* $\mathcal{I}$ will always be a type respecting function from constants to values. For PCF$_v$ we define[3]

$$\begin{aligned} \mathcal{I}(\underline{n}) &= n, \\ \mathcal{I}(succ)n &= \eta^\iota(n+1), \\ \mathcal{I}(pred)n &= \eta^\iota(n \dot{-} 1), \\ \mathcal{I}(\mathrm{Y}_{\sigma\to\tau})f &= \eta^{\sigma\to\tau}(fix(\underline{\lambda} g \in V^{\sigma\to\tau}.\ \underline{\lambda} v \in V^\sigma.\ app^{\sigma,\tau}(fg, \eta^\sigma v))), \end{aligned}$$

where $fix : (D \to D) \to D$ denotes the least fixed point operator for any pointed cpo D. Note that $V^{\sigma\to\tau}$ is indeed a pointed cpo whose least element is the constant function $\underline{\lambda} v \in V^\sigma.\bot$ (which

[3] Here we explicitly mention the lifting operators η^τ, because this allows us to use the same definition in section 5.

should not be confused with the least element $\bot$ of C), hence the fixed point in the definition of $\mathcal{I}(\mathrm{Y}_{\sigma\to\tau})$ exists. Also note that this definition is exactly tailored after the rule (FIXP-V).

An *environment* ρ will always be a type respecting function from variables to values. *Env* denotes the set of all environments, and $\rho[v/x]$ is the environment which assigns v to x and coincides with ρ on all other variables. The meaning of an expression $M : \tau$ is a function $[\![M]\!] : Env \to C^\tau$, which is defined as follows

$$\begin{aligned}
[\![c^\tau]\!]\,\rho &= \eta^\tau(\mathcal{I}(c));\\
[\![x^\tau]\!]\,\rho &= \eta^\tau(\rho x);\\
[\![\lambda x^\sigma.M]\!]\,\rho &= \eta^{\sigma\to\tau}(\underline{\lambda} v \in V^\sigma.\,[\![M]\!]\,\rho[v/x]);\\
[\![MN]\!]\,\rho &= app^{\sigma,\tau}([\![M]\!]\,\rho, [\![N]\!]\,\rho);\\
[\![\mathrm{if}_\tau MNP]\!]\,\rho &= \begin{cases} [\![N]\!]\,\rho & \text{if } [\![M]\!]\,\rho = n > 0,\\ [\![P]\!]\,\rho & \text{if } [\![M]\!]\,\rho = 0,\\ \bot & \text{otherwise;}\end{cases}\\
[\![\mathrm{pif}\, MNP]\!]\,\rho &= \begin{cases} [\![N]\!]\,\rho & \text{if } [\![M]\!]\,\rho = n > 0,\\ [\![P]\!]\,\rho & \text{if } [\![M]\!]\,\rho = 0,\\ n & \text{if } [\![M]\!]\,\rho = \bot \text{ and } [\![N]\!]\,\rho = [\![P]\!]\,\rho = n,\\ \bot & \text{otherwise.}\end{cases}
\end{aligned}$$

As usual $[\![M]\!]\,\rho$ does not depend on ρ if M is closed; then we abbreviate $[\![M]\!]\,\rho$ by $[\![M]\!]$.

Note that $[\![V]\!]\,\rho$ is of the form $\eta^\tau v \neq \bot$ for each value expression $V : \tau$. This corresponds to the fact that a value expression V is never reduced to any other expression M by the interpreter, hence in particular its evaluation can never diverge.

3 Adequacy and Full Abstraction

The denotational semantics in section 2 is computationally adequate; more precisely:

Theorem 1 (Computational Adequacy for PCF$_\mathrm{v}$) *For each PCF$_\mathrm{v}$-program P: $[\![P]\!] = n$ iff $P \xrightarrow{*} \underline{n}$.*

A proof is already contained in [19], even for a recursively typed language, an alternative proof can be found in [22].

We now turn to the proof of full abstraction. As in [17], the main idea is to show that all finite elements of the denotational model are definable by closed expressions of the language. We briefly repeat the technical definitions and theorems; some of them slightly differ from [17], because they must also make sense for bottomless cpos.

An element d of a cpo D is *finite* if $d \sqsubseteq \bigsqcup\Delta$ implies $\exists e \in \Delta.\ d \sqsubseteq e$, for every nonempty directed set $\Delta \subseteq D$. D is *algebraic*, if every $d \in D$ is the lub of a directed set of finite elements. D is *consistently complete* if any two elements with an upper bound also have a least upper bound.

For finite elements $d \in D, e \in E$ the *threshold function* $(d \Rightarrow e) \in D \to E_\bot$ is defined by

$$(d \Rightarrow e)u = \begin{cases} e & \text{if } d \sqsubseteq u,\\ \bot & \text{otherwise.}\end{cases}$$

Lemma 1 *Let D and E be consistently complete algebraic cpos. Then $D \to E_\bot$ is also consistently complete and algebraic, and its finite elements are exactly the (existing) lubs of the form $\bigsqcup_{i=1}^n (d_i \Rightarrow e_i)$ with $n \geq 0, d_i \in D, e_i \in E$ finite.*

For $n = 0$ this lub denotes the least element of $D \to E_\perp$, i.e. the constant function $\underline{\lambda}d \in D.\ \perp$. Note that other constant functions are not necessarily finite, if D is not pointed.

Lemma 1 implies immediately that V^τ is consistently complete and algebraic for each type τ and that each finite element $v \in V^{\sigma\to\tau}$ is of the form

$$v = \bigsqcup_{i=1}^{n}(u_i \Rightarrow w_i) \tag{1}$$

with $n \geq 0, u_i \in V^\sigma, w_i \in V^\tau$ finite. This form can be expanded as follows. If $v \in V^{\sigma_1\to\cdots\to\sigma_k}$ with $\sigma_k = \iota$, then

$$v = \bigsqcup_{i=1}^{n}(u_{i1} \Rightarrow \cdots \Rightarrow u_{ik_i}) \tag{2}$$

with $n \geq 0, 2 \leq k_i \leq k, u_{ij} \in V^{\sigma_j}$ finite. Note that—in contrast to [17]—the threshold functions in (2) do not necessarily have the full length k. The simplest example is $v = (1 \Rightarrow \underline{\lambda}u.\perp) \in V^{\iota\to\iota\to\iota}$, which cannot be the lub of threshold functions of length 3.

Theorem 2 (Definability of finite elements) *For each finite element $v \in V^\tau$ there is a closed Y-free PCF$_v$-expression M with $[\![M]\!] = v$.*

Sketch of the Proof:

By induction on τ we show that not only v itself is definable by a closed Y-free expression, but also the following elements (provided they exist):

- $(v \Rightarrow 1)$,
- $(v \Rightarrow 1) \sqcup (u \Rightarrow 0)$ for finite u,
- $v \sqcup \underline{\lambda}u.w$ for finite w.

The last clause allows us to use the simple form (1) in the induction step instead of form (2). The details of the induction are similar as in [17].

Lemma 2 (Main Lemma) *Let $d, e \in C^\tau, d \neq e$. Then there is a closed Y-free PCF$_v$-expression $M : \tau \to \iota$ such that $[\![M]\!] \bullet d \neq [\![M]\!] \bullet e$.*

Proof:

Without loss of generality we may assume that $d \not\sqsubseteq e$. Then $d \in V^\tau$, and because V^τ is algebraic, there is a finite element $v \in V^\tau$ with $v \sqsubseteq d, v \not\sqsubseteq e$. Hence $(v \Rightarrow 1)$ is also finite, and we can take the closed Y-free expression $M : \tau \to \iota$ with $[\![M]\!] = (v \Rightarrow 1)$, which exists by Theorem 2.

Theorem 3 (Full Abstraction for PCF$_v$) *For any two PCF$_v$-expressions M_1, M_2: $M_1 \approx M_2$ iff $[\![M_1]\!] = [\![M_2]\!]$.*

Proof:

If $[\![M_1]\!] \neq [\![M_2]\!]$, then $[\![\lambda\bar{x}.M_1]\!] \neq [\![\lambda\bar{x}.M_2]\!]$, where $\bar{x}$ is the list of free variables of M_1 and M_2. Hence $[\![M(\lambda\bar{x}.\ M_1)]\!] \neq [\![M(\lambda\bar{x}.\ M_2)]\!]$ for the closed expression M of the Main Lemma. By computational adequacy this means $beh(M(\lambda\bar{x}.\ M_1)) \neq beh(M(\lambda\bar{x}.\ M_2))$, hence $M_1 \not\approx M_2$.

4 Lazy PCF

Syntactically PCF_l is obtained from PCF_v by adding a constant

$$up?_\tau : \tau \to \iota$$

for each type τ. Its operational semantics can be obtained by changing the rules (BETA-V) and (FIXP-V) to the more familiar call-by-name rules

(BETA) $(\lambda x^\sigma.M)N \to M[x := N]$

(FIXP) $Y_{\sigma\to\tau}V \to V(Y_{\sigma\to\tau}V)$

and adding two rules for the *up?*-operators [2], namely:

(UP 1) $\dfrac{M \to M'}{up?_\tau M \to up?_\tau M'}$

(UP 2) $up?_\tau M \to \underline{1}$ if M is a constant or an abstraction.

In the denotational semantics for a call-by-name language there is no need to distinguish between values and computations, because each expression can be passed as a parameter without being evaluated first. Nevertheless we stick to our general framework for the sake of uniformity. The cpo's V^τ and C^τ are defined by

$$\begin{aligned} V^\iota &= Nat_\perp, \\ V^{\sigma\to\tau} &= (V^\sigma \to V^\tau)_\perp, \\ C^\tau &= V^\tau; \end{aligned}$$

η^τ is the identity and $app^{\sigma,\tau}$ is defined by

$$app^{\sigma,\tau}(d,e) = \begin{cases} \perp & \text{if } d = \perp, \\ de & \text{otherwise.} \end{cases}$$

The new interpretation of the constants is

$$\begin{aligned} \mathcal{I}(\underline{n}) &= n; \\ \mathcal{I}(succ)v &= \begin{cases} \eta^\iota\perp & \text{if } v = \perp, \\ \eta^\iota(v+1) & \text{otherwise;} \end{cases} \\ \mathcal{I}(pred)v &= \begin{cases} \eta^\iota\perp & \text{if } v = \perp, \\ \eta^\iota(v\dot{-}1) & \text{otherwise;} \end{cases} \\ \mathcal{I}(Y_\tau)v &= \begin{cases} \eta^\tau\perp & \text{if } v = \perp, \\ \eta^\tau(fix\, v) & \text{otherwise;} \end{cases} \\ \mathcal{I}(up?_\tau)v &= \begin{cases} \eta^\iota\perp & \text{if } v = \perp, \\ \eta^\iota 1 & \text{otherwise.} \end{cases} \end{aligned}$$

These are the only necessary changes in the denotational semantics.

As mentioned in the introduction we may assume that we only have ground type observations. Hence computational adequacy can be expressed as before.

Theorem 4 (Computational Adequacy for PCF$_l$) *For each PCF$_l$-program P:* $[\![P]\!] = n$ *iff* $P \stackrel{*}{\rightarrow} \underline{n}$.

For the proof we refer to [2].

We will now derive full abstraction for PCF$_l$ from full abstraction for PCF$_v$, as sketched in the introduction. The first step is to define the 'embedding functions' φ^τ which map elements of the lazy model to their corresponding thunks in the call-by-value model.[4]

For each type τ let the types τ° and τ^* be defined by

$$\begin{aligned} \iota^\circ &= \iota, \\ (\sigma \to \tau)^\circ &= \sigma^* \to \tau^\circ, \\ \tau^* &= \iota \to \tau^\circ, \end{aligned}$$

and functions $\varphi^\tau : V_l^\tau \to V_v^{\tau^*}, \psi^\tau : V_v^{\tau^*} \to V_l^\tau$ by

$$\begin{aligned} \varphi^\iota v &= \underline{\lambda} n \in V_v^\iota .\ v; \\ \psi^\iota v &= v0; \\ \varphi^{\sigma\to\tau} f &= \begin{cases} \underline{\lambda} n \in V_v^\iota .\ \bot & \text{if } f = \bot, \\ \underline{\lambda} n \in V_v^\iota .\ \underline{\lambda} v \in V_v^{\sigma^*} .\ \varphi^\tau(f(\psi^\sigma v))0 & \text{otherwise;} \end{cases} \\ \psi^{\sigma\to\tau} f &= \begin{cases} \bot & \text{if } f0 = \bot, \\ \underline{\lambda} v \in V_l^\sigma .\ \psi^\tau(\underline{\lambda} n \in V_v^\iota .\ f0(\varphi^\sigma v)) & \text{otherwise.} \end{cases} \end{aligned}$$

τ^* is the 'thunk type' corresponding to τ, and φ^τ maps each element of type τ in the lazy model to its corresponding thunk of type τ^* in the call-by-value model.

Lemma 3 *φ^τ and ψ^τ are well-defined continuous functions. $\psi^\tau \circ \varphi^\tau$ is the identity on V_l^τ, hence φ^τ is one-to-one.*

The proof is a straightforward induction on τ.

The next step is to simulate the functions φ^τ in the language PCF$_l$. Using $\lambda_s x.M$ as an abbreviation for $\lambda x.\mathrm{if}(up?\,x)M\Omega$ we define closed PCF$_l$-expressions $I^\tau : \tau \to \tau^*$ and $J^\tau : \tau^* \to \tau$ by

$$\begin{aligned} I^\iota &\equiv \lambda x^\iota .\lambda_s z^\iota .x, \\ J^\iota &\equiv \lambda_s x^{\iota^*} .x\underline{0}, \\ I^{\sigma\to\tau} &\equiv \lambda x^{\sigma\to\tau} .\lambda_s z^\iota .\mathrm{if}(up?\,x)(\lambda_s y^{\sigma^*} .I^\tau(x(J^\sigma y))\underline{0})\Omega, \\ J^{\sigma\to\tau} &\equiv \lambda_s x^{(\sigma\to\tau)^*} .\mathrm{if}(up?\,(x\underline{0}))(\lambda y^\sigma .J^\tau(\lambda_s z^\iota .x\underline{0}(I^\sigma y)))\Omega. \end{aligned}$$

These expressions define functions $i^\tau \in V_l^{\tau\to\tau^*}$ and $j^\tau \in V_l^{\tau^*\to\tau}$ by

$$[\![I^\tau]\!] = \eta^{\tau\to\tau^*} i^\tau, [\![J^\tau]\!] = \eta^{\tau^*\to\tau} j^\tau.$$

I^τ and J^τ are exactly tailored after φ^τ and ψ^τ. In order to express that they simulate these functions we define relations $R^\tau \subseteq V_v^\tau \times V_l^\tau, S^\tau \subseteq C_v^\tau \times C_l^\tau$ by

$$\begin{aligned} R^\iota(u,v) &\Leftrightarrow u = v, \\ R^{\sigma\to\tau}(f,g) &\Leftrightarrow (g \neq \bot \wedge g\bot = \bot \wedge \forall u \in V_v^\sigma, v \in V_l^\sigma .\ R^\sigma(u,v) \Rightarrow S^\tau(fu, gv)), \\ S^\tau(d,e) &\Leftrightarrow ((d = \bot \wedge e = \bot) \vee (d \in V_v^\tau \wedge R^\tau(d,e))). \end{aligned}$$

[4]From now on we must distinguish between the two models; we will do this by using indices v and l whenever necessary.

The definition of these relations is very similar to the definition of logical relations [16]. Indeed we have

$$S^{\sigma\to\tau}(d_1, d_2) \wedge S^{\sigma}(e_1, e_2) \Rightarrow S^{\tau}(d_1 \bullet e_1, d_2 \bullet e_2).$$

The simulation is now expressed by

Lemma 4 *For each type* τ

- $R^{\tau^*}(\varphi^\tau v, i^\tau v)$ *for all* $v \in V_1^\tau$.
- $R^{\tau^*}(u, v) \Rightarrow \psi^\tau u = j^\tau v$ *for all* $u \in V_c^{\tau^*}, v \in V_1^{\tau^*}$.

Again the proof is a straightforward induction on τ.

Finally we define the translation. For each PCF$_v$-expression M let $\bar{M}$ be the PCF$_l$-expression obtained from M by replacing each λ by λ_s. Then—with the obvious generalization of the relations R^τ to environments—we get

Lemma 5 *For each* Y*-free PCF$_v$-expression $M : \tau$ and each pair of environments $\rho_1 \in Env_v, \rho_2 \in Env_l$*

$$R(\rho_1, \rho_2) \Rightarrow S^{\tau}([\![M]\!]_v \rho_1, [\![\bar{M}]\!]_l \rho_2).$$

This implies in particular $S^{\tau}([\![M]\!], [\![\bar{M}]\!])$ for each closed Y-free expression M.

Theorem 5 **(Full Abstraction for PCF$_l$)** *For any two PCF$_l$-expressions M_1, M_2: $M_1 \approx M_2$ iff $[\![M_1]\!] = [\![M_2]\!]$.*

Proof:

As usual, it is sufficient to consider closed expressions. Hence let $M_1, M_2 : \tau$ be closed PCF$_l$-expressions with $[\![M_1]\!]_l \neq [\![M_2]\!]_l$. Then $\varphi^\tau [\![M_1]\!]_l \neq \varphi^\tau [\![M_2]\!]_l$ in $V_v^{\tau^*}$, hence by the Main Lemma there is a closed Y-free PCF$_v$-expression $M : \tau^* \to \iota$ with $[\![M]\!]_v \bullet (\varphi^\tau [\![M_1]\!]_l) \neq [\![M]\!]_v \bullet (\varphi^\tau [\![M_2]\!]_l)$. By the last two lemmata $S^{\tau^*}(\varphi^\tau [\![M_i]\!]_l, [\![I^\tau M_i]\!]_l)$ for $i = 1, 2$ and $S^{\tau^*\to\iota}([\![M]\!]_v, [\![\bar{M}]\!]_l)$, and this implies $S^{\iota}([\![M]\!]_v \bullet (\varphi^\tau [\![M_i]\!]_l), [\![\bar{M}(I^\tau M_i)]\!]_l)$. But S^ι is just the equality on V_l^ι, hence we obtain $[\![\bar{M}(I^\tau M_1)]\!]_l \neq [\![\bar{M}(I^\tau M_2)]\!]_l$. By computational adequacy this implies $M_1 \not\approx M_2$.

5 PCF and Continuations

PCF$_c$ is obtained from PCF$_v$ by adding the constants

$$\begin{aligned} \mathcal{A}_\tau &: \ \iota \to \tau, \\ \mathcal{K}_\tau &: \ ((\tau \to \iota) \to \tau) \to \tau, \end{aligned}$$

and the new formation rule

$$\%M : \iota \text{ if } M : \iota.$$

$\mathcal{A}_\tau$ is an abort or exit operator, $\mathcal{K}_\tau$ is the typed version of SCHEME's call/cc and % is a control delimiter or *prompt*. More about their semantics will be said below.

We do not present an interpreter for PCF$_c$ here, but simply refer to [22], where computational adequacy for the following denotational semantics is proved (cf. Theorem 6 below).

The denotational semantics is defined in continuation passing style. For each type τ the cpos V^τ and C^τ and an additional cpo $Cont^\tau$ of *continuations* of type τ are defined by

$$\begin{aligned} V^\iota &= Nat, \\ V^{\sigma\to\tau} &= V^\sigma \to C^\tau, \\ Cont^\tau &= V^\tau \to V^\iota_\perp, \\ C^\tau &= Cont^\tau \to V^\iota_\perp, \end{aligned}$$

and the functions $\eta^\tau, app^{\sigma,\tau}$ by

$$\begin{aligned} \eta^\tau v &= \underline{\lambda}\kappa \in Cont^\tau.\ \kappa v, \\ app^{\sigma,\tau}(d,e) &= \underline{\lambda}\kappa \in Cont^\tau.\ d(\underline{\lambda} u \in V^{\sigma\to\tau}.\ e(\underline{\lambda} v \in V^\sigma.\ uv\kappa)). \end{aligned}$$

Note that continuations of type τ map values of type τ to 'final answers' in $V^\iota_\perp$, and computations of type τ (which serve as meanings of expressions) map continuations to final answers. The trivial computation $\eta^\tau v$ simply passes v as an argument to the current continuation κ, and the computation $app^{\sigma,\tau}(d,e)$ can roughly be understood as follows: First the computation d is executed, returning a function $u \in V^{\sigma\to\tau}$, then e is executed and returns a value $v \in V^\sigma$; finally u is applied to v, followed by the given continuation κ.

The new constants are interpreted as follows.

$$\begin{aligned} \mathcal{I}(\mathcal{A}_\tau)n &= \underline{\lambda}\kappa \in Cont^\tau.\ n, \\ \mathcal{I}(\mathcal{K}_\tau)f &= \underline{\lambda}\kappa \in Cont^\tau.\ f(\underline{\lambda} v \in V^\tau.\ \underline{\lambda}\kappa' \in Cont^\iota.\ \kappa v)\kappa. \end{aligned}$$

The interpretation of the old constants is 'literally the same' as for PCF$_v$, but of course with the new definition of η^τ and $app^{\sigma,\tau}$. The meaning of $\%M$ is defined by

$$[\![\%M]\!]\rho\kappa = \kappa([\![M]\!]\rho(\lambda m \in V^\iota.m)).$$

We must also give new definitions for the conditional expressions, namely

$$[\![\mathbf{if}_\tau MNP]\!]\rho\kappa = \begin{cases} [\![N]\!]\rho\kappa & \text{if } [\![M]\!]\rho(\underline{\lambda} m.m) = n > 0, \\ [\![P]\!]\rho\kappa & \text{if } [\![M]\!]\rho(\underline{\lambda} m.m) = 0, \\ \perp & \text{otherwise;} \end{cases}$$

$$[\![\mathbf{pif}\, MNP]\!]\rho\kappa = \begin{cases} [\![N]\!]\rho\kappa & \text{if } [\![M]\!]\rho(\underline{\lambda} m.m) = n > 0, \\ [\![P]\!]\rho\kappa & \text{if } [\![M]\!]\rho(\underline{\lambda} m.m) = 0, \\ n & \text{if } [\![M]\!]\rho(\underline{\lambda} m.m) = \perp \text{ and } [\![N]\!]\rho\kappa = [\![P]\!]\rho\kappa = n, \\ \perp & \text{otherwise.} \end{cases}$$

The meaning of the remaining expressions is 'the same' as for PCF$_v$.

These semantic definitions can be understood as follows:

The abort operator $\mathcal{A}_\tau$ ignores the current continuation κ and simply returns its argument n, i.e. it stops evaluation of the program, returning n. The call/cc operator $\mathcal{K}_\tau$ first transforms its current continuation κ into the corresponding function $\underline{\lambda} v.\ \underline{\lambda}\kappa'.\ \kappa v \in V^{\tau\to\iota}$ and then applies its argument f to it. In this sense, f is indeed 'called with the current continuation'. $\%M$ evaluates M with the trivial continuation $\underline{\lambda} m \in V^\iota.\ m$, i.e. it runs M as an independent program. This means that each control action in M is restricted to M, e.g. an abort action in M only stops evaluation of M and not of the whole program. Similarly, control actions in the test position of conditional expressions are delimited.

This denotational semantics is computationally adequate with respect to the interpreter in [22]; more precisely:

Theorem 6 (Computational Adequacy for PCF$_c$) *For each PCF$_c$-program P:* $P \to \underline{n}$ *iff* $[\![P]\!]\,(\underline{\lambda} m \in V^{\iota}.\ m) = n$.

The proof can be found in [22].

Now we give a full abstraction proof along the same lines as in section 4. For each type τ the type τ^* is defined by

$$\begin{aligned}\iota^* &= \iota,\\ (\sigma \to \tau)^* &= \sigma^* \to (\tau^* \to \iota) \to \iota,\end{aligned}$$

and the functions $\varphi^\tau : V_c^\tau \to V_v^{\tau^*}, \psi^\tau : V_v^{\tau^*} \to V_c^\tau$ by

$$\begin{aligned}\varphi^\iota n &= n,\\ \psi^\iota n &= n,\\ \varphi^{\sigma\to\tau} f &= \underline{\lambda} v \in V_v^{\sigma^*}.\ \underline{\lambda} k \in V_v^{\tau^*\to\iota}.\ f(\psi^\sigma v)(\underline{\lambda} u \in V_c^\tau.\ k(\varphi^\tau u)),\\ \psi^{\sigma\to\tau} f &= \underline{\lambda} v \in V_c^\sigma.\ \underline{\lambda} \kappa \in Cont^\tau.\ f(\varphi^\sigma v) \bullet (\underline{\lambda} u \in V_v^{\tau^*}.\ \kappa(\psi^\tau u)).\end{aligned}$$

The definition of the closed PCF$_c$-expressions $I^\tau : \tau \to \tau^*$ and $J^\tau : \tau^* \to \tau$ is somewhat more sophisticated than for PCF$_l$:

$$\begin{aligned}I^\iota &\equiv \lambda y^\iota.y,\\ J^\iota &\equiv \lambda y^\iota.y,\\ I^{\sigma\to\tau} &\equiv \lambda y^{\sigma\to\tau}.\lambda x^{\sigma^*}.\lambda k^{\tau^*\to\iota}.\%k(I^\tau(y(J^\sigma x))),\\ J^{\sigma\to\tau} &\equiv \lambda y^{(\sigma\to\tau)^*}.\lambda x^\sigma.\mathcal{K}_\tau(\lambda k^{\tau\to\iota}.\mathcal{A}_\tau(y(I^\sigma x)(\lambda z^{\tau^*}.\%k(J^\tau z))).\end{aligned}$$

i^τ and j^τ are defined as before by

$$[\![I^\tau]\!] = \eta^{\tau\to\tau^*} i^\tau, [\![J^\tau]\!] = \eta^{\tau^*\to\tau} j^\tau,$$

and the relations $R^\tau \subseteq V_v^\tau \times V_c^\tau, S^\tau \subseteq C_v^\tau \times C_c^\tau$ by

$$\begin{aligned}R^\iota(m,n) &\Leftrightarrow m = n,\\ R^{\sigma\to\tau}(f,g) &\Leftrightarrow (\forall u \in V_v^\sigma, v \in V_c^\sigma.\ R^\sigma(u,v) \Rightarrow S^\tau(fu, gv)),\\ S^\tau(d,e) &\Leftrightarrow ((d = \bot \wedge e = \underline{\lambda}\kappa.\bot) \vee (\exists v \in V_c^\tau.\ R^\tau(d,v) \wedge \forall \kappa.e\kappa = \kappa v)).\end{aligned}$$

Finally the translation is just the identity, i.e. we define $\bar{M} = M$ for each PCF$_c$-expression M. With these new definitions we obtain the same lemmata as in section 4, and again these lemmata imply

Theorem 7 (Full Abstraction for PCF$_c$) *For any two PCF$_c$-expressions M_1, M_2:* $M_1 \approx M_2$ *iff* $[\![M_1]\!] = [\![M_2]\!]$.

6 Conclusion

In the last two sections we have derived full abstraction theorems for two—fairly different—languages from the full abstraction theorem for PCF$_v$. Of course the question arises, whether we can obtain further (new) results with the same method.

It is crucial for our proofs—like for almost all studies of full abstraction—that we consider programming languages with sufficient computational power: In PCF_l the *up?*-operators allow us to compute with thunks; in PCF_c the call/cc mechanism and first class prompts allow us to compute with continuations as if they were objects of function type. The really hard full abstraction problems have to do with some lack of computational power. The famous example is sequential PCF, i.e. PCF *without* parallel conditional. So far, no 'tasteful' fully abstract model has been found for this language, although much research has been done in this direction [1,13,5]. A similar problem arises for ALGOL-like languages [8,11], when procedures may have global as well as local variables. One must then know that a global procedure has no access to a local variable, and this is again a lack of computational power which is hard to express semantically. We cannot expect that our method—by itself—delivers solutions to such problems.

What we *can* expect is to find full abstraction results for some further extensions of PCF_v. (Note that PCF_l can be indeed considered as an extension of PCF_v, because a call-by-value mechanism comes as syntactic sugar with the *up?*-operators—cf. the definition of λ_s in section 4.) A first candidate might be a language in which functions have side effects only on a *global* store. As the next step we can try to combine side effects and control facilities. We believe that PCF_v is the basic language from which full abstraction for such extensions can be derived.

Last but not least, we think that our method is interesting in its own, because it reveals an unexpected connection between fully abstract models of different programming languages.

Acknowledgments

I'm grateful to Joachim Philippi, Matthias Felleisen and Jon Riecke for helpful comments.

References

[1] G. Berry, P. Curien, and J. Lévy. Full abstraction for sequential languages: the state of the art. In M. Nivat and J. C. Reynolds, editors, *Algebraic Methods in Semantics*, pages 89–132, Cambridge Univ. Press, 1985.

[2] B. Bloom and J. G. Riecke. LCF should be lifted. In *Proc. Conf. Algebraic Methodology and Software Technology*, pages 133–136, Department of Computer Science, University of Iowa, 1989.

[3] S. S. Cosmadakis. Computing with recursive types. In 4th *Symposium on Logic in Computer Science*, pages 24–38, IEEE, June 1989.

[4] S. S. Cosmadakis, A. R. Meyer, and J. G. Riecke. Completeness for typed lazy equalities. In 5th *Symposium on Logic in Computer Science*, pages 312–320, IEEE, 1990.

[5] P. Curien. *Categorical Combinators, Sequential Algorithms and Functional Programs. Research Notes in Theoretical Computer Science*, Pitman, Wiley, 1986.

[6] M. Felleisen. The theory and practice of first-class prompts. In 15th *Symposium on Principles of Programming Languages*, pages 180–190, 1988.

[7] D. P. Friedman, C. T. Haynes, and E. Kohlbecker. Programming with continuations. In P. Pepper, editor, *Program Transformations and Programming Environments*, pages 263–274, Springer-Verlag, 1985.

[8] J. Y. Halpern, A. R. Meyer, and B. A. Trakhtenbrot. The semantics of local storage, or what makes the free-list free? In 11th *Symp. on Principles of Programming Languages*, pages 245–257, ACM, 1984.

[9] H. Langmaack. *Über vollständig operationell adäquate denotationelle Semantik funktionaler Programmiersprachen.* Bericht 8901, Institut für Informatik und Praktische Mathematik der Christian–Albrechts–Universität Kiel, 1989.

[10] A. R. Meyer. Semantical paradigms: Notes for an invited lecture, with two appendices by Stavros Cosmadakis. In 3rd *Symposium on Logic in Computer Science*, pages 236–253, IEEE, 1988.

[11] A. R. Meyer and K. Sieber. Towards fully abstract semantics for local variables: preliminary report. In 15th *Symp. on Principles of Programming Languages*, pages 191–203, ACM, 1988.

[12] E. Moggi. Computational lambda calculus and monads. In 4th *Symposium on Logic in Computer Science*, pages 14–23, IEEE, 1989.

[13] K. Mulmuley. *Full Abstraction and Semantic Equivalence.* PhD thesis, Carnegie-Mellon University, 1985.

[14] C. L. Ong. Fully abstract models of the lazy lambda calculus. In 29th *Symposium on Foundations of Computer Science*, pages 368–376, IEEE, 1988.

[15] G. D. Plotkin. Call-by-name, call-by-value and the λ-calculus. *Theoretical Computer Science*, 1:125–159, 1975.

[16] G. D. Plotkin. Lambda-definability in the full type hierarchy. In J. Seldin and J. Hindley, editors, *To H. B. Curry: Essays on Combinatory Logic, Lambda Calculus and Formalism*, pages 363–374, Academic Press, 1980.

[17] G. D. Plotkin. LCF considered as a programming language. *Theoretical Computer Science*, 5:223–256, 1977.

[18] G. D. Plotkin. *A Structural Approach to Operational Semantics.* Technical Report DAIMI FN-19, Aarhus University, Computer Science Department, Denmark, 1981.

[19] G. D. Plotkin. (Towards a) logic for computable functions, CLSI summer school notes. 1985. Unpublished Manuscript.

[20] J. Rees and W. Clinger. The revised^3 report on the algorithmic language Scheme. *SIGPLAN Notices*, 21(12):37–79, 1986.

[21] J. G. Riecke. A complete and decidable proof system for call-by-value equalities. In 17th *International Colloqium on Automata, Languages, and Programming*, pages 20–31, Warwick, England, 1990.

[22] D. Sitaram and M. Felleisen. Reasoning with continuations II: Full abstraction for models of control. In *Conference on Lisp and Functional Programming*, Nice, France, 1990.

Appendix: Operational Semantics for PCF$_v$

(IF 1) $$\frac{M \to M'}{\mathbf{if}_\tau MNP \to \mathbf{if}_\tau M'NP}$$

(IF 2) $\mathbf{if}_\tau \underline{n+1}\, MN \to M$

(IF 3) $\mathbf{if}_\tau \underline{0}\, MN \to N$

(APPL 1) $$\frac{M \to M'}{MN \to M'N}$$

(APPL 2) $$\frac{N \to N'}{VN \to VN'}$$

(BETA-V) $(\lambda x^\sigma.M)V \to M[x := V]$

(FIXP-V) $\mathrm{Y}_{\sigma\to\tau} V \to \lambda x^\sigma.V(\mathrm{Y}_{\sigma\to\tau}V)x \quad (x \notin FV(V))$

(SUCC) $\mathit{succ}\, \underline{n} \to \underline{n+1}$

(PRED) $\mathit{pred}\, \underline{n} \to \underline{n \dot{-} 1}$

(PIF 1) $$\frac{M \to M'}{\mathbf{pif}\, MNP \to \mathbf{pif}\, M'NP}$$

(PIF 2) $$\frac{N \to N'}{\mathbf{pif}\, MNP \to \mathbf{pif}\, MN'P}$$

(PIF 3) $$\frac{P \to P'}{\mathbf{pif}\, MNP \to \mathbf{pif}\, MNP'}$$

(PIF 4) $\mathbf{pif}\, \underline{n+1}\, MN \to M$

(PIF 5) $\mathbf{pif}\, \underline{0}\, MN \to N$

(PIF 6) $\mathbf{pif}\, M\, \underline{n}\, \underline{n} \to \underline{n}$

TOWARDS A THEORY OF COMMONSENSE VISUAL REASONING

B. Chandrasekaran N. Hari Narayanan
Laboratory for Artificial Intelligence Research
Department of Computer and Information Science
Ohio State University, Columbus, OH 43210, USA

Abstract: In this paper we propose a cognitive architecture underlying visual perception and mental imagery that explains analog mental imagery as well as symbolic visual representations. This architecture has an inherent duality: it can represent and manipulate visual aspects of objects in both symbolic and imaginal forms. It is argued that this architecture resolves many issues raised by the analogic-propositional debate in cognitive psychology. Then we discuss a computational theory, inspired by this architecture, for solving a class of commonsense spatial problems. This involves a novel approach to spatial reasoning that advocates the use of representations with both symbolic and imaginal aspects and visual cases.

1. Introduction

The subject of this paper is closely related to many of Professor R. Narasimhan's concerns about how intelligence (natural and artificial) operates. One hallmark of human intelligence is its capability to reason about the physical world using only approximate, imprecise, and incomplete information from the senses. This mode of reasoning is often called qualitative or commonsense reasoning. Clearly this capacity is deeply rooted in sensory perception, with visual perception being the most prominent. Therefore, to understand and model this capacity artificially (computationally) it is essential to investigate the nature of sensory representations, how sensory modality-specific mental mechanisms operate on such representations, and how such modality-specific mechanisms integrate with the more conscious and deliberate thought processes involving abstract symbolic representations. We believe that only such an endeavor can lead to fruitful hypotheses about the cognitive architecture of the mind which can explain how percepts and concepts are interrelated and how symbols in the mind are grounded in perception.

However, research in artificial intelligence (AI) so far has concentrated on representations that are so abstractly symbolic that they are not grounded in anything. In a typical AI system the exact semantics of symbols, for the most part, is based on how human users interpret the symbols and symbol manipulating inference steps of the system. For instance, current work on "qualitative reasoning about physical systems" (Weld & deKleer, 1990), to the extent that it is intended to emulate or be inspired by human qualitative reasoning capacities, is open to this criticism. Consider, for example, the problem of predicting the motion of one of a set of interlocked gears shown in a diagram, given the other's motion. Existing methods for its solution (Faltings, 1987) transform the initial symbolic and quantitative problem description into a description in a multi-dimensional parameter space and then abstract salient information from this to form a symbolic description of possible motions of all gears involved. Most of the "reasoning" is accomplished through the use of symbolic algebra. In contrast, anyone familiar with how gears operate will be able to "pick out" the solution from the diagram by imagining the rotary motion of one gear being transmitted to the other. While solving such problems from diagrams, humans do not seem to engage in any explicit numerical or algebraic computations. How do they accomplish this?

We believe that part of the answer is the direct use of images, for simulating spatial events and for reasoning by means of visual cases embodying commonsense experiential knowledge. In order to develop this notion further, it is first necessary to describe how images may be represented so that both symbolic properties such as compositionality, naming and abstraction *and* pictorial properties are preserved by the representations. Therefore the central ideas in this paper are divided into two parts and presented in the following two sections. Section 2 describes a cognitive architecture for visual representations and section 3 provides an outline of a computational theory of commonsense visual reasoning in which dual representations and visual cases play a prominent role. Section 4 concludes the paper by putting this research in perspective.

2. Mental Representation of Visual Information

2.1 Motivation

A close introspective look at thought processes behind our reactions to, and reasoning about, everyday situations is certain to reveal rich and complex interactions between concepts and images. Situations in which a mental image is generated and processed to arrive at a conclusion are not uncommon. We can also reason with pure concepts that have no pictorial content. These two modalities (perceptual and conceptual) are very closely related, as is evident from the ease with which we perform transformations across modalities such as generating verbal descriptions of mental images. Mental representations of conceptual knowledge are considered to be propositional in nature (Pylyshyn, 1984). However, the nature of perceptual representations, especially visual, and its relation to the phenomenon of mental imagery have been centers of a debate in cognitive psychology (Anderson, 1978; Kosslyn & Pomerantz, 1977; Kosslyn, 1981; Pylyshyn, 1981). The representation of visual information must be "picture-like", in some sense of the term, to one camp (whom we call analogists) because they see evidence that some aspects of human reasoning are better explained by exploiting special properties of this modality. Their motivation is to be able to explain operations, such as scanning, relative distance estimation, and direction finding, that humans seem to apply to mental imagery. For this purpose they claim that mental representations of images are distinct from mental representations of conceptual knowledge and that these reside in an analog medium. For researchers subscribing to this view, what is important is that any ultimate proposal for mental representations should be able to explain this differential use of modality-specific operations. On the other side there are people, whom we call propositionalists, who view propositions as the basic currency of mental representations. They believe that mental representations are uniformly propositional across modalities and that this is the property uniting conceptual and sensory-specific perceptual processes. They view the advocacy of image-like representations as a rejection of their claims about the generality of propositional representations. They argue that the use of visual operations can be explained by propositional representations and processes as well and that the experience of mental imagery and of performing operations on it are epiphenomenal to the actual cognitive processes involved. Many such arguments are given in (Anderson, 1978; Pylyshyn, 1981).

To further clarify these distinctions, consider the following two scenarios. In one a subject is asked to study a picture of two apples on a plate and the picture is removed afterwards. Then (s)he is asked to answer questions such as "was there a red apple on the plate?" and "was the green apple the biggest?". In the other, the subject is told how interest rates and inflation are related in an economy, and then asked questions about the narrative. It is very unlikely that the subject used mental imagery to answer questions about economics. In the first scenario, however, analogists would claim that the subject would tend to use mental imagery, implying that a representation and processes different from those in the economics case were used to generate correct answers. Propositionalists would argue that the very process of studying the picture created propositions such as (color apple1 red), (size apple1 big) etc., and that these were in fact used to generate answers. They would dismiss the experience of mental imagery, if any, by the subject as merely a side-effect of accessing propositions whose semantic content referred to visual knowledge. Suppose two of the questions (one for each scenario) asked are:

1. Was the red apple to the right of the green one?
2. Will higher interest rates reduce inflation?

To answer question 2 one has to reason with the known relations between interest rates and inflation to derive the effect of increasing one on the other and this reasoning is certainly not imaginal. Propositionalists would say that a similar process operating on propositions derived from the image applies to question 1 as well. Analogists would reply that spatial relations such as "right-of" are implicit in the image and so a more efficient way to answer 1 is to "pick out the answer directly" from a separate analogic representation, namely, one's mental image.

This is the dichotomy between positions taken by proponents of analogic and propositional representations. But are these two views really mutually exclusive contenders for the position of the "ultimate" theory of visual representations? Maybe what is missing is the realization that a mechanism that preserves the significant properties of both analogic and propositional representations can account for supportive experimental evidence presented by researchers on both sides of the issue. This is the insight that led to the ideas presented in the rest of this section.

2.2 Visual Representations

In the literature, representations that result from seeing objects are called perceptual representations and representations that underlie mental imagery are called imaginal representations. We refer to these collectively as visual representations in this paper. A visual representation is a mental representation that results from visual processing and contains information about all (and only) visual aspects.

The analogic-propositional debate centered around two kinds of representations. One is called an analogic representation and the motivation for it stemmed from the phenomenon of mental imagery. While few deny the existence of mental imagery, the hypothesis that analogic representations underlie mental imagery has been questioned. Analogists are impressed by what they see as evidence for subjects' preferential use of pictorial operations (e.g., scanning) on mental imagery and to account for this they ascribe to this representation certain properties that are usually associated with pictures. Such operations have a special status in analog representational theories, but not in propositional theories. Kosslyn (1981) presents a concrete explication of an analogic theory of visual representation. He proposes two levels of representations: one "deep" representation that is abstract and not experienced directly and a "surface" representation that supports mental imagery. A surface representation is pictorial in nature since it depicts an object by regions of activation in the visual buffer which is an analog medium. This two level view of imagery (i.e., surface displays generated by comparison and/or transformation processes from a deep structure) is used in (Kosslyn & Schwartz, 1977; Kosslyn & Pomerantz, 1977; Pinker, 1980) as well. Considering a wide spectrum of literature on the analog position, Anderson (1978) concludes that the essence of all analog models of imagery is the "pictorial representation", i.e., some format that represents information either as a spatially structured array of light information or in a form that is directly transformable to such an array.

The other type of representation is called propositional. It is made up of propositions. A proposition consists of symbols, but it is more than a mere collection of symbols. Propositions have identifiable predicate and argument constituents, bear truth values, and have rules of formation (Anderson, 1978). Thus a proposition has both a fixed syntactic form and a fixed semantic content. In the propositional view of mental representations, propositions encode knowledge about objects in a perceived scene and require interpretation for their semantic contents to be accessed by processes operating on them. Propositional theories have an underlying implication that the rules which govern how propositions are interpreted are independent of the perceptual or cognitive modality that produced the propositions. In other words, a general purpose mechanism that is not modality-specific is assumed to operate on propositional representations. For example, according to propositionalists, the propositions (left-of A B), (smell-of C pungent) and (rate-of inflation high) will be handled by mental processes in a uniform manner that does not reflect the distinction that one describes a visual attribute, another an olfactory attribute, and the third is a conceptual assertion. Thus the intrinsic property of propositional representations is their uniformity of representation and processing across modalities or "faculties".

There is a third type of representation, called a discrete symbolic representation, which originated in computer science. A discrete symbolic representation comprises structures of discrete or atomic symbols composed according to well-defined rules of formation. A symbol is just a token: binary values corresponding to on/off pixels in an image on a computer screen and tokens in the proposition (color apple1 red) all qualify as symbols. By itself, a symbol is devoid of any meaning. Its semantics derives from the *architecture* of the system it resides in and from *how* it is used by programs operating on it. Therefore it is conceivable that the same symbol may be interpreted differently by different processors and processes. This is an important distinction. Consider the symbol "end" appearing in a program. To a Pascal compiler it denotes the end of a program block. Had the program been in a different language, the same symbol might have a different meaning to that language's compiler. Thus the meaning of a program (a program is nothing but a discrete symbol structure) is given by its operational semantics which specifies the operations performed and their effects on the inputs (which are also discrete symbol structures) and the compiler enforces this semantics. We propose that the discrete symbolic representation in the general sense is also a contender for the mental representation of visual information. The operational semantics of such a visual representation specifies the operations allowed by the visual modality-specific architecture and their effects on the representation and the architecture enforces this semantics.

Both propositional and discrete symbolic representations are made up of symbols and composed according to specific rules of formation. However, unlike propositional representations, a discrete symbolic representation does not necessarily need to have a truth value or have predicates and arguments as constituents. In other words, a proposition is a special type of discrete symbolic structure whose operational semantics is truth-preserving. Thus discrete symbolic representations are more general than propositional representations. The only commitment entailed by the discrete symbolic representation is that it is composed, in a principled manner, of discrete symbols and interpreted consistently by the underlying architecture and processes operating on the representation. While the discrete symbolic representation has a fixed syntactic form, its semantic content is defined relative to the underlying architecture and the processes that operate on it. Properties exhibited by such a representation are not intrinsic to the representation itself, but stem from mechanisms (which may well be sensory-modality specific; this is one of the claims made later in this section) that support and operate on the representation.

2.3 The Image Representational System

The central issue of the analogic-propositional debate is the following question.

1. Are visual representations analog *or* propositional?

In the light of the previous discussion we can see that this issue may be addressed in two other ways as well.

2. Are visual representations analog *or* symbolic?
3. Are visual representations and their interpreter sensory modality-specific *or* sensory modality-independent and uniform?

In the literature on this debate, discrete symbolic representations are equated with propositional representations, i.e., 1 and 2 above are considered to be the same question. However, as we just discussed, propositional representations are a special form of discrete symbolic representations. Additionally, because of the uniformity of interpretation that applies to propositional representations, propositionalists are necessarily led to a sensory modality-independent view of representation. The machinery that interprets propositions and formulae involving them operates by the rules of truth tables and thus is independent of what sensory modality the information represented by the propositions is in. Therefore, to the extent that analogic representations involve interpretations that give a privileged status to some operations over others in each sensory modality, there is a genuine opposition between analogists and propositionalists.

However, the central thesis of this section is that on the contrary, there is no real opposition between a belief in the need for some form of analogic representations and a belief in the realization of such a representation from symbolic structures. The facile equation of propositional representations and symbolic representations has, in our view, set up a false opposition in 2 above. The root of this misconception arises from the assumption that symbolic representations necessarily need to run on general purpose computers. We argue that in fact one can have analogic, i.e., visual modality-specific, representations which are also in principle symbol structures. The key to this possibility is that representations for different sensory modalities are run on interpreters which give pride of place to operations that are specific to that modality. Of course, these representations, to the extent possible and relevant, need to be coordinated with corresponding representations in other sensory modalities as well as the general cognitive architecture.

We propose that properties exhibited by visual representations stem from an underlying mechanism, which we call the Image Representational System (IRS). The IRS contains a special purpose architecture that is specific to the visual modality. Visual representations reside in this architecture and the architecture interprets the representations in a way that allows visual operations (e.g., scanning, relative position estimation etc.) to be performed on them. It is this interpretation that gives rise to mental imagery. Thus the analog nature of mental imagery arises from the interaction between visual representations and the visual modality-specific architecture.

The central components of the IRS are the visual representations that result from vision, called Image Symbol Structures (ISS), the underlying specialized (to the visual modality) architecture in which these structures reside, the interpretation of ISS (which gives rise to mental imagery) that the architecture produces, and the visual operations that it provides.

An ISS is a hierarchical discrete symbolic representation, similar in spirit to the 3-D sketch of Marr and Nishihara (1978). It is the end product of visual processing that starts from the retinal image. The ISS has both syntactic form and semantic content. When an ISS is interpreted by the architecture, its semantic content may be experienced as mental imagery. These interpretations and the ISS function as inputs to high level visual processes for object recognition etc. The ISS itself is neutral with respect to recognition; it represents objects in terms of visual attributes, but does not "name" the objects that it represents. When high level visual processes recognize and label an object represented in the ISS, that facilitates the evocation of non-visual (conceptual) knowledge about it. The visual modality-specific architecture of the IRS also provides basic operations such as scanning on the ISS. These have concomitant effects on its interpretation as well. Visual processes can manipulate the Image Symbol Structures by invoking these operations. Figure 1 illustrates this role of the IRS. A mechanism like the IRS can account for the preferential use of visual operations on mental images with underlying non-analogic representations.

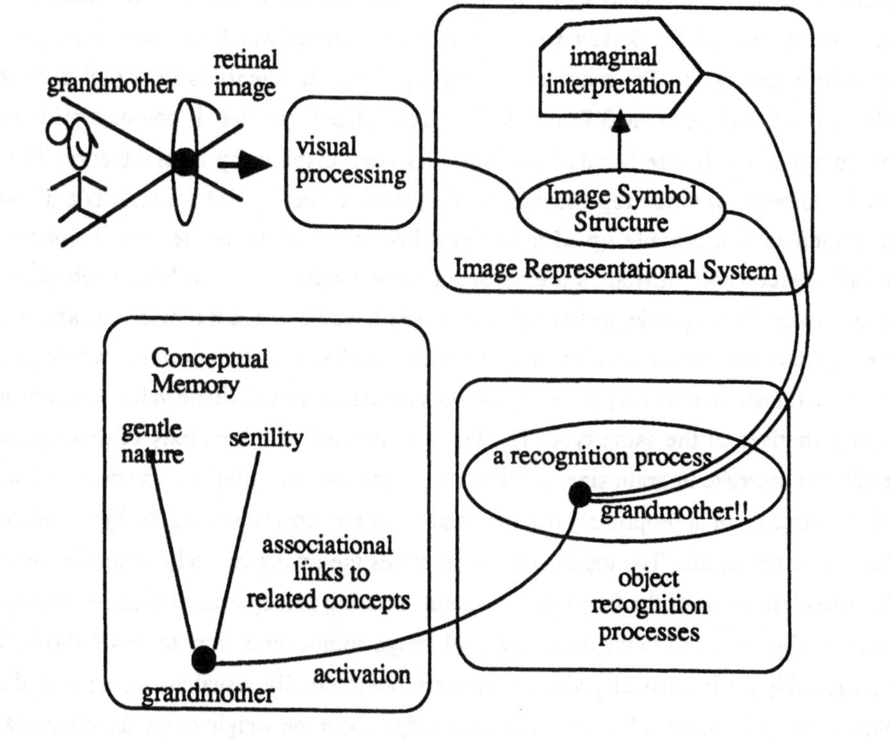

Figure 1. Role of the Image Representational System in Visual Perception

As an aside, note that even though we argue how visual representations can be discrete symbolic while preserving analogic properties, the discrete symbolic form is not essential. The same argument can be extended to representations that are connectionist or neural. Representational requirements necessary for our argument are the informational content of the representations, how this visual information is organized (e.g., structured as hierarchical composites built up from primitives of visual attributes, as explained later), and how the representations get interpreted by the architecture. Connectionist representations can also satisfy these (Chandrasekaran, Goel, & Allemang, 1988).

2.4 The Image Symbol Structure

Marr and Nishihara (1978) propose three structures called the primal sketch, the 2 1/2-D sketch and the 3-D sketch for the representation of visual information. Visual perception, according to this theory, consists of the transformation of the primal sketch obtained from the retinal image into a 2 1/2-D sketch and then into a 3-D sketch which feeds into shape and object recognition processes. The most interesting aspect of this theory is its use of parametrized volumetric primitives in the 3-D sketch. The "generalized cylinder" is one such primitive. Our conception of the Image Symbol Structure has been inspired by Marr's theory. The ISS is defined to be the internal representation of a perceived real world scene. It is a hierarchical compound structure made up of primitives. Primitives of shape, texture, color and other visually perceivable attributes are assumed to be available to the IRS. Each primitive is parametrized. For example, a shape primitive may have its relevant dimensions as parameters. These parameters are not absolute measurements, but have relative meaning within an internal reference frame. That is, they serve as yardsticks that facilitate attribute value comparisons with other primitives of the same type. The ISS is structured as a hierarchy of descriptions with levels that decrease in grain size, or alternately, increase in resolution. The description at each level is made up of appropriately parametrized primitives corresponding to objects delineative at that level's resolution. The topmost level describes the image coarsely while the lowest level describes it in terms of the finest details captured during perception. At each intermediate level more details get added to the descriptions of image components from the level above. The ISS encodes only the intrinsically visual (and therefore internally visualizable) aspects of a scene. Non-visualizable aspects (for example, knowledge about the weight of an object) are part of the conceptual knowledge associated with the scene and not part of the ISS.

We term those parts of an ISS that together correspond to an object or a delineative part of an object, an S-percept ("symbolic percept"). An ISS is thus made up of multiple S-percepts and an S-percept may itself be composed of other S-percepts. It is essentially a description that contains (only) visual aspects of a delineative object or its part, in terms of parametrized primitives. For example the S-percept corresponding to an apple will consist of primitives that describe its shape, color, shiny texture etc., but not its taste or nutritional value. In addition to parametrized primitives an S-percept also contains descriptions of spatial relations among the primitives. For example, figure 2 shows what an S-percept representing the side view of a chair may look like. It is not intended to show what S-percepts actually are, rather to show a simplified version of what they may be. For instance, the spatial relations among primitives are shown by connecting arcs in the figure whereas in an actual S-percept these will also be encoded symbolically. This example assumes parametrized cylinders as shape primitives and color names as color primitives.

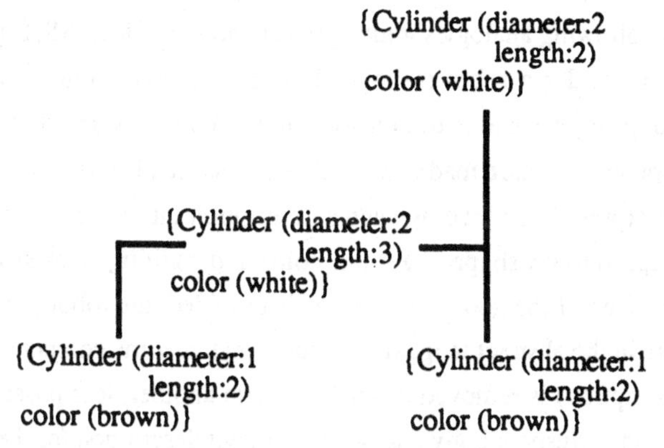

Figure 2. An S-Percept

Each S-percept has a corresponding mental image that results from its interpretation. This entity is called an A-percept ("analogic percept"). An A-percept is the analogic equivalent of an S-percept. It is an entity that has pictorial properties and which appears in the mind's eye as an image which has all visual attributes and spatial orientations described by the corresponding S-percept. For instance, an A-percept corresponding to an S-percept of the form {cylinder (diameter:2, length:4), color(red)} will be the image of a red cylinder of diameter 2 units and length 4 units. Thus the S-percept is a symbolic entity whereas the A-percept is an imaginal entity, and the two may be thought of as two sides of the same coin. Therefore the ISS is both an internal representation of a perceived scene that functions as a symbolic description *and* an algorithm for the composition of a mental image by the visual modality-specific architecture.

Operations performed on S-percepts (A-percepts) have concomitant effects on A-percepts (S-percepts). The mental image of a scene results from accessing the ISS corresponding to that scene and bringing into the IRS a description of the scene from the appropriate level in the ISS hierarchy. Some examples of basic operations performed on mental images are changing the relative position of an object, enlarging or zooming in on an object, scanning, and replacing an object with another. In the IRS these are not analogic operations. Rather, changing the position of an object (moving it from one place to another in the mental image) can be achieved by appropriately modifying spatial relations among S-percepts in the ISS. Zooming in on an object corresponds to selectively bringing in a more detailed (lower level) description of the corresponding S-percept from the ISS hierarchy. Scanning is the process of moving one's fixation point from object to object in the mental image and bringing in more material (from the ISS) as the fixation point approaches the mental horizon (Pinker, 1980). Replacing an object with another in an image can be effected by replacing its S-percept with that of the new object in the ISS.

The following analogy should explicate how the IRS, ISS, S-percepts, and A-percepts are related. Consider a robot standing beside bins containing cubes, cylinders and other geometric objects of various dimensions and colors. Assume that it is possible to write a description of any structure made up of these geometric objects in an abstract language that the robot can interpret. Upon loading such a description into the robot it is capable of picking up objects of appropriate shape, size and color and building that structure. Conversely, if a structure made up of the geometric objects is provided, the robot can produce a description of that structure in the abstract language. Assume that if some component in this structure (or the abstract description) is removed or replaced with another, it is possible for the robot to sense the change and correspondingly change the abstract description (or the structure). This situation is similar to the mechanism comprising IRS and ISS. The robot is analogous to the special architecture of the IRS, the abstract description is analogous to an ISS, parts of the abstract description are analogous to S-percepts, the geometric objects are analogous to A-percepts, and the structure built by the robot is analogous to the interpretation of an ISS.

2.5 Related Work

Work by Kosslyn and Schwartz (1977) on two dimensional mental images and by Pinker (1980) on 3-D images report similar models. Kosslyn (1981) provides a cognitive theory that utilizes two distinct representations - deep non-pictorial representations and surface representations (patterns) in a visual buffer. The ISS and A-percepts may be viewed as deep and surface representations respectively. However, the ISS is a hierarchical multi-resolution representation that consists of object descriptions composed of visual primitives, unlike the propositional and literal encodings which constitute the deep representation of Kosslyn. While the IRS can have a visual buffer as a medium for A-percepts, it is more than a medium; it is an architecture specialized for the visual modality.

Pylyshyn (1981; 1984) has also made significant contributions to the imagery debate. He uses the concepts of tacit knowledge and cognitive penetrability to argue against a purely "analog" position. The IRS is not in opposition to these concepts. In fact, some cognitive processes that operate on ISS or A-percepts may be (and some may not be) cognitively penetrable and thus influenced by tacit knowledge, overt instructions etc. However, we postulate that the interpretation of the ISS by the visual modality-specific architecture and the basic operations that the architecture provides on ISS and A-percepts are not cognitively penetrable and that these are in fact properties of the functional architecture (as defined by Pylyshyn) of visual perception and mental imagery.

Our proposal is related to the question about how a purely syntactic system, such as a Turing Machine, can make connections to semantics, except in an arbitrary way. This question lies at the heart of Searle's Chinese Room argument (Searle, 1980) which seeks to show that computer programs cannot understand the meanings of symbols they manipulate. Harnad (1988), in an answer to Searle, suggests that symbols are grounded in perception. This limitation of purely symbolic programs has also led Shrager (1989) to conclude that conceptual knowledge must be grounded in sensory experience. The IRS shows how modality-specific architectures preserve some aspects of the semantics of the world in such a way that the symbols (S-percepts) can be seen to be grounded in sensory modality-specific entities (A-percepts).

2.6 Summary

In this section we have suggested that visual knowledge can be represented within the framework of discrete symbolic representations in such a way that both mental images and symbolic thought processes can be explained. We argue that if a special purpose architecture, providing privileged visual operations, underlies visual representations, then the phenomenon of mental imagery arising from symbolically represented percepts is explainable. We propose a mechanism called an Image Representational System that provides interpretations of and visual modality-specific operations on symbolic visual representations, called Image Symbol Structures. An Image Symbol Structure is a hierarchical multi-resolution structure composed of S-percepts. S-percepts are made up of parametrized symbolic primitives of visual attributes such as texture and color. S-percepts represent delineative objects or parts of objects in a scene. A-percepts are interpretations of S-percepts that give rise to mental imagery. S-percepts and A-percepts may be viewed as dual facets of a single entity, namely, information gleaned from seeing an object. According to this theory, both symbols and images play equally important roles in visual perception and reasoning, rather than the latter being merely an epiphenomenon. The IRS affords dual perspectives (symbolic and imaginal) on visual representations and similar mechanisms may underlie human visual perception and mental imagery.

3. Commonsense Visual Reasoning

3.1 Motivation

Computational modeling of spatial reasoning is one of the fundamental problems of artificial intelligence. This is a problem of great practical significance as well, since its solution is a prerequisite to building robots that can navigate and manipulate objects in the environment. One restricted, yet interesting, aspect of spatial reasoning is the ability to predict motions of rigid objects. Anyone who has played billiards can testify to the apparent ease with which humans perform this task. Recently there has been a surge of research interest in endowing machines with such a capability, albeit for simple rigid body pairs like gears and clock escapement mechanisms (Faltings, 1987; Nielsen, 1988). While progress has been made, current approaches to this problem suffer from many limitations. For example, the problem posed in figure 3 will take hours to solve on a computer using current qualitative methods. This made us look for new ways of solving the motion prediction problem. The initial inspiration came from introspective reports of people, when given diagrams like figure 3 and asked to predict motions, that by looking at the diagram they were able to visualize the motion of one object causing that of another through physical contact. They appeared to be using the image of the diagram in front of them directly to simulate motions in their minds. In fact, there is considerable evidence in cognitive psychology for the use of mental images by people when solving spatial problems (Shepard & Cooper, 1982; Kosslyn, 1980). Besides, the cognitive architecture described in section 2 also motivated our current research efforts towards developing a new computational theory of commonsense visual reasoning.

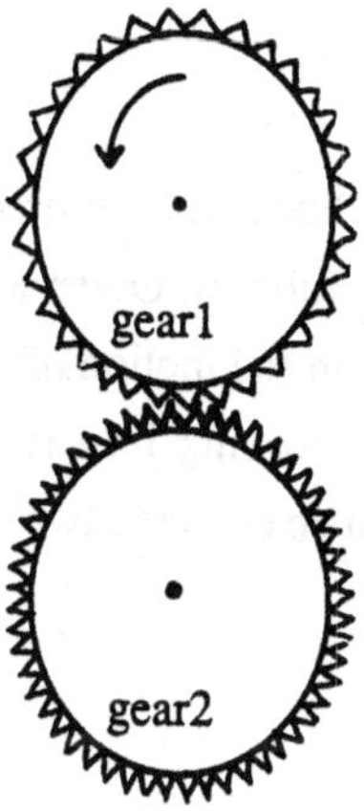

Figure 3. A Kinematic Pair

We started by placing two constraints on such a theory. The first was that it should involve the direct use of images for spatial reasoning. This, in turn, required a representation with both symbolic and imaginal aspects and the cognitive architecture for visual representations, discussed in the previous section, provided a natural foundation. Thus we are developing a machine representation, termed "direct representation" (Narayanan & Chandrasekaran, 1990c), which is a computer model of the ISS and the IRS. A theory of reasoning requires not just representations, but also an account of how the representations are used in reasoning. So the second constraint was that our theory should have a process model which utilizes direct representations and is inspired by how humans reason about common spatial problems encountered in everyday life, such as objects sliding down, motion transmission through collisions, etc. Clearly, images have a direct causal role in such a model. Furthermore, observations of humans have led us to conclude that experiential knowledge (e.g., "hinged objects under collision tend to rotate") as well as mental simulation of motion are used to generate predictions during reasoning. So we have developed visual cases to encode experiential knowledge and a technique called analogical simulation (Narayanan & Chandrasekaran, 1990b) to generate predictions. These aspects of our theory are outlined in the following subsections.

3.2 The Domain

The domain of the theory is rigid body motion prediction. The general rigid body motion prediction problem can be stated as follows. Given a kinematic tuple of rigid objects, their relative spatial configurations, and the initial motion of one of them, predict the resulting motions of all objects. Currently we are working in a restricted version of this domain, obtained by limiting objects to pairs that can be depicted two dimensionally. Figure 3 shows an example.

3.3 Direct Representations

The direct representation (DR) of a scene (or a diagram) is a hierarchical multi-level description in which all but the lowest levels are symbolic and the lowest level is imaginal. The resolution increases with levels, so the top level contains the coarsest description. Each level of the representation contains descriptions of shapes of objects in the scene being represented and their relative spatial configurations. A small set of shape descriptors are used to represent object shapes and a small set of configuration descriptors are used to represent spatial configurations. Both shape and configuration descriptors are parametrized. At a level of low resolution an object may be represented by a single shape descriptor while at a level of high resolution it may be represented in terms of shapes of its delineative parts. At still lower levels each part may in turn be represented in terms of its subparts. The imaginal part of a DR is a 2-dimensional pixel array of fixed width and height in which a scene is depicted by the boundaries of objects in the scene. Thus the "image" is a boundary-based rendering. The lowest symbolic level of a DR contains pointers to the image. The symbolic part of a DR corresponds to the ISS and the imaginal part corresponds to the imaginal interpretation of ISS by IRS. For illustration, the direct representation of a block sitting on an inclined surface is shown in figure 4.

3.4 Visual Cases: Representation of Experiential Knowledge

A widely accepted view on experiential knowledge is that memory is an organized and indexed collection of cases, which in turn are previously experienced episodes or abstractions of them (Schank, 1982). In our opinion, human ability to reason about the world is the result of building a good repertoire of such cases. Therefore knowledge derived from prior experience about how objects typicaly behave in various spatial situations is represented as visual cases. Each case represents a typical spatial configuration. These are called "visual" because the configurational information encoded in a case is visual in nature and this visual information is the "key" by which relevant cases get selected during reasoning. Since cases are acquired from experience, they may not be logically parsimonious or mutually exclusive. Thus visual cases may be viewed as an application of the theory of case-based reasoning to the perceptual world.

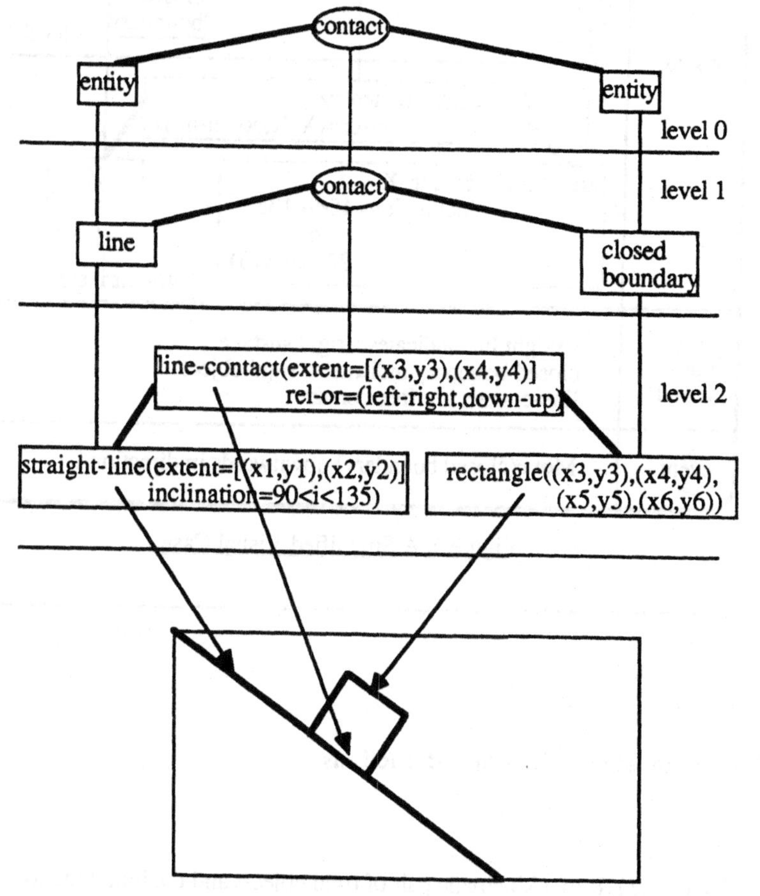

Figure 4. A Direct Representation

A visual case has three parts. One is the visual information. The second is non-visual knowledge that qualifies the visual part further in determining the applicability of a case to a particular situation. The third part is an event affecting objects in the spatial configuration represented by the case. This event may specify a state change (e.g., a directional force being applied on an object), a continuous change (e.g., an object moving in a particular direction), etc. A sample visual case, which encodes the experiential knowledge "a rigid object resting on a rigid inclined surface and free to move downwards will tend to slide down", is shown in figure 5. We are currently developing a representative set of such cases for our domain.

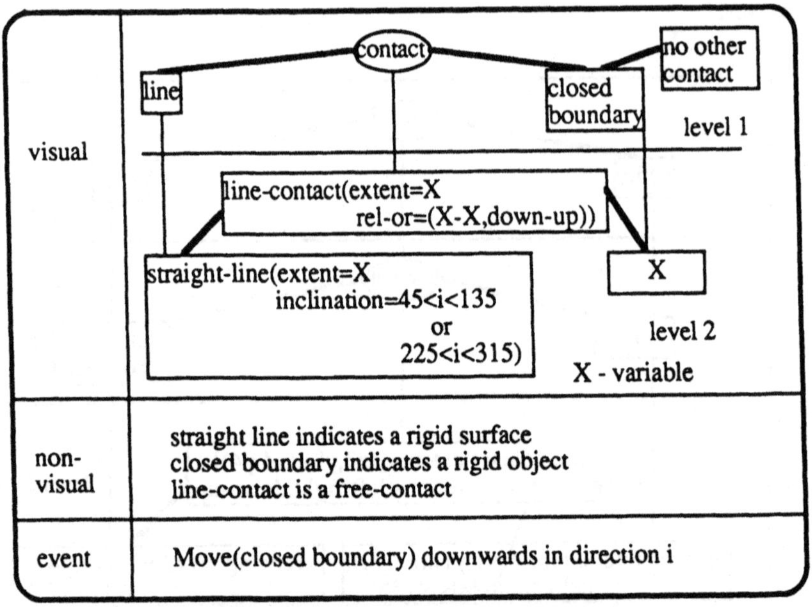

Figure 5. A Simplified Visual Case

3.5 Reasoning about Spatial Interactions

Given the DR of a kinematic pair of rigid objects and the initial motion of one of them, the reasoning process proceeds as enumerated below.

1. Compute the locus of the given motion.
2. Simulate the motion on the imaginal part of DR while changing the symbolic part correspondingly.
3. Continue simulation until a significant state change is reached.

4. Select relevant visual cases by matching visual aspects of the current configuration with visual parts of cases.
5. Use general knowledge and object-specific knowledge to determine applicable cases from the relevant ones.
6. Prune events predicted by the applicable cases by using current configurational information, and thus determine the next event(s).
7. Simulate object behavior according to results from the previous step, until a significant state change is reached. Then go to step 4.

A key component of this process is the simulation of motion (rotation and translation) using the imaginal part of a DR (Narayanan & Chandrasekaran, 1990a). A significant state change indicates a new configuration in which simulation requires guidance by knowledge-based reasoning to proceed. Occurrence of inter-object contact due to collision and removal of a previously established contact are examples of significant state changes. The nature of the significant state change determines applicable visual cases. Then general knowledge, object-specific knowledge, current configuration, and the cases together are used to determine resulting motions and this guides subsequent simulation. This interaction between simulation and knowledge-based reasoning occurs in steps 5 and 6. This process yields motion predictions.

3.6 Related Work

Significant research in rigid body motion prediction under the rubric of qualitative kinematics has been done by Forbus and colleagues (Forbus, Nielsen & Faltings, 1987; Faltings, 1987; Nielsen, 1988). The basis of their work is the Metric Diagram/Place Vocabularies model. The metric diagram is a symbolic and quantitative description of the spatial mechanism under analysis. This may contain algebraic and predicate-based descriptions of object shapes, boundaries, vertices etc. The configuration space (C-space) of the mechanism (Lozano-Perez, 1983), which is a multi-dimensional space spanned by the free motion parameters of objects under consideration, is computed from the metric diagram. Salient points, boundaries and areas in the C-space form the place vocabularies. Each place corresponds to a particular spatial configuration of objects. The places are computed from the C-space and organized as a place graph. This graph represents possible object motions as place transitions. To predict motion from a given configuration the place graph and axiomatic laws about motion constraints are used to obtain free directions, laws of motion transfer are used to obtain transferred motions, and the intersection of the two yields motion predictions. This approach is limited by the complexity of C-space computation and the computation of the place graph from the C-space. Extensive use of symbolic algebra is involved in both. So the computation remains tractable only for pair-wise analysis of regular objects with at most one degree of freedom each. But the C-space of a general object pair can be arbitrarily complex. Thus, this approach does not scale up well. In comparison, a DR is more compact since spatial information is implicitly encoded in the image. Also, the reasoning process is more direct, less complex, and knowledge-intensive (rather than computation-intensive) since it utilizes spatial knowledge about motion constraints directly from the image as well as object-specific knowledge and general knowledge.

A predecessor of this work is the program WHISPER (Funt, 1977) which was concerned with rotation, sliding, and stability of blocks-world structures. Others have investigated the use of analogical representations for reasoning about the physical world (Steels, 1988; Gardin & Meltzer, 1989) and our motivation for using a representation with an imaginal part is similar to theirs- to exploit the fact that spatial aspects are manifest in this type of representation. The computational model of the theory of commonsense perception (Shrager, 1990), which casts theory formation as an act of reinterpretation of knowledge grounded in imagery, has many similarities with our approach to visual reasoning. Direct representations have the same symbolic-imaginal duality as the iconic and propositional stores of Shrager's laser model, but direct representations are more structured and encode *only* visual aspects. The instantiation of process views and the resulting mental imagery-like animation in the laser model is similar to the application of visual cases to configurations depicted in the imaginal parts of direct representations. However, process views are commonsense concepts related to the theory being reformulated (e.g., spontaneous emission is a process view in the laser model) and these have considerable knowledge content and serve to ensure consistency of theory reinterpretations. Visual cases have a different intent, namely to encode simple chunks of experiential knowledge about typical spatial events that humans have.

3.7 Discussion

We have proposed a novel and intuitive technique to predict qualitative motions of objects in a kinematic pair. As Forbus and colleagues (Forbus, Nielsen & Faltings, 1987) rightly points out, there can be no *purely qualitative general purpose* kinematics. What is required is to develop qualitative and quantitative methods and integrate them; qualitative ones to provide rough solutions that serve to reduce ambiguities while more precise and computation-intensive quantitative methods can be applied to those rough solutions to refine them. We believe that such a combination will result in robust and computationally efficient engineering systems capable of spatial reasoning about objects. In this context our approach makes a contribution to the qualitative aspect of spatial reasoning.

Our current work is on implementing analogical simulation and motion prediction for simple kinematic pairs. We have observed that while solving motion prediction problems humans focus on potential areas of interaction (like meshing gear teeth) and do local motion simulations rather than simulating entire objects involved. Development of similar focussing mechanisms will greatly improve simulation efficiency and this is an area of current research. We are also developing a taxonomy of visual operations in which complex visual processes such as simulation of motion, detection of contact and obstacles, etc. are composed of a small number of operations (e.g., scanning) that seem basic to the human visual system.

Areas of future research include extending the method to handle kinematic n-tuples and kinematic chains. Another avenue is the extension to 3-dimensional configurations either by using 3-D graphical representations instead of the current 2-D pixel array, or by combining multiple 2-D views. Moreover, we believe that this technique can be applied to more complex situations such as reasoning about the function of mechanical devices like door stoppers from cross-sectional diagrams.

4. Concluding Remarks

During his illustrious research career Professor Narasimhan has often turned to natural intelligence for solution to problems that he has investigated. In this paper we discuss two research problems, one cognitive and the other computational, while addressing which we have been inspired by how human intelligence solves them robustly. The cognitive problem involves visual representations and mental imagery, and the computational problem is rigid body motion prediction by visual reasoning.

There is an ongoing debate in cognitive psychology about the nature of representations that underlie visual perception and mental imagery. We have proposed a type of visual representation and a specialized cognitive architecture to support and interpret it, which together can explain many issues raised in this debate. Then we described a problem of current interest in artificial intelligence, particularly qualitative physics. This is the rigid body motion prediction problem. We have proposed a new approach to this problem and this approach has been inspired by observations of humans and by our previous proposal about visual representations. While much more research remains to be done on these topics, we believe that what we have presented here constitutes a significant first step towards a theory of commonsense visual reasoning that will have far reaching implications.

Acknowledgments: This research has been supported by DARPA & AFOSR contract F-49620-89-C-0110 and AFOSR grant 890250. Ideas in this paper have benefited from our discussions with Stephen Kosslyn and Jeff Shrager, and many have previously appeared in (Chandrasekaran & Narayanan, 1990).

References

Anderson, J. R. (1978). Arguments concerning representations for mental images. *Psychological Review*, 85, 249-277.

Chandrasekaran, B., Goel, A., & Allemang, D. (1988). Connectionism and information processing abstractions: the message still counts more than the medium. *AI Magazine*, 9:4, 24-34.

Chandrasekaran, B., & Narayanan, N. H. (1990). Integrating imagery and visual representations. *Proc. 12th Annual Conference of the Cognitive Science Society*, Boston, MA, 670-678.

Faltings, B. (1987). Qualitative kinematics in mechanisms. *Proceedings IJCAI-10*, Milano, Italy, 436-442.

Forbus, K. D., Nielsen, P., & Faltings, B. (1987). Qualitative kinematics: a framework. *Proceedings IJCAI-10*, Milano, Italy, 430-436.

Funt, B. V. (1977). WHISPER: a problem solving system utilizing diagrams and a parallel processing retina. *Proceedings IJCAI-5*, Cambridge, MA, 459-464.

Gardin, F., & Meltzer, B. (1989). Analogical representations of naive physics. *AI Journal*, 38, 139-159.

Harnad, S. (1988). Mind, machine, and Searle. *Journal of Experimental and Theoretical Artificial Intelligence*, 1, 5-27.

Kosslyn, S. M., & Pomerantz, J. R. (1977). Images, propositions, and the form of internal representations. *Cognitive Psychology*, 9, 52-76.

Kosslyn, S. M., & Schwartz, S. P. (1977). A simulation of visual imagery. *Cognitive Science*, 1, 265-295.

Kosslyn, S. M. (1980). *Image and mind.* Cambridge, MA: Harvard University Press.

Kosslyn, S. M. (1981). The medium and the message in mental imagery: a theory. *Psychological Review*, 88, 46-66.

Lozano-Perez, T. (1983). Spatial planning: a configuration space approach. *IEEE Transactions on Computers*, C-32, 108-120.

Steels, L. (1988). Steps towards common sense, *Proc. ECAI-88*.

Marr, D., & Nishihara, H. K. (1978). Representation and recognition of the spatial organization of three dimensional shapes. *Proceedings of the Royal Society*, 200, 269-294.

Narayanan, N. H., & Chandrasekaran, B. (1990a). Qualitative simulation of spatial mechanisms: a preliminary report. *Proc. 21st Annual Conference on Modeling & Simulation*, Pittsburgh, PA.

Narayanan, N. H., & Chandrasekaran, B. (1990b). Rigid body motion prediction by analogical simulation. *Proc. AAAI-90 Workshop on AI & Simulation*, Boston, MA, 69-74.

Narayanan, N. H., & Chandrasekaran, B. (1990c). A visual approach to qualitative kinematics. *Proc. AAAI-90 Workshop on Qualitative Vison*, Boston, MA, 72-76.

Nielsen, P. (1988). A qualitative approach to mechanical constraint. *Proc. AAAI-88*, St. Paul, MN, 270-274.

Pinker, S. (1980). Mental imagery and the third dimension. *Journal of Experimental Psychology: General*, 109, 354-37.

Pylyshyn, Z. W. (1981). The imagery debate: analogue media versus tacit knowledge. *Psychological Review*, 88, 16-45.

Pylyshyn, Z. W. (1984). *Computation and cognition: towards a foundation for cognitive science*. Cambridge, MA: MIT Press.

Schank, R. (1982). *Dynamic memory: a theory of learning in computers and people*. New York: Cambridge University Press.

Searle, J. R. (1980). Minds, brains, and programs. *Behavioral and Brain Sciences*, 3:3, 417-458.

Shepard, R. N., & Cooper, L. A. (1982). *Mental images and their transformations*. Cambridge, MA: MIT Press.

Shrager, J. (1989). Reinterpretation and the perceptual microstructure of conceptual knowledge: cognition considered as a perceptual skill. *Proc. Annual Conference of the Cognitive Science Society*, Ann Arbor, MI, 876-883.

Shrager, J. (1990). Commonsense perception and the psychology of theory formation. J. Shrager & P. Langely, (Eds.), *Computational models of scientific discovery and theory formation*. San Mateo, CA: Morgan Kaufmann.

Weld, D. S., & deKleer, J. (Eds.), (1990). *Readings in qualitative reasoning about physical systems*. San Mateo, CA: Morgan Kaufmann.

Natural Language Processing, Complexity Theory and Logic

(*Extended Abstract*)

Akshar Bharati

Rajeev Sangal

Vineet Chaitanya

Department of Computer Science & Engg

Indian Institute of Technology Kanpur

1. Introduction

Goal of Natural Language Processing (NLP) is to construct computational models of natural language production, comprehension, acquisition, etc. One of the central problem being addressed by the field currently, is the assignment of meaning to sentences in natural language (NL).

In some models, this assignment process is broken up into two stages. Let us call these syntactic and semantic stages, for want of better terms (Fig. 1).

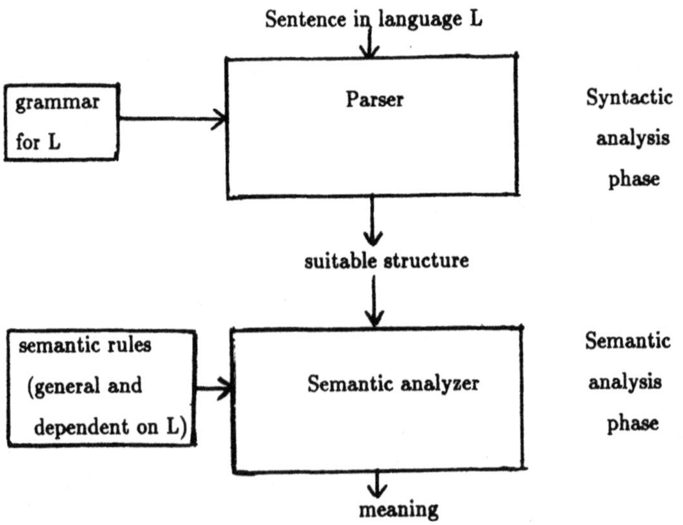

Fig. 1 Meaning assignment to a sentence

A large amount of work has been done in the last fifteen years on the syntactic phase. Several grammar formalisms have been developed for which parsers have been built and substantial NL grammars have been written.

Work on semantic phase is relatively recent. Here, the Focus has been on quantifiers, word sense disambiguation, finding referents of pronouns and definite phrases, use of background knowledge, discourse models, etc.

In the alternative models, no distinction is made between the syntactic and semantic phases. There is a single phase with no intermediate structure (in principle) between the sentence and its meaning. Examples here are Wilks (1975) and Schank (1980).

In this paper, we will discuss some solved and some open problems in NLP that have a direct relationship with Theoretical Computer Science. At times we will also bring the perspective of Indian languages and traditional Indian grammar. All this is with the hope that theoretical computer scientists will find problems of their interest in NLP and work on them.

We can best honour Prof. R. Narasimhan by identifying important inter-disciplinary areas and working in them. He has always emphasized the importance of inter disciplinary work, encouraged others to work in such areas and himself made insightful contributions, for instance, in language acquisition, psychology and cognition (Narasimhan (1981)), orality versus literacy (Narasimhan(1985)), epistemology of AI, philosophy of science (Narasimhan (1971) and (1973)).

2. Grammar Formalisms

Grammar is a crucial component of any NLP system. Consequently, much effort has gone in developing formalisms which are suitable for writing grammars for NLs. Most of the formalisms are innovative extensions of the context free grammar. We will look at some of the important ones, and the problems they pose to a computer science theorist. Grammar is used here in the narrow sense, pertaining only to the syntactic phase (same as in Fig.1).

It is desirable from complexity point of view that the grammar formalism be as weak as possible. In general, weaker the formalism, the lower will be its upper bound. The upper bounds guarantee that no matter what the grammar, what the sentence, the parsing task would take less time or space as the case may be than the upper bound. (Although, there are differing points of view (Shieber (1988)) that for development of grammar it is desirable that the formalism be powerful. Here we will not go into those aspects.)

Coupled with the grammar formalism is the related problem of where do you draw the line separating syntax from semantics. What language phenomena are handled by syntactic phase and what are left for semantic phase? Drawing of the line will have major affect on efficiency. A similar problem appears in programming languages. If scopes of variables (determined from their declaration) and their use is considered, a programming language is not context free. As a result their parsers should operate in exponential time. However, by moving the above out of syntax, the programming language becomes context free, and its parser operates in polynomial (even linear) time. The scope of declaration and use check is performed separately by a special purpose mechanism which operates in polynomial time. The result: overall time complexity is low order polynomial.

There has been much debate in the last five years on whether NLs are context free (see Pullum (1986) for an interesting account of its recent history). Approaching the problem from the other end, namely looking at language phenomena and characterizing their complexity is immensely useful, because it might tell the formalism designers whether their formalism has any hope of handling the phenomena. For example, Barton, Berwick and Ristad (1987, pp 93) show that agreement and ambiguity in combination in NL produce computational intractability: the universal recognition problem with agreement and ambiguity is NP- complete. Thus, trying to construct a CFG to solve the above is an exercise in futility. Therefore, it might be prudent to exclude the above phenomena out of the purview of one's grammar (or syntax).

Let us now look at some of the novel grammar formalisms.

One of the most interesting grammar formalisms is tree adjoining grammar (TAG) by Joshi et al. (1975), (1985). It consists of initial trees and auxiliary trees. The initial trees correspond to the surface structure of kernel sentences (Perrault (1986)). The auxiliary trees on the other hand are like rules: they derive new trees by adjunction operation when applied to the initial trees or other derived trees. TAGs capture some complex linguistic phenomena elegantly, for example, PRO and wh-movement in English, and cross-serial dependencies in Dutch.

TAGs define a new class of languages called mildly context sensitive, which is properly contained in class of context sensitive languages and properly contains CFLs. The interesting property is that it has a polynomial time recognition algorithm (O (n4)). It is open whether an O(n3) algorithm exists.

Generalized Phrase Structure Grammar (GPSG) by Gazdar et al. (1982) contains productions in which no order is implied on grammar symbols on the right hand side of a production. It only shows immediate dominance; the precedence relations are given separately. There are devices for specifying constraints among features (where a set of feature value pairs can be considered equivalent to a non-terminal). Also there are meta-rules which operate on productions to yield finite number of additional productions. It has been shown that all these additional devices do not increase the power of the formalism and it is equivalent to CFG. The devices do help in capturing certain linguistic generalizations though, and hence increase its expressive power.

Recognition problem is of polynomial complexity for CFG, hence GPSG should be efficient. It seems to be giving the best of both worlds: Linguistic generalizations through devices without having to pay a price for the recognition time. But as Barton et al. (1987, p. 251) show, hidden dangers lie waiting. The size of the grammar also plays a part in complexity (square of grammar size, times cube of sentence length). If a CFG is obtained from GPSG by expanding out the productions, it leads to "literally trillions" of rules (Shieber (1983, p. 137)). Hitherto the size was ignored as a constant in the complexity analysis. But now it will completely dominate the time complexity. In fact, the size of resulting CFG is a hyper exponential on the size of the given GPSG (Barton et al. (1987, p. 251)), a function which grows at a frightening rate.

The complexity analysis of GPSG also tells us what devices contribute to hyper complexity, and in what ways GPSG framework ought to be changed as in Barton et al. (1987, p. 255). Again complexity theory comes to the aid of NLP.

It needed GPSG and Barton et al. to alert us to the importance of grammar size. In hind sight, even for other CFG based models, the size of grammar dominates the time taken in real life. Note that in NLP, a typical grammar would have thousands of rules and a typical sentence only tens of words. (Whereas in programming languages, a typical grammar is hundreds of rules, and a typical program is thousands of tokens.)

3. A Framework for Indian Languages

Virtually all of the major grammar formalisms in Linguistics and NLP have been designed with English in the background. As a result they have a strong bias towards configurational languages (i.e., fixed word order languages, for the purposes of this paper). Even the formalisms that try to relax word ordering (e.g., GPSG), end up paying a penalty in recognition time for the relaxation. More importantly, there are virtually no devices to handle (or take advantage of) the richness of inflections in non- configurational languages.

Moreover, there may be specific features that can be exploited in a specific languages or groups of languages. For example, languages in the Indian linguistic area, share several common properties, the most important being the karaka structure. There also happens to be a well developed framework for analysis, namely the Paninian framework. A grammar for Sanskrit exists in this framework.

Work at IIT Kanpur has concentrated on adapting the Paninian framework to modern Indian languages. Purpose is to develop an efficient formalism for which parsers can be developed and in which grammars can be written for Indian languages (to start with).

The notion of karaka relation is central to the framework. These are semantico-syntactic relations between the verb(s) and the nominals in a sentence. The computational grammar specifies a mapping from the nominals and the verb(s) in a sentence to karaka relations between them. Similarly, other rules of grammar provide a mapping from karaka relations to (deep) semantic relations between the verb(s) and the nominals. Thus, the karaka relations by themselves do not give the semantics. They specify relations which mediate between vibhakti of nominals and verb form on one hand and semantic relations on the other (Bharati, Chaitanya and Sangal, (1990a) (1990b)).

For each verb group in a sentence, for one of its forms called as basic, there is a default karaka chart. The default karak chart specifies a mapping from vibhaktis to karakas when that verb-form is used in a sentence. (Vibhakti contains information from inflection of noun together with its post- positions.) Karaka chart has additional information besides vibhakti pertaining to 'yogyata' of the nominals. This serves to reduce the possible parses. Yogyata gives the semantic type that must be satisfied by the word group that serves in the karaka role.

When a verb-form other than the basic occurs in a sentence, the applicable karaka chart is obtained by taking the default karaka chart and transforming it using the verb type and its form. The new karaka chart defines the mapping from vibhakti to karaka relations for the sentence.

The above principle allows us to handle active passives among other things. The verb forms for active passives are just two special cases of the forms a verb can take.

Two quite different methods have been used for building parsers : constraint logic programming (Ramesh (1990)) and integer programming (Bharati et al.(1990c)). The parser sets up constraints between the verbs and the nominals, which can then be solved by any of the above two methods. To speed up the parser, lexical ambiguity is resolved separately by a special purpose efficient mechanism. More work is needed to constrain the formalism further, and to do the complexity analysis.

Non-configurational languages need the development of a separate model different from CFL. A sentence in such languages will possibly consist of a set of words each containing the root and vibhakti. The grammar rules may contain words or non- terminals on the right-hand side where instead of order there would be constraints on vibhaktis. Perhaps there will be a hierarchy of such languages. Theoretical results in this area would be useful to NLP for such languages.

4. Logic

We will now pick up some issues in semantics of NL and point out some problems they raise for logicians. Their study will not only be useful to NLP but it will also enrich logic.

4.1 Generalized Quantifiers

Barwise and Cooper (1981) point out that "there are sentences (in NL) which simply cannot be symbolized in a logic which is restricted to the first-order quantifiers ∀ and ∃." Consider the following sentences for example,

All arrows hit the target.

More than half of the arrows hit the target.

Writing them in first-order logic, we get:

∀a (arrow (a) -----> hit-target (a))

MHa (arrow (a) -----> hit-target (a))

But there is a problem with the latter. When we give an interpretation to it using the usual method, we find that the meaning of quantifier MH (more than half) depends on arrow(a), that is, on some predicate in the scope of MH.

The first suggestion is to include arrow(a) in the quantifier. In other words the quantifier becomes MH arrow(a) or the NL phrase 'More than half of the arrows':

MH arrow (a): a (hit-target (a))

We are now able to at least symbolize the quantifier and can give it a suitable meaning. Barwise and Cooper give it a Montague style semantics:

arrow - set of arrows

MH arrow - Collection of sets such that each set contains more than half of the arrows (plus possibly other things in the universe).

hit-target - set of things which hit the target.

The proposition is true if hit-target is a member of MH arrow, false otherwise.

Other specifiers such as most, almost all, few, none, exactly two, hardly any, etc. can be similarly defined in Montague semantics, except now suitable definitions will have to be supplied for each of the specifiers.

There is a need to develop this logic further. In particular, a proof theory needs to be developed.

4.2 Branching Quantifiers

It is well known that when an existential quantifier is in the scope of a universal quantifier(s), its bound variable can be replaced by a function which depends on the bound variable(s) of the universal quantifier(s). For example,

$$\forall x\ \exists y\ \forall z\ \exists w\ (.....x.....y.....z.....w.....)$$

can be changed to

$$\forall x\ \forall z\ \ (.....x......f(x)......z.....g\ (x,z)....)$$

where f and g are the skolem functions. There are sentences in NL where such a linear nesting of quantifiers is absent. For instance, how would one express the following dependence in a wff:

$$\forall x\ \forall z\ \ (.....x.....f(x)....z....g\ (z)....)$$

Consider the following NL sentence as an example:

Every townsman admires a friend (of his) and every villager envies a cousin (of his) who have met each other.

It could be written as (as claimed by Hintikka (1977)):

$\forall x\ \forall z$ [(x is a townsman $\wedge$ y is a villager)
f(x) is a friend of x $\wedge$
x admires f(x) $\wedge$
g(y) is a cousin of y $\wedge$
y envies g(y) $\wedge$
f(x) and g(y) have met each other]

Diagrammatically the independence of the quantifiers can be shown as:

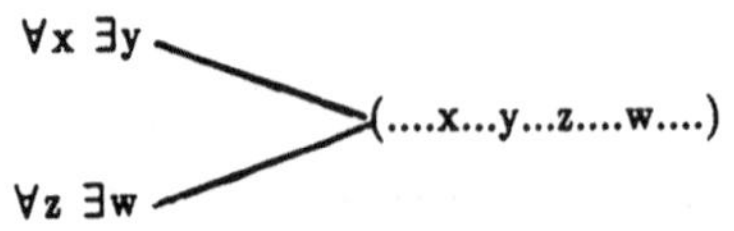

These are called branching quantifiers. Notion of branching quantifiers can be combined with generalized quantifiers resulting in generalized branching quantifiers (Westerstahl (1987)).

4.3 Scopes of Quantifiers

If we consider NL text or discourse we find that the scope of quantifiers goes upto arbitrary distance. A quantifier might occur in a sentence with appropriate relative scope in the sentence. However, its scope might extend upto several sentences. The occurrence of a pronoun referring to an entity in the scope of a quantifier in an earlier sentence serves to extend the scope to the pronoun and the sentenee. For example, one might say 'a boy' or 'some pony' in a sentence. After that one can keep referring to 'him' or 'it' for as long as one wants (Hintikka (1977)).

A natural language processing system needs capability of representing flexible scopes and changing them easily. The ease with which we deal with scope in NL without bracketing, without delimters of any kind, suggests that we must explore radically different proposals for dealing with scopes of quantifiers. In this light, there is a proposal for game-theoretic semantics by Hintikka (1977).

4.4 Belief Spaces

In NL communication, it is natural and necessary for the speaker to have a model of the listener, to have a model of the listener's model of the speaker, and so on. The same is necessary for the listener. For this we need, among other things, to maintain beliefs, maintain beliefs about beliefs, etc. In other words, we need the ability to deal with belief spaces.

There is in fact a sense of urgency for this kind of research because of the need to build proper dialogue systems and user models in general.

4.5 Other Aspects

We have not mentioned several important and difficult issues which are already under active consideration of researchers in Logic and Knowledge Representation. For example, dealing with time, space, hypotheticals, counter factuals, contingent truths, common sense reasoning, etc. In some of the ongoing work, the emphasis is on making logic closer to NL, but without introducing latter's ambiguity.

NLP has served as a driving application for knowledge representation research for a long time. But of late, it has been used to delimit the scope of the problem, and define focus of work. For instance, rather than build a general semantic type hierarchy, build one which captures the intuitions of language. The intuitions of language are to be obtained by careful analysis of language possibly by looking at more than one NL.

5. Conclusion

In this paper, we have focussed on assignment of meaning to sentences in NL. We have tried to say that theoretical Computer Science in general, and computational complexity theory and logic in particular, have a lot to contribute to NLP. On the other hand NLP has a number of challenging problems which require new ways of thinking and may thus lead to radically new frameworks in theoretical CS, particularly logic. Recent history has several instances where theoretical CS has helped shape research in NLP. At the same time, several open problems in NLP await work, some of which have the potential to throw up radically new frameworks in theoretical Computer Science.

References

Barton, G. Edward, Robert C. Berwick, and Eric S. Ristad, Computational Complexity and Natural Language, MIT Press, Cambridge, MA, 1987.

Barwise, Jon, and Robin Cooper, "Generalized Quantifiers and Natural Language," Linguistics and Philosophy 4, 1981, pp.159-219. (Also in Kulas et al. (1988)).

Bharati, Akshar, Vineet Chaitanya, and Rajeev Sangal, A Computational Grammar for Indian Languages Processing, Tech. Report TRCS-90-96, Dept of Computer Sc. & Engg, I.I.T. Kanpur, 1990a.

Bharati, Akshar, Vineet Chaitanya, and Rajeev Sangal, A Computational Framework for Indian Languages, Tech. Report TRCS-90-100, Dept of Computer Sc. & Engg, I.I.T. Kanpur, 1990b.

Bharati, Akshar, and Rajeev Sangal, "A Karaka Based Approach to parsing of Indian Languages," COLING-90: Int. Conf. on Computational Linguistics, Assoc. of Computational Linguistics, 1990c (forthcoming).

Chomsky, N., Aspects of Theory of Syntax, MIT Press, Cambridge, MA, 1965.

Dowty, David R., Lauri Karttunen and Arnold M. Zwicky, (eds.), Natural Language Parsing, Cambridge University Press, Cambridge, UK, 1985.

Gazdar, Gerald E., E. Klein, G. Pullum, and I. Sag, Generalized Phrase Structure Grammar, Basil Blackwell, Oxford, 1985.

Grosz, Barbara J., Karen Sparck Jones, Bonnie Lynn Webber, (eds.), Readings in Natural Language Processing, Morgan Kaufmann, Los Altos, CA, 1986.

Hintikka, Jaakko, "Quantifiers in Natural Languages: Some Logical Problems," in Essays on Mathematical and Philosophical Logic, J. Hintikka et al., (eds.), D. Reidel, Dordrecht, 1977. (Also in Kulas et al. (1988)).

Joshi, Aravind K., "Tree Adjoining Grammars: How Much Context Sensitivity is Required to Provide Reasonable Structural Descriptions ?," in Dowty et al. (1985).

Joshi, Aravind K., Leon S. Levy, and M. Takahashi, "Tree Adjunct Grammars," Journal of Computer and Systems Sciences, 1975.

Kulas, Jack, James H. Fetzer, and Terry L. Rankin, (eds.), Philosophy, Language and Artificial Intelligence, Kluwer Academic, Dordrecht, 1988.

Kaplan, Ronald M., and Joan Bresnan, "Lexical Functional Grammar," The Mental Representation of Grammatical Relations, Joan Bresnan, (ed), MIT Press, Cambridge, MA, 1982.

Narasimhan, R., "On the Nature of Scientific Activity," Tech. Report, Computer Sc. Group, Tata Inst. of Fundamental Res., Bombay, 1971.

Narasimhan, R., "What is Science Really About," Science Today, Nov.-Dec.1973.

Narasimhan, R., Modeling Language Behaviour, Springer Verlag, Berlin, 1981.

Narasimhan, R., "The Orality Literacy Contrast," Keynote Address to National Seminar on Human Communication, I.I.T. Kanpur, 1985. (Appeared in Aspects of Human Communication, L. Krishnan, B.N. Patnaik and N.K. Sharma, (eds.), Mittal Publicatons, New Delhi, 1989.)

Pullum, Geoffrey K., "Footloose and Context Free," Natural Language and Linguistic theory 4, 1986, pp. 409-414. (Also in Kulas et al.(1988).)

Perrault, C.R., "On the Mathematical Properties of Linguistic Theories," Computational Linguistics 10, 1984, pp. 165-176. (Also in Grosz et al. (1986).)

Ramesh, P.V., Constraints in Logic Programming, M.Tech. thesis, Dept. of Computer Sc. & Engg., I.I.T. Kanpur, 1990.

Reyle, U., and C. Rohrer, (eds.), Natural Language Parsing and Linguistic Theories, D. Reidel, Dordrecht, 1989.

Schank, Roger C., "Language and Memory," Cognitive Science 4,(3), 1980, pp. 243-284. (Also in Grosz et al. (1988).)

Shieber, Stuart M., "Direct Parsing of ID/LP Grammars," Linguistics and Philosophy 7(2), 1983. pp. 135-154.

Shieber Stuart M., "Separating Linguistic Analysis from Linguistic Theories," in Reyle and Rohrer (1988).

Westerstahl, Dag, "Branching Generalized Quantifiers and Natural Language", in Generalized Quantifiers, Peter Gardenfors, (ed.), D. Reidel, Dordrecht, 1987, pp. 269-298.

Wilks, Yorick, "An Intelligent Analyzer and understander of English," Communications of ACM 18(5), 1975, pp. 264-274. (Also in Grosz et al. (1988).)

Vol. 437: D. Kumar (Ed.), Current Trends in SNePS – Semantic Network Processing System. Proceedings, 1989. VII, 162 pages. 1990. (Subseries LNAI).

Vol. 438: D.H. Norrie, H.-W. Six (Eds.), Computer Assisted Learning – ICCAL '90. Proceedings, 1990. VII, 467 pages. 1990.

Vol. 439: P. Gorny, M. Tauber (Eds.), Visualization in Human-Computer Interaction. Proceedings, 1988. VI, 274 pages. 1990.

Vol. 440: E.Börger, H. Kleine Büning, M.M. Richter (Eds.), CSL '89. Proceedings, 1989. VI, 437 pages. 1990.

Vol. 441: T. Ito, R.H. Halstead, Jr. (Eds.), Parallel Lisp: Languages and Systems. Proceedings, 1989. XII, 364 pages. 1990.

Vol. 442: M. Main, A. Melton, M. Mislove, D. Schmidt (Eds.), Mathematical Foundations of Programming Semantics. Proceedings, 1989. VI, 439 pages. 1990.

Vol. 443: M.S. Paterson (Ed.), Automata, Languages and Programming. Proceedings, 1990. IX, 781 pages. 1990.

Vol. 444: S. Ramani, R. Chandrasekar, K.S.R. Anjaneyulu (Eds.), Knowledge Based Computer Systems. Proceedings, 1989. X, 546 pages. 1990. (Subseries LNAI).

Vol. 445: A.J.M. van Gasteren, On the Shape of Mathematical Arguments. VIII, 181 pages. 1990.

Vol. 446: L. Plümer, Termination Proofs for Logic Programs. VIII, 142 pages. 1990. (Subseries LNAI).

Vol. 447: J.R. Gilbert, R. Karlsson (Eds.), SWAT 90. 2nd Scandinavian Workshop on Algorithm Theory. Proceedings, 1990. VI, 417 pages. 1990.

Vol. 448: B. Simons, A. Spector (Eds.), Fault-Tolerant Distributed Computing. VI, 298 pages. 1990.

Vol. 449: M.E. Stickel (Ed.), 10th International Conference on Automated Deduction. Proceedings, 1990. XVI, 688 pages. 1990. (Subseries LNAI).

Vol. 450: T. Asano, T. Ibaraki, H. Imai, T. Nishizeki (Eds.), Algorithms. Proceedings, 1990. VIII, 479 pages. 1990.

Vol. 451: V. Mařík, O. Štěpánková, Z. Zdráhal (Eds.), Artificial Intelligence in Higher Education. Proceedings, 1989. IX, 247 pages. 1990. (Subseries LNAI).

Vol. 452: B. Rovan (Ed.), Mathematical Foundations of Computer Science 1990. Proceedings, 1990. VIII, 544 pages. 1990.

Vol. 453: J. Seberry, J. Pieprzyk (Eds.), Advances in Cryptology – AUSCRYPT '90. Proceedings, 1990. IX, 462 pages. 1990.

Vol. 454: V. Diekert, Combinatorics on Traces. XII, 165 pages. 1990.

Vol. 455: C.A. Floudas, P.M. Pardalos, A Collection of Test Problems for Constrained Global Optimization Algorithms. XIV, 180 pages. 1990.

Vol. 456: P. Deransart, J. Maluszyński (Eds.), Programming Language Implementation and Logic Programming. Proceedings, 1990. VIII, 401 pages. 1990.

Vol. 457: H. Burkhart (Ed.), CONPAR '90 – VAPP IV. Proceedings, 1990. XIV, 900 pages. 1990.

Vol. 458: J.C.M. Baeten, J.W. Klop (Eds.), CONCUR '90. Proceedings, 1990. VII, 537 pages. 1990.

Vol. 459: R. Studer (Ed.), Natural Language and Logic. Proceedings, 1989. VII, 252 pages. 1990. (Subseries LNAI).

Vol. 460: J. Uhl, H.A. Schmid, A Systematic Catalogue of Reusable Abstract Data Types. XII, 344 pages. 1990.

Vol. 461: P. Deransart, M. Jourdan (Eds.), Attribute Grammars and their Applications. Proceedings, 1990. VIII, 358 pages. 1990.

Vol. 462: G. Gottlob, W. Nejdl (Eds.), Expert Systems in Engineering. Proceedings, 1990. IX, 260 pages. 1990. (Subseries LNAI).

Vol. 463: H. Kirchner, W. Wechler (Eds.), Algebraic and Logic Programming. Proceedings, 1990. VII, 386 pages. 1990.

Vol. 464: J. Dassow, J. Kelemen (Eds.), Aspects and Prospects of Theoretical Computer Science. Proceedings, 1990. VI, 298 pages. 1990.

Vol. 466: A. Blaser (Ed.), Database Systems of the 90s. Proceedings, 1990. VIII, 334 pages. 1990.

Vol. 467: F. Long (Ed.), Software Engineering Environments. Proceedings, 1989. VI, 313 pages. 1990.

Vol. 468: S.G. Akl, F. Fiala, W.W. Koczkodaj (Eds.), Advances in Computing and Information – ICCI '90. Proceedings, 1990. VII, 529 pages. 1990.

Vol. 469: I. Guessarian (Ed.), Semantics of Systems of Concurrent Processes. Proceedings, 1990. V, 456 pages. 1990.

Vol. 470: S. Abiteboul, P.C. Kanellakis (Eds.), ICDT '90. Proceedings, 1990. VII, 528 pages. 1990.

Vol. 471: B.C. Ooi, Efficient Query Processing in Geographic Information Systems. VIII, 208 pages. 1990.

Vol. 472: K.V. Nori, C.E. Veni Madhavan (Eds.), Foundations of Software Technology and Theoretical Computer Science. Proceedings, 1990. X, 420 pages. 1990.